P9-DWP-800

DATE DUE

JY 5 0 '98			
DE 2 0 '00			

DEMCO 38-296

U.S. Trade,
Foreign Direct Investments,
and Global Competitiveness

INTERNATIONAL BUSINESS PRESS
Erdener Kaynak, PhD
Executive Editor

New, Recent, and Forthcoming Titles:

U.S. Trade, Foreign Direct Investments, and Global Competitiveness

Rolf Hackmann

International Business Press
An Imprint of The Haworth Press, Inc.
New York • London

Published by

International Business Press, an imprint of The Haworth Press, Inc., 10 Alice Street, Binghamton, NY 13904-1580

Cover design by Donna M. Brooks.

Library of Congress Cataloging-in-Publication Data

Hackmann, Rolf.
    U.S. trade, foreign direct investments, and global competitiveness / Rolf Hackmann.
        p.   cm.
    Includes bibliographical references and index.
    ISBN 0-7890-0085-7
    1. Investments, American. 2. Balance of payments–United States. I. Title.
HG4538.H225   1996
332.6'73'0973–dc20   96-14338
                                                                                                         CIP

CONTENTS

Figures and Tables

Figures

Tables

Chapter 14

ABOUT THE AUTHOR

Rolf Hackmann, Dr.rer.pol, MA, is Associate Professor of International Marketing in the Department of Marketing and Finance at Western Illinois University. Educated in the United States, Germany, and Austria, he worked for leading American pharmaceutical companies in both the United States and Europe for 20 years. He held positions in market research, marketing planning, sales management, and general management. He became an expert in market development functions in Eastern Europe, enabling him to note interesting contrasts with similar functions performed in Western Europe. With such a diverse background, Mr. Hackmann has found that the teaching of international subjects comes naturally. He teaches a wide range of courses, including International Business, World Markets and International Marketing, Consumer Behavior, and Marketing Decision Making.

Preface

The following study addresses America's development and growth in the economic world since World War II. This seems an appropriate starting point for such an undertaking because it signifies the beginning of the country's rise to global power and stewardship of a new world order. All major events and developments since then carry the handwriting of American influence and leadership in the political, military, cultural, and economic arenas of our global society. Obviously, not all these areas of interest can be addressed at once, even though their mutual interdependence is recognized. Rather, the focus is on economic matters, which alone may be considered the major domain where national creativity and competitiveness are free to measure each other.

Competitive rankings and their changes are determined by three forces: research and development, capital investments in productive and commercial infrastructures, and international trade. For traditional reasons, this latter factor has become the yardstick by which a nation's competitive prowess is judged. It is a concept that is still useful to a limited degree, but outmoded at a time when direct investments determine measurable national market shares in a visionary global market. Direct investments carry competition to the local level of use and consumption, represent national capital control over marketing processes, increasingly shape international trade flows, and thereby determine national market shares much better than trade information can. To illustrate this point, the U.S. situation is quite useful. About 90 percent of its merchandise exports are handled by companies related to foreign direct investment, as are roughly two-thirds of its imports. This includes both inward and outward direct investment enterprises. Each of these command business volumes far in excess of trade figures, and generate more value-added and income than trade is able to produce.

This is not always recognized, unfortunately, and leads to an official trade bias in shaping policies or voicing concerns over international relations. Major international organizations like GATT and the IMF reveal the same trade orientation and receive more public attention by officials and the media than investment facilitators.

America's focus on international trade and investment interests is best described by the following policy statements made by the International

Trade Administration section of the U.S. Department of Commerce. Quoting from the introductory comments to the "U.S. Trade Performance in 1988," the government position on foreign trade is clearly spelled out:

> *Continued strength of U.S. exports will depend on preserving and improving U.S. access to foreign markets. A priority U.S. trade policy objective is a successful conclusion to the Uruguay Round of multilateral trade negotiations. Our efforts include expanding the scope of international trade rules to "new" areas such as intellectual property, services and investment. U.S. Government priorities also include working on successful implementation of the United States-Canada Free Trade Agreement, which came into effect at the beginning of 1989; efforts to ensure U.S. access to Western Europe's markets while the European Community attempts to unify its markets by 1992; and continuing our efforts to open the Japanese market. We will continue our aggressive use of bilateral and multilateral negotiations, GATT procedures, and U.S. trade laws to deal with the unfair trade practices of other countries to ensure that all trading nations play by the same rules.*
>
> *At the same time, a major U.S. objective is the further strengthening of macroeconomic policy cooperation among the key trading nations to help increase trade flows and promote adjustment of trade and current account imbalances. The "Plaza Agreement" of 1985 marked the beginning of a concerted effort to strengthen macroeconomic coordination among major trading nations. The success of this agreement in realigning exchange rates which, coupled with stronger economic growth abroad, has created increased export opportunities for U.S. firms. The sharp rise in U.S. exports in 1988 indicated that U.S. firms are taking advantage of the opportunities created by our international economic policy effort.*
>
> *Achievement of these objectives will continue the trend toward reducing the U.S. trade deficit. The road to deficit reduction, however, will not be easy. . . .*
>
> *Reduction of our trade deficit will become more and more difficult. As U.S. firms recapture increasing shares of domestic and foreign markets, an unfortunate result of this adjustment process could be increased protectionist pressures and bilateral tensions in world trade. This will pose a great challenge to the openness of the multilateral trading system.*

This rather forceful pronouncement of the U.S. position on trade is echoed by a more reflective, if not subdued, assessment of the country's direct investment role as quoted from the introduction to the study by the same government agency entitled: International Direct Investment, Global Trends and the U.S. Role, 1988 Edition.

> *The international investment policy of the United States is that the U.S. Government should not actively promote or restrict U.S. investment abroad or foreign investment in the United States. This policy is based on the belief that free market forces will generally allocate international investment capital flows in the most economically efficient manner.*
>
> *However, as international payments imbalances have grown large and have lingered in the 1980s, international flows of capital have surged. The large current account deficits incurred by the United States since 1982 have been "financed" by a combination of accepting deposits from foreigners, selling U.S. assets to foreigners, and by a slowdown in U.S. investment abroad. The rather sudden surge of foreign investment in the 1980s has invoked fears among some writers who say America is mortgaging its future. Although most of the foreign capital inflow has been in the form of deposits in U.S. banks, U.S. bank borrowing abroad and portfolio investment, FDI has also increased rapidly. The policy debate waged in the U.S. Congress over the growing level of foreign investment in the United States is likely to continue, especially if large U.S. trade deficits linger. Undoubtedly, many of the arguments heard in the past in host countries of U.S. direct investment abroad concerning the costs and benefits of FDI will now be renewed in the United States.*
>
> *The Administration has reiterated its policy position on international investment, based on the belief that an open, nondiscriminatory international investment system is essential for continuing world economic growth. As a part of that system, foreign direct investment in the United States contributes significantly to the U.S. economy, particularly through the introduction of new technology and know-how, inflows of financial assets and other capital, and increased employment opportunities.*

This sober evaluation of the increasingly balanced U.S. inward and outward investment situation could not contrast more harshly with the ebullient tone of the earlier statement on trade policy. Uncertainty about the correct course to follow in the country's foreign economic relations shines through which, by hindsight, takes on the aura of premonition. Policy rhetoric aside, the American position in trade and direct investment has not improved since these passages were written in 1989. Foreigners are expanding their footholds in the U.S. economy and trade, creating the lion's share in the U.S. trade deficit, and America's leadership in the global economy is becoming less absolute.

After seven years of extensive negotiations, the Uruguay Round of GATT talks (now considered the General Agreement to Talk and Talk) was brought to a successful conclusion in April 1994, long after its third declared deadline on December 15, 1993. The trade advantages wrestled from the treaty appear to fall far short of U.S. expectations, even if all parties stick to the spirit and letter of the treaty. The economist Lester Thurow wrote the organization's obituary years ago by declaring, "GATT is dead." NAFTA is now in place after its ratification by the three member states: the United States, Canada, and Mexico. However, bitter exchanges over alleged trade barriers and violations continue between its three members. Japan is still far from being the open market for U.S. goods which was envisioned, and the EC of twelve has turned into the EU of fifteen, if not actually into a solid Western European alliance. Regional trading blocs seem to become stepping stones to a global market, and increasingly self-determined, instead of the direct transformation envisioned by America.

It is the purpose of the following analysis to explore the dynamics affecting the U.S. role and position in the world from a global perspective since the 1950s. The collection and processing stage of the background information made it obvious–how the interpretation of the data material would require new approaches to adequately portray, measure, and weigh structural changes in the world economy, as well as the major players in this new environment.

America's pioneering initiative and vision, for example, caused foreign direct investments to reach proportions not seen before in history, with effects more far-reaching than imaginable for a world built mainly on trade transactions. Despite this, historic views handed down from the trade era are still determining the focus of discussion.

Outward U.S. FDI, for example, has created an extraterritorial yet American-owned or -controlled economy that rivals many nations' in size, employs the equivalent of 18 percent of the U.S. manufacturing labor force, and produces a revenue volume exceeding U.S. exports of goods and services. In addition, merchandise exports of majority-controlled overseas affiliates are equal to or even higher than total U.S. exports. None of this becomes apparent in official policy declarations emphasizing concerns over domestic exports alone, assuming they could be treated in total separation from new economic structures built in the meantime. The reality of this has developed faster than the full appreciation of this fact and its related consequences.

A trade-oriented mentality misses an important point if full participation in the world economy is the ultimate national goal. Trade pursues arm's length transactions in the space between nations with little possibility or intention to get directly involved in national economies. Direct investment specifically seeks such internal involvement, and with it full control over foreign production and marketing activities in the pursuit of national and indeed, global markets. In the process, it accounts for a growing share of world trade.

The difference is like focusing on the wholesale channel rather than the much broader retail market of a national economy. Participation in both is important, but the battle for the global market is fought and won by directly competing within national economies, not by trade alone. When measuring a nation's status in the world economy, it is important to take this new situation into account. Required are new evaluation processes and yardsticks to complement, but not replace, those developed for trade relations. In other words, the step from historic channel vision to macroeconomic perspectives has to be taken.

International trade data are essentially sales-related. They are easily supplemented with macroeconomic indicators for a striking visualization of foreign competitive roles in host economies. Balance of payments data, output of gross product or value added, employment, and related shares by national industrial sectors provide additional dimensions for this purpose. They are especially useful if based on national currencies, free of the distortion effect of exchange rate vacillations.

The horizontal and vertical integration process unfolding for the world economy through direct investment affects all parties involved in three distinct ways not seen with foreign trade, and demands a fundamental change in the perception and interpretation of the world's economic environment.

The first effect is that all investor companies and in turn, their domestic economies, face basic adjustments in the areas of production, foreign trade, capital needs and allocations, and human resources. In the American experience, outward direct investment may have produced abundant economic benefits for the investors, but not necessarily for the nation. Its exports seem to have lost ground in world trade during the period of high external investment activity, as has manufacturing employment. At the same time, inward FDI activities have brought a sizable part of the American economy under foreign control, and related trade has become a major contributor to its high and persistent trade deficits. Is this development linked to the establishment or acquisition of American-owned trade and production facilities abroad? If so, are there any redeeming benefits to balance the loss of jobs, exports, and outflow of capital which would no longer be available for domestic investment? Also, what about potentially adverse implications for the U.S. economy from investment-related trade of products with lower value-added (primary materials, semiprocessed products, or products requiring foreign assembly) over formerly upgraded, finished products? Or the suspected-more-than-proven profit strategies employed by the foreign investment firms, both outward and inward, to take advantage of fluctuating exchange rates, government incentives, or international tax havens?

Obviously, satisfactory answers cannot be found to these and related questions by looking at the picture in an undifferentiated way conveniently offered by published statistics, or picking out a single aspect at a time as used to be possible in the trade period. Direct investments, unlike exports, must be seen as a projection of a national economy into world markets; that is to say, a country's economic weight today must be viewed in a global context rather than a national frame of reference.

This fact is most impressively illustrated by the widely accepted "decline" of U.S. exports as measured in the traditional national accounting and interpretation of trade. It is a judgement flowing from trade-related past terms and points of reference whose unsophisticated use can lead to very misleading conclusions. Is the fact of a falling U.S. national share in world trade really a sign of weakness and a reason for alarm or resignation? Exports by U.S. parents, for instance, to foreign customers and subsidiaries alike are constantly growing in absolute terms–a very positive development. Equally clear is the fact that they fall behind the growth in world trade, but this can be partially explained with rapidly growing shipments of lower value-added materials, and transfer pricing involving their subsidiaries. How much of this results from tax legislation rather than competitive considerations?

The role of the subsidiaries is pivotal to the discussion. They may indeed be implicated in America's loss of trade share by reasons given above, and a substitution effect because of their own trading activities. But they make up for it by providing gains in market shares within foreign economies either through acquisition of foreign business entities (which may be responsible for loss of U.S. trade with foreigners by conversion to affiliate trade), or establishment of their own production units.

Viewing the combined effect of economic resource commitments in the trade and economic output spheres enables the researcher to see the true share of the world economy controlled by a nation. Applying the output of GDP as the yardstick and ultimate criterion of a nation's international strength rebukes the notion that the U.S. export performance is even remotely indicative of its overall position in the global economy. The superficial and undifferentiated impression of a weakening position in world trade is contradicted by offsetting gains in the generation of foreign gross domestic product.

Foreign direct investment cuts two ways. Outward investment can enter into a race with inward investment trying to stay ahead of the latter, lest it turn into a net drain on the balance of payments. From this angle, direct investments become another test of a nation's competitiveness, its economic viability. Once the race has been entered, there seems to be no turning back. The score is kept in terms of comparable flows of trade, capital, and profits among the contestants. Citing the U.S. example once more; foreign ownership of U.S. enterprises at this moment comes closer to the value of U.S. holdings abroad. Present trends continuing, foreigners will also substantially widen the U.S. trade deficit, thereby adding another problem on top of that seen developing from their profit management.

The second effect is that from the traditional point of view, world trade between independent countries is still seen as a comparative national accomplishment, but totally misses the important points made above. More and more of the traditional trade is pushed into the background by transactions among direct investment members. The concept of national share in world trade on the basis of geographical origin does not reflect the country's weight in this trade because of national capital control extending to foreign shores. A change of vision is needed, or the implications of the changing power structures are lost to the observer.

The third effect of integration is that trade in the traditional view relates to products with direct and immediate economic benefits for the exporter. The products usually lose their national identity upon importation, producing expected and useful economic functions, but normally exert only minimal influence over other aspects of life in the importing nation. Classic economic doctrine saw the sole cause of such trade in the existence of resource inequities among nations without any motive other than increasing the welfare of all.

By contrast, direct investments, which normally follow established trade contacts, require capital exports, which produce profits only indirectly for the investor, and involve extra risks. An investor's readiness to accept these drawbacks is explained by one element not seen in a trade relationship: control. For the recipient nation, capital imports retain their national identity and are capable of controlling to some degree, their external and internal trade, production, employment, political, financial, fiscal, and cultural life.

Direct investment is the transplantation of economic influence; a deliberate projection of economic and, perhaps even national power, into the world to a degree that may have been intended, but was never achieved by international trade. Imagined or real, direct investment's potential for dominance over that of simple trade is best reflected in the relative volumes of national legislation spawned in both areas and not only by less-privileged nations.

The United States has been both the champion and major beneficiary of a liberalized world economy. Basically practicing what it preached for so long, the nation now finds itself at a crossroad. Free trade is still the official guidelines for America's foreign trade policy, but tougher-than-expected competition and allegations of unfair trade practices are moderating the unqualified support for a persuasive theoretical principle whose application is often beset with practical inequities.

The enthusiasm for global cooperation prevailing in earlier years has given way to more regionally focused interests: tariff and nontariff barriers for alleged infractions of accepted trade rules and unfair industry subsidies are reimposed or threatened, charges of deliberate strictures on market access are flung, and retaliatory threats over alleged dumping practices increase in frequency. In short, the whole Pandora's box of mercantile protectionism reappears. Surprisingly, after all these years of growing liberalization in spirit and action, all sides are found equally adept and willing to make use of its contents.

America's leadership of the proclaimed new world order is unquestioned, but clearly being challenged by the success of two of its declared political aims: the defeat of the communist system, and the integration of Western Europe as an integral part of U.S. strategy.

With the end of the East/West confrontation, the pressing necessity for a unified free-world military alliance has disappeared, and as a realistic consequence, America's global military deployment is being reduced. Will the voluntary military disengagement have a tandem effect on America's global economic interests, given the close recent relationship between both? One persuasive reason for this could be the sudden disintegration of the Eastern power bloc shattering the relative stability of the cold war and leading back to regional fractionalization and, predictably, the reappearance of smoldering political, ethnic, tribal, and religious conflicts. Such factors destabilize the previous climate for foreign trade and investment by creating new risks and uncertainties.

The end of the cold war has quite unexpectedly cast a shadow over the process of global integration, which was so carefully and successfully orchestrated under the auspices of the United States, instead of providing a more forceful impetus for its continuance. Now the time has come for a careful reassessment of all options. Under the visible and audible rise of dissension, the United States is given the choice of maintaining, expanding, or cutting back on its global engagement. It must face the possibility that opting for the first two could prove to be very costly, even for the greatest economic power in the world. Economic worries at home over a drop in the American standard of living, a lingering recession, unending industrial downsizing, unclear employment trends, unmanageable fiscal and trade deficits, mounting internal and external debts, coupled with a visible loss in power to shape international consensus and cooperation, may ultimately force a more inward orientation. Indeed, the pursuit of NAFTA as a counterweight to the EC, plus a visible decline in outward FDI capital flows during the 1980s, may be indications of a more regional and less global vision taking hold.

The most persuasive argument in favor of a continuation along the path of progress taken since World War II is the record of tangible advances made under U.S. leadership and guidance. At the same time, a growing number of new borders, the proliferation of regionalized economies, and the hardening spirits of cooperation and narrow self-interests cannot be overlooked, as they are good reasons for a sober assessment. The intriguing, futuristic vision of a borderless world economy integrated through business initiative and leading to a parallel political evolution may have become somewhat utopian for the moment, but is definitely more comforting to look at than any of its alternatives.

The following discussion attempts to unearth facts, relationships, and consequences of America's direct investment activities for the donor as well as the host countries, and world trade linking both. Rather than studying all players in the field at once, the focus of this analysis centers on the United States, not only because of its role as the largest trader and direct investor for the post–World War II period, but because of the ample documentation available. Much preparation has gone into condensing four decades of U.S. FDI into a few pages of information. It was not so much the absence of information as the time-consuming collecting, sorting, recording, updating, and analyzing of vast stores of information in the archives, which would have been virtually impossible without the help of dedicated assistants, and at this point their generous support is gratefully acknowledged. Special thanks go to the group whose international background is a credit to the topic discussed: Ms. Kazue Watanabe, Mr. Jaesin Yoo, Mr. Mushabab M. Al Saad, Mr. Tahir Raza S. Kazmi, Mr. Stephan Weber, Mr. Steve Myers, and Mr. Stefan Kopp.

PART I:
THE U.S. PARENT SIDE

Chapter 1

Historical Overview

BACKGROUND

The roots of American foreign direct investment (FDI) are likely to reach back to the time when the country was still making its transition from colony to independent nation. This is suggested by the first official records of such activity published in 1897 (see Table 1.1) that reported the total FDI stock at $600 million (1950 FDI census, p. 4). While it is difficult to visualize such an amount in terms of today's purchasing power, it can be related to the GNP of $14.6 billion for that same year (*The Statistical History of the United States*, p. 224). The volume indicates an extended period of accumulation, and the 4.1 percent share of GNP in those days comes impressively close to FDI's 7.7 percent share of GNP reached in 1990. Considering the development status of the fledgling republic, both the amount and the diversity of industries involved come as a surprise. After all, investments are documented for diverse industries such as manufacturing, petroleum, mining, railroads, utilities, agriculture, and numerous others.

Geographically, investments were concentrated in the Western Hemisphere for nearly a century, which is to be expected in view of the political distance the United States maintained toward other regions of the world prior to World War II. Canada and Latin America combined accounted for more than 70 percent of U.S. FDI as late as the 1950s, but then gradually ceded their position as American businesses discovered investment opportunities in other parts of the world. Had it not been for the war, the world map of U.S. FDI might still look essentially the same, which is to say that direct investment activities up to the middle of this century do portray very regional interests, but certainly not a dynamic and deliberate universal diffusion around the world.

This changed with the cessation of hostilities even though there was a period of cautious reorientation before capital started to flow freely into

TABLE 1.1. Geographical Development of U.S. Foreign Direct Investment ($ billion)

Year	Total	Canada	%	Latin America	%	Europe	%	Africa	%	Asia	%	Oceania	%
1897	$0.6	$0.2	33	0.3	50	$0.1	17	N/A	—	N/A	—	N/A	—
1914	2.7	0.6	22	1.3	48	0.6	22	N/A	—	N/A	—	N/A	—
1919	3.9	0.8	21	2.0	51	0.7	18	N/A	—	N/A	—	N/A	—
1929	7.5	2.0	27	3.5	47	1.3	17	$0.1	1	$0.4	5	$0.1	1
1936	6.7	2.4	36	2.6	39	1.2	18	0.1	1	0.4	6	0.1	1
1943	7.9	3.6	46	2.8	35	1.8	23	0.1	1	0.4	5	0.1	1
1950	11.8	3.6	31	4.9	42	1.7	14	0.4	3	1.0	8	0.2	2
1960	31.9	11.2	35	8.4	26	6.7	21	0.9	3	2.4	8	0.9	3
1970	75.5	21.0	28	13.0	17	25.3	34	3.2	4	5.3	7	3.3	4
1980	215.4	45.1	21	38.8	18	96.5	45	6.2	3	16.9	8	8.3	4
1981	228.3	47.1	21	38.8	17	101.6	45	6.8	3	19.8	9	9.4	4
1982	207.8	43.5	21	28.2	14	92.4	44	6.5	3	22.1	11	9.7	5
1983	207.2	44.3	21	24.1	12	92.2	44	6.1	3	25.2	12	9.6	5
1984	211.5	46.7	22	24.6	12	91.6	43	5.8	3	28.0	13	9.4	4
1985	230.3	46.9	20	28.3	13	105.2	46	5.9	3	29.2	13	9.3	4
1986	259.8	50.6	19	36.9	14	120.7	46	5.4	2	31.7	12	9.9	4
1987	314.3	57.8	18	47.6	15	150.4	48	5.9	2	36.8	12	12.1	4
1988	335.9	62.7	19	53.5	16	157.1	47	5.5	2	40.3	12	12.9	4
1989	381.8	63.9	18	62.1	17	189.5	50	3.9	1	41.2	11	15.4	4
1990	430.5	69.5	16	71.4	17	214.7	50	3.7	1	46.4	11	18.3	4
1991	467.8	70.7	14	77.7	16	235.2	48	4.4	1	53.2	11	19.0	4
1992	502.1	68.7	14	91.3	18	248.7	50	4.5	1	67.2	13	20.2	4
1993	559.7	69.6	12	101.6	18	280.5	50	5.5	1	77.0	14	22.1	4
1994	612.1	72.8	12	115.0	19	300.2	49	5.5	1	91.0	15	24.1	4

Note: Data do not always add to 100 percent due to an "International" category for funds that cannot be attributed to specific regions.

Sources: U.S. Direct Investment Abroad, End of 1950, p. 4. Selected Data on U.S. Direct Investment Abroad, 1950-76, pp. 1, 11, 21. SOCB, November 1984, pp. 24-7; August 1987, pp. 81-2; August 1988, pp. 65-6; August 1989, pp. 85-6; August 1990, pp. 96-7; August 1991, pp. 104-5; July 1993, pp. 121-2; August 1994, pp. 134-7; June 1995, p. 63; August 1995, p. 95.

the vacuum left by the devastations of the war. It is very much in evidence in Europe where the investment volume did not change substantially between 1929 and 1950, but then burst forth to become the leading investment area for U.S. business today. As success in previously uncharted environments grew, so did the self-confidence and determination to aggressively move into other world markets. The change in investor attitude was encouraged by the American government through sweeping postwar economic rehabilitation programs, and its determination to provide the umbrella of political and military leadership for the free world.

According to census data available for the first half of this century, U.S. foreign investments grew vigorously for three decades, stagnated and even retrenched temporarily during the depression, but snapped back during, and literally exploded after, the war. The unprecedented boom period for U.S. trade and investment ushered in by the new era of geopolitics has continued for four full decades now, and still is on an expansionary course.

The amounts of resources involved and the speed of their growth are incredible. The universal investment void created by World War II had an effect on U.S. capital transfers resembling the impact of a black hole on celestial matter. It took the U.S. more than one century to invest $10 billion abroad, a milestone reached in the late 1940s. It took less than twenty-five years to reach $100 billion in 1973. Only seven short years later, this amount had doubled to $200 billion. Exactly one decade later, the net direct investment stock had doubled once more to surpass $400 billion in 1990. At this pace, U.S. firms will add yet another $100 billion to their foreign direct investment holdings in less than five years. Such amounts are difficult to visualize, but they take on perspective if one realizes that they cover more than 150 countries, support the employment of about 6.5 million people, generate over $1 trillion in sales, and account for an annual value-added that rivals the GNP of many well-known industrialized nations.

Without doubt, American investment activities can continue at a fast pace given a continuation of the, until now, favorable investment climate in developing and developed countries alike. Only once did its momentum suffer a temporary slowdown during the 1980s through a combination of factors, the most important of which was OPEC and its disruptive impact on the world economy. But in 1984, investments started a new upward trend following a selective course toward the future centers of economic activity. This may very well include the former communist orbit of Eastern Europe, if and when the present destabilization process can be halted and prevent chaos or a total reversal to the old order. The teetering metamorphosis of these societies from Moscow's centralism to economic and political pluralism comes at a time when the industrialized nations are faced with economic uncertainties of their own, leaving their ability and willingness to aid these nations under scrutiny. Tracing the history of U.S. direct investment from World War II to the present is the subject of the following analysis.

GEOGRAPHICAL DISTRIBUTION

Canada has historically been the nation favored by American direct investors for political, cultural, and obvious geographical reasons. It maintained its leading position until the end of the 1980s, when it was replaced by England, and now ranks in second place. America's investment attention has not always been fully appreciated north of the border for fear of economic and political domination by its overpowering neighbor. But even though both nations have had more or less friendly family disputes, Canada has remained open and receptive to American investors. This is clearly reflected in Canada's growth over the years, the conclusion of the Free Trade Agreement of 1989 between both nations, and its accession into the expanded North American Free Trade Area (NAFTA) set up in the fall of 1992. The fact that the Canadian share in overall American FDI fell from 31 percent in 1950 to 12 percent in 1994 is no indication to the contrary, but rather a result of the country's limited investment potential.

The same factors that are helpful in forging close bonds between the United States and Canada were not always visible between the United States and its Latin American neighbors. Long-standing and deep historic discords due to cultural, political, and ethnic differences have left these nations wary of U.S. designs and intentions. American businesspeople see the area as prone to social, economic, and political upheavals which are potentially harmful to sound investment interests. A history of expropriations (notably in Mexico, Cuba, and Chile) delays in debt service to American banks, and capital flight from the area have caused a waning investment interest in Latin America for some time now. As a consequence, it is the only region with a large potential for economic development where U.S. investments are, in effect, stagnant, and have been for at least a decade, which accounts for the area's rapid loss of investment share to other regions of the world. Between 1950 and 1994, investment share has dropped from 42 percent to only 19 percent. The decline in investment interest should come to an end, and eventually reverse itself with the recovery of the presently seriously debilitated NAFTA agreement signed at the end of 1993 between the United States, Canada, and Mexico. Even before the treaty has reached the stage of full implementation, there is talk of a NAFTA extension to include other Latin American partners.

While basically correct, this superficial assessment needs to be qualified because the situation of this region is characterized by factors which tend to distort the overall investment picture. For one thing, the term Latin America covers two heterogeneous geographical areas: the nations of Central and South America in one, and what is officially called the "Other Western Hemisphere," which comprises the island nations in the Caribbean basin. The two areas are divided not only by cultural, political, and historical heritage, but also by vastly different endowments of natural resources. For this reason, that they have played completely separate roles in U.S. FDI as evidenced by a comparison of their sectoral structures (see Table 1.10).

Latin America's continental republics show a diversified investment picture commensurate with their population and resource potential. In 1994, emphasis was on manufacturing with 44 percent of all investments, followed by finance and banking with 27 percent, oil 8 percent, trade 3 percent, and all others 10 percent respectively in 1994. In the same year, 86 percent of all investments in the Caribbean were concentrated in finance and banking, in order to take advantage of favorable local tax laws. Oil affiliates and manufacturing with 2 percent each, and trade with 6 percent, practically made up the rest (*SOCB*, July 1993, p. 98).

The Caribbean finance affiliates, excluding banking, are not only the most important single investment group there (76 percent), but also the cause of a distorted FDI picture. This applies in particular to the finance affiliates located in the Netherlands Antilles whose primary function is to borrow funds from overseas for their U.S. parent organizations. As explained in greater detail later on, these funds flowing into the United States have been subject to fundamentally different statistical treatment before and after 1977. The change in accounting procedures against the prior period not only reduced the investment stock for the Latin American area in a significant way, but for global U.S. FDI as well.

In the early 1980s, the negative fund flows produced by the new procedure, as seen from an outward investment point of view, rapidly gained momentum and reached more than $40 billion, which essentially reduced the total U.S. FDI stock by about 8 percent in 1984. In the context of the small Latin American investments, such amounts had a drastic impact causing a 42 percent drop in the area's investment position from $48 billion in 1977 to $28 billion in 1982. At the peak of the Netherlands Antillean borrowing, with $42.5 billion in 1984, the total Latin American investment stock had been cut by 50 percent on the strength of this accounting procedure alone. In the early 1990s, the lopsided situation had almost returned to normal through sweeping reductions in the outstanding net debt of U.S. parent companies to $6.3 billion in 1994 (*SOCB*, August 1995, p. 92).

Looking at the continental Latin republics per se, shows them to have suffered a net loss in investment share from 38 percent in 1950 to 11 percent in 1994 on account of a practically stagnant investment volume between 1980-1987. The Caribbean affiliates on the other side expanded their share in total U.S. FDI from 1 percent to 8 percent in the same period.

Canada and Latin America combined shared 69 percent of all investment funds in 1950, but less than half that figure with 31 percent in 1994. Their loss turned into Europe's gain, whose share grew from 14 percent to 49 percent in the same time period. It has more or less come to rest around the 50 percent level as of late, but this could change in view of the scheduled consolidation of the European Union and the opening of Eastern Europe.

Despite its rapid growth and accounting for half of all U.S. direct investment funds, Europe does not stand alone in expanding at the expense of the traditional investment areas. U.S. business interests are being lured to new horizons, in particular to the Pacific Basin covering the Asian rim nations and Oceania, which includes Australia and New Zealand.

Asia's share in U.S. FDI has grown from 8 percent in 1950 to 15 percent in 1994, while that of Oceania doubled from 2 percent to 4 percent. Together, both areas now carry the same weight as all of the Latin American investments put together with the difference being that the former are expanding while the latter are really not. Asia's share is still fairly modest considering the enormous economic potential lying dormant in its vast expanse, resources, and population. Barriers blocking that potential are: the area's low level of economic development, political volatility in the Middle East, and remaining restrictions on foreign participation in the more important national economies of the area, despite declared and officially more open investment policies (such as those in China, India, and Japan). In this part of the world, American investments have met spectacular setbacks to date—from the confiscation of property in Iran, the nationalization of the oil industry in Saudi Arabia, the war in Vietnam, chilled relations with India and China, to the loss of military bases in the Philippines; all have been compelling reasons to put American investment activities on hold in major areas of Asia for some time to come (see Table 1.2).

Geographical shifts in U.S. investment flows have been substantial since 1950. This is even more pronounced in individual countries, as documented in Table 1.3, which lists the twenty leading countries in rank order of dollars committed, and comprising at least 80 percent of total

TABLE 1.2. Investment Position by Area and Major Country ($ billion)

Area/Country	1950	1960	1970	1980	1990
World	**11.8**	**31.9**	**75.5**	**215.4**	**430.5**
Canada	**3.6**	**11.2**	**21.0**	**45.1**	**69.5**
Europe	**1.7**	**6.7**	**25.3**	**96.5**	**214.7**
Belg./Lux.	0.1	0.2	1.5	6.9	11.2
Denmark	nil	0.1	0.4	1.3	1.7
France	0.2	0.7	2.6	9.3	19.2
Germany	0.2	1.0	4.3	15.4	27.6
Greece	N/A	N/A	N/A	0.3	0.3
Ireland	N/A	nil	0.2	2.3	5.9
Italy	0.1	0.4	1.5	5.4	14.1
Netherlands	0.1	0.3	1.6	8.0	19.1
Portugal	nil	N/A	N/A	0.3	0.9
Spain	nil	0.1	0.7	2.7	7.9
Switzerland	nil	0.3	2.6	11.3	25.1
UK	0.8	3.2	8.0	28.5	72.7
EC (12)	N/A	N/A	13.0	80.4	180.5
Latin America	**4.9**	**8.4**	**13.0**	**38.8**	**71.4**
Argentina	0.4	0.5	1.0	2.5	2.5
Bahamas	nil	nil	0.4	2.7	4.0
Bermuda	N/A	0.4	0.2	11.0	20.2
Brazil	0.6	1.0	1.5	7.7	14.4
Chile	0.5	0.7	0.8	0.6	1.9
Colombia	0.2	0.4	0.6	1.0	1.7
Mexico	0.4	0.8	1.9	6.0	10.3
Nether. Antilles	N/A	N/A	N/A	−4.3	−4.5
Panama	0.3	0.4	1.2	3.2	9.3
UK Caribbean	N/A	N/A	N/A	0.7	5.9
Venezuela	1.0	2.6	2.2	1.8	1.1
Africa	**0.4**	**0.9**	**3.2**	**6.1**	**3.7**
South Africa	0.1	0.3	0.8	2.4	0.8
Asia	**1.0**	**2.4**	**5.3**	**16.9**	**46.4**
Hong Kong	N/A	N/A	N/A	2.1	6.1
Indonesia	0.1	0.2	0.2	1.3	3.2
Japan	nil	0.3	1.5	6.2	22.6
Korea	N/A	N/A	N/A	0.6	2.7
Malaysia	N/A	N/A	N/A	0.6	1.5
Middle East	0.7	1.1	1.5	2.2	4.0
Singapore	N/A	N/A	N/A	1.2	4.0
Taiwan	N/A	N/A	N/A	0.5	2.2
Oceania	**0.2**	**0.9**	**3.3**	**8.2**	**18.3**
Australia	0.2	0.9	3.1	7.7	15.1
New Zealand	nil	nil	0.1	0.6	3.2

TABLE 1.3. The Twenty Top-Ranking Investment Countries ($ million)

1950			1970			1990		
	$	%		$	%		$	%
World	11,788	100.0	World	75,480	100.0	World	430,521	100.0
1 Canada	3,579	30.4	Canada	21,015	27.8	UK	72,707	16.9
2 Venezuela	993	8.4	UK	8,016	10.6	Canada	69,508	16.1
3 UK	847	7.2	Germany	4,313	5.7	Germany	27,609	6.4
4 Brazil	644	5.5	Australia	3,148	4.2	Switzerland	25,099	5.8
5 Cuba	642	5.4	France	2,643	3.5	Japan	22,599	5.2
Subtotal	6,705	56.9		39,135	51.8		217,522	50.4
6 Chile	540	4.6	Switzerland	2,631	3.5	Bermuda	20,169	4.7
7 Mexico	415	3.5	Venezuela	2,241	3.0	France	19,164	4.5
8 Argentina	346	2.9	Mexico	1,912	2.5	Netherlands	19,120	4.4
9 France	217	1.8	Netherlands	1,550	2.1	Australia	15,110	3.5
10 Germany	204	1.7	Belg./Lux.	1,546	2.0	Brazil	14,384	3.3
Subtotal	8,427	71.5		49,015	64.9		305,469	70.8
11 Australia	201	1.7	Brazil	1,526	2.0	Italy	14,063	3.3
12 Colombia	193	1.6	Japan	1,482	2.0	Belg./Lux.	11,161	2.6
13 Philippines	149	1.3	Italy	1,464	1.9	Mexico	10,313	2.4
14 Peru	145	1.2	Panama	1,190	1.6	Panama	9,289	2.2
15 S. Africa	140	1.2	Argentina	1,022	1.4	Spain	7,868	1.8
Subtotal	9,255	78.4		55,699	73.8		358,163	83.1
16 Netherlands	84	0.7	Libya	896	1.2	Hong Kong	6,055	1.4
17 Belg./Lux.	69	0.6	S. Africa	778	1.0	UK Carib.	5,929	1.4
18 Italy	63	0.5	Chile	758	1.0	Ireland	5,894	1.4
19 Sweden	58	0.5	Peru	744	1.0	Bahamas	4,004	0.9
20 Panama	58	0.5	Spain	696	0.9	Singapore	3,975	0.9
Subtotal	9,587	81.2		59,571	78.9		384,020	89.1

Sources: *U.S. Direct Investment Abroad, 1950-76*, pp. 1, 21. *SOCB*, August 1994, p. 134.

U.S. FDI at various time intervals. The fact that twenty countries out of roughly 150 held 89 percent of all investment stock in 1990 is a rather forceful demonstration of the 80/20 rule and is proof of a growing investment concentration.

Canada remained at the top for three decades of the postwar period, but the constant erosion of its share from 30 percent in 1950 to 16 percent in 1990 put it in second place after the UK. It is interesting to speculate whether it can return to the former position after the conclusion of the

1993 NAFTA agreement. The accession of Mexico into the original United States-Canadian Free Trade Agreement, which was seen as a major investment stimulus, turned into the opposite after the unexpected devaluation of the Mexican peso almost before the ink on the NAFTA pact had dried. Comforting to the Canadians should be the certainty of a second place position for a long time, as the next most important country, Germany, had reached only a 6 percent share in 1990.

Latin America furnished nine out of the twenty top nations in 1950. Of the oldtimers, only two–Brazil and Mexico–remained on the list while Panama, Bermuda, the Bahamas, and the UK Caribbean islands joined their ranks as newcomers for a total of six Latin American nations in the top twenty by 1990. Cuba became a spectacular fatality of cold war politics, but may expect renewed American investment interest following the recent East/West detente. Mexico is still assured a star performance in the long run, because none of the original NAFTA agreement's provisions, such as elimination of all trade and investment barriers over a fifteen-year period, have been affected by its one-sided jolt to its partners.

Europe provided seven countries to the list in 1950 despite the relatively weak position of the whole continent at the time. Their number had grown to ten by 1990, with generally improved levels in ranking for all. The former EC (European Community) of twelve countries accounted for a combined share of 42 percent. For all practical purposes, the time has come to see Europe as one economic block. Its historic integration process is almost complete with fifteen of the eighteen West European countries now full-fledged members of the EU (European Union) and the rest closely associated via the European Economic Area (EEA).

Asia and Africa were represented in the top twenty by one nation each in 1950. With South Africa's disappearance from the list, the whole continent dropped out of the picture, despite large petroleum investments in several other areas. Asia shows three entries at the latest count. The most important is Japan, which emerged slowly over the years, and is now holding a respectable fifth place, followed by Hong Kong and Indonesia.

Striking is the overwhelming presence of developed nations in the list. What is not immediately visible though, is the fact that investments in developed countries accounted for only 48 percent in 1950, owing to the heavy orientation towards Latin America, but has grown to 75 percent of the total over time.

English-speaking countries hold a particular appeal for U.S. investors, which is not surprising in view of a common language and historic ties between these members of the former British empire. Despite their similarities, the countries fall into two distinctively different groups, each of which is playing a special role in the scheme of things. From the comments made above, it is evident that the investments in the Caribbean area serve purely financial interests, while those in the other countries address primarily commercial and production purposes.

Of the eight countries listed, two represent economies of world rank: Canada and England. Both have moved in opposite directions in the investment picture. Canada's share has been cut in half, while England's has doubled with the net effect of both having reached almost identical investment levels by the end of the period. Considering their relative economic weight in terms of population, GNP, foreign trade, industrial depth, etc., England is moving in the right direction, but is still underrepresented. Canada, more in the same league with Australia, enjoys its exalted position because of its geographical proximity and long-standing ties between both nations which also applies to Australia to some degree. The preferential investment status accorded Commonwealth nations appears to be limited only by economic potential (a question common to all) and political considerations as those in South Africa (apartheid) and to some degree, Canada, as mentioned above (trade issues) (see Table 1.4).

The twenty leading countries attract a growing share of the investment funds. As a matter of interest, they do not consist exclusively of developed nations, as might be assumed. Part of the concentration process is due to a change in investment character which de-emphasizes traditional manufacturing industries in favor of service-related enterprises such as trade, finance, holding companies, etc. This trend is evidenced by the appearance

TABLE 1.4. Investment Share of Anglo-Saxon Countries

	1950	1960	1970	1980	1990
	%	%	%	%	%
Australia	1.7	2.7	4.2	3.6	3.5
Canada	30.4	35.1	27.8	20.9	16.1
New Zealand	0.2	0.2	0.2	0.3	0.7
South Africa	1.2	0.9	1.0	1.1	0.2
UK	7.2	10.1	10.6	13.3	16.9
Bahamas	0.0	0.0	0.5	1.3	0.9
Bermuda	0.0	1.2	0.3	5.1	4.7
UK Carib.	N/A	N/A	N/A	0.5	1.4
Total	40.7	50.2	44.6	46.1	44.4

Sources: *U.S. Direct Investment Abroad, 1950-76*, pp. 1, 11, 21. *International Direct Investment, Global Trends, and the U.S. Role*, pp. 50-1. *SOCB*, August 1994, p. 134.

on the list of countries such as Switzerland, Bermuda, the Bahamas, Panama, and British Caribbean which are industrial dwarfs. Their principal role is to serve as tax havens and profit centers, which will repeatedly be discussed in various sections of this study.

The same group of countries accounted for around 80 percent of all U.S. investments in the 1950s, 1960s, and 1970s, but then shot up to almost 90 percent by 1990. Such concentration of investment capital coincides with a very noticeable contraction in the number of U.S. parent companies and their foreign affiliates, in addition to a temporary slowdown in the growth of the overall investment stock in the early 1980s for the first time since World War II. Factors playing a role include: the uncertainties overshadowing the world economy after two OPEC coups, the merger mania gripping U.S. companies during the Reagan/Bush years of deregulation, and the distortion effect of the investments in the Netherlands Antilles described earlier (see Table 1.5).

DIRECT INVESTMENT BY INDUSTRY

Two industries have dominated the FDI scene practically from the beginning of recorded activity: manufacturing and natural resources. Of the original investments in agriculture, mining, smelting, and petroleum, only the latter has retained a noteworthy presence. For the last fifty years, the manufacturing sector has led all other industries in total amounts of dollars invested. During the depression and immediate prewar period, this industry commanded a 25 percent share of the direct investments made by U.S. companies. After the war, its share gradually increased to reach a peak of 45 percent during the mid-1970s, but the advent and subsequent growth of financial, trade, and other service industries reduced it to 36 percent by 1994 (see Tables 1.6 and 1.7).

TABLE 1.5. Key Data of U.S. Foreign Direct Investment

	1950	1957	1966	1977	1982	1989
Parents	2,363	2,812	3,354	3,540	2,245	2,272
Affiliates	7,417	10,272	23,120	24,666	18,339	18,899
FDI ($ bil.)	$11.8	$25.4	$51.8	$146.0	$207.3	$381.8

Sources: 1950 FDI census, pp. 4, 44-5; 1957 FDI census, pp. 90, 98, 144; 1966 FDI census, pp. 29, 232, 234; 1977 FDI census, pp. 2, 10-1; 1982 FDI census, p. 6; 1989 FDI census, p. M-7.

TABLE 1.6. U.S. Foreign Direct Investment Position by Industry ($ billion)

Year	Total	Mfg.	Pet.	Trade	Banks	Fin./Ins.*	Mining	Utilities**	Services	Other
1950	$11.8	$3.8	$3.4	$0.8	N/A	N/A	$1.1	1.4	N/A	$1.3
1955	19.4	6.6	5.9	1.3	N/A	N/A	2.2	1.6	N/A	1.7
1960	32.8	11.2	10.9	2.4	N/A	N/A	3.0	2.2	N/A	2.4
1965	49.5	19.3	15.3	4.2	N/A	N/A	3.9	2.1	N/A	4.6
1970	75.5	31.0	19.8	6.2	N/A	7.2	5.4	2.8	N/A	3.1
1975	124.1	55.9	26.0	12.5	N/A	14.6	6.5	3.2	N/A	5.3
1980	215.4	89.3	47.6	25.8	7.3	27.9	6.8	N/A	N/A	11.0
1981	228.3	92.4	53.2	28.3	8.5	26.6	N/A	N/A	N/A	12.1
1982	207.8	83.5	57.8	24.5	10.3	18.0	5.2	2.3	4.6	1.6
1983	207.2	82.9	57.6	25.2	12.4	15.1	5.5	2.4	4.7	1.5
1984	211.5	85.9	58.1	24.8	13.5	15.7	4.9	2.4	4.4	1.8
1985	230.3	94.7	57.7	26.8	14.5	22.5	4.9	2.7	4.7	1.8
1986	259.8	105.1	58.5	30.8	14.5	36.4	5.1	2.6	5.1	1.7
1987	314.3	131.6	59.8	36.9	18.0	53.0	4.7	1.9	6.7	1.5
1988	335.9	138.7	57.8	40.4	19.1	63.4	4.9	2.1	7.9	1.7
1989	381.8	147.9	48.3	44.7	19.4	101.1	4.7	2.7	11.7	1.2
1990	430.5	170.2	52.8	50.7	20.7	109.7	5.0	6.8	13.4	1.2
1991	467.8	179.2	57.7	57.1	21.3	120.6	5.3	8.2	15.8	1.7
1992	499.0	186.3	58.5	61.5	24.7	137.2	5.6	9.2	17.2	1.9
1993	559.7	194.3	63.5	66.4	27.1	168.9	6.0	11.7	19.7	2.0
1994	612.1	220.3	65.7	77.0	29.5	175.0	6.5	13.6	23.0	1.5

Notes: Trade data include wholesale and retail. *Finance/Insurance includes real estate from 1977 on and bank data from 1950 through 1976. **Includes transportation, communication, and public utilities.

Sources: *Selected Data on U.S. Direct Investment Abroad, 1950-76*, pp. 1-27. 1977 FDI census, p. 46. 1982 FDI census, pp. 13-4. *SOCB*, August 1980, p. 26; August 1981, p. 31; August 1982, p. 21; August 1983, p. 23; August 1985, p. 34; August 1987, pp. 83-4; August 1988, pp. 67-8; August 1990, pp. 97-8; August 1991, pp. 106-7; July 1993, pp. 123-4; August 1995, pp. 115-6.

TABLE 1.7. Industry Share in U.S. Foreign Direct Investment Position (percentages)

Year	Mfg.	Pet.	Trade	Fin./Ins.	Mining	Utilities	Services	Banking	Other
1950	32.5	28.8	6.5	N/A	9.6	12.1	N/A	N/A	10.6
1955	34.1	30.4	6.7	N/A	11.3	8.5	N/A	N/A	8.9
1957	31.5	35.7	6.6	N/A	9.3	8.4	N/A	N/A	8.5
1960	34.0	33.4	7.2	N/A	9.1	6.8	N/A	N/A	7.4
1965	39.1	30.9	8.5	N/A	7.9	4.5	N/A	N/A	9.2
1966	40.0	26.8	8.4	8.8	7.7	4.4	N/A	N/A	4.0
1970	41.1	26.2	8.2	9.5	7.2	3.7	N/A	N/A	4.1
1975	45.1	20.9	10.1	11.8	5.3	2.6	N/A	N/A	4.3
1977	42.5	19.2	11.5	14.4	4.1	1.5	2.7	3.0	1.1
1980	41.4	22.1	12.0	13.0	3.1	N/A	N/A	N/A	5.1
1981	40.5	23.3	12.4	11.7	N/A	N/A	N/A	N/A	5.3
1982	40.1	27.8	11.8	8.7	2.5	1.1	2.2	5.0	0.8
1983	40.0	26.1	12.2	7.3	2.7	1.2	2.3	6.0	0.7
1984	40.5	27.4	11.7	7.4	2.3	1.1	2.1	6.4	0.8
1985	41.1	25.1	11.7	9.8	2.1	1.2	2.0	6.3	0.8
1986	40.4	22.5	11.8	14.0	2.0	1.0	2.0	5.6	0.7
1987	42.0	19.1	11.8	16.9	1.5	0.6	2.1	5.7	0.5
1988	41.3	17.2	12.0	18.9	1.5	0.6	2.4	5.7	0.5
1989	38.7	12.6	11.6	26.4	1.2	0.7	3.1	5.1	0.3
1990	39.5	12.2	11.8	25.5	1.2	1.6	3.1	4.9	0.3
1991	38.3	12.3	12.2	25.8	1.0	1.8	3.4	4.6	0.4
1992	37.1	11.7	12.3	27.5	1.1	1.8	3.4	5.0	0.4
1993	34.6	11.3	11.9	30.2	1.1	2.1	3.5	4.8	0.4
1994	35.9	10.7	12.6	28.6	1.1	2.2	3.8	4.8	0.2

Manufacturing covers a wide range of industries, but chemicals, machinery, and transportation equipment combined held 59 percent of the total in 1994. That share would be even larger if petroleum processing were shown under the chemical industry, where it is customarily included. However, in U.S. practice, data that monitor FDI activities for the petroleum industry cover all aspects from exploration, basic extraction of crude and processing, to the marketing of the end products. Details for the individual manufacturing industries are not available prior to 1966 with the exception of the census years 1950 and 1957 (see Table 1.8).

Data that provide details of major subsidiary manufacturing sectors are somehow reminiscent of the fate these industries met in the United States where chemicals and machinery expanded, while primary metals (steel,

TABLE 1.8. Major Subgroups in Manufacturing–Percentages (all manufacturing = 100)

Year	Food	Chemical	Prim. Metals	Machinery*	Trans. Equip.	Other
1950	12.6	13.4	10.0	21.1	12.7	30.3
1957	9.0	17.2	11.7	20.7	15.0	26.3
1966	8.5	18.5	7.0	24.3	18.9	22.8
1970	8.6	18.9	7.7	25.3	16.3	23.2
1980	9.3	21.2	7.1	26.2	13.8	22.3
1985	9.6	21.1	4.8	28.7	14.2	21.4
1988	9.6	22.6	5.7	26.9	13.7	21.3
1989	8.0	22.7	5.5	27.1	14.5	22.2
1990	9.1	22.3	6.2	27.4	12.6	22.4
1991	9.6	22.7	5.3	26.5	13.0	23.0
1992	11.3	24.1	5.2	23.4	13.7	22.5
1993	13.2	24.1	5.2	22.6	12.1	23.0
1994	13.0	23.5	5.0	23.3	12.7	22.5

Note: *Includes machinery except electric plus electric/electronic equipment.

fabricated metals, etc.) and transportation equipment stagnated or even declined. Such parallel developments affecting companies in the United States and abroad alike may be viewed as shifts in sectoral competitiveness among nations, which is confirmed by the annual battles fought over alleged illegal trade practices.

Fortunately, these examples are not indicative of the competitiveness of U.S. industries in general. Many branches compete directly and successfully with foreign industries in areas such as chemicals, pharmaceuticals, telecommunications, medical equipment, office equipment, computers, high-tech electronics, etc. There are other areas where U.S. leadership is not contested, yet never led to investments overseas for obvious reasons. Such areas are aerospace, defense, aircraft, mainframe computers and other high-tech, but security-sensitive industries.

Fluctuations in relative investment shares illustrate the pursuit of profits by U.S. industries in an increasingly open international business environment. However, they say little about the actual business rationale behind the final decision to invest or disinvest in each case. Relative levels of profitability, growth prospects, superior technology and management skills developed by the investor (aggressive rationale) or by competition (defensive rationale), political and tax considerations, and a host of other reasons may play a role either singly or in combination. Students of the field have studied a selection of investment motivators ranging across a fair number of theoretical possibilities. One school of thought sees monopolistic competition as the primer spurred by competitive advantages of one business over domestic competitors (Hymer, 1960; Kindleberger, 1965; Caves, 1971). Others find clues in theories of international trade (Dollar, 1987), the search for diversification (Calvert, 1983 and Shapiro, 1989), a combination of firm-specific/location-specific factor advantages as found in the eclectic theory (Dunning, 1977, 1979, 1980, 1981, and Ethier, 1986) and finally, imbalance theory (Moon and Roehl, 1993).

Petroleum, the second most important investment sector, had an episode of trading leadership positions with manufacturing in the late 1950s. After reaching a peak of 35.1 percent in 1961, it gradually declined to around 11 percent in 1994–a downward development that actually predates the OPEC impact.

After 1970, there was a pronounced shift of U.S. oil investments away from OPEC countries which coincided with fundamental changes in the investment structure for this industry as shown in Table 1.8. In very general terms, U.S. foreign direct investment moved from exploration and crude production to processing, marketing, and service activities for a while. According to the latest information, this trend may be reversing. These moves may have been imposed upon the industry more by OPEC actions and policies than by deliberate management decisions. The expropriations in Iran, Saudi Arabia, and Libya come to mind.

The statistical treatment of the petroleum industry as an autonomous industrial complex by the U.S. Department of Commerce makes comparisons with international data difficult. Foreign countries, international agencies, as well as U.S. domestic statistics normally break this industry down into three major segments. Each is listed under a different industrial sector. Exploration and crude production are thus included with extractive industries under such headings as mining, quarrying, etc. Refining is shown under the chemical industry and selling/marketing operations are shown under wholesale or retail trade data (see Table 1.9).

The third key investment area is the trade industry which includes wholesale and retail channels. Wholesaling accounted for 87 percent of all dollars invested in both industries in 1994 and represented traditional domestic wholesale functions in the majority of countries. However, there are situations where business volume in relation to the local market is so unusually large that it can only be generated from global trading activities. For example, industry sales in nations such as Switzerland, Hong Kong, Panama, the Bahamas, etc., would completely dominate the national economy, if taken at face value. Their role is repeatedly explored in different

TABLE 1.9. Structural Changes in Petroleum Investments ($ billion)

	1957		1966		1977		1989	
	$	%	$	%	$	%	$	%
Total Position	9.1	100	13.9	100	28.0	100	48.3	100
Crude Production/Explor.	5.4	60	3.1	22	12.3	44	23.1	48
Refin./Processing	1.1	12	1.4	10	8.1	29	15.8	33
Distribution/Marketing	1.2	13	1.8	13	5.4	19	5.4	11
Tanker Oper.	.7	8	1.0	7	2.1	7	0.9	2
Pipelines	.5	5	.1	1	.1	–	0.4	–
Field Service	.1	1	.5	3	.3	1	2.2	5
Other	.1	1	6.1*	44	.02	–	.4	1

Note: *Refers to integrated companies that are broken down by extraction and refining functions for all other years.

Sources: 1957 FDI census, p. 94; 1966 FDI census, p. 42; 1977 FDI census, p. 45; 1982 FDI census, p. 13; *SOCB*, July 1993, p. 123.

sections of this study under the subjects of sales, exports, and tax havens. The industry gradually expanded its share of global investments from 6.5 percent in 1950 to 12.6 percent in 1994, putting it slightly ahead of the oil industry into the number two spot for the time being.

During the 1960s and 1970s, two additional industries emerged as major investment centers. In rank order of investment size, they are: (1) Finance, Insurance, and Real Estate and (2) Banking.

Finance and insurance, as it was called until 1976, comprised banking, holding companies, other finance, and insurance but excluded real estate. In the 1977 census, it was changed to cover finance, insurance, real estate, holding companies, and nonbusiness entities except government, but excluded banking. For that year, the group held an investment share of 14 percent which increased to 26 percent in 1990.

Banking was assigned a separate statistical group in 1977 for several reasons. One was that banking developed into a major investment worthy of separate attention; and second, it represented an industry with essential differences in the area of assets and sales that set it apart from all others. Banks, for instance, do not generate sales, only income. Their assets include customer deposits which have nothing to do with assets which represent equity or debt capital. Depositary assets share the name but do not fit the definition of direct investment assets. For these reasons, all statistics covering other industries state in their headings that they are based on nonbank parents and nonbank affiliates starting with the 1977 census.

Separate statistics for finance, insurance, and real estate are not available prior to 1966. The same goes for banking prior to 1977, except for the census years 1950, 1957, and 1966. Banks maintained a very low profile in the investment picture, at least until 1966, when they appeared for the first time with a tiny 0.5 percent share. Details which became available on a regular basis since 1977 show a 3 percent share for that very same year and only a modest 4.8 percent for 1994.

Among other industries worth mentioning are services covering a wide spectrum of activities such as: (1) business services including advertising, management consulting and public relations, equipment rental exclusive of automotive and computers, computer and data processing, research and development, testing laboratories, employment and office help agencies; and (2) all other services such as: motion pictures inclusive of television tape and film, engineering, architecture and surveying, health services, automotive rental and leasing, accounting, auditing, bookkeeping, legal services, educational services, plus lodging services (1982 FDI Census, p. 17).

Roughly one-half of service investments are in business services. The all services category has established a small but fairly steady share of around 2.5 percent of total investments between 1977-88, but has been on a definite growth path since 1989. It would be interesting to find out how much of the increase was due to Walt Disney's theme park in Paris, which was financed with plenty of French government subsidies.

Other industries shown separately include mining, with a once important 11 percent share (1955), but down to 1.1 percent in 1994; utilities comprising transportation, communications, and public utilities with an equally important 12 percent share of all investments in 1950, but again reduced to only 2 percent in 1994. The all other category, representing a larger mixture of industries and accounting for around 10 percent in the earlier period, has been reduced to the agricultural and construction sector today, with under one-half of 1 percent combined.

DISTRIBUTION OF U.S. FDI BY INDUSTRY AND GEOGRAPHIC AREA

Direct investments made during the four decades since World War II have reached tidal wave proportions. But like all waves, its outward dimensions hide a multitude of crosscurrents which must be looked at separately in order to appreciate their impact on major world areas. For analytical purposes, the flow volume and direction of investments have been broken down and analyzed by major industry, world region, and ultimately, by single country. The evolutionary process is captured by statistical still pictures made at regular time intervals and tracing two key features.

The first set of data focuses on the regional distribution of total direct investments and their breakdown by major industries over the four decades. Expressed in percentages, it provides insight into a region's importance for individual industries, and its changes over time. As FDI is attracted to the most promising business opportunities under given environmental conditions, the history also provides a useful tool for forecasting future focal points of investment. Areas of high investment concentration are not necessarily a consequence of equally concentrated local business volume, but rather a mixture of favorable tax legislation, low production costs, and a minimum of political exposure. The first point applies more to service industries, the second more to manufacturing, and the last to all. Finally, the regional dispersion of U.S. investments can also be viewed as a demonstration of an increasingly integrating world economy (see Table 1.10).

The second analysis traces the changing mix of total American investments in a given area over time and answers the question of how important an industry is in the context of total U.S. commitment there. The conclusions of this analysis, again expressed in percentage form, are laid down in Table 1.11.

THE DEFINITION
OF FOREIGN DIRECT INVESTMENT

Today, U.S. FDI is defined as the cumulative net book value of investors' equity in, and outstanding loans to, their foreign affiliates, in which each investor owns at least 10 percent of the voting securities, or an equivalent interest. Net book value in this context refers to claims of U.S. parent companies against subsidiary assets on a historical cost basis. It neither includes funds borrowed from foreign lenders, nor does it represent current cost or current market value of those or any other assets controlled by these affiliates.

Estimates of the cumulative value of the FDI stock or position are made on a current basis by measuring capital flows to and from these affiliated organizations. They are periodically adjusted with information from benchmark surveys taken every five to eleven years to get an update on the actual position. The surveys include changes in the dollar value of the investment stock resulting from inflation, exchange rate changes, new accounting methods, taxes, or a whole range of other factors, which are

TABLE 1.10. Area Share in Worldwide Investments by U.S. Industries

CANADA (Percentages)

	1950	1957	1970	1980	1990
All Industries	30.4	34.5	27.8	20.9	16.2
Petroleum	12.3	22.3	22.0	23.0	19.8
Manufacturing	49.5	49.0	28.9	21.3	19.7
Food	47.0	44.2	31.1	22.4	16.3
Chemicals	38.7	47.0	22.5	18.0	16.1
Primary Metals	64.7	71.3	28.1	26.0	25.7
Nonelectric Mach.	48.5	35.3	N/A	11.5	9.8
Elec. Equip.	36.4	45.1	N/A	17.9	11.8
Trans. Equip.	33.0	33.1	32.6	29.0	33.4
Other	62.0	58.4	37.8	26.2	26.4
Trade	31.5	29.9	18.7	15.1	12.3
Finance, Insurance, and Real Estate	73.6	58.8	37.9	22.4	10.7
Banking	N/A	N/A	N/A	N/A	5.3
Mining	29.6	36.2	47.6	45.2	N/A

LATIN AMERICA (Percentages)

	1950	1957	1970	1980	1990
All Industries	41.8	31.7	17.2	18.0	16.5
Petroleum	38.4	33.1	13.7	9.2	8.0
Manufacturing	20.4	16.0	14.6	16.3	13.9
Food	32.7	27.8	17.6	20.5	19.2
Chemicals	40.0	24.2	19.2	19.0	12.9
Primary Metals	5.7	6.4	18.3	21.8	16.0
Nonelectric Mach.	3.1	5.6	N/A	8.6	10.1
Elec. Equip.	18.8	18.6	N/A	13.9	10.0
Trans. Equip.	17.1	11.1	12.2	15.4	17.5
Other	13.3	9.0	16.2	18.0	15.0
Trade	32.2	34.3	18.3	15.0	6.2
Finance, Insurance, and Real Estate	16.7	27.8	19.6	36.6	27.6
Banking	N/A	N/A	N/A	34.2	28.9
Mining	59.0	52.2	31.7	24.1	N/A

not captured by capital flow statistics alone. It is worth noting that U.S. balance of payment (BOP) flow data do also include reinvested earnings, which is not a common practice for all nations, and whose implications will be discussed later on.

TABLE 1.10 (continued)

L.A. REPUBLIC (Percentages)

	1950	1957	1970	1980	1990
All Industries	37.6	29.2	14.7	12.3	10.1
Petroleum	36.4	29.8	11.7	6.4	5.6
Manufacturing	20.3	15.9	13.6	15.8	13.4
Food	32.7	27.7	17.1	18.5	18.9
Chemicals	40.0	23.9	17.1	18.0	12.1
Primary Metals	5.7	6.4	N/A	N/A	12.5
Nonelectric Mach.	3.1	5.6	N/A	8.6	10.0
Elec. Equip.	20.4	18.6	N/A	13.6	9.8
Trans. Equip.	17.1	11.2	12.2	15.4	9.7
Other	19.0	17.0	N/A	N/A	14.6
Trade	31.8	32.7	15.5	11.0	3.9
Finance, Insurance, and Real Estate	16.7	16.3	15.6	9.9	10.0
Banking	N/A	N/A	N/A	11.7	6.4
Mining	55.6	47.1	23.4	19.4	N/A

CARIBBEAN (Percentages)

	1950	1957	1970	1980	1990
All Industries	N/A	N/A	N/A	N/A	6.5
Petroleum	N/A	N/A	N/A	N/A	2.3
Manufacturing	N/A	N/A	N/A	N/A	0.3
Food	N/A	N/A	N/A	N/A	0.3
Chemicals	N/A	N/A	N/A	N/A	0.8
Primary Metals	N/A	N/A	N/A	N/A	N/A
Nonelectric Mach.	N/A	N/A	N/A	N/A	N/A
Elec. Equip.	N/A	N/A	N/A	N/A	0.1
Trans. Equip.	N/A	N/A	N/A	N/A	nil
Other	N/A	N/A	N/A	N/A	N/A
Trade	N/A	N/A	N/A	N/A	2.4
Finance, Insurance, and Real Estate	N/A	N/A	N/A	N/A	17.5
Banking	N/A	N/A	N/A	22.5	22.4
Mining	N/A	N/A	N/A	N/A	N/A

The definition evolved over the period covered by this report which leaves data shown not always entirely comparable. From 1950 to 1961, direct investment ownership was defined on the basis of percentage control over voting stock in foreign enterprises by: (1) a single U.S. investor (including an associated group of investors) holding at least 25 percent of

EUROPE (Percentages)

	1950	1957	1970	1980	1990
All Industries	15.5	16.3	33.5	44.8	49.9
Petroleum	12.9	13.8	27.7	42.2	40.3
Manufacturing	25.4	27.4	44.5	50.7	50.2
Food	13.3	20.6	38.3	45.5	50.3
Chemicals	14.4	23.1	41.8	50.6	52.8
Primary Metals	28.8	18.9	44.1	40.3	46.7
Nonelectric Mach.	41.7	52.6	N/A	66.6	63.5
Elec. Equip.	39.5	29.3	N/A	50.3	37.4
Trans. Equip.	39.6	39.5	44.3	48.1	31.4
Other	14.2	18.2	36.9	45.8	42.5
Trade	24.4	26.0	46.3	54.4	59.2
Finance, Insurance, and Real Estate	8.7	7.1	29.3	36.0	55.4
Banking	N/A	N/A	N/A	44.9	44.4
Mining	2.7	2.3	0.6	0.5	N/A

ASIA (Percentages)

	1950	1957	1970	1980	1990
All Industries	8.7	8.2	7.0	7.8	10.8
Petroleum	22.7	16.8	13.8	N/A	19.6
Manufacturing	1.6	2.4	5.0	6.5	12.2
Food	N/A	2.1	5.3	5.1	7.4
Chemicals	N/A	2.9	N/A	7.6	11.4
Primary Metals	N/A	2.1	2.4	3.4	4.8
Nonelectric Mach.	N/A	1.6	N/A	8.7	14.5
Elec. Equip.	N/A	1.6	N/A	13.7	38.7
Trans. Equip.	N/A	1.9	N/A	3.2	6.7
Other	N/A	3.3	N/A	2.6	7.1
Trade	6.4	5.2	5.1	9.3	17.8
Finance, Insurance, and Real Estate	N/A	2.9	1.2	3.3	5.0
Banking	N/A	N/A	N/A	N/A	15.9
Mining	1.9	1.4	N/A	N/A	N/A

the voting stock or (2) collective ownership of at least 50 percent of the voting interest in a publicly held business in which no single U.S. investor owned as much as 25 percent.

In 1962, this definition was expanded to include ownership interests of 10 percent in the voting stock of foreign companies. Share ownership of

TABLE 1.10 (continued)

AFRICA (Percentages)

	1950	1957	1970	1980	1990
All Industries	3.0	2.6	4.2	2.9	0.8
Petroleum	N/A	3.0	N/A	N/A	3.8
Manufacturing	1.4	1.3	1.6	1.7	0.5
Food	N/A	1.4	N/A	2.1	N/A
Chemicals	N/A	0.9	2.0	1.8	0.5
Primary Metals	N/A	0.5	N/A	3.7	1.5
Nonelectric Mach.	N/A	1.8	N/A	1.2	0.5
Elec. Equip.	N/A	0.7	N/A	1.6	0.3
Trans. Equip.	N/A	N/A	N/A	N/A	0.2
Other	N/A	0.3	1.8	N/A	N/A
Trade	3.1	2.6	2.0	N/A	0.3
Finance, Insurance, and Real Estate	0.7	2.3	0.9	0.7	0.2
Banking	N/A	N/A	N/A	N/A	0.5
Mining	5.7	7.7	N/A	9.2	N/A

OCEANIA (Percentages)

	1950	1957	1970	1980	1990
All Industries	1.9	2.5	4.4	3.8	4.2
Petroleum	N/A	N/A	N/A	N/A	5.9
Manufacturing	2.8	3.9	5.3	3.5	3.4
Food	N/A	3.9	N/A	4.4	6.1
Chemicals	N/A	2.0	7.0	3.0	6.0
Primary Metals	N/A	0.9	N/A	4.8	3.4
Nonelectric Mach.	N/A	2.8	N/A	3.3	1.7
Elec. Equip.	N/A	4.7	N/A	2.5	1.9
Trans. Equip.	N/A	12.1	N/A	N/A	1.3
Other	N/A	1.2	N/A	N/A	3.3
Trade	2.4	2.0	2.5	N/A	4.1
Finance, Insurance, and Real Estate	N/A	0.8	N/A	2.5	1.3
Banking	N/A	N/A	N/A	N/A	5.3
Mining	1.0	0.9	N/A	19.1	N/A

less than 10 percent is considered to represent portfolio investment. Revised again in 1977, the definition determined that from that year forward, only investors with a single 10 percent interest are considered for inclusion under foreign direct investment. The interpretation of "single person" allows the inclusion of a group of associated investors, each of which holds less than 10 percent but, in the aggregate, meets the 10 percent limit. Independent investors with a share of less than 10 percent each are not included, even though in the aggregate they exceed 10 percent of the voting stock. The rationale for this position is not completely clear. Corporate laws in many countries assign minority holdings over 25 percent legal significance by giving them "blocking" powers. Holdings under that limit do not exercise any legal control–the key criterion for the U.S. definition–which makes it difficult to see the justification for this step. This conceptual difficulty may have been the reason for introducing a technical refinement through the establishment of three distinct affiliate categories in the 1966 census:

a. "Associated" subsidiaries in which a single parent holds at least a 10, but less than 25 percent, ownership. Also, the combined ownership of all U.S. investors must be less than 25 percent.
b. "Allied" affiliates are those where combined U.S. ownership exceeds 25 percent. It includes the third and next class of affiliates:
c. "Majority-owned" foreign affiliates (Mofas for short), which were permanently established. Table 1.12 reveals a strong preference of U.S. parents for majority control (1966 FDI Census, p. 3).

The terms "associated" and "allied" are no longer used. Instead, subsidiaries as discussed in the following are now simply referred to as "nonbank affiliates," and may be broken down into all affiliates and Mofas, which is a very practical division for all purposes.

A final change introduced in the 1982 census concerned the time frame which served as the basis for census reports. Up to that time, all FDI data were collected on a basis of or close to a calendar year, whereas affiliates now were permitted to also report on a fiscal year basis. It was established that 59.8 percent of the affiliates and 63.0 percent of the parents operated on a calendar year basis. Their share of assets was 80 percent, and 90 percent and for sales, 74 percent and 78 percent respectively (1982 FDI census, p. 6).

NUMBER OF PARENT COMPANIES
AND THEIR FOREIGN SUBSIDIARIES

Numbers on parent companies and their foreign subsidiaries are available only for the census years 1950, 1957, 1966, 1977, 1982, and 1989. In interpreting the respective growth patterns for both, and the affiliates in particular, it is well to keep in mind the definitional changes of foreign direct investments introduced in 1961 as discussed above. The inclusion of

TABLE 1.11. Industry Share of Total U.S. Foreign Direct Investments by Area

CANADA (Percentages)

	1950	1957	1970	1980	1990
All Industries	100	100	100	100	100
Petroleum	12	23	21	24	15
Manufacturing	53	45	43	42	48
Food	6	4	4	4	4
Chemicals	6	7	6	8	9
Primary Metals	7	8	3	4	4
Nonelectric Mach.	6	4	N/A	4	4
Elec. Equip.	4	4	N/A	7	3
Trans. Equip.	4	5	8	8	10
Other	20	14	13	12	14
Trade	7	6	6	9	8
Finance, Insurance, and Real Estate	9	6	13	14	17
Banking	N/A	N/A	N/A	N/A	2
Mining	9	10	12	7	N/A

LATIN AMERICA (Percentages)

	1950	1957	1970	1980	1990
All Industries	100	100	100	100	100
Petroleum	29	37	21	11	6
Manufacturing	16	16	35	38	33
Food	3	2	4	4	4
Chemicals	4	4	9	9	7
Primary Metals	nil	1	3	4	2
Nonelectric Mach.	nil	1	N/A	4	4
Elec. Equip.	2	2	N/A	3	2
Trans. Equip.	2	2	5	5	5
Other	3	2	9	9	8
Trade	5	7	9	10	4
Finance, Insurance, and Real Estate	1	3	11	26	43
Banking	N/A	N/A	N/A	6	8
Mining	13	15	13	4	N/A

holdings between 10 to 25 percent in the investment position must be at least partially responsible for the very strong surge in the numbers between 1957 and 1966, but published data do not permit a discussion of this particular point.

L.A. REPUBLIC (Percentages)

	1950	1957	1970	1980	1990
All Industries	100	100	100	100	100
Petroleum	28	36	21	12	7
Manufacturing	18	17	38	53	53
Food	4	3	4	6	7
Chemicals	5	4	9	13	11
Primary Metals	1	1	N/A	N/A	3
Nonelectric Mach.	nil	1	N/A	5	7
Elec. Equip.	2	2	N/A	4	4
Trans. Equip.	2	2	6	7	9
Other	5	5	N/A	N/A	13
Trade	5	7	9	11	4
Finance, Insurance, and Real Estate	2	2	10	10	25
Banking	N/A	N/A	N/A	5	3
Mining	14	15	11	5	N/A

CARIBBEAN (Percentages)

	1950	1957	1970	1980	1990
All Industries	100	100	100	100	100
Petroleum	53	48	21	10	4
Manufacturing	1	2	17	4	3
Food	N/A	N/A	1	1	nil
Chemicals	N/A	N/A	6	1	1
Primary Metals	N/A	N/A	N/A	N/A	nil
Nonelectric Mach.	N/A	N/A	N/A	N/A	N/A
Elec. Equip.	N/A	N/A	N/A	nil	nil
Trans. Equip.	N/A	N/A	N/A	N/A	nil
Other	N/A	N/A	N/A	N/A	nil
Trade	2	4	9	8	4
Finance, Insurance, and Real Estate	N/A	N/A	16	59	69
Banking	N/A	N/A	N/A	28	17
Mining	29	19	24	3	N/A

While the term "Mofas" was officially introduced by the 1966 census, their existence has been documented from 1957 onward, with some startling fluctuations in their numbers. Although Mofas more than doubled between 1957 and 1966 from 9,672 to 20,544, they suffered an unexplained and drastic setback to 11,941 Mofas in the 1977 survey, only to recover to 15,654 by 1989. The strong dip in Mofa numbers in the 1977

TABLE 1.11 (continued)

EUROPE (Percentages)

	1950	1957	1970	1980	1990
All Industries	100	100	100	100	100
Petroleum	25	24	21	21	10
Manufacturing	54	53	55	47	40
Food	4	4	4	4	4
Chemicals	4	8	10	10	9
Primary Metals	6	4	4	3	2
Nonelectric Mach.	10	12	N/A	11	9
Elec. Equip.	9	5	N/A	4	3
Trans. Equip.	11	11	9	6	4
Other	9	9	11	9	8
Trade	11	10	11	15	12
Finance, Insurance, and Real Estate	2	1	8	10	28
Banking	N/A	N/A	N/A	3	4
Mining	2	1	nil	nil	N/A

ASIA (Percentages)

	1950	1957	1970	1980	1990
All Industries	100	100	100	100	100
Petroleum	75	73	51	N/A	26
Manufacturing	6	9	30	34	42
Food	N/A	1	3	3	2
Chemicals	N/A	2	N/A	9	9
Primary Metals	N/A	1	1	1	1
Nonelectric Mach.	N/A	1	N/A	8	9
Elec. Equip.	N/A	1	N/A	6	12
Trans. Equip.	N/A	2	N/A	2	3
Other	N/A	3	N/A	3	5
Trade	5	4	6	14	16
Finance, Insurance, and Real Estate	N/A	1	2	5	11
Banking	N/A	N/A	N/A	N/A	7
Mining	2	1	N/A	N/A	N/A

survey is not observed for all affiliates, whose number actually increased between those same years. Even when allowing some adjustments for banking affiliates included in the 1957 to 1966 period versus only nonbank Mofas of all parents in the years 1977 to 1982, this drop cannot be reconciled because banking affiliates do not account for more than 1,100 units

AFRICA (Percentages)

	1950	1957	1970	1980	1990
All Industries	100	100	100	100	100
Petroleum	N/A	41	N/A	N/A	56
Manufacturing	16	16	16	25	23
Food	N/A	2	N/A	3	N/A
Chemicals	N/A	2	4	6	6
Primary Metals	N/A	1	N/A	4	4
Nonelectric Mach.	N/A	3	N/A	3	4
Elec. Equip.	N/A	1	N/A	2	1
Trans. Equip.	N/A	N/A	N/A	N/A	1
Other	N/A	1	4	N/A	3
Trade	16	6	4	N/A	4
Finance, Insurance, and Real Estate	7	3	2	3	6
Banking	N/A	N/A	N/A	N/A	3
Mining	18	27	N/A	10	N/A

OCEANIA (Percentages)

	1950	1957	1970	1980	1990
All Industries	100	100	100	100	100
Petroleum	N/A	N/A	N/A	N/A	17
Manufacturing	47	50	50	38	32
Food	N/A	4	N/A	4	5
Chemicals	N/A	4	12	7	12
Primary Metals	N/A	1	N/A	4	2
Nonelectric Mach.	N/A	4	N/A	6	3
Elec. Equip.	N/A	5	N/A	2	2
Trans. Equip.	N/A	23	N/A	N/A	1
Other	N/A	4	N/A	N/A	7
Trade	8	5	5	N/A	10
Finance, Insurance, and Real Estate	N/A	1	N/A	8	8
Banking	N/A	N/A	N/A	N/A	6
Mining	5	3	N/A	16	N/A

Sources: See Table 1.6.

in total for the two latest surveys, and are not likely to ever exceed numbers achieved in earlier years.

Mofa share in total U.S. FDI has fluctuated slightly over most of the study period, but eventually dropped below 90 percent according to data

TABLE 1.12. Breakdown of U.S Foreign Direct Investment by Affiliate Type ($ million)

Year	Total Investment Position	Nonbank Mofas of Nonbank Parents	Mofa Share of Total Stock
1950	$11,788	N/A	95.0e
1957	25,394	$23,949	94.3
1966	51,792	48,005	92.7
1977	145,990	128,156	90.5
1982	207,320	185,259	94.0
1989	381,781	333,688	87.4

Note: e = estimate.

Sources: FDI census data: 1950, p. 2; 1957, p. 101; 1966, pp. 29, 44; 1977, p. 20; 1982, p. 27; 1989, p. M-25.

shown in Table 1.12. This information seems to contradict the picture conveyed by the data on affiliate numbers or, at least, is difficult to reconcile.

A significant break in the number of parents and total affiliates alike occurred between 1977 and 1989. Parents dropped from a high of 3,540 in 1977 to 2,378 in 1982, and dropped further to 2,272 in 1989, a 36 percent decline that put their numbers below the 1950 level. It coincided with a 23 percent drop in affiliate numbers from 24,666 in 1977 to 18,899 in 1989, and a 9 percent constriction in total investments between 1977 and 1982. While the drop in the number of affiliates and parents is real, the reduction in investment stock stems partly from new accounting principles and practices as explained previously. It proved to have only a temporary effect, as investments have strongly recovered since then.

The number of parents is surprisingly small in view of the enormous volume invested abroad. Representing an estimated 2 percent of all U.S. businesses with more than 100 employees, they make up in financial weight what they lack in numbers. The decline in both parent and affiliate numbers plus the increase in actual investments overseas translates into a massive concentration of economic power in the hands of fewer and fewer companies. The average parent had eight affiliates in 1982 and 1989 versus three during the 1950s. Each affiliate averaged 372 (1982) and 357 (1989) employees versus 114 in 1957, owned assets worth $108.8 million (1989) versus $9.6 million in 1950, accounted for $21.5 and $20.2 million of total FDI capital accumulated in 1982 and 1989 versus $1.6 million in 1950, and produced twenty times more in after-tax profits than it did in the beginning. The respective figures are: $231,400 (1950), $2.0 million (1982), and $4.6 million (1989). In short, with each affiliate employing three times the number of people over four decades, each increased assets and profits more than tenfold (see Table 1.13).

In 1957, 45 companies (1.6 percent of all parent companies) shared 57 percent of the total FDI stock. While similar data are unavailable for the other census years, interim studies by the Department of Commerce estimated that in 1966, only 298 multinationals (9 percent of all parents) accounted for no less than 64 percent of all sales by affiliates operating in overseas markets (*SOCB*, January 1973, p. 39).

INTERNATIONAL COMPARABILITY
OF FDI DATA

Nations engaging in FDI measure its scope in different ways. Often they do not follow the American practice of showing reinvested earnings as concurrent BOP flow items on the income side of the current account and on the outflow side of the capital account. In addition, some countries do not even include retained earnings in their stock estimates at all. Belgium-Luxemburg, France, Germany, Iceland, Italy, Japan, and Spain are representative examples of this school of thought (OECD, 1993 Yearbook, p. 10). All of this not only complicates the comparability of such data among countries, it can also lead to biased conclusions unless full compatibility of the reporting practices is assured.

A beautiful illustration of this point is offered by Japan. A Japanese source puts the 1992 FDI position at $387 billion, whereas the OECD shows only $248 billion for the same year. The discrepancy arises from the OECD practice of counting only cumulative capital flows shown in national BOP statistics converted at year-end exchange rates into dollars. The Japanese use accumulated values of approvals and notifications published by the Ministry of Finance (OECD, *International Direct Investment Statistics Yearbook 1994*, p. 16. Japan 1994, An International Comparison, p. 54).

In the U.S. case, adoption of such accounting practices would cause the 1994 FDI position to shrink by roughly 65 percent, from $612 billion to only $217 billion, the cumulative equity and debt flow for the 1950 to 1994 period (see Table 2.2). Simultaneously, receipts of FDI income and capital outflows registered in the BOP would be reduced by $357 billion, the cumulative reinvestment volume for the same period. In addition, all of this would shatter the apparently positive U.S. service account balances portrayed by official statistics, magnifying the perennial current account problems for the United States. For the capital account, the reduction in flows would be less serious, but would sharply lower the U.S. profile in

TABLE 1.13. Number of Foreign Direct Investment Parents and Affiliates

Year	1950	1957	1966	1977	1982	1989
Parents Total	2,363	2,812	3,354	3,540	2,245	2,272
Bank Parent	N/A	N/A	N/A	111	133	89
Nonbank Parents	N/A	N/A	N/A	3,429	2,138	2,183
Affiliates Total	7,645	10,272	23,120	24,666	18,339	18,889
of Bank Parents	N/A	N/A	N/A	968	1,061	1,027
of Nonbank Parents	N/A	N/A	N/A	23,698	17,278	17,872
Mofas	N/A	9,672	20,544	11,941	14,589	15,654
of Bank Parents	N/A	N/A	N/A	32	114	273
of Nonbank Parents	N/A	N/A	N/A	11,909	14,475	15,381
Mofa % of Affiliates	N/A	94.2%	88.9%	48.4%	79.6%	82.8%
Affiliates/Parent	3.1	3.7	6.9	7.0	8.2	8.3
Number of Affiliates by Industry						
Manufacturing	2,501	3,481	9,300	9,712	7,005	7,552
Petroleum	621	1,090	1,865	1,933	1,801	1,443
Trade	1,846	2,268	4,310	5,799	3,976	4,019
Finance, Insurance, and Real Estate	550	783	1,814	2,466	2,423	2,564
Trans., Utilities, and Communications	550	602	1,016	613	348	328
Mining	269	336	485	292	180	142
Banks	N/A	N/A	N/A	884	882	729
Services	N/A	N/A	N/A	2,300	1,336	1,625
Other	1,120	1,538	4,330	687	665	825

Sources: FDI census data: 1950, pp. 4, 45; 1957, pp. 74, 98-102; 1966, pp. 234-5; 1977, pp. 2, 10-1, 20; 1982, pp. 13-4, 27; 1989, pp. M-25, 4.

actual world exports of capital (see Tables 2.2 and 2.3). Conversely, applying the U.S. FDI accounting system to all those nations that presently do not share the U.S. methodology would definitely lead to a sizeable downscaling of the U.S. role in global FDI, which is predominantly financed from reinvestments. For the purpose of this discussion, it is sufficient to point out that international FDI accounting ranges from the inclusion of capital flows exclusive of reinvestments, to the much more complex American practice of establishing the position estimate on such diverse factors as actual capital flows, reinvestments, and various kinds of valuation adjustments explained in Table 2.7. Other countries may follow a system of calculation that falls anywhere in between these extremes.

Chapter 2

FDI-Related Capital Flows
in the U.S. Balance of Payments

GENERAL COMMENTS

Foreign direct investment activities lead to a number of two-way fund flows across the borders of investor nations which are traced in their balance of payments (BOP). Some of them represent capital transfers, some relate to income derived from those foreign investments, while still others are trade related. Depending on their origin or purpose, they lead to entries in the capital account or the current account, the latter being subdivided into a service and trade section. These distinctly different flow components are discussed under three separate headings in the following:

  a. Capital flows which directly determine the overseas investment position. They are customarily recorded in the capital account proper. In U.S. practice they also include reinvestments, which for technical reasons appear again as an offsetting entry in the services account of the BOP's current account (Chapter 2).
  b. Income type flows derived from the investment stock including reinvestments, which are found exclusively in the services part of the current account (Chapter 3).
  c. Trade flows comprising exports and imports of merchandise relating to all FDI partners including parents, affiliates, and their third-party customers or suppliers (Chapter 4).

CAPITAL FLOWS

In U.S. accounting practice, three distinctly separate fund flows determine the FDI volume, rate of growth, and direction. Only the first one involves actual fund flows across international borders, and thus represents a bona fide entry in the capital account of the country's BOP. They are:

1. Flows of equity and debt capital. Outflows of both forms of capital add to the country's outward investment position, while inflows or capital repatriation lead to its reduction. Often the opposing flows are shown in their net form. Net outflows of equity capital, that is, outflows of ownership capital from parents to their foreign affiliates in excess of repatriated funds or inflows, add to the FDI equity stock held overseas, while net inflows reduce the same. Net flows of debt capital refers to all flows of intercompany loans which do not affect the parents' equity position in their affiliates. Again, net means: parents' payments minus parents' receipts. Similar to the equity capital situation, net outflows add to the FDI position while net repatriations detract from the FDI position.

2. Reinvested or retained earnings increase the direct investment stock. Unlike equity and debt flows, they do not represent actual capital flows even though some countries, including the United States, treat them as such. As their name implies, they are profits that were not paid out to investors but stay in the country where they were generated, and are automatically added to the owner country's FDI position. In the U.S. BOP, they appear as an offsetting double entry, once as income (inflow) in the current account, and then as a capital export (outflow) in the capital account. Both are labeled "reinvested earnings." Until 1982, they were narrowly defined as:

   > *Reinvested earnings are the total earnings (U.S. parent equity in the net income after foreign income taxes) of incorporated affiliates less gross dividends (dividends declared before deduction of foreign withholding taxes) on common and preferred stock held by the parent (SOCB, August 1982, p. 18).*

   This definition denied branch earnings (of unincorporated affiliates) a role in the formation of investment stock via reinvestments, because it was always assumed that branch earnings flow totally into their parents' pockets. Once this position had proven to be untenable, it was abandoned, and branch earnings are now treated like those from incorporated affiliates: they are divided into remitted and reinvested earnings. Remitted funds from both subsidiary categories are furthermore split into payments for the use of equity capital under the name of dividends or, sometimes, branch earnings and payments for the use of intercompany debt capital listed as interests (1982 FDI census, p. 22).

3. Valuation adjustments, which include all changes in the investment position not stemming from any of the above components. They are

derived, generally speaking, from very diverse factors best described by the following quotation.

> *For example, they include differences between the proceeds from and book value of affiliates that are sold or liquidated; differences between the purchase price and book value of affiliates that are acquired by U.S. parents; and write-offs resulting from uncompensated expropriations of affiliates. Valuation adjustments may also arise from reclassification of investments from (to) direct investments to (from) portfolio investments; revisions made in conjunction with benchmarking, such as the correction of errors or changes in definition, and revaluations of affiliate assets. For individual areas and industries, they include reclassification of investments between areas and industries. Valuation adjustments were a relatively small component of the change in the position in most years. However, they were quite large in the benchmark years, 1957 and 1966, and in 1960, when the expropriated investments in Cuba were removed from the position; the adjustments were negative in all three years. Relatively large negative adjustments were also made for 1962 and 1972; these adjustments resulted from the reclassification of several Canadian investments from direct to portfolio investments. The largest positive adjustments were made for 1978, when several affiliates were sold for more than their book value, and when, partly as a byproduct of the 1977 benchmark survey, several previously unreported affiliates were included in the position for the first time.* (SOCB, February, 1981, pp. 42, 43)

These direct valuation adjustments of the investment stock are not to be confused with adjustments in capital flow estimates based on transaction and translation gains/losses. Translation gains/losses arise when positions on affiliate balance sheets expressed in foreign currency are periodically translated into U.S. dollars. Valuation changes arising from currency fluctuations lead to gains or losses which are not a result of regular business transactions. They are accounting income that is not subject to local taxation and, for that matter, cannot lead to foreign tax credits or liabilities. Gains established by these accounting procedures also cannot be remitted as actual profits and thus were added to reinvested earnings for the period between 1982 and 1989. Losses, on the other hand, were deducted from them.

Transaction gains/losses arise when assets are actually sold at prices different from book values, or when standard exchange rates used by the company differ from market rates at the time of the transaction. Gains establish taxable income and may be remitted, while losses lead to tax credits.

In order to appreciate the complexity of this subject, another quotation is added reflecting the attempts by government statisticians to come to grips with the vexing problem of currency translations. The subject is the 1982 survey, but the comments apply to later accounting periods as well. To quote:

Use of generally accepted accounting principles. In the benchmark survey data were required to be reported as they would have been for purposes of preparing stockholders' reports, rather than for tax or other purposes. Thus, U.S. generally accepted accounting principles (GAAP) were followed unless otherwise indicated by the survey instructions. The survey instructions departed from GAAP in cases where the departure would have resulted in data that were conceptually or analytically more useful or appropriate for direct investment purposes. This was the case, for example, with the unique consolidation rules discussed above for affiliates and for U.S. parents.

Exchange gains and losses and translation adjustments. Monetary amounts were reported to BEA (Bureau of Economic Analysis) in U.S. dollars. The report forms specified that, when a foreign affiliate's assets, liabilities, revenues, and expenses were denominated or measured on the affiliate's financial statement in a foreign currency, they must be translated into dollars using GAAP. Under GAAP, either Financial Accounting Standards Board Statement No.8 or 52 (FASB 8 or 52) could be used to translate 1982 data (GAAP required companies to use FASB 52 for fiscal years beginning on or after December 15, 1982. For earlier years, use of FASB 52 was encouraged but not required; thus, for 1982, some companies had switched to FASB 52 while others continued to use FASB 8).

Under FASB 8, the balance sheet is divided into monetary and nonmonetary accounts. Monetary accounts, which consist of cash and items settled in cash, are translated at current exchange rates, that is, at rates in effect on the balance sheet date. Nonmonetary accounts are translated at historical exchange rates, that is, at rates in effect when the asset was acquired or liability incurred. Most income statements are translated at weighted-average exchange rates for the period, as a proxy for using the rate in effect on the date each revenue or expense transaction occurred; however, revenues and expenses related to non-monetary assets or liabilities, such as depreciation, are translated at historical exchange rates. Under FASB 8, the entire effect of changes in exchange rates on affiliates' balance sheets and income statements is included in affiliates' net income.

Under FASB 52, all assets, liabilities, revenues, and expenses are translated at current exchange rates. For assets and liabilities, the exchange rate at the balance sheet date is used. For revenues and expenses, weighted average exchange rates for the period are used. Under FASB 52, gains and losses resulting from translating foreign currency-denominated assets, liabilities, revenues, and expenses into the affiliates' principal, or functional, currency at exchange rates that differ from those used in the prior period are included in net income. Also included in the net income are gains and losses from translating foreign affiliates' income statements from their functional currency into U.S. dollars at exchange rates different from those in the prior period. Most other gains and losses, whether realized or unrealized, are excluded from affiliates' net income and, instead, are taken directly to a separate component of owner's equity, entitled "translation adjustments." Gains and losses taken directly to the translation adjustment account include gains and losses resulting from translating opening balances for foreign affiliates' assets and liabilities at exchange rates different from those for closing balances, and from foreign currency transactions that hedge the net investment in a foreign affiliate against changes in exchange rates. For a more complete description of translation procedures, refer to FASB 8 and FASB 52.

In this publication, the treatment of exchange gains and losses and translation adjustments in the income statements of foreign affiliates is as reported in the benchmark survey. Thus, for the companies that used FASB 8, all effects of exchange rate changes on affiliates' financial statements are included in affiliates' net income, whereas, for companies that used FASB 52, only a portion of those effects are included. The effects of exchange rate changes that are not included in net income under FASB 52 were reported in the benchmark survey, together with certain extraordinary gains and losses, as a separate item, outside the income statement. That item, "capital gains/losses not included in income," is shown as an addendum to the income statements of foreign affiliates in tables . . . of this publication.

For balance of payments purposes, all exchange gains and losses and translation adjustments are included in direct investment income, even though they may be excluded from net income for income statement purposes. Direct investment income is intended to reflect all the benefits a U.S. parent receives from its investments in affiliates, whether in form of ordinary income, extraordinary income, or other income-type items. Thus, exchange gains and losses, translation adjustments, and extraordinary gains and losses that are excluded from affiliates' reported net income for income statement purposes are added to reported net income by DX in computing direct investment income for balance of payment purposes.

In the 1977 benchmark survey, all companies had to translate their financial statements in accordance with FASB 8, because FASB 52 had not yet been instituted. Thus, in that survey, all exchange gains and losses were included in net income for income statement purposes, as well as in direct investment income for balance of payment purposes.

For companies that switched from FASB 8 to FASB 52 during 1982, income statement accounts were calculated in conformance with FASB 52. In the balance sheet, the opening balances were translated based upon FASB 8 and the closing balances were translated based upon FASB 52. The one-time revaluation of U.S. parents' equity in their foreign affiliates that resulted from the switch is considered to be a valuation adjustment to the direct investment position and, therefore, is excluded from direct investment income and capital flows. (1982 FDI census, p. 5)

The 1982 change in accounting rules was in effect until 1990 when in a sharp reversal of standing policy, all translation gains or losses were completely removed from income type and capital flow accounts and added to the valuation adjustments of the FDI position. It led to drastic retroactive alignments in the following accounts: income, capital outflows, and reinvestments. All three appear now in two substantially different versions for the time period 1982 to 1989, and the student of the subject matter does well to understand the reasons for their existence. Data incorporated in this study reflect the most recent change which is best paraphrased by this quotation:

As part of the annual revision of the U.S. international transactions accounts in June 1990, capital gains/losses associated with currency translation adjustments for U.S. direct investment abroad have been removed from direct investment income and from the reinvested earnings component of capital outflows. These gains/losses which arise because of changes from the end of one accounting period to the next in exchange rates applied in translating affiliates' assets and liabilities from foreign currencies into dollars, are now classified as valuation adjustments to the direct investment position. The change in the direct investment position is not affected because translation adjustments have been reclassified from one component of the change (capital outflows) to another (valuation adjustments). (SOCB, August 1990, p. 57)

The net flows of equity and intercompany debt capital were called "net capital outflows" during the 1950s and 1960s before being renamed "equity and intercompany account outflows." Under either heading, the flows were inseparably combined until the end of 1981. Starting with 1982, data details became available for each account separately. The entries are designated as positive positions as long as they add to the foreign direct investment stock. A minus sign preceding a fund outflow entry signifies a net capital inflow into parent accounts which reduces the investment stock. This is contrary to generally accepted BOP accounting practices where minus signs represent outward fund flows and plus signs fund inflows.

Government statistics combine "equity and intercompany account out-flows" with reinvested earnings to form the new account "capital out-flows" for a full accounting of the three factors bearing on the development of the investment position.

The division of actual capital outflows from the United States into an equity and debt category is carried through to capital inflows upon repatriation of capital. The equity portion of the reverse capital flows now includes the former reinvested earnings which lose their identity quite unceremoniously after their fusion with the equity account.

Balance of payment flows and value adjustments are the basic factors used in establishing the FDI stock estimate according to the formula: position at beginning of a year plus/minus net capital flows and valuation adjustments establish the position for the end of that year which serves also as the starting position for the following year. However, despite very meticulous accounting efforts, it is impossible to keep track of all elements affecting the position, and it becomes necessary to periodically correct the estimates by conducting special benchmark surveys. For the time period covered by this study, such census surveys were undertaken in 1950, 1957, 1966, 1977, 1982, and 1989.

A major element affecting the accuracy of such annual estimates are exchange rate fluctuations as mentioned previously. In and by themselves, the market oscillations of the dollar value may be of more financial consequence than many investment and marketing decisions made in executive suites. Illustrating this point is the following quote:

Second, the sharp depreciation of the dollar against major currencies in 1985 resulted in capital gains of $4.9 billion, primarily from *translating affiliate financial statements from foreign currencies into dollars. (SOCB, June 1986, p. 30)*

It might be added that these $4.9 billion amounted to 28 percent of the total net capital outflow from the United States for the year 1985. Since then, the amounts have increased substantially, establishing valuation adjustments as a major source of financing.

SCOPE OF DIRECT INVESTMENT FLOWS

Both major components of direct investment–reinvested earnings and net capital flows from the United States–have synergistically propelled the FDI stock to higher levels for each year until and including 1981. In 1982, this unbroken trend was disrupted, mainly under the influence of the 1977 change in accounting procedures for the foreign borrowing activities of American finance affiliates located in the Netherlands Antilles. Contrary to the previous practice, borrowed funds were treated as repatriated FDI capital, which caused a serious, if only temporary, reversal in the otherwise positive outflows of equity and debt capital from the United States (*International Direct Investment*, 1984, pp. 16, 38).

More important, it led to a defacto reduction in the U.S. FDI position. Repayment of these funds later on generated exactly the opposite effect by accelerating the fund outflows and adding to the FDI position. Available statistics make it possible to give an impression of the size and impact of these procedural changes. The development in the parent payables account is the pivotal information to focus on, as it is the decisive factor in the movement of the net debt position, and indirectly, the FDI position.

Placing the data into perspective, the cumulative $42 billion borrowed by 1984 almost equalled the entire net capital outflow from parent companies during the 1970s ($43.5 billion). Any changes in this account, or the accounting process alone, can and does affect the overall U.S. FDI position in a significant way. This becomes visible in the data on capital flows and the overall FDI position. As the Netherlands Antillean position is being worked down, mainly on account of parent net debt reduction, both overall U.S. flow and position statistics have begun to grow rapidly. The gradual decline in the Netherlands Antilles investment position from a peak of $–25 billion in 1984 to $–4.7 (1990), $–5.3 (1991), $–2.2 (1992) billion, and an actual reversal to $45 million in 1993, to $2.0 billion in 1994 turned into a positive factor for the overall FDI picture by adding $10.5 billion nominally to growth in the overall U.S. FDI position between 1989 and 1993, without a real effect on the physical direct investment already in place (see Table 2.1).

TABLE 2.1. Position in Netherlands Antillean Finance Affiliates ($ billion)

Year	1983	1984	1985	1986	1987	1988
FDI Position	−23.3	−25.1	−20.8	−17.2	−14.5	−10.3
Equity	15.0	16.9	16.7	16.4	15.3	12.1
Debt, net	−38.3	−42.0	37.5	−33.7	−29.8	−24.5
Parents'						
Receivables	.4	.5	1.2	.5	.6	.7
Payables	38.7	42.5	39.6	34.2	30.4	23.1

Year	1989	1990	1991	1992	1993	1994
FDI Position	−8.5	−4.7	−5.3	−2.1	nil	2.0
Equity	9.1	8.5	9.0	8.5	7.6	8.3
Debt, net	−17.6	−13.1	−14.4	−10.6	−7.6	−6.3
Parents'						
Receivables	1.2	3.1	.3	.2	.2	.1
Payables	18.8	16.2	14.7	10.7	8.9	6.3

Sources: *SOCB*, August 1992, p. 120; July 1993, p. 94; August 1995, p. 92.

As pointed out, reinvested earnings always affect the FDI position of investor countries in a positive manner. For the United States, they became the decisive factor behind its sustained FDI growth by largely compensating for the negative development of equity and debt flows since 1981 as described above. The only year when reinvestments failed to neutralize these reverse capital flows was 1982, which produced an additional impetus for the downward adjustment in the investment stock.

Condensing the annual information on capital movements provided in Table 2.6 into one number for each decade or fraction thereof makes the relative contribution of each capital source to the expansion of the investment base transparent. In the first two decades after World War II, America's FDI was financed predominantly through net capital outflows from the States, even though there were already five years during the 1950s (1951-1955) where reinvestments exceeded U.S. capital flows in value. However, this flow pattern changed during the early 1970s (see Table 2.2).

The turning point came in 1972 and coincided, accidentally or not, with the 1971 abandonment of the fixed exchange rate system. Since then, capital exports have consistently been smaller than reinvested earnings for each and every year with the exceptions of 1989 and 1992. The sudden

TABLE 2.2. Development of Reinvested Earnings and Net Equity/Debt Flows ($ million + outflow)

Decade	A. Reinvestments	B. Equity/Debt	Ratio A/B
1950-59	$9,210	$11,153	42 : 58
1960-69	16,816	25,360	34 : 66
1970-79	79,266	43,455	64 : 36
1980-89	132,414	30,789	81 : 19
1990-94	119,343	106,028	53 : 47
1950-94	357,049	216,785	62 : 38

reversal in the reinvestment and capital export ratio during the early 1990s is to some extent related to the Netherlands Antilles situation described above. The fairly heavy net outflows of intercompany debt from the Netherlands Antilles during that period added to the debt/equity portion of the FDI position in full accord with the accounting procedures established. For the period 1990 to 1994, these additional funds amount to $10.5 billion or 10 percent of the equity/debt flows recorded.

The free float of all currencies and the gradual depreciation of the dollar have helped to bolster reinvestments simply by making it increasingly expensive to finance foreign acquisitions or expansions with weaker dollars. Also, in view of the post-OPEC inflation and rising interest rates, the development of profits and return on investments became uncertain. Technically, profits and write-offs in foreign currency were on an automatic upswing, but there was a growing uneasiness and risk awareness which fostered an attitude of caution. For this reason, it was prudent to play with foreign money and keep American dollars at home. This uncertainty is reflected in the reported shift from purchases to sales of capital stock in incorporated affiliates by U.S. parents (see Table 2.3).

Also, the shrinking dollar had a ballooning effect on overseas profits which was in sharp contrast to depressed domestic earnings in the wake of oil-induced stagflation. Deemphasizing capital transfers in favor of reinvestments in financing, the expanding investment base helped to conserve cash needed at home, allowed dynamic investment activities abroad, and still left room for growing dividend payments.

Contributing elements may also be seen in the automatic asset appreciation as balance sheets benefitted from upward valuation adjustments upon translation of foreign currency holdings into the depreciating dollar, and in the maturing investment stock, which produced sufficient investment funds to render capital transfers superfluous. The period of seed

TABLE 2.3. Acquisitions and Sales of Capital Stock in Affiliates from or to Foreigners Other Than Affiliates in Which Investment Was Made, 1963-1978 ($ million)

Year	Acquisitions	Sales	Net Acquisitions
1963	$228	$52	$176
1964	434	106	328
1965	369	90	279
1966	591	29	562
1967	508	318	190
1968	800	220	580
1969	847	164	683
1970	855	157	698
1971	656	196	460
1972	854	152	702
1973	666	627	39
1974	525	573	−48
1975	502	546	−44
1976	311	1,055	−744
1977	491	647	−156
1978	721	2,331	−1,610

Source: *SOCB*, February 1981, p. 42.

capital had temporarily, at least, come to an end for the bulk of investments. Whether or not the revival of capital exports during the early 1990s sets a lasting new trend for America's FDI engagement remains to be seen. Whatever motivated U.S. businessmen to do one thing or another at any given moment, their investment decisions favored retained earnings over capital exports to the tune of 1.7:1 for the whole period. This appearance of a clear-cut preference is obviously biased somewhat by the change in the accounting treatment of the Netherlands Antillean affiliates. Even by eliminating their negative impact on the ratio by reversing the total debt position and adding it to the investment stock would still leave the balance in favor of reinvested earnings at 1.6:1.

U.S. NET CAPITAL OUTFLOWS
VERSUS DISTRIBUTED INCOME

Another way of looking at the actual money flows registered in the BOP, but exclusive of reinvested earnings which in reality do neither touch U.S. territory nor the BOP proper, is to compare net intercompany capital flows with parent receipts of disbursed income from their affiliates. A sort of parental cash flow resulting from their foreign investments and balancing net income receipts with net capital exports (see Table 2.4).

Parents enjoyed a very favorable cash flow from their subsidiaries throughout the whole period, netting approximately $2.50 for each dollar sent abroad. This figure does not include reinvestments or the income-type flows represented by royalties, license fees, and service fees which will be discussed later. Adding reinvested funds alone to this balance sheet would result in $4.15 returned for each invested dollar. All that is documented here is the actual operating income flowing into the parents' bank accounts in the United States against their real cash outflows.

FDI AND THE U.S. GDP

Capital flows can be related to the U.S. output of goods and services to establish their hypothetical weight in that economy. Following the U.S. practice of including reinvestments as part of the calculation indicates that they amount to less than one percent of GDP over the four decades. Narrowing it down to actual capital transfers, exclusive of reinvestments, reveals how surprisingly small U.S. spending in that area has been. It never exceeded one-half of 1 percent of its GDP over the whole period.

The figures convey the impression of a rapid development in overall investment outflows from the United States, but at second glance, actual capital transfers from the United States, after almost doubling during each of the first three decades, have fallen back rather dramatically during the fourth decade to the level seen during the 1960s. Considering the depreciation of the currency in the interim years, the $30.8 billion equity/debt outflow during the 1980s is certainly not equivalent to the purchasing

TABLE 2.4. U.S. Parent Net Cash Flow ($ million)

Period	Remitted Income*	Net Interco. Capital Flow	Balance
1950-59	$18,032	$11,153	$6,879
1960-69	35,217	25,360	9,857
1970-79	103,572	43,455	60,117
1980-89	219,634	30,789	188,845
1990-94	165,277	106,028	59,249
1950-94	541,732	216,785	324,947

Note: *Net income less reinvestments.

power of the $25.4 billion during the 1960s. The sharp decline in actual capital outflows from the U.S. during the 1980s is explained by a variety of factors. Citing the U.S. DOC, the list of factors includes:

- the reduction in affiliate earnings during the early 1980s due to the widespread oil recession around the globe;
- a slower recovery in Canada and Europe than the United States;
- lower interest rates abroad encouraging intercompany fund flows to the United States;
- the reduction in America's corporate tax rate, increased depreciation allowances, lower inflation leading to higher aftertax returns on new investments at home;
- the international debt crisis resulting in currency devaluations and austerity programs in major LDCs;
- the dramatic increase in large mergers, acquisitions, and leveraged buyouts in the United States requiring huge funds; and
- the continuing appreciation of the dollar between 1980 and 1985 resulting in exchange-rate-conditioned transaction or translation losses (*International Direct Investment*, 1988, p. 19). (See Table 2.5.)

In view of the weak capital export situation in the last full decade under review, the very strong rebound of investment flows during the early 1990s comes as a surprise. The impression is created to a good part by the developments in the Netherlands Antillean finance subsidiaries discussed above. Between 1989 and 1994, U.S. parents' payables, or capital imports, which produced the negative impact on the growth of the total investment stock according to the adopted accounting rules, were reduced by $17

TABLE 2.5. FDI Capital Outflows Compared to U.S. GDP ($ billion)

Years	U.S. Business GDP	Total Capital Outflows*	%	Debt/Equity Outflows	%
1950-59	$3,606	$19.1	0.53	$11.2	0.31
1960-69	6,180	38.2	0.62	25.4	0.41
1970-79	13,823	119.8	0.87	43.5	0.32
1980-89	33,527	163.1	0.49	30.8	0.09
1990-94	25,757	225.4	0.87	106.0	0.41

Note: *Debt/Equity plus reinvested earnings.

Sources: *GNP: Economic Report of the President*, February 1990, p. 294, Table C-1. *GNP: Economic Report of the President*, February 1995, pp. 286-8. Flows: Table 2.6.

billion from $18.8 to $6.3 billion. The net effect of this change is a surge in intercompany debt flows and an increase in the FDI stock by the same amount. These payables stood at $–42.5 billion in 1984, reducing the investment position by that amount, but adding to it as they were gradually worked down. In other words, the total cumulative effect of this account alone for the FDI position between 1984 and 1993 amounted to a $36.2 billion boost in the FDI stock, and to $10.5 billion during the early 1990s as mentioned earlier (see Table 2.1).

CAPITAL FLOWS BY WORLD REGION

A review of the official capital flows to the various geographical regions demonstrates the complementary interplay of capital outflows from the United States and reinvestments. They move at different speeds and levels to the corners of the globe, constantly changing their mix in response to the respective maturity of direct investments, and changes in political, economic, or other strategic constellations. Table 2.6 suggests a number of interesting facts. First, it confirms the distinct two-stage pattern in financing U.S. FDI mentioned before. Seed capital forms the early stages of expansion. After reaching a critical mass and the capacity to produce sufficient profits, capital exports are gradually replaced by reinvestments. The subsidiaries are moving from the nursing stage to financial self-sufficiency.

The gradual transition from seed capital dependence (imports) to the autarky stage is indicated by the horizontal percentage shares representing the respective shares of capital imports and locally generated funds in total investments. As long as fund inflows maintain a better than 50 percent share of investments, the affiliates are still strongly dependent on capital injections from abroad.

Once equity/debt inflows drop below the 50 percent level of total committed expansion funds, the investment needs are financed predominantly through retained earnings rather than capital transfers. The offspring has been weaned, and stands on its own feet. The time required to go through the parent-dependent growth stage lasted between one and two decades on average in the case of American investments after World War II, if very generalized conclusions can be drawn from the data. An interesting and first-time investment phenomenon is presented by Canada where reinvestments feed a still-growing investment stock during the same time that capital transfers went into reverse, leading to capital repatriation on a large scale during the 1980s.

The second point of interest in Table 2.6 lies in the vertical percentage figures which relate to the share of global investments going to a particular

TABLE 2.6. Capital Flows by Region ($ million)

Decade	Total Capital Outflow*		Equity/Debt Flow		Reinvested Earnings	
Total World						
1950-59	$19,127	100%	$11,153	58%	$9,210	42%
1960-69	38,267	100%	25,360	66%	16,816	34%
1970-79	119,764	100%	43,455	36%	79,266	64%
1980-89	163,144	100%	30,789	19%	132,414	81%
1990-94	225,371	100%	106,028	47%	119,343	52%
Canada						
1950-59	7,187	100%	4,234	59%	2,953	41%
	38%		38%		32%	
1960-69	10,746	100%	5,034	47%	5,712	53%
	28%		20%		34%	
1970-79	21,936	100%	3,676	17%	18,260	83%
	18%		8%		23%	
1980-89	18,180	100%	−7,026	NMF	25,565	138%
	11%		NMF		19%	
1990-94	14,785	100%	9,171	75%	5,614	25%
	7%		9%		5%	
Latin America						
1950-59	5,403	100%	3,386	63%	2,017	37%
	28%		30%		22%	
1960-69	5,568	100%	2,723	49%	2,845	51%
	15%		11%		17%	
1970-79	23,969	100%	11,189	47%	12,780	53%
	20%		26%		16%	
1980-89	30,038	100%	3,611	12%	24,423	81%
	18%		12%		19%	
1990-94	62,668	100%	26,063	42%	36,605	58%
	28%		25%		31%	
L.A. Republics						
1950-59	4,983	100%	3,201	64%	1,782	36%
	26%		29%		19%	
1960-69	N/A	N/A	N/A	N/A	2,573	N/A
	−		−		15%	
1970-79	13,877	100%	4,622	33%	9,255	67%
	11%		11%		12%	
1980-89	18,164	100%	6,225	34%	10,787	59%
	11%		20%		8%	
1990-94	36,982	100%	11,455	27%	25,527	74%
	16%		11%		22%	
Other Western Hemisphere						
1950-59	421	100%	186	44%	235	56%
	2%		1%		3%	
1960-69	N/A	N/A	N/A	N/A	272	N/A
	−		−		3%	
1970-79	10,265	100%	6,403	62%	3,862	38%
	9%		15%		5%	
1980-89	16,806	100%	−2,712	NMF	13,637	81%
	10%		NMF		10%	
1990-94	25,687	100%	14,609	61%	11,078	39%
	11%		14%		9%	

TABLE 2.6 (continued)

Decade	Total Capital Outflow*		Equity/Debt Flow		Reinvested Earnings	
	Europe					
1950-59	3,997	100%	1,851	46%	2,146	54%
	21%		17%		23%	
1960-69	16,608	100%	11,804	71%	4,804	29%
	43%		47%		29%	
1970-79	57,936	100%	23,408	40%	34,528	60%
	48%		54%		44%	
1980-89	91,478	100%	31,507	34%	62,438	69%
	56%		102%		47%	
1990-94	104,556	100%	55,152	53%	49,404	47%
	46%		52%		42%	
	Africa					
1950-59	649	100%	267	41%	382	59%
	3%		2%		4%	
1960-69	1,429	100%	903	63%	526	37%
	4%		4%		3%	
1970-79	4,067	100%	1,623	40%	2,444	60%
	3%		4%		3%	
1980-89	1,534	100%	1,887	121%	54	NMF
	1%		6%		nil	
1990-94	500	100%	454	90%	46	NMF
	—		—		NMF	
	Asia					
1950-59	1,413	100%	747	53%	666	47%
	7%		1%		7%	
1960-69	2,757	100%	1,762	64%	995	36%
	7%		7%		6%	
1970-79	13,519	100%	6,803	50%	6,716	50%
	11%		16%		8%	
1980-89	17,561	100%	667	4%	16,935	96%
	11%		2%		14%	
1990-94	32,980	100%	10,836	39%	22,150	61%
	15%		10%		19%	
	Oceania					
1950-59	672	100%	275	41%	397	59%
	4%		2%		4%	
1960-69	2,094	100%	1,306	62%	788	38%
	5%		5%		5%	
1970-79	4,385	100%	1,767	40%	2,618	60%
	4%		4%		3%	
1980-89	6,481	100%	1,194	19%	5,260	81%
	4%		4%		4%	
1990-94	8,630	100%	3,670	55%	4,960	45%
	4%		3%		4%	

Notes: *Total flows are correct but may differ from sum of regional equity/debt plus reinvested earnings flows due to value adjustments and only partially revised data in the original government sources. Table excludes valuation adjustments for regions. Valuation adjustments were removed from total flow estimates starting with 1982.

Sources: See References for Table 2.6 and Table 2.7 at end of Chapter 2.

region during the decade in question. Indicating an area's relative investment maturity they disclose trends that make future FDI flows predictable.
Areas with rising shares of U.S. capital exports in particular, as well as
reinvestments, are future growth centers; those whose shares are stagnant
or declining have reached their potential, or are of lesser interest for other
reasons. Typical examples for each of these situations are represented as
follows:

a. Canada typifies the mature investment situation with a tendency
   toward decline in relative but also absolute investment terms during
   the 1980s. All indications point to a lack of major investment interest. Noteworthy is the rebound in the intercompany capital flow
   account during the 1990s, after the negative performance for the
   1980s, and the complete reversal in the role played by capital transfers and reinvestments. While the first account seems to signal
   renewed investment interest in Canada, the development in the reinvestment account leads to exactly the opposite conclusion. It will be
   interesting to watch the long-term effect of the Free Trade Agreement concluded between Canada and the United States in 1992, and
   its expanded version ratified to include Mexico at the end of 1993,
   NAFTA will alter the investment picture for the country.
b. Africa appears to be in a situation of permanently declining investment
   interest. Total investment activity is shrinking from previous levels
   during the 1980s, but turned into outright disinvestment during the
   early 1990s. Capital transfers and reinvestments indicate future expansion into this area to be unlikely. The picture here is very much
   affected by the very concentrated investment base in a few industries.
   Actually, the whole continent has always been questionable for U.S.
   investors due to economic stagnation, relative market size, political
   considerations, etc.
c. Clear-cut growth areas are represented by Europe, Latin America,
   Asia, and Oceania (Australia and New Zealand). Investment growth
   follows distinctly different financing patterns. Europe stands out
   with a dynamic expansion of both seed capital flows and reinvestments, while all other areas grow predominantly on the strength of
   reinvestments with the conspicuous exception of the Western Hemisphere affiliates. The very strong commitment of seed capital in this
   area at almost twice the level of reinvestments during the early
   1990s only emphasizes the special character of these financial centers in the American FDI context. The European situation could turn
   even more dynamic with the final integration of all of Western
   Europe and its admission of interested Central European nations.

This optimistic view is predicated upon the assumption that the increasing frequency of trade disputes between Washington and the EC do not deteriorate into a serious confrontation among the two most powerful economic blocs. For the moment, this appears to be a potential but remote possibility, as the successful conclusion of the GATT Round in December of 1993 injected a new and conciliatory spirit of international cooperation. It may be helpful in overcoming the controversies over European farm and industrial subsidies, opening of service industries, reduction of nontariff barriers, harmonization of industrial property rights, or other protective measures. At the other end of the world, similar sentiments appear in the Japanese and Korean concessions on American rice and automotive imports, and more vigorous attention to patent protection.

d. The very sharp increase of seed capital outflows in the beginning of the 1990s, both in absolute terms and relative to reinvested funds, is a fortunate development for America's future status in the world market. It is still impressive when considering the 10 percent boost these figures received from the Netherlands Antilles accounting practices discussed in the beginning. Eliminating this factor still indicates U.S. capital exports equal to the combined three decades of the 1960s, 1970s, and 1980s. As will be shown later–the true, that is capital-controlled, U.S. share in global output of value-added is waning–a direct consequence of two factors. One is the fact that inward FDI is increasingly eroding the U.S.-controlled part of its domestic market. The other is the fact that American outward FDI, despite all its vigorous expansion in monetary terms, is not keeping pace with the exploding world economy. A particular contributing point to this latter situation is the visible slowdown of seed capital exports during the 1980s (see Table 2.7).

TABLE 2.7. U.S. FDI Capital Flows by Region

WORLD—($ million)

Year	Total Capital Outflows*	Equity/Debt Flows Total	Equity	Debt	Reinvest- ments	Value Ad- justments
1950	$1,088	$621	N/A	N/A	$475	$−8
1951	1,191	508	"	"	752	−68
1952	1,742	853	"	"	923	−34
1953	1,533	735	"	"	826	−28
1954	1,376	667	"	"	702	−7
1955	1,766	823	"	"	962	−19
1956	3,108	1,951	"	"	1,175	−18
1957	2,890	2,442	"	"	1,363	−915
1958	2,015	1,181	"	"	944	−111
1959	2,418	1,372	"	"	1,089	−43
1960	2,039	1,675	"	"	1,266	−902
1961	2,852	1,599	"	"	1,054	199
1962	2,559	1,654	"	"	1,198	−293
1963	3,460	1,976	"	"	1,507	−23
1964	3,744	2,328	"	"	1,431	−15
1965	4,994	3,468	"	"	1,542	−66
1966	2,318	3,625	"	"	1,791	−3,098
1967	4,768	3,050	"	"	1,757	−39
1968	5,347	2,855	"	"	2,440	52
1969	6,186	3,130	"	"	2,830	266
1970	7,387	4,413	"	"	3,176	−202
1971	7,280	4,441	"	"	3,176	−337
1972	7,118	3,214	"	"	4,532	−628
1973	11,435	3,195	"	"	8,158	82
1974	8,765	1,275	"	"	7,777	−287
1975	13,971	6,196	"	"	8,048	−273
1976	12,759	4,253	"	"	7,696	810
1977	11,893	5,497	"	"	6,396	−2,712
1978	16,056	4,713	"	"	11,343	681
1979	25,222	6,258	"	"	18,964	−91
1980	19,222	2,205	"	"	17,017	8,482
1981	9,624	−3,803	"	"	13,483	1,304
1982	1,078	−3,728	9,708	−13,436	4,806	−2,081
1983	6,686	−6,766	4,903	−11,669	13,453	−275
1984	11,649	−5,626	1,347	−6,973	17,276	1,933
1985	12,724	−941	−2,210	1,269	13,665	1,001
1986	17,706	8,657	551	8,106	9,048	1,501
1987	28,980	11,331	4,635	6,696	17,650	3,988
1988	17,871	4,553	−6,112	10,665	13,319	2,976
1989	37,604	24,907	6,395	18,512	12,697	810
1990	30,982	9,546	8,739	807	21,436	17,555
1991	32,696	14,369	17,682	−3,313	18,327	1,899
1992	42,647	26,352	14,647	11,705	16,294	−10,440
1993	71,349	41,110	22,265	18,845	30,240	−13,679
1994	47,698	14,642	11,697	2,945	33,046	4,678

TABLE 2.7 (continued)

CANADA—($ million)

Year	Total Capital Outflows*	Equity/Debt Flows			Reinvest- ments
		Total	Equity	Debt	
1950	$433	$287	N/A	N/A	$146
1951	416	235	"	"	181
1952	669	430	"	"	239
1953	705	404	"	"	301
1954	682	408	"	"	274
1955	695	353	"	"	342
1956	1,042	601	"	"	441
1957	1,035	678	"	"	357
1958	700	421	"	"	279
1959	810	417	"	"	393
1960	860	471	"	"	389
1961	567	301	"	"	266
1962	685	314	"	"	371
1963	898	365	"	"	533
1964	798	582	"	"	500
1965	1,502	962	"	"	540
1966	1,612	985	"	"	627
1967	1,022	372	"	"	650
1968	1,218	384	"	"	834
1969	1,584	582	"	"	1,002
1970	1,462	763	"	"	699
1971	1,087	64	"	"	1,023
1972	1,755	376	"	"	1,379
1973	2,448	581	"	"	1,867
1974	2,857	643	"	"	2,214
1975	2,592	419	"	"	2,173
1976	2,471	20	"	"	2,451
1977	1,581	−49	"	"	1,630
1978	1,206	−615	"	"	1,821
1979	4,477	1,474	"	"	3,003
1980	3,906	317	"	"	3,589
1981	−761	−2,681	"	"	1,920
1982	−1,796	−2,359	−2,005	−356	563
1983	905	−2,705	−428	−2,277	3,610
1984	3,333	−272	−25	−247	3,605
1985	173	−2,705	−2,625	−80	2,878
1986	2,400	726	−120	846	1,674
1987	6,470	3,309	1,499	1,540	3,161
1988	2,641	344	15	329	2,297
1989	1,268	−1,000	−969	−31	2,268
1990	3,902	3,614	863	2,751	288
1991	1,337	896	2,485	−1,589	461
1992	2,068	2,103	498	1,605	−36
1993	3,226	1,541	1,509	32	1,685
1994	4,252	1,035	1,205	−170	3,216

LATIN AMERICA—($ million)

Year	Total Capital Outflows*	Equity/Debt Flows			Reinvest-ments
		Total	Equity	Debt	
1950	$154	$51	N/A	N/A	$103
1951	397	187	"	"	210
1952	587	322	"	"	265
1953	283	142	"	"	141
1954	180	53	"	"	127
1955	357	169	"	"	188
1956	883	647	"	"	236
1957	1,550	1,220	"	"	330
1958	520	329	"	"	191
1959	492	266	"	"	226
1960	427	149	"	"	278
1961	498	219	"	"	279
1962	337	29	"	"	308
1963	417	235	"	"	182
1964	363	113	"	"	250
1965	616	271	"	"	345
1966	612	303	"	"	309
1967	513	311	"	"	202
1968	1,069	708	"	"	361
1969	716	385	"	"	331
1970	1,032	579	"	"	453
1971	1,069	696	"	"	373
1972	917	272	"	"	645
1973	1,645	654	"	"	991
1974	3,353	2,244	"	"	1,109
1975	2,866	1,245	"	"	1,621
1976	1,762	439	"	"	1,323
1977	3,949	2,526	"	"	1,423
1978	4,014	2,096	"	"	1,918
1979	3,362	438	"	"	2,924
1980	2,833	−533	"	"	3,366
1981	−37	−3,534	"	"	3,497
1982	−4,864	−6,142	6,303	−12,445	1,277
1983	−2,932	−5,485	1,672	−7,157	2,553
1984	275	−2,701	1,308	−4,009	2,977
1985	4,436	2,201	−1,646	3,847	2,009
1986	7,445	5,488	660	4,828	1,956
1987	8,132	4,891	1,010	3,881	3,236
1988	6,042	1,709	−4,083	5,792	2,174
1989	9,094	7,717	2,981	4,736	1,378
1990	10,141	5,267	571	4,696	4,874
1991	7,194	2,199	6,180	−3,981	4,994
1992	12,751	5,821	2,432	3,389	6,931
1993	16,859	8,279	3,409	4,870	8,579
1994	15,723	4,496	1,097	3,399	11,227

TABLE 2.7 (continued)

L.A. REPUBLICS—($ million)

Year	Total Capital Outflows*	Equity/Debt Flows			Reinvest- ments
		Total	Equity	Debt	
1950	$145	$45	N/A	N/A	$100
1951	391	182	"	"	209
1952	567	302	"	"	265
1953	264	137	"	"	127
1954	186	70	"	"	116
1955	343	167	"	"	176
1956	823	618	"	"	205
1957	1,402	1,163	"	"	239
1958	442	299	"	"	143
1959	420	218	"	"	202
1960	N/A	N/A	"	"	215
1961	N/A	N/A	"	"	255
1962	N/A	N/A	"	"	268
1963	N/A	N/A	"	"	173
1964	N/A	N/A	"	"	216
1965	N/A	N/A	"	"	306
1966	464	180	"	"	284
1967	394	207	"	"	187
1968	796	482	"	"	314
1969	676	321	"	"	355
1970	750	348	"	"	402
1971	745	451	"	"	294
1972	610	74	"	"	536
1973	1,178	371	"	"	807
1974	1,369	345	"	"	1,024
1975	2,048	672	"	"	1,376
1976	731	−219	"	"	950
1977	1,243	401	"	"	1,167
1978	2,209	844	"	"	1,570
1979	2,704	1,335	"	"	1,129
1980	3,498	1,370	"	"	2,128
1981	3,416	1,614	"	"	1,802
1982	2,058	2,694	1,651	1,043	−635
1983	−829	−468	441	−909	−361
1984	221	34	284	−250	188
1985	−742	−943	−474	−469	200
1986	1,761	634	649	−15	1,126
1987	2,024	−9	680	−689	1,934
1988	2,017	−1,067	−1,105	38	2,069
1989	4,703	2,366	1,556	810	2,336
1990	4,572	1,485	953	532	3,077
1991	5,652	2,460	2,326	134	3,194
1992	5,827	675	1,126	−451	5,151
1993	8,719	2,074	1,825	249	6,644
1994	12,222	4,761	2,039	2,722	7,461

OTHER WESTERN HEMISPHERE–($ million)

Year	Total Capital Outflows*	Equity/Debt Flows			Reinvest-ments
		Total	**Equity**	**Debt**	
1950	$8	$6	N/A	N/A	$2
1951	7	5	"	"	2
1952	N/A	20	"	"	N/A
1953	19	5	"	"	14
1954	−5	−16	"	"	11
1955	14	2	"	"	12
1956	60	29	"	"	31
1957	148	57	"	"	91
1958	78	30	"	"	48
1959	72	48	"	"	24
1960	N/A	N/A	"	"	63
1961	N/A	N/A	"	"	23
1962	N/A	N/A	"	"	40
1963	N/A	N/A	"	"	10
1964	N/A	N/A	"	"	34
1965	N/A	N/A	"	"	39
1966	148	123	"	"	25
1967	120	105	"	"	15
1968	273	226	"	"	47
1969	41	65	"	"	−24
1970	282	231	"	"	51
1971	324	245	"	"	79
1972	307	198	"	"	109
1973	468	284	"	"	184
1974	1,984	1,899	"	"	85
1975	818	573	"	"	245
1976	1,031	658	"	"	373
1977	2,705	2,020	"	"	415
1978	1,805	1,360	"	"	526
1979	658	−1,065	"	"	1,795
1980	−713	−2,000	"	"	1,239
1981	−3,620	−5,149	"	"	1,695
1982	−6,922	−8,835	4,653	−13,488	1,913
1983	−2,103	−5,017	1,231	−6,248	2,914
1984	53	−2,735	1,024	−3,759	2,789
1985	4,952	3,144	−1,171	4,315	1,809
1986	5,683	4,835	11	4,843	829
1987	6,107	4,900	330	4,570	1,302
1988	4,025	2,776	−2,978	5,754	105
1989	4,392	5,350	1,425	3,925	−958
1990	5,580	3,783	−382	4,165	1,798
1991	1,541	−260	3,854	−4,114	1,801
1992	6,924	5,145	1,305	3,840	1,779
1993	8,140	6,205	1,584	4,621	1,935
1994	3,502	−263	−942	678	3,765

TABLE 2.7 (continued)

EUROPE—($ million)

Year	Total Capital Outflows*	Equity/Debt Flows Total	Equity	Debt	Reinvest- ments
1950	$272	$121	N/A	N/A	$151
1951	245	64	"	"	181
1952	169	−6	"	"	175
1953	221	48	"	"	173
1954	243	45	"	"	198
1955	349	130	"	"	219
1956	739	488	"	"	251
1957	311	287	"	"	294
1958	428	190	"	"	238
1959	750	484	"	"	266
1960	1,325	962	"	"	363
1961	1,057	725	"	"	332
1962	1,161	869	"	"	292
1963	1,443	930	"	"	513
1964	1,796	1,388	"	"	408
1965	1,867	1,479	"	"	388
1966	2,249	1,835	"	"	414
1967	1,858	1,435	"	"	423
1968	1,601	984	"	"	617
1969	2,251	1,197	"	"	1,054
1970	3,030	1,894	"	"	1,136
1971	3,424	2,209	"	"	1,215
1972	3,030	1,139	"	"	1,891
1973	6,577	3,070	"	"	3,507
1974	6,432	3,664	"	"	2,768
1975	4,584	2,239	"	"	2,345
1976	5,492	2,408	"	"	3,084
1977	5,289	2,908	"	"	2,381
1978	7,820	2,245	"	"	5,574
1979	12,259	1,632	"	"	10,627
1980	13,011	5,401	"	"	7,610
1981	5,278	676	"	"	4,515
1982	4,114	2,150	3,777	−1,627	1,963
1983	5,141	299	1,185	−886	4,841
1984	5,825	−1,053	1,010	−2,063	6,879
1985	7,592	−22	1,321	−1,343	7,615
1986	7,587	1,543	−515	2,058	6,044
1987	11,397	2,631	1,525	1,106	10,060
1988	7,854	3,065	395	2,670	6,048
1989	23,679	16,817	3,494	13,323	6,863
1990	10,194	−2,153	7,016	−9,169	12,347
1991	19,563	10,295	7,321	2,974	9,267
1992	18,931	14,654	10,014	4,640	4,277
1993	40,586	27,772	14,873	12,899	12,814
1994	15,282	4,584	8,062	−3,478	10,699

AFRICA–($ million)

Year	Total Capital Outflows*	Equity/Debt Flows Total	Equity	Debt	Reinvestments
1950	$49	$33	N/A	N/A	$16
1951	43	14	"	"	29
1952	67	33	"	"	34
1953	41	3	"	"	38
1954	37	4	"	"	33
1955	95	45	"	"	50
1956	92	49	"	"	43
1957	56	9	"	"	47
1958	81	38	"	"	43
1959	88	39	"	"	49
1960	129	79	"	"	50
1961	N/A	N/A	"	"	33
1962	56	8	"	"	48
1963	55	12	"	"	43
1964	59	17	"	"	42
1965	78	30	"	"	48
1966	148	87	"	"	61
1967	226	187	"	"	39
1968	365	295	"	"	70
1969	280	188	"	"	92
1970	541	413	"	"	128
1971	327	194	"	"	133
1972	264	132	"	"	132
1973	−226	−573	"	"	347
1974	889	523	"	"	366
1975	337	92	"	"	245
1976	454	237	"	"	217
1977	−127	10	"	"	201
1978	591	396	"	"	272
1979	576	199	"	"	403
1980	1,067	489	"	"	578
1981	736	311	"	"	425
1982	626	1,058	463	595	−432
1983	42	15	876	−861	26
1984	364	−89	105	−194	453
1985	−10	−63	189	−252	53
1986	−365	394	−325	719	−759
1987	240	182	−199	381	133
1988	−592	−87	−439	352	−280
1989	−554	−412	−364	−48	−143
1990	−450	−296	109	−405	−153
1991	75	106	124	−18	−31
1992	−84	N/A	N/A	N/A	−431
1993	866	558	360	198	308
1994	93	−259	67	−326	352

TABLE 2.7 (continued)

ASIA–($ million)

Year	Total Capital Outflows*	Equity/Debt Flows Total	Equity	Debt	Reinvest-ments
1950	$109	$80	N/A	N/A	$3
1951	67	−3	"	"	70
1952	177	67	"	"	110
1953	241	169	"	"	72
1954	N/A	56	"	"	N/A
1955	86	14	"	"	72
1956	172	109	"	"	63
1957	268	144	"	"	124
1958	176	108	"	"	68
1959	61	3	"	"	58
1960	45	−20	"	"	65
1961	205	141	"	"	64
1962	50	27	"	"	23
1963	202	130	"	"	72
1964	195	120	"	"	75
1965	334	273	"	"	61
1966	327	179	"	"	148
1967	460	304	"	"	156
1968	402	225	"	"	177
1969	537	383	"	"	154
1970	506	304	"	"	202
1971	693	469	"	"	224
1972	900	659	"	"	241
1973	−140	−812	"	"	672
1974	−346	−1,014	"	"	668
1975	3,706	2,374	"	"	1,332
1976	1,371	1,400	"	"	−29
1977	892	518	"	"	796
1978	1,862	369	"	"	1,169
1979	3,867	2,536	"	"	1,441
1980	−2,300	−3,426	"	"	1,126
1981	3,243	1,447	"	"	1,771
1982	2,433	1,271	847	424	1,161
1983	3,120	1,302	1,305	−3	1,816
1984	2,378	−579	−22	−557	2,956
1985	654	−641	341	−982	1,295
1986	2,233	841	677	164	1,393
1987	2,397	246	757	−511	2,649
1988	1,660	−279	−1,803	1,524	2,503
1989	1,743	478	141	337	1,265
1990	4,485	1,533	56	1,477	3,090
1991	3,581	−636	387	−1,023	3,875
1992	6,407	2,292	971	1,321	4,140
1993	8,068	N/A	N/A	N/A	5,265
1994	10,447	4,434	1,109	3,325	5,781

OCEANIA–($ million)

Year	Total Capital Outflows*	Equity/Debt Flows Total	Equity	Debt	Reinvest- ments
1950	$42	$25	N/A	N/A	$17
1951	60	32	"	"	28
1952	60	33	"	"	27
1953	13	−28	"	"	41
1954	71	34	"	"	37
1955	105	62	"	"	43
1956	57	16	"	"	41
1957	44	−4	"	"	48
1958	74	22	"	"	52
1959	90	27	"	"	63
1960	113	41	"	"	2
1961	107	89	"	"	18
1962	160	119	"	"	41
1963	182	100	"	"	82
1964	203	125	"	"	78
1965	113	33	"	"	80
1966	246	172	"	"	74
1967	415	323	"	"	92
1968	277	158	"	"	119
1969	278	146	"	"	132
1970	358	235	"	"	123
1971	395	268	"	"	127
1972	427	228	"	"	199
1973	397	37	"	"	360
1974	480	238	"	"	242
1975	378	112	"	"	266
1976	418	107	"	"	311
1977	474	65	"	"	148
1978	650	275	"	"	411
1979	617	202	"	"	431
1980	532	−24	"	"	556
1981	665	28	"	"	637
1982	347	363	184	179	−15
1983	258	108	99	9	150
1984	69	−417	−824	407	487
1985	365	40	199	−159	324
1986	137	−191	184	−375	328
1987	1,070	315	N/A	N/A	723
1988	779	−144	−157	13	1,034
1989	2,159	1,124	994	130	1,036
1990	2,813	1,857	400	1,457	954
1991	794	N/A	1,046	N/A	−370
1992	1,829	524	502	12	1,314
1993	1,479	107	444	−337	1,372
1994	1,715	23	140	−117	1,691

Notes: Breakdown between equity and debt capital not provided prior to 1982.*
+ sign = outflow; − sign = inflow.
Sources: See References for Table 2.6 and Table 2.7 at end of Chapter 2.

REFERENCES FOR TABLES 2.6 AND 2.7

Reinvested Earnings

1950-76 *Selected Data on U.S. Direct Investment Abroad*, February 1982, pp. 55-81.
1950-79 *SOCB*, February 1981, pp. 52-3.
1977 Ibid., August 1979, p. 30.
1978 Ibid., August 1980, p. 30.
1979 Ibid., August 1981, p. 35.
1980 Ibid., August 1982, p. 25.
1981 Ibid., August 1983, p. 27.
1982-89 Ibid., August 1990, pp. 76-83. Ibid., August 1992, p. 122.
1988-89 Ibid., August 1991, pp. 95-6.
1989-92 Ibid., July 1993, pp. 96, 109-112.
1990-93 Ibid., August 1994, pp. 146-9.
1992-94 Ibid., August 1995, pp. 104-6.

Capital Outflows Total

1950-79 *SOCB*, February 1981, pp. 52-3.
1950-81 *International Direct Investment, Global Trends and the U.S. Role*, August 1984, p. 54.
1966-76 *Selected Data on U.S. Direct Investment Abroad*, 1950-76, February 1982, pp. 204-6.
1977-81 Ibid., November 1984, pp. 24-7. Ibid., August 1991, p. 85.
1982-89 Ibid., August 1990, pp. 65-72.
1988-89 Ibid., August 1991, pp. 89-90.
1987-88 Ibid., August 1992, pp. 141-2.
1989-92 Ibid., July 1993, pp. 101-4, 121-2.
1989-93 Ibid., August 1994, pp. 138-41, 158-9.
1992-94 Ibid., August 1995, pp. 98-100
Up to 1982 this account was called "equity and intercompany account outflows."

Equity Capital and Intercompany Debt Outflows

1982-83 *SOCB*, August 1986, pp. 54-5, 62-3.
1984 Ibid., August 1987, pp. 69, 75.
1985-87 Ibid., August 1988, pp. 53-5, 59-61.
1986-88 Ibid., August 1989, pp. 73-5, 79-81.
1987-89 Ibid., August 1990, pp. 73-5, 84-6.
1988-89 Ibid., August 1991, pp. 92-3, 98-9.
1982-88 Ibid., August 1992, pp. 129-132, 135-7.
1989-92 Ibid., July 1993, pp. 96, 105-8, 113-6.
1989-93 Ibid., August 1994, pp. 142-5, 146-9.
1992-94 Ibid., August 1995, pp. 101-3, 107-9.

Valuation Adjustments

These adjustments include translation gains/losses plus other adjustments and are used in the calculation of annual changes in the FDI position. They played a role similar to capital flows until 1981. Starting with 1982, they have been strictly separated from all flow statistics.

1950-79 *International Direct Investment, Global Trends and the U.S. Role*, August 1984, p. 54.
1980 *SOCB*, August 1982, p. 12.
1981 Ibid., August 1983, p. 15.
1982 Ibid., August 1984, p. 19.
1983 Ibid., August 1985, p. 31.
1984 Ibid., August 1986, p. 41.
1985 Ibid., August 1987, p. 59.
1986 Ibid., August 1988, p. 43.
1987 Ibid., August 1989, p. 63.
1988 Ibid., August 1990, p. 58.
1989 Ibid., August 1991, p. 82.
1990 Ibid., August 1992, p. 119.
1991-92 Ibid., July 1993, p. 93.
1992-93 Ibid., August 1994, p. 128.
1993-94 Ibid., August 1995, p. 91.

Chapter 3

FDI-Related Income Type Flows in the U.S. Balance of Payments

Interesting as the development of the U.S. FDI position over four decades may be, it says absolutely nothing about the achievement of its primary purpose–profits. Their evolution over the same time period is the ultimate measuring stick of investment success and, therefore, needs to be explored in detail. Doing research in this area leads to the immediate discovery that the term "profit" is not termed as such in official publications. In its stead appear words such as income, earnings, dividends, etc., which evoke fewer philosophical, political, and emotional sensitivities, and are much more pragmatic than the undifferentiated term "profit."

There is a vast store of information on this subject. Data are published and revised in BOP statistics where they are meticulously monitored on a monthly and annual basis. Details are available for aggregate income, as well as its various components by industry, country, year, type of affiliate, etc. The volume and diversity of official data is an accountant's delight, but for the novice, a few introductory comments and explanations should be quite helpful.

To begin with, the discussion of the profit complex in the following chapter has adopted the descriptive terms of the official nomenclature for very practical reasons. A major reason is the realization that the generic word "profit" does not adequately reflect the existence of widely different profit categories. In other words, such terms as earnings, reinvested earnings, income, other income, dividends, interests, and branch earnings carry very specific meanings and are partial aspects of, but not necessarily synonymous with, overall profits. For a full appreciation of the statistical data on hand, a precise definition of the terms is, therefore, essential.

DIRECT INVESTMENT EARNINGS AND INCOME

Researchers encounter two basic headings in government publications covering profit data: earnings and income. Both look similar, with earnings always being slightly larger, which leads to the correct assumption that the first is a gross profit of sorts and the second an adjusted net figure. This insight does not explain their precise relationship. It is best to approach the intricacies of FDI profits from the parent company's perspective which is primarily interested in disposable net income after all foreign income and withholding taxes have been paid. Net income, as shown in Table 3.1, is the result of a stepwise transformation of subsidiary gross earnings as explained in Figure 3.1.

Earnings are thus the technical term for the profits generated by subsidiaries in their gross or net form as long as they are held abroad. They turn into income of the parent organizations as soon as they are actually remitted or considered remitted. As was pointed out earlier, reinvested earnings, even though technically not remitted, are still treated as such in U.S. BOP accounting practice. The only difference between affiliate net earnings and parental income is the withholding tax levied on remitted dividends and interests by the country where the earnings were generated.

Remitted earnings were formerly divided into dividends and branch earnings. Dividends refer to parent income derived from equity capital invested in their incorporated subsidiaries net of all withholding taxes; and branch earnings were designated as income from equity capital invested in unincorporated affiliates that makes both comparable except for the legal form of the payer. This division of income was abandoned in 1990, when it was established that branch earnings are not always remitted in full, as previously assumed, but may be paid out as dividends or plowed back into

FIGURE 3.1. The Earnings Transformation Scheme

a. <u>Subsidiary Gross Earnings</u>
   adjusted for capital gains/losses from business transactions
   minus foreign income taxes equal:
b. <u>Subsidiary (Net) Earnings</u>
   which turn into:
   1. distributed earnings to parents after deduction of foreign withholding taxes plus
   2. reinvested earnings plus
   3. interest net of foreign withholding taxes to equal:
c. <u>(Net) Income of parents</u>

Source: Adapted from *SOCB*, August 1990, p. 60.

TABLE 3.1. U.S. Foreign Direct Investment Income ($ million)

Year	Total Income	Interests, Dividends, Branch Earnings	Reinvested Earnings
1950	$1,769	$1,294	$475
1951	2,244	1,492	751
1952	2,343	1,420	923
1953	2,268	1,442	826
1954	2,427	1,725	702
1955	2,874	1,912	962
1956	3,346	2,171	1,175
1957	3,612	2,249	1,363
1958	3,065	2,121	944
1959	3,295	2,206	1,089
1960	3,621	2,355	1,266
1961	3,822	2,768	1,054
1962	4,241	3,044	1,198
1963	4,636	3,129	1,507
1964	5,106	3,674	1,431
1965	5,506	3,963	1,542
1966	5,260	3,467	1,791
1967	5,603	3,847	1,757
1968	6,592	4,152	4,152
1969	7,649	4,819	2,830
1970	8,168	4,992	3,176
1971	9,159	5,983	3,176
1972	10,949	6,416	4,532
1973	16,542	8,384	8,158
1974	19,156	11,379	7,777
1975	16,595	8,547	8,048
1976	18,999	11,303	7,696
1977	19,673	13,277	6,396
1978	25,458	14,115	11,343
1979	38,183	19,219	18,964
1980	37,146	20,129	17,017
1981	32,549	18,963	13,483
1982	24,828	20,022	4,806
1983	26,813	13,360	13,453
1984	30,046	12,770	17,276
1985	27,858	14,193	13,665
1986	29,927	20,879	9,048
1987	38,523	20,873	17,650
1988	50,429	37,110	13,319
1989	53,929	41,232	12,697
1990	58,004	36,568	21,436
1991	52,087	33,760	18,327
1992	50,565	34,271	16,294
1993	59,175	28,240	30,240
1994	64,789	31,743	33,046

Sources: *Selected Data on U.S. Direct Investment Abroad*, 1950-76, pp. 55-81 (Reinvested Earnings); pp. 82-108 (Interests, Dividends, Branch Earnings); pp. 109-35 (Total Income). *SOCB*, June 1982, pp. 42-3 (Reinvested Earnings, 1960-80); March 1982, p. 54 (Reinvested Earnings, 1980-81).

the business. Now, both forms of income are statistically treated as equal in all respects and appear either under dividends or reinvested earnings.

For many years, it was believed that all disbursed earnings are uniformly subject to withholding taxes. Upon closer inspection however, it was discovered that the remittance of branch earnings is tax free in the majority of countries (*SOCB*, August 1984, p. 25). This is a fact that may have led to overstated historic income figures.

Interest is the technical term for parental income derived from debt capital furnished to their subsidiaries, or vice versa, the net of applicable withholding taxes. It is treated in the above figure as a separate form of income, and is normally stated in its net form, the equation being affiliate payments to their parents minus parent payments to their affiliates. It is then added to earnings, a term that is strictly reserved to income from equity capital, to yield the total parent income in accordance with the accounting formula shown in Figure 3.1 on page 64.

Earnings that are not remitted and, therefore, not subject to withholding taxes appear in U.S. BOP statistics as reinvested earnings in two separate accounts; once in the current account, where they appear together with remitted funds under "direct investment income." As they are not truly a fund inflow (+ sign), they appear again in the capital account of the BOP as a fund outflow (− sign) to counterbalance the first, and purely hypothetical entry. Reinvestments always, and correctly, add to the equity portion of direct investments.

Between 1982 and 1989, income used to be reported inclusive of capital gains or losses arising from the translation of balance sheet data (as opposed to capital gains/losses derived from business transactions shown above) under fluctuating exchange rates. Such gains/losses are, obviously, not included in the local tax returns of affiliates because they do not arise from regular business operations. While they were not taxable, they also cannot be remitted. Nonetheless, as mere accounting entries, they add to or reduce investment stock. Adjustments of this sort were credited or debited to the reinvested earnings portion of overall income which, conceptually and in reality, remained in the accounts of the overseas subsidiaries. During the 1980s, these accounting gains or losses reached dramatic proportions.

This reporting system was changed in 1990. All previously reported income data were adjusted from 1982 forward to conform to new accounting procedures for translation gains/losses. They were completely removed from all income (including reinvestment) data and now appear as direct valuation adjustments to the investment position. Thus, two sets of official income statistics exist side-by-side which show very different values for that period (see Table 3.2).

The procedural correction did, of course, have no effect on the erratic swings in the valuation adjustments in subsequent periods, which went from $17,555 million in 1990 to $1,899 million (1991), $–11,406 million (1992), $–13,679 million (1993), and $4,678 million (1994). All income figures appearing in this report are based on the new interpretation, which is closer to reality. Previously, translation adjustments to earnings reached as high as 25 to 30 percent of total income for these years, causing grave distortions because of their weight and wide swings (from reference in "U.S. International Transactions, First Quarter 1990" in *SOCB*, June 1990).

The relative size of distributed versus retained earnings, condensed into one figure per decade, is shown in the following table. Reinvestments have maintained a fairly steady one-third share in the picture over the whole period after a brief rise to over 40 percent during the 1970s. Interesting is the fact that during the late 1980s, income per year began to approach the level achieved during the whole decade of the 1960s–consequence of the general growth in investments, but also inflation (see Table 3.3).

INCOME BY WORLD REGION

Owing to shifts in investment emphasis, profitability, and exchange rates, income flows have undergone significant geographical changes over time. In 1950, Canada accounted for 30 percent of the U.S. FDI stock and 25 percent of total income. By 1994, its investment share had dropped to 12 percent and only 8 percent for income.

Latin America's share in total U.S. FDI stood at 42 percent in 1950, and its income share at 35 percent. By 1994, these shares had declined to 19 percent and 25 percent respectively. This superficially negative impression must be corrected in line with a similar point made in the investment section. The Spanish-speaking nations south of the U.S. border need to be looked at separately from the English-, French-, and Dutch-speaking island nations in the Caribbean basin. While the cultural aspect is of minor

TABLE 3.2. Capital Gains/Losses from Asset Translation ($ million)

1982	1983	1984	1985	1986	1987	1988	1989
3,337	−6,323	−8,766	4,907	7,633	14,877	−901	−1,040

Sources: *SOCB*, August 1990, p. 57; August 1991, p. 82.

TABLE 3.3. Cumulative Income Volumes per Decade ($ million)

Period	Total Income	Dividends, Interests, Branch Earnings	%	Reinvested Earnings	%
1950-59	$27,242	$18,032	66.2	$9,210	33.8
1960-69	52,033	35,217	67.7	16,816	32.3
1970-79	182,838	103,572	56.7	79,266	43.3
1980-89	351,919	219,505	62.4	132,414	37.6
1990-94	284,620	161,847	56.9	119,343	43.1
Total	898,652	538,173	59.9	357,049	40.1

Source: See Table 3.1.

importance, the completely different investment structure of both regions definitely is of major importance (see Table 3.4).

The continental nations of the region, or Latin America proper, derive their income from a highly diversified investment base in comparatively large economies. Their share in total FDI stood at 38 percent in 1950, but only 11 percent in 1994 with similar income shares of 35 percent and 16 percent, respectively.

The Caribbean economies are small, less diversified, and accommodate a much narrower range of FDI industries, but have a financial impact on the income side that seems completely out of proportion to their own economic stature, as well as that of their host nations. Their share in overall direct investments grew from 4 to 8 percent between 1950 and 1994. On the income side, they held a share of 0.6 percent in 1950 and 7 percent in 1994 with an interim high of 9 percent in 1979. While this looks rather modest, it is an artificial situation because it is heavily impacted by the previously mentioned affiliate operations in the Netherlands Antilles. Had it not been for the $1.7 billion in interest payments on their foreign borrowings in 1990, income of the area would be higher by that amount, reaching 8 percent, and closer to the current level of income (see Table 3.5).

Their prominence in the U.S. direct investment picture rests entirely on favorable legislation which turns them into tax havens par excellence, whose special role is undetectable from Latin America's aggregate data. Consisting of a mere handful of island nations, these subsidiary institutions display common features. Investments there are highly concentrated in banking, insurance, financial and other service industries, which makes their position much more pivotal than is suggested by their share in the overall investment stock.

TABLE 3.4. FDI Income

WORLD AREA ($ million)

Year	Canada	Europe	Latin America	Africa	Asia	Oceania
1950	$440	$269	$626	$53	$328	$30
1951	417	310	853	87	459	41
1952	462	315	847	88	489	38
1953	509	325	714	87	509	57
1954	512	395	724	93	595	66
1955	635	486	882	121	623	71
1956	767	565	1,063	115	654	69
1957	691	575	1,241	88	755	85
1958	596	536	879	51	827	94
1959	739	659	897	55	790	107
1960	750	759	997	33	919	108
1961	731	818	1,103	31	979	84
1962	847	818	1,199	82	1,034	116
1963	988	1,020	1,139	165	1,084	139
1964	1,134	1,067	1,261	343	1,057	138
1965	1,243	1,157	1,340	375	1,101	142
1966	1,294	1,050	1,326	377	858	128
1967	1,341	1,153	1,322	391	963	142
1968	1,567	1,352	1,546	564	1,043	193
1969	1,643	2,008	1,568	665	1,120	257
1970	1,518	2,401	1,421	636	1,226	316
1971	1,871	2,721	1,434	572	1,628	356
1972	2,174	3,577	1,560	599	2,150	417
1973	2,844	5,751	2,511	883	3,175	728
1974	3,394	5,713	3,145	1,286	4,145	661
1975	3,412	4,989	3,201	674	3,180	735
1976	3,837	6,169	3,479	807	3,375	840
1977	3,253	7,211	3,712	724	4,022	650
1978	3,516	10,350	4,779	805	4,906	948
1979	5,517	17,086	6,520	1,642	6,041	1,116
1980	5,855	15,991	6,968	2,072	4,359	1,286
1981	4,253	11,837	6,143	1,546	6,385	1,423
1982	2,799	10,217	3,768	736	5,393	769
1983	5,209	11,823	1,794	1,072	5,146	787
1984	5,984	13,178	1,941	1,286	5,902	1,131
1985	5,184	13,771	2,465	1,114	4,567	932
1986	4,898	16,504	3,520	358	5,236	769
1987	5,487	20,932	3,848	955	6,219	1,208
1988	7,260	25,722	7,544	805	7,488	2,035
1989	6,501	27,637	9,245	775	7,526	2,093
1990	4,793	32,647	8,685	902	8,782	1,966
1991	3,208	27,963	8,993	1,143	9,415	879
1992	2,766	21,758	12,073	1,172	10,067	2,444
1993	3,941	26,659	14,203	1,223	10,255	2,418
1994	4,925	28,311	16,051	1,318	11,294	2,711

TABLE 3.4 (continued)

WORLD AREA (Percentages: World = 100)

Year	Canada	Europe	Latin America	Africa	Asia	Oceania
1950	24.9	15.2	35.4	3.0	18.5	1.7
1951	18.6	13.8	38.0	3.9	20.5	1.9
1952	19.7	13.4	36.2	3.8	20.9	1.6
1953	22.4	14.3	31.5	3.8	22.4	2.5
1954	21.1	16.3	29.8	3.8	24.5	2.7
1955	22.1	17.0	30.7	4.2	21.7	2.5
1956	22.9	16.9	31.8	3.4	19.5	2.1
1957	19.1	16.0	34.4	2.4	21.0	2.4
1958	19.4	17.5	28.7	1.7	27.0	3.1
1959	22.4	20.0	27.2	1.7	24.0	3.2
1960	20.7	21.0	27.5	0.9	25.4	3.0
1961	19.1	21.4	28.9	0.8	25.7	2.2
1962	20.0	19.3	28.3	1.9	24.4	2.7
1963	21.3	22.0	24.6	3.6	23.3	3.0
1964	22.2	20.9	24.7	6.7	20.7	2.7
1965	22.6	21.0	24.3	6.7	20.0	2.6
1966	24.6	20.0	25.2	7.2	16.3	2.4
1967	23.9	20.6	23.6	7.0	17.2	2.5
1968	23.8	20.6	23.5	8.6	15.8	2.9
1969	21.5	26.2	20.5	8.7	14.6	3.4
1970	18.6	29.4	17.4	7.8	15.0	3.9
1971	20.4	29.7	15.7	6.2	17.8	3.9
1972	19.8	32.7	14.2	5.5	19.6	3.8
1973	17.2	34.8	15.2	5.3	19.2	4.4
1974	17.7	29.9	16.4	6.7	21.6	3.5
1975	20.6	30.1	19.3	4.1	19.2	4.4
1976	20.2	32.5	18.3	4.2	17.8	4.4
1977	16.5	36.7	18.9	3.7	20.4	3.3
1978	13.8	40.7	18.8	3.2	19.3	3.7
1979	14.5	44.8	17.1	4.3	15.8	2.9
1980	15.8	43.0	18.8	5.6	11.7	3.5
1981	13.1	36.4	18.9	4.7	19.6	4.4
1982	11.3	41.3	15.4	3.0	21.8	3.1
1983	19.4	44.0	6.7	4.0	19.2	2.9
1984	20.1	44.1	6.4	4.3	19.7	3.8
1985	18.4	48.8	8.8	3.9	16.1	3.3
1986	15.8	52.8	11.4	1.2	16.9	2.4
1987	14.2	54.3	12.6	2.5	16.2	3.1
1988	14.4	51.0	15.0	1.6	14.9	4.0
1989	12.1	51.2	17.2	1.4	14.0	3.9
1990	8.3	56.3	15.0	1.6	15.1	3.4
1991	6.2	53.6	17.3	2.2	18.1	1.7
1992	5.5	43.1	23.9	2.3	20.0	4.8
1993	6.7	45.1	24.0	2.1	17.3	4.1
1994	7.6	43.7	24.8	2.0	17.4	4.2

WESTERN EUROPE ($ million)

Year	Belg./Lux.	France	Germany	Italy	Nether.	Spain
1950	$12	$29	$27	$9	$15	$3
1951	15	40	21	13	14	3
1952	15	36	18	10	13	4
1953	14	31	22	9	15	3
1954	16	41	27	13	14	5
1955	18	50	51	12	16	5
1956	22	54	57	23	23	3
1957	30	54	63	21	30	2
1958	24	59	88	17	7	3
1959	19	46	123	36	13	4
1960	31	70	142	37	19	5
1961	39	54	170	29	29	8
1962	28	55	179	31	34	11
1963	43	68	203	29	34	11
1964	48	79	197	16	34	11
1965	51	74	194	−4	49	26
1966	31	73	153	22	49	21
1967	50	53	180	49	70	7
1968	83	99	225	47	54	16
1969	130	206	491	83	63	32
1970	158	237	588	85	180	53
1971	197	299	563	58	177	57
1972	192	426	826	141	155	110
1973	426	585	1,415	225	413	146
1974	375	383	1,079	205	753	232
1975	270	657	956	90	540	168
1976	263	484	1,945	290	664	100
1977	447	392	1,491	301	1,028	117
1978	510	816	2,668	547	1,171	120
1979	980	972	2,898	925	1,934	370
1980	637	1,253	1,864	1,298	1,853	225
1981	267	148	849	385	1,218	−81
1982	577	184	1,129	532	1,061	139
1983	534	555	1,421	730	1,532	−59
1984	574	983	1,177	848	1,272	160
1985	600	917	1,719	948	1,539	262
1986	1,112	1,234	2,434	1,752	2,407	468
1987	1,143	1,517	2,856	1,341	2,922	816
1988	1,362	2,040	3,126	1,667	2,902	1,236
1989	1,351	2,163	3,530	1,408	3,129	1,501
1990	1,774	2,484	4,609	2,070	4,117	1,424
1991	1,884	2,171	4,693	2,256	3,609	1,210
1992	1,358	1,498	2,761	1,790	3,062	867
1993	1,394	1,173	3,118	1,265	2,436	42
1994	1,965	2,197	3,867	1,588	2,571	695

TABLE 3.4 (continued)

WESTERN EUROPE ($ million)

Year	UK	Denmark	Ireland	Norway	Sweden	Switzerl.
1950	$142	$1	$1	$3	$7	$4
1951	164	3	1	3	8	5
1952	176	3	1	4	7	6
1953	187	2	1	4	9	6
1954	226	5	1	5	10	7
1955	280	3	1	5	7	10
1956	330	3	1	3	5	14
1957	333	5	1	3	8	13
1958	302	4	1	4	5	18
1959	371	1	1	2	7	23
1960	377	6	1	5	6	49
1961	361	6	2	6	10	84
1962	303	2	2	6	11	122
1963	418	4	1	12	17	155
1964	448	8	3	8	20	153
1965	512	8	11	6	15	159
1966	420	7	15	3	13	177
1967	429	1	19	6	17	213
1968	537	N/A	24	3	17	187
1969	526	9	35	9	25	313
1970	626	21	24	5	37	333
1971	825	−5	21	−2	38	396
1972	1,049	13	39	−5	44	467
1973	1,278	64	67	19	72	779
1974	1,081	66	99	45	141	1,028
1975	936	26	144	92	94	853
1976	842	85	182	191	60	874
1977	1,787	24	140	243	28	1,021
1978	2,174	83	318	343	40	1,363
1979	5,765	170	397	248	214	1,988
1980	5,408	111	392	565	198	1,865
1981	5,411	93	573	944	−2	1,896
1982	3,639	88	407	940	35	1,437
1983	4,012	140	521	799	64	1,417
1984	4,822	163	543	777	124	1,632
1985	4,317	148	748	575	120	1,647
1986	3,645	189	788	405	151	1,759
1987	5,657	143	1,037	288	118	2,662
1988	8,167	132	1,148	491	175	2,685
1989	7,672	163	1,286	738	275	3,805
1990	8,237	234	1,433	815	315	4,423
1991	5,427	189	1,556	962	155	3,216
1992	4,587	121	1,817	660	−19	2,711
1993	9,965	113	1,755	677	−61	4,284
1994	8,165	167	1,849	696	198	3,625

LATIN AMERICA ($ million)

Year	L.A. Rep.	Argentina	Brazil	Chile	Colombia	Mexico
1950	$614	$18	$97	$41	$16	$43
1951	838	29	143	57	15	64
1952	834	30	150	54	20	61
1953	688	20	112	34	13	47
1954	695	31	83	41	45	45
1955	848	27	71	74	23	66
1956	1,005	20	67	96	22	66
1957	1,118	29	74	51	20	57
1958	785	12	46	46	−2	58
1959	802	25	59	82	18	55
1960	856	46	84	80	27	62
1961	986	100	75	61	34	55
1962	1,029	76	87	75	21	75
1963	974	54	71	64	32	62
1964	1,111	93	63	86	33	95
1965	1,340	137	103	86	25	103
1966	1,152	107	108	127	34	108
1967	1,143	78	95	155	17	109
1968	1,327	123	144	159	21	135
1969	1,343	148	154	169	39	155
1970	1,206	109	208	81	43	146
1971	1,166	80	213	2	60	126
1972	1,247	79	308	7	31	198
1973	2,000	71	426	6	46	268
1974	2,297	47	464	20	90	394
1975	2,155	103	657	N/A	53	455
1976	1,906	246	731	22	79	731
1977	2,111	257	589	28	89	243
1978	2,512	135	910	30	96	581
1979	2,965	520	247	37	22	843
1980	3,689	695	499	7	68	1,167
1981	3,606	104	499	161	59	1,362
1982	1,627	464	803	−68	195	−951
1983	1,375	350	185	48	183	−275
1984	2,131	61	569	43	249	−377
1985	2,282	127	551	63	268	664
1986	3,106	375	836	95	194	216
1987	3,685	327	1,294	125	101	688
1988	5,497	369	2,346	226	164	1,253
1989	6,484	43	3,505	303	82	1,417
1990	5,666	405	1,427	337	342	1,850
1991	5,792	500	931	321	374	2,267
1992	7,865	518	2,325	359	457	2,457
1993	10,296	647	4,953	256	311	2,392
1994	11,547	848	4,818	659	327	2,631

TABLE 3.4 (continued)

LATIN AMERICA ($ million)

Year	Panama	Peru	Venezuela	O.W.H.	Bahamas	Bermuda
1950	$13	$21	$232	$12	$0	$0
1951	44	36	297	14	0	0
1952	33	31	329	12	0	0
1953	14	21	334	27	0	0
1954	23	29	346	29	0	0
1955	28	40	434	34	0	0
1956	44	34	551	58	0	0
1957	55	36	680	123	0	56
1958	51	18	484	95	0	29
1959	60	27	426	95	0	16
1960	64	58	430	141	0	55
1961	100	60	469	117	0	20
1962	109	52	506	169	0	40
1963	86	65	512	165	0	36
1964	69	79	548	150	0	38
1965	82	92	498	165	0	60
1966	61	123	417	173	19	29
1967	75	90	453	179	16	22
1968	94	106	474	220	46	N/A
1969	72	109	431	225	35	29
1970	93	74	395	215	37	N/A
1971	122	39	449	268	51	64
1972	163	30	342	313	79	90
1973	288	90	623	512	129	106
1974	346	47	573	848	166	333
1975	405	−88	344	1,047	358	428
1976	226	46	262	1,573	695	N/A
1977	435	35	329	1,601	692	704
1978	257	164	277	2,267	810	1,014
1979	449	508	142	3,555	1,422	1,627
1980	488	N/A	108	3,280	1,003	1,551
1981	587	405	297	2,537	1,054	1,264
1982	578	255	306	2,141	1,209	1,451
1983	826	120	−160	419	1,168	1,241
1984	382	113	185	−190	668	1,439
1985	487	−31	65	183	974	1,293
1986	972	−3	242	415	833	1,498
1987	868	−43	153	163	240	1,592
1988	696	−108	270	1,547	308	2,096
1989	929	−131	111	2,761	63	2,652
1990	1,075	−122	152	3,019	438	2,067
1991	955	−17	276	3,201	306	2,016
1992	909	30	487	4,208	756	2,090
1993	833	18	548	3,907	84	3,029
1994	1,212	119	391	4,504	173	2,893

LATIN AMERICA/AFRICA ($ million)

Year	Nether. Antilles	UK Caribbean	Egypt	Libya	Nigeria	South Africa
1950	N/A	N/A	N/A	$0	$1	$25
1951	N/A	N/A	N/A	0	12	33
1952	N/A	N/A	N/A	0	10	35
1953	N/A	N/A	N/A	N/A	14	40
1954	N/A	N/A	N/A	N/A	14	43
1955	N/A	N/A	N/A	N/A	14	58
1956	N/A	N/A	N/A	−6	2	59
1957	N/A	N/A	N/A	−20	1	64
1958	N/A	N/A	N/A	−29	−1	42
1959	N/A	N/A	N/A	−34	−1	43
1960	N/A	N/A	N/A	−65	9	50
1961	N/A	N/A	N/A	−53	−8	61
1962	N/A	N/A	N/A	6	−7	72
1963	N/A	N/A	N/A	85	−11	79
1964	N/A	N/A	N/A	258	−30	84
1965	N/A	N/A	N/A	232	5	96
1966	N/A	N/A	N/A	230	−11	101
1967	N/A	N/A	N/A	265	−30	99
1968	N/A	N/A	N/A	405	2	97
1969	N/A	N/A	N/A	498	19	104
1970	N/A	N/A	N/A	373	46	114
1971	N/A	N/A	N/A	309	N/A	96
1972	N/A	N/A	N/A	253	173	102
1973	N/A	N/A	N/A	N/A	N/A	215
1974	N/A	N/A	N/A	373	496	257
1975	N/A	N/A	N/A	N/A	285	140
1976	N/A	N/A	N/A	N/A	198	197
1977	−$147	$170	$97	188	206	176
1978	−6	217	177	166	153	217
1979	−107	123	364	519	227	366
1980	33	258	N/A	N/A	199	666
1981	−405	255	689	135	213	491
1982	−1,935	1,213	648	155	136	212
1983	−3,228	1,041	610	244	228	273
1984	−3,426	868	588	109	335	197
1985	−3,196	754	494	96	423	142
1986	−2,735	609	85	−24	573	235
1987	−2,196	314	218	−2	216	244
1988	−1,986	565	205	3	143	179
1989	−1,309	701	286	−7	200	122
1990	−932	789	407	−2	197	163
1991	−888	1,073	324	−5	642	158
1992	−417	946	343	−2	620	156
1993	−377	514	243	−1	573	174
1994	−92	801	274	−3	579	187

TABLE 3.4 (continued)

ASIA & MIDDLE EAST ($ million)

Year	M. East	Bahrain	S. Arabia	U.A.E.	Hong Kong	Indonesia
1950	$219	N/A	N/A	N/A	N/A	$36
1951	343	N/A	N/A	N/A	N/A	38
1952	388	N/A	N/A	N/A	N/A	28
1953	409	N/A	N/A	N/A	N/A	32
1954	482	N/A	N/A	N/A	N/A	26
1955	491	N/A	N/A	N/A	N/A	37
1956	526	N/A	N/A	N/A	N/A	37
1957	607	N/A	N/A	N/A	N/A	55
1958	678	N/A	N/A	N/A	N/A	56
1959	621	N/A	N/A	N/A	N/A	59
1960	736	N/A	N/A	N/A	N/A	73
1961	771	N/A	N/A	N/A	N/A	68
1962	852	N/A	N/A	N/A	N/A	73
1963	904	N/A	N/A	N/A	N/A	60
1964	846	N/A	N/A	N/A	N/A	58
1965	839	N/A	N/A	N/A	N/A	46
1966	597	N/A	N/A	N/A	N/A	44
1967	665	N/A	N/A	N/A	N/A	N/A
1968	707	N/A	N/A	N/A	N/A	N/A
1969	677	N/A	N/A	N/A	N/A	70
1970	711	N/A	N/A	N/A	N/A	82
1971	1,033	N/A	N/A	N/A	N/A	101
1972	1,346	N/A	N/A	N/A	N/A	245
1973	1,730	N/A	N/A	N/A	N/A	699
1974	2,092	N/A	N/A	N/A	N/A	1,094
1975	1,643	N/A	N/A	N/A	N/A	921
1976	1,941	N/A	N/A	N/A	N/A	404
1977	2,116	89	1,459	125	384	596
1978	1,867	131	1,257	101	461	825
1979	2,720	222	N/A	140	537	1,170
1980	-22	149	-369	165	564	2,080
1981	1,456	179	1,128	89	679	2,159
1982	1,269	N/A	790	227	680	1,756
1983	656	N/A	233	219	642	1,672
1984	907	N/A	536	202	629	1,990
1985	414	-42	278	150	512	1,389
1986	592	-195	341	79	646	676
1987	528	-105	375	155	1,024	939
1988	773	-18	461	91	997	848
1989	646	-18	370	93	1,282	1,057
1990	1,071	-27	454	133	1,200	1,886
1991	978	17	472	140	1,540	1,785
1992	1,028	55	256	259	1,855	1,509
1993	867	52	249	123	2,100	1,251
1994	923	125	225	161	1,664	1,308

ASIA/OCEANIA ($ million)

Year	Japan	Malaysia	Philip.	Singap.	S. Korea	Taiwan	Australia	New Zeal.
1950	$2	N/A	$39	N/A	N/A	N/A	$27	$3
1951	8	N/A	35	N/A	N/A	N/A	37	4
1952	3	N/A	33	N/A	N/A	N/A	34	4
1953	8	N/A	29	N/A	N/A	N/A	51	6
1954	15	N/A	34	N/A	N/A	N/A	60	6
1955	21	N/A	38	N/A	N/A	N/A	64	7
1956	19	N/A	43	N/A	N/A	N/A	62	7
1957	23	N/A	40	N/A	N/A	N/A	77	8
1958	10	N/A	54	N/A	N/A	N/A	85	9
1959	23	N/A	57	N/A	N/A	N/A	98	9
1960	32	N/A	49	N/A	N/A	N/A	97	11
1961	35	N/A	57	N/A	N/A	N/A	71	13
1962	34	N/A	37	N/A	N/A	N/A	102	14
1963	51	N/A	36	N/A	N/A	N/A	122	17
1964	65	N/A	41	N/A	N/A	N/A	118	20
1965	97	N/A	46	N/A	N/A	N/A	124	18
1966	87	N/A	51	N/A	N/A	N/A	116	12
1967	109	N/A	56	N/A	N/A	N/A	131	11
1968	147	N/A	52	N/A	N/A	N/A	185	8
1969	177	N/A	73	N/A	N/A	N/A	243	14
1970	228	N/A	54	N/A	N/A	N/A	301	15
1971	270	N/A	54	N/A	N/A	N/A	337	19
1972	334	N/A	25	N/A	N/A	N/A	389	28
1973	514	N/A	50	N/A	N/A	N/A	671	57
1974	393	N/A	65	N/A	N/A	N/A	624	37
1975	233	N/A	30	N/A	N/A	N/A	726	9
1976	417	N/A	77	N/A	N/A	N/A	819	21
1977	598	45	91	$97	$47	$61	623	27
1978	1,199	106	111	160	54	70	895	53
1979	833	265	136	237	63	94	1,099	17
1980	839	314	168	332	−43	89	1,217	69
1981	939	265	202	482	33	89	1,362	61
1982	572	284	51	503	80	128	738	31
1983	926	379	99	513	59	149	743	44
1984	841	397	176	521	177	188	1,066	65
1985	948	332	134	383	184	92	876	56
1986	2,040	162	205	493	114	93	686	83
1987	1,988	227	167	670	125	307	1,100	108
1988	2,580	382	230	765	192	334	1,951	84
1989	2,070	231	270	727	245	443	2,006	87
1990	1,722	469	227	1,127	269	341	1,888	78
1991	2,293	505	232	1,138	70	414	749	130
1992	1,979	666	369	1,539	143	411	2,234	210
1993	1,723	701	409	1,835	218	423	2,233	185
1994	2,894	583	440	1,593	339	583	2,371	340

TABLE 3.5. Income Share of Selected Profit Centers in the Caribbean

Year	Income $ million	% of Total FDI Income
1982	$3,873	15.7
1983	3,450	12.9
1984	2,975	9.9
1985	3,021	10.6
1986	2,940	9.5
1987	2,146	5.6
1988	3,169	6.3
1989	3,416	6.3
1990	3,294	5.7
1991	3,395	6.5
1992	3,792	7.5
1993	3,627	6.1
1994	3,867	6.0

Note: Includes Bahamas, Bermuda, UK Islands, and Caribbean.

Sources: *SOCB*, August 1990, pp. 87-94; August 1992, p. 141; July 1993, p. 121; August 1994, p. 158; August 1995, p. 113.

Islands of interest are the Bahamas, Bermuda, British possessions in the Caribbean, and the Netherlands Antilles. The special role of these profit centers is best illustrated by a comparison of their profit contributions with that of a regular investment center like Canada, for example. The latter, representing the typical mature, fully developed, and highly diversified investment situation, produced $5,100 of income for each and every one of its almost one million employees in 1990. The Bahamas affiliates returned over $53,000 for each of its 8,200 employees in financial and other services in the same year, a rather poor showing compared to the $120,000 produced only five years earlier. The UK possessions reached a more respectable $537,000 for each of their 1,500 employees, but were dwarfed by Bermuda with a record-setting $761,000 for each of their 2,700 people. These three tiny islands harbored 0.2 percent of total FDI employment, but accounted for the shares of total direct investment income shown in Table 3.5. It is worth noting another profit center in Central America which is not included here: Panama. The country produced on the level of the Bahamas with $52,600 for each of the 19,800 employees in the same year (Employment data from *SOCB*, July 1993, p. 52).

The significance of the Caribbean affiliates to the overall FDI operations and profits would be inadequately projected without a thorough understanding of the role played by the finance affiliates in the Netherlands Antilles. In sharp contrast to the islands mentioned above, which are heavy net contributors to direct investment profits, the Netherlands Antilles are just the opposite up to the point where they wipe out a great portion of the positive income flows produced by the other islands in the region.

Established to tap the international capital markets for their parents, The Netherlands Antilles owe their existence to a tax treaty with the United States exempting them from the 40 percent source tax on interest payments by U.S. companies to foreigners. With the revocation of this tax in December of 1982, they were not really needed any longer, but remain in operation.

Before 1977, funds channeled through the affiliates to their parents were statistically treated as if the parents had directly borrowed in Euro-bond markets. As mentioned before, starting with 1977 this was changed, and the affiliates began to be treated like all other finance companies in that any funds flowing from them back to the United States were considered repatriations of FDI capital.

Statistically, such inflows have the effect of reducing the investment stock, and this is why they are shown with a minus sign in front within official publications, even though fund inflows are normally treated as positive BOP entries. Repayment of such massive debts produces exactly the opposite effect on the stock position.

Interest payments on these borrowed funds now became a part of the FDI income picture where they displayed an equally negative force. Had parent companies either borrowed directly in international capital markets, or had the treatment of borrowings through these affiliates continued as before 1977, both the income picture and the size of the direct investment stock would look totally different. The positive aspect of the situation lies in the fact that the gradual reduction in the parents' indebtedness (Table 2.1) leads to a simultaneous decline in interest payments. The trend of these flows is shown below for the years 1983 through 1994 (see Table 3.6).

Income produced by affiliates in the Latin American republics was surprisingly stable until 1981. In view of the continent's history of political and economic turmoil, currency instabilities, import substitution policies and even expropriations, this is quite an accomplishment. Mexico upset this picture of tranquility twice with its jolting Peso devaluations of 100 percent in 1982, and 50 percent at the end of 1993. The sudden collapse of the exchange rate, plus the ensuing economic uncertainties caused a $2.3 billion loss of income from Mexico in 1982 alone, which effectively wiped out one-third of total Latin America's profits (including the Caribbean islands) or fully two-thirds of the income generated by affiliates from the continental republics alone. Aftershocks of the Mexican debacle were felt through 1984 to 1985, but a short-lived improvement became visible from 1985 forward

TABLE 3.6. Income Flows through Affiliates in Netherlands Antilles ($ billion)

Year	1983	1984	1985	1986	1987	1988
Income	−3.2	−3.4	−3.2	−2.7	−2.2	−2.0
Earnings	1.4	1.8	1.6	1.2	1.1	0.8
Interest	−4.6	−5.2	−4.8	−3.9	−3.3	−2.8

Year	1989	1990	1991	1992	1993	1994
Income	−1.3	−1.0	−0.8	−0.4	−0.3	−0.1
Earnings	0.8	0.8	0.7	0.6	0.5	0.4
Interest	−2.1	−1.7	−1.5	−1.0	−0.8	−0.5

Sources: *SOCB*, August 1992, p. 120; July 1993, p. 94; August 1994, p. 131; August 1995, p. 92.

until the freshly signed NAFTA agreement was shaken to the core in 1994. Surprisingly, the latest and totally unexpected devaluation has not visibly hurt the profit picture, but neither did it help to improve it (see Table 3.4).

Europe's share of the investment stock rose from 16 to 49 percent between 1950 and 1994 and income shares from 15 to 43 percent, with a high of 56 percent in 1990, indicating a very positive development in the return on investments over four decades. Europe used to be the only area besides Asia producing income shares which were above underlying investment shares. This came to an end in 1992, when income ratios started to slip below those for investment stock. Only four countries out of eighteen countries in total accounted for 61 percent of Europe's income in 1994. In rank order of importance they were: the United Kingdom (31 percent), Switzerland (12 percent), Germany (10 percent), and the Netherlands (8 percent).

England's profit contribution, now strongly dependent on oil revenues, has been even more spectacular in the past. During the early 1980s, when a combination of recession and strong dollar devastated the profit performance of most affiliates operating in terms of other currencies, the United Kingdom saved the day with its oil profits which are mostly unaffected by dollar swings, as they are mostly earned in dollars.

Switzerland plays a tax shelter role very similar to that of the Caribbean islands in that its income per employee exceeds by far the levels generated by surrounding European countries. In France, the 1990 figure reached $5,900; in Germany, $7,600; in the UK, $8,800; but, in Switzerland, a phenomenal $79,600 was reached.

Asia's share in the U.S. FDI stock grew from 9 percent in 1950 to 15 percent in 1994, while the respective shares in income stayed around 19 percent–a reflection of the investment emphasis on oil affiliates in the Middle East and Indonesia, with their typical ups and downs overshadowing otherwise positive developments of lesser industries in that region.

Asia also seems to have its own profit centers, even though nothing on the scale of the Caribbean or Swiss affiliates. Hong Kong with 82,400 employees and $1.2 billion in profits averaged $14,500 per employee in 1990, or twice the $7,000 for the region as a whole. Typically, 42 percent of the enclave's profits in 1990 came from wholesaling, and 28 percent from manufacturing. It will be interesting to see how U.S. businesses will fare in this city after its return to China in 1997.

Singapore may become a logical successor to Hong Kong, if and when worse comes to worst after Hong Kong's return to China. Singapore is presently the number two profit center in Asia after Japan with an income of $1.0 billion in 1990 or $11,700 for each of its 87,000 employees. With a predominantly Chinese population, it harbors considerable manpower as well as financial, technical, and managerial resources, and seems to be predestined for a vital role in China's future independent of Hong Kong's fate.

Africa has maintained a pretty consistent 1 to 3 percent share in total direct investments for the whole period. Income has, in general, produced shares at about double that level, even with some fluctuations owing to concentrated investments in petroleum ventures and politically sensitive areas. Libya has practically disappeared from the U.S investment map, Nigeria appears to barely hold its own, and South Africa is now stabilizing after a period of major declines with the wholesale withdrawal of American companies for political reasons.

Reference was made to the prominent role of the Anglo-Saxon countries in the FDI position (see Table 1.4). Their role is more or less repeated on the income side, with the exception that income shares, by and large, tended to be much lower than investment shares. This fact is temporarily obscured by the strong showing of the UK affiliates during the early 1980s due to lofty oil prices at the time. As they returned to lower levels under recessionary pressures, so did Anglo-Saxon income figures return to their historic norms. The largest members in this group, Canada and the UK, earned a surprisingly large portion of their income from traditional smoke-stack industries. Manufacturing accounted for 55 percent of total affiliate income in Canada and 39 percent in England in 1990 (see Table 3.7).

Worldwide income is concentrated in a handful of countries. In 1950, only four countries produced 51 percent of the total. That was the year

TABLE 3.7. Income Share of Anglo-Saxon Countries (percentages)

Year	1950	1960	1970	1980	1985	1990	1994
Australia & N. Zeal.	2	3	4	4	3	3	4
Canada	24	21	19	16	18	8	7
South Africa	1	1	1	2	nil	nil	nil
UK	8	10	8	15	15	14	14
Bahamas	0	0	1	3	3	1	nil
Bermuda	0	2	N/A	4	5	4	5
UK Caribbean	N/A	N/A	N/A	1	3	1	1
Grand Total	**35**	**37**	**33**	**45**	**47**	**31**	**31**

when Brazil alone generated more income ($97 million) than the six members of the European Economic Community ($92 million) for a total share of 5 percent; and Cuba with $56 million in turn produced more than half of all European affiliates put together.

By 1970, it took a slightly larger number of countries to produce more than half of all income. The seven countries accounting for 51 percent of the total for the year also showed a wider geographical dispersion than twenty years earlier. In 1950, the Western Hemisphere dominated the statistics. By 1970, this area was still strongly represented, but Europe, Africa, and Australia were pushing their way to the top of the list. By 1990, the situation had changed altogether. Still, only seven nations accounted for a slightly higher 53 percent of all FDI income. This time, Europe and Canada dominated. Despite the appearance of a rather one-sided income concentration created by Table 3.8, collected data in Table 3.4 reveal a more balanced situation with a growing set of countries around the world approaching the magic $1 billion mark.

INCOME BY INDUSTRY

The bulk of income has traditionally been generated by two industries: manufacturing and petroleum, whose share in the total has maintained a level between 60 to 70 percent for most of the four decades under study. Their starting share of 70.8 percent in 1950, was gradually reduced to 70 percent in 1960, 68.4 percent in 1970, 65.2 percent in 1980 and, finally, 51 percent in 1990 (see Table 3.9).

Manufacturing has maintained a fairly steady pace in total income flows for the period. The performance of the petroleum industry, on the

TABLE 3.8. Leading Income Countries ($ million)

1950	$	%	1970	$	%	1990	$	%
Total	1,769	100	Total	8,169	100	Total	57,746	100
Canada	440	25	Canada	1,518	19	UK	8,224	14
Venez.	232	13	UK	626	8	Canada	4,738	8
UK	142	8	Germany	588	7	Germany	4,493	8
Brazil	97	5	Venez.	395	5	Switzer.	4,410	8
N/A			Libya	373	5	Nether.	4,120	7
N/A			Switzer.	333	4	France	2,480	4
N/A			Australia	301	4	Italy	2,067	4
Subtotal	911	51		4,134	51		30,532	53

Sources: *Selected Data on U.S. Direct Investment Abroad, 1950-76*, pp. 109, 129 (1950, 1970). *SOCB*, July 1993, p. 118 (1990).

other hand, rapidly deteriorated after 1984 and there seems to be no true recovery in sight. This is surprising even for an industry with a history of very erratic development patterns. At any rate, petroleum has been solidly replaced as an income producer by the financial sector since 1989, and there is a chance that it may slip further to fourth place in the rankings behind the trade affiliates if present trends continue. In the beginning, income from oil affiliates led the profit flow, but was surpassed by income from manufacturing in 1964. It regained its leading position in 1979, but lost it again in 1985. This seesaw pattern of competitive ranking demonstrates how the fate of both industries was affected by two major yet uncontrollable forces. One was OPEC's pricing dictate, which led to a temporary income boost for oil affiliates during the early 1970s and again during the late 1970s. The other is the strong rise of the dollar's exchange value during the 1980 through 1985 period in the aftermath of the second oil crisis. Oil profits were automatically boosted by the twin effect of rising prices and the fact that oil is exclusively traded in dollars, which sheltered revenues and profits from the negative impact of currency conversion. With oil prices in the early 1990s at less than half of their peak compared to a decade earlier and the dollar's exchange value greatly reduced, it is not difficult to pinpoint the major causes for the industry's decline.

The fluctuating dollar usually had the opposite effect on other industries, whose earnings were counted in foreign currencies. The strong dollar between 1980 and 1985 boosted oil income, but produced the flat to declining

TABLE 3.9. Development of Income by Industry ($ million)

Year	Pet.	Mfg.	Trade*	Banks	Finance	Services	Other
1950	$629	$623	$116	N/A	N/A	N/A	$401
1951	900	690	141	N/A	N/A	N/A	512
1952	1,015	683	145	N/A	N/A	N/A	499
1953	994	718	133	N/A	N/A	N/A	423
1954	1,029	764	148	N/A	N/A	N/A	485
1955	1,231	860	174	N/A	N/A	N/A	609
1956	1,454	908	207	N/A	N/A	N/A	777
1957	1,744	883	262	N/A	N/A	N/A	723
1958	1,324	924	237	N/A	N/A	N/A	580
1959	1,188	1,130	304	N/A	N/A	N/A	673
1960	1,319	1,177	349	N/A	N/A	N/A	777
1961	1,485	1,167	387	N/A	N/A	N/A	783
1962	1,698	1,259	406	N/A	N/A	N/A	878
1963	1,835	1,527	419	N/A	N/A	N/A	855
1964	1,821	1,826	456	N/A	N/A	N/A	1,001
1965	1,854	1,989	489	N/A	N/A	N/A	1,173
1966	1,496	1,868	456	N/A	$405	N/A	1,034
1967	1,765	1,863	412	N/A	465	N/A	1,100
1968	1,983	2,411	472	N/A	515	N/A	1,211
1969	2,026	3,113	650	N/A	544	N/A	1,316
1970	2,456	3,133	789	N/A	642	N/A	1,349
1971	2,878	3,492	884	N/A	906	N/A	999
1972	3,095	4,740	1,077	N/A	1,089	N/A	947
1973	5,717	6,579	1,448	N/A	1,444	N/A	1,355
1974	6,963	6,684	1,821	N/A	1,922	N/A	1,766
1975	4,795	5,998	1,678	N/A	2,432	N/A	1,692
1976	5,123	7,223	1,685	N/A	2,767	N/A	2,200
1977	5,331	6,655	2,041	1,819	2,220	674	932
1978	6,010	9,980	2,555	N/A	4,246	N/A	2,084
1979	13,292	13,054	3,905	1,800	3,634	N/A	2,522
1980	13,181	11,053	4,003	2,044	3,777	N/A	3,088
1981	13,330	8,194	3,331	2,241	3,009	N/A	2,385
1982	9,455	6,417	1,575	3,787	2,032	788	648
1983	10,421	8,217	1,997	3,308	854	735	1,227
1984	10,673	10,709	2,741	3,176	943	645	972
1985	9,403	11,208	3,070	2,406	933	608	673
1986	7,271	13,832	4,192	1,906	2,517	619	563
1987	7,317	18,617	5,965	322	4,919	846	537
1988	7,727	25,963	6,897	1,727	6,206	1,074	835
1989	5,454	27,034	6,857	219	11,547	1,732	1,085
1990	9,889	24,774	7,425	380	12,830	1,748	977
1991	10,299	20,133	6,249	250	12,137	1,463	1,176
1992	7,416	19,074	6,526	2,234	12,667	1,386	1,260
1993	8,438	21,784	7,273	3,736	15,222	1,769	953
1994	7,440	28,595	9,300	3,278	12,586	1,897	1,693

Note: *Includes wholesale/retail for all years except 1982-84 (wholesale only).

Sources: *Selected Data on U.S. Direct Investment Abroad, 1950-76*, pp. 109-35. 1977 FDI census, p. 84. *SOCB*: 1978, August 1980, p. 34; 1979, August 1981, p. 37; 1980, August 1982, p. 27; 1981, August 1983, p. 29; 1977-81, August 1985, p. 34; 1982-89, August 1990, pp. 87-9, 97-8; 1986-89, August 1991, pp. 106-7; 1987-88, August 1992, pp. 143-4; 1989-92, July 1993, pp. 123-4; 1990-93, August 1994, pp. 154-7; August 1995, pp. 114-5.

performance evident in other industries. The dollar's decline after 1985 contributed to oil's weakening and the rather dramatic profit recovery of all other industries during the remainder of the period with the exception of banks, which suffered from imprudent lending policies in developing markets.

The generally weak and very erratic income performance of the banking branch toward the end of the period is a sharp contrast to that of the finance industry, which showed an almost perfect earnings record. Undoubtedly, the accounting changes for the Netherlands Antilles affiliates mentioned above played an important role here. Borrowing large amounts at high interests during and following the second oil embargo had a negative impact on parent income early on, but with declining liabilities and interest rates later on, the pressure on the industry's income was greatly reduced.

TAX ASPECTS OF FDI INCOME

Two kinds of taxes are levied against earnings of U.S. affiliates: corporate (income) taxes and withholding taxes on remittances (distributed earnings and interests). Data presented below reflect the impact of effective tax rates rather than statutory rates. Differences between the two are normal because of modifying factors such as tax credits, concessions, holidays, etc. All information consists of Mofa data alone which explains why they are lower than previously shown BOP figures covering all affiliates.

Affiliate income is established on the basis of a standard profit and loss accounting formula developed by Department of Commerce (DOC) researchers. It measures affiliate earnings after income taxes but before withholding taxes on distributed earnings and interest payments (see Figure 3.2).

Adding the actual foreign income taxes paid (which are provided by the benchmark surveys) to this figure results in total taxable income and allows the calculation of the effective tax rate on corporate earnings as shown in Table 3.10.

Effective tax rates vary between 1 and 90 percent depending on the country and industry involved. A real revelation is the fact that high rates are by no means an exclusive of developed nations whose average effective rate in 1982 stood at 54.5 percent against 53.6 percent for developing nations. In an environment of seemingly universal high rates, there are nations that levy incredibly low income taxes: the tax havens attracting foreign business with favorable tax legislation. It is a successful strategy, as proven by Switzerland and the Caribbean islands which produced more than 21 percent of all Mofa net income in 1982 on a sales share of only 9.8 percent. Compared to tax levels averaging 55 percent for the rest of

Europe, tax shelters such as Switzerland, Ireland, and Luxemburg demonstrate a striking contrast with effective tax rates below 20 percent.

Equally incredible tax levies at the other end of the spectrum are documented for oil-producing nations which are practically confiscatory by comparison. Nigeria and the UAE are prime examples of nations in this category. Somewhere in between lie the highly socialized countries such as the UK, France, Norway, Italy, Sweden, and also Japan. The English

FIGURE 3.2. Income Calculation Scheme

Income	less Costs/Expenses	equals Net Income*
Sales + Equity in net income of other affiliates + Income from other equity investments + Exchange gains/losses from translating financial statements (FASB 8) + Other capital gains/losses + All other	Cost of goods sold + Selling, general, and administrative expenses + Foreign income taxes + Other	*net income (excluding capital gain/loss according to FASB 52)

Source: 1982 FDI census, p. 216.

TABLE 3.10. 1989 Income Tax Rate by Mofa Industry ($ million)

Industry	Net Income	Income Tax	Gross Income	% Tax Rate
Total	$72,142	$33,291	$105,433	31.5
Petroleum	7,659	8,088	15,747	51.5
Manufacturing	34,025	17,341	51,366	33.8
Trade*	8,704	4,413	13,117	33.7
Finance (except banking), Insurance, and Real Estate	17,543	1,541	19,084	8.1
Services	2,614	935	3,549	26.4
Other	1,597	973	2,570	37.8

Note: *Includes wholesale/retail.

Source: 1989 FDI census, p. 179.

and Norwegian rates could be a mixture of welfare and oil taxation, as both have developed into major petroleum producers (see Table 3.11).

A less significant set of taxes imposed by most countries on top of corporate taxes consists of withholding charges on distributed earnings and interest payments. They can be estimated with the help of two sets of figures from the annual *SOCB* tables covering U.S. FDI which provide details on distributed earnings and actual withholding taxes paid. The latest information available from these sources is shown in Table 3.12. There is no explanation for the wide fluctuations of these rates within a relatively short time span.

OTHER INCOME

Operating income composed of remitted funds (dividends and interests) and reinvestments is the most important, but not the only form of income generated by subsidiaries. Two additional categories represent genuine income for parents and add substantially to their cash flow. They appear in the export section of the BOP's current account under these headings:

1. "Royalties and license fees from affiliated foreigners" in older publications and, since 1982, changed to simply read "royalties and license fees" in the special section of the international transaction tables dealing with U.S. direct investment abroad.
2. "Other private services from affiliated foreigners" again changed in 1982 to "other private services" on U.S. direct investment abroad.

Both entries measure the net flow of funds among U.S. parents and their affiliates. They should not be confused with two very similar positions found in the import section of the current account labeled:

3. "Royalties and license fees to affiliated foreigners" changed in 1982 to simply be called "royalties and license fees."
4. "Other private services to affiliated foreigners" changed in 1982 to "other private services" on FDI in the United States.

These latter two accounts deal strictly with transactions of affiliates located in the United States and their foreign parents. All four of the above accounts are reserved only for members of the FDI community. Separate accounts exist for similar information on nonaffiliated U.S. and foreign business partners. They are briefly dealt with in the following discussion, but are no of immediate interest to the student of foreign direct investment.

TABLE 3.11. Effective Income Tax Rates for Selected Countries, 1989 ($ million)

Country	Net Income	Income Tax	Gross Income	% Tax Rate
Canada	$7,694	$4,470	$12,164	36.7
Europe	40,239	14,277	66,277	21.5
Belgium	1,653	552	2,205	25.0
Denmark	180	98	278	35.3
France	2,412	1,526	3,938	38.8
Germany	4,950	2,870	7,820	36.7
Ireland	3,084	58	3,143	1.8
Italy	1,761	1,383	3,144	44.0
Luxemburg	236	51	287	17.8
Netherlands	5,585	1,055	6,640	15.9
UK	11,033	3,938	14,971	26.3
Norway	706	924	1,630	56.7
Spain	2,018	740	2,758	26.8
Sweden	359	201	560	35.9
Switzerland	5,475	435	5,910	7.4
Latin America	11,537	4,204	15,741	26.7
Argentina	−265	59	−206	NMF
Brazil	3,010	2,373	5,383	44.1
Colombia	11	197	208	94.7
Peru	−57	184	127	NMF
Venezuela	27	105	132	79.5
Mexico	1,174	671	1,950	34.4
Panama	1,655	39	1,694	2.3
Bahamas	253	5	258	1.9
Bermuda	2,957	71	3,028	2.3
Nether. Antilles	1,166	67	1,233	5.4
UK Carib. Islands	547	7	554	1.3
Africa	911	2,060	2,971	69.3
South Africa	160	150	310	48.3
Nigeria	304	963	1,267	76.0
Asia	8,756	6,802	15,558	43.7
Saudi Arabia	187	14	191	7.3
UAE	79	630	709	88.9
Hong Kong	1,737	281	2,018	13.9
Indonesia	1,290	1,623	2,913	55.7
Japan	2,348	2,891	5,239	55.2
Malaysia	377	281	658	42.7
Singapore	1,128	130	1,258	10.3
Taiwan	661	112	773	14.5
Australia	2,368	1,374	3,742	36.7
New Zealand	76	61	137	44.5
World	72,142	33,291	105,433	31.6

Note: Data cover Mofas only.

Source: 1989 FDI census, p. 178.

TABLE 3.12. Effective Withholding Tax Rates on Distributed Earnings ($ million)

Year	Distributed Earnings		Effective % Tax Rate
	Before Tax	After Tax	
1990	$35,802	$34,192	4.5
1991	36,549	35,167	3.8
1992	35,431	34,256	3.3
1993	29,358	28,390	3.3
1994	32,099	31,065	3.2

Sources: *SOCB*, August 1992, pp. 120-1; July 1993, pp. 94-5; August 1994, pp. 131-2; August 1995, pp. 92-3.

For the investigation of outward U.S. FDI income flows, only points 1 and 2 above are relevant. Each position reflects net flows between parents and subsidiaries; that is to say, they establish the balance between subsidiary payments to parents and parent payments to their subsidiaries.

While this part of the flows is well defined, its informational value is still limited in that it does not provide for full disclosure of the FDI role in the overall flows of these funds. For instance, transactions between U.S. parents and unaffiliated foreigners, as well as those between subsidiaries and unaffiliated U.S. businesses, cannot be filtered out of the aggregate accounts published.

Details on such transactions would be of interest because the chance of FDI members being involved in the generation of further income flows to the United States are considerably greater than for non-FDI companies. Availability of such information would also permit an accurate assessment of the true role played by U.S. FDI companies in the outward dissemination of technology, as U.S. parent companies are known to maintain parallel licensing agreements with foreigners and affiliates alike, often in the same country. As a rule, they cover unrelated products and/or processes so both licensees doing business in the same market are not in competition, and exists as a result of:

1. A contract entered into before a subsidiary was formed or acquired;
2. The affiliates' business character not permitting the use of a particular technology;
3. The license helping to put a foot in the door of a potential acquisition;
4. A move to block the entry of a competitor;
5. A quid pro quo in a lucrative cross-licensing deal; and
6. A subsidiary not being possible for any reason.

Looking at the other side of the situation, firms that were acquired overseas may have had preexisting licensing agreements with U.S. nationals, which in the absence of antitrust violations would normally be continued. In such a case, the parent company has become an indirect licensor in its home territory.

Licensing and service contracts with unrelated business partners seem fair and square, as they were entered into on a perfectly voluntary basis. The same contracts between members of the same company however, carry the aura of a captive situation. They are not questionable from a legal point of view, but seem artificial and contrived because the affiliate partner has no choice in the matter, so to speak, and may have to accept conditions that could not be demanded of independent third parties. Many of these licensing and service contracts owe their existence to tax advantages or other concessions not applicable to regular operating income. They are very helpful in cases of exchange restrictions or other limitations on income remittances. Because of their often disputed nature, licensing agreements among affiliated companies are watched very closely by fiscal authorities around the globe, particularly in less-developed nations. Here licensing agreements are seen as one side of the "triangle of domination"– a reference to the perceived forced imposition of capital, management, and technology strictures by the industrialized nations. This attitude explains the constant pressure on the United Nations to alter laws governing property rights in developing countries' favor.

A final point concerns the technical differentiation of income from direct capital investments, and other income in the form of royalties, license fees, and service fees. The first category is shown in the form of dividends, interest, or retained earnings for the use of equity or debt capital after payment of applicable corporate and withholding taxes. The second category is legally considered a business expense paid for the use of property rights or business services and, as such, subject to a different tax treatment. The stiff corporate taxes are avoided and if any, only moderate withholding taxes are levied in the payor country. Remittance of regular income disguised in this form has a very practical appeal–it reduces the volume of regular operating income exposed to much higher tax rates.

ROYALTIES AND LICENSE FEES

The BOP position covering receipts of royalties/license fees from affiliated foreigners is defined by the U.S. Department of Commerce (DOC) as follows:

net receipts or payments for the use or sale of intangible property rights, including: patents, industrial processes, trademarks, copyrights, franchises, designs, know-how, formulas, techniques, and manufacturing rights. (*SOCB*, June 1987, p. 53, footnotes to the U.S. International Transaction Tables)

Adopted for data published from 1960 forward, this definition renders similar information for prior years incomparable, and is thus excluded from the tables below. All data presented are net transactions between parents and their affiliates, and net of withholding taxes applicable in the United States or foreign nations. Table 3.13 gives a summary view of the U.S. net flows by individual component in this BOP account for the years from 1960 forward, which allows an objective assessment of the relative importance of each entry as follows:

- Column A details U.S. parent net receipts from their foreign affiliates (receipts minus payments) after withholding taxes. It is the foreign direct investment information proper.
- Column B records receipts by all U.S. companies from foreign nonaffiliates. This would include, of course, parent and subsidiary transactions with their respective nonaffiliated business partners.
- Column C shows net payments between subsidiaries located in the United States and their foreign parents (affiliate payments minus affiliate receipts). This column was added to allow a comparison of FDI inflows and outflows for the United States.
- Column D finally records payments by all U.S.-based companies to nonaffiliated foreigners. This account again could conceivably include U.S. parent companies and their foreign subsidiaries.

U.S. parents are the main recipients of total royalty and license fee net inflows. Their share has remained at a level between 70 and 80 percent between 1960 and 1994 with the exception of the years 1977 through 1985, when it dipped into the 40 to 50 percent range. No explanation is given for this setback and the subsequent recovery. Parent receipts of income from this payment category could, in reality, be higher for the reasons explained above.

In comparison to operating income of U.S. parents, royalties and license fees are much smaller in size, and relatively volatile. They accounted for 16 percent of U.S. parent income in 1960, 22 percent in 1970, 10 percent in 1980, and 24 percent in 1990–a seemingly rather modest accomplishment. But patent agreements are subject to specific

TABLE 3.13. Royalty and License Fee Flows (U.S. BOP Data–$ million)

Year	All*	U.S. Net Receipts: Parents A	%	Other B	U.S. Net Payments: Affil. C	Other D
1960	$837	$590	70%	$247	−$35	−$40
1961	906	662	73	244	−43	−46
1962	1,056	800	76	256	−57	−44
1963	1,162	890	77	273	−61	−51
1964	1,314	1,013	77	301	−67	−60
1965	1,534	1,199	78	335	−68	−67
1966	1,516	1,162	77	353	−64	−76
1967	1,747	1,354	77	393	−62	−104
1968	1,867	1,430	77	437	−80	−106
1969	2,019	1,533	76	486	−101	−120
1970	2,331	1,758	75	573	−111	−114
1971	2,545	1,927	76	618	−118	−123
1972	2,770	2,115	75	655	−155	−139
1973	3,225	2,513	78	712	−209	−176
1974	3,821	3,070	80	751	−160	−186
1975	4,300	3,543	82	757	−287	−186
1976	4,353	3,531	80	822	−293	−189
1977	4,920	2,173	44	2,747	−243	−262
1978	5,885	2,697	46	3,188	−393	−277
1979	6,184	3,002	49	3,182	−523	−309
1980	7,085	3,693	52	3,392	−428	−296
1981	7,284	3,658	50	3,626	−362	−288
1982	5,603	3,507	63	2,096	−325	−470
1983	5,778	3,597	62	2,181	−405	−538
1984	6,177	3,921	63	2,256	−597	−571
1985	6,678	4,096	61	2,582	−466	−704
1986	8,113	5,412	67	2,701	−602	−799
1987	10,183	6,889	68	3,294	−896	−961
1988	12,146	8,333	69	3,813	−1,001	−1,600
1989	13,818	10,014	72	3,804	−1,249	−1,279
1990	16,634	11,998	72	4,636	−1,499	−1,636
1991	18,114	12,970	72	5,144	−2,098	−1,937
1992	20,015	14,286	72	5,729	−2,282	−2,792
1993	20,637	14,511	70	5,826	−2,290	−2,573
1994	22,436	15,781	70	6,655	−2,461	−3,205

Note: *The series was put on a new basis in 1981.

Sources: SOCB, August 1988, p. 46; June 1989, pp. 62, 78; June 1990, pp, 61, 77, 96; June 1991, pp. 45, 58, 60; August 1991, p. 85; August 1992, pp. 92, 122; July 1993, p. 96; June 1992, pp. 79, 100; June 1993, pp. 71, 88; July 1993, pp. 64, 96; August 1994, p. 103, 133; June 1995, pp. 84-5; August 1995, pp. 58, 94.

dimensions not encountered in the development of operating income. Patents have a limited lifespan and normally cease to be applicable before the natural death of a product, which means that regular revenues are still being produced by the product, but property rights and related payments have expired. Also, licenses with third parties are revoked, neglected, abandoned or repudiated before expiration of the patent rights, which again impacts negatively on the continuous derivation of a "second" income. Even so, the relatively small size of the development of royalty/fee flows is an encouraging sign of the innovative vigor of U.S. industry, and an expression of foreigners needs for U.S. technology, especially where third parties are involved.

The volume of these flows belies their true importance. Very often the existence of licensing arrangements is tied to exports of essential raw materials to the licensee, causing a positive effect in a country's trade account whose course is not directly evident. In addition, their existence may require entering into long-term consulting or other service contracts, which in turn reflect positively on the development of fund flows in the service accounts.

Comparing inflows and outflows of fees relating to technological use rights by U.S. parents with those of foreign parents operating in the United States (Column A versus Column C) leaves the United States with a very favorable balance albeit a progressively diminishing one. Whereas U.S. parents received $17 in 1960 for each dollar paid by subsidiaries in the United States to their foreign parents, this lead narrowed to $16 in 1970, $14 in 1980, and only $6 in 1994. This was a consequence of the rather slow start, but later accelerating pace of FDI activities in the United States. The flow balance for U.S. parents has obviously been favored by exchange rate developments since 1985, which could cause a deterioration in their competitive fund flows once the dollar enters a prolonged phase of appreciation.

When discussing these counterflows and their competitive implications, it is well to remember that 15 percent of U.S. parents are partially or wholly owned by foreign FDI investors. In other words, the information is technically correct but from a true ownership point of view, too favorable to the American side. Unfortunately, no details have ever been published which allow a quantification of the impact on the U.S. outward FDI picture beyond the sheer numbers of parents involved.

On the payment side of the balance sheet, foreign affiliates hold a fairly steady and important share of around 45 to 50 percent of all outflows, which in view of the above discussion could be an understated figure. At any rate, their progress is a serious indicator of their competitiveness.

Actually, the same could be said for all foreign licensors whose receipts from U.S. partners are advancing quite strongly against similar U.S. inflows. Between 1960 and 1980, outflows stood at about 10 percent of related inflows. However, during the early 1990s, their share has shifted upward to around 16 percent (see Table 3.13).

OTHER SERVICE FEES

The final income category found in the current account of the BOP relates to "other private services" and is structured similar to the royalty account. Again, four entries are found clearly dividing the information for outward and inward FDI accounts. They are listed in the perennially updated "U.S. International Transaction" tables and read:

Receipts or Exports

- Column A *"other private services from affiliated foreigners"* or since 1982, simply *"other private services"* on U.S. direct investment abroad reflects the net balance of U.S. parent receipts.
- Column B *"other private services from unaffiliated foreigners"* refers to receipts from independent foreign business partners. This column may again include parent companies and affiliates as discussed under the royalty section. Since 1982, it has been renamed *"unaffiliated services"* in the BOP section headed *"exports of selected services."*

Payments or Imports

- Column C *"other private services to affiliated foreigners"* show the net balance of flows among foreign parents and their U.S. subsidiaries. Since 1982, this information is found under *"other private services"* on FDI in the United States.
- Column D *"other private services to unaffiliated foreigners"* cover U.S. payments to nonaffiliated foreign companies, which again could involve parents and their affiliates abroad. Since 1982, it is headed *"unaffiliated services"* under *"imports of selected services."*

Service fees become clearly visible in published statistics like those following below. Often, however, they are disguised as a sales figure when they are included in the price of a major project, machinery or component. They are defined and reported by the DOC net of all U.S. or foreign withholding taxes and intercompany transactions, and contain:

> *fees for management, professional and technical services; charges for the use of tangible property, film and television tape rentals, and all other charges and fees.* (1982 FDI census, p. 25)

Aggregate U.S. flows of service fees are much larger than flows for royalties and license fees. In 1994, U.S. receipts of service fees amounted to $59.0 billion, or more than twice the $22.4 billion received for the latter. On the other hand, payments of service fees to the outside world by all U.S accounts were roughly seven times the volume of royalties and license fee outflows—$35.6 billion vs. $5.7 billion.

The balance on service fee flows was less dramatic than that for royalties and license fees, which showed a clearcut gain for foreigners. Over the period of 1981 to 1994, the United States averaged receipts of just about two dollars for each dollar remitted abroad. But, once again, flows to foreigners seem to be gaining against U.S. receipts. In 1980, they reached only 46 percent of inflows compared to 60 percent in 1994.

What makes this account noteworthy is the fact that parents account for a much smaller share in U.S. receipts of service fees than they do for royalties, and that share is sharply declining where it seems to increase or, at least, hold steady for the latter. Again, one must suspect that the exclusion of parent receipts from third parties represents a major distortion factor for the data shown.

A real curiosity is the information concerning service fee flows relating to foreign subsidiaries in the United States. From the beginning of available records, they show a positive contribution to U.S. BOP flows–a situation which, quite frankly, is contrary to all expectations after looking at all other accounts. But for all years documented, foreign affiliates in the United States had receipts in excess of payments. Once again, it would be nice to find out what the factual foreign ownership of U.S. parent companies means in this context. To some degree, there is double-counting involved as in previous statistics presented. Data for foreign companies correctly reflect foreign ownership of the respective fund flows traced here. But an unknown part of these very same flows are also contained in the series for U.S. parent companies. At any rate, it is intriguing to realize that foreign FDI interests receive payments of service charges in the United States. Were these inflows a reason for their acquisition of U.S. companies?

Similar to the U.S. parent role on the inflow side, foreign FDI companies in the United States played a very small to insignificant role in service fee flows. They accounted for less than 2 percent of total, and there seems to be little change, if any. It is a sharp contrast to their 50 percent weight on the royalty outflow side and to the fact that these flows are growing. Given their weak overall stature in service fee flows, it pays to look at the relative roles of both FDI parties. Between 1981 and 1989, U.S. parents received approximately five dollars for each dollar earned by foreign affiliates in the United States. In one exceptional case, there were even eighty-seven dollars in favor of U.S. parents (1989). But for the beginning of the 1990s, U.S. parents received approximately thirteen dollars for each dollar imported by foreign subsidiaries. Clearly, there is no sign of a serious competitive inroads by foreigners in this account (see Table 3.14).

While royalty/license fees and service fees taken separately are relatively modest in comparison to regular operating income of U.S. parents, they take on quite respectable proportions if combined into total "other income." Available data allow a glimpse of the complete picture only from 1977 forward, when parent receipts of service fees were published for the first time on a separate basis.

Table 3.15 reveals how total U.S. FDI income measured in this fashion was in a strong upward drift until 1990. Then its growth began to falter, and actually turned negative for two years before resuming its rise in 1993. The temporary slowdown comes exclusively from developments in the operating income sector which, for all practical purposes, stagnated between 1988 and 1993. This was a very vivid contrast to the vigorous upward movement of the other income category, which was becoming ever more important in the picture. Its share in all income has grown from roughly 15 percent during the late 1970s to 25 percent during the early 1990s, undoubtedly aided by the weakness in the operating income group, but also by its own resilience in face of factors which had a negative effect on the fate of the former. In view of earlier comments made, the development may have been more than sheer coincidence. For instance, the awareness and understanding of tax avoidance possibilities must have grown over time and provided a key incentive for large-scale shifts of funds from regular income to tax-advantaged service fees.

TOTAL RETURN ON INVESTMENT

All previously displayed income flows generated by U.S. FDI, whether in the form of regular operating income or all other income, can now conveniently be employed for the purpose of establishing a picture of the profitability of U.S. FDI efforts over the years. The following analysis

TABLE 3.14. Net Flows of Other Private Service Fees ($ million)

	U.S. Net Receipts:				U.S. Net Payments:	
Year	All*	Parents A	%	Other B	Affil. C	Other D
1960	$570	N/A	–	$570	N/A	–$593
1961	607	N/A	–	607	N/A	–588
1962	585	N/A	–	585	N/A	–528
1963	613	N/A	–	613	N/A	–493
1964	651	N/A	–	651	N/A	–527
1965	714	N/A	–	714	N/A	–461
1966	814	N/A	–	814	N/A	–506
1967	951	N/A	–	951	N/A	–565
1968	1,024	N/A	–	1,024	N/A	–668
1969	1,160	N/A	–	1,160	N/A	–751
1970	1,294	N/A	–	1,294	N/A	–827
1971	1,546	N/A	–	1,546	N/A	–956
1972	1,764	N/A	–	1,764	N/A	–1,043
1973	1,985	N/A	–	1,985	N/A	–1,180
1974	2,321	N/A	–	2,321	N/A	–1,262
1975	2,920	N/A	–	2,920	N/A	–1,551
1976	3,584	N/A	–	3,584	N/A	–2,006
1977	3,848	1,710	45	2,138	N/A	–2,190
1978	4,717	2,008	43	2,709	N/A	–2,573
1979	5,439	1,978	37	3,461	N/A	–2,822
1980	6,276	2,087	33	4,189	N/A	–2,909
1981	10,250	2,136	21	8,114	$400	–3,162
1982	17,444	1,816	10	15,628	403	–7,756
1983	18,192	2,532	14	15,660	471	–7,530
1984	19,255	2,483	13	16,712	478	–8,562
1985	20,036	2,490	12	17,546	696	–9,507
1986	27,514	3,024	11	24,490	1,284	–12,657
1987	28,688	2,446	8	26,242	530	–16,798
1988	30,812	3,091	10	27,721	178	–18,476
1989	36,450	4,333	12	32,117	50	–19,848
1990	39,535	4,199	11	35,336	306	–22,844
1991	46,770	4,434	9	42,336	92	–26,424
1992	50,997	4,839	8	46,117	1,766	–24,448
1993	55,101	4,789	9	50,312	796	–31,203
1994	59,022	5,171	9	53,851	441	–35,164

Note: *New series starting with 1981.

Sources: *SOCB*, August 1987, p. 62; August 1988, p. 46; June 1989, pp. 62, 78; June 1990, pp. 76-7, 94, 96; August 1990, p. 61; June 1991, pp. 45, 60; August 1991, p. 85; August 1992, pp. 92, 122; June 1993, pp. 70-1; July 1993, pp. 64, 96; August 1994, pp. 103, 133; June 1995, pp. 84-5; August 1995, pp. 58, 94.

TABLE 3.15. Aggregate U.S. Parent Company Income ($ million)

Year	Total Income	Operating Income	%	Other Income*	%
1977	$23,556	$19,673	83	$3,883	17
1978	30,163	25,458	85	4,705	15
1979	43,163	38,183	88	4,980	12
1980	42,926	37,146	86	5,780	14
1981	38,343	32,549	85	5,794	15
1982	30,151	24,828	82	5,323	18
1983	32,942	26,813	81	6,129	19
1984	36,450	30,046	82	6,404	18
1985	34,444	27,858	81	6,586	19
1986	38,363	29,927	78	8,436	22
1987	47,858	38,523	80	9,335	20
1988	61,853	50,429	81	11,424	19
1989	68,276	53,929	79	14,347	21
1990	74,201	58,004	78	16,197	22
1991	69,491	52,087	75	17,404	25
1992	69,731	50,565	73	19,166	28
1993	78,475	59,175	75	19,300	25
1994	85,741	64,789	76	20,952	24

Notes: *Comprises royalties, license fees, and other private service fees. The series has been put on a new base starting with 1982.

Sources: See Tables 3.1, 3.13, and 3.14.

provides details for the returns on total funds invested, categorized by industry, and also for major geographical areas or countries.

Table 3.16 gives a breakdown of such ROI separately for: operating income, other income, and both combined. It should be mentioned that the return rate has been established on a net basis after payment of all income and withholding taxes in the generating country, and on the year-end FDI position. This represents a deviation from the official practice of calculating the return on the averaged positions at the beginning and the end of the year, which leads to somewhat higher rates of return. Data to this effect are regularly published in the August issues of the Survey of Current Business in articles covering U.S. Direct Investment Abroad.

The data emphasize two points: (1) a very rewarding overall level of return after taxes. It must be remembered that all years prior to 1977 excluded other private service fees from affiliates which, if they were available, would have increased the return rate for those years; and (2) the upward trend which appeared from about 1973 for the return ratios despite

TABLE 3.16. Return on U.S. FDI Position ($ billion)

Year	Position	Income $	Income %	Other Income* $	Other Income* %	Total $	Total %
1960	32.8	$3.6	10.9	$0.6	1.8	$4.2	12.8
1961	34.7	3.8	11.0	0.7	2.0	4.5	13.0
1962	37.3	4.2	11.3	0.8	2.1	5.0	13.4
1963	40.7	4.6	11.3	0.9	2.2	5.5	13.5
1964	44.5	5.1	11.5	1.0	2.2	6.1	13.7
1965	49.5	5.5	11.1	1.2	2.4	6.7	13.5
1966	51.8	5.3	10.2	1.2	2.3	6.5	12.5
1967	56.6	5.6	9.9	1.4	2.5	7.0	12.4
1968	61.9	6.6	10.7	1.4	2.3	8.0	12.9
1969	68.1	7.6	11.2	1.5	2.2	9.1	13.4
1970	75.5	8.2	10.9	1.8	2.4	10.0	13.2
1971	82.8	9.2	11.1	1.9	2.3	11.1	13.4
1972	89.9	10.9	12.1	2.1	2.3	13.0	14.5
1973	101.3	16.5	16.3	2.5	2.5	19.0	18.8
1974	110.1	19.2	17.4	3.1	2.8	22.3	20.3
1975	124.1	16.6	13.4	3.5	2.8	20.1	16.2
1976	136.8	19.0	13.9	3.5	2.6	22.5	16.4
1977	146.0	19.7	13.5	3.9	2.7	23.6	16.2
1978	162.7	25.5	15.7	4.7	2.9	30.2	18.5
1979	187.9	38.2	20.3	5.0	2.7	43.2	23.0
1980	215.4	37.1	17.2	5.8	2.7	42.9	20.0
1981	228.3	32.5	14.2	5.8	2.5	38.3	16.8
1982	207.8	24.8	11.9	5.3	2.5	30.2	14.5
1983	207.2	26.8	12.9	6.1	2.9	32.9	15.9
1984	211.5	30.0	14.2	6.4	3.0	36.5	17.2
1985	230.3	27.9	12.1	6.6	2.9	34.4	15.0
1986	259.8	29.9	11.5	8.4	3.2	38.4	14.7
1987	314.3	38.5	12.2	9.3	3.0	47.9	15.2
1988	335.9	50.4	15.0	11.4	3.4	61.9	18.4
1989	381.8	53.9	14.1	14.3	3.7	68.3	17.9
1990	430.5	58.0	13.5	16.2	3.8	74.2	17.2
1991	467.8	52.1	10.6	17.4	3.6	69.5	14.2
1992	502.1	50.6	10.1	19.2	3.8	69.7	13.9
1993	559.7	59.7	10.7	19.3	3.4	78.5	14.0
1994	612.1	64.8	10.6	20.9	3.4	85.7	14.2

Note: *Represents royalties and license fees from 1960 forward and starting with 1977 includes other private services fees.

Sources: See Tables 3.1, 3.13, and 3.14.

currency fluctuations, business cycles, expropriations, etc., for the remainder of the period may, therefore, not be correct for that very reason.

Excepting the OPEC years because of artificially induced spurts, the return rates were very steady–around 15 percent of invested capital. The temporary strong showing of the ROI at the end of the 1980s may have been the result of the declining dollar in conjunction with improving business conditions worldwide. The historic level of performance was excellent, revealed good profit management, and must have exceeded what American investors could have realized at home. Otherwise, the extra risks would not have been faced.

This is essentially confirmed by the share increase produced by U.S. FDI vis-à-vis U.S. corporate profits. Taking only FDI income figures displayed in Table 3.3 and measuring them against American corporate profits of $653 billion (1960-69), $1,213 billion (1970-79), $2,013 billion (1980-89), and $1,309 billion (1990-93) yields the following results: 8.0 percent, 15.1 percent, 17.5 percent, and 16.8 percent (U.S. data: *Economic Report of the President*, February 1995, p. 380). Adding all other income to the picture raises the FDI share to 21.4 percent for the 1980s–and 22.3 percent for the 1990 to 1993 period–phenomenal results compared to the approximately 8 percent size of FDI relative to the U.S. business sector as discussed later.

The sudden downward shift in return rates for operating income starting with 1991 should not yet be declared a cause for concern. It may only be a transient phenomenon connected with the sharp rise in investment activity after the period of stagnation during the early 1980s. As the increase comes from a real expansion of the investment stock based on capital transfers, as opposed to reinvestment activities, a lag period for income flows has to be expected. It takes time before income developments reflect the new situation. This explanation seems to be reasonable in view of the fact that the weaker performance is shaped entirely by the operating income side, whereas the other income side maintains a very steady share against the FDI position.

Another factor to be remembered from previous discussions may also play a role in the development. It is the accounting effect caused by the Netherlands Antilles financing affiliates, which depressed FDI stock data while they increased their borrowings in the world market to be transferred to their parents in the United States–a negative factor for the FDI position. As these debts are reversed by capital exports, they add to the FDI stock. For the ROI discussion, the first step is positive because it does not materially touch on the income produced, but vice versa, it increases the position without again affecting the income stream to any important extent, thus producing the visible decline in the rates (see Tables 2.1 and 3.6).

RETURN ON INVESTMENT
BY INDUSTRY AND AREA

In contrast to the previous table, returns by industry are based solely on operating income as a percentage of the investment position. Leaving all other income out of the calculation understates returns on industry totals by roughly three percentage points. The effect on individual industries, with exception of manufacturing and petroleum, is unknown as no details for other income are provided by the above-mentioned international transaction tables of the DOC (see Table 3.17).

Returns of the petroleum industry would have increased by less than one percentage point in 1988 and 1989 if other income had been added to the equation. The increase for manufacturing would have been more significant with an additional return of 5.5 percent in 1988 and 6.0 percent in 1989. Also, in both years manufacturing accounted for a surprising 67 percent of all other income, which left very little volume to share for the remaining industries.

The petroleum industry's rate of return has to be regarded separately from all other industries because its business is conducted to a large extent in dollars, and thus not as susceptible to currency fluctuations. Oil subsidiaries have, therefore, been able to show a more consistent rate of return, except for the OPEC years and their aftermath which produced substantially higher rates. A similar short-term effect was created by the war against Iraq in 1991.

The return rates for the petroleum industry have been subject to pressures originating from various quarters. One example is the loss of the Saudi Arabian oil fields in 1980, which lead to investment shifts from crude production and exploration to processing and marketing and, consequently, more exposure to competitive pressures. A second example is the increased income tax burden facing the industry, and squeezing both profit margins and rates of return. The industry's 1966 effective tax rate stood at 55.5 percent at a time of increasing demand and pricing flexibility (1966 FDI census, pp. 174, 177). After the first jump in oil prices, the tax rate shot up to 88.6 percent and the pricing elasticity disappeared with lower oil demand and growing supplies–a situation that prevails until today (1977 FDI census, pp. 286-7). In 1989 the effective tax rate was still the highest for all industries shown, but at a much reduced level of 52 percent (see Table 3.10). Interesting to see are the differences in taxation between the various oil nations where Mofas are doing business: Indonesia (55.7 percent), Nigeria (76.0 percent), Norway (56.7 percent), UAE (88.9 percent) (see Table 3.11).

TABLE 3.17. Return on Investment by Major Industries (percentages)

Year	Pet.	Mfg.	Trade	Banks	Finance*	Services	Other
1950	18.4	16.3	15.2	N/A	N/A	N/A	11.1
1951	24.4	15.9	16.1	N/A	N/A	N/A	16.5
1952	23.8	13.8	15.1	N/A	N/A	N/A	11.1
1953	20.2	13.4	12.7	N/A	N/A	N/A	10.9
1954	19.4	13.0	12.6	N/A	N/A	N/A	10.8
1955	20.9	13.0	13.4	N/A	N/A	N/A	11.0
1956	19.8	12.0	14.0	N/A	N/A	N/A	11.3
1957	19.3	11.0	15.7	N/A	N/A	N/A	11.1
1958	13.5	10.7	13.3	N/A	N/A	N/A	8.2
1959	11.5	11.6	14.9	N/A	N/A	N/A	10.9
1960	12.0	10.6	14.8	N/A	N/A	N/A	11.0
1961	12.2	9.7	14.5	N/A	N/A	N/A	11.0
1962	13.3	9.5	13.6	N/A	N/A	N/A	11.1
1963	13.4	10.2	12.7	N/A	N/A	N/A	11.0
1964	12.7	10.8	12.4	N/A	N/A	N/A	11.1
1965	12.1	10.3	11.6	N/A	N/A	N/A	11.1
1966	10.8	9.0	10.5	N/A	8.9	N/A	11.2
1967	11.6	8.2	8.9	N/A	9.6	N/A	10.0
1968	12.0	9.6	9.7	N/A	9.6	N/A	11.2
1969	11.5	11.0	11.9	N/A	8.6	N/A	11.2
1970	12.4	10.1	12.7	N/A	8.9	N/A	11.2
1971	13.2	10.2	12.9	N/A	11.6	N/A	10.8
1972	13.2	12.4	13.8	N/A	13.3	N/A	10.8
1973	22.9	14.8	15.6	N/A	14.8	N/A	10.5
1974	32.5	13.1	16.1	N/A	15.3	N/A	13.1
1975	18.5	10.7	13.4	N/A	16.7	N/A	11.2
1976	17.8	11.8	12.4	N/A	16.5	N/A	13.3
1977	19.0	10.7	12.1	41.6	10.6	17.4	9.5
1978	19.7	14.3	14.7	N/A	17.7	N/A	11.2
1979	34.0	16.5	17.2	27.6	14.5	N/A	16.6
1980	27.7	12.4	15.5	27.4	13.6	N/A	17.4
1981	25.0	8.9	11.7	25.9	11.3	N/A	19.8
1982	16.4	7.7	6.5	36.9	11.1	17.1	7.1
1983	18.1	9.9	7.9	26.6	5.7	15.6	13.0
1984	18.4	12.5	10.9	23.7	6.0	14.7	10.7
1985	16.3	11.8	11.6	16.6	4.1	12.9	7.2
1986	12.2	13.1	13.6	13.1	6.9	12.1	6.0
1987	12.2	14.1	16.3	1.9	9.2	12.6	6.6
1988	13.3	18.7	17.1	8.9	9.8	12.9	9.6
1989	11.3	18.2	15.4	1.1	11.4	14.5	12.6
1990	18.7	14.6	15.6	1.8	11.7	13.0	12.2
1991	17.9	11.2	12.0	1.2	10.0	9.2	13.1
1992	12.7	10.3	10.6	9.0	9.3	8.1	7.5
1993	13.3	11.2	11.2	13.8	9.0	9.0	4.8
1994	11.3	13.0	12.1	11.1	7.2	8.2	7.9

Notes: *Finance includes insurance and real estate. Trade includes wholesale and retail.

Manufacturing as oil's traditional rival has generally seen lower rates of return over the decades. But the rate compression caused by the strong dollar during the early 1980s has disappeared and rates have recovered to levels comparable to those prevailing in the oil industry. Interestingly, affiliates in manufacturing have also gained from the aftereffects of the oil crises. They helped to push up their rates to levels not seen since the early 1950s; in 1973 and again in 1979. If there is a pattern to the success of these two industries, it is that both thrive on upheavals in the oil fields. The effects may be shortlived, but they are clearly visible. As indicated before, the financial performance of all non-oil industries is strongly influenced by the dollar's exchange moves. They become particularly visible in the case of the manufacturing rates dropping during the early 1980s, but then peaking in 1988 and 1989.

The trade industry, with its twin components of wholesale and retail, displays generally high and relatively stable return rates. They are obviously equally sensitive to strong currency fluctuations as experienced during the beginning of the 1980s. After the rather severe depression of that period, rates have made a nice comeback attesting to the pricing resilience of this industry in the long run.

Banks showed the highest rates for any industry, for a short while at least. The prosperous years came to a sudden end during the mid-1980s with a collapse of catastrophic proportions. Unfortunately, their documented history is too short to draw any conclusions about their long-term chances. From available evidence, it appears that the oil crises generated their high return rates with all the OPEC billions flowing through their hands. Oil made banks kings for a while, but within a short decade, they paid a steep price for their careless fund management, which became the major cause of the debt crisis in developing nations. Their inability to repay oversized loans or even service the debt burden has severely slashed return rates for banks. For the moment at least, the industry ranks visibly behind all other industries with returns so low that a return to prosperity is inconceivable without massive outside intervention.

Affiliates in finance, insurance, and real estate suffered from a feast or famine syndrome which let them go through cycles from average returns to very low ones, and back up again. The poor showing in the 1982 through 1985 period is a direct consequence of the debt burden accumulated by parents through the Netherlands Antillean financing subsidiaries and the high interest rates prevailing at that time (see Table 2.1).

With some exceptions, the data reflect the meticulous attention to return on investment typical for American managers. It cannot always prevent a certain volatility of the rates around historical norms–an aspect surfacing even more strikingly when looking at geographic areas or selected countries where prevailing economic, fiscal, and political factors often play rough and tumble with established returns. A good example is provided by oil affiliates who often produced astronomical returns. As a matter of fact, some of their annual returns are large enough to pay for the investment in that country and then some (Indonesia 1980). Small wonder then, that these countries want a larger slice of the business. For the oil industry it meant profit sharing through payments of royalties for resource depletion (not to be confused with royalties from use of technology), very high income taxes, and often nationalization.

TABLE 3.18. Return on Investment by Geographic Area (percentages)

Area/Country	1950	1960	1970	1980	1990
Canada	12.3	6.7	7.2	13.0	6.8
Europe	15.5	11.3	9.5	16.6	15.3
Belg./Lux.	17.4	13.4	10.2	10.2	16.0
France	13.4	9.5	9.0	6.8	13.2
Germany	13.2	14.1	13.6	12.1	16.4
Italy	14.3	9.6	5.8	24.1	14.9
Netherlands	17.9	6.7	11.6	22.8	21.9
Switzerland	16.0	18.8	12.7	16.5	17.5
UK	16.8	11.7	7.8	19.0	11.3
Latin America	12.9	11.9	11.0	18.0	12.1
Argentina	5.1	9.7	10.7	27.4	16.1
Bahamas	0	0	9.1	37.0	11.2
Bermuda	0	14.2	N/A	14.1	10.2
Brazil	15.1	8.8	13.6	6.5	9.9
Mexico	10.4	7.8	7.6	19.5	17.9
Panama	3.7	15.8	7.8	15.4	11.6
UK Caribbean	N/A	N/A	N/A	26.3	13.7
Venezuela	23.4	16.7	17.6	5.7	14.1
Africa	15.1	3.6	19.9	33.8	25.0
South Africa	17.9	17.5	14.7	28.3	21.3
Asia	31.8	38.2	23.2	25.9	17.6
Indonesia	62.1	41.0	37.6	158.3	59.1
Middle East	31.7	64.6	46.0	NMF	27.5
Japan	10.5	12.6	15.4	13.5	7.6
Philippines	26.2	11.8	8.4	13.3	16.8
Oceania	13.3	11.9	9.6	15.6	10.8
Australia	13.4	11.3	9.6	15.9	12.5

Chapter 4

FDI-Related U.S. Merchandise Trade

FDI AND U.S. TRADE FLOWS

Measuring the full extent of FDI-related trade in the U.S. balance of trade (BOT) is difficult for several reasons. First of all, the BOT is set up to record trade with foreigners in general, but does not routinely break out FDI information. Second, the appearance of affiliates adds new dimensions to formerly bilateral trade relationships between U.S. and foreign trading partners. Prior to their existence, foreign trade was a simple two-way exchange among unaffiliated business entities.

Enter affiliates, and the picture becomes more complex, as U.S. parent companies suddenly face two separate customers overseas: foreigners and the affiliates with whom they maintain regular trade exchanges. On the surface, both may appear to be identical, but in reality, they are not. The differences arise in such areas as intercompany and market pricing, shipments of raw materials or goods at various stages of processing versus finished goods only, control over foreign marketing operations, strategic profit management, operating in several legal environments, etc.

That is not all. Affiliates obviously trade not only with their parents, but also with unaffiliated companies in the United States, particularly in such cases where they were acquired with preexisting trade ties to the United States. By adding affiliates to the picture, three different sets of trading relations emerge directly or indirectly for FDI parents where there was only one before: parents with foreigners, parents with affiliates, and affiliates with U.S. independents.

The complete picture for FDI trade relations is even more intricate as subsidiaries trade with other subsidiaries and unaffiliated foreigners in third countries, adding two more trade relationships to those mentioned above. The term third country is used by the DOC to mean countries besides the United States and the country where the affiliates are located. But since this does not concern U.S. trade directly, its discussion is relegated to a later section on affiliate trade.

Considering the complex trading patterns outlined, it would be desirable to have a complete record of each. Unfortunately, this is not available. Trade data of affiliates with parents and other customers in the United States are sketchy to begin with and even more so for U.S. exports than imports. Table 4.1 outlines all the information provided by official statistics on this subject.

In addition to the lack of a detailed and coherent time series covering U.S. FDI trade by customer group, there is often an equally large data deficit on details by industry and country. Yet, in spite of these shortcomings, an attempt is made in the following pages to piece the picture together. Actual data have at times been supplemented by estimates when they seem justified. A simultaneous discussion of all FDI trading connections relating to the U.S. BOT is not an ideal way to tackle the subject. In order to put the information into focus, it is arbitrarily divided into two separate parts which seem to flow naturally from the statistical material at hand: U.S. trade with affiliates comprising parents and other U.S. companies and parent trade with unaffiliated foreigners.

U.S. TRADE WITH AFFILIATES

All data refer to shipments of merchandise rather than sales, both of which are available, but sufficiently different to cause potentially significant distortions and misinterpretations of the trade taking place. The principal advantage of using shipments is that they permit a direct comparison with official U.S. trade statistics maintained on the same basis. Data prior to 1966 refer to all foreign subsidiaries. Mofas were introduced in the 1966 census and data provided from that year forward refer strictly to them unless otherwise indicated. A third point is that all transactions between parents and their affiliates, as well as between affiliates and their U.S. nonaffiliated business partners, are based on documentation from the affiliates themselves with the following consequences:

1. All affiliate shipments to the United States are shown as U.S. imports, which tends to underestimate their weight in official trade statistics because of the FOB/CIF and customs differential.
2. Conversely, U.S. shipments to affiliates are overstated vis-à-vis official export statistics as they are reported on a CIF rather than FOB basis.

Parent company trade with foreigners is entirely based on parent documents and conforms fully with official U.S. trade reports. A final comment

TABLE 4.1. Total U.S. Trade with Affiliates (shipments/$ billion)

Year	Affil. Type	U.S. Exports to Affiliates by: All	Parents	Other	U.S. Imports from Affiliates by: All	Parents	Other
1950	All	$1.5	N/A	N/A	$2.5	N/A	N/A
1957	All	3.0	N/A	N/A	3.8*	N/A	N/A
1962	All	4.9	$4.0	$0.9	N/A	N/A	N/A
1963	All	5.3	4.3	1.0	N/A	N/A	N/A
1964	All	6.3	5.1	1.2	N/A	N/A	N/A
1966	Mofa	7.7	6.3	1.4	6.3	$4.6	$1.7
1977	All	40.8	32.4	8.4	41.5	32.6	8.9
	Mofa	35.8	29.3	6.5	38.0	30.9	7.1
1982	All	56.7	46.6	10.2	51.4	41.6	9.8
	Mofa	52.8	44.3	8.4	46.1	38.5	7.6
1983	All	57.5	N/A	N/A	53.2	N/A	N/A
	Mofa	54.5	N/A	N/A	48.3	N/A	N/A
1984	All	66.2	N/A	N/A	62.5	N/A	N/A
	Mofa	63.4	N/A	N/A	57.2	N/A	N/A
1985	All	69.6	N/A	N/A	68.2	N/A	N/A
	Mofa	66.5	N/A	N/A	60.3	N/A	N/A
1986	All	71.3	N/A	N/A	65.6	N/A	N/A
	Mofa	68.0	N/A	N/A	57.2	N/A	N/A
1987	All	78.9	N/A	N/A	75.9	N/A	N/A
	Mofa	74.9	N/A	N/A	65.5	N/A	N/A
1988	All	94.9	N/A	N/A	87.3	N/A	N/A
	Mofa	90.8	78.2	12.6	75.6	65.5	10.1
1989	All	102.1	89.2	12.9	93.7	76.0	17.7
	Mofa	97.1	85.6	11.5	84.8	72.4	12.4
1990	All	106.4	94.6	11.8	102.2	N/A	N/A
	Mofa	100.2	88.4	11.8	88.6	75.3	13.4
1991	All	115.3	102.2	13.1	102.8	N/A	N/A
	Mofa	108.8	95.7	13.1	90.5	77.6	12.9
1992	All	122.0	105.9	16.0	108.4	93.9	14.5
	Mofa	115.5	100.7	14.8	97.9	84.9	13.1
1993	All	130.7	111.1	19.6	122.2	102.9	19.3
	Mofa	122.8	104.9	17.8	111.3	95.9	15.4

Note: *Excludes trade and finance.

Sources: FDI census data: 1950, p. 29; 1957, pp. 110-1, 114, 121; 1966, pp. 82, 86-8, 198, 209; 1977, pp. 154-61, 336-62; 1982, pp. 127-34, 264-91. *SOCB*, December 1965, pp. 14-16 (1962-64); September 1986, pp. 33, 36-7 (1983-84); June 1988, pp. 90-1, 94-5 (1985-86); June 1990, pp. 36, 40-1 (1987-88); October 1991, pp. 36, 50, 54 (1988-89); July 1993, pp. 45, 52-4 (1990-91); June 1995, pp. 39, 54-6 (1992-93).

refers to the time factor underlying all statistics: up to 1982, all census data were shown on a calendar year basis. Starting with that year, companies were allowed to report on their fiscal year basis where applicable. It is not known what practical effect this has on the comparability of data among the two periods.

Affiliate trade data in Table 4.1 show Mofas maintaining a 90 percent or even higher share in these transactions between 1977 and 1988. It is believed that this ratio also applied to prior years. Even though records supporting this hypothesis are not available, it is reasonable to assume that Mofas have held a pretty steady 90 percent share in the FDI position for all years, which makes a strong correlation between position and trade shares very likely.

The data suggest that trade with the affiliates may have had a negative impact on the U.S. BOT, at least during the 1950s; but that problem was corrected by 1966 when the balance had turned positive. It has remained so ever since. This is true despite the dollar fluctuations, and is particularly remarkable in view of the persistent and growing trade deficits facing the United States since 1971. The deficit position with foreign affiliates in the immediate post-World War II period was consistent with U.S. policy in those days: to make much-needed dollars available to financially weak economies.

Table 4.1 documents the existence of two very different growth trends for affiliate trade with the United States. America's export volume to affiliates grew seventy-three times between 1950 and 1991, which is more or less a performance similar to the growth in total world trade over the period. American imports from affiliates, on the other hand, grew only forty-one times—an important factor contributing to the favorable trade balance.

As far as the affiliate share in total U.S. trade is concerned, it again follows entirely different patterns of development on the export and import side over the four decades. Tables 4.3 and 4.4 give the overall picture plus details for affiliates located in major world regions. According to the information, between 25 and 32 percent of total U.S. merchandise imports were supplied by affiliates up until the 1982 FDI census. Mofas then started to lose ground and ended up with a 19 percent share through 1991.

Exports reveal exactly the opposite picture. U.S. parent and nonaffiliated business shipments to affiliates abroad accounted for 15 percent of all U.S. exports during the 1950s. It increased gradually to around 30 percent by the late 1970s before settling back to 27 percent in 1989 (see Table 4.3). Except for the 1950s, this trade also contributed positively to the U.S. BOP and furnished a solid argument in favor of U.S. FDI, even though it is not dynamic enough to neutralize unfavorable trade aspects discussed in the section evaluating FDI's overall role for America's trade.

Factors contributing to the relative decline of affiliates on the U.S. import side include first and foremost, the 11 percent drop in total affiliate oil exports to the United States between 1977 ($17.8 billion) and 1982 ($15.8 billion), partly due to reduced domestic demand and partly to the expropriation of the oil subsidiaries in the Middle East. Shipments from these subsidiaries declined 45 percent from $2.9 billion to $1.6 billion between those two years, accounting for two-thirds of the decline in affiliate shipments to the United States alone (FDI census data: 1977, p. 158; 1982, p. 131). Other contributing factors were the growing U.S. consumer preference for foreign products, rapidly expanding foreign direct investments in the United States, and the export pressure by developing nations to earn dollars for their debt service. Finally, it is safe to assume that deliberate trade policies of major FDI corporations were synchronized with Washington to shore up the trade balance.

Parents consistently account for the bulk of all U.S. trade with affiliates. On the export side, that share has gone up from 82 to 88 percent with no important difference by affiliate type over a 30-year period. Very much the same pattern holds true for the import side. Here, parents evidently took more and more control over affiliate exports to the United States by consolidating their share from 73 to 85 percent within more or less the same time span (see Table 4.2).

U.S. TRADE WITH AFFILIATES BY WORLD REGION

Trade between the United States and its subsidiaries in various parts of the world reveals lively trends and crosscurrents as one would expect from the discussion of changing direct investment flows over the years. During the 1950s, affiliates accounted for close to 30 percent of all U.S. merchandise imports. That share was down to around 20 percent during the early 1990s. Those same nonbank U.S. subsidiaries reversed that record by increasing their share of total U.S. merchandise exports from about 15 to 28 percent in the same time span. Their trade assured a positive influence on the U.S. BOT for practically all these years (see Tables 4.1, 4.3, and 4.4).

Looking at how that trade developed uncovers some interesting aspects. For one thing, a close and consistent correlation between investment and trade levels that might theoretically exist cannot be demonstrated in all cases. Where it does exist, it appears more as an exception rather than the rule.

TABLE 4.2. Parent Share of U.S. Trade with Affiliates

Year	Affiliate Type	Share of Exports	Share of Imports
1962	All	81.6%	N/A
1963	All	81.1	N/A
1964	All	80.9	N/A
1966	Mofa	81.8	73.0%
1977	All	79.4	78.5
	Mofa	81.8	81.3
1982	All	82.2	80.9
	Mofa	83.9	83.5
1990	All	88.9	N/A
	Mofa	88.2	85.0
1991	All	88.7	N/A
	Mofa	88.0	85.7
1992	All	86.8	86.6
	Mofa	87.2	86.7
1993	All	85.0	84.2
	Mofa	85.4	86.2

Source: See Table 4.1.

Canada and Europe illustrated this point very well. Europe accounted for about 50 percent of total U.S. FDI in the 1989-93 period, but affiliates located there reached only 16 percent of total U.S. imports from affiliates and about 30 percent of all U.S. exports to affiliates. Canada, on the other hand, held a 15 percent share in U.S. FDI, supplied 41 percent of all U.S. imports from affiliates, and took up 35 percent of all U.S. exports to the same. In other words, Canadian affiliates clearly outranked their European sister organizations in U.S. trade despite their much lower investment profile. They actually appear to have been set up for this role, a fact that applies fully to the automotive industry.

Latin American subsidiaries accounted for about 18 percent of direct investments. They also accounted for equal shares of 15 percent each in U.S. exports to and imports from affiliates, indicating a fairly close correlation between all three factors. Investment shares of Asian affiliates held a steady 12 percent level in the latter period, but exceeded that level with a 17 percent share in U.S. exports to all affiliates, and even more so with a 25 percent share in U.S. imports from the same (see Tables 4.3C and 4.4C).

Reasons for these perplexing relationships lie in the history of U.S. direct investment. Canada was, and still is a principal raw material supplier to the United States, despite its important role as a coproducer of automotive products for the U.S. market. Europe's primary attractiveness for U.S. investors lies in its enormous consumer potential, advanced technology, and last but not least, its role as a gateway to parts of the world where American firms had not yet established a foothold before World War II or could not, for political reasons, after it was over. Eastern Europe comes to mind, but also the sixty-six nations around the globe with preferential trade concessions from the EU.

Asian affiliates, on the other hand, are located in the developing part of the world, and as such are more dependent on sourcing from the United States. Being tied to oil and labor intensive industries explains their high rating in U.S. import receipts. Different investment strategies and economic conditions lead to very different consequences for U.S. trade with affiliates.

Another aspect gleaned from the published data is that overall affiliate share development in total U.S. trade does not necessarily parallel that of regional affiliates. This is to say that while the affiliate share in total U.S. exports has risen from 15 to 28 percent during the study period, regional affiliates may have run counter to the trend. Thus, affiliates in Latin America, Africa, and Oceania did not contribute to that growth and show practically no change in their share of total U.S. exports. The increase in total affiliate share were produced by subsidiaries in Canada, Europe, and Asia (see Table 4.3B).

On the other hand, affiliate share in overall U.S. imports has declined sharply from 28 to 20 percent in four decades. But this downward trend is not shared by European and Asian subsidiaries. The Europeans held on to a minuscule but remarkable steady 2 to 3 percent, whereas shares of Asian affiliates doubled from 2 to 4 percent over the same period (see Table 4.4B).

According to the accounts, Canadian affiliates have consistently taken the lion's share of U.S. trade with subsidiaries, except during the 1950s when this dominant position was briefly challenged by affiliates in Latin America. This was the time when U.S. FDI was still concentrating on both areas and far from reaching its global position of today. Canadian affiliates provided 11 to 16 percent of total American imports until the mid-1970s, but that figure declined gradually to 8 percent in 1982 where it stayed for the rest of the period. The drop may be explained by the fact that trade among the two neighbors depends so heavily on materials and manufactures sensitive to economic cycles and international competition. Mining, paper, and lumber, oil, basic metals, and in particular the automotive industry, are prime examples. This general decline makes their share in total U.S. imports from affiliates appear all the more remarkable. It stood at 37 percent during the 1950s, grew to about 60 percent during the 1970s,

TABLE 4.3. U.S. Exports to Affiliates by Region (shipments/$ billion)

Year	Total U.S. Exports	A. U.S. Exports to Affiliates in:						
		World	Canada	Lat. Am.	Europe	Africa	Asia	Oceania
1950	$9.9	$1.5	N/A	N/A	N/A	N/A	N/A	N/A
1957	19.3	3.0	$0.9	$0.9	$0.4	$0.1	$0.2	$0.1
1962	20.8	4.9	1.7	1.0	1.5	N/A	N/A	N/A
1963	22.3	5.3	1.9	1.2	1.5	N/A	N/A	N/A
1964	25.5	6.3	2.2	1.4	1.8	N/A	N/A	N/A
1966M	29.3	7.7	3.3	1.0	2.1	0.3	0.6	0.3
1977A	120.8	40.8	17.3	4.7	12.3	0.8	4.2	1.3
M		35.8	16.2	3.7	10.9	0.6	3.2	1.1
1982A	211.2	56.7	19.5	7.3	18.1	1.1	8.2	2.3
M		52.8	19.4	6.5	17.2	1.0	6.7	1.9
1989A	362.1	102.1	38.2	12.5	30.1	0.6	17.1	3.5
M		97.1	37.8	11.1	29.5	0.4	14.5	3.4
1990A	389.3	106.4	38.1	13.4	32.8	0.6	18.4	3.1
M		100.2	37.0	11.9	32.0	0.6	15.7	3.0
1991A	416.9	115.3	40.8	15.9	35.2	0.5	19.5	3.3
M		108.8	39.5	14.4	34.3	0.5	16.7	3.3
1992A	440.4	122.0	42.0	18.4	36.9	0.4	20.8	3.4
M		115.5	40.9	16.7	36.0	0.4	18.2	3.3
1993A	456.8	130.7	44.6	20.7	37.3	0.5	24.1	3.5
M		122.8	43.2	18.3	36.1	0.4	21.3	3.4
B. Regional Affiliate Share of Total U.S. Exports – Percentages								
1950	100	15	N/A	N/A	N/A	N/A	N/A	N/A
1957	100	16	5	5	2	1	1	1
1962	100	24	8	5	7	N/A	N/A	N/A
1963	100	24	9	5	7	N/A	N/A	N/A
1964	100	25	9	6	7	N/A	N/A	N/A
1966M	100	27	11	3	7	1	2	1
1977A	100	34	15	4	10	1	4	1
M	100	30	14	3	9	1	3	1
1982A	100	27	9	4	9	1	4	1
M	100	26	9	3	8	1	3	1
1989A	100	28	10	3	8	nil	5	1
M	100	27	10	3	8	nil	4	1
1990A	100	27	10	3	8	nil	4	1
M	100	26	10	3	8	nil	4	1
1991A	100	28	10	4	8	nil	5	1
M	100	26	9	3	8	nil	4	1
1992A	100	28	10	4	8	nil	5	1
M	100	26	9	4	8	nil	4	1
1993A	100	29	10	5	8	nil	5	1
M	100	27	9	4	8	nil	5	1

Year	Total U.S. Exports	C. Regional Affiliate Share of Total U.S. Exports to Affiliate						
		World	Canada	Lat. Am.	Europe	Africa	Asia	Oceania
1950		100	N/A	N/A	N/A	N/A	N/A	N/A
1957		100	30	30	13	3	6	3
1962		100	35	20	31	N/A	N/A	N/A
1963		100	36	23	28	N/A	N/A	N/A
1964		100	35	22	29	N/A	N/A	N/A
1966M		100	43	13	27	.4	8	4
1977A		100	42	12	30	2	10	3
M		100	45	10	30	2	9	3
1982A		100	34	13	32	2	14	4
M		100	37	12	32	2	13	4
1989A		100	37	13	30	1	17	3
M		100	39	11	30	nil	15	4
1990A		100	36	13	31	1	17	3
M		100	37	12	32	1	16	3
1991A		100	35	14	31	nil	17	3
M		100	36	13	31	nil	15	3
1992A		100	34	15	30	nil	17	3
M		100	35	14	31	nil	16	3
1993A		100	34	16	28	nil	18	3
M		100	35	15	29	nil	17	3

Notes: M = Mofas. A = All Affiliates. U.S. Exports include U.S. merchandise excluding military.

Sources: *Business Statistics*, 1973 Edition, p. 111; *Business Statistics*, 1984 Edition, p. 78 (Total U.S. Exports). FDI census data: 1950, p. 29; 1957, p. 121; 1966, p. 86; 1977, pp. 154, 336; 1982, pp. 127, 264. *SOCB*, June 1993, pp. 70-1 (1960-91); June 1995, pp. 84-5 (1960-91); October 1991, pp. 50-4 (1989); June 1993, pp. 52-4 (1989); June 1995, pp. 43-5 (1989).

and currently retains a relatively high share of around 43 percent (see Table 4.4B).

The same affiliates accounted for a rising share of total U.S. exports by actually tripling their share from 5 to 15 percent between 1957 and 1977, but then settled back to 9 to 10 percent after 1982 (see Table 3.4B). The reason for the temporary softness in demand for U.S. products stemmed from low levels of imports by the manufacturing sector in general and again the automotive affiliates, which alone accounted for almost two-thirds of all Canadian affiliate imports from the United States. The Canadian share in total U.S. exports to affiliates moved up from 30 percent during the 1950s to over 40 percent during the 1970s before currently settling at 35 percent.

TABLE 4.4. U.S. Imports from Affiliates by Region (shipments/$ billion)

Year	Total U.S. Imports	A. U.S. Imports from Affiliates in:						
		World	Canada	Lat. Am.	Europe	Africa	Asia	Oceania
1959A	$8.9	$2.5	N/A	N/A	N/A	N/A	N/A	N/A
1957A	13.0	3.8	$1.4	$1.7	$0.2	$0.1	$0.3	nil
1966M	25.5	6.3	2.9	1.8	0.8	0.1	0.5	nil
1967M	26.9	7.2	3.7	1.7	0.9	0.1	0.4	N/A
1968M	33.0	8.6	4.6	1.9	1.1	0.1	0.5	N/A
1969M	35.8	9.5	5.4	1.9	1.1	0.1	0.6	N/A
1970M	39.9	9.9	5.9	1.8	1.3	0.1	0.5	N/A
1971M	45.6	12.8	7.2	2.4	1.6	0.2	1.1	N/A
1972M	55.8	14.4	8.0	2.6	1.8	0.2	1.5	N/A
1973M	70.5	19.6	9.8	3.8	2.4	0.5	2.4	N/A
1974M	103.8	31.8	11.4	6.4	3.1	1.5	6.9	N/A
1975M	98.2	31.6	12.7	6.7	3.1	1.8	6.3	N/A
1977A	151.9	41.5	15.6	5.8	5.1	4.7	10.0	N/A
M		38.0	14.3	5.2	4.7	4.6	8.9	N/A
1982A	247.6	51.4	21.4	7.5	6.1	2.9	12.7	0.9
M		46.1	20.4	7.0	5.8	2.8	9.3	0.8
1989A	477.4	93.7	40.1	11.9	15.8	2.3	21.9	1.5
M		84.8	38.9	10.4	15.2	2.3	16.6	1.4
1990A	498.3	102.2	41.1	12.6	15.8	3.4	27.5	1.8
M		88.6	40.1	11.4	14.3	3.4	18.0	1.5
1991A	490.9	102.8	41.8	13.8	15.4	3.1	27.3	1.4
M		90.5	39.5	12.8	14.3	3.1	18.4	1.2
1992A	536.5	108.4	43.9	17.2	16.6	3.3	27.5	N/A
M		97.9	43.2	15.9	15.5	3.3	18.8	1.2
1993A	589.4	122.2	50.1	18.8	19.0	N/A	31.0	N/A
M		111.3	48.8	17.5	18.2	3.1	22.9	0.9

Canadian affiliates thus hold the uncontested pole position in U.S. trade with affiliates (see Table 4.3C).

Latin American affiliates briefly played a role as the leading subsidiary supplier to the United States during the 1950s. This position, however, was lost when the direction of U.S. global interests and investments shifted to Canada, Europe, and later, Asia. Being predominantly exporters of oil and mining products to the U.S. in the beginning, Latin America has since graduated to products with higher value-added content. Raw materials typically accounted for more than two-thirds of their total exports in 1957, with oil shipments alone reaching 67 percent of their exports to the United States. By 1970, oil had dropped to 46 percent and was well on its way to

Year	Total U.S. Imports	B. Regional Affiliate Share of Total U.S. Imports – Percentages						
		World	Canada	Lat. Am.	Europe	Africa	Asia	Oceania
1950M	100	28	N/A	N/A	N/A	N/A	N/A	N/A
1957A	100	29	11	13	2	1	2	nil
1966M	100	25	11	7	3	nil	2	nil
1967M	100	27	14	6	3	nil	1	nil
1968M	100	26	14	6	3	nil	2	nil
1969M	100	26	15	5	3	nil	2	nil
1970M	100	25	15	5	3	nil	1	nil
1971M	100	28	16	5	3	nil	2	nil
1972M	100	26	14	5	3	nil	3	nil
1973M	100	28	14	5	3	1	3	nil
1974M	100	31	11	6	3	1	7	nil
1975M	100	32	13	7	3	2	6	nil
1977A	100	27	10	4	3	3	7	nil
M	100	25	9	3	3	3	6	nil
1982A	100	21	9	3	2	1	5	nil
M	100	19	8	3	2	1	4	nil
1989A	100	20	8	3	3	nil	5	nil
M	100	18	8	2	3	nil	4	nil
1990A	100	20	8	3	3	1	6	nil
M	100	18	8	2	3	1	4	nil
1991A	100	21	9	3	3	1	6	nil
M	100	18	8	3	3	1	4	nil
1992A	100	20	8	3	3	1	5	nil
M	100	18	8	3	3	1	4	nil
1993A	100	21	9	3	3	N/A	5	nil
M	100	19	8	3	3	1	4	nil

below 20 percent during the last decade. It was replaced by manufactures holding about 70 percent by the end of the 1980s. The switch to processed products could not prevent a sharp reduction in their share of total U.S. imports which slipped from a very respectable 13 percent in 1957 to 3 percent at the latest count (see Table 4.4B). They were simply displaced by Canadian, European, and Asian sisters which was the reason for a similar decline in their position among U.S. imports from affiliates only where their share dropped from 45 to 15 percent over the period (see Table 4.4C).

On the U.S. export side, these Latin American companies maintained their share at a very steady 5 percent level for the whole period (see Table 4.3B). Trade goods and manufactures make up about 90 percent of affiliate

TABLE 4.4 (continued)

Year	Total U.S. Imports	C. U.S. Imports from Affiliates in:						
		World	Canada	Lat. Am.	Europe	Africa	Asia	Oceania
1950M		100	N/A	N/A	N/A	N/A	N/A	N/A
1957A		100	37	45	5	3	8	nil
1966M		100	46	29	13	2	8	nil
1967M		100	51	24	13	1	6	nil
1968M		100	53	22	13	1	6	nil
1969M		100	57	20	12	1	6	nil
1970M		100	60	18	13	1	5	nil
1971M		100	56	19	14	2	9	nil
1972M		100	55	18	13	1	10	nil
1973M		100	50	19	12	3	12	nil
1974M		100	36	20	10	5	22	nil
1975M		100	40	21	10	6	20	nil
1977A		100	38	14	12	11	24	nil
M		100	38	14	12	12	23	nil
1982A		100	42	15	12	6	25	2
M		100	44	15	13	6	20	2
1989A		100	43	13	17	2	23	2
M		100	46	12	18	2	20	2
1990A		100	40	12	15	3	27	2
M		100	45	13	16	4	20	2
1991A		100	41	13	15	3	27	1
M		100	44	14	16	3	20	1
1992A		100	41	16	15	3	25	nil
M		100	44	16	16	3	19	1
1993A		100	41	15	16	nil	25	nil
M		100	44	16	16	3	21	1

Notes: M = Mofas. A = All Affiliates. U.S. Imports include U.S. merchandise excluding military.

Sources: *Business Statistics*, 1977 Edition, p. 113 (Total U.S. Imports). *SOCB*, June 1990, pp. 76-7; June 1995, pp. 84-5 (Total U.S. Imports). FDI census data: 1950, p. 29; 1957, pp. 110-1; 1966, p. 198; 1977, pp. 158, 352; 1982, pp. 131, 283. *SOCB*, August 1975, pp. 26-9 (1966-73); February 1977, pp. 31-5 (1966-75); October 1991, pp. 36, 50, 54 (1989); June 1993, pp. 52-4 (1990-91); June 1995, pp. 43-5 (1992-93).

imports. Focusing on U.S. exports to all affiliates only, they show a serious loss with their share cut in half from 30 percent during the 1950s to 15 percent during the 1990s (see Table 4.4C).

European affiliates with close to half of all investment dollars and accounting for 58 percent share in all affiliate exports play a surprisingly weak role in U.S. trade. Never once in four decades did they exceed 3.5 percent of all U.S. imports. Thus, they rank visibly behind their Canadian and Asian peers, and practically on the same level with those in Latin America (see Table 4.4B). Up to the mid-1970s, U.S. imports from that corner of the globe consisted 90 percent of manufactures and trade items, and only 10 percent of oil. Oil then grew temporarily to about one-third of total volume in 1982 before settling back to the more historic 12 percent level in 1988.

Their role in U.S. imports from affiliates is more impressive, but still lacks the weight commensurate with their investment profile. Advancing from rank four during the 1950s to second place behind Canada during the beginning of the 1990s was paralleled by their share increase from 5 to 15 percent. While not noticeably superior to the ranking of the Latin American affiliates, it is another demonstration of the pointed imbalance between investment and trade importance of the Europeans (see Table 4.4C).

As customers for U.S. exports, Europe has done better, but again not very convincingly. After increasing their share of the total from 2 percent in 1957 to around 8 percent in the end, they still trailed the leader: Canada (see Table 4.3B). Manufactures in the form of machinery, chemicals, processed foods and trade goods were the leading items on the subsidiary shopping list, which largely reflected their investment structure. Narrowing the discussion down to U.S. exports to affiliates only shows an advance from third to second position and a growth in share from 13 to 30 percent, again far short of their investment rank (see Table 4.3C).

Asian affiliates enjoyed a period of success by raising their share of total U.S. imports from 2 to 7 percent between 1957 and 1974 before falling back to 5 percent (see Table 4.4B). Oil shipments were mainly responsible for the ups and downs. Manufactured goods accounted for less than 15 percent of their exports to the U.S. market until 1974, but since then have advanced to more than 60 percent of the shipments, bolstered by strong expansions in the electronics and automotive fields (Japan). Their share of total U.S. exports quadrupled from 1 to 4 percent between 1957 and 1993–only a very modest result which put them slightly ahead of the Latin American affiliates with whom they competed for third place for so long. Manufactures, mainly machinery and chemicals, account for about one-half and trade goods for another third of all shipments (see Table 4.3B).

As far as their position in affiliate trade with the United States is concerned, Latin America fared much better. Here they were able to expand from 6 to 17 percent of all U.S. shipments to affiliates (see Table 4.3C) and from 8 to 25 percent of total affiliate shipments to the United States between 1957 and 1993. In the first category, they now rank third behind

TABLE 4.5. U.S. Trade Balances with Regional Mofas (shipments/$ billion)

Year:	1957	1966	1977	1982	1990	1993
Total U.S. Trade with Affiliates						
U.S. Exports to	$3.0	$7.7	$35.8	$52.8	$100.2	$122.8
U.S. Imports from	3.8	6.3	38.0	46.1	88.6	111.3
Balance	(0.8)	1.4	(2.2)	6.7	11.6	11.5
With Canadian Affiliates						
U.S. Exports to	0.9	3.3	16.2	19.4	37.0	43.2
U.S. Imports from	1.4	2.9	14.3	20.4	40.1	48.8
Balance	(0.5)	0.4	1.9	(1.0)	(3.1)	(5.6)
With European Affiliates						
U.S. Exports to	0.4	2.1	10.9	17.2	32.0	36.1
U.S. Imports from	0.2	0.8	4.7	5.8	14.3	18.2
Balance	0.2	1.3	6.2	11.4	17.7	17.9
With Latin American Affiliates						
U.S. Exports to	0.9	1.0	3.7	6.5	11.9	18.2
U.S. Imports from	1.6	1.8	5.2	7.0	11.4	17.5
Balance	(0.7)	(0.8)	(1.5)	(0.5)	0.5	0.7
With African Affiliates						
U.S. Exports to	0.1	0.3	0.6	1.0	0.6	0.4
U.S Imports from	0.1	0.1	4.6	2.8	3.4	3.1
Balance	0.0	0.2	(4.0)	(1.8)	(2.8)	(2.7)
With Asian Affiliates						
U.S. Exports to	0.2	0.6	3.2	6.7	15.7	21.3
U.S. Imports from	0.3	0.5	8.9	9.3	18.0	25.4
Balance	(0.1)	0.1	(5.7)	(2.6)	(2.3)	(4.1)
With Affiliates in Oceania						
U.S. Exports to	0.1	0.3	1.1	1.9	3.0	3.4
U.S. Imports from	0.0	0.0	0.1	0.8	1.5	0.9
Balance	0.1	0.3	1.0	1.1	1.5	2.5

Note: Mofas recorded as of 1966.

Sources: FDI census data: 1957, pp. 110-1, 146; 1966, pp. 91, 198; 1977, pp. 336, 352; 1982, pp. 264, 281. *SOCB*, June 1993, pp. 52-4; June 1995, p. 45 (1990).

Canadian and European subsidiaries, and in the second category, they have pushed the Europeans from second place behind Canada to third (see Tables 4.3C and 4.4C).

Trade with African subsidiaries is of little consequence, even though it reached a temporary prominence based on oil exports to the United States, which accounted for about 90 percent of affiliate exports from that region.

The continent's peak position was reached in 1977 with an affiliate share of 3 percent in all U.S. imports, but has since declined to less than 1 percent in 1988. On the U.S. export side, they never exceeded 1 percent of the total and by 1990, had virtually disappeared altogether.

Africa's share of U.S. exports to affiliates only went from 3 to 1 percent, marking the weakest level achieved among regional affiliates. Among U.S. imports from affiliates, they reached a temporary peak of 12 percent; but at the end of the study period, this share was down to 3 percent, equal to the level they held during the 1950s.

Another noteworthy aspect of the U.S. merchandise trade with affiliates concerns the trade balances maintained over the four decades. Not so much because they are mostly favorable in total for the United States as indicated, but because there are strong regional variations from this norm. Actually, of the six regions covered, half contributed to the U.S. trade deficit with some persistent regularity. Intended or not, they occur mostly in and for the benefit of less developed areas, where trade balances provide much-needed development funds.

Interesting in this regard is Canada's changing picture. Since 1982, the United States has been running almost annual trade deficits with affiliates up north, a situation not encountered since the 1950s. It results from strong imports of Canadian raw materials and upgraded automotive products which cannot be compensated for with U.S. exports of mostly manufactures and wholesale goods.

Other trade deficits occur in the trade with Latin American, African, and Asian affiliates. The latter two are strongly affected by the trade in petroleum products for which the United States has been a longtime and very large net importer. Asian affiliates also contribute to the deficit with huge exports of textiles, as well as electrical and electronic equipment.

The only areas which consistently provide a trade surplus for the United States are Australia, New Zealand, and Europe. Were it not for the latter, there would not be a favorable trade balance for the United States, at all. U.S. exports to those affiliates consist of a very diversified product range for manufactured and wholesale goods. In turn, in addition to exports of similar product groups, these affiliates ship large quantities of petroleum products to the U.S. market, most likely from their North Sea oil fields.

The Australian subsidiaries import mostly manufactured and durable wholesale goods from the United States. Their exports include about 75 percent manufactures with no one group reaching particularly important dimensions.

PARENT TRADE WITH FOREIGNERS

The second major FDI imprint in the U.S. BOT is left by trade between parents and nonaffiliated foreigners. Such trade precedes direct investment, and one would expect to see it shrink once affiliates start operating in closer proximity to those customers. Even if it does not eliminate this trade entirely, there should be a noticeable shift in that direction. Wouldn't it be paradox to find parents continuing significant trade with foreigners after they had set up subsidiaries to deal with them locally? A cursory glance at available data seems to dispel such a hypothesis for a major part of the period under study, even though there is support for it in the end. Parent trade with foreigners did grow all along rather than shrink or remain steady despite the existence of subsidiaries. As a matter of fact, it was expanding even faster than parent trade with affiliates for a while, which is absolutely contrary to expectations.

Census data document that for each dollar worth of merchandise shipped to their own subsidiaries, parents shipped merchandise to foreigners valued at $1.83 in 1966, $1.89 in 1977, $2.30 in 1982, $1.36 in 1989, and $1.25 in 1993. In addition, these shipments went from 39 percent of total U.S. merchandise exports in 1966 to 50 percent in both 1977 and 1982, returned to 38 percent in 1989, and declined to an all time low of 30 percent in 1993.

A similar situation can be seen on the import side where total parent imports from foreigners not only top those from their own affiliates, but again were doing so at an accelerating pace in the beginning, but slowing down towards the end. In 1977, parent purchases from unaffiliated foreigners amounted to $1.39 for each dollar worth of merchandise bought from affiliates. By 1982, the spread had grown to $1.67, mainly because of the drop in oil imports from Middle Eastern affiliates and expanded parent sourcing from foreign oil producers. In 1989, the parent trade between subsidiaries and foreigners approached a more balanced position with the latter accounting for only $1.05 for each dollar's worth of merchandise purchased from affiliates. The situation remained constant thereafter, with parent imports at $1.06 for each dollar's worth from foreigners in 1993.

There are a number of plausible explanations for this situation that at first glance, does not seem to make much sense. The period which the above data related to was one of extraordinary circumstances, of wrenching adjustments in the international economy which almost twenty years later, appear as only a fleeting phenomenon—a temporary distortion that is returning to normal. At least that is what the latest ratios indicate. The expected trade shift in favor of subsidiaries is finally taking hold. On both the export and import side, parent trade approaches a ratio of 1:1 between affiliates and foreigners–well below levels seen during the 1960s before affiliates were as well developed.

OPEC plunged the world into economic turmoil of unprecedented proportions. With two jolting moves in less than a decade, it caused worldwide inflation, recession, stagflation in the United States, political volatility, and huge shifts in international liquidity. Immediately preceded by the breakdown of the international monetary system in 1971 and the loss of stable exchange rates, the period affected parent companies, affiliates, and foreigners in different ways.

The first oil crisis in 1973 produced a fourfold increase in oil prices which initially hit all nations with full force, but continued to affect the United States far more deeply and much longer than foreign economies–a direct result of oil being invoiced in dollars and the erosion of the U.S. currency in the aftermath of the crisis which lasted roughly from 1972 to 1980.

The appreciation of foreign currencies cushioned the oil shock for many nations, allowing them to tackle the oil recession much sooner than the United States. With domestic markets in a slump, U.S. companies turned their attention to more vibrant overseas markets. World demand rose on a wave of international liquidity produced by a flood of petroleum dollars to OPEC and other third world nations, where excess funds were invested on a large scale. Idle industrial capacity and the declining dollar made U.S. goods very competitive in world markets. Many industries had only limited or no affiliate operations at all. Parents as the leading exporters from the United States were able to make the best of the favorable circumstances, and boosted their exports to unaffiliated foreigners tenfold between 1966 and 1982.

The dollar's decline caused an automatic and substantial improvement in affiliate sales and profits after their translation into dollars. Deliberate lowering of U.S. transfer prices to affiliates created a synergistic profit leverage from pricing on top of the currency effect–a unique opportunity that parents quickly learned to take advantage of. U.S. businesses also discovered tax havens for additional profit opportunities, which had really come into their own during this period. The net effect of this constellation is evidenced by the sevenfold rise in U.S. exports to affiliates between 1966 and 1982 (see Table 4.1).

These fortuitous circumstances evaporated with the second oil crisis. The threefold jump in oil prices between 1979 and 1985 led to more inflation and recession. Rising foreign demand for dollars to pay for bloated energy imports drove up the dollar during those same years, exacerbating the price explosion for importing countries beyond the impact of the crisis on the United States. Strengthening the dollar further were relatively high American interest rates to combat renewed inflation pressures, but also to attract funds for financing bulging budget deficits at a time when other countries were pursuing easy money policies. Considering this last point, the previously mentioned huge parent debt that floated in international markets through the Netherlands Antilles affiliates may have contributed substantially to the upward pressure on the dollar, rather than work in the opposite direction as is normal. Though helpful from a financial management point of view, those borrowing activities worked against trading interests.

Being tied to U.S. sources for at least part of their material and equipment needs, affiliates suffered a double-barrelled effect on profits. On one hand, by way of their U.S. purchases, they were exposed to U.S. inflation fortified by the dollar's rise. On the other, the resulting cost pressure on profits was intensified by translation losses on sales and profits resulting from the exchange rate factor–a combination of factors that led to a deemphasis of U.S. exports to affiliates, whose share in total U.S. exports dropped from a high of 34 percent in 1977 to 27 percent in 1982, where it has remained since (see Table 4.3).

With a slight change in the database, the trade effect is even more pronounced. By removing agricultural exports from the global data, as they are of little relevance in this discussion, U.S. exports to affiliates go from 21.4 percent of nonagricultural exports in 1950, to 34.4 percent (1966), 42.0 percent (1977), 42.6 percent (1982), but are down to 27.8 percent in 1991. More to the point, parent exports to foreigners rose 75 percent between 1977 and 1982, while those to affiliates went up only 47 percent as a consequence of these intricate crosscurrents (see Tables 4.1 and 4.6).

On the U.S. import side, similar developments are visible but for very different reasons. Affiliate exports to the United States went up throughout the early 1970s. From 1977, they went on a lasting decline relative to overall U.S. imports, which took them from a high of 32 percent in 1975 to around 20 percent in the following years (see Table 4.4). It can be explained partly with the explosive growth of U.S. imports by inward FDI companies, non-FDI related importers, and also parent (oil) sourcing from nonaffiliated foreigners. The rapid decline in affiliate import share may also have been aided further by the dollar's decline after 1985, making affiliate merchandise relatively expensive for parents, their major customer.

The concentrated pursuit of foreign customers could also be interpreted as a deliberate parent move to shift exports from affiliates to the United States in an attempt to alleviate the American trade situation–a step that certainly would put parent strategy in line with Washington's trade promotion efforts.

TABLE 4.6. U.S. Parent Trade with Foreigners (shipments/$ billion)

Year	U.S. Total	Parents	%	U.S. Parent Trade with Foreign Parent Group	%
I. Exports					
1966	29.3	11.5	39.1	N/A	N/A
1977	120.8	61.1	47.4	N/A	N/A
1982	211.2	106.7	50.6	N/A	N/A
1989	363.1	139.4	37.2	10.4	2.9
1990	389.3	134.9	34.7	13.7	3.5
1991	416.9	142.6	34.2	14.8	3.5
1992	440.4	143.9	32.7	14.9	3.4
1993	456.8	139.3	30.5	13.0	2.8
II. Imports					
1977	151.9	45.2	29.7	N/A	N/A
1982	247.6	69.4	28.0	N/A	N/A
1989	477.4	98.9	20.7	32.4	6.8
1990	498.3	111.2	22.3	36.8	7.4
1991	490.9	109.9	22.4	35.9	7.3
1992	536.5	111.3	20.7	33.8	6.3
1993	589.4	108.9	18.5	35.1	6.0

Sources: *SOCB*, June 1993, pp. 70-1; June 1995, pp. 84-5 (U.S. merchandise import/export data excluding military). FDI census data: 1966, p. 83; 1977, pp. 186, 189, 395, 398; 1982, pp. 153, 156, 332, 336. *SOCB*, August 1992, p. 68; July 1993, p. 45; June 1994, p. 51; June 1995, p. 39.

Data provided in Table 13.1 point in that direction. The U.S. position in world trade has held steady over a long time, while that of the subsidiaries has gone into a percentage decline since the mid-1980s. In view of the strong dollar during the first half of the 1980s, this decline should have occurred on the parent and not the affiliate side if unrestricted market forces were at play.

It has to be assumed that the major part of parent trade is totally conducted in dollars, unlike that of affiliates with the exception of their sales of crude oil. This is why such a business policy offers distinct advantages for the United States. First, it relieves pressure on the BOT. Second, it improves the U.S. share in world trade by weakening foreign exports per se, but also in comparison with the U.S. trade record. Lastly, it diminishes affiliate and parent exposure to often painful exchange rate variations.

A secondary factor contributing to the uneven trade volumes for foreigners and affiliates are growing pricing differentials for both markets: market prices for products bought from or sold to independent foreigners vs. transfer prices on intercompany business. Furthermore, from sketchy information available, it may be assumed that exports of manufactures to foreigners consist largely of finished merchandise, while trade with affiliates increasingly moves in the direction of raw materials or semifinished goods. Inherent pricing differentials emerge from varying processing stages of traded products and materials.

Based on official statistics, it must be emphasized that there are compelling reasons for continuing parent trade with foreigners, perhaps even on a fairly large scale, and not necessarily to the detriment of affiliates–a mistake parents have little reason to commit. The situation in markets where no subsidiaries exist is obvious. But even in markets where the same have been established or acquired, opening or continuing direct channels between parents and foreigners can be very advantageous. Often affiliates cannot or may not offer all parent products or services for reasons like: (preexisting) licensing agreements, marketing and production specialization, competition, technology transfer problems, political or economic reasons, size of the local market, internal and external trade barriers, etc.

The conclusion to be drawn from all evidence presented so far is that parent trade with foreigners bolsters the U.S. BOT, which is known to be unfavorable for more than two decades now. The United States ships more to foreigners, both in terms of actual dollars and percentage of total U.S. exports, than they import from them in terms of dollars or percentage of total U.S. imports. Once more, the net effect is a very substantial surplus for the country's trade balance.

The above discussion makes valid points, but appears in a totally new light when adding information which surfaced only quite recently. It relates to the use of the term "foreigners" in government statistics. While technically correct, it includes so-called "foreign parent groups of U.S. parents," a reference to the fact that foreigners own equity capital positions of 10 percent or more in U.S. outward FDI corporations. That in itself is not as surprising as the fact that official recognition of this fact came for the first time with the 1989 census, even though it must have existed before.

In 1995, it was disclosed that this previously unknown ownership affects an estimated 15 percent of U.S. FDI parents, 5 percent of FDI-associated exports, and 15 percent of like imports (*SOCB*, June 1995,pp. 39, 40). Details on the subject provided in Table 4.6 allow these percentages to be quantified in actual dollars, pointing not only at big volumes, but also at big trade deficits.

The DOC's Bureau of Economic Analysis (BEA), the source of this disclosure, considers this trade to be an "intra-MNC" transaction, meaning between outward FDI group members, a debatable contention from the capital control point of view. Obviously, such a position also leads to duplication of trade figures insofar as they are included in trade information concerning U.S. inward FDI companies. All available data are broken down in Table 4.6.

All the above comments and observations are strictly adhering to the official version of the trade figures published. Any change in the official position will be long in coming, as it would cause disturbing differences in the way the trade picture is presented owing to the magnitude of the figures involved. Overall, the favorable effect of parent trade on the U.S. BOT remains intact, but the role of the parents' trading partners is upset. Parent trade with foreigners would shrink in volume, yet turn even more favorable for the United States, while trade balances with affiliates would turn negative because foreign parent groups use their affiliated U.S. parents mainly as importers and to a lesser extent as suppliers.

The change in the accounting procedure would have the hypothetical effect of turning the parent/affiliate trade from a surplus of $12.0 billion into a $6.9 billion deficit for 1992, and from a surplus of $8.2 billion into an even larger $13.9 billion deficit for 1993. In a reversal of previously made observations, U.S. parents would now contribute to instead of alleviating the trade deficit. The only redeeming aspect of the new situation is that taking this trade as intra-affiliate business would clearly result in the above postulated parent preference for trading with their foreign affiliates.

FDI EFFECT ON U.S. MERCHANDISE TRADE

The foregoing discussion of trade by U.S. nonaffiliates and parents with affiliates plus parents with foreigners allows the assembly of a complete picture of outward FDI's role in U.S. foreign trade. The next table establishes that between two-thirds and three-fourths of all U.S. merchandise exports are connected with these parties in one form or another. Estimates on this table for 1950 and 1957 may be understated, as they are based on the assumption that parent exports to nonaffiliates reached the same 50 percent of total U.S. exports found for later years. How realistic this is may never be determined. It may be equally reasonable to argue that they were much higher, but certainly not lower, because affiliates were not as numerous or as developed at that time. Higher nonaffiliated shares in U.S.

exports may actually have provided the primer for direct investment activities of later years.

In reading Table 4.7, one should remember that exports to affiliates combine parent and U.S. nonaffiliated exports to outward FDI companies, while exports to foreigners consist solely of U.S. parent shipments. The growth of both combined is definitely lagging behind total U.S. export growth, owing to significant share reductions from 50 to 30 percent in the trade with foreigners, while exports to affiliates increased rapidly from 15 to 28 percent, where they may be currently levelling off.

All the above data confirm a very positive effect of outward FDI on the U.S. BOT. For each year shown, there is a very healthy surplus in the trade account. Furthermore, subsidiaries may well continue to provide a growing market for U.S. goods not only from their expanding share in total U.S. exports, but from the successful conclusion of the latest GATT round and also from NAFTA.

On the U.S. import side, outward FDI companies play a less prominent role. Again, the findings are influenced heavily by estimates for the early

TABLE 4.7. FDI Share in Total U.S. Exports (shipments/$ billion)

Year	Total U.S. Exports	FDI Share in Total U.S. Exports by Customer Group:					
		Total	%	Affiliates	%	Nonaffil.	%
1950	$9.9	$6.5e	66	$1.5A	15	$5.0e	51e
1957	19.3	12.8e	66	3.0A	15	9.8e	50e
1966	29.3	19.2	73	7.7M	26	11.5	39
1977	120.8	101.9	84	40.8A	34	61.1	50
		93.2	77	35.8M	30	57.4	47
1982	211.2	163.5	78	56.7A	27	106.7	50
		147.7	70	52.8M	25	94.9	45
1989	362.1	241.5	67	102.1A	28	139.4	38
				97.1M	27		
1990	389.3	241.3	62	106.4A	27	134.9	35
				100.2M	26		
1991	416.9	257.9	62	115.3A	28	142.6	35
				108.8M	26		
1992	440.4	265.9	60	122.0A	28	143.9	33
				115.5M	26		
1993	456.8	270.0	59	130.7A	29	139.3	30
				122.8M	27		

Notes: M = Mofas. A = All Affiliates. e = estimate.

Sources: See Tables 4.3, 4.4, and 4.6.

years rather than documented facts due to the weak database. Estimates for total FDI trade volumes in 1950, 1957, and 1966 rest on the basis of parent imports from nonaffiliated foreigners reaching the same 30 percent share they showed in 1977. According to these estimates, between 50 and 60 percent of all U.S. imports were related to FDI until the late 1970s. Its share started to slide to about 40 percent at latest count, and may continue in that vein. BOP information discloses a huge inflow of FDI capital into the United States, which is historically tied to increasing imports, and which may very well cause a further decline in the role of U.S. parents in this trade segment.

In comparison to the export side, the role of affiliates in American imports appears reversed. In the first instance, they were gaining–actually doubling their share. Here they are declining, losing about one-third of their earliest share estimate. Combined with equally shrinking FDI purchases from foreigners, the gradual erosion of the FDI position on the import side of America's foreign trade is easy to understand, but not necessarily a negative factor (see Table 4.8).

TABLE 4.8. FDI Share in Total U.S. Imports (shipments/$ billion)

Year	Total U.S. Imports	FDI Share in Total U.S. Imports by Supplier					
		World	%	Affiliates	%	Nonaffil.	%
1950	$8.9	$5.2e	58	$2.5A	28	$2.7e	30e
1957	13.0	7.7e	59	3.8A	29	3.9e	30e
1966	25.5	14.7e	58	6.3M	25	8.4e	33e
1977	151.9	86.8	57	41.5A	27	45.2	30
		79.6	52	38.0M	25	41.6	27
1982	247.6	120.8	49	51.4A	21	69.4	28
		106.1	43	46.1M	19	60.0	24
1989	477.4	192.6	40	93.7A	20	98.9	21
				84.8M	18		
1990	498.3	213.4	43	102.2A	20	111.2	22
				88.6M	18		
1991	490.9	212.7	43	102.8A	21	109.9	22
				90.5M	18		
1992	436.5	219.7	41	108.4A	20	111.3	21
				97.9M	18		
1993	589.4	231.1	39	122.2A	21	108.9	18
				111.3M	19		

Note: M = Mofas. A = Affiliates. e = estimate.
Sources: See Tables 4.3, 4.4, and 4.6.

During the 1950s, there was a trade imbalance between affiliates and their parents which has since been completely eliminated, causing the earlier negative effect on the U.S. BOT to change to a permanent surplus for the United States. (See Table 4.1.) The same clearcut contribution cannot be registered for affiliates trading with unaffiliated U.S. businesses, which reaches a trade volume standing at roughly 25 percent of that between parents and affiliates after 1965. This trade shows a very changeable pattern with alternating positive and negative results for the U.S. BOT. In 1966, 1977, 1989, and 1990, affiliates registered a surplus causing a trade deficit for the United States. In 1982 and the 1991 to 1993 period, affiliates bought more than they had shipped to them, effectively creating a negative trade balance for themselves, but a surplus for the Untied States. The concurrent generation of a U.S. BOT surplus by parents and offspring during the later years may again be a deliberate effort by the outward FDI companies to support the official export policy and thus relieve pressures on the U.S. BOP and the dollar (see Table 4.9).

Mofas dominate the FDI trade with parents with shares, exceeding 90 percent for imports and exports alike. Their 76 to 80 percent share of trade

TABLE 4.9. Trade Between Affiliates and U.S. Nonaffiliates (shipments/$ billion)

Year	Affil. Exports to U.S.	Percent of U.S. Imports	Affil. Imports from U.S.	Percent of U.S. Exports	Affiliate Trade Balance
1966M	$1.7	6.7%	$1.4	4.8%	$0.3
1977A	8.9	5.9	8.4	7.1	0.5
M	7.1	4.7	6.5	5.5	0.6
1982A	9.8	4.0	10.2	4.9	(0.4)
M	7.6	3.1	8.4	4.1	(0.8)
1989A	17.7	3.7	12.9	3.6	4.8
M	12.4	2.6	11.5	3.2	0.9
1990A	N/A	N/A	11.8	3.0	N/A
M	13.4	2.7	11.8	3.0	1.6
1991A	N/A	N/A	13.1	3.1	N/A
M	12.9	2.6	13.1	3.1	(0.2)
1992A	14.5	2.7	16.0	3.6	(1.5)
M	13.1	2.4	14.8	3.4	(1.7)
1993A	19.3	3.3	19.6	4.3	(0.3)
M	15.4	2.6	17.8	3.9	(2.4)

Notes: M = Mofas. A = All Affiliates.

Source: See Table 4.1.

with U.S. nonaffiliates clearly demonstrates the tight parent control over Mofas, which is obviously not possible in the case of minority holdings.

In summary, U.S. foreign direct investment companies have established a very proud and exemplary record by maintaining a favorable external trade balance for themselves. In doing so, they have contributed positively to the regular trade surpluses of the United States in earlier years, and indirectly also in those crucial years where the overall U.S. trade shows persistent and large deficits–essentially all years from 1971 forward with the exception of 1973. That it is based on a deliberate and determined effort by the companies themselves, and perhaps to some degree also to government prodding, is evident (see Table 4.10).

The foregoing discussion of U.S. trade involving FDI members can be amplified with details for major industries. They are available for the census years 1966, 1977, 1982, and 1989 for U.S. exports, plus several additional years for U.S. imports. Development patterns by industry can deviate substantially from aggregate totals. In the following, all FDI trade, as it affects the U.S. BOT, will be analyzed from two different angles. First, imports and exports involving parents, affiliates, and unaffiliated partners of both are looked at separately and isolated from total U.S. trade. The same data will be used to establish FDI's role in total U.S. trade for selected industries. Slight variations in the following data may appear, as they are based on FDI census results.

U.S. imports from affiliates received a more comprehensive statistical coverage than exports, so they are introduced at this point. Table 4.11 captures each industry's share development since 1957. Manufacturing

TABLE 4.10. Overall FDI Balance of Trade with United States ($ billion)

Year	FDI Exports	FDI Imports	Balance
1950	$6.5e	$5.2e	$1.3e
1957	12.8e	7.7e	5.1e
1966	21.3e	14.7e	6.6e
1977	101.9	86.8	15.1
1982	163.5	120.8	42.7
1989	241.5	201.2	40.3
1990	241.3	213.4	27.9
1991	257.9	216.5	41.4
1992	265.9	219.7	46.2
1993	269.9	231.1	38.8

Note: e = estimate.
Sources: See Tables 4.7 and 4.8.

TABLE 4.11. U.S. Imports from Affiliate Industries (shipments/$ billion)

Year	Total $	Pet. $	%	Mfg. $	%	Trade $	%	Other $	%
1957A	$3.8	$1.4	37	$1.1	29	N/A	N/A	$1.2	32
1966M	6.3	1.5	24	2.7	43	$0.5	8	1.6	25
1967M	7.2	1.5	21	3.2	44	0.6	8	1.9	26
1968M	8.6	1.6	19	4.1	48	0.7	8	2.2	26
1969M	9.5	1.7	18	5.0	53	0.7	7	2.1	22
1970M	9.9	1.7	17	5.4	55	0.8	8	2.0	20
1971M	12.8	3.3	26	6.5	51	1.0	8	2.0	16
1972M	14.4	3.9	27	7.8	54	1.1	8	1.6	11
1973M	19.6	6.4	33	9.5	49	1.5	8	2.2	11
1974M	31.8	16.0	51	11.2	35	1.4	4	3.2	10
1975M	31.6	15.1	48	11.4	36	2.6	8	2.5	8
1977A	41.5	17.8	43	19.6	47	1.8	4	2.3	6
M	38.0	16.8	44	17.7	47	1.7	5	1.8	5
1982A	51.4	15.8	31	31.1	61	2.7	5	1.8	4
M	46.1	15.5	34	26.4	57	2.6	6	1.6	4
1988A	87.3	9.0	10	69.0	79	7.3	8	2.0	2
M	78.6	8.9	11	57.7	73	7.2	9	1.8	2
1989A	93.7	10.7	11	72.4	77	8.4	9	2.2	2
M	84.8	10.6	12	64.3	75	8.3	10	1.6	2
1990A	102.2	11.8	12	81.1	80	7.4	7	1.8	2
M	88.6	11.7	13	68.3	77	7.2	8	1.5	2
1991A	102.8	11.7	11	80.6	78	8.8	9	1.7	2
M	90.5	11.5	13	68.9	76	8.6	9	1.4	2
1992A	108.4	12.1	11	85.4	79	8.9	8	1.8	2
M	97.9	12.0	12	75.7	77	8.8	9	1.5	2
1993A	122.2	13.0	11	97.2	80	10.2	8	1.8	1
M	111.3	12.8	12	87.0	78	10.0	9	1.5	1

Notes: M = Mofas. A = All Affiliates.

Source: See Table 4.4.

affiliates emerged as the number one industry for practically the whole period with the possible exception of the years prior to 1957, and the period of the oil crisis which catapulted the oil affiliates to brief prominence between 1974 and 1976.

Manufacturing's trade share rose from about 30 percent during the 1950s to over 50 percent during the early 1970s on its way to almost 80 percent during the 1990s. Without the upheaval in the oil sector, these affiliates would most likely have maintained their steady lead and growth pattern without interruption. OPEC caused a temporary setback in both, but may actually be credited with their rebound to an even higher import share.

Petroleum affiliates were simultaneously the beneficiaries and victims of OPEC's policies, which resulted in their wide swings of import shares from 20 percent during the 1960s to over 50 percent during the 1970s, and back down to 11 to 12 percent in the end. Oil sold for an average of $2.65 per barrel during the early 1970s; jumped to $11.65 at the end of 1973; practically doubled in 1979; reached its peak of $34 at the end of 1981; retreated to $20 by 1989, and fell to around $16 in 1995. Such violent price gyrations set off secondary inflation waves in other areas, whose impact on manufactures and services, for instance, proved to be more permanent than for the more volatile oil.

Trade affiliates represented the third most important group among U.S. imports from affiliates, yet held only a comparatively modest share that barely touched 10 percent in 1989. Its historic level appears to be around 8 percent, despite a dip below 5 percent during the late 1970s from where it seems to be recovering (see Table 4.11). The industry includes both wholesale and retail operations except for the period of 1990 to 1993 which shows wholesale only. Wholesale accounted for 99 percent of the total.

The rather strong performance of the "Other" category early on with a share between 25 and 32 percent is due to the prominence of agriculture, mining and utilities in those years whose development could not keep up with other investment fields and, as a consequence, saw their share decline to a mere 2 percent or less of all affiliate exports to the United States.

TOTAL U.S. FDI-RELATED IMPORTS
BY INDUSTRY

The information presented in this section is limited to benchmark survey years alone. Total FDI-related imports including parents, affiliates and foreign trading partners of both more than doubled between 1977 and 1989. Dominated by the same three industries that play leading roles on the investment side, they are in rank order of their 1989 importance: manufacturing, petroleum, and trade with respective 1989 shares of 14 percent, 62 percent, and 18 percent, for a combined total of 94 percent. Between 1977 and 1989, petroleum shares were reduced significantly from 48 to 14 percent, a loss that led to equally impressive gains for manufactures from 38 to 60 percent, and all other industries from 18 to 24 percent (see Table 4.12A).

U.S. imports from affiliates underwent a practically similar change in pattern as a result of scaled back oil investments in 1980 and crude oil's price erosion in later years. Manufacturing remained the leader at this time with a share expansion from 47 to 82 percent. Petroleum ranked second, but its share declined from 43 to 9 percent, with all others furnishing around 9 percent of the total. The overall position of these three key industries was not materially affected by the internal shifts among the members, leading to their aggregate share remaining at 95 percent of subsidiary exports. Overall, affiliates have maintained their share in total American FDI imports at around 45 percent (see Table 4.12B).

Total parent imports from affiliates and foreigners reached over 90 percent of overall FDI-related imports, with equally high shares holding true for petroleum, trade, manufactures, and the rest of affiliate industries at the end of 1989 (see Table 4.12C).

Parent imports from affiliates accounted for a very steady 36 to 37 percent of all FDI-related imports. But sourcing from oil affiliates has dropped from 42 to 9 percent of their total imports, which in turn led to sharp rises for manufactures, where parents increased their purchases from 48 to 84 percent of total. In 1989, parent imports of manufactures from affiliates broke down as follows: 52 percent transport equipment, 20 percent nonelectrical machinery, 8 percent electrical and electronic machinery, and 20 percent for all others. The remaining proportion of the affiliates is of declining importance for parents, with a share dropping from 26 percent in 1966 to 7 percent in 1989 (see Table 4.12D).

Parent imports from foreigners held fairly steady between 1977 and 1989 with a share between 52 and 57 percent of all FDI-related imports. There has been a significant change, though, for the oil business. Here, parent sourcing increased from 54 to 67 percent of all FDI-related oil imports (see Table 4.12E). But oil's once-leading share in parent imports was virtually obliterated after falling from 46 to 18 percent with an interim peak of 60 percent in 1982. For manufactures, exactly the opposite development can be observed, with the share declining from 30 to 23 percent between 1977 and 1982, then shooting up to 44 percent in 1989. The net share loss for both affiliate categories in parent imports from 76 percent in 1977 to 62 percent in 1989 led to gains for the rest of the affiliate suppliers.

All of this left the trade between affiliates and unrelated U.S. customers, with a stagnant share of 10 percent in FDI-related U.S. imports. The oil affiliates held on to a pretty level import share with 10 percent, but at a greatly reduced dollar volume. In this they parallel the development seen for parent imports from affiliates and foreign suppliers alike. But this is not surprising in view of their shrinking supply basis after the Middle East expropriation in 1980. Manufacturing and trade affiliates held their own with a steady 12 percent and 3 percent share, respectively. All other affiliate categories suffered a pronounced setback with their share plummeting from 18 to 11 percent between 1977 and 1989 (see Table 4.12F).

The information set forth in Table 4.12 summarizes all census information available in detail for the four FDI trading partners: affiliates, parents, and nonaffiliated trading partners of both in the United States as well as abroad. While it is available in complete form for only three years, 1977, 1982, 1989, and partially for 1966, it gives a good account of changes effected. Horizontal percentages in the table indicate an industry's share in U.S. imports from that particular source. Vertical percentages refer to the supplier's share in total U.S. FDI-related imports for a particular industry, that is to say, they are only a part of overall U.S. imports.

The table in conjunction with Table 4.13 permits a closer look at the previously noted shift of parent imports from affiliates to foreign suppliers. It appears that the oil, trade, and the all other category are mainly responsible for this development. The parent share of oil import from affiliates declined drastically from 36 percent in 1977 to 24 percent in 1989. Similarly, it declined from 12 to 7 percent for trade affiliates, and from 52 to 24 percent for all others (see Table 4.12D). It automatically caused parent imports from foreigners to rise from 54 to 67 percent for oil, from 85 to 90 percent in the case of the trade sector, and from 30 to 63 percent for all others (see Table 4.12E).

All of this coincided with a reduction in the number of petroleum affiliates from 1,933 in 1977 to 1,801 in 1982, and to 1,443 in 1989. The dollar amount spent by parents and U.S. nonaffiliates on oil imports from affiliates fell between 1977 and 1982, as may be expected after the expropriation of U.S. holdings in the Middle East, while parent purchases from foreigners doubled at a time when the price of oil did the same. The data translate into the fact that in terms of barrels of oil, affiliates slashed their shipments to the United States by more than half, while foreigners held their volume at steady to slightly increasing.

Foreign suppliers have always played important roles in parent imports, even though the sketchy evidence does not allow a reconstruction of what the actual levels may have been or what trends they were subject to in the past. Their gains in the indicated sectors are obvious and could actually continue. The only encouraging trend is set by the manufacturing segment where parent imports from affiliates are steady to slightly rising.

In view of the previously mentioned disclosure–that the term foreigners includes foreign parent groups of U.S. parents which are not accepted as affiliated companies by the DOC–it would be interesting to see how the picture would change if the official interpretation were abandoned.

TABLE 4.12. U.S. FDI Imports by Industry, Supplier, and Customer (shipments/ $ billion)

Year	Total $	Pet. $	%	Mfg. $	%	Trade $	%	Other $	%
A. TOTAL U.S. FDI IMPORTS BY INDUSTRY									
1977A	$86.8	$38.6	44	$34.4	38	$11.8	14	$3.3	4
%	100	100		100		100		100	
1977M	79.6	37.6	47	30.2	38	9.0	11	2.8	4
%	100	100		100		100		100	
1982A	120.8	56.5	47	48.4	40	13.7	11	2.2	2
%	100	100		100		100		100	
1982M	106.1	51.7	48	42.0	40	10.4	10	2.0	2
%	100	100		100		100		100	
1989A	201.1	27.1	14	125.4	62	35.9	18	12.7	5
%	100	100		100		100		100	
1989M	188.1	27.0	14	113.4	60	35.8	19	11.9	6
%	100			100		100		100	
B. TOTAL U.S. IMPORTS FROM AFFILIATES **(Parents and Nonaffiliates)**									
1977A	41.5	17.8	43	19.6	47	1.8	4	2.3	6
%	48	46		59		15		70	
1977M	38.0	16.8	44	17.7	47	1.7	5	1.8	5
%	48	45		59		19		64	
1982A	51.4	15.8	31	31.1	61	2.7	5	1.8	4
%	43	27		66		20		82	
1982M	46.1	15.5	34	26.4	57	2.6	6	1.6	3
%	43	30		63		25		80	
1989A	97.4	8.9	9	80.0	82	3.8	4	4.7	5
%	48	33		64		11		37	
1989M	84.3	8.8	10	68.0	81	3.7	4	3.8	5
%	45	33		60		10		32	
C. TOTAL PARENT IMPORTS **(from Affiliates and Nonaffiliates)**									
1977A	77.8	34.6	44	29.1	37	11.4	15	2.7	3
%	90	90		88		97		82	
1977M	72.5	34.4	47	27.0	37	8.6	12	2.5	3
%	91	91		90		96		89	
1982A	111.0	54.5	49	41.5	37	13.3	12	1.7	2
%	92	94		88		97		77	
1982M	98.5	48.6	49	38.4	39	10.0	10	1.5	2
%	93	94		91		96		75	
1989A	181.1	24.8	14	110.4	61	34.7	19	11.2	6
%	90	92		88		97		88	
1989M	175.1	24.7	14	104.9	60	34.6	20	10.9	6
%	93	91		93		97		92	

Year	Total $	Pet. $	%	Mfg. $	%	Trade $	%	Other $	%
D. PARENT IMPORTS FROM AFFILIATES									
1966M	4.6	1.2	26	2.2	48	0.3	7	0.9	19
1977A	32.6	13.8	42	15.7	48	1.4	4	1.7	5
%	38	36		47		12		52	
1977	30.9	13.6	44	14.4	47	1.3	4	1.6	5
%	39	36		48		14		57	
1982A	41.6	12.6	30	25.4	61	2.3	6	1.3	3
%	34	22		54		17		59	
1982M	38.5	12.5	32	22.8	59	2.1	5	1.1	3
%	36	24		54		20		55	
1989A	77.3	6.6	9	65.1	84	2.5	3	3.1	4
%	38	24		52		7		24	
1989M	71.3	6.5	9	59.5	83	2.4	3	2.9	4
%	38	25		53		7		20	
E. PARENT IMPORTS FROM FOREIGNERS									
1977	45.2	20.8	46	13.4	30	10.0	22	1.0	2
%	52	54		41		85		30	
1982	69.4	41.9	60	16.1	23	11.0	16	0.4	1
%	57	73		34		80		18	
1989	103.8	18.2	18	45.4	44	32.2	31	8.0	8
%	52	67		36		90		63	
F. U.S. NONAFFILIATE IMPORTS FROM AFFILIATES									
1966M	1.7	0.3	18	0.5	29	0.2	12	0.7	41
1977A	8.9	4.0	45	3.9	44	0.4	4	0.6	7
%	10	10		12		3		18	
1977M	7.1	3.2	45	3.2	45	0.4	6	0.3	4
%	9	9		11		4		11	
1982A	9.8	3.1	32	5.7	58	0.4	4	0.6	6
%	8	5		12		3		3	
1982M	7.6	3.0	39	3.6	47	0.4	5	0.6	8
%	7	6		9		4		3	
1989A	20.1	2.4	12	15.0	75	1.3	6	1.4	7
%	10	9		12		4		11	
1989M	13.0	2.3	18	8.5	65	1.3	10	0.9	7
%	7	9		8		4		8	

Notes: M = Mofas. A = All Affiliates. All data by industry of affiliate.

Sources: FDI census data: 1966, pp. 198, 201, 205-6; 1977, pp. 158, 160-1, 188, 352, 358, 362, 398; 1982, pp. 131, 133-4, 155, 283, 287, 291, 335; 1989, pp. 87, 115, 255, 259, 262.

TABLE 4.13. U.S. Import Shares of FDI Customers and Suppliers (percentages)

Year	FDI Imports by Supplier			FDI Imports of Customer	
	All	Affil.	Foreign	Parents	U.S. Nonaffil.
Total Imports					
1977 All	100	48	52	90	10
Mofa	100	48	52	91	9
1982 All	100	43	57	92	8
Mofa	100	43	57	93	7
1989 All	100	48	52	91	9
Mofa	100	45	55	89	11
Petroleum					
1977 All	100	46	54	90	10
Mofa	100	45	55	91	9
1982 All	100	27	73	92	8
Mofa	100	30	70	93	7
1989 All	100	33	67	92	8
Mofa	100	33	67	92	8
Manufacturing					
1977 All	100	59	41	88	12
Mofa	100	59	41	90	10
1982 All	100	66	34	88	12
Mofa	100	63	37	91	9
1989 All	100	64	36	88	12
Mofa	100	60	40	93	7
Trade					
1977 All	100	15	85	97	3
Mofa	100	19	81	96	4
1982 All	100	20	80	97	3
Mofa	100	25	75	96	4
1989 All	100	11	89	97	3
Mofa	100	10	90	97	3

FDI ROLE IN TOTAL
U.S. MERCHANDISE IMPORTS BY INDUSTRY

In addition to the above information, it is possible to give an impression of the role played by all FDI members in total U.S. imports of major commodity groups for five of the six census years. The five groups selected accounted for 91 percent of all nonmilitary merchandise imports in 1989. Table 4.14 points out two interesting facts. One is that the FDI position is quite changeable between census years and probably declining in general. A regrettable development, but one that has to be expected in view of the much lower ranking of this group in overall U.S. imports seen before.

The other fact is that in three sectors, all parties connected with FDI maintained an unchallenged leadership in oil, chemicals, and transporta-

TABLE 4.14. FDI Position in Total U.S. Imports by Major Industry (shipments/ $ billions)

Year	1957*	1966*	1977	1982	1989
Petroleum					
Total	$1.5	$2.3	$48.1	$62.7	$38.8
FDI	1.4	1.5	38.6	56.5	27.1
%	93	65	80	90	70
Manufacturing					
Total	4.6	13.5	81.9	150.6	396.9
FDI	1.1	2.7	34.4	48.4	125.4
%	24	20	42	31	32
Transport Equipment					
Total	0.4	2.2	19.2	33.9	87.9
FDI	0.1	N/A	13.4	17.3	54.6
%	25	N/A	70	51	62
Chemicals					
Total	0.3	1.0	5.0	9.5	20.1
FDI	0.1	0.2	3.1	5.4	13.2
%	33	18	62	57	66
Machinery					
Total	0.4	2.6	17.7	39.5	109.4
FDI	0.1	0.4	6.0	11.8	32.9
%	21	17	34	30	30

Note: *Excludes parent imports from foreigners.

Sources: FDI census data: 1957, pp. 110-1; 1966, p. 197; 1977, p. 188; 1982, p. 155; 1989, p. 115. *U.S. import data: U.S. Exports/Imports, 1923-68,* Supplement to *SOCB,* 1970, pp. 21-32. *Statistical Abstract of the United States,* 1987, p. 800. *Statistical Abstract of the United States,* 1992, p. 806.

tion equipment. All three represent important pillars of the U.S. economy, and play similar roles in U.S. outward FDI. Their share, if adjusted for the missing parent import data from foreigners in 1957 and 1966, probably never fell below 50 percent of total U.S. imports. In other industries, the FDI participation is much less impressive, which could be taken as sign of reduced emphasis on these sectors, but not necessarily a weaker competitive position.

What applies to the total FDI position in foreign trade of the United States must not necessarily apply to U.S. parents as such. As one would expect from the parent companies' role in U.S. trade seen earlier, they command important positions in total merchandise imports as well as those of individual industries. Noteworthy is their almost uniform decline in total imports, oil, manufactures, as well as machinery, and their very strong position in transport equipment and chemicals, where they not only hold their ground, but seem to be gaining territory. For the all-important transport equipment sector, this means gaining on automotive imports by Japanese and European competitors (see Table 4.15).

TABLE 4.15. Parent Shares in Total U.S. Imports by Industry (based on parent imports from affiliates and foreigners)

Year	Total	Oil	Manufact.	Machinery	Transp. Equip.	Chemicals
1977	53%	72%	36%	34%	63%	51%
1982	46%	87%	28%	30%	44%	50%
1989	38%	64%	28%	29%	54%	61%

U.S. FDI-RELATED EXPORTS BY INDUSTRY

As mentioned before, FDI-related exports exceed similar FDI imports for all years where such data have been published, which is in sharp contrast to the perpetually unfavorable balance of trade for the United States since 1971. They also are structured very differently from FDI imports due to a weak presence of the oil industry in the database. Manufactures now are solidly in first place accounting for over 70 percent of the total versus 60 percent on the import side; trade ranks second with a 15 to 20 percent share (imports: 10 to 18 percent); and petroleum is in a distant third place with 5 to 13 percent of the total (imports: 44 to 48 percent in earlier years but only 14 percent in 1989) (see Table 4.16A).

The following summary view of all U.S. shipments condenses the roles played by parents and nonaffiliated U.S. businesses in exports made to overseas affiliates or foreign clients in 1966, 1977, 1982, and 1989.

Exports by parents and U.S. nonaffiliates to overseas affiliates show a relative decline in overall FDI exports until 1982 to recover their pre-OPEC shares by 1989. Between 1966 and 1982, that share moved down from 41 to 35 percent, but returned to 42 percent in 1989. This temporary weakness was not shared by all industries. The affiliate share in manufacturing exports actually held pretty steady in the 42 to 47 percent range from 1966 to 1982 before moving up to 49 percent in 1989. Trade behaved similarly by maintaining a level between 13 to 16 percent from 1966 to 1982, but then took a decisive downturn to only 10 percent in 1989. Oil and all other categories were responsible for the affiliate dip in the export picture with dramatically falling shares from 1966 to 1982, and ending up with lower shares in 1989 than those held in 1966 (see Table 4.16B).

Parents have generally maintained their leading position in all FDI related exports with a share of 90 percent or higher for more than two decades. This applies to all categories with the exception of the small all other group where their share moved up from 75 to 86 percent between 1966 and 1989 (see Table 4.16C). Parents always have shipped more to foreigners than to their own affiliates at the rate of 2:1, unless the term foreigner will be redefined someday for that part covering foreign parent groups of U.S. parents alluded to on page 122. This is particularly true for trade with a ratio of 90:10; oil, 75:25; all other, 70:30; and manufactured goods, 55:45 (see Tables 4.16D and E).

The weakening of the parent/affiliate links in all U.S. FDI exports between 1966 and 1982 may have been a temporary phenomenon, if 1989 data are indicative of a firm trend reversal. The possibility certainly exists, but one year's results are just too small a sample to establish this as a fact. It would be a welcome sign, as subsidiaries should reach and maintain the most important place in parent strategies aiming at a firm foothold in global markets. A long-term parent preference for foreign business partners over affiliates, as suggested by the data between 1966 and 1982, is no realistic approach to that end.

FDI ROLE IN TOTAL U.S. EXPORTS BY INDUSTRY

Much like on the import side, it is possible to establish the role of FDI-related exports in the country's total external trade, though only with difficulty. U.S. FDI export data, with the exception of parent exports to foreigners, are actually affiliate import data which are substituted for

TABLE 4.16. Total U.S. FDI Exports by Industry, Supplier, and Customer (shipments/$ billion)

Year	Total Exports	Mfg.	%	Trade	%	Pet.	%	Other	%
colspan-A. TOTAL U.S. FDI EXPORTS BY INDUSTRY
1966M	$19.2	$14.7	77	$2.7	14	$1.0	5	$0.8	4
%	100	100		100		100		100	
1977A	101.8	73.2	72	18.9	19	5.2	5	4.5	4
%	100	100		100		100		100	
1977M	96.9	70.5	73	17.4	18	5.2	5	3.8	4
%	100	100		100		100		100	
1982A	163.4	112.1	69	26.2	16	20.8	13	4.3	3
%	100	100		100		100		100	
1982M	151.4	110.6	73	23.2	15	13.3	9	4.3	3
%	100	100		100		100		100	
1989A	236.4	190.6	79	29.9	13	8.9	4	7.0	2
%	100	100		100		100		100	
1989M	231.3	186.4	81	29.7	13	8.7	4	6.5	3
%	100	100		100		100		100	
colspan-B. TOTAL U.S. EXPORTS TO AFFILIATES (Parents and U.S. Nonaffiliates)
1966M	7.7	6.3	82	0.4	5	0.6	8	0.4	5
%	41	43		15		60		50	
1977A	40.8	34.0	83	2.5	6	2.2	5	2.1	5
%	40	47		13		42		47	
1977M	35.8	30.7	86	2.1	6	1.8	5	1.2	3
%	37	44		12		35		32	
1982A	56.7	47.0	82	4.1	7	4.2	7	1.4	2
%	35	42		16		20		33	
1982M	52.8	44.3	84	3.8	7	3.5	7	1.2	2
%	35	40		16		26		28	
1989A	102.6	92.8	90	3.1	3	3.6	4	3.1	3
%	44	49		10		40		44	
1989M	97.5	88.6	91	3.0	3	3.4	3	2.5	3
%	42	48		10		39		38	
colspan-C. TOTAL PARENT EXPORTS
1966M	17.8	13.7	77	2.7	15	0.8	4	0.6	3
%	93	93		96		80		75	
1977A	93.5	67.5	72	18.0	19	4.9	5	3.1	3
%	92	92		95		92		69	
1977M	86.7	62.9	73	16.4	19	4.4	5	3.0	3
%	89	89		94		85		79	
1982A	153.3	105.2	69	25.0	16	19.4	13	3.7	2
%	94	94		95		93		86	
1982M	139.3	102.0	73	21.9	16	11.8	8	3.6	3
%	92	92		94		88		84	
1989A	223.4	179.9	79	29.3	13	8.2	4	6.0	3
%	94	94		98		92		86	
1989M	219.9	176.7	80	29.2	13	8.1	4	5.9	3
%	95	95		98		93		91	

Year	Total Exports	Mfg.	%	Trade	%	Pet.	%	Other	%
D. PARENT EXPORTS TO AFFILIATES									
1966M	6.3	5.3	84	0.4	6	0.4	6	0.2	3
%	33	36		15		40		25	
1977A	32.4	28.3	87	1.6	5	1.8	6	0.7	2
%	32	39		8		35		16	
1977M	29.3	25.8	88	1.4	5	1.4	5	0.7	2
%	30	37		8		27		18	
1982A	46.6	40.1	86	2.9	6	2.8	6	0.8	2
%	29	36		11		13		19	
1982M	44.3	38.3	86	2.7	6	2.6	6	0.7	2
%	29	35		12		20		16	
1989A	89.5	82.1	92	2.6	3	2.8	3	2.0	2
%	38	43		9		31		29	
1989M	86.1	78.9	92	2.5	3	2.8	3	1.9	2
%	37	42		8		32		29	
E. PARENT EXPORTS TO FOREIGNERS									
1966	11.5	8.4	73	2.3	20	0.4	4	0.4	3
%	61	57		85		40		50	
1977	61.1	39.2	64	16.4	27	3.1	5	2.4	4
%	60	54		87		60		53	
1982	106.7	65.1	61	22.1	21	16.6	16	2.9	3
%	65	58		84		80		67	
1989	133.8	97.8	73	26.7	20	5.3	4	4.0	3
%	57	51		90		60		57	
F. U.S. NONAFFILIATE EXPORTS TO AFFILIATES									
1966M	1.4	1.0	71	0.1	7	0.2	14	0.1	7
%	7	7		4		20		13	
1977A	8.4	5.8	69	0.9	11	0.4	5	1.3	15
%	8	8		5		8		29	
1977M	6.5	5.0	77	0.7	11	0.3	5	0.5	8
%	7	7		4		6		13	
1982A	10.2	6.9	68	1.2	12	1.4	14	0.7	7
%	6	6		5		7		16	
1982M	8.4	6.0	71	1.0	12	0.9	11	0.5	6
%	6	5		4		7		12	
1989A	13.0	10.7	82	0.6	5	0.8	6	0.9	7
%	6	6		2		9		13	
1989M	11.4	9.7	85	0.2	2	0.6	5	0.9	8
%	5	5		1		7		14	

Notes: M = Mofas. A = All Affiliates. All data by industry of parent.

Sources: FDI census data: 1966, p. 82; 1977, pp. 185, 395; 1982, pp. 152, 332. 1989, p. 112.

actual U.S. exports as explained before, because there is no other practical way to accurately record U.S. unaffiliated exports to affiliates. This accounting method raises some problems with affiliate data, which may fall into a very different industrial class in the host country than that applying to the U.S. exporter. All of which means that products from different export industries in the United States suddenly reappear as U.S. exports under a single and potentially totally unrelated affiliate nomenclature. In addition, subsidiary imports are inflated by the normal logistic charges such as customs, shipping and handling, etc. This problem appears to have been corrected with the 1989 census, where exports and imports were maintained by industry of U.S. parent.

Table 4.17 establishes that the previous practice results in higher export volumes for the petroleum and transport equipment industry than shown by official U.S. export statistics. For the oil industry, the discrepancy arises from the inclusion of trade, service, and extraction data in affiliate imports that are not part of the U.S. export category used. The problem is by now familiar from earlier observations and comments on this point as just one of the peculiar features of FDI reporting. Removal of these data from the table would result in FDI-related oil exports showing $4.0 billion for 1977 and a total U.S. export share of 93 percent. For 1982, the same figures would stand at $9.8 billion and 77 percent. While overall more in line of what could be expected, there is still no full assurance of the data being fully compatible with each other.

Similar discrepancies in the transportation equipment sector cannot be pinpointed exactly. They seem to arise from what is called "other" affiliate imports without further details. It is probably legitimate to assume that the "other" refer to capital goods imported in conjunction with regular parts and assemblies. Again, the removal of this category indicates a more reasonable relationship between total U.S. exports and FDI related exports. The 1977 data would show FDI exports of $15.6 billion and 83 percent of total U.S. exports, and figures for 1982 would show $17.5 billion and 66 percent.

Finally, the role of parents in total U.S. exports by industry can be established. The development of their share in total as well as selected manufacturing exports should be a matter of concern, while their performance in the transport and machinery sector is outstanding. There is no ready explanation for the sudden parent prominence in the latter category unless large exporters decided to establish foreign subsidiaries between 1982 and 1989 which, once more, brings up the point about foreign business interests holding capital shares in U.S. FDI parents (see Table 4.18).

TABLE 4.17. FDI Position in Total U.S. Exports by Major Industries ($ billion)

Year	1957*	1966	1977*	1982	1989
Petroleum					
Total	$1.8	$1.0	$4.3	$12.8	$10.1
FDI	1.2	1.0	5.2	20.8	8.9
%	44	60	**	**	89
Manufacturing					
Total	9.5	16.4	94.9	168.4	290.5
FDI	1.2	14.7	73.2	112.1	190.6
%	12	38	77	67	66
Chemicals					
Total	1.4	2.7	10.7	20.1	35.8
FDI	N/A	2.1	9.9	16.8	26.7
%	N/A	33	93	84	75
Nonelectrical Machinery					
Total	3.2	6.2	21.4	39.9	55.5
FDI	N/A	2.8e	12.8	19.9	32.9
%	N/A	18	60	50	59
Electrical Machinery					
Total	0.8	1.9	10.3	18.1	32.7
FDI	N/A	1.5e	8.2	17.0	21.3
%	N/A	32	80	94	65
Transportation Equipment					
Total	1.8	3.7	18.9	26.7	58.9
FDI	N/A	3.9	23.6	31.3	62.3
%	N/A	54	**	**	**

Notes: *Excludes parent exports to foreigners. **See comments in text. e = estimate.

Sources: FDI census data: 1957, pp. 121, 146; 1966, p. 82; 1977, p. 185; 1982, p. 152. *U.S. export data: Census data: 1957*, p. 113. All other years: *Statistical Abstract of the U.S.*, 1987, p. 800; 1992, p. 806.

TABLE 4.18. Parent Share in Total U.S. Exports by Industry (based on parent exports to affiliates and foreigners)

Year	Total	Oil	Mfg.	Machinery		Chemical	Trans. Equip.
				Nonelectric	Electric		
1966	68%	85%	84%	18%	25%	74%	95%
1977	77	N/A	71	24	26	86	70
1982	72	69	62	25	29	78	56
1989	62	81	62	58	63	70	98

Chapter 5

FDI and the U.S. Balance of Payments

The early 1970s became a turning point for America. Internally, they marked the beginning of decades of mounting financial and fiscal woes, mushrooming budget deficits, and rapidly expanding public, corporate, and consumer debt. Externally, the postwar order and stability fostered under U.S. leadership began to disintegrate. On August 13, 1971, the Bretton Woods agreement on fixed exchange rates and the establishment of the dollar as the world's key currency after World War II was abandoned. Its termination by President Nixon led to the first devaluation of the dollar in December of the same year, and its slow depreciation until 1980. In 1973, OPEC began to assert itself, orchestrating the first of two major oil price escalations during the decade, which shook the world economy to its foundation. Following up with a traumatic blow to American oil interests in 1980, Saudi Arabia expropriated ARAMCO, the jointly held Arab-American Corporation. The year 1971 also marked the beginning of persistent and growing U.S. trade deficits. From a fairly moderate level, the trade imbalances have assumed annual proportions rivaling those of their domestic twin, the budget deficits. This caused wide dollar fluctuations and destabilization of the international exchange markets.

A country's internal and external developments leave an imprint on its BOP, which is nothing more than a barometer for the economy's health relative to other nations. The following pages are devoted to discussing all previously collected information on U.S. outward FDI in the broader BOP context, that is, relating it to the competitive developments for inward FDI activities in the current and capital accounts. The current account, with its twin entries of merchandise trade and flow of services, usually evokes very different perceptions. Because of highly publicized big and unwieldy deficits, the trade account is generally held to represent the key problem for America's economic relations with other nations, while the services account is conveniently assumed to produce more favorable surplus flows.

Because the BOP is the arbiter of America's external business relations, it may be very beneficial to bring all facts registered for the three accounts to the surface at this point, in order to arrive at a balanced judgement about the country's international viability, or competitiveness. As it turns out, this is largely a matter of interpretation of documented facts and the statistical methods employed in their establishment.

Beginning with the trade account problems and their negative impact on the current account, it is interesting to watch its unresponsiveness to traditional cures ranging from deliberate currency depreciation and deflation of the economy, to export incentives such as subsidies, and even diplomatic armtwisting at periodic economic summits. Forceful appeals for easier access of U.S. goods to foreign markets have been blended with restraints on U.S. imports of some commodities. Well-known examples are the voluntary Japanese car quotas, textile quotas, and the threats of imposing a total ban on the imports of steel and a whole host of other goods.

The above are urgent measures to stem the flow of red ink and correct what could become an ominous prelude to the future of free trade. Their ineffectiveness in correcting or eliminating the persistent problem suggests that factors are at work which cannot be addressed with trade policies alone. The only positive aspect of the debacle, until now, has been the steadfast refusal of the United States to openly break its free trade policy, and chance the collapse of world trade and cause political upheaval.

The public discussion of the situation in the domestic and foreign press, the statements by U.S. officials, and the comments and advice by economic experts generally agree on one point: they all are quick to point the finger at oversized U.S. imports as the culprit for the trade deficits. Such unanimity is comforting to those who stand in the public limelight, but forces the focus of discussion and corrective action dangerously into only one and, perhaps, the wrong direction. Above all else, it could conceivably lead to the treatment of symptoms without a solid diagnosis of the underlying ailment, which might exactly be the reason why actions taken so far remained without positive results (see Table 5.1).

To declare highly visible imports as the source of all problems is understandable and convenient, as it allows finger-pointing at foreign traders. Prominence by itself, however, is only a symptom, which does not necessarily establish a legitimate cause. After all, the principle of free trade is supposed to prevent persistent trade imbalances, which in this case could indicate a serious lack of national competitiveness. What is needed in this situation is a balanced and unemotional look at both sides of trade to decide how much each contributes to the problem.

TABLE 5.1. Basic Data Relating to the U.S. Balance of Trade ($ billion)

		Merchandise Trade				
		Adjusted, excl. military		Percent of GDP		Balance of Trade
Year	GDP	Exports	Imports	Exports	Imports	
1960	$513.3	$19.7	−$14.8	3.8	2.9	$4.9
1961	531.8	20.1	−14.5	3.7	2.7	5.6
1962	571.6	20.8	−16.3	3.6	2.8	4.5
1963	603.1	22.3	−17.0	3.6	2.8	5.2
1964	648.0	25.5	−18.7	3.9	2.9	6.8
1965	702.7	26.5	−21.5	3.8	3.0	5.0
1966	769.8	29.3	−25.5	3.8	3.4	3.8
1967	814.3	30.7	−26.9	3.8	3.3	3.8
1968	889.3	33.6	−33.0	3.8	3.7	0.6
1969	959.5	36.4	−35.8	3.8	3.7	0.6
1970	1,010.7	42.5	−39.9	4.2	3.9	2.6
1971	1,097.2	43.3	−45.6	3.9	4.1	−2.3
1972	1,207.0	49.4	−55.8	4.0	4.6	−6.4
1973	1,349.6	71.4	−70.5	5.2	5.2	0.9
1974	1,458.6	98.3	−103.8	6.7	7.1	−5.5
1975	1,585.9	107.1	−98.2	6.7	6.1	8.9
1976	1,768.4	114.7	−124.2	6.4	7.0	−9.5
1977	1,974.1	120.8	−151.9	6.1	7.6	−31.1
1978	2,232.7	142.1	−176.0	6.3	7.8	−33.9
1979	2,488.6	184.5	−212.0	7.4	8.5	−27.5
1980	2,708.0	224.3	−249.7	8.2	9.2	−25.5
1981	3,030.6	237.1	−265.1	7.8	8.7	−28.0
1982	3,149.6	211.2	−247.6	6.7	7.8	−36.4
1983	3,405.0	201.8	−268.9	5.9	7.9	−67.1
1984	3,777.2	219.9	−332.4	5.8	8.8	−112.5
1985	4,038.7	215.9	−338.1	5.3	8.3	−122.2
1986	4,268.8	223.3	−368.4	5.2	8.6	−145.1
1987	4,539.9	250.2	−409.8	5.5	9.0	−159.6
1988	4,900.4	320.2	−447.2	6.5	9.1	−127.0
1989	5,250.8	362.1	−477.4	6.9	9.1	−115.2
1990	5,546.1	389.3	−498.3	7.0	9.0	−109.0
1991	5,724.8	416.9	−490.9	7.3	8.6	−74.1
1992	6,020.2	440.4	−536.5	7.3	8.9	−96.1
1993	6,343.3	456.8	−589.4	7.2	9.3	−132.6
1994	6,736.8	502.5	−668.6	7.5	9.9	−166.1

Sources: *Economic Report of the President*, February 1995, p. 274. *SOCB*, June 1993, pp. 70-1; June 1995, pp. 84-5.

IMPORTS TOO HIGH OR EXPORTS TOO LOW?

The discussion of the relative importance of exports and imports to the U.S. trade deficit can be addressed in a straightforward manner. A comparison of U.S. trade with that of other industrialized nations makes it abundantly clear that both imports and exports of the United States are comparatively low relative to its GNP.

Taking a look at OECD countries as representative of the industrialized nations of today, one finds import and export shares ranging from 12 to 35 percent of their respective GDP (*OECD*, 1988). This is more than double the U.S. figures where merchandise imports have never exceeded 10 percent of GDP. For the past decade, they have consistently fluctuated around the 9 percent mark–quite a modest ratio by international standards.

Merchandise exports, on the other hand, of around 7 percent of GDP are abnormally low by the same set of criteria, and the prime cause of the trade shortfalls. Very alarming is the fact that imports have shown a tendency to grow against GNP, while exports seem to be in a holding pattern.

Seen from this perspective, merchandise trade is only of limited consequence for the economic prosperity of the country, and out of proportion with the tough official trade initiatives taken. In addition, the negative trade situation for goods has to be viewed in conjunction with America's trade in services that have produced annual surpluses since 1971. While the positive balance in this account is not yet sufficient to completely offset the trade deficit on the merchandise side, it still has a strongly mitigating influence on the BOP's current account balance.

POSSIBLE CAUSES OF THE PROBLEM

Declaring U.S. merchandise exports, and not its imports, as the primary suspect in the nation's trade problem is a position which is at odds with conventional thinking on the subject. However, it may lead away from the present trade myopia that is so heavily tinged with political sentiments, and pave the way for an unbiased search for hidden contributory causes. The situation calls for definitive answers to very specific questions. Is it, for instance, possible to identify major U.S. or even foreign business interests playing a role in the country's trade development? Could such information lead to a partial or full explanation of why they have not been more responsive to the nation's problem? Could trade interests even be in conflict with official trade policies, which would make finding a solution to the problem all the more difficult? If light can be shed on the role they play on the export side, it is only natural to apply the same line of questioning to the import side, and thus establish their specific contributions to the trade deficit. If the parties effecting the fate of U.S. exports and imports of goods are not the same, who else of importance can be identified? Finally, can the responsible parties be persuaded to align their business strategies with official trade policies?

Merchandise trade flows are but one aspect of a country's economic bond with the outside world. Traditionally viewed as commercial transactions among independent trading partners to balance resource differentials for the unquestionable benefit of all, merchandise trade has become the standard measure of international business success. These days, trade is so preoccupied with classical and modern economic thinking that it effectively clouds the vision for its complement: direct overseas investments, and the growing interdependence between the two. From Adam Smith to the middle of the twentieth century, direct investments were embryonic at best, and thus not given much thought. Their growing prominence in today's national and international economics, however, deserves the same attention trade has ever been accorded. The following analysis of the trade situation demonstrates very vividly how FDI shapes the composition and developments of the U.S. current account balances.

FDI AND THE U.S. MERCHANDISE TRADE DEFICITS

Taking a closer look at the U.S. BOT reveals how outward and inward FDI parties dominate the country's trade flows. On the export side, all parties connected with outward FDI are controlling the lion's share of that business. Included are U.S. parent companies exporting to affiliates and foreigners, as well as unrelated American business shipping to the same U.S.-owned overseas subsidiaries. Their combined share in total U.S. exports reached 66 percent in 1966, 84 percent in 1977, 78 percent in 1982, and 59 percent in 1993. 1966 data are understated as they cover Mofas only, unlike for all other years where they pertain to all nonbank affiliates and their parents (see Table 4.7). Foreign-owned, inward FDI companies account for another 20 to 25 percent of all U.S. merchandise exports as documented below, such that both FDI parties combined reach between 80 and 90 percent of all U.S. nonmilitary merchandise exports (see Table 5.2).

On the import side, similar information indicates a much-reduced role for outward FDI members, yet a disproportionately stronger position for foreign companies operating in the United States. The column "Outward

TABLE 5.2. U.S. Export Data ($ billion)

Year	Total U.S. Exports	U.S. Outward FDI-Related Exports $	%	U.S. Inward FDI-Related Exports $	%	FDI Share %
1966	$29.3	$19.2	65.5	N/A	N/A	N/A
1974	98.3	N/A	N/A	N/A	N/A	N/A
1977	120.8	101.9	84.4	$24.9	20.6	105.0
1978	142.1	N/A	N/A	32.2	22.6	N/A
1979	184.5	N/A	N/A	44.3	24.1	N/A
1980	224.3	N/A	N/A	52.2	23.2	N/A
1981	237.1	N/A	N/A	64.1	27.0	N/A
1982	211.2	163.5	77.4	60.2	28.5	105.9
1983	201.8	N/A	N/A	53.9	26.7	N/A
1984	219.9	N/A	N/A	58.2	26.5	N/A
1985	215.9	N/A	N/A	56.4	26.1	N/A
1986	223.3	N/A	N/A	49.6	22.2	N/A
1987	250.2	N/A	N/A	48.1	19.2	N/A
1988	320.2	215.2	67.2	69.5	21.7	88.9
1989	362.1	241.5	66.7	86.3	23.8	90.5
1990	389.3	241.3	62.0	92.3	23.7	85.7
1991	416.9	257.9	61.9	96.9	23.2	85.1
1992	440.4	265.9	60.5	103.9	23.6	84.1
1993	456.8	270.0	59.1	105.1	23.0	82.1

Note: Data of merchandise excluding military.

Sources: U.S. BOP exports: *SOCB*, June 1991, pp. 44-5; June 1995, pp. 84-5. U.S. outward FDI exports: See Table 4.7. U.S. inward FDI exports: *SOCB*, May 1995, p. 62.

U.S. FDI Imports" represents subsidiary shipments to all U.S. customers plus U.S. parent imports from foreigners, whose combined volume ranges between 40 and 50 percent of overall U.S. merchandise imports. Comparable information for foreign subsidiaries in the United States indicates they are responsible for another one-third of all U.S. imports (see Table 5.3).

Even though not quite matching their combined performance on the export side, both parties together still accounted for a respectable 70 to 75 percent of overall U.S. nonmilitary imports. While outward FDI-related imports hold a very steady share of around 40 percent of U.S. merchandise imports, those connected with foreign affiliates in the United States showed an equally steady share in the vicinity of 35 percent. The net effect of both developments is a trade surplus in the U.S. BOT for outward FDI companies alluded to before, while foreign subsidiaries contribute heavily to the U.S. trade deficits.

TABLE 5.3. U.S. Merchandise Imports by FDI Companies (excluding military — $ billion)

Year	Total U.S. Imports	Outward U.S. FDI Imports $	Outward U.S. FDI Imports %	Inward U.S. FDI Imports $	Inward U.S. FDI Imports %
1977	$151.9	$79.6	52.3	$43.9	28.9
1982	247.6	106.1	42.7	84.3	34.0
1987	409.8	N/A	N/A	143.5	35.0
1988	447.2	180.9	40.5	155.5	34.8
1989	477.4	192.6	40.4	171.8	36.0
1990	498.3	213.4	42.9	182.9	36.7
1991	490.9	212.7	43.3	178.7	36.4
1992	536.5	219.7	41.0	184.5	34.4
1993	589.4	231.1	39.2	198.5	33.7

Sources: Total U.S. Imports: *SOCB*, June 1993, pp. 70-1; June 1995, pp. 84-5. Inward U.S. FDI Imports: *SOCB*, May 1995, p. 62. Outward U.S. FDI Imports: See Table 4.8.

The existence of a consistent surplus production does not fully absolve U.S. parents from, at least, indirect responsibility for the trade debacle. By building an affiliate export capacity matching or even exceeding that of the United States proper, they certainly have created a direct and forceful substitution effect for U.S. exports. For most years since 1971, affiliate exports have exceeded total U.S. exports. If agricultural exports are eliminated from U.S. statistics because affiliates are not engaging in this sector, then the U.S. was already surpassed in 1966. The respective parent vs. affiliate trade volumes for specific industries come into sharper focus in Table 5.4. A related phenomenon is outward FDI's decreasing share in total U.S. exports (see Table 5.2).

Raising the subject of foreign capital participation in U.S. parent companies again, as discussed before, proves the need for a revision of all outward FDI trade data presented so far, if capital control becomes the guiding principle for these discussions. It would lead to across-the-board reductions in their trade data by the amounts shown in Table 4.6. They should be seen as foreign-controlled business entities that also happen to be former U.S.-controlled firms.

How much do inward FDI members specifically contribute to the U.S. balance of trade difficulties? Table 5.5 shows subsidiaries of foreign parents averaging two-thirds to three-fourths of the annual trade deficits. Thus, they are not only a major problem for America's balance of trade, as stated before, they are beyond all doubt the most important cause of these deficits.

TABLE 5.4. Relative U.S. Parent/Subsidiary Export Volumes ($ billion)

Year	Parent Export Shipments	Mofa Export Sales of Goods	Subsid./Parent %
Grand Total			
1966	$17.8	$24.4	137
1977	86.7	194.3	223
1982	139.3	252.3	181
1988	198.5	295.8	149
1989	225.1	298.9	132
1990	229.4	366.0	160
1991	244.8	384.0	157
1992	249.9	398.0	159
1993	250.4	391.3	156
Petroleum			
1966	0.8	8.2	1,025
1977	4.5	98.3	2,184
1982	11.8	94.2	798
1989	8.2	45.9	560
Manufactures			
1966	13.7	8.8	64
1977	62.8	59.8	95
1982	102.0	91.8	90
1989	179.9	192.7	107
Chemicals			
1966	2.0	1.0	50
1977	8.8	8.4	95
1982	15.2	17.4	114
1989	24.9	31.6	127
Machinery, electric & nonelectric			
1966	4.1	2.5	61
1977	18.6	16.8	91
1982	34.6	26.7	89
1989	52.7	62.9	119
Transport Equipment			
1966	3.5	2.7	77
1977	20.1	18.9	94
1982	27.8	24.7	89
1989	57.8	53.6	93
Trade			
1966	2.7	4.1	152
1977	16.4	26.7	163
1982	21.8	47.8	219
1989	29.3	61.2	209

Sources: *U.S. Direct Investment Abroad*, 1966, pp. 87-9, 201-2; 1977, pp. 319, 395; 1982, pp. 235, 333; 1989, pp. 112, 191. *SOCB*, October 1991, pp. 36, 40; August 1992, p. 68; July 1993, pp. 45-6; June 1994, p. 51; June 1995, pp. 39, 40.

TABLE 5.5. FDI Contributions to the U.S. Trade Balance ($ billion)

Year	Total Exports	Total Imports	Balance	% of Deficit
I. U.S. Outward FDI				
1966	$19.2	N/A	N/A	N/A
1977	101.9	$86.8	$15.1	NMF
1982	163.5	120.8	42.7	NMF
1988	215.2	180.9	34.3	NMF
1989	241.5	192.6	48.9	NMF
1990	241.3	213.4	27.9	NMF
1991	257.9	212.7	45.2	NMF
1992	265.9	219.7	46.2	NMF
1993	270.0	231.1	38.9	NMF
II. Foreign Subsidiaries in United States				
1974	$24.2	$30.5	−$6.3	115
1977	24.9	43.9	−19.0	61
1978	32.2	56.6	−24.4	72
1979	44.3	63.0	−18.7	67
1980	52.2	75.8	−23.6	93
1981	64.1	82.3	−18.2	65
1982	60.2	84.3	−24.1	69
1983	53.9	81.5	−27.6	42
1984	58.2	100.4	−42.2	38
1985	56.4	113.3	−56.9	47
1986	49.6	125.7	−76.1	52
1987	48.1	143.5	−95.4	60
1988	69.5	155.5	−86.0	68
1989	86.3	171.8	−85.5	74
1990	92.3	182.9	−90.6	83
1991	96.9	178.7	−81.8	110
1992	103.9	184.5	−80.6	84
1993	105.1	198.5	−93.4	70

Sources: U.S. Outward FDI: See Tables 4.7 and 4.8. Foreign Subsidiaries in United States: *SOCB*, May 1995, p. 62.

Firms not related to either inward or outward U.S. FDI account for only a relatively modest export volume with about 15 to 20 percent of total. With 25 to 30 percent of imports, however, they command not only an important share here but, at the same time, one of similar magnitude in the trade deficits. It is entirely possible that foreign parents are also involved in this trade by exporting to unaffiliated U.S. customers, which would increase their involvement in the U.S. deficit–a point that cannot be clarified from existing records.

Other observations about FDI's impact on the U.S. trade balances are relevant to the topic. One observation concerns the role played by parent products in overall affiliate sales. Here the difference between U.S. outward and inward FDI companies is striking, even though a closing of the gap becomes evident when looking at the late 1980s. Parent and other U.S. supplier shipments to U.S. subsidiaries abroad, even though reaching about 20 percent of total U.S. exports, accounted for no more than 11 percent of affiliate sales.

Imports by U.S. inward FDI subsidiaries from their parents and other foreigners, on the other hand, have accounted for double to triple those levels. They are still about 50 percent higher at the latest count. In other words, foreigners are using their affiliates intensively, as export conduits—more so than U.S. parents do employ theirs (see Table 5.6).

Another noteworthy aspect concerns the mix of raw materials, semifinished, and finished merchandise in intercompany trade, and corresponding valuation differences. Available statistics indicate a relatively low and declining portion of U.S. exports going to overseas subsidiaries in finished form, while foreign shipments to subsidiaries in the United States show exactly the reverse: a relatively high level of finished merchandise in their imports. Such differences in the processing status and concurrent valuations have one common effect: they not only produce negative effects for the U.S. BOP, but for the national economy as well by significantly curtailing upgrading operations.

U.S. parent shipments of materials ready for resale without further processing by their affiliates amounted to $3.2 billion or 51 percent in 1966, $18.5 billion or 63 percent in 1977, $19.4 billion or 44 percent in 1982, and $36.3 billion or 42 percent of all such parental shipments in 1989. If all U.S. exports to affiliates are taken into consideration, the figures reached $3.4 billion or 45 percent for 1966, $20.5 billion or 57 percent for 1977, $21.0 billion or 40 percent for 1982, and $38.4 billion or 39 percent in 1989. Both sets of data indicate a relatively low-level and distinct drop in finished exports going into the affiliate sales mix overseas (FDI census sources: 1966, p. 91; 1977, p. 347; 1982, p. 275. 1989, p. 248). Similar information on the importation of finished or semiprocessed goods by U.S. parents is not available.

In terms of sales share, these finished products reached 3.3, 2.9, 2.1, and 2.8 percent of all nonbank affiliate sales in 1966, 1977, 1982, and 1989.

Similar import data for American affiliates of foreign parents exist for three years, and allow a comparison of the trade patterns between both FDI parties. With total imports of $59.3 billion for resale without further processing, assembly, or manufacture in 1980, this group represented

TABLE 5.6. Affiliate Imports and Share of Affiliate Sales ($ billion)

Year	Parents to Affiliates	Affiliate Sales of Goods	Parent Share of Sales	All Affiliate U.S. Imports	% Sales
U.S. Exports to U.S. Subsidiaries					
1966M	$6.3	$97.8	6.4	$7.7	9.3
1977A	32.4	648.0	5.0	40.8	6.3
M	29.3	507.0	5.8	35.8	7.1
1982A	46.6	935.8	5.0	56.7	6.1
M	44.3	730.2	6.1	52.8	7.2
1988A	81.2	1,194.7*	6.8	94.9	7.9
M	78.2	816.6	9.6	90.8	11.1
1989A	91.2	1,284.9*	7.1	102.6	8.0
M	86.1	889.9	9.6	97.5	11.0
1990A	94.6	1,493.4*	6.3	106.4	7.1
M	88.4	1,208.3	7.3	100.2	8.3
1991A	102.2	1,543.5*	6.6	115.3	7.5
M	95.7	1,240.9	7.7	108.8	8.8
1992A	105.9	1,574.1*	6.7	122.0	7.8
M	100.7	1,291.6	7.8	115.5	8.9
1993A	111.1	1,573.9*	7.1	130.7	8.3
M	104.9	1,279.1	8.2	122.8	9.6
U.S. Imports by Subsidiaries of Foreign Parents					
1977	30.9	194.0	15.9	43.7	22.5
1980	47.0	412.4	11.4	75.8	18.4
1986	93.4	672.0	13.9	125.7	18.8
1987	108.2	744.6	14.5	143.5	19.3
1988	118.4	886.4	13.3	155.5	17.6
1989	129.9	1,056.6	12.3	171.8	16.3
1990	137.5	1,175.9	11.7	182.9	15.6
1991	132.2	1,185.9	11.1	178.7	15.1
1992	137.8	1,231.9	11.2	184.5	15.0
1993	148.5	1,302.1	11.4	198.5	15.3

Notes: *Includes services. A = All Affiliates. M = Mofas.

Sources: U.S. outward FDI: *U.S. Foreign Direct Investment Abroad*, 1966, pp. 83, 197; 1977, pp. 138, 185, 282; 1982, pp. 111, 128-9, 217, 271. *SOCB*, October 1991, pp. 39, 40; August 1992, p. 68; July 1993, pp. 45-6; June 1994, p. 51; June 1995, pp. 39, 40. For U.S. Inward FDI: *SOCB*, May 1981, pp. 47-8; October 1983, pp. 29, 32; July 1990, p. 128; July 1991, pp. 82-3; May 1993, pp. 100-1; May 1995, p. 62.

78.2 percent of aggregate affiliate imports. In 1987, on a volume of $109.4 billion these imports stood at 76.2 percent of total affiliate foreign purchases, and by 1992, with a volume of $127.5 billion, this product category still held a slightly reduced total import share of 70 percent. The relatively high finished component, presumably at high valuations, is partly explained by the nature of the leading import categories such as road motor vehicles, machinery and equipment, and other manufactures, which were shipped predominantly in assembled form (see Table 5.8).

Expressed in terms of share in affiliate U.S. sales, these data indicate levels of 14.4, 14.6, and 10.4 percent for the three census years–levels three to five times above their American counterparts in overseas markets.

Such sharp contrasts in trading patterns concerning FDI affiliates are not accidental, but symptomatic for deliberate marketing and financial strategies by both inward and outward FDI parent organizations, whose divergent appearance betrays a convergence of purpose. Profit considerations dictate avoidance of high U.S. production costs and taxes on one hand, and in view of the declining dollar, allocation of profits in hard currencies and foreign tax shelters.

Logically, these considerations lead to increasing exports of unfinished U.S. materials from parents and other U.S. suppliers for upgrading by overseas affiliates, visible in Table 5.7. In combination with the eroding dollar, an effect magnified by transfer pricing strategies, significant savings in affiliate costs can be achieved. Parents will maximize their global income by reducing affiliate expenditures, strategically inflating their local profits, and then converting those profits made in foreign currencies at a more favorable exchange rate into dollars, if conditions are right. Deliberately depressed export values in pursuit of such windfall profits are the key factor driving the apparent low value ratio of U.S. parent materials in the affiliate sales mix. Obviously, such value-based ratios have the additional effect of artificially understating the real usage of U.S. materials in subsidiary operations.

TABLE 5.7. U.S. Parent Exports of Goods to Mofas (shipments/$ billion)

Year	Total Parent Exports	Parents to Mofas	%	For Further Processing	%
1966	$17.8	$6.3	35.4	$2.5	39.7
1977	86.7	29.3	33.8	9.6	32.8
1982	139.3	44.3	31.9	22.4	50.6
1989	225.1	86.1	38.2	47.7	55.4

TABLE 5.8. Imports of Goods by Inward FDI Companies in United States (shipments/$ billion)

Year	Total Imports	For Direct Resale	%	For Further Processing	%
1980	$75.8	$59.3	78.2	$16.1	21.2
1987	143.5	109.4	75.6	33.1e	23.0e
1992	182.2	127.5	70.3	52.9	29.1

Note: e = estimate.

Sources: *FDI Investment in the United States*, 1980, p. 171; 1987, p. 154; 1992, Table G-36.

Incremental profit gains from favorable tax rates offered by a number of foreign tax shelters expand the list of strategic profit management options. Their combined net effect of these actions on the U.S. balance of trade and, indeed, the whole current account is manifestly negative. Profit strategies based on transfer pricing are difficult to prove as companies take every precaution to avoid problems with the IRS and, for that matter, their foreign counterparts, which very emphatically disapprove of such practices. Their existence thus has to be inferred more than it can be proven. Representative of the existence of such tax-dodging devices is the decline in parent exports of finished products to their affiliates, indicative of a transfer pricing strategy per se, which is not documented in the same manner for overall parent exports to foreigners. A second argument in support of this hypothesis rests on the large business volume and income streams produced by FDI trading centers set up in low tax countries, which are not reconcilable with that specific country's economic importance.

This line of reasoning is very real. In 1987, for instance, U.S. parents showed capital gains of $15.6 billion on affiliate earnings of $36.7 billion, or an increase of 42.5 percent (*SOCB*, June 1988, p. 55). Similar gains were made in other years as a result of combined transaction and translation adjustments, meaning international income is affected by more factors than found in domestic operations. Here, profits can be determined by regular business operations, expense manipulations, and inventory valuations. Overseas profit management options expand this domestic arsenal by transfer pricing, changing the value-added status of exported materials, use of exchange rate fluctuations, employment of tax havens, etc.

The realities of international profit management are not lost on foreigners operating in the United States, and have led to exactly opposite strategies such as importing finished form or advanced stages of product upgrading at high transfer prices, all leading to deliberately reduced profit margins in the United States (see Table 5.7). This point is fully supported by a comparison of outward and inward FDI income streams reported in Table 5.8, which are not reconcilable with the relatively close sales volumes produced by outward and inward FDI members to be discussed later. Depicting a David and Goliath situation, they are by no means a valid indicator of good American profit management, and poor profit management practices by foreigners as a superficial evaluation might suggest. The consequences of these competitive strategies for the U.S. BOP are visible in relatively high income flows for outward parents in contrast to low flows to foreigners, but the real impact is felt in the trade account. The trade deficits generated by foreign FDI companies doing business in the United States are the high price America's economy is paying for its tenacious adherence to the official and unconditional free trade policy.

Probably more important to profit management decisions by foreigners dealing with the American market is the dollar's fluid exchange rate. Its long-term decline has produced windfall profits for U.S. businesses active in the international market, but had the effect of an extra, almost confiscatory tax burden on foreign direct and portfolio investors. Recent estimates put Japanese investment losses alone from this exchange effect at $600 to $800 million. No wonder that all investors take a more cautious stance in doing business with the United States. Aspects relating to this situation are further discussed below in the section dealing with FDI's role in the U.S. services and capital accounts.

The export sector controlled by these foreign companies operating in the United States is quite diverse. Twenty-two percent of all affiliate exports in 1986 were shipped by manufacturing and 68 percent by wholesale organizations. The remaining 10 percent were handled by all other industries. Among the latter group, agricultural raw materials, and metals and minerals predominated with 36 and 19 percent of total affiliate exports, respectively. It is safe to assume that at least 55 percent of all their exports were in unfinished form. No such information on the finishing status of other export shipments is available.

The majority of U.S. inward FDI is of fairly recent origin, and it is overwhelmingly used as an import vehicle for advanced finish or finished goods from their parents. Their role as exporters from the United States is not only relatively insignificant, by comparison, it seems composed of products with a relatively low upgrade status, and is also definitely shrinking in relation to their growing import volume as illustrated by the following numbers. In 1974, their exports from the United States reached 79 percent of their imports. By 1980, they were down to 69 percent, and for the 1986 to 1989 period, that share had dropped further to between 40 to 50 percent, with an interim dip to 33 percent in 1987. During the early 1990s, exports stood at a slightly improved level of 53 percent against affiliate imports. This improvement was no doubt prompted by the falling dollar. It proved, on one hand, the effectiveness of America's official policy to employ the dollar as an export subsidy against foreign traders which, on the other hand, led to an unintended strengthening of exactly those same foreign competitors. It was to some degree, a self-defeating policy.

A final comment concerns a trade development that casts light on fundamental economic, trade, and competitive changes caused by the vigorous expansion of FDI in the United States and abroad. American exports to affiliates always included shipments of capital goods. In the beginning they accounted for a fairly large percentage of all exports to overseas affiliates for three reasons: the expanding investment volume, the superior quality and technology of American machinery, and the rumored existence of an official trade directive requiring the use of American equipment in overseas plants. Over the period covered in these pages American exports declined both in relative and absolute dollar terms, eroded by emerging foreign competitors, including perhaps even other U.S. subsidiaries, and the quiet withdrawal of the trade directive despite a constantly expanding investment base. In and by itself, the decline is a clear statement about the competitiveness of the American machine tool industry with important consequences for the domestic economy, employment, and trade.

At any rate, this is the general picture: in 1957, capital equipment for use by affiliates reached $657 million or 33 percent of U.S. exports to all affiliates. In 1966, the figures stood at $711 million or 9 percent (of which from parents $329 million). In 1977, $1.6 billion or 4 percent (of which from parents $1.2 billion). In 1982, $3.2 billion or 6 percent (parents $2.1 billion), and in 1989 $2.4 billion or 2 percent of all U.S. shipments to Mofas (parents $1.5 billion) (1957 Benchmark Survey, p. 121; 1966 Benchmark Survey, p. 91; 1977 Benchmark Survey, p. 347; 1982 Benchmark Survey, p. 248; 1989 Benchmark Survey, p. 252).

In view of an estimated 500 percent inflation rate over the four decades, and a forty times larger investment stock, the 1989 figures represent only a minuscule remnant of the once exclusive relationships shown for earlier years. Had the 1957 percent share been maintained throughout the period, 1989 U.S. shipment of machinery and equipment to Mofas should have reached $31 billion, offering employment for an additional 600,000 U.S. workers, and a significant reduction in the trade deficit.

Again, it is possible to contrast this information with figures for foreign companies in the United States. According to the three benchmark surveys conducted in 1980, 1987, and 1992, capital goods imported by these affiliates reached 0.5 percent in 1980, an estimated 0.7 percent in 1987, and 0.9 percent of all nonbank affiliate imports reported for 1992. Such low volume is probably explained by foreigners avoiding sourcing machinery and equipment locally since the high rate of finished product imports minimizes the necessity of employing highly specialized equipment for extensive upgrading operations.

FDI ROLE IN SERVICES
AND CAPITAL ACCOUNTS OF THE U.S. BOP

From the beginning of this discussions it became evident that FDI's role is not limited to business activities registered in the trade account of the U.S. BOP. Now, information has to be gathered and analyzed in detail for FDI-related developments in the services and capital accounts by again tracing their movement going in both directions. Of the two accounts, the BOP's current account records the flow of services, or trade in intangibles, where they establish a country's total trade picture in conjunction with the merchandise trade covered above. They will thus be addressed first.

FDI AND THE SERVICES ACCOUNTS

The statistical treatment of international services transactions in the U.S. current account has been covered before in connection with fund flows involving outward U.S. FDI. Information about U.S. inward FDI is subject to the same accounting principles, and is added here to afford a broader vision of the overall BOP impact of both FDI parties. In order to cut through the maze of BOP, or more precisely, its current account information, and focus on the respective roles played by both in the services sector, the official data have been rearranged. All pertinent FDI data were filtered out of the various subaccounts, and combined under the new heading: "FDI Services Transactions." The new accounts are the sum total of aggregate FDI income data (dividends, interests, and reinvestments), royalties and license fees, and other private services as discussed before (Chapter 3).

Restating official statistics in this condensed manner spotlights the key role of outward FDI services transactions in generating steady and big surplus flows for the services account. They go a long way in offsetting the negative trade balances, where outward FDI plays an equally remedial role, and preventing the total current account deficit from being even larger than it has been since 1977. In this respect, the performance of U.S. outward FDI companies has been impeccable.

FDI services flows are generated either by way of direct imports and exports of the same, or indirectly through prior investment activities, including two-way direct and portfolio investments.

Table 5.9 focuses on officially recorded U.S. income flows from services connected with inward and outward FDI in their net form. Depending on their balances, they produce positive or negative effects on the current account and, indirectly, the exchange rate of U.S. currency. Mimicking a struggle for financial superiority, the relative size and growth rates of inward FDI against the same data for outward FDI is pivotal for the future health of the U.S. current account.

On the surface, these official data are good cause for a feeling of relief in view of the situation on the trade side, because U.S. outflows of income in the form of interests, dividends, royalties and license fees plus other services to foreign direct investors have not produced a serious offset effect on the same fund inflows generated by outward American direct investments. As a matter of fact, the balance of the FDI services account has been in a strong updrift since 1985.

INCOME EFFECT
OF REINVESTMENTS ON THE BOP

Once again, the question of how U.S. BOP accounting practices affect the picture by treating reinvested earnings as if they were real flows for inward and outward FDI accounts which, in reality, they are not, has to be raised. It is realized that their dual entry in the current and capital account neutralizes their overall BOP effect. They distort those accounts where they are registered by affecting their volumes in very disproportionate ways.

Not all countries follow the U.S. BOP accounting model for reasons of their own, which renders unadjusted international statistics on the subject not directly comparable. Without questioning or extolling the theoretical merits of either practice, official services account data have been revised for this factor in order to isolate the real fund flows, and interpret any significant discrepancies between both sets of data. The step leads to a uniform reduction of income and capital flows for both inward and outward FDI, causing a general deflation of the U.S. BOP.

At this point it is necessary to introduce a summary review of the income history for inward FDI. The balances shown in Table 5.10 include reinvestments. They are shown separately with the reverse valuation sign

TABLE 5.9. Official Balances on Services Accounts ($ million)

Year	Balances on Services	FDI Services Flows for:			Other
		Total FDI	Outward	Inward	
1960	−1,385	3,782	4,211	−429	−5,167
1961	−1,376	4,010	4,484	−473	−5,386
1962	−1,151	4,585	5,041	−456	−5,736
1963	−1,014	5,006	5,526	−520	−6,020
1964	−779	5,523	5,649	−596	−6,302
1965	−287	5,980	6,705	−725	−6,267
1966	−877	5,647	6,422	−775	−6,524
1967	−1,196	6,074	6,957	−883	−7,270
1968	−385	7,065	8,022	−956	−7,450
1969	−516	8,233	9,182	−949	−8,749
1970	−349	8,941	9,927	−986	−9,290
1971	957	9,805	11,086	−1,282	−8,848
1972	973	11,625	13,064	−1,439	−10,652
1973	989	17,236	19,055	−1,819	−16,247
1974	1,213	20,736	22,226	−1,491	−19,523
1975	3,501	17,617	20,138	−2,521	−14,116
1976	3,401	19,127	22,530	−3,403	−15,726
1977	3,845	20,479	23,556	−3,077	−16,634
1978	4,164	25,559	30,163	−4,604	−21,395
1979	3,003	36,283	43,163	−6,880	−33,280
1980	6,093	33,863	49,926	−9,063	−27,770
1981	11,852	31,084	38,343	−7,259	−19,232
1982	12,329	27,074	30,151	−3,077	−14,745
1983	9,335	27,839	32,942	−5,103	−18,504
1984	3,419	26,894	36,450	−9,556	−23,475
1985	294	27,126	34,444	−7,318	−26,823
1986	5,530	31,562	38,363	−6,801	−26,032
1987	6,861	38,833	47,858	−9,025	−31,972
1988	11,635	48,256	61,853	−13,597	−36,621
1989	23,863	59,586	68,276	−8,690	−35,723
1990	29,037	70,072	74,201	−4,129	−41,035
1991	44,664	70,349	69,491	850	−25,345
1992	56,626	67,806	69,731	−1,925	−6,748
1993	57,777	71,287	78,475	−7,188	−9,803
1994	59,887	60,685	85,741	−25,056	−798

Sources: BOP services balance: *SOCB*, June 1993, pp. 70-1; June 1995, pp. 84-5. FDI balances: See Tables 3.15, 5.10. *SOCB*, August 1991, p. 51; August, 1992, p. 92; August 1994, p.103; August 1995, p. 58.

TABLE 5.10. Balances of U.S. Inward FDI Income Flows ($ million)

Year	Aggregate Income	Operating Income	Reinvestments	Other Income*
1960	$–429	$–394	$–174	$–35
1961	–473	–432	–238	–43
1962	–456	–399	–214	–57
1963	–520	–459	–236	–61
1964	–596	–529	–327	–67
1965	–725	–657	–358	–68
1966	–775	–711	–339	–64
1967	–883	–821	–440	–62
1968	–956	–876	–488	–80
1969	–949	–848	–431	–101
1970	–986	–875	–434	–111
1971	–1,282	–1,164	–542	–118
1972	–1,439	–1,284	–569	–155
1973	–1,819	–1,610	–910	–209
1974	–1,491	–1,331	–1,065	–160
1975	–2,521	–2,234	–1,189	–287
1976	–3,403	–3,110	–1,659	–293
1977	–3,077	–2,834	–1,586	–243
1978	–4,604	–4,211	–2,583	–393
1979	–6,880	–6,357	–3,955	–523
1980	–9,063	–8,635	–5,177	–428
1981	–6,860	–6,898	–2,945	38
1982	–3,096	–3,174	2,361	78
1983	–5,103	–5,169	340	66
1984	–9,556	–9,437	–3,105	–119
1985	–7,318	–7,548	–90	230
1986	–6,751	–7,433	239	682
1987	–9,025	–8,659	–579	–366
1988	–13,957	–12,774	–1,963	–823
1989	–8,690	–7,491	7,390	–1,199
1990	–4,129	–2,936	14,156	–1.193
1991	850	2,856	18,684	–2,006
1992	–1,925	–1,409	12,103	–516
1993	–7,188	–5,694	8,686	–1,494
1994	–25,056	–23,036	–8,212	–2,020

Note: *Royalties and license fees plus other service fees.

Sources: Income: *SOCB*, June 1991, pp. 44-5 (1960-89); August 1992, p. 92; July 1993, p. 64; August 1995, p. 58. *Reinvestments: International Direct Investment*, August 1984, p. 65 (1960-79). *SOCB*, August 1991, p. 51; August 1992, p. 92; July 1993, p. 64; August 1994, p. 103; August 1995, p. 58 (1980-94). All other data: See Tables 3.13 and 3.14.

they carry in the capital account, where they are broken out. In agreement with current accounting procedures income figures are established in a two-step operation. First, total earnings in the United States are determined by adding distributed and reinvested earnings. The latter carry + signs for years of positive earnings and – signs in case of losses, which are reversed for BOP flow purposes. The latter amounts minus withholding taxes on distributed earnings plus interest net of withholding taxes results in a global income figure accruing to parent organizations.

By treating reinvestments as a flow entry, the actual income flows to both outward and inward parents are boosted artificially. It will be remembered from previous discussions of a similar approach in the case of outward FDI income accounting that this step is neutralized by entering the reinvested amount with the reverse sign in front in the capital account as a capital outflow. This practice again has an inflationary effect on actual capital flows. In case of divestments, the reinvestment amount entered in the capital account carries a dollar sign as it reduces the FDI position.

The relative flows between inward and outward FDI members led to the impression of inward investment flows not only being much smaller, but also structured differently from those for outward FDI. Cumulative income for the outward group totaled $352 billion between 1980 and 1989 with an average share of 38 percent for reinvestments. In turn, these reinvested earnings contributed $132 billion or 80 percent of the $166 billion increase in the investment stock during that same time (see Tables 1.1 and 3.3).

Inward FDI expanded its investment base by $285.9 billion during that same decade from $83.0 to $368.9 billion with reinvestments accounting for $3.5 billion or only 1.2 percent of the total investment volume. With cumulative income of $79 billion reported for the decade, reinvestments reached only a paltry 5 percent of that figure (*SOCB*, August 1985, p. 65; August 1994, p. 124, Table 5.10).

The different financing strategy pursued by foreigners is understandable in light of previous observations made in connection with their diligent income management. Expansion of their investment stock in the U.S. market by means of reinvested earnings would expose them unnecessarily to U.S. taxation, while capital transfers from abroad offer only tax advantages through interest payments and write-offs, leading to a concomitant reduction in taxable income produced.

Two facts emerge from this analysis. Total inward FDI income would have financed only one-fourth of the actual investment expansion seen during the 1980s, which rested on capital transfers on a scale never seen for U.S. outward FDI during any single decade, as it is primarily financed with reinvestments. The low reinvestment rate of foreigners in the United States versus the very high reinvestments of U.S. investors overseas lends further support to the previous observation, that both parties pursue the same tax avoidance scheme, and prefer to take their profits outside the United States. It is very likely that both parties use tax shelters for that purpose, even though this is not verified from the above sources for the foreign companies.

Trimmed of reinvestments as being somewhat hypothetical, BOP flows for both outward and inward FDI accounts, and total services take on different dimensions for America's BOP. This is particularly evident for the inward FDI side. In line with previous discussions of the point, it should be remembered that a minus sign in front of reinvestments in the services account signifies a fund outflow, which is balanced by the same amount with a plus sign in the capital account. The result is overstated outflows in the services account and overstated inflows in the capital account. Conversely, if the sign is positive for the services account it leads to understated income outflows and overstated repatriation of capital or understated capital inflows. This accounting process is identical to the one used for outward FDI data.

The resulting changes for the U.S. BOP are shown in Table 5.11 which restates the official data provided in Table 5.9. The contrast in both sets of information dealing with essentially the same subject could not be more drastic. For one thing, the records of the balances on the services account turn negative for many years, while they were previously producing a surplus for the BOP. It also shows greatly reduced positive flows where they occur. Foreign investors are impacting the BOP more heavily than was visible before, because they carry relatively more weight compared to U.S. parent data once reinvestment has been removed as a distortion factor. Adjusted and more realistic income flows to foreigners now show a level averaging about 8 percent of the flow to U.S. parents between 1960 and 1975, rising to 15 percent until 1980 to 1981, but then jumping to between 25 and 35 percent for the rest of the period. Their advance can become a critical factor in the future, if and when the dollar gains considerable strength. The decline of the dollar after 1985 gave U.S. parent income a significant boost, and any dollar appreciation could suddenly reverse this favorable situation by reducing U.S. parent income in absolute terms and strengthening foreigners' income in the United States, not necessarily in absolute but definitely in relative terms (see Table 5.11).

FDI AND THE CAPITAL ACCOUNT

Similar adjustments for reinvestments can be introduced for official capital account flows. Table 5.12 summarizes the impact of such BOP

TABLE 5.11. Services Account Balances Excluding Reinvestments ($ million)

Year	Balances on Services	FDI Services Transactions: Total	Outward	Inward	Other
1960	$-2,477	$2,690	$2,945	$-255	$-5,167
1961	-2,193	3,193	3,430	-235	-5,386
1962	-2,135	3,601	3,843	-242	-5,736
1963	-2,285	3,735	4,019	-284	-6,020
1964	-2,353	3,949	4,218	-269	-6,302
1965	-1,471	4,796	5,163	-367	-6,267
1966	-2,329	4,195	4,631	-436	-6,524
1967	-2,513	4,757	5,200	-443	-7,270
1968	-4,048	3,402	3,870	-468	-7,450
1969	-2,915	5,834	6,352	-518	-8,749
1970	-3,091	6,199	6,751	-552	-9,290
1971	-1,678	7,170	7,910	-740	-8,848
1972	-2,990	7,662	8,532	-870	-10,652
1973	-6,259	9,988	10,897	-909	-16,247
1974	-5,509	14,023	14,449	-426	-19,523
1975	-3,358	10,758	12,090	-1,332	-14,116
1976	-2,636	13,090	14,834	-1,744	-15,726
1977	-965	15,669	17,160	-1,491	-16,634
1978	-4,596	16,799	18,820	-2,021	-21,395
1979	-12,006	21,274	24,199	-2,925	-33,280
1980	-5,747	22,023	25,909	-3,886	-27,770
1981	1,713	20,945	24,860	-3,915	-19,232
1982	5,134	19,888	25,345	-5,457	-14,745
1983	-4,458	14,046	19,489	-5,443	-18,504
1984	-10,752	12,723	19,174	-6,451	-23,475
1985	-13,272	13,461	20,779	-7,318	-26,823
1986	-3,707	22,325	29,315	-6,990	-26,032
1987	-10,210	21,762	30,208	-8,446	-31,972
1988	279	36,900	48,534	-11,634	-36,621
1989	3,776	39,499	55,579	-16,080	-35,723
1990	-6,555	34,480	52,765	-18,285	-41,035
1991	7,216	33,330	51,164	-17,834	-25,337
1992	29,948	39,410	53,438	-14,028	-6,748
1993	19,857	32,361	48,235	-15,874	-9,803
1994	35,053	35,851	52,695	-16,844	-798

Sources: See Tables 3.1, 5.9, and 5.10.

cosmetics. Of the original three components, only equity and intercompany debt capital remain as genuine BOP flows. As pointed out elsewhere, reinvestments used to be heavily bloated by translation gains/losses required by earlier accounting practices, which were abandoned in 1990. All data shown here have been revised retroactively for this factor and refer strictly to capital flows without such extraneous valuation adjustments, which are still part of the official transaction tables (see Chapter 2 and Table 2.7).

In the following table, official capital flows that include reinvestments are contrasted with adjusted figures that exclude them to get an unobstructed view of the true FDI capital movements into and out of the United States. A hypothetical operation, it leaves the relative investment positions of both FDI parties intact, but aids the comparability of international statistics which may not record reinvestments in their BOP flows. Table 5.12 reveals a number of points previously obscured. First, official data show U.S. FDI capital exports in excess of imports until 1981. Freed of reinvestments, equity and intercompany debt outflows from the United States outpaced the same fund inflows from foreigners only until 1977. The flows then sharply reversed, with foreigners pumping tens of billions more into the U.S. economy than vice versa. Also, during the 1970s, U.S. actual capital exports exceeded capital imports by a factor of only 1.6:1 compared to official data indicating a 3:1 ratio. For the 1980s, official data show a 33 percent increase in U.S. capital exports during the 1970s where, in actuality, they were shrinking by about 30 percent. Official capital import statistics for the same period are shown at twice the level of official U.S. exports when, in reality, they exceeded actual exports by a factor of 8.5:1. In the early 1990s this information inversion continues with real capital imports at twice the level of exports, but official statistics show an export surplus of 26 percent (see Table 5.12).

Several observations about these findings are appropriate. First, actual U.S. capital exports were contracting sharply in absolute terms during the 1980s compared to the preceding decade. This means that American investors were spending a decreasing fraction of U.S. GNP on direct investments in contrast to foreign spending gains in the United States. The renewed investment vigor by American business since 1989 may change this trend, ushering in a period of lasting commitment to foreign markets now that NAFTA is in place. The funds actually leaving the United States are, however, less than one-half the size of capital inflows, leaving the foreigners with a strong and growing positive balance in capital flows which eventually translates into pressures for the services account.

TABLE 5.12. U.S. Inward and Outward FDI Capital Flows ($ million)

Year	U.S. Outward FDI Fund Flows Net*		U.S. Inward FDI Fund Flows Net*	
	Official	Adjusted	Official	Adjusted
1970	$-7,590	$-4,414	$1,464	$1,030
1971	-7,618	-4,442	367	-175
1972	-7,747	-3,215	949	380
1973	-11,353	-3,195	2,800	1,890
1974	-9,052	-1,275	4,760	3,695
1975	-14,244	-6,196	2,603	1,414
1976	-11,949	-4,253	4,347	2,688
1977	-11,890	-5,494	3,728	2,142
1978	-16,056	-4,713	7,897	5,314
1979	-25,222	-6,258	11,877	7,922
Total	-122,721	-43,455	40,792	26,300
Difference	$-79,266		$-14,492	
1980	-19,222	-2,205	16,918	11,638
1981	-9,624	3,803	25,195	22,250
1982	-1,078	3,728	13,810	16,171
1983	-6,686	6,766	11,518	11,858
1984	-11,649	5,626	25,567	22,462
1985	-12,724	941	20,490	20,400
1986	-17,706	-8,657	36,145	36,384
1987	-29,980	-11,331	59,581	59,002
1988	-17,871	-4,553	58,571	56,608
1989	-37,604	-24,907	69,010	76,400
Total	-164,144	-30,789	336,805	333,173
Difference	$-133,355		$3,632	
1990	-30,982	-9,546	48,422	62,580
1991	-32,696	-14,369	22,799	41,483
1992	-42,647	-26,353	18,885	30,988
1993	-71,349	-41,109	41,738	50,424
1994	-47,698	-14,652	50,066	41,854
Total	-225,372	-106,029	181,910	227,329
Difference	$-119,343		$45,419	

Notes: + sign = fund outflows; − sign = fund inflows. *Official fund flows include reinvested earnings; adjusted data exclude reinvested earnings. Data deviate from totals in Table 2.6 because different government sources were used.

Sources: *SOCB*, June 1993, pp. 70-1; June 1995, pp. 84-5; August 1995, p. 58; Tables 2.7 and 5.10.

America's economic future is actually at stake to some extent. During the late 1980s, the United States came dangerously close to being outspent by foreign direct investors and developing a negative direct investment position. Its overall international investment position had been negative for some time, and the recovery in the balance of direct investments goes a long way in slowing its further deterioration. In 1989, the spread between inward and outward FDI positions was down to a 4 percent lead for the United States in monetary terms, with $382 billion versus $369 billion. By 1994, that lead had widened to 21 percent with $612 billion against $504 billion thanks to much larger U.S. capital transfers than in the past. Active capital exports are the most important guarantee America has against being overtaken by aggressive foreign interests. While not an absolute defense, it can be a strong factor in case of adverse exchange rate developments for the dollar, which in the past has been more beneficial to the investment balance than actual capital movements.

Further information coming to the surface in Table 5.12 confirms the previously stated fact that the development of outward U.S. FDI is predominantly fed by reinvested earnings, often enlarged by favorable exchange rate developments, with an estimated 81 percent of total during the 1980s. Foreign investment flows to the United States reveal exactly the opposite situation with 99 percent of the incremental flows coming from the equity/debt component at that time. Here lies the key for the wide gaps between official data including reinvestments and adjusted data excluding them.

The differences in the financing methods of both sides open the door for multiple interpretations. They could be a consequence of different maturity stages in their respective investment cycles; or retained earnings providing all the capital needed for a static, if not actually declining, number of active investors; or an indicator of a seriously lower investment interest on the U.S. side due to perceived higher risks, lack of competitiveness, or failure to appreciate the potential of international markets and tax considerations.

All of them could be involved, playing changing roles over time. The latter two sets of possible reasons have special merits, because real flows of U.S. outward investment capital declined from a benchmark of 36 percent against official BOP flow figures inclusive of reinvestments during the 1970s to only 19 percent during the 1980s, before recovering to 47 percent during the early 1990s (see Table 2.2). While definitely encouraging, it is too early to call the newly invigorated actual capital transfers since 1989 a permanent reversal of past trends. Further support for the hypothesis is provided by the $21 billion repatriation of funds reported for the early 1980s, which effectively reduced the real flows in that decade to only 72 percent of the level reached in the 1970s. Whatever the reasons, the situation is clearly a concession to the highly competitive stance adopted by foreigners throughout the world economy with as yet unclear long-term consequences for the United States.

Another possible explanation for the slack period in U.S. outward FDI flows may be the reported fact of 15 percent of U.S. parent companies being controlled by foreign capital participation. Not much is known beyond this cursory statistic, although in theory, at least, these foreign landlords could have put the brakes on potentially growing competition from their own affiliates. It may also be a gamble on the dollar. By borrowing dollars on favorable terms and investing in growth areas of the world, these debts could be easier repaid from higher capital returns, especially if the dollar is expected to fall further.

The scenario depicted in Table 5.12 is still good news of sorts for the U.S. economy despite the potentially more precarious future of the current account. The switch from a net exporter to a hefty net importer of capital eases the pressure on the beleaguered dollar, injects new vitality into the domestic investment scene, improves the domestic employment outlook, introduces new technologies and, management expertise, as well as competition. The Americanization of international markets after World War II is followed by the internationalization of the U.S. market with long-term advantages arising from technical and managerial cross-fertilization.

The future health of the U.S. BOP rests entirely on two factors: the dollar's exchange rate, and decisions by FDI companies concerning their pace of investment expansion. The pivotal issue here is the dollar, because an upswing of 50 percent or more in its value as seen in the past can drastically upset all balances in a very short time. Dollar gains generally work against the U.S. side in both sectors of the current account and may stimulate investment interests visible in the capital account, while the currency's decline has the reverse effect. This leverage effect does not exist for foreign investors in the United States because they are based on the dollar, whose external gyrations do not make any difference as far as the investors are concerned.

In summary, probing into the impact of FDI on the services and capital sector of the U.S. BOP leads to interesting yet conflicting findings. The undifferentiated inclusion of reinvestments in official income flow data is a disturbance factor clouding the picture of the actual roles played by outward and inward investment for the United States. Their basic purpose as a determinant of total investment stock (positional concept) cannot be disputed, and gives them a legitimate place in the calculation of America's international investment position. However, there is good reason to question their inclusion in the BOP (flow concept), as they neither cross national borders nor do they affect exchange markets, a fact tacitly acknowledged by the use of self-neutralizing double entries in official BOP data. Such accounting practice portrays a very strong American services account. Removing them from the statistics shows a very different BOP situation that could lead to further and decisive evisceration of the dollar owing to the compounding effects of perpetually weak services and trade balances in the current account which, at best, are only temporarily relieved by capital inflows.

In the ultimate analysis, the discussion points to diagonally opposed investment and profit strategies pursued by American and foreign investors in addition to those mentioned earlier for production and trade. Retained earnings play only a relatively small role as a feeder source for inward direct investors. Exactly the reverse is true for U.S. investments, which decidedly deemphasize capital exports by comparison. This ping-pong game between inward and outward FDI is of greater importance for the U.S. economy than appears from the relative flow patterns traced in its BOP. The latter are actually only of minor significance in the context of the country's GNP. But while inward FDI takes on a much larger and positive dimension in the American economy by generating internal employment and value added, it also shrinks American ownership of its own economy. In the previous discussion of U.S. trade developments, the possibility of outward FDI's implication in the loss of U.S. employment was raised. Regardless of how big or how real this possibility is judged to be, the following figures on both FDI partners offer some food for thought.

In 1993, outward U.S. investors employed a total of 6.7 million people worldwide versus the 4.7 million Americans employed by inward FDI. If Mofas are singled out as more relevant indicators of actual capital control over foreign ventures, the figures read 5.3 for outward against 4.0 million for inward investors. Assuming hypothetically that both outward FDI figures represent actual losses for the U.S. economy, the negative balance for U.S. employment should be reduced quite rapidly by the more vigorous investment posture of inward investors coming to light in Table 5.12.

A more critical look at the economic relationship among outward and inward FDI expressed by the ebbs and flows in the U.S. BOP suggests that BOP really stands for Battle of Powers.

PART II:
THE FOREIGN AFFILIATE SIDE

Chapter 6

Leading FDI Companies
by Industry

The introductory section covering the development of U.S. FDI provided global census numbers for parent organizations and their affiliates without disclosing individual companies. U.S. law protects the anonymity of investor companies in official publications, and thus renders their identification from the official source impossible. But several business publications allow an indirect and partial glimpse at the leading names in the investment scene, and permit that information to be linked to the benchmark surveys on U.S. outward FDI.

Use of these sources leads to some complications. Articles in business magazines covering financial data of U.S. multinationals appear with some regularity. Their drawback is that they invariably provide details on overseas operations only for a very limited number of FDI parents. Another major drawback is their lack of company classification by industry, which requires the enlistment of several information sources to piece the picture together. Whether or not this results in a complete overlap with government data is not known, even though the close fit of the results obtained suggests a reasonable correlation of the data.

The following information was adapted from material published by *Forbes* magazine on July 23, 1990, with kind permission from the publishers. Covered are the 100 largest U.S. multinationals, which were then linked to the 1989 FDI benchmark survey of U.S. outward FDI members. Banks are excluded, because the census statistics refer to nonbank subsidiaries of U.S. nonbank parents only. Company classification by industry, which is not provided by Forbes, is based on Dun & Bradstreet's *Million Dollar Directory*, *Business Week's* quarterly *Corporate Scoreboard*, and *The Value Line Investment Survey* which in combination furnished the needed information.

Collecting information from these different media and relating it to census data required yet another adaptation in order to achieve an acceptable degree of comparability. Affiliate data throughout this study are set up by industry of affiliate. This is basically a foreign classification, which obviously does not fully satisfy the purpose at hand. Therefore, they had to be replaced with census data for affiliates classified by industry of U.S. parent.

A further point concerns the use of census data for all affiliates and majority holdings only. As it is impossible to distinguish between minority and majority holdings in the media sources, totals for both are covered in the following tables. Company shares, however, are based on Mofas alone. Finally, it is believed with a high degree of certainty that company reports and census information share a common base in that both are reported on a fiscal year basis. It will be remembered from previous comments on the evolution of FDI statistics that the 1989 survey broke with the traditional treatment of FDI statistics on the calendar year, and allowed companies to report on a fiscal year basis for the first time.

With these caveats in mind, the following information was pieced together revealing the identity of ninety-two major nonbank FDI companies. Their number in total and in relation to the dimensions of their specific industry of affiliation is small, yet their impact in economic terms is often surprising. The ninety-two companies represented only 4 percent of all FDI parents including banks in 1989, but controlled over 50 percent of foreign revenues and overseas profits generated by Mofas, and the total assets controlled by them (see Table 6.1).

TABLE 6.1. Selected Indicators for Company Shares in Industry Group ($ million)

	Foreign Revenues	%	Foreign Profits	%	Foreign Assets	%
Industry: Petroleum Affiliate Survey Data (1989):						
All	$249,095		$15,679		$287,191	
Mofa	$185,590	100	$12,238	100	$226,938	100
Company Reports:						
Exxon	$63,429	34	$2,888	24	$46,417	20
Mobil	33,003	18	1,648	14	19,972	9
Texaco	13,710	7	2,054	17	6,827	3
Amoco	6,354	3	322	3	9,960	4
Chevron	6,047	3	793	7	7,653	3
Sun Co.	1,774	1	−7	−	2,992	1
Phillips Pet.	1,835	1	308	3	2,232	1
Tenneco	4,285	2	198	2	4,884	2
Atlantic Richf.	2,932	2	119	1	3,986	2
Halliburton	1,734	1	57	−	1,124	1
Union Oil Cal.	1,532	1	351	3	1,669	1
Dresser Ind.	1,678	1	61	1	820	−
Company Total	138.313	74	8,792	72	108,536	48
Total number in 1989 survey: Parents: 85. Affiliates, 1,618. Number of oil-related companies listed: 12 = 14% of all parents in industry.						
Industry: Manufacturing Affiliate Survey Data (1989):						
All	$789,699		$56,712		$706,300	
Mofa	$657,769	100	$50,201	100	$593,808	100
Company Reports:						
IBM	$36,965	6	$4,145	8	$37,793	6
General Motors	33,768	5	2,952	6	43,576	7
Ford Motors	31,964	5	2,208	4	43,218	7
El du Pont	14,152	2	896	2	10,244	2
ITT	10,944	2	453	1	11,502	2
Dow Chemical	9,516	1	1,127	2	9,943	2
Proctor & Gamble	8,529	1	355	1	5,260	1
Philip Morris	7,630	1	560	1	5,714	1
Eastman Kodak	7,529	1	540	1	6,628	1
Digital Equipment	6,893	1	690	1	4,719	1

TABLE 6.1 (continued)

	Foreign Revenues	%	Foreign Profits	%	Foreign Assets	%
	Industry: Manufacturing Affiliate Survey Data (1989):					
General Electric	$6,769	1	$773	2	$11,346	2
United Tech.	6,501	1	377	1	3,901	1
Hewlett Packard	6,338	1	486	1	3,897	1
Xerox	6,093	1	385	1	7,657	1
3M	5,389	1	485	1	3,712	1
Unisys	4,961	1	44	–	3,353	1
Motorola	4,910	1	304	1	2,605	–
Coca-Cola	4,886	1	819	2	2,840	–
Johnson & John.	4,876	1	600	1	3,656	1
Goodyear	4,448	1	95	–	3,162	1
Chrysler	4,172	1	181	–	5,615	1
Bristol-Myers	3,685	1	149	–	2,104	–
NCR	3,514	1	313	1	1,824	–
Alcoa	3,416	1	1,051	2	4,899	1
American Brands	3,360	1	310	1	2,683	–
Colgate-Palmol.	3,211	1	157	–	1,672	–
Sara Lee	3,201	1	190	–	2,854	–
Monsanto	3,091	–	294	1	2,449	–
Merck	3,064	–	397	1	2,146	–
Whirlpool	3,032	–	93	–	1,944	–
Caterpillar	2,993	–	97	–	2,116	–
Union Carbide	2,951	–	91	–	3,250	–
CPC Int.	2,844	–	182	–	2,129	–
GTE	2,763	–	246	–	4,559	1
Pepsico	2,723	–	416	1	3,070	–
Allied Signal	2,603	–	137	–	2,066	–
Pfizer	2,575	–	451	1	2,565	–
Gillette	2,471	–	210	–	1,949	–
Kimberly Clark	2,344	–	172	–	2,112	–
HJ Heinz	2,328	–	182	–	1,622	–
Rockwell Int.	2,208	–	147	–	1,768	–
W. R. Grace	2,129	–	143	–	1,742	–
TRW	2,054	–	103	–	1,471	–
Texas Inst.	2,047	–	9	–	1,551	–
Am. Home Prod.	1,992	–	152	–	1,474	–
Warner-Lambert	1,947	–	162	–	1,099	–
Deere & Co.	1,902	–	114	–	1,635	–
Scott Paper	1,884	–	89	–	1,796	–
Am. Cyanamid	1,861	–	183	–	1,225	–

	Foreign Revenues	%	Foreign Profits	%	Foreign Assets	%
Industry: Manufacturing **Affiliate Survey Data (1989):**						
Abbott Labs	1,838	–	125	–	1,255	–
Ralston Purina	1,832	–	68	–	1,023	–
Borden	1,824	–	80	–	1,559	–
PPG Industries	1,771	–	124	–	1,677	–
Avon Products	1,724	–	106	–	787	–
Honeywell	1,712	–	117	–	1,269	–
Kellogg	1,711	–	125	–	1,531	–
Quaker Oats	1,650	–	59	–	658	–
Baxter Int.	1,623	–	125	–	1,435	–
Emerson Elec.	1,621	–	132	–	1,221	–
Int. Paper	1,590	–	98	–	1,984	–
Westinghouse Elec.	1,539	–	68	–	736	–
Eli Lilly	1,517	–	325	–	1,840	–
AMP	1,515	–	164	–	1,141	–
Black & Decker	1,458	–	93	–	2,298	–
Intel	1,352	–	331	–	1,167	–
Company Total	327,703	50	26,855	53	313,696	53

Total number in 1989 survey: Parents: 1,312. Affiliates: 12,078. Number of companies listed above: 65 = 5.0% of all parents in industry.

Industry: Food & Kindred **Affiliate Survey Data (1989):**						
All	$79,614		$5,691		$76,661	
Mofa	$57,477	100	$4,908	100	$62,515	100
Company Reports:						
Coca-Cola	$4,886	8	$819	17	$2,840	4
Sara Lee	3,201	6	190	4	2,854	4
CPC International	2,844	5	182	4	2,129	3
Pepsico	2,723	5	416	8	3,070	5
H J Heinz	2,328	4	182	4	1,622	3
Ralston Purina	1,832	3	68	1	1,023	2
Borden	1,824	3	80	2	1,559	2
Kellogg	1,711	3	125	3	1,531	2
Quaker Oats	1,650	3	59	1	658	1
Company Total	22,999	40	2,121	43	17,286	28

Total number in 1989 survey: Parents: 63. Affiliates: 1,083. Number of food companies listed above: 9 = 14.3% of all parents in industry.

TABLE 6.1 (continued)

	Foreign Revenues	%	Foreign Profits	%	Foreign Assets	%
Industry: Chemicals **Affiliate Survey Data (1989):**						
All	$146,028		$13,418		$147,230	
Mofa	$130,442	100	$12,320	100	$129,024	100
Company Reports:						
El du Pont	$14,152	11	$896	7	$10,244	8
Dow Chemical	9,516	7	1,127	9	9,943	8
Proctor & Gamble	8,529	7	355	3	5,260	4
Union Carbide	2,951	2	91	1	3,250	3
Colgate-Palmol.	3,211	2	157	1	1,672	1
Johnson & John.	4,876	4	600	5	3,656	3
Monsanto	3,091	2	294	2	2,449	2
Bristol-Myers	3,685	3	149	1	2,104	2
Merck	3,064	2	397	3	2,146	2
Pfizer	2,575	2	451	4	2,565	2
Am. Home P.	1,992	2	152	1	1,474	1
Gillette	2,471	2	210	2	1,949	2
W. R. Grace	2,129	2	143	1	1,742	1
Warner Lambert	1,947	1	162	1	1,099	1
Am. Cyanamid	1,861	1	183	1	1,225	1
Abbott Labs	1,838	1	125	1	1,255	1
Avon Products	1,724	1	106	1	787	1
Baxter Int.	1,623	1	125	1	1,435	1
Eli Lilly	1,517	1	325	3	1,840	1
Company Total	72.752	56	6,048	49	56,095	43

Total number in 1989 survey: Parents: 173. Affiliates: 3,067. Number of companies listed above: 19 = 10.4% of all parents in industry.

Industry: Primary and Fabricated Metals **Affiliate Survey Data (1989):**						
All	$32,288		$3,349		$38,662	
Mofa	$24,056	100	$2,481	100	$25,930	100
Company Reports:						
Alcoa	3,416	14	1,051	42	4,899	19

Total number in 1989 survey: Parents: 163. Affiliates: 842. Total number of companies listed above: 1 = 0.6% of all parent companies in industry.

	Foreign Revenues	%	Foreign Profits	%	Foreign Assets	%
**Industry: Machinery, Except Electrical Affiliate Survey Data (1989):**
All	$162,913		$12,591		$136,336	
Mofa	$152,117	100	$11,949	100	$124,625	100
Company Reports:						
IBM	$36,965	24	$4,145	35	$37,793	30
Xerox	6,093	4	385	3	7,657	6
Hewlett-Packard	6,338	4	486	4	3,897	3
Unisys	4,961	3	44	–	3,353	3
NCR	3,514	2	313	3	1,824	1
Honeywell	1,712	1	117	1	1,269	1
Deere	1,902	1	114	1	1,635	1
Digital Equip.	6,893	5	690	6	4,719	4
Caterpillar	2,993	2	97	1	2,116	2
Company Total	71,371	47	6,391	54	64,263	51

Total number in 1989 survey: Parents: 253. Affiliates: 2,075. Number listed above: 9 = 3.6% of all parents in industry.

	Foreign Revenues	%	Foreign Profits	%	Foreign Assets	%
**Industry: Electric and Electronic Equipment Affiliate Survey Data (1989):**
All	$52,193		$2,931		$47,105	
Mofa	$44,960	100	$2,530	100	$41,085	100
Company Reports:						
General Elec.	$6,769	15	$773	31	$11,346	28
Texas Inst.	2,047	4	9	–	1,551	4
Motorola	4,910	11	304	12	2,605	6
Whirlpool	3,032	7	93	4	1,944	5
Rockwell	2,208	5	147	6	1,768	4
Emerson Elec.	1,621	4	132	5	1,221	3
Westinghouse Elec.	1,539	3	68	3	736	2
AMP	1,515	3	164	7	1,141	3
Black & Decker	1,458	3	93	4	2,298	6
Intel	1,352	3	331	13	1,167	3
Company Totals	26,451	59	2,114	84	25,777	63

Total number in 1989 survey: Parents: 161. Affiliates: 1,299. Number of companies listed above: 9 = 5.6% of all parents in industry.

TABLE 6.1 (continued)

	Foreign Revenues	%	Foreign Profits	%	Foreign Assets	%
	**Industry: Transportation Equipment** **Affiliate Survey Data (1989):**						
All Mofa	$199,863 $146,911	 100	$9,943 $8,232	 100	$159,822 $122,312	 100
Company Reports:						
Ford Motor	$31,964	22	$2,208	27	$43,218	35
General Motors	33,768	23	2,952	36	43,576	36
United Tech.	6,501	4	377	5	3,901	3
Chrysler	4,172	3	181	2	5,615	5
Allied Signal	2,603	2	137	2	2,066	2
TRW	2,054	1	103	1	1,471	1
Company Total	81,062	55	5,958	73	99,847	82
	Total number in 1989 survey: Parents: 81. Affiliates: 1,017. Number of companies listed above: 6 = 7.4% of all parents in industry.						
	**Industry: Other Manufacturing** **Affiliate Survey Data (1989):**						
All Mofa	$116,803 $101,806	 100	$8,789 $7,782	 100	$100,484 $88,317	 100
Company Reports:						
Philip Morris	$7,630	7	$560	7	$5,714	6
Eastman Kodak	7,529	7	540	7	6,628	8
3M	5,389	5	485	6	3,712	4
Goodyear	4,448	4	95	1	3,162	4
American Brands	3,360	3	310	4	2,683	3
Scott Paper	1,884	2	89	1	1,796	2
Kimberly-Clark	2,344	2	172	2	2,112	2
PPG	1,771	2	124	2	1,677	2
Int. Paper	1,590	2	98	1	1,984	2
Company Total	35,945	35	2,473	32	29,468	33
	Numbers in 1989 survey: Parents: 418. Affiliates: 2,695. Number listed above: 9 = 2.2% of all parents in industry.						

	Foreign Revenues	%	Foreign Profits	%	Foreign Assets	%
Industry: Finance (excl. banks), Insurance, and Real Estate Affiliate Survey Data (1989):						
All	$89,985		$7,057		$251,999	
Mofa	$58,024	100	$4,773	100	$171,597	100
Company Reports:						
American Int.	$5,432	9	$893	19	$18,510	11
American Family	1,783	3	94	2	5,351	3
Cigna	2,327	4	−93	–	6,119	4
American Express	4,859	8	171	4	28,201	16
Salomon	2,567	4	559	12	36,422	21
Merrill Lynch	1,650	3	−65	–	7,884	5
Company Total	18,618	32	1,559	33	102,487	60
Number of companies in 1989 survey: Nonbank parents: 205. Affiliates: 1,284. Number of finance companies listed above: 6 = 3% of all parents in industry.						
Industry: Retail Trade Affiliate Survey Data (1989):						
All	$41,907		$1,235		$27,384	
Mofa	$22,886	100	$700	100	$17,094	100
Company Reports:						
Sears Roebuck	$4,135	18	$67	10	$3,171	19
Woolworth	3,790	17	117	17	1,697	10
K-mart	3,512	15	N/A	N/A	1,217	7
Company Total	11,437	50	184	26	6,085	36
Number of companies listed in 1989 survey: All retail trade parents: 50. Affiliates: 211. Number of companies listed above: 3 = 6.0% of all parents in industry.						
Industry: Services Affiliate Survey Data (1989):						
All	$25,499		$2,061		$34,182	
Mofa	$21,318	100	$1,827	100	$28,260	100
Company Reports:						
McDonald's	$2,219	10	$219	12	$3,529	12
Dun & Bradstreet	1,428	7	139	8	1,463	5
Company Total	3,647	17	358	19	4,992	18
Number of companies in 1989 survey: Parents: 202. Affiliates: 1,175. Number of service companies listed above: 2 = 1% of all parents in industry.						

TABLE 6.1 (continued)

	Foreign Revenues	%	Foreign Profits	%	Foreign Assets	%
Industry: Other Industries Affiliate Survey Data (1989):						
All	$91,726		$3,086		$54,755	
Mofa	$74,379	100	$2,402	100	$42,750	100
Company Reports:						
ITT	$10,944	15	$453	41	$11,502	27
Pan Am	2,559	3	−159	−	N/A	N/A
GTE	2,763	4	246	10	4,559	11
UAL	2,179	3	N/A	N/A	N/A	N/A
Company Total	18,445	25	540	23	16,061	38
Number of companies in 1989 survey: Parents: 329. Affiliates: 1,524. Total number of companies listed above: 4 = 1.2% of all parents in industry.						
Industry: All Industries Affiliate Survey Data (1989):						
All	$1,368,097		$86,925		$2,055,299	
Mofa	$1,019,966	100	$72,142	100	$1,080,247	100
Company Reports:						
Total listed	$518,163		$38,288		$551,857	
All		38		44		27
Mofa		51		53		51
Total number in 1989 survey: All parents: 2,272. Affiliates: 18,899. Total number of companies listed above: 92 = 4.0% of all parents listed in 1982 benchmark survey.						

Sources: *Forbes*, July 23, 1990; Forbes Inc., 160 Fifth Avenue, New York, NY 10011 provided financial information by company. Restating the information by industry of company was accomplished with the help of: *Business Week*, Corporate Scoreboard, Fourth Quarter 1989, pp. 67-94, March 19, 1990; McGraw-Hill, Inc., P.O Box 430, Hightstown, NJ 08520. *The Value Line Investment Survey*, Value Line Publishing, Inc., 711 3rd Avenue, New York, NY, 10017-4064. 1989 Benchmark Survey, pp. 4, 5, 156, 185. *Million Dollar Directory*, Dun's Marketing Services, Inc. Dun & Bradstreet Corp. Parsippany, NJ. 1988.

Chapter 7

Macroeconomic Dimensions of U.S. FDI

MOFA GROSS PRODUCT

The following sections collect and analyze available information on the most commonly used macroeconomic business indicators in order to measure the development of quantitative relationships between Mofas and parent organizations, both with the U.S. economy, and most importantly, their dimensions in international trade and foreign economies. These indicators include domestic and international sales, income, assets, employment, and gross product or value-added.

Being fully integrated into national economies, Mofas contribute their gross product (GP) to the host nation's output of gross domestic product (GDP). GDP data are widely available and show themselves as one important indicator of the competitive performance of Mofas. Both national GDP and Mofa GP reflect the basic value added concept, be it for the transformation of tangible natural resources through manufacturing, or the generation of private and public services. Economists define such output of value in two principal ways with essentially equivalent results:

1. sales plus inventory changes minus cost of intermediaries and services, the value-added concept proper; or
2. by adding up all charges against production.

Calculation of the Mofa GP for 1989 by either method yields a 5 percent difference in volume. Published government figures are calculated by the first method and show a level of $320 billion. The same calculation done by employing the second method results in a volume of only $304 billion, a discrepancy of little practical significance (see Table 7.1).

The principles of national accounting are sufficiently standardized by international organizations to assure a high degree of comparability among

TABLE 7.1. Mofa Gross Product in Relation to Sales and FDI Stock ($ billion)

Year	Total GDP	Sales	GP/Sales	FDI Stock	GP/Stock
1957	16.1	38.2	42.1%	$25.3	63.6%
1966	36.8*	97.8	37.6	48.0	76.6
1977	161.1	507.0	31.8	128.1	125.8
1982	223.7	730.2	30.6	185.2	120.8
1989	319.9	1,019.9	31.4	333.7	95.9
1990	356.0	1,242.6	28.6	N/A	N/A
1991	355.9	1,240.9	28.7	N/A	N/A
1992	361.5	1,291.6	28.0	N/A	N/A
1993	357.9	1,279.1	28.0	N/A	N/A

Note: *Includes affiliates with a parent ownership interest of at least 25 percent, which renders data not directly comparable with 1966 sales and investment position, as well as data for all other years that related strictly to Mofas.

Sources: 1957 FDI census, pp. 92, 110, 115 (data related to all affiliates except trade and finance). *SOCB*, February 1977, pp. 17-28 (1966); February 1994, pp. 50, 53-55; June 1994, p. 51; June 1995, pp. 38, 40.

nations. The same methods have been employed in the calculation of Mofa GP, which allows linking those data directly to national series (see Table 7.2). Reliable estimates for all affiliate GP are available for the census years 1957 and 1966, and for Mofa GP for 1977, 1982, and 1989, as presented in Table 7.1. These five benchmark figures are sufficient to reveal some interesting undercurrents in the development of Mofa GP over a period of four decades. For one thing, Mofa gross product is growing slower than sales. Expressed in different terms, it means that over a period of thirty-two years, each sales dollar has contributed less and less value added. In the base year 1957, one sales dollar produced $0.43 worth of GP, $0.38 in 1966, $0.32 in 1977, and $0.31 in both 1982 and 1989. For the period after 1989, estimates have been provided that are not based on official benchmark surveys, but indicate a further decline in the ratios to around $0.28 of GP per dollar.

The fact that 1957 and 1966 data cover all affiliates versus Mofas only in later census years is not considered to be of major importance for this development because Mofas consistently account for over 87 percent of the affiliate universe (see Table 1.12). As a rule of thumb, today roughly 30 percent of Mofa sales represents value-added or GP. While true for all Mofas, there are considerable variations in the ratios for the various industrial subgroups as presented in Table 7.2. Data show how some industries maintain quite stable GP production rates against sales, while others document substantial

TABLE 7.2. GP Share of Sales and Investment Position by Mofa Industry

	GP Percent of Sales				GP Percent of Investment			
	1966 %	1977 %	1982 %	1989 %	1966 %	1977 %	1982 %	1989 %
All Mofas	37.6	31.8	30.6	31.4	76.6	125.8	120.8	95.9
Petroleum	43.1	31.2	32.3	42.0	91.8	246.0	157.5	167.1
Manufacturing	37.9	36.9	37.2	32.4	94.4	127.2	131.6	121.6
Foods	26.2	25.7	27.5	25.2	87.9	105.8	126.6	118.5
Chemicals	36.1	31.1	30.2	31.9	77.8	97.1	100.4	102.7
Primary & fabricated metals	43.4	36.7	36.2	32.2	133.3	115.6	111.4	97.3
Machinery except elec.	N/A	47.7	43.7	30.2	N/A	127.4	131.8	117.4
Electric/electronic equipment	N/A	43.2	39.5	26.4	N/A	161.1	149.4	84.0
Transport equipment	34.1	28.6	32.7	28.4	103.3	155.8	184.2	169.3
Other manufacturing	43.7	49.4	51.6	45.9	86.4	130.3	131.2	134.0
Trade	14.8	18.5	16.9	16.8	49.4	94.2	95.9	90.3
Finance, Insurance, Real Estate	NMF	19.5	4.2	1.6	5.0	9.7	5.5	0.9
Services	N/A	N/A	45.5	42.5	N/A	N/A	188.3	126.6
Other	52.3	37.3	16.3	33.5	61.5	100.3	80.2	115.1

declines in areas such as nonbank finance and the electric/electronic equipment sector.

Curiously enough, exactly the reverse took place when measuring GP against FDI stock over most of the period. Here every dollar invested produced significantly increasing amounts of GP for a while. Starting again with 1957, when one FDI dollar generated $0.65 of GP, the ratio grew to $0.77 in 1966, $1.26 in 1977, $1.21 in 1982 before falling back to $0.96 in 1989. No such data are available for the nonsurvey years after 1989.

Putting the observed relationship once more into a handy formula, one may be tempted to state that GP falls within a range of +/–30 percent of the FDI value. The movements of the ratios, however, seem to suggest a natural or historic GP/FDI ratio of under 1:1 which applies to three out of the five years shown. The fact that GP in 1957 and 1966 covered all affiliates whereas, in 1977, 1982 and 1989 Mofas only is again not considered to be of significance. The question of why this presumably normal relationship was upset for 1977 and 1982 leads to a number of plausible explanations. First, the sharp rise in world prices following the oil price escalation in the 1970s, which spread from crude revenues to all other industries, resulted in rapidly mushrooming Mofa sales volumes. The same happened to Mofa GP, which automatically and opportunistically ballooned faster than the more sluggish investment volume. In addition, GP is increasingly determined by strongly expansive components, and that did not carry the same weight in earlier years as direct and indirect business taxes (see Table 7.3).

The picture is also deeply affected by the 1977 change in the definition of FDI stock. As explained earlier, the DOC's decision to treat the international borrowings of U.S. parents through affiliates in the Netherlands Antilles as an investment related transaction rather than debt financing operation led to a de facto reduction in the U.S. FDI position. It caused the

TABLE 7.3. Mofa Gross Product by Component ($ billion)

Year	Total	Employee Compens.	Profit Returns	Net Interest	Indirect Taxes	CCA
1957	$16.1	$6.9	$6.2	$0.4	$2.1	$1.7
1966	36.8*	15.6	9.7	0.9	6.3	4.3
1977	161.1	59.5	52.2	2.8	35.4	11.2
1982	223.7	89.4	54.9	-.4	62.3	17.5
1989	320.0	132.6	86.5	-5.0	78.9	27.0
1990	N/A	N/A	N/A	N/A	N/A	N/A
1991	356.0	160.4	74.5	-7.2	96.3	32.1
1992	361.5	169.6	71.4	-10.1	95.6	35.1
1993	358.0	167.0	75.2	-12.5	92.6	35.8
Percentages						
1957	100.0	42.8	38.5	2.4	12.7	10.3
1966	100.0	41.4	26.4	2.4	17.2	11.7
1977	100.0	37.0	32.4	1.7	22.0	7.0
1982	100.0	40.0	24.5	NMF	27.8	7.8
1989	100.0	41.6	27.0	NMF	24.7	8.4
1991	100.0	45.1	20.9	NMF	27.1	9.0
1992	100.0	46.9	19.7	NMF	26.4	9.7
1993	100.0	46.6	21.0	NMF	25.9	10.0

Note: *Includes affiliates with 25 percent or higher parent ownership interest.

Sources: U.S. Business Investments in Foreign Countries (1957 FDI census), p. 115 (data cover all affiliates). SOCB, February 1977, pp. 22-3 (1966); February 1994, pp. 53-4 (1977, 1982, 1989, and 1991); June 1995, p. 38 (1992-3).

islands' investment picture to turn negative (–$792 million in 1977) where it had been positive in all prior years. By 1982, the investment position of that money center had run a cumulative deficit of $20.1 billion, which reduced the aggregate investment position by an equal amount. Adding this amount in accordance with previous accounting policy would raise the 1982 Mofa position to $205 billion and lower the gross product/investment ratio to $1.10:1. By 1989, the islands' net investment position had been reduced to –$8.5 billion thus presenting a much smaller disturbance factor for overall U.S. FDI which had nearly doubled in size (see Table 2.1).

Another major contributor to the uneven relationships of GP and FDI stock lies in the FDI stock accounting practices themselves. While annual data are ostensibly established on a historic cost basis comprising actual equity/debt flows and reinvestments, the latter are subject to major valuation adjustments caused by currency fluctuations and the periodic benchmark surveys–the results of which are reconciled retroactively with annual estimates of the stock for the interim years (see Table 2.7).

COMPOSITION OF MOFA GROSS PRODUCT

As pointed out above, Mofa GP may be calculated in one of two ways. The first of these alternatives is applied in the development of the following official information, which determines Mofa GP by five major expense categories: employee compensation, profit-type returns before tax, net interest, indirect business taxes, and capital consumption allowances (CCA) (*SOCB*, February 1983, p. 29).

Of these, employee compensation is the most important determinant, with approximately 40 percent of total GP. The account covers wages, salaries, and supplemental employee benefit plans (1982 FDI census, p. 323). It is followed by two accounts with fairly equal weight of about 25 percent each. One measures "profit-type returns" consisting of net income plus foreign income taxes (the same as earnings before taxes) minus equity in net income of other affiliates, income from other equity investments, exchange gains/losses from translation of financial statements, and other capital gains/losses (direct communication from the DOC).

Another account headed "indirect business taxes, etc." is a collection of taxes and tax-like charges on business other than income and payroll deductions. It includes production royalties paid by the petroleum industry. They are similar to a depletion charge for the use of natural resources by foreign governments, and despite the similarity in name, should not be confused with business royalties and license fees maintained separately. It also includes sales, consumption, excise, property, capital, and asset taxes plus customs (import/export) levies, license fees, penalties and fines, etc. Subsidies received are deducted from the total (1982 FDI census, p. 368; footnotes to Table II.R 3). The account is the most rapidly expanding component of affiliate GP, growing from 13 to 25 percent between 1957 and 1989, and identifying affiliates as tax collectors is of increasing importance.

The two remaining accounts are "net interest"–the difference of interest paid and received, and "capital consumption allowances" (CCA) relating to depreciation, depletion, and like charges (1982 FDI census, p. 312). In combination, they used to contribute more than 10 percent of affiliate GP, but were reduced below that threshold during the last two census years.

The various tables summarize the development of Mofa GP from different angles. Standing alone, such information may not say much, but a comparison with the GDPs of individual nations makes it very real. In 1989, for example, the Mofa GP put them ahead of the total GDP, including the public sector, of India ($273 billion), the Netherlands ($224 billion), Australia ($294 billion), Sweden and Norway ($280 billion), Mexico ($205 billion), and on the same level with a combined Austria and Switzerland ($304 billion) (*UN Statistical Yearbook*, Thirty-eighth Issue, pp. 225-38, 1993).

MOFA GROSS PRODUCT BY INDUSTRY

Also available for the five benchmark years 1957, 1966, 1977, 1982, and 1989 are details by Mofa industry, which establish an uncontested leading share between 44 and 54 percent for manufacturing. Major sectors in this group are transportation equipment, chemicals, and machinery, which provided roughly two-thirds of the industry's total in 1982 and 1989. Manufacturing Mofas would assume an even more impressive position if the processing part of the oil industry were added here following the usual practice of U.S. and international record keeping. The figures would now read $129.5 billion and 80.4 percent for 1977, $170.4 billion and 75.9 percent for 1982, and $242.0 billion and 75.6 percent for 1989.

As officially reported, oil affiliates commanded second place with a 32 to 39 percent share in total Mofa gross product for most of the period, but a very weak 24 percent share in 1989. Third place was held by the trade affiliates with around 10 percent of the total, while the rest contributed less than 10 percent. Incorporating the oil industry's trading GP in the trade category would again, like for the manufacturing sector, dramatically change the distribution of Mofa GP. To start with, a reduction of the industry to its extractive activities alone would cut its contribution to global Mofa GP to $838 million and 0.5 percent for 1977, $3.4 billion and 1.5 percent in 1982, and $1.0 billion and 0.3 percent in 1989. The trade GP would correspondingly increase to 11 percent each in 1977 and 1982, and 13 percent in 1989.

Such realignment of the data in a more conventional manner would leave the combined shares of these three leading industries (oil, trade, and manufacturing) in total Mofa GP unaltered with 86.8 percent in 1966, 89.9 percent in 1977, 91.4 percent in 1982, and 89.8 percent in 1989. Among the rest of the industries, services stand out not so much for their absolute size, but for the rate of growth they experienced between 1977 and 1989, which lifted their share from less than 1 percent to 5 percent.

The finance, insurance, and real estate group has seen its GP go on a roller coaster ride that took it from a 0.6 percent share in 1966 to 1.1 percent in 1977, down to less than 0.5 percent in 1982, and back up to 1.1 percent in 1989. These bizarre results were thanks to the aforementioned Caribbean financial operations, which showed very large negative entries in the net interest account in connection with receipts/payments on the heavy loan burden of their parent companies, and thus obscured otherwise positive developments of the industry in other regions of the world. All other industries play a declining part in the generation of Mofa GP. Between 1966 and 1989 their share went from 13 to 5 percent, owing to a number of branches with reduced economic potential and accelerating downward trends (see Table 7.4).

MOFA GROSS PRODUCT
BY INDUSTRY AND COMPONENT

Aggregate GP data by component presented in Table 7.3 can be combined with individual industry GPs shown in Table 7.4 to yield further information laid down in Table 7.5. As could be expected, single GP components contribute in completely different ways to the GP generated by all industries. Some are mainly determined by employee compensation (services, manufacturing, etc.), others by taxes and profits, as for petroleum affiliates. The finance, insurance and real estate industry is in a completely separate league again, with most of its GP derived from profit-type returns. Table 7.5 summarizes the constellation of GP components by individual industry and in actual dollar terms for 1977 through 1989. Conversion of the above data into percentage figures brings out these relationships even more clearly, demonstrating at the same time how all ratios can shift substantially over time for any industry (see Table 7.6).

TABLE 7.4. Mofa Gross Product by Industry ($ billion)

Year	1966	%	1977	%	1982	%	1989	%
All Mofas	$36.8*	100	$161.1	100	$223.7	100	$320.0	100
Petroleum	11.8	32	62.0	39	85.6	38	77.2	24
Manufacturing	17.9	49	71.6	44	99.8	45	173.3	54
Foods	1.5	4	5.6	4	8.9	4	13.6	4
Chemicals	2.7	7	10.1	6	16.4	7	32.1	10
Primary & fabricated metals	1.7	5	4.2	3	5.4	2	7.6	2
Machinery except elec.	N/A	NMF	13.6	8	17.6	8	31.7	10
Electric/electronic equipment	N/A	NMF	8.1	5	9.9	4	12.6	3
Transport equipment	3.8	10	13.9	9	18.1	8	33.8	11
Other manufacturing	3.7	10	16.2	10	23.5	10	41.8	13
Trade**	2.1	6	11.3	9	19.4	9	36.8	12
Finance, Insurance, Real Estate	.2	1	1.9	1	1.2	NMF	3.4	1
Services	N/A	NMF	3.9	NMF	8.0	4	14.5	5
Other	4.6	13	10.3	7	9.8	4	14.8	5

Notes: *Includes affiliates with 25 percent or higher parent ownership interest. **Wholesale only.

Sources: *SOCB*, February 1977, pp. 22-5 (1966); February 1983, pp. 26-7, 29 (1977); February 1994, pp. 53, 58 (1982, 1989).

Major transformations of the GP subcomponents occurred in the oil industry between 1977 and 1982, and there is no realistic explanation other than the liquidation of the Saudi Arabian investment holdings, which forced a reorientation of the industry to other parts of the world, and fundamental restructuring of its assets. Setting the oil industry's GP = 100 percent shows extraction remaining practically unchanged at 30 percent in 1977 and 28 percent in 1989. The same is true for the "all other" category with its much smaller 3 percent level. But the refining and processing part dropped from 53 to 48 percent, while trade grew from 14 to 18 percent.

The oil industry does not stand alone in this respect, though. To some degree, all industries follow a similar pattern of shifting ratios, a point that was unidentified before. In manufacturing, trade, finance, and services, all accounts changed relative weights, with the most pronounced movements shown by employee compensation, profits, and indirect taxes.

Common to the majority of Mofa industries is the declining importance of profits in the formation of GP, while indirect taxes are going in just the opposite direction. Interest does not play an important role in any of the industries except finance excluding banking where it is the dominant factor in the formation of the industry's GP and, unfortunately, only a negative one. The huge losses apparent in this account not only affect the industry's GP itself adversely, but that for all Mofas as well. Paradoxical as it may sound, this is not necessarily a bad situation from a business point of view, because the deficits arise from the difference between interest receipts (a negative GP entry) and payments (a positive GP entry). The basically healthy state of the industry is confirmed by the rapid growth of all other accounts, notwithstanding the fact that total industry GP has not risen much.

MOFA GROSS PRODUCT
BY COUNTRY AND INDUSTRY

Information on this topic was published by U.S. government researchers in complete form for the census years 1977, 1982, 1989, and on a more or less regular basis during the years thereafter. The following table also provides additional GP estimates for major industries and selected countries based on the census years 1957 and 1966. These latter figures include minority-held affiliates, and thus are not fully comparable with later Mofa data. The information provided is valuable as a monitoring device for America's economic presence and growth in selected nations, and will be used in subsequent chapters to draw conclusions about its competitive implications by linking these data to national outputs of GDP (see Table 7.7).

MOFA GROSS PRODUCT AND U.S. GDP

FDI parents accounted for 29.6, 29.2, and 23.7 percent of total U.S. industrial GDP in 1977, 1982, and 1989 respectively. Their share in manufacturing GDP was even more impressive with 64.7, 65.2, and 60.8 percent for the same years. The available information is sufficient to compare affiliates, which have attained quite respectable dimensions of their own, directly with their parents and the U.S. economy itself. Mofa GP can be used for a comparison in two areas: for all industries and manufacturing, provided the relevant GP of the petroleum processing Mofas is included in the latter. The U.S. Standard Industrial Classification (SIC) code agrees with international statistical practice on this point, and includes that part of the oil industry in manufacturing or, more precisely, in its chemical sector.

TABLE 7.5. Composition of Mofa Gross Product by Industry ($ million)

	Total	Employee Compens.	Profit-type Return	Net Interest	Indirect Taxes	CCA*
Petroleum						
1977	$62,010	$4,876	$28,978	$848	$24,143	$3,165
Extrac.	18,639	N/A	N/A	N/A	N/A	N/A
Proc.	32,621	N/A	N/A	N/A	N/A	N/A
Trade	8,897	N/A	N/A	N/A	N/A	N/A
Other	1,854	N/A	N/A	N/A	N/A	N/A
1982	85,608	10,336	28,933	977	40,754	4,607
Extrac.	36,332	3,068	20,310	753	8,585	3,616
Proc.	37,201	5,719	5,907	370	23,420	1,785
Trade	10,595	1,139	1,442	−42	7,773e	283
Other	1,898	410	−257	313	976e	456
1989	77,195	9,277	15,176	1,935	44,769	6,038
Extrac.	21,845	2,725	8,274	1,420	3,885	5,541
Proc.	37,078	4,985	1,373	611	28,407	1,702
Trade	14,072	1,316	1,036	91	11,190	439
Other	2,196	252	330	87	1,286	241
Manufacturing						
1977	71,609	40,416	14,852	1,929	8,837	5,575
1982	99,756	56,436	14,254	3,715	16,141	9,210
1989	173,298	81,732	48,877	1,273	26,251	15,164
Food and kindred products						
1977	5,598	3,136	1,415	205	521	321
1982	8,884	4,716	2,065	419	1,102	581
1989	13,643	6,147	4,269	290	1,948	988
Chemicals and allied products						
1977	10,075	5,366	2,624	511	693	882
1982	16,429	8,794	3,693	811	1,604	1,527
1989	30,059	13,615	11,716	217	2,583	3,928
Primary and fabricated metals						
1977	4,231	2,271	890	152	158	311
1982	5,402	3,698	558	291	364	491
1989	7,623	4,135	2,161	212	523	592
Machinery except electrical						
1977	13,555	7,551	3,520	200	630	1,654
1982	17,619	10,182	3,907	592	688	2,251
1989	31,720	16,663	10,374	634	1,480	2,570

	Total	Employee Compens.	Profit-type Return	Net Interest	Indirect Taxes	CCA*
Electric and electronic equipment						
1977	8,062	5,404	1,373	209	657	419
1982	9,876	6,715	1,330	300	848	683
1989	12,643	7,651	2,839	173	615	1,369
Transportation equipment						
1977	13,921	8,127	2,387	225	2,105	1,077
1982	18,055	11,240	−166	745	3,853	2,383
1989	33,764	16,598	8,068	−556	6,461	3,193
Other manufacturing						
1977	16,165	8,109	2,643	429	4,074	910
1982	23,491	11,091	2,867	557	7,683	1,293
1989	41,843	16,923	9,450	305	12,641	2,525
Trade						
1977	11,301	5,010	3,511	226	1,399	1,156
1982	19,409	9,534	4,119	255	3,837	1,663
1989	36,760	18,324	10,493	−307	5,951	2,299
Finance (except banking), insurance, and real estate						
1977	1,948	855	1,604	−657	90	56
1982	1,180	1,800	4,524	−5,676	291	240
1989	3,439	4,928	6,046	−8,767	504	728
Services						
1977	3,929	2,530	987	5	140	268
1982	8,009	5,250	1,584	−87	453	809
1989	14,509	10,046	2,593	141	510	1,219
Other industries						
1977	10,339	5,847	2,265	427	800	998
1982	9,757	6,088	1,437	409	814	1,008
1989	14,793	8,258	3,339	738	918	1,541

Notes: *Capital Consumption Allowance. e = estimate.

Sources: See Tables 7.3 and 7.4.

TABLE 7.6. Composition of Mofa Gross Product by Industry (Percentages; Gross Product = 100)

	Employee Compens.	Profit Returns	Net Interest	Indirect Taxes	CCA
Petroleum 1977	7.9	46.6	1.4	38.9	5.1
Petroleum 1982	12.1	33.8	1.1	47.6	5.4
Extraction	8.5	55.9	2.1	23.7	10.0
Processing	15.3	15.9	1.0	63.0	4.8
Trade	10.7	13.6	NMF	73.3	2.7
Other	21.6	NMF	16.5	51.4	24.0
Petroleum 1989	12.0	19.7	2.5	57.9	7.8
Extraction	12.5	38.1	6.5	17.9	25.2
Processing	13.4	3.8	1.6	76.5	4.6
Trade	9.3	7.4	0.6	79.4	2.5
Other	11.5	15.0	4.0	58.6	11.0
Manufacturing 1977	56.4	20.7	2.7	12.3	7.8
Manufacturing 1982	56.5	14.3	3.7	16.1	9.2
Manufacturing 1989	47.2	28.3	0.8	15.2	8.8
Trade 1977	44.2	31.0	2.0	12.4	10.2
Trade 1982	49.0	21.1	1.3	19.6	8.6
Trade 1989	49.7	28.5	NMF	16.2	6.2
Finance 1977	43.9	84.2	NMF	4.6	2.9
Finance 1982	152.5	383.1	NMF	24.7	20.3
Finance 1989	143.3	175.6	NMF	14.5	21.2
Services 1977	64.9	25.4	0.1	3.6	6.8
Services 1982	65.6	19.8	NMF	5.7	10.1
Services 1989	69.0	17.9	1.0	3.5	8.4

In the following analysis, 1977, 1982, and 1989 figures are presented in two ways: one set of Mofa manufacturing data is based on the DOC's official statistics exclusive of the petroleum industry, while a second set incorporates the necessary adjustments. This latter figure is considered to reflect the true size of Mofas in relation to the U.S. manufacturing industry.

Going beyond these broad categories leads to definitional and procedural problems due to the fact that Mofa data are based on their industrial classification in the host country, which may not be compatible with U.S. standards and thus had to be eliminated from further consideration here.

Total Mofa GP reached a level between 8 and 10 percent of U.S. industrial GDP during the 1970s and early 1980s. By the end of the

TABLE 7.7. Mofa Gross Product by Industry and Country of Affiliate ($ million)

	Total	Pet.	Mfg.	Trade	Finance	Other
World						
1957	$16,129	$6,525	$7,088	N/A	N/A	N/A
1966	36,752	11,838	17,977	N/A	N/A	N/A
1977	161,136	62,010	71,609	$11,301	$1,948	$14,268
1982	223,717	85,608	99,756	19,409	1,180	17,766
1989	319,994	77,195	173,298	36,760	3,439	29,405
1990	356,033	86,987	187,573	40,233	5,637	35,603
1991	355,963	88,775	182,082	40,832	4,788	39,486
1992	361,524	92,526	181,927	39,754	5,290	42,028
1993	357,972	91,408	181,610	38,357	6,398	40,199
Canada						
1957	4,703	812	3,140	N/A	N/A	N/A
1966	8,237	952	5,299	N/A	N/A	N/A
1977	27,783	6,110	15,151	875	910	4,735
1982	34,017	10,998	16,413	1,795	341	4,411
1989	52,114	9,509	28,885	3,291	1,165	9,264
1990	50,820	9,853	27,391	3,444	1,752	7,179
1991	47,192	7,634	23,813	3,598	2,559	9,588
1992	44,938	7,796	21,615	3,547	2,671	9,210
1993	45,034	8,507	22,067	3,523	2,342	8,595
Europe						
1957	4,234	1,531	2,480	N/A	N/A	N/A
1966	14,464	4,407	8,509	N/A	N/A	N/A
1977	69,360	16,944	40,441	8,897	276	4,071
1982	112,577	38,413	54,727	12,058	701	6,678
1989	179,758	41,596	99,389	24,463	1,137	13,173
1990	213,419	48,825	116,180	27,436	2,205	6,785
1991	217,355	53,048	115,337	27,444	948	20,578
1992	217,652	55,116	112,146	26,415	1,771	22,204
1993	206,432	53,192	104,914	24,370	2,496	21,461
Austria						
1977	844	N/A	226	313	0	N/A
1982	981	N/A	246	297	1	N/A
1989	2,021	582	695	659	3	82
1990	2,380	N/A	733	694	nil	N/A
1991	2,364	824	759	594	37	151
1992	2,628	946	909	562	43	167
1993	2,669	868	880	510	57	354

TABLE 7.7 (continued)

	Total	Pet.	Mfg.	Trade	Finance	Other
Belgium/Luxemburg						
1957	151	50	96	N/A	N/A	N/A
1966	653	170	392	N/A	N/A	N/A
1977	4,442	566	2,780	912	17	167
1982	5,362	972	2,590	1,446	−19	373
1989	9,127	1,432	5,471	1,521	−28	676
1990	10,811	1,524	6,117	2,101	261	808
1991	10,570	1,662	6,068	1,747	226	867
1992	11,389	1,970	6,559	1,641	128	1,091
1993	10,871	2,031	6,183	1,402	87	1,168
Denmark						
1957	52	34	14	N/A	N/A	N/A
1966	145	84	30	N/A	N/A	N/A
1977	672	N/A	123	227	N/A	N/A
1982	1,334	749	231	294	34	26
1989	1,243	128	369	605	18	128
1990	1,476	153	429	733	28	131
1991	1,875	532	476	709	8	150
1992	1,858	558	457	648	24	171
1993	1,896	488	467	448	33	460
France						
1957	680	313	345	N/A	N/A	N/A
1966	2,378	N/A	1,384	N/A	N/A	N/A
1977	9,688	N/A	6,203	1,177	N/A	N/A
1982	12,196	1,784	7,423	1,972	34	983
1989	22,625	4,725	11,794	4,008	160	1,938
1990	27,410	5,418	13,993	4,593	183	3,223
1991	27,309	5,557	13,776	4,503	145	3,329
1992	28,665	5,651	14,209	4,635	242	3,927
1993	27,923	5,353	14,083	4,800	281	3,406
Germany						
1957	631	187	424	N/A	N/A	N/A
1966	2,995	816	1,966	N/A	N/A	N/A
1977	18,115	4,424	12,058	1,240	78	315
1982	24,756	7,137	15,292	1,333	30	964
1989	35,683	5,116	25,804	2,479	−38	2,328
1990	46,969	6,795	33,620	3,084	313	3,157
1991	49,192	7,519	34,539	3,476	92	3,568
1992	52,220	8,859	35,587	3,634	174	3,965
1993	50,102	9,218	33,011	3,198	262	4,414

	Total	Pet.	Mfg.	Trade	Finance	Other
Ireland						
1966	94	N/A	40	N/A	N/A	N/A
1977	762	188	485	83	−2	8
1982	1,893	404	1,336	143	−11	−1
1989	4,473	569	3,502	298	18	87
1990	5,416	672	4,270	393	−16	97
1991	5,325	660	4,226	290	51	97
1992	5,800	698	4,563	353	89	97
1993	5,521	556	4,325	384	80	76
Italy						
1957	345	243	97	N/A	N/A	N/A
1966	1,310	639	573	N/A	N/A	N/A
1977	5,825	3,183	3,928	903	23	138
1982	8,481	2,992	4,028	862	174	471
1989	16,487	6,148	7,760	1,881	54	633
1990	18,967	6,250	9,227	2,271	169	1,050
1991	20,268	7,077	9,288	2,459	139	1,304
1992	19,981	7,182	8,899	2,500	108	1,292
1993	16,549	6,137	7,123	2,002	160	1,128
Netherlands						
1957	162	109	47	N/A	N/A	N/A
1966	565	N/A	271	N/A	N/A	N/A
1977	4,209	887	2,235	678	19	390
1982	5,392	1,496	2,553	808	17	518
1989	13,214	1,677	7,761	2,421	−171	1,526
1990	13,724	2,392	6,931	2,748	−31	1,684
1991	13,465	2,602	6,714	2,965	−458	1,642
1992	13,828	2,489	6,987	2,843	−212	1,722
1993	13,035	2,400	6,734	2,744	−399	1,557
Norway						
1957	49	24	20	N/A	N/A	N/A
1966	134	43	57	N/A	N/A	N/A
1977	1,655	1,207	178	233	−5	42
1982	4,440	3,732	257	345	4	102
1989	4,164	3,497	120	436	23	88
1990	5,120	4,314	177	518	−1	112
1991	4,926	4,288	115	412	3	109
1992	4,870	4,219	121	394	11	127
1993	4,236	3,404	202	483	9	136

TABLE 7.7 (continued)

	Total	Pet.	Mfg.	Trade	Finance	Other
Portugal						
1977	178	N/A	84	53	N/A	N/A
1982	341	17	191	94	0	39
1989	997	258	342	308	N/A	89
1990	1,269	357	420	381	8	103
1991	1,503	461	465	446	4	126
1992	1,857	616	589	485	13	193
1993	1,858	553	628	527	49	150
Spain						
1957	34	1	29	N/A	N/A	N/A
1966	242	−1	195	N/A	N/A	N/A
1977	2,019	8	1,479	433	7	92
1982	2,571	88	1,854	309	2	318
1989	7,398	106	5,723	1,120	−3	452
1990	8,428	146	6,353	1,215	55	659
1991	8,482	149	6,366	1,232	69	666
1992	8,017	197	5,781	1,077	98	864
1993	6,697	201	4,762	844	43	846
Sweden						
1957	89	53	34	N/A	N/A	N/A
1966	222	N/A	119	N/A	N/A	N/A
1977	1,103	294	518	239	N/A	N/A
1982	1,889	765	626	391	6	101
1989	2,229	590	1,008	N/A	15	N/A
1990	2,128	N/A	1,049	810	29	N/A
1991	2,415	352	1,076	N/A	37	N/A
1992	2,265	339	885	743	61	248
1993	2,151	349	846	817	N/A	N/A
Switzerland						
1957	58	16	38	N/A	N/A	N/A
1966	371	71	169	N/A	N/A	N/A
1977	2,015	321	449	1,064	42	139
1982	3,198	803	721	1,284	67	323
1989	5,106	768	1,215	2,407	273	442
1990	6,072	984	1,728	2,825	28	507
1991	6,761	725	2,228	2,765	450	583
1992	4,896	682	1,620	2,190	−313	716
1993	5,599	771	1,695	2,322	−78	888

	Total	Pet.	Mfg.	Trade	Finance	Other
UK						
1957	1,891	469	1,316	N/A	N/A	N/A
1966	4,804	1,226	3,191	N/A	N/A	N/A
1977	16,861	3,793	10,679	1,483	18	888
1982	38,465	16,418	17,254	2,010	552	2,231
1989	52,703	15,514	27,423	4,703	749	4,314
1990	60,123	17,322	30,545	4,205	1,143	6,908
1991	59,532	19,046	28,422	4,320	119	7,624
1992	55,343	18,978	23,679	4,001	1,237	7,449
1993	52,824	19,331	21,885	3,367	1,807	6,433
Latin America						
1957	4,350	1,980	882	N/A	N/A	N/A
1966	6,187	1,699	2,404	N/A	N/A	N/A
1977	16,036	3,072	9,533	1,495	348	1,588
1982	27,930	5,974	17,531	2,199	−159	2,385
1989	29,601	3,561	21,684	2,553	−208	2,031
1990	31,080	5,699	21,621	1,883	−671	1,877
1991	28,396	4,756	20,939	2,122	−1,572	2,171
1992	33,635	5,117	25,150	2,196	−1,779	2,952
1993	38,714	5,570	29,388	2,114	−1,523	3,165
Latin America Republics						
1957	4,196	1,870	879	N/A	N/A	N/A
1966	5,701	1,546	2,372	N/A	N/A	N/A
1977	13,806	1,901	9,397	1,352	83	1,073
1982	25,285	3,897	17,260	2,083	10	2,035
1989	28,051	2,751	21,492	2,235	141	1,428
1990	29,729	4,943	21,392	1,500	188	1,706
1991	28,164	3,888	20,777	1,745	25	1,728
1992	33,633	4,357	24,992	1,971	98	2,214
1993	37,988	4,570	29,211	1,761	−52	2,498
Argentina						
1957	169	N/A	129	N/A	N/A	N/A
1966	717	65	562	N/A	N/A	N/A
1977	1,449	306	945	143	3	52
1982	2,902	664	1,859	190	22	167
1989	1,577	454	973	75	4	72
1990	2,603	765	1,397	256	N/A	N/A
1991	3,365	921	1,950	372	N/A	N/A
1992	3,748	962	2,279	376	N/A	N/A
1993	4,138	973	2,682	340	1	142

TABLE 7.7 (continued)

	Total	Pet.	Mfg.	Trade	Finance	Other
Brazil						
1957	405	83	234	N/A	N/A	N/A
1966	744	73	576	N/A	N/A	N/A
1977	6,485	736	5,169	311	26	243
1982	11,199	475	9,572	665	11	476
1989	16,618	849	14,167	1,273	62	266
1990	16,093	2,602	12,938	83	N/A	N/A
1991	11,509	1,221	9,880	82	N/A	N/A
1992	14,457	1,662	12,369	86	N/A	N/A
1993	18,188	1,863	15,753	151	N/A	N/A
Chile						
1957	275	N/A	20	N/A	N/A	N/A
1966	605	N/A	51	N/A	N/A	N/A
1977	162	N/A	62	30	0	N/A
1982	468	135	122	88	88	35
1989	681	135	364	101	19	62
1990	801	N/A	359	127	N/A	N/A
1991	887	176	325	151	20	194
1992	1,310	218	369	250	79	394
1993	1,286	242	420	138	100	386
Colombia						
1957	163	82	46	N/A	N/A	N/A
1966	241	72	121	N/A	N/A	N/A
1977	532	113	320	84	6	9
1982	1,361	434	720	102	−1	106
1989	1,150	489	650	101	4	−94
1990	1,399	581	588	111	2	117
1991	1,350	525	639	99	−2	88
1992	1,545	526	740	98	1	180
1993	1,708	666	840	105	−25	123
Mexico						
1957	418	7	237	N/A	N/A	N/A
1966	891	10	630	N/A	N/A	N/A
1977	2,050	21	1,646	293	7	83
1982	3,561	41	2,879	421	−5	225
1989	4,883	30	4,123	388	68	274
1990	5,800	39	4,984	450	32	295
1991	7,546	52	6,503	594	58	340
1992	8,664	61	7,419	648	107	428
1993	8,745	71	7,660	510	60	444

	Total	Pet.	Mfg.	Trade	Finance	Other
Panama						
1957	23	12	3	N/A	N/A	N/A
1966	92	14	5	N/A	N/A	N/A
1977	289	89	26	73	27	74
1982	433	197	45	64	−22	149
1989	530	164	182	72	N/A	N/A
1990	522	130	193	85	N/A	N/A
1991	549	154	182	N/A	−38	N/A
1992	540	162	201	N/A	−25	N/A
1993	303	68	65	N/A	−47	N/A
Peru						
1957	127	41	23	N/A	N/A	N/A
1966	465	N/A	112	N/A	N/A	N/A
1977	404	114	74	49	N/A	N/A
1982	1,116	707	108	86	N/A	215
1989	397	167	90	21	0	119
1990	412	N/A	60	67	N/A	N/A
1991	344	N/A	61	69	−9	N/A
1992	361	N/A	71	19	−5	N/A
1993	471	107	84	61	−6	224
Venezuela						
1957	1,782	1,544	98	N/A	N/A	N/A
1966	1,614	1,173	227	N/A	N/A	N/A
1977	1,370	97	745	304	10	214
1982	2,394	300	1,401	384	−1	310
1989	736	64	509	129	−2	35
1990	694	76	439	148	−5	36
1991	1,080	107	713	209	−5	56
1992	1,309	133	952	173	−5	56
1993	1,505	165	1,105	171	−10	73
Other Western Hemisphere						
1957	154	110	3	N/A	N/A	N/A
1966	486	153	32	N/A	N/A	N/A
1977	2,230	1,170	136	142	266	516
1982	2,654	2,076	251	115	−168	381
1989	1,549	807	172	318	−349	602
1990	1,351	1,055	229	383	−860	545
1991	232	868	162	377	−1,597	423
1992	2	760	157	225	−1,877	737
1993	727	1,000	178	353	−1,471	678

TABLE 7.7 (continued)

	Total	Pet.	Mfg.	Trade	Finance	Other
Bahamas						
1966	39	6	4	N/A	N/A	N/A
1977	157	39	6	55	5	52
1982	209	30	14	86	7	86
1989	425	61	8	62	178	117
1990	286	39	8	43	41	149
1991	279	59	9	42	−9	178
1992	249	56	7	23	3	159
1993	231	47	11	28	3	142
Bermuda						
1966	35	N/A	1	N/A	N/A	N/A
1977	398	56	0	49	268	25
1982	82	67	0	23	−38	30
1989	−113	49	1	54	−231	14
1990	−210	17	1	134	−383	21
1991	−732	8	1	77	−859	40
1992	−817	−11	1	−50	−847	90
1993	−567	19	1	72	−723	64
Netherlands Antilles						
1977	89	N/A	1	4	−14	N/A
1982	189	20	6	4	N/A	13
1989	−244	−16	7	8	−244	1
1990	−506	4	8	9	−544	17
1991	−793	4	8	10	−672	−143
1992	−859	3	8	−20	−871	20
1993	−588	5	8	11	−598	−14
Africa						
1957	419	119	101	N/A	N/A	N/A
1966	1,689	N/A	257	N/A	N/A	N/A
1977	8,020	N/A	801	329	0	N/A
1982	10,055	7,881	1,345	515	2	312
1989	5,299	3,232	883	117	−15	1,082
1990	6,162	4,659	868	144	21	480
1991	6,098	4,594	898	173	30	405
1992	6,241	4,700	972	148	29	393
1993	5,961	4,495	900	200	29	338

	Total	Pet.	Mfg.	Trade	Finance	Other
South Africa						
1957	419	N/A	97	N/A	N/A	N/A
1966	460	N/A	206	N/A	N/A	N/A
1977	1,317	N/A	546	213	8	N/A
1982	2,330	826	1,011	377	−2	118
1989	701	151	441	55	0	54
1990	698	N/A	423	75	0	N/A
1991	754	N/A	460	68	0	N/A
1992	802	N/A	492	78	0	N/A
1993	782	N/A	418	73	9	N/A
Libya						
1966	696	690	1	N/A	N/A	N/A
1977	2,934	2,927	N/A	N/A	0	N/A
1982	3,150	3,057	0	13	0	18
1989	N/A	N/A	N/A	N/A	N/A	N/A
Nigeria						
1966	44	31	N/A	N/A	N/A	N/A
1977	1,848	1,736	54	N/A	2	N/A
1982	2,219	2,138	65	19	0	−3
1989	1,733	1,701	18	12	N/A	1
1990	2,222	2,185	22	12	1	24
1991	2,249	2,197	39	N/A	1	N/A
1992	2,225	2,153	57	11	4	1
1993	2,215	2,140	61	11	2	1
Asia						
1957	1,855	1,755	159	N/A	N/A	N/A
1966	4,539	3,415	730	N/A	N/A	N/A
1977	32,664	N/A	3,066	955	N/A	N/A
1982	25,863	18,568	5,164	1,893	235	3
1989	36,879	18,568	14,024	5,422	1,274	−2,409
1990	37,900	13,083	14,949	5,540	1,941	2,387
1991	40,562	12,001	15,597	6,357	2,479	2,471
1992	42,665	14,633	16,725	5,911	2,229	4,604
1993	46,603	14,939	18,973	6,726	2,674	3,941

TABLE 7.7 (continued)

	Total	Pet.	Mfg.	Trade	Finance	Other
Japan						
1957	−44	N/A	57	N/A	N/A	N/A
1966	922	463	384	N/A	N/A	N/A
1977	3,065	N/A	1,468	434	94	N/A
1982	4,587	1,613	2,178	777	97	−78
1989	14,940	3,471	7,668	3,249	613	−61
1990	14,565	N/A	7,305	2,845	992	N/A
1991	16,547	N/A	7,955	3,552	1,310	N/A
1992	15,747	N/A	7,883	2,903	1,059	N/A
1993	17,958	N/A	8,993	3,346	1,141	N/A
Hong Kong						
1977	542	71	199	174	24	74
1982	959	95	246	342	75	201
1989	2,926	240	751	910	302	723
1990	3,122	294	856	933	417	562
1991	3,192	380	810	950	483	569
1992	3,485	428	920	975	357	805
1993	4,163	502	931	1,234	557	940
India						
1957	117	N/A	32	N/A	N/A	N/A
1966	339	N/A	133	N/A	N/A	N/A
1977	210	1	205	3	−1	2
1982	229	15	209	0	1	4
1989	157	−9	161	3	1	1
1990	136	−9	141	3	N/A	1
1991	123	−11	130	3	N/A	N/A
1992	121	−16	122	13	N/A	N/A
1993	176	−10	176	N/A	N/A	N/A
Indonesia						
1977	4,661	4,394	106	N/A	N/A	N/A
1982	6,317	5,998	146	35	4	135
1989	3,999	3,591	100	42	−1	268
1990	4,987	4,529	111	42	N/A	N/A
1991	5,031	4,590	114	46	N/A	N/A
1992	5,100	4,447	145	48	N/A	N/A
1993	4,753	4,307	173	20	N/A	N/A

	Total	Pet.	Mfg.	Trade	Finance	Other
Malaysia						
1977	333	161	122	28	1	21
1982	1,691	1,095	373	62	4	165
1989	1,749	795	477	80	35	362
1990	1,825	1,006	612	119	72	15
1991	2,016	N/A	813	131	89	N/A
1992	3,117	N/A	1,209	164	184	N/A
1993	3,151	1,616	1,136	171	197	31
Philippines						
1957	150	N/A	47	N/A	N/A	N/A
1966	245	79	93	N/A	N/A	N/A
1977	549	N/A	278	42	N/A	N/A
1982	1,074	418	447	51	67	91
1989	1,006	240	625	69	54	96
1990	1,015	N/A	571	53	N/A	N/A
1991	1,189	283	688	68	N/A	N/A
1992	1,413	N/A	848	48	N/A	84
1993	1,586	N/A	928	64	N/A	117
Singapore						
1977	400	105	210	55	−1	131
1982	1,109	309	570	183	5	42
1989	2,353	463	1,453	293	51	92
1990	3,547	652	2,372	242	101	180
1991	3,345	802	1,921	308	110	204
1992	3,298	574	2,117	325	70	213
1993	4,784	778	3,121	499	70	306
Taiwan						
1977	260	9	224	24	N/A	N/A
1982	616	50	514	39	2	11
1989	1,938	4	1,531	239	−41	205
1990	2,256	5	1,526	489	N/A	N/A
1991	2,396	13	1,573	563	205	52
1992	2,678	18	1,744	654	214	48
1993	2,559	12	1,480	612	314	142

TABLE 7.7 (continued)

	Total	Pet.	Mfg.	Trade	Finance	Other
Thailand						
1977	254	N/A	58	59	N/A	N/A
1982	657	446	96	52	N/A	63
1989	1,815	1,132	476	99	56	52
1990	1,832	1,045	496	161	N/A	N/A
1991	2,195	1,367	472	178	N/A	N/A
1992	2,130	1,243	450	207	N/A	N/A
1993	2,324	1,310	536	212	N/A	N/A
Oceania						
1957	520	138	319	N/A	N/A	N/A
1966	1,274	N/A	263	N/A	N/A	N/A
1977	5,962	N/A	2,616	697	184	N/A
1982	10,687	3,558	4,576	948	64	1,541
1989	14,887	3,915	7,163	2,100	214	1,495
1990	15,092	4,845	6,564	1,884	389	1,410
1991	14,566	N/A	5,498	1,138	342	N/A
1992	15,043	N/A	5,319	1,439	368	N/A
1993	13,651	N/A	5,367	1,425	378	N/A
Australia						
1957	461	N/A	297	N/A	N/A	N/A
1966	1,136	171	721	N/A	N/A	N/A
1977	5,578	1,158	2,485	633	178	1,151
1982	10,069	3,351	4,295	844	62	1,517
1989	13,902	3,691	6,861	1,927	203	1,221
1990	14,178	4,445	5,321	1,713	359	2,340
1991	12,302	4,124	5,312	1,032	303	1,531
1992	13,148	4,630	5,126	1,290	317	1,784
1993	12,814	4,153	5,111	1,272	328	1,750
New Zealand						
1957	50	N/A	23	N/A	N/A	N/A
1966	138	N/A	57	N/A	N/A	N/A
1977	384	N/A	158	64	6	N/A
1982	618	207	281	104	2	24
1989	985	132	302	173	11	367
1990	914	N/A	243	171	30	N/A
1991	2,264	N/A	186	106	39	N/A
1992	1,895	N/A	193	149	51	N/A
1993	947	N/A	256	153	52	N/A

Sources: 1957 FDI census, pp. 110-1, 118 (calculated on basis of sales less expenditures on materials and services; inventory changes not available and not included; data exclude trade and finance sectors). *SOCB*, February 1977, pp. 22-3 (1966); February 1994, pp. 59-63; June 1994, p. 61; June 1995, pp. 50-1 (1977, 1982, and 1989).

decade, its share had dipped slightly to 7 percent. In the manufacturing sector, they reach twice and even three times that level with oil refining included, but the information seems to be more ambiguous (see Table 7.8).

The apparent drop of total Mofa manufacturing GP including oil processing vis-à-vis the U.S. industry figures from 28 percent (1977) to 25 percent in 1989 is clearly influenced by developments in the oil sector, because industry data excluding oil affiliates established a clear share gain. Factors behind the oil Mofa developments were the 1980 disinvestments in Saudi Arabia, the strong rise of the dollar from 1980 to 1985 and its subsequent decline, the weakness in the oil price during the same period, and the weak demand for oil products in general. All events combined caused petroleum Mofa GP to grow by only 25 percent from $62.0 to $77.2 billion between 1977 and 1989, which was not nearly sufficient to keep pace with the 108 percent expansion of the U.S. manufacturing GDP in the same time span.

Exclusion of the oil subsidiaries reveals a clear-cut gain of manufacturing Mofas against their U.S. counterpart from 8 to 18 percent between 1966 and 1989. Nothing here suggests that Mofas are sharing the alleged decline of the U.S. rust belt (see Table 7.9).

Other factors may have been involved in the relative drop of total Mofa GP against U.S. industrial GDP. This appears likely when studying employment figures. Total subsidiary manpower and that of U.S. industry run different courses for the time period in question. The civilian labor

TABLE 7.8. U.S. Industrial GDP and Mofa Gross Product ($ billion)

Year	Total Industrial GDP/Mofa GP			Manufacturing		
	U.S.A.*	Mofas	%	U.S.A.*	Mofas	%
1966	$644.4	$36.8	5.7	$217.4	$18.0	8.3
1977	1,673.0	161.1	9.6	465.3	71.6 129.5**	15.4 27.8**
1982	2,634.4	223.7	8.5	634.6	99.8 170.4**	15.7 26.8**
1989	4,413.7	320.0	7.2	966.0	173.3 242.0**	17.9 25.1**

Notes: *Total U.S. Business GDP. Excludes agricultural, household, and government accounts. **Adjusted or petroleum data.

Sources: *Economic Report of the President*, February 1988, Table B-10; February 1995, p. 286.

TABLE 7.9. Industrial Employment in the United States and by Mofas (000)

	All Industries*			Manufacturing		
Year	U.S.A.*	Mofas	%	U.S.A.*	Mofas	%
1966	63,900	3,874	6.1	19,214	2,615	13.6
					2,796**	14.6
1977	67,344	5,369	8.0	19,682	3,773	19.2
					3,912**	19.8
1982	73,707	5,022	6.8	18,781	3,358	17.9
					3,538**	18.8
1989	90,116	5,114	5.7	19,442	3,247	16.7
					3,351**	17.3

Notes: *Total employees on nonagricultural payroll less government. **Adjusted for petroleum industry.

Sources: *Economic Report of the President,* January 1993, p. 394; February 1995, pp. 324-5. FDI census data: 1966 pp. 190-2; 1977, pp. 294-5; 1982, pp. 244-5; 1989, p. 217.

force in all U.S. industries, excluding agriculture, expanded steadily between 1966 and 1989 from 63.9 to 90.1 million employees (plus 41 percent), while that of Mofas grew between 1966 and 1977, but was down through 1989 from its 1977 peak, with an actual increase in numbers from 3.9 to 5.1 million (plus 31 percent) over the same period (*Economic Report of the President,* January 1995, pp. 324-5).

Employment in manufacturing, of both the United States and Mofas, showed temporary parallels by increasing both for the United States and subsidiaries from 1966 to 1977, settling back by 1982, only to recover slightly by 1989. For the United States, it meant a recovery to previous levels, and for Mofas. actual growth. For the period as a whole, U.S. employment was flat with 19.2 and 19.4 million employees versus a 24 percent increase for affiliates. Adjusting manufacturing information for oil data alters subsidiary trend figures little. They still grew by only 27 percent for the period.

In summary, the relatively modest growth of total Mofa GP compared to U.S. GDP was partly a result of the dollar's exchange gyrations, different economic growth patterns and, ultimately, the structural changes of the oil Mofas between 1977 and the end of the period.

Comparing employment data and gross product information leads to striking conclusions. With only 6 to 8 percent of the total U.S. industrial labor force, Mofas generate a GP in the range of 7 to 10 percent of America's industrial GDP. Valid though it is, the statement does not permit the across-the-board conclusion of all subsidiary industries enjoying technological and productive superiority. Such an impression is not intended, nor can it be fully supported with available data. Many more variables would have to be critically evaluated before a meaningful conclusion can be reached.

It is probably fair to say that all evidence points to the oil subsidiaries as being the main factor behind the positive picture. When comparing affiliate and parent GP in other industries, there are cases where affiliates lead parents in a per capita performance, but definitely not as a rule. As parents are the industry leaders in America, the relative output levels documented for parents and subsidiaries in Table 7.12 can be taken as an indicator of the affiliate performance level vis-à-vis their American counterparts in general, as laid down in Table 7.10. Analysis of the manufacturing side uncovers a similar picture. In 1977, 1982, and 1989, Mofas reached between 17 and 19 percent of U.S. employment, but turned out a GP volume, after adjustment for the oil industry, in the range of 22 to 28 percent of the U.S. manufacturing GDP.

COMPARATIVE PARENT/MOFA PROFILES

Parents and their offspring can be compared on a wide range of issues such as: sales, income, assets, employment, and gross product. This discus-

TABLE 7.10. Comparative Levels of Gross Product/Employee (dollars)

	Industrial GP			Manufacturing GP		
Year	U.S.A.	Mofas	%	U.S.A.	Mofas	%
1966	$10,085	$9,499	94	$11,315	$6,883	61
1977	24,859	30,006	121	23,641	18,977 33,103*	80 140
1982	35,739	44,544	125	33,789	29,720 48,163*	88 137
1989	48,985	62,573	128	49,686	53,372 72,217*	107 145

Note: *Adjusted for petroleum data and comparable to U.S. official data.

Sources: Calculated from data in Tables 7.8 and 7.9.

sion requires the introduction of a minor technical change in data presentation. So far, all statistical information for parents and subsidiaries covered their industry affiliation in their respective countries of domicile.

When making direct comparisons between parents and their subsidiaries, these data become less logical and actually misleading, because quite often, U.S. parents acquire companies in industries different from their own, and not subject to the general American industrial classification. For example, a U.S. automobile manufacturer takes over a French producer of hydraulic presses. Putting everything on an equal footing then requires a restatement of affiliate data by industry of the parent, a step which, theoretically, may cause a subsidiary to lose its identity as a member of a particular industry in its own country.

The affiliates are thus forced to change their foreign official classification by being reclassified on the basis of their parent's industrial category, or in the official terminology, "by industry of parent." Information of this kind is published for the census years 1977, 1982, and 1989, either partially (Mofa GP for 1977 only) or completely (all affiliate sales, assets, employment, and net profits for the latter years). One might expect to find structural parallels in the percentage distribution of the above parameters among parents and affiliates, but there are none. Instead of presenting a miniature replica of their parents' industrial profile, Mofas can differ substantially in practically all aspects, variances that reflect the different stages of internationalization achieved by U.S. investors, and probably also in the economic structures of foreign markets against the United States, as well as other factors.

The structural variations introduced by reclassifying affiliates by parental ownership, rather than by industry of affiliate, affect practically all industries, with the most pronounced case represented by petroleum affiliates which in the FDI realm carry twice the weight of their parents in the United States.

Complementary information on the structural composition of parent and offspring industries in terms of percentage distribution (see Table 7.11) is provided by actual data on the relative size and weight of Mofas in comparison to their parents. It confirms the previous impression of Mofas having reached more or less one-third the size of their parents, when measured in terms of sales, employment, and gross product. Such generalization hides important differences between parents and Mofas, which appear only after assembly of serial information with a common denominator, in this case resources committed and output achieved per respective parent and affiliate employee (see Table 7.12).

Thus, the average Mofa employee aided greatly, with assets reaching 95 percent of U.S. levels, and receiving compensation at roughly one-third

TABLE 7.11. Structural Differences Among Parents and Subsidiaries (percentages)

Year	Total	Pet.	Mfg.	Trade	Finance	Service	Other
Sales							
Parents							
1977	100.0	16.6	52.6	11.9	8.6	1.4	8.9
1982	100.0	24.0	44.0	11.1	8.7	2.0	10.2
1989	100.0	9.9	46.7	6.9	11.8	3.3	15.8
Mofas							
1977	100.0	39.8	45.8	6.2	3.5	0.8	3.2
1982	100.0	37.0	47.9	7.5	3.6	1.1	2.9
1989	100.0	18.2	64.5	5.7	5.7	2.1	4.0
Employment							
Parents							
1977	100.0	4.9	62.9	12.4	4.6	3.3	14.6
1982	100.0	6.7	56.4	13.5	5.5	5.2	12.6
1989	100.0	3.0	51.6	2.2	5.7	8.7	24.5
Mofas							
1977	100.0	5.7	74.1	6.2	6.3	2.1	5.7
1982	100.0	7.5	74.0	6.6	6.2	2.5	3.2
1989	100.0	4.0	69.5	2.9	5.9	6.2	9.4
Gross Product							
Parents							
1977	100.0	10.6	61.4	6.4	4.7	2.0	14.9
1982	100.0	17.3	53.7	7.0	1.5	3.2	17.4
1989	100.0	8.8	56.2	2.2	4.9	5.5	22.5
Mofas							
1977	100.0	38.5	50.3	0.6	3.7	1.2	5.6
1982	100.0	34.8	54.7	1.8	4.0	1.3	3.6
1989	100.0	22.8	64.7	1.9	3.8	3.1	3.8
Assets							
Parents							
1977	100.0	14.7	41.1	4.9	24.7	1.2	13.3
1982	100.0	17.8	37.0	5.1	24.9	1.9	14.3
1989	100.0	9.7	39.4	1.9	33.1	2.8	13.6
Mofas							
1977	100.0	27.8	53.1	4.1	8.6	1.1	5.5
1982	100.0	31.6	51.2	3.8	8.8	1.5	3.2
1989	100.0	21.0	55.0	1.9	15.9	2.6	3.6

Note: All data by industry of parents.

Source: Based on Table 7.12.

TABLE 7.12. Comparative Benchmarks of Parents and Mofas

Year	All Indus.	Pet.	Mfg. Total	Food	Chem.	Prim. metals	Mach. nonelec.	Elec. equip.	Trans. equip.	Mfg. Other	Trade ***	Finance	Services	Other
Parents														
							SALES ($ billion)							
1977	$1,326	$220	$698	$78	$94	$87	$77	$57	$162	$142	$157	$114	$19	$118
1982	2,250	540	991	112	168	98	114	125	180	194	250	196	44	229
1989	3,015	330	1,524	175	233	103	170	145	362	335	373	383	105	301
1990	3,244	396	1,575	207	252	88	176	157	351	344	412	396	113	352
1991	3,274	347	1,574	199	265	86	170	170	342	359	443	411	121	378
1992	3,331	359	1,640	224	267	86	178	144	367	374	397	415	120	429
1993	3,495	345	1,697	232	266	89	193	157	392	368	468	430	130	436
Mofas by industry of parent														
1966	$98	$28	$57	$6	$9	$6	$14*	N/A	$13	$10	$7	$1	N/A	$5
1977	507	202	232	23	41	14	38	$15	63	38	34	18	$4	16
1982	730	270	350	38	80	22	60	29	69	52	54	26	8	22
1989	1,020	186	658	54	130	24	152	45	147	102	79	58	21	18
Mofa %														
1977	38.2	92.2	33.2	30.0	43.1	15.8	50.0	27.0	38.5	27.0	21.7	15.8	21.1	13.6
1982	39.7	50.1	35.3	34.2	47.5	22.6	52.2	23.2	38.5	26.8	21.8	13.5	17.7	9.2
1989	32.5	52.7	42.6	30.0	56.0	23.1	87.4	32.8	38.1	29.5	21.2	15.4	18.9	5.9
Mofas by industry of affiliate														
1977	$507	$199	$194	$22	$32	$12	$28	$19	$49	$33	$77	$10	$9	$18
1982	730	266	271	33	55	15	40	25	57	46	129	24	18	22
1989	1,020	179	509	51	95	21	100	40	114	88	204	51	32	43
1990	1,208	238	581	62	108	23	114	46	124	105	227**	58	43	61
1991	1,241	238	596	68	113	22	113	48	128	105	227**	66	46	68
1992	1,292	239	623	72	124	23	112	49	135	108	241**	71	51	67
1993	1,279	220	623	80	121	24	109	52	132	107	247**	76	53	60

Notes: *Both machinery sectors. **Excludes retail. ***Wholesale plus retail.

Sources: FDI census data: 1966, p. 207; 1977, pp. 319, 323, 391; 1982, pp. 226, 230, 315; 1989, pp. 191, 211, 278. *SOCB*, October 1991, pp. 49, 55; July 1993, pp. 50-1, 53-4; June 1995, pp. 41-2, 44-5.

EMPLOYMENT (million)

Year	All Indus.	Pet.	Mfg. Total	Food	Chem.	Prim. metals	Mach. nonelec.	Elec. equip.	Trans. equip.	Mfg. Other	Trade***	Finance	Services	Other
Parents														
1977	17.5	0.9	11.0	1.0	1.2	1.4	1.5	1.2	2.2	2.6	2.2	0.8	0.6	2.6
1982	18.2	1.2	10.3	1.0	1.4	1.0	1.4	1.6	1.7	2.3	2.5	1.0	1.0	2.3
1989	18.2	0.6	9.9	1.0	1.2	0.7	1.2	1.1	2.1	2.6	2.6	1.1	1.7	2.3
1990	18.4	0.6	9.8	1.2	1.3	0.6	1.2	1.1	2.0	2.5	2.7	1.1	1.6	2.6
1991	18.0	0.6	9.5	1.1	1.2	0.6	1.1	1.0	1.9	2.6	2.7	1.0	1.7	2.5
1992	17.5	0.6	9.2	1.2	1.2	0.6	1.1	0.9	1.8	2.6	2.6	1.0	1.6	2.5
1993	17.7	0.5	9.0	1.2	1.1	0.6	1.1	0.8	1.8	2.4	2.9	1.1	1.7	2.4
Mofas by industry of parent														
1966	3.9	0.3	3.0	0.3	0.4	0.3	0.9*	N/A	0.5	0.6	0.1	0.1	N/A	0.6
1977	5.4	0.3	4.0	0.4	0.6	0.2	0.6	0.4	0.9	0.8	0.3	0.3	0.1	0.3
1982	5.0	0.4	3.7	0.4	0.7	0.2	0.5	0.5	0.6	0.7	0.3	0.3	0.1	0.2
1989	5.1	0.2	3.7	0.3	0.6	0.2	0.7	0.4	0.7	0.8	0.5	0.3	0.3	0.2
Mofa %														
1977	30.7	35.1	36.2	43.2	48.9	16.7	40.7	37.0	39.8	31.9	15.2	41.1	19.1	12.0
1982	27.6	30.7	36.2	43.6	49.3	26.0	35.6	30.5	39.1	31.8	13.6	31.5	13.2	7.0
1989	28.0	35.5	36.8	32.4	50.2	23.6	52.7	35.7	35.6	29.5	17.9	27.6	18.7	7.1
Mofas by industry of affiliate														
1966	3.9	0.3	2.6	0.2	0.4	0.2	0.8*	N/A	0.5	0.5	0.3	0.1	N/A	0.6
1977	5.4	0.3	3.8	0.4	0.5	0.2	0.5	0.6	0.7	0.8	0.6	0.1	0.2	0.3
1982	5.0	0.3	3.4	0.4	0.5	0.2	0.4	0.6	0.6	0.7	0.7	0.1	0.3	0.3
1989	5.1	0.2	3.2	0.3	0.5	0.2	0.5	0.5	0.6	0.7	0.8	0.1	0.4	0.3
1990	5.4	0.2	3.4	0.3	0.5	0.2	0.5	0.5	0.6	0.8	0.5**	0.1	0.4	0.7
1991	5.4	0.2	3.3	0.3	0.5	0.2	0.5	0.5	0.6	0.7	0.5**	0.1	0.5	0.8
1992	5.3	0.2	3.3	0.4	0.5	0.2	0.4	0.5	0.6	0.8	0.5**	0.1	0.5	0.7
1993	5.3	0.2	3.3	0.4	0.5	0.2	0.4	0.5	0.6	0.7	0.5**	0.1	0.5	0.7

Notes: *Both machinery sectors. **Excludes retail. ***Wholesale plus retail.

Sources: FDI census data: 1966, pp. 190, 194; 1977, pp. 295, 302, 392; 1982, pp. 245, 252, 323; 1989, pp. 215, 223, 278. *SOCB*, October 1991, pp. 49, 55; July 1993, pp. 50-1, 53-4; June 1995, pp. 41-2, 44-5.

TABLE 7.12 (continued)

Year	All Indus.	Pet.	Mfg. Total	Food	Chem.	Prim. metals	Mach. nonelec.	Elec. equip.	Trans. equip.	Mfg. Other	Trade +	Finance	Services	Other
						GROSS PRODUCT ($ billion)								
Parents														
1977	$491	$52	$301	$22	$39	$35	$42	$27	$71	$65	$31	$23	$10	$73
1982	796	134	421	36	66	37	61	59	71	91	14	23	26	178
1989	1,045	93	587	60	97	38	71	56	121	143	23	51	57	235
Mofas by industry of parent														
1977	161	62	81	6	12	5	18	5	17	17	1	6	2	9
1982	224	78	122	10	27	6	23	10	20	25	4	9	3	8
1989	320	73	207	19	44	8	45	12	39	39	6	12	10	12
Mofa %														
1977	32.8	119.2	26.9	27.2	30.8	14.3	42.9	18.5	23.9	26.2	3.2	26.1	20.0	12.3
1982	28.1	58.2	29.0	27.8	40.9	16.2	37.8	16.9	28.2	27.5	28.6	39.1	11.5	4.5
1989	30.6	78.5	35.3	31.7	45.4	21.1	63.3	21.4	32.2	27.3	26.1	23.5	17.5	5.1
Mofas by industry of affiliate														
1977	$161	$62	$72	$6	$10	$4	$14	$8	$14	$16	$11	$2	$4	$10
1982	224	86	100	9	16	5	18	10	18	24	19	1	8	10
1989	320	77	173	14	32	8	32	13	34	42	37	3	15	15
1990	356	87	188	16	33	8	33	13	37	47	40	6	17	19
1991	356	89	182	18	33	7	30	13	34	47	41	5	18	21
1992	362	93	182	19	37	8	26	13	34	45	40	5	21	22
1993	358	91	182	21	36	7	26	15	33	44	38	6	22	19
Mofa %														
1977	32.8	119.1	26.9	28.0	31.7	13.6	42.6	20.2	24.1	26.3	12.7	28.1	17.3	13.7
1982	28.1	64.2	23.8	25.0	24.2	13.5	29.5	16.9	25.4	26.4	135.7	4.3	30.8	5.6
1989	30.6	82.8	29.5	23.3	33.0	21.1	45.1	23.2	28.1	29.4	160.9	5.9	26.3	6.4

Note: +Wholesale only.

Sources: See Table 7.4 for Mofas. SOCB, June 1995, pp. 44-5. Parent data: SOCB, February 1994, pp. 47, 58, 62-3; June 1995, pp. 44-5.

ASSETS ($ billion)

Year	All Indus.	Pet.	Mfg. Total	Food	Chem.	Prim. metals	Mach. nonelec.	Elec. equip.	Trans. equip.	Mfg. Other	Trade***	Finance	Services	Other
Parents														
1977	$1,475	$217	$606	$46	$95	$82	$80	$43	$131	$128	$73	$365	$18	$196
1982	2,703	482	1,000	78	178	112	131	126	190	185	137	673	51	360
1989	4,702	454	1,854	168	295	105	212	215	451	406	253	1,534	135	472
1990	4,951	478	1,910	184	308	84	215	241	451	426	294	1,600	142	528
1991	5,183	405	1,969	178	326	84	207	252	456	467	368	1,729	152	561
1992	5,580	521	2,076	199	343	87	213	274	475	483	304	1,931	147	600
1993	6,085	514	2,171	212	363	94	210	327	500	464	316	2,267	162	655
Mofas by industry of parent														
1977	352	98	187	14	36	14	35	11	41	35	14	30	4	20
1982	580	183	297	25	67	29	49	25	55	46	22	51	8	20
1989	1,080	227	594	63	129	26	125	41	122	88	37	172	28	23
Mofa %														
1977	24.2	45.6	30.9	30.4	37.9	17.1	43.8	25.6	31.3	27.3	19.2	8.2	22.2	10.2
1982	21.5	37.9	29.7	32.1	37.6	25.9	37.4	19.8	28.9	24.4	16.1	7.5	15.7	5.6
1989	23.0	50.0	32.0	37.5	43.7	24.8	59.0	19.1	27.1	21.7	14.6	11.2	20.7	4.9
Mofas by industry of affiliate														
1977	$352	$86	$138	$12	$27	$10	$24	$14	$24	$28	$38	$61	$9	$21
1982	580	154	190	18	41	12	30	18	34	38	59	139	17	20
1989	1,080	151	371	33	77	19	73	31	64	75	119	376	37	26
1990	1,275	170	441	45	95	22	81	36	72	90	122**	444	45	53
1991	1,376	172	458	49	99	21	86	37	73	93	125**	503	54	63
1992	1,474	178	475	58	108	21	83	39	71	95	136**	659	59	68
1993	1,743	184	491	66	109	22	85	41	70	98	144**	793	62	69

Notes: **Excludes retail. ***Wholesale plus retail.

Sources: FDI census data: 1977, pp. 230, 246, 384; 1982, pp. 187, 196, 310; 1989, pp. 141-3, 149, 156. SOCB, October 1991, pp. 49, 55; July 1993, pp. 50-1, 53-4; June 1994, pp. 52, 55; June 1995, pp. 41-2, 44-5.

TABLE 7.12 (continued)

Year	All Indus.	Pet.	Mfg. Total	Food	Chem.	Prim. metals	Mach. nonelec.	Elec. equip.	Trans. equip.	Mfg. Other	Trade***	Finance	Services	Other
NET INCOME ($ billion)														
Parents														
1977	$78	$16	$42	$3	$8	$3	$7	$4	$8	$9	$4	$6	$1	$9
1982	101	25	41	5	11	-2	8	6	2	10	5	13	3	15
1989	166	24	83	13	23	5	10	7	8	17	7	25	6	21
1990	134	21	68	13	22	3	9	6	4	11	8	11	7	21
1991	92	14	36	13	22	1	-6	5	-5	6	8	17	5	12
1992	39	7	-2	13	14	-2	-10	6	-32	8	3	14	5	13
1993	105	15	40	10	15	3	-7	7	7	6	12	26	5	5
Mofas by industry of parent														
1977	20	6	12	1	2	1	3	1	2	2	1	1	.2	1
1982	26	8	14	2	4	1	4	2	1	2	1	2	.5	1
1989	72	12	50	5	12	2	12	3	8	8	2	5	1.8	1
Mofa %														
1977	25.8	37.3	27.3	29.4	27.8	26.9	44.6	22.9	19.3	22.5	16.2	15.5	16.7	12.0
1982	25.9	31.9	35.2	31.3	35.4	NMF	53.2	25.0	20.8	19.8	15.2	12.0	19.2	7.4
1989	43.4	50.0	60.2	38.5	52.2	40.0	120.0	42.9	100.0	47.1	28.6	20.0	30.0	4.8
Mofas by industry of affiliate														
1977	$20	$5	$8	$1	$1	$.5	$2	$1	$1.0	$1	$3	$3	$1	$1
1982	26	8	8	1	2	.1	2	1	0.3	1	2	6	1	1
1989	72	8	34	4	8	1.7	7	2	5.7	7	9	18	3	1
1990	73	12	31	4	7	1.1	7	2	3.8	6	8**	17	3	2
1991	66	13	25	4	7	.7	4	2	2.9	5	7**	17	2	2
1992	63	10	23	5	8	.8	1	1	1.9	5	7**	19	2	2
1993	67	10	26	6	8	.7	1	2	2.7	5	7**	21	3	1

Notes: **Excludes retail. ***Wholesale plus retail.

Sources: FDI census data: 1977, pp. 288, 291, 391; 1982, pp. 221-2, 315; 1989, pp. 184-5, 278. *SOCB*, October 1991, pp. 49, 55; July 1993, pp. 50-1, 53-4; June 1994, p. 52, 55; June 1995, pp. 41-2, 44-5.

SALES/EMPLOYEE ($ thousand)

Year	All Indus.	Pet.	Mfg. Total	Food	Chem.	Prim. metals	Mach. nonelec.	Elec. equip.	Trans. equip.	Mfg. Other	Trade ***	Finance	Services	Other
Parents														
1977	$76	$244	$63	$78	$78	$62	$51	$48	$74	$55	$71	$143	$31	$45
1982	124	450	96	112	120	98	81	78	106	84	100	196	44	100
1989	168	562	153	170	185	151	127	135	172	128	151	348	64	142
1990	176	662	161	180	197	148	148	143	176	138	150	365	69	141
1991	182	603	166	174	212	151	152	153	180	140	164	405	73	151
1992	190	650	177	192	224	155	161	170	203	146	153	404	76	160
1993	198	674	188	188	232	153	184	188	221	152	160	394	78	170
Mofas by industry of parent														
1977	94	673	58	58	68	44	63	38	70	49	113	60	40	53
1982	146	675	95	95	114	49	120	58	115	74	180	87	80	105
1989	199	930	178	180	217	120	217	113	210	128	158	193	70	90
Mofa %														
1977	124	276	92	74	87	71	124	79	95	89	159	42	129	118
1982	118	150	99	85	95	50	148	74	108	88	180	44	182	105
1989	118	165	116	106	117	79	171	84	122	100	105	55	109	63
Mofas by industry of affiliate														
1977	$94	$663	$51	$55	$64	$60	$56	$32	$70	$41	$128	$100	$45	$60
1982	146	887	80	83	110	75	100	42	95	66	186	240	60	73
1989	199	895	159	170	190	105	200	80	190	125	255	430	80	57
1990	224	1,246	172	188	220	125	222	92	207	137	446+	460	101	83
1991	230	1,293	181	196	226	129	238	99	215	144	435+	528	100	85
1992	245	1,337	190	195	244	142	250	100	251	142	474+	575	110	91
1993	243	1,187	191	195	242	136	253	106	255	143	505+	573	109	85

Notes: +Wholesale only. ***Wholesale plus retail.

219

TABLE 7.12 (continued)

Year	All Indus.	Pet.	Mfg. Total	Food	Chem.	Prim. metals	Mach. nonelec.	Elec. equip.	Trans. equip.	Mfg. Other	Trade***	Finance	Services	Other
EMPLOYEE COMPENSATION ($ billion)														
Parents														
1977	$306	$17	$205	$13	$23	$27	$29	$19	$53	$40	$21	$14	$7	$42
1982	509	44	306	22	16	31	44	46	63	58	38	26	17	78
1989	648	27	388	26	54	26	56	40	95	91	49	46	40	98
1990	689	29	402	31	58	24	57	43	98	91	51	49	44	113
1991	707	30	411	31	60	24	57	41	98	99	52	51	46	117
1992	725	32	421	33	61	24	57	40	101	104	52	54	46	121
1993	753	31	426	36	63	25	55	39	104	104	65	59	49	124
Mofas by industry of parent														
1966	14	2	11	1	1	1	3*	—	2	2	.4	.3	N/A	1
1977	60	5	43	4	7	3	9	3	10	8	2	4	1	4
1982	89	10	64	6	12	4	13	6	12	11	4	7	2	3
1989	133	8	98	7	18	4	24	7	19	18	6	10	7	4
Mofa %														
1977	19.4	29.2	21.2	26.9	28.7	10.3	32.4	16.7	18.5	20.3	11.0	28.9	16.9	8.7
1982	17.5	22.1	20.9	26.1	72.2	14.1	29.0	13.6	19.6	18.9	10.3	26.2	12.9	3.3
1989	20.5	29.6	25.3	26.9	33.3	15.3	42.9	17.5	20.0	19.8	12.2	21.7	17.7	4.1
Mofas by industry of affiliate														
1977	$60	$5	$40	$3	$5	$3	$8	$5	$8	$8	$7	$1	N/A	$5
1982	89	10	57	5	9	1	10	7	12	11	12	2	$5	4
1989	133	9	82	6	14	4	17	8	17	17	22	5	10	4
1990	151	8	94	7	15	5	19	9	19	20	21**	6	12	11
1991	160	8	98	8	17	5	19	9	20	20	22**	6	13	13
1992	170	9	104	9	19	5	19	9	20	22	23**	6	15	13
1993	167	8	102	10	19	5	18	10	19	21	22**	7	16	12

Notes: *Both machinery sectors. **Excludes retail. ***Wholesale plus retail.

Sources: FDI census data: 1966, p. 195; 1977, pp. 301, 392; 1982, pp. 220, 223, 278. *SOCB*, October 1991, p. 55; July 1993, pp. 50-1, 53-4; June 1994, pp. 52, 55; June 1995, pp. 41-2, 44-5.

COMPENSATION/EMPLOYEE ($ thousand)

Year	All Indus.	Mfg. Total	Pet.	Food	Chem.	Prim. metals	Mach. nonelec.	Elec. equip.	Trans. equip.	Mfg. Other	Trade***	Finance	Services	Other
Parents														
1977	$17	$19	$19	$13	$19	$20	$19	$16	$24	$16	$10	$18	$12	$16
1982	28	30	37	22	12	31	32	28	37	25	15	26	17	34
1989	35	39	47	26	43	39	45	37	45	36	18	43	24	44
1990	37	41	48	27	45	41	48	39	49	36	19	45	27	44
1991	39	43	51	28	49	43	51	41	51	38	20	50	28	46
1992	41	46	58	29	51	43	52	47	56	40	20	52	29	48
1993	43	47	60	29	55	43	52	47	59	43	22	54	30	52
Mofas by industry of parent														
1977	11	11	17	9	11	14	16	8	11	10	8	14	12	12
1982	18	17	24	14	17	22	26	12	21	16	13	23	22	13
1989	26	26	40	12	30	20	34	18	27	23	12	33	23	20
Mofa %														
1977	65	58	89	69	58	70	84	50	46	63	80	78	100	75
1982	64	57	65	64	142	71	81	43	57	64	87	88	129	38
1989	74	67	85	46	70	51	76	49	60	64	67	77	96	45
Mofas by industry of affiliate														
1977	$11	$11	$17	$8	$10	$15	N/A	N/A	$11	$10	$12	$10	N/A	$17
1982	18	17	33	13	18	20	$25	$12	20	16	17	20	$17	13
1989	26	25	45	20	28	20	36	17	28	24	28	41	25	13
1990	28	28	41	22	32	25	37	18	32	26	40++	45	28	15
1991	30	30	44	24	33	27	41	19	33	28	43++	47	29	16
1992	32	32	48	24	31	30	42	19	37	29	45++	52	33	18
1993	32	31	44	26	38	29	42	20	36	29	45	55	32	17

Notes: ++Retail only. ***Wholesale plus retail.

TABLE 7.12 (continued)

Year	All Indus.	Pet.	Mfg. Total	Food	Chem.	Prim. metals	Mach. nonelec.	Elec. equip.	Trans. equip.	Mfg. Other	Trade***	Finance	Services	Other
NET INCOME/EMPLOYEE (dollars)														
Parents														
1977	$4,457	$17,780	$3,818	$3,000	$6,670	$2,143	$4,667	$3,333	$3,637	$3,462	$1,818	$7,500	$1,667	$3,461
1982	5,549	20,830	3,980	5,000	7,857	NMF	5,714	3,750	1,176	4,348	2,000	13,000	3,000	6,522
1989	8,877	40,000	8,218	11,800	19,167	7,143	7,692	7,000	3,810	6,296	2,500	22,727	3,529	8,750
1990	7,283	35,000	6,939	10,830	16,923	5,000	7,500	5,455	2,000	4,400	2,963	10,000	4,375	8,077
1991	5,111	23,330	3,895	11,818	18,330	NMF	NMF	5,000	NMF	2,308	2,963	17,000	2,941	4,800
1992	2,242	13,585	-2,020	11,467	11,796	-3,255	-9,064	7,482	-1,784	3,239	1,018	13,121	3,153	5,000
1993	5,945	31,355	4,472	8,482	13,275	5,246	-6,409	8,234	3,288	2,361	4,094	24,242	2,978	2,167
Mofas by industry of parent														
1977	3,704	20,000	3,000	2,500	3,333	5,000	5,000	2,500	2,222	2,500	3,330	3,333	2,000	3,330
1982	5,200	20,000	7,833	5,000	5,714	5,000	8,000	2,500	1,670	2,857	3,330	6,670	5,000	5,000
1989	14,117	60,000	13,514	16,667	20,000	10,000	17,143	7,500	11,429	10,000	4,000	16,667	6,000	5,000
Mofa %														
1977	83.1	112.5	78.9	83.3	50.0	233.3	107.3	75.1	61.2	72.3	183.2	44.4	120.0	96.2
1982	93.7	96.0	195.9	100.0	72.7	NMF	140.4	66.7	142.0	65.7	166.5	51.3	166.7	76.7
1989	158.5	150.0	164.6	141.3	104.2	140.0	222.9	107.1	300.0	158.7	160.0	73.4	170.5	57.1
Mofas by industry of affiliate														
1977	$3,704	$16,667	$2,105	$2,500	$2,000	$2,500	$4,000	$1,667	$1,429	$1,250	$5,000	$3,000	$5,000	$3,330
1982	5,200	26,667	2,353	2,500	4,000	1,000	5,000	1,667	500	2,857	2,857	6,000	3,333	3,330
1989	14,117	40,000	10,625	13,333	16,000	8,500	14,000	4,000	9,500	10,000	11,250	18,000	7,500	3,330
1990	13,519	60,000	9,118	13,333	14,000	5,500	14,000	4,000	6,330	7,500	16,000++	17,000	7,500	2,857
1991	12,220	65,000	7,879	13,333	14,000	1,400	8,000	4,000	4,833	7,143	14,000++	17,000	4,000	2,500
1992	11,908	55,000	7,017	13,561	15,183	4,783	3,107	2,618	3,579	6,384	13,258++	15,319	5,280	2,764
1993	12,757	53,540	7,837	14,000	15,431	4,442	3,065	4,746	5,273	6,927	14,591++	15,567	5,432	1,454

Notes: ++Retail only. ***Wholesale plus retail.

Year	All Indus.	Pet.	Mfg. Total	Food	Chem.	Prim. metals	Mach. nonelec.	Elec. equip.	Trans. equip.	Mfg. Other	Trade +	Finance	Services	Other
						GP/EMPLOYEE ($ thousand)								
Parents														
1977	$28	$58	$27	$22	$33	$25	$28	$23	$32	$25	$14	$24	$17	$28
1982	42	111	40	35	47	37	43	37	41	38	22	11	25	58
1989	58	155	62	55	81	63	65	56	64	55	9	51	34	94
Mofas by industry of parent														
1977	30	207	20	15	20	25	30	13	19	21	33	20	20	30
1982	45	195	33	25	39	30	46	20	33	36	13	30	30	40
1989	63	365	56	33	73	40	64	30	56	49	12	40	33	60
Mofa %														
1977	107	357	74	68	61	100	107	57	59	84	236	83	118	107
1982	107	176	83	71	83	81	107	54	80	95	59	273	120	69
1989	109	235	90	60	90	63	98	54	88	89	133	78	97	64
Mofas by industry of affiliate														
1977	$30	$207	$27	$15	$20	$25	$30	$13	$19	$27	$13	$20	$20	$20
1982	45	215	27	23	24	25	36	20	32	34	60	3	80	50
1989	63	375	45	43	50	35	43	30	46	51	68	3	47	70
Mofa %														
1977	107	357	100	68	61	100	107	57	59	108	93	83	118	71
1982	107	194	68	66	51	68	84	54	78	89	273	27	320	86
1989	109	242	73	78	62	56	66	54	71	93	756	6	138	74

Note: +Wholesale only.

223

below U.S. standards. This produced sales levels 20 to 25 percent higher than that for their U.S. counterparts, income levels three to five times parent levels, and a GP up to 10 percent above U.S. standards. The maverick petroleum industry provides a first striking example of one extreme with Mofas employing one-third the number of people on the parents' payroll, but selling between 50 and 90 percent of their parents' volume, for a per capita differential of up to 200 percent in favor of affiliates.

The manufacturing sector demonstrates a generally more balanced situation. Overall, affiliates generate 33 to 43 percent of parental sales with employment levels of around 36 percent. Again, there are important deviations from the norm. Industries with relatively high Mofa employment levels, but disproportionately low output vis-à-vis their parents are represented by primary metals, electric and electronic equipment, and other manufacturing. A complete reversal is visible in the nonelectric machinery sector, where relatively small numbers of Mofa employees produce much higher sales in comparison to their parents. In all other sectors employee and sales levels seem to be more evenly matched.

Causes for the observed variations are seen in product specialization, and relative pay and resource levels where Mofas are definitely at a disadvantage. In the nonelectrical machinery group, the lower parent productivity might result from affiliate sales of more specialized equipment (the reason for their acquisition?) and/or a different employment structure. In the electronics industry, on the other hand, affiliate employment reaching one-third of parent levels produces only one-fourth of parent sales, leading to exactly the opposite conclusion. Parents are concentrating on high-tech products, while subsidiaries produce labor intensive consumer electronics.

As a rule, average sales per employee in all manufacturing industries remain under comparable parent output. Notable exception is the nonelectric machinery sector, where Mofas register levels of output from 50 to 100 percent above parent levels and rising.

All other affiliate industries deserve mentioning in only two cases. Trade Mofas, including wholesale and retail operations, show a markedly superior performance against their parents by employing around 15 percent of their numbers, but selling 20 to 22 percent of their volume. This may be due to generally higher price levels and margins in foreign markets. Alternately, there is the extensive use of those affiliates as profit centers for intracorporate transactions such as the Swiss subsidiaries, for instance. The end effect is that Mofas tower over their parents on a sales/employee basis for most of the period (1977 to 1989) with levels of 100 to 180 percent.

On the surface, finance affiliates present a fairly atypical account of themselves by employing between 28 and 41 percent of parent numbers, but generating sales totals reaching only 14 to 16 percent of comparable parent levels. This is a deceptive picture, as Mofas, which are measured on a per capita basis, generally produce at levels between 42 and 55 percent of their respective parent results, and net incomes ranging between 44 and 73 percent of parent levels.

A further breakdown of parent and Mofa GP by major components quickly points at considerable structural dissimilarities arising mainly from the employee compensation account, which accounts for two-thirds of parental, but only 40 percent of Mofa GP. Surprising at first glance perhaps, it appears realistic when seen against the following background: parents have to maintain typical overhead staff not found in affiliates at all or at least not to the same extent, ranging from financial functions through research and development to legal, promotional, and ultimately even the production area with quality control, etc.

Also, U.S. compensation levels were 30 to 50 percent higher between 1977 and 1989. Another area where Mofa GP ranks visibly below parent shares is in the CCA category due to the much higher asset levels maintained by parents.

All other GP accounts play more important roles for Mofas than parents. Indirect taxes, which in dollar terms are almost equal for parents and affiliates, carry three times the weight in the affiliate picture. They reflect different taxing philosophies between the United States and outside world. The value-added tax (VAT), for example, is an extra burden on all levels of industry outside the United States, as is the existence of production royalties levied on resource depletion by many oil nations. Affiliate profit type returns also rank about twice as high as they do in parent GP. In summary, Mofa GP is driven by profits and taxes, and parent GP primarily by employee compensation (see Table 7.13).

The discussion provides other interesting insights into the forces driving American FDI in the past. The obvious sales stagnation of parents and Mofas alike during the late 1980s and early 1990s, which reflected the global recession, resulted in a 77 percent reduction in parent income between 1989 and 1992, but only 10 percent for Mofas.

By linking all these pieces of information together and proving that total Mofa output per employee averages often dramatically rise above parent achievements, with compensation and asset levels substantially below those of their parents, reveals the true rationale behind FDI. Given the very same competitive management know-how, U.S. FDI can develop markedly higher levels of productivity and profitability, as well as a more stable economic performance because of market diversification than is possible at home. In its ultimate consequence, this is also an eye-opening revelation about the comparative competitiveness of parents and their own affiliates.

TABLE 7.13. GP Components for Parents and Mofas

	Total	Employee Compens.	Profit-type Return	Net Interest	Indirect Taxes	CCA
($ billion)						
1977						
Parents	$490.5	$305.5	$103.4	$9.8	$32.6	$39.2
Mofas	161.1	59.5	52.2	2.8	35.4	11.2
1982						
Parents	796.0	520.4	121.1	10.7	63.0	80.9
Mofas	223.7	89.4	54.9	−.4	62.3	17.5
1989						
Parents	1,044.9	666.2	164.9	26.3	66.6	120.8
Mofas	319.9	132.6	86.5	−5.0	78.9	27.0
Percentages						
1977						
Parents	100.0	62.3	21.1	2.0	6.6	8.0
Mofas	100.0	37.0	32.4	1.7	22.0	7.0
1982						
Parents	100.0	66.0	14.9	0.2	8.0	10.8
Mofas	100.0	40.0	24.5	NMF	27.8	7.8
1989						
Parents	100.0	63.8	15.8	2.5	6.4	11.6
Mofas	100.0	41.6	27.0	NMF	24.7	8.4
Mofa %						
1977	32.8	19.5	50.5	28.6	108.6	28.6
1982	28.1	17.2	45.3	NMF	98.9	21.6
1989	30.6	19.9	52.4	NMF	118.5	22.4

Sources: Parent and Mofa data: *SOCB*, February 1994, pp. 47, 53.

Chapter 8

Commercial Dimensions
of U.S. FDI

AFFILIATE SALES

Pursuing profits internationally leaves the choice between trading or investment activities. If deciding for the latter, portfolio or direct investments are the avenues of choice. Investors seeking a direct return on their exported capital in the form of dividends or interest income opt for the portfolio type of investment, that is, ownership of stocks, bonds, or municipal/government securities. Active participation in the management of the investment is neither desired nor exercised.

Foreign direct investment, though motivated by the same quest for profits, differs in several key aspects: it expressedly seeks to exercise full or partial ownership control over foreign production and marketing organizations, active rather than passive resource management, and risk taking in order to achieve potentially more rewarding returns on the funds committed.

Unlike portfolio investment, foreign direct investment can generate profits only indirectly through sales of goods and services, which are the lifeblood of all business organizations because they carry life-sustaining profits. This is a fundamental relationship whose importance was not properly recognized by government accountants, especially not in the earlier years, with the consequence that a great deal of financial information on earnings, income, taxes, other expenses, etc., is available but not on sales.

Unfortunately, this has led to the partial or total loss of such vital data for many years under study. As far as can be established, sales statistics were tabulated for the first time ever in the 1955 census of Latin American affiliates, and the first fairly complete worldwide sales report appeared in the 1957 survey. It initiated a nearly regular flow of such information until the 1977 census, when it stopped completely for four years. Reporting resumed with the 1982 census. All in all, complete sales information exists for five census years, no data are available for thirteen years, and only partial information for the remainder of the period (1950-1994).

The 1966 survey became a landmark in sales reporting. It marked the beginning of a relatively complete, detailed and consistent annual sales series. It also introduced Mofas, the affiliate group highlighted throughout this report. Mofas accounted for 93 percent of all direct investment dollars, and an 88 percent share in total affiliate sales in 1966.

Besides Mofa sales, the 1966 census provided details not seen before for exports to parents and other U.S. customers, as well as affiliates and foreigners in third markets. Information value was also enhanced by details for local sales to affiliates and unrelated foreigners in the country of affiliate location.

The 1977 census introduced another refinement in sales reporting by separating bank and nonbank businesses to account for the fact that banks do not produce sales, but only income.

As time went on, government researchers not only increased the amount and detail of information available, but also its quality. Until 1977, for instance, affiliate exports to all destinations, including the United States, were reported under the assumption that export sales and shipments were synonymous. This notion was dispelled at the time of the 1977 census, when monumental differences between the two values were unearthed by researchers trying to reconcile affiliate sales to U.S. customers with official trade statistics.

Small discrepancies are nothing unusual. First, there is always a time lag between sale, shipment, and arrival of merchandise. Second, affiliate export sales may also contain services, which usually do not lead to shipments. Third, the same can be said for merchandise sales to other countries, which are mere paper transactions not followed by actual export shipments from the seller. There is also a theoretical possibility, that the buyer takes possession in the country of sale and handles the shipments within his own country. In both cases, affiliates would not get involved in shipping and produce no export records. All of this is familiar to the experienced international executive. What makes these latter transactions interesting is the relationship between buyer and seller. If it involves unrelated companies, they are transactions as usual. If, however, separate divisions of the same company are involved, it touches the cryptic subject of international profit management.

Another point concerns the industry breakdown of sales. The oil industry's treatment as one integrated unit instead of three separate ones is by now a familiar topic. It makes direct comparisons with U.S. domestic and international statistics difficult, not to mention the distortions caused for the extractive, manufacturing, and trade industries which normally harbor these components.

DEVELOPMENT OF AFFILIATE SALES BY AREA

Between 1950 and 1993, sales of all affiliates grew more than seventy-fold from an estimated $21.0 billion to over $1.5 trillion–a growth which compares positively with a fourty-seven-fold increase in the direct investment stock. Both figures reflect monetary values which are subject to the effects of inflation, currency fluctuations, and changing accounting procedures.

In order to get a reasonable footing in understanding affiliate sales, an estimate had to be developed for the base year 1950. For this purpose, the 1957 benchmark survey was used, despite minor flaws indicated earlier. Parameters used in this face-lifting exercise included the asset/sales ratio (1957: 1.06:1) which put 1950 sales at $20.9 billion; the direct investment stock to sales ratio (1957: 1:1.8) which suggests 1950 sales of $21.2 billion; and finally, the income/sales ratio (1957: 1:12.2) resulting in estimated sales of $21.6 billion for 1950. Averaging all three numbers led to the final estimate of $21.2 billion.

The underlying assumption is, of course, that the basic relationship of all parameters did not change significantly during those seven short years which, in view of the very stable economic and political conditions as well as the practically fixed exchange markets, appears to be fairly realistic.

Doing this kind of reconstruction work inevitably leads to the observation of parallels in the development of sales and direct investment levels by geographical areas, while the time periods are measured in decades rather than shorter time spans. In the latter case, wide variations between the two may exist, but ultimately they are forced to converge.

Latin America and Canada, for instance, tended to have a higher share in the investment stock than in affiliate sales from the 1950s to the 1980s. Canadian shares for both categories narrowed their gap during the late 1980s, while Latin America's shares were as far apart as ever, even though they temporarily narrowed during the early 1980s. The strongly diverging series in the later years were caused by the special investment situation of this area documented before. Europe exhibited exactly the opposite picture. Here as the sales share was consistently above the investment share until the middle of the 1970s, when both began to narrow, only to open the gap again toward the end of the period (early 1990s). Africa and Oceania have always maintained a close correlation among both levels. Because of the distorting oil factor, Asia displayed a completely separate pattern. Sales shares were far above investment shares until the late 1970s, when they abruptly fell into line as a consequence of the Middle Eastern disinvestments. At that time, more capital was repatriated than had historically been accumulated on the books.

While the relative area shares in total sales and investments may diverge considerably for lengthy periods of time, they normally tend to travel in the same direction. That is to say, they both go up or down in unison. The only exception is the Middle East and in its wake, Asia, where oil investments have created a very unique situation.

These observations raise the question about the chicken and the egg. Which factor triggers the development of the other? Are investments the dependent variable or sales? From a superficial glance at the tables, it appears that sales are pushing or, better yet, pulling investments whose share developments trail those of sales. This is very evident in all geographical areas, but Latin America is a perfect demonstration of the point. Here, the steady decline in sales shares from 20 percent in 1957 to 10 percent in 1993 eventually pulls down the less responsive investment shares from 32 to 19 percent.

The reverse situation is found in Europe where disproportionately high and fast growing sales shares still run ahead of laggard investment shares. Such share imbalances tend to drift toward an equilibrium after prolonged adjustment processes which, for U.S. investments, have empirically lasted about two decades (see Table 8.1).

Support for the hypothesis of sales leading investments comes also from other quarters. Import substitution policies, for example, have forced investments in a country or face loss of established markets. Also, in the section discussing the development and uses of FDI income, it was shown that after a certain development stage, U.S. FDI tends to be funded predominantly from retained earnings, which can only come from local sales. Sales serve a proxy function in their observed tandem relationship with investments as, in actuality, it is the profit portion of those sales that triggers investments.

Global affiliate sales grew for all years with the exception of the early 1980s which, no doubt, was caused by the strong dollar and the recession after OPEC. The general upward movement of sales prior to that time, and thereafter, was not shared uniformly by all regions though, as evidenced by their share development. In view of the uneven investment patterns discussed earlier, this is not unexpected (see Table 8.2).

Europe is the growth area that sets the pace for the rest of the world in both data series. Canada's investment base is still shrinking in relative

TABLE 8.1. Geographical Distribution of Affiliate Sales and Investments (percentages/world = 100%)

Year	Canada		Lat. America		Europe		Africa		Asia		Oceania	
	Inv.	Sales	Inv.	Sales	Inv.	Sales	Inv.	Sales	Inv.	Sales	Inv.	Sales
1957	34.6	31.1	31.7	20.2	16.3	29.6	2.6	2.7	8.2	9.5	2.5	3.2
1966	30.3	24.4	18.8	14.6	31.6	41.4	3.5	3.2	6.8	9.6	3.8	3.9
1967	29.5	24.6	18.2	14.6	32.2	40.7	3.5	3.4	7.2	9.4	4.2	3.9
1968	29.0	24.8	18.3	14.4	32.1	40.4	3.9	3.6	7.6	9.8	4.3	3.9
1969	28.8	24.2	17.6	14.0	32.6	41.4	4.0	3.7	7.0	10.1	4.3	4.0
1970	27.8	22.3	17.2	12.8	33.5	43.8	4.2	3.7	7.0	10.1	4.4	4.1
1971	26.3	23.3	16.9	11.6	34.6	44.0	4.2	3.4	6.6	11.7	4.5	4.0
1972	25.6	22.9	16.6	13.5	35.3	45.2	4.2	3.3	1.2	12.7	4.6	3.7
1973	25.2	19.4	16.3	11.4	37.9	43.7	3.5	3.2	4.0	15.3	4.5	3.7
1974	25.6	16.3	17.7	11.8	40.6	37.9	3.4	N/A	4.7	23.6	4.6	N/A
1975	25.0	17.1	17.9	12.5	39.8	40.7	3.2	3.2	4.1	20.3	4.4	3.2
1977	24.0	16.7	18.8	11.5	42.8	43.4	2.6	3.7	4.7	18.7	4.7	3.1
1982	20.9	14.8	13.5	14.2	47.9	49.9	3.1	3.2	10.6	12.5	4.7	4.2
1983	21.3	16.9	11.6	12.2	44.5	50.3	N/A	N/A	12.1	12.4	N/A	N/A
1984	22.0	18.2	11.8	11.6	43.4	49.7	N/A	N/A	13.2	12.6	N/A	N/A
1985	20.4	18.3	12.3	11.1	45.7	51.1	2.6	N/A	12.7	12.0	4.1	N/A
1986	19.5	17.4	14.2	10.3	46.5	55.1	2.1	N/A	12.2	11.2	3.8	N/A
1987	18.4	16.7	15.2	9.1	47.7	56.7	1.9	N/A	11.7	11.8	3.9	N/A
1988	18.7	16.8	15.9	9.0	46.7	56.5	1.6	N/A	12.0	12.0	4.1	N/A
1989	16.7	16.9	16.2	8.6	49.6	56.2	1.0	1.1	11.5	12.6	4.0	4.0
1990	16.2	12.7	16.6	8.7	49.9	54.2	0.8	1.1	12.1	18.4	4.2	4.3
1991	16.1	12.2	16.6	8.2	50.3	54.5	0.9	1.1	12.4	19.3	4.1	4.1
1992	13.8	11.7	18.2	9.5	49.3	54.2	0.9	1.1	13.1	18.9	4.0	4.2
1993	12.8	12.2	18.6	10.2	49.0	51.5	1.0	1.0	14.1	20.4	3.9	4.1

TABLE 8.2. Affiliate Sales by World Area ($ billion)

Year	Total	Canada	Lat. Am.	Europe	Africa	Asia	Mid. East	Oceania
1950	$21.2e	N/A	N/A	N/A	N/A	N/A	N/A	N/A
1957	43.8	$13.6	$8.9	$13.0	$1.2	$4.2	$1.8	$1.4
1966	97.8	23.9	14.3	40.5	3.2	9.4	4.0	3.9
1967	108.5	26.7	15.8	44.2	3.7	0.3	4.2	4.2
1968	120.8	29.9	17.4	49.0	4.3	11.9	4.7	4.7
1969	134.3	32.5	18.8	55.8	4.9	13.6	5.3	5.3
1970	155.9	34.8	20.0	68.4	5.7	15.7	5.8	6.4
1971	184.4	42.9	21.4	81.2	6.4	21.5	8.9	7.4
1972	212.3	48.7	28.7	95.9	7.0	26.9	11.1	7.9
1973	291.4	56.5	33.3	127.3	9.3	44.6	22.2	10.7
1974	437.7	71.4	51.6	165.8	N/A	103.4	64.1	N/A
1975	458.3	78.5	57.2	186.5	14.5	93.2	53.7	14.8
1977	507.0	84.7	58.2	220.2	19.0	94.9	62.9	15.6
1982	730.2	108.0	103.9	364.4	23.6	91.4	16.7	30.8
1983	705.8	119.6	86.3	355.3	N/A	87.8	15.7	N/A
1984	717.4	130.4	83.0	355.7	N/A	90.2	15.0	N/A
1985	702.8	129.1	78.3	358.7	N/A	84.3	12.2	N/A
1986	720.2	124.9	74.0	396.6	N/A	80.9	9.5	N/A
1987	815.5	135.5	74.0	463.1	N/A	95.9	9.1	N/A
1988	928.4	156.3	83.4	525.1	N/A	111.6	7.9	N/A
1989	1,019.9	173.3	87.0	573.3	11.6	128.7	8.0	40.9
1990	1,208.3	178.7	102.9	712.4	13.8	130.8	6.7	43.8
1991	1,242.6	177.0	103.0	733.9	13.5	166.3	8.2	42.6
1992	1,291.6	174.9	115.5	758.5	14.1	181.5	9.3	41.4
1993	1,279.1	182.4	120.5	716.0	13.6	200.4	7.9	40.0

Notes: Data for 1950 and 1970 cover all affiliates; other years represent Mofa sales; 1957 data exclude finance, insurance, and trade. e = estimate.

Sources: 1957 FDI census, pp. 110-2. 1966 FDI census, p. 199. *SOCB*, August 1975, p. 26 (1966-72); February 1977, p. 32 (1973-75). 1977 FDI census, p. 318. 1982 FDI census, p. 225. *SOCB*, September 1986, pp. 36-7 (1983-84); June 1988, pp. 94-6 (1985-86); June 1990, pp. 40-1 (1987-88); August 1992, p. 75 (1989-92); July 1993, pp. 53-4; June 1994, p. 55; June 1995, pp. 44-5.

terms, bringing it into line with declining sales shares. Both have fallen substantially from their historic highs, but may be revived again with the implementation of NAFTA. Asia's role as a growth promoter during the 1970s has gained new vigor after a hiatus in both categories during the 1980s. Oceania is pretty much following suit with no special trends visible in either direction.

Africa is the only real loser as both investment and sales shares are steadily falling. Latin America plays a very ambiguous role with investment shares rising, but sales declining. This is not as paradoxical as it may seem, because of the rising investments in the Caribbean service industries and the relatively declining importance of the continental affiliates mentioned before (see Table 8.1).

Affiliates in the Middle East are atypical of any of the above instances as they not only lost shares, but lost heavily in actual dollar volume as well. Historically part of the Asian area, their sales went into a decline after the mid-1970s and produced the negative effect for the whole area. Published data do not make it clear which country or countries were responsible for this setback, but they identify the petroleum industry as the chief cause whose sales volume plummeted from $62.5 billion in 1974 to barely $8 billion in 1993 for an 88 percent loss. Saudi Arabia must have been the chief cause of the decline, but a complementary role for other countries cannot be ruled out (see Table 8.2).

Asian sales statistics do reflect the full impact of these developments, even though some of the petroleum business was shifted to other countries in the region, notably Indonesia, Singapore, Malaysia, Hong Kong, and the Philippines. Actual dollar sales of petroleum products by these Asian affiliates were down from $85.5 billion in 1974 to $28.7 billion in 1986 despite the second OPEC price increase between the two periods. Adjusted for Middle East data, Asian sales in 1986 of $23.4 billion were around the 1974 level of $23.0 billion. The stagnation in the petroleum sector was partially offset by the strong expansion of investments in other industries such as manufacturing and trade.

Previous discussions mentioned the special status of Anglo-Saxon countries. They are noteworthy in this discussion in that, taken as a group, they do not show the stated close correlation between sales and investment levels, even over extended periods of time. Comparing the sales data below with Table 1.4 in the investment section shows them to remain constantly and significantly below those suggested by their relative investment levels except for 1957.

Looking at individual countries, a very mixed picture emerges. The UK, Australia, New Zealand, and South Africa tend to conform nicely to the expected affinity of sales and investment shares over time. However, Canada has a history of deviating strongly from the rule for most of the four decades, even though in the end it shows the typical narrowing of the tenacious gaps, all of which leaves the affiliates in the Caribbean as the cause of the group's atypical profile. Their low sales to investment ratio can largely be explained by the fact that the vast majority of investments here are concentrated in financial institutions, and thus far removed from the typical industry mix prevailing in the other nations. The group's decline in overall affiliate sales is led by Canada and the UK, with serious share losses of their own (see Table 8.3).

Of interest is the fact that only twelve countries have persistently accounted for two-thirds or more of affiliate sales, even though the list of names and the rank order has changed over time. More remarkably, the four leaders of the group remained the same between 1957 and 1993. They were Canada and the UK, which traded the number one and two spot; Germany and France, whose aggregate sales share went from 51.8 percent in 1957 to 51.3 in 1966, 39.3 in 1977, 44.5 in 1982, and finally, back up to 47.7 percent in 1993. Canada's 50 percent loss of share between 1957 and 1993 explains the interim dip, as the other three countries did not grow fast enough to fully offset the decline.

Phenomenal gains in sales shares have been posted by Japan, Italy, Germany, Switzerland, and the Netherlands, each whose share has at least doubled over four decades. Latin American countries in general fared poorly. They were represented by four countries in 1957, of which only Mexico remained on the list in 1993. A really distinguished fatality is Cuba, whose once prominent position in the investment and sales area has disappeared altogether with the nationalization of foreign assets after the communist takeover. It should play a more important role once more in the near future, even though it can never reach a position comparable to the one it had then. South Africa was the continent's sole representative in the earlier years, but has disappeared completely from the list with political reasons outweighing its economic potential.

Asia was represented by two countries, despite strong development in the area as a whole. Despite this, too many nations share in the overall sales position to help individual ones appear on the list. Japan's rank is

TABLE 8.3. Affiliate Sales in Anglo-Saxon Countries (percentage of all affiliate sales)

	1957	1970	1977	1982	1989	1993
Australia	2.7	3.8	2.8	3.9	3.7	3.7
Canada	31.1	22.3	16.7	14.8	16.9	12.3
New Zealand	0.4	0.3	0.2	0.3	0.3	0.4
South Africa	1.3	1.3	0.9	1.1	0.3	0.3
United Kingdom	10.7	11.9	11.0	14.8	16.5	12.9
Bahamas	N/A	0.2	0.5	0.8	0.2	0.1
Bermuda	N/A	0.2	2.3	2.7	1.1	0.1
UK Caribbean	N/A	N/A	N/A	0.1	0.1	0.1
Grand Total	46.2	40.0	34.4	38.5	39.1	29.9

notably small in view of its economic stature in the world, but climbing rapidly. Somehow, it does not fit the picture of a nation closing itself to outside influences, as Washington's official rhetoric tries to portray it.

The unexpected reduction in sales share experienced by the twelve leading affiliate countries between 1966 and 1977 from 73 to 66 percent is due to the explosive jump in Middle Eastern sales in 1977, sparked by OPEC inflation and possibly, also, in anticipation of the U.S. disinvestment noted for 1980. Country details are not available for that region, but Saudi Arabia must be assumed to be the main cause of the temporary decline in the group's share (see Table 8.4).

PROFILE OF AFFILIATE SALES

Available sales statistics permit the coverage of a variety of related topics which will be discussed in the following sequence:

1. Sales by type of affiliate–all affiliates versus Mofas
2. Sales by customer group–other affiliates and foreigners
3. Sales by destination–domestic sales versus exports
4. Sales by industry of affiliate
5. Combinations of the above

In view of the variability of the database, not all of the suggested topics can be presented in the same format for all years, which imposes some restrictions on the comparability of the information.

SALES BY TYPE OF AFFILIATE

Aggregate sales data for all affiliates exist for a total of fifteen years. Mofa sales, introduced in 1966, have been published more frequently and are available for fully twenty-four years between 1966 and 1993, roughly half of the time period covered in this study. They have the advantage of being all-inclusive for more years than total affiliate data and, therefore, are more useful. It is for this reason, and also the fact that Mofas alone represent the true American element in foreign countries, that their data will be given preferential attention in the following (see Table 8.5).

A major modification in the data for both affiliate categories came with the 1977 survey, which introduced the strict separation of bank and non-bank data for all FDI statistics as mentioned earlier. Table 8.5 displays all

TABLE 8.4. The Twelve Leading Affiliate Countries in Sales ($ billion)

1957			1966		
Total	$43.8	100.0%	Total	$97.8	100.0%
Canada	13.6	31.1	Canada	23.9	24.4
UK	4.7	10.7	UK	13.4	13.7
Germany	1.8	4.1	Germany	7.7	7.9
France	1.6	3.7	France	5.3	5.4
Brazil	1.3	3.0	Australia	3.5	3.6
Australia	1.2	2.7	Venezuela	3.2	3.3
Mexico	1.0	2.3	Italy	3.2	3.3
Italy	0.8	1.8	Switzerland	2.8	2.9
Cuba	0.7	1.6	Brazil	2.2	2.2
South Africa	0.6	1.4	Netherlands	2.1	2.2
Japan	0.6	1.4	Japan	2.1	2.1
Argentina	0.5	1.1	Belg./Lux.	2.0	2.0
Subtotal	28.4	64.7%	Subtotal	71.4	73.0%
1977			**1993**		
Total	507.0	100.0%	Total	1,279.1	100.0%
Canada	84.7	16.7	UK	186.5	14.6
UK	55.9	11.0	Canada	182.4	14.3
Germany	48.0	9.5	Germany	147.8	11.6
France	28.5	5.6	France	92.3	7.2
Netherlands	17.1	3.4	Japan	81.9	6.4
Brazil	16.6	3.3	Netherlands	60.4	4.7
Switzerland	16.6	3.3	Italy	50.0	3.9
Belg./Lux.	15.4	3.0	Switzerland	47.1	3.7
Australia	14.5	2.9	Singapore	38.3	3.0
Italy	14.1	2.8	Belg./Lux.	36.8	2.9
Japan	13.2	2.6	Australia	36.4	2.8
Bermuda	11.9	2.3	Mexico	32.7	2.6
Subtotal	336.5	66.4%	Subtotal	992.6	77.6%

Notes: Total and Canada data include trade industry; all other countries do not, which underrepresents their share. With the exception of 1957, all data represent Mofa sales.

Sources: 1957 FDI census, pp. 40, 110-1. 1966 FDI census, p. 198. 1977 FDI census, p. 318. *SOCB*, June 1995, p. 45 (1993).

accessible information, which divulges two surprising facts. For one thing, it discloses Mofa sales to be steadily declining relative to those of all affiliates from 88 percent in 1966 to around 81 percent in 1993. Equally unexpected was the stagnant sales picture for both affiliate categories between 1990 and 1993, which was hard to reconcile with the 44 percent

TABLE 8.5. Summary of Sales by Type of Affiliate ($ million)

Year	All Affiliates	Mofas	Mofa Share
1957	$43,795	N/A	N/A
1966	110,686	$97,783	88.3%
1967	N/A	108,509	N/A
1968	N/A	120,758	N/A
1969	N/A	134,316	N/A
1970	N/A	155,914	N/A
1971	N/A	184,411	N/A
1972	N/A	212,334	N/A
1973	N/A	291,354	N/A
1974	N/A	437,685	N/A
1975	N/A	458,310	N/A
1977	647,969	507,019	78.2
1982	935,780	730,235	78.0
1983	886,314	705,811	79.7
1984	898,558	716,410	79.6
1985	895,460	702,837	78.5
1986	928,915	720,069	77.5
1987	1,052,795	815,541	77.5
1988	1,194,733	928,417	77.7
1989	1,284,894	1,019,966	79.3
1990	1,493,426	1,208,349	80.9
1991	1,541,566	1,242,635	80.6
1992	1,574,069	1,291,649	82.1
1993	1,573,891	1,279,119	81.3

Sources: FDI census data: 1957, pp. 110-1; 1966, pp. 167, 197; 1977, pp. 138, 282, 319, 352; 1982, pp. 110-2, 226, 281. *SOCB*, August 1975, pp. 26-7 (1967-72); February 1977, p. 32 (1973-75); September 1986, pp. 33, 36 (1983); June 1988, p. 96 (1984-86); June 1990, pp. 36, 40-3 (1987-88); August 1992, pp. 62, 68 (1989-93); July 1993, pp. 42, 46; June 1994, pp. 54-6; June 1995, pp. 43-5.

expansion in the investment position during the 1989 to 1993 period. It is hard to imagine that the $167 billion were spent only for upgrading existing plant, equipment, and for more efficient operations. But it looks very much like this is exactly what happened–an explanation that fits also smoothly with information provided in Table 7.12 which shows Mofa employment to be unchanged between 1977 and 1993. If the main goal of all that investment activity was increased operating efficiency rather than expansion in the market coverage and competitive stature, then that same table provides discouraging news, as it shows net income per employee to be equally stagnant since the late 1980s. But that performance is still better than the decline in the per capita data shown for their parent organizations (see page 248).

AFFILIATE SALES BY CUSTOMER GROUP

Mofa sales may be further desegregated into sales made to other affiliates and unrelated foreigners. The term affiliate covers parents, local subsidiaries of U.S. corporations in overseas markets, and affiliates in third countries. The terms nonrelated, nonaffiliated, and unaffiliated foreigners on the other hand, are interchangeable and designate all those customers that are not U.S. FDI members. Similar to the affiliate situation they may be located in the country of the selling affiliate, the United States, or in other export markets. Information to this effect is on record for the four census years 1966, 1977, 1982, 1989, the noncensus years 1984-88 and 1990-93, and covers only Mofas.

Mofa business with other affiliates amounts to a steady 20 to 25 percent of their overall sales in the latest period (early 1990s). The term other affiliates should be interpreted to mean inclusion of sales to affiliates of the same, but also unrelated American companies. In the first case, transfer pricing may affect the valuation of merchandise shipped or services rendered. This does not infer that pricing is always (and uniformly) higher or lower than among unaffiliated customers, which in any individual case would depend on a number of different factors. All that is pointed out here is the possibility of transfer pricing being invoked if it leads to higher profits for the organization. In all cases of trading with nonaffiliates, this point is moot, and normal market pricing may be assumed.

Interesting is the fairly even progression in Mofa business with affiliates from 19 to 25 percent over almost three decades. The sudden and atypical peak of 33 percent recorded in 1977 must have been caused by the escalation in oil prices during that period, when the U.S. investment base in this industry was still intact. Oil may again be suspected as influencing the pronounced slowdown of Mofa sales to affiliates and foreigners alike during the early 1990s, which were marked by crude prices at half the level prevailing during OPEC's reign.

Sales of goods normally are followed by shipments to domestic and export customers. As will be shown later, this is not necessarily the case, thus providing one of the more puzzling aspects of American FDI. Sometimes discrepancies between the two figures are so large that America's real position in international trade, for instance, cannot be defined with an acceptable degree of believability. But this subject will be raised again in more detail in the following pages (see Table 8.6).

TABLE 8.6. Mofa Sales to Major Customer Groups ($ billion)

Year	Total	Affiliates	%	Foreigners	%
1966	$97.8	$18.7	19.1	$79.1	80.9
1977	507.0	168.0	33.1	338.9	66.9
1982	730.2	159.9	21.9	570.4	78.1
1984	717.4	173.5	24.2	543.9	75.8
1985	702.8	171.5	24.4	531.3	75.6
1986	720.1	171.3	23.8	548.7	76.2
1987	815.5	198.9	24.4	616.7	75.6
1988	927.9	226.6	24.5	701.3	75.5
1989	1,109.9	246.2	24.1	773.8	75.9
1990	1,208.3	287.7	23.8	920.6	76.2
1991	1,242.6	296.7	23.9	945.9	76.1
1992	1,291.6	320.2	24.8	971.5	75.2
1993	1,279.1	319.7	25.0	959.4	75.0

Sources: FDI census data: 1966, p. 198; 1977, pp. 318, 352; 1982, pp. 225, 281. *SOCB*, June 1988, p. 96 (1984-86); June 1990, p. 43 (1986-88); October 1991, p. 40 (1988-89); August 1992, p. 68 (1989-93); July 1993, p. 46; June 1994, p. 51; June 1995, p. 40.

INTERAFFILIATE SALES

Information about the two basic customer groups shown above can be expanded to offer more details for three major affiliate categories involved. Sales among affiliates, which account for about 24 percent of all Mofa sales, are addressed first to provide insights on the following topics:

1. Sales to affiliates domiciled in the same country
2. Sales to parent companies in the United States
3. Sales to affiliates in other countries

Business transactions among affiliates have obviously undergone important changes. Over the twenty-seven-year period covered, sales to local affiliates have dropped from 25 percent to around 13 percent during the beginning of the 1990s. Mofa sales to U.S. parents have grown from 25 to 35 percent regarding the all-time high of 50 percent in 1977 as nonrepresentative. This left businesses with affiliates in third countries within a farily steady range of 45 to 55 percent with the noted exception of 1977.

In other words, between 85 to 90 percent of all interaffiliate business is conducted between Mofas and affiliate organizations outside their own home territory, thus contributing substantially to international trade in goods and services.

Looking at the developments in actual dollars reveals another interesting facet about the interaffiliate business. After 1977, Mofa sales to local affiliates and U.S. parents lost ground to rapidly growing business with affiliates in third countires, which reduced their share in total sales practically until the present (see Table 8.7).

The shifts cannot directly be explained with the data provided, which leaves their interpretation open to speculation, as a number of diverse factors may have affected the developments. Sales to affiliates in the same country, for instance, were certainly reduced by recessionary pressures following the double OPEC onslaught during the 1970s. Invoiced in local currencies, they were further subjected to the depressive effect of the strong dollar during the first half of the 1980s. Economic recovery and the falling dollar in the second half of the decade set the stage for steadier, and slightly growing, actual dollar sales and shares toward the end of the period (late 1980s, early 1990s).

TABLE 8.7. Mofa Sales to Affiliates by Area ($ billion)

Year	World	Country*	%	U.S.A.	%	Other	%
1966	$18.7	$4.6	24.6	$4.6	24.6	$9.5	50.8
1977	168.0	34.1	20.3	84.2	50.1	49.8	29.6
1982	159.9	28.1	17.6	63.6	39.8	68.2	42.6
1984	173.5	24.3	14.0	75.8	43.6	73.4	42.2
1985	171.5	23.8	13.9	74.7	43.4	73.1	42.6
1986	171.3	21.4	12.5	66.6	38.9	83.3	48.7
1987	198.9	25.7	12.9	73.8	37.1	99.4	49.9
1988	226.6	30.9	13.7	82.2	36.2	113.5	50.1
1989	246.2	39.0	15.8	92.9	37.8	114.2	46.3
1990	297.7	37.9	12.7	98.5	33.1	151.4	52.6
1991	296.7	39.8	13.4	98.9	33.3	158.0	53.3
1992	320.2	42.5	13.3	103.2	32.2	174.5	54.5
1993	319.7	41.6	13.0	110.3	34.5	167.8	52.5

Note: *of the Mofa location.

Sources: See sources for Table 8.6.

Mofa sales to their U.S. parents and affiliates in the rest of the world follow a different line of reasoning. With the exception of oil affiliates, their business can be conducted in any chosen currency. In the case of a stronger dollar, sales to the U.S. market will most likely be invoiced in U.S. currency, which makes sourcing from affiliates ever more attractive for U.S. customers, as now they are getting more for each dollar spent, but also for the affiliates themselves whose earnings are aided by business transactions in an appreciating currency. All of which leads to the visible trade expansion in relative terms during the early 1980s. Facing a weaker dollar, affiliates are likely to abandon that strategy and invoice in local currency where possible, as now additional profits are to be made in dollars by holding on to the appreciating currency. This causes their products to become expensive for U.S. customers and, consequently, results in a relatively reduced trade volume, which again is clearly demonstrated for the years after 1985. Further, there can be no doubt that the oil price extremes for the whole period have left their mark in the development of all these shares.

The Mofa trade pattern with third country affiliates probably follows a similar course. Currency strategies are certainly part of their trade relations, but may be much more flexible than in the U.S. case, again, with the exception of the oil business which is solely conducted in dollars. To some degree, the picture is also influenced by affiliate business exposed to the ups and downs in all the markets they deal with, including that of the United States. As that trade grows in terms of total Mofa sales to all affiliates, it leads to a relative deemphasis of all other business shares by definition (see Table 8.7).

AFFILIATE SALES TO FOREIGNERS

Sales to unrelated business partners account for 75 percent of Mofa sales; this is three times the volume generated by sister affiliates, as mentioned earlier. They may be subdivided in a manner similar to the interaffiliate business by stressing affiliate sales to: (a) foreigners in the affiliate's country; (b) nonrelated business partners in the United States; and (c) foreigners in the rest of the world.

The first and most striking difference between interaffiliate and unrelated customer sales lies in the complete role reversal of the local market. While sales to affiliates in the same country were not only the smallest part of Mofa sales to other American subsidiaries, declining at that in relative terms from 25 to 13 percent, there is a steady and high 80 percent share for local transactions in the total business with foreigners.

The second inversion concerns the business conducted with the United States where nonaffiliates maintain a very small but rock solid share just under 3 percent of the total compared to the 33 percent parent share in the interaffiliate business. Parents obviously maintain strict control over all transactions within their home markets by carefully channeling most affiliate business to or through their own organization. Finally, sales to foreigners in export markets reach between 10 and 20 percent of the total, and do not even come close to the 50 percent of the business transacted among affiliates in this market segment.

In summary, the paramount purpose of Mofas is selling to independent customers. Those in the affiliate's country come first, those in third countries second, and U.S. customers last. In their business with affiliates, Mofas serve third world markets first, the United States second, and the home market last (see Table 8.8).

AFFILIATE SALES BY INDUSTRY

Sales for all affiliates by industry have been published irregularly since 1957. Complete coverage is available for twenty-four years between 1950 and 1993, or slightly more than 50 percent of the time span covered, with another seven years of data for the manufacturing industries only provided

TABLE 8.8. Mofa Sales to Nonaffiliates by Area ($ billion)

Year	World	Country	%	U.S.A.	%	Other	%
1966	$79.1	$68.8	87.0	$1.7	2.1	$8.6	10.9
1977	338.9	279.2	82.3	9.4	2.8	50.4	14.9
1982	570.4	449.8	78.9	13.2	2.3	107.3	18.8
1984	543.9	431.7	79.4	13.3	2.4	98.9	18.1
1985	531.3	424.8	80.0	14.3	2.7	92.1	17.3
1986	548.7	450.4	82.1	13.3	2.4	85.0	15.5
1987	616.7	513.7	83.4	15.2	2.5	87.9	14.2
1988	701.3	575.4	82.0	19.2	2.7	106.7	15.2
1989	773.8	651.5	84.2	21.8	2.8	100.5	13.0
1990	920.6	771.6	83.8	25.4	2.8	123.6	13.4
1991	945.9	784.7	83.0	26.7	2.8	134.6	14.2
1992	971.5	814.3	83.7	26.1	2.7	131.1	13.6
1993	959.4	803.2	83.7	27.9	2.9	128.3	13.4

Sources: See sources for Table 8.6.

for the period 1959 to 1965. Mofa data were introduced in the 1966 benchmark survey and are available in complete form covering fifteen years, and in partial form covering another nine years. As in the previous sections, Mofa data will be shown exclusively for all years after 1966.

Between 80 and 90 percent of all Mofa sales fall into three major industrial groups: manufacturing, petroleum, and trade. The trade industry includes both wholesaling and retail outlets up to and including 1977. After that date, only wholesaling data are covered unless otherwise noted. This presents no serious problem, as they reach more than 90 percent of the trade industry when both are combined.

Historically, manufacturing was the sales leader with close to half of the total until the early 1970s, when the first oil crisis brought major changes. After the OPEC debacle, manufacturing's share declined from 50 percent in 1970 to a low of 34 percent in 1985 before recovering its former position by 1988. Most of the loss was petroleum's gain whose share went from 27 percent in 1970 to a high of 42 percent in 1974 before settling back to under 20 percent by the end of the period. The data demonstrate how the fates of both industries are intertwined to a degree not shown for the rest of the industries (see Table 8.13).

Official accounting procedures and industrial classification in use play a significant role in this picture. As mentioned throughout, trade and manufacturing affiliate data are really underreported by pulling all oil subsidiaries together in one group which encompasses extraction, manufacturing, and trade activities. Table 8.9 highlights the different components of oil sales as reported in official statistics, which are then regrouped in Table 8.10 to provide a corrected picture for manufacturing and trade affiliates.

Allocating the basic components of the oil affiliates in this manner is consistent with the U.S. Standard Industrial Classification (SIC) code and

TABLE 8.9. Breakdown of Petroleum Sales ($ billion)

	1977	%	1982	%	1989	%
Oil/Gas Extraction Petroleum/Coal Prod.	$26.9	13.5	$52.5	19.7	$36.1	20.1
Manufacturing	88.2	49.4	97.2	36.5	71.9	40.0
Wholesale Trade	73.0	36.8	107.6	40.4	65.6	36.5
Other	10.5	5.3	9.0	3.4	6.2	3.4
Total	198.6	100.0	266.3	100.0	179.9	100.0

Note: Mofa data.

Sources: 1977 FDI census, p. 283. 1982 FDI census, p. 226. *SOCB*, October 1991, p. 55.

international practice. It thus becomes a legitimate correction, and one that alters dollar volumes and shares among the three industries in a fundamental way for the census years 1977, 1982, and 1989. With this change, manufacturing's lead was never seriously challenged, with trade affiliates moving into a solid second, and crude extraction into a distant third position.

Manufacturing sales are comprised of several subgroups led by non-electric and electric machinery, which are closely followed by transportation equipment (basically automotive), chemicals, foods, and all others. All of them have contributed in varying degrees to affiliate growth. Pacesetters have been chemicals and machinery, while other groups have held their shares or show slightly declining tendencies. Transportation equipment is a prime example of the latter, which is surprising in view of the globally entrenched U.S. automobile industry after World War II. Europe and Japan later exacted their toll on an industry that considered itself immune to competition for too long. Such complacency prevented America from contributing to the advances in automotive technology exemplified by radial tires, fuel injection, fuel economy, wheel suspension, board computers, turbo chargers, all-wheel drivetrains, effective corrosion protection, air bags, ABS brakes, etc. But the past focus on frills, annual model changes, planned obsolescence, and poor aerodynamics is gradually being forced back to attention on innovation and quality.

The example of the automotive industry raises the question as to what degree U.S. FDI was undertaken to commercialize superior American know-how and technology, and to what extent it was prompted by the desire and, indeed, necessity to acquire foreign technology. Or, more precisely, when did

TABLE 8.10. Revised Industry Shares ($ billion)

Year	Petroleum	%	Manufacturing	%	Trade	%
Published Statistics						
1977	$198.6	39	$194.2	38	$77.4	15
1982	266.3	36	271.1	37	113.6	16
1989	179.9	18	504.6	50	204.1	20
Revised Statistics						
1977	37.4	7	282.4	56	150.4	30
1982	61.5	8	368.3	50	221.2	30
1989	36.1	4	576.5	57	269.7	27

the transition from one position to the other occur? In the early period, it was certainly America's technological lead and financial potential that filled the vacuum left by the war. When foreigners gradually caught up, the acquisition of foreign know-how must have become an increasingly important investment factor. Besides market size, of course, this is one of the primary reasons for the concentration in Europe. It also becomes visible in demands for more American access to the Japanese market, whose pioneering and innovative products and production methods have imprinted deeply on U.S. and European auto industries with the kanban system, quality circles, total quality concept, and styling. A brand new lead seems to emerge there in dual-purpose technology–applications equally suited for war and peace.

How America's technological position is changing vis-à-vis the rest of the world can be illustrated by the following information. In 1960, 49,900 patents were issued in the United States, of which 4,700, or 9.4 percent, went to foreigners. The 1970 figures stood at 67,900 and 12,300 or 18.1 percent; in 1980, a total of 66,200 faced 25,400 foreign registrations or 38.4 percent; in 1990, foreigners claimed 46,200 or 46.7 percent of 99,200 patents granted during that year (*Statistical Abstract of the United States*: 1970, p. 528; 1975, p. 556; 1990, p. 535; 1994, p. 552). But there is hope. In 1991, American business, for the first time in twenty-eight years, had more patents issued in the United States than in the previous year, increasing its share to 54 percent of the total of 106,800 issued (see Table 14.4).

Affiliate industries show strong structural variations by geographic area, and by individual country within each, as measured by their regional distribution in census years. They also display significant fluctuations in their industrial mix for a given area when looking at the whole period covered (see Table 8.11).

All of Latin America, for instance, shows a decline in manufacturing, but a relatively increasing oil industry. Focusing on the continental economies of that area, however, reveals exactly the opposite trend. Manufacturing posted strong gains, and the oil industry lost ground during the 1970s and 1980s. The distorted picture for the whole region was caused by affiliates in the Caribbean basin, whose manufacturing industry was insignificant to begin with, and was dwarfed by the growth in oil affiliates. It was an unreal situation, as the islands do not produce one single drop of oil, nor do they offer the market potential for such tremendous sales volumes. Tax advantages created the lopsided business, which consists most likely of paper transactions without physical movement of goods into or through the territories.

TABLE 8.11. Leading Groups in the Manufacturing Industry (% share of industry)

Year	Manufacturing	Food	Chemical	Machinery	Transp. Equipment	Other
1957	100	13.4	13.2	21.6	23.0	28.9
1960	100	12.4	14.0	20.2	26.1	27.2
1965	100	9.5	16.3	22.1	25.4	26.8
1970	100	9.6	16.0	25.6	21.5	27.3
1975	100	9.5	19.6	26.5	19.8	24.7
1982	100	12.0	20.2	24.3	21.1	22.4
1989	100	10.0	18.6	27.5	22.4	21.5
1990	100	10.6	18.6	27.5	18.1	25.2
1991	100	11.8	19.0	26.8	17.6	24.8
1992	100	11.6	19.8	25.8	21.7	21.0
1993	100	12.8	19.3	25.9	17.2	20.8

Affiliate industries in Canada, Europe, the Latin American republics, and Oceania (Australia and New Zealand) as a rule are led by manufacturing, even though there may be major national deviations from the area norm. A good illustration is presented by three European economies that are very similar in size. In the UK, oil affiliates compete with their manufacturing cousins for first place in sales while they engage in integrated production, refining, and marketing activities. Germany, without any oil production of its own, shows sales of manufactured goods running at twice the level of oil affiliates, and in France, there is practically no U.S. oil investment at all, due to a state monopoly.

Asia, Africa, and the Caribbean islands, as typical representatives of developing countries, are dominated by oil. Falling into the same group of nations, the Latin American republics would probably look very similar were it not for the fact that American interests play virtually no role in the area's two major oil-producing countries, Mexico and Venezuela. In the following pages, all available sales information has been organized in three ways to compress the vast data material found in the original documentation into a more readable form.

A first series of data sets total Mofa sales in each major geographical area equal to 100 percent, and establishes the shares held by each individual industry, or the industrial sales mix for that area. Expressed in percentage terms, the tables simultaneously reflect actual changes that have taken place over four decades (see Table 8.13).

In a second configuration, this part then is adapted to identify the leading countries for each industry throughout the world for all census years except 1950, which adds significance to the information. Not only do these figures allow a glimpse of the traditionally preferred locations for the various affiliate industries, but they also may be used to forecast future moves with reasonable accuracy. Unlike the previous series, this section is based on actual dollars (see Table 8.14).

The information contained in this section sometimes raises questions which cannot be answered from the statistics at hand. Petroleum sales, for instance, are a mixture of crude, intermediate, and final products. For oil producers such as Indonesia and the Middle East, it is reasonable to expect the shown dollar volumes to mainly represent sales of crude petroleum. In the Caribbean situation where total sales in 1982 amounted to $26.2 billion of which only $2.8 billion were made locally, there is no telling what the dollar amounts really refer to. Most likely, though, they reflect sales of crude, which the islands neither produce nor process to any large extent. For a market such as Germany, sales relate predominantly to finished end products, but when it comes to the UK and Norway, which are sizable producers and exporters, it certainly must be a blend of both. Published data just do not allow a statement about the stage of the refining process at which products are sold locally or to export markets, which makes interaffiliate sales even more difficult to interpret.

Another point is this: Latin American oil sales, for example, fall into a rather steady range of 15 to 23 percent of the industry's global sales over the four decades investigated. But, the share of the Latin American republics (Venezuela in particular) who are actual producers has dropped sharply, while that of the affiliates in the islands–the traders–has increased significantly. The statistics do not divulge where the Caribbean affiliates source all the oil they sell, but there can be little doubt about their function as conduits for major profit shifts within the region. A similar scenario is at work in the Far East, where Indonesian and Malaysian basic production affiliates develop sales volumes that are easily matched by trading affiliates located in Hong Kong and Singapore where tax rates, once again, are very favorable.

Close parallels to the petroleum industry may be found among trade affiliates. Some data obviously refer strictly to local sales while others are so far out of proportion to the real market potential, that they can only be the result of profit strategies. Countries in question include Switzerland, the ubiquitous Caribbean islands, Singapore, and Hong Kong (see Table 8.12).

The unmistakable downward trend of Mofa shares in sales of all U.S. affiliates throughout the 1980s has come to a halt. With the exception of

TABLE 8.12. Mofa Share in Total Affiliate Sales by Industry (percentages)

Year	Total	Petroleum	Manufacturing	Trade	Finance	Other
1966	88.3	94.5	87.5	94.6	N/A	87.7
1977	78.2	83.7	78.8	75.1	68.0	78.1
1982	78.0	80.9	75.5	92.6	82.0	73.3
1983	79.7	81.9	77.6	92.9	82.9	61.5
1984	79.6	83.6	77.2	92.9	88.8	59.3
1985	78.5	82.4	76.0	90.2	85.3	58.1
1986	77.5	79.5	74.7	90.7	84.9	61.0
1987	77.5	78.9	74.6	90.8	84.8	62.9
1988	77.7	79.8	74.8	91.6	85.8	61.8
1989	79.3	78.5	77.1	91.9	85.0	60.6
1990	80.9	80.4	78.4	93.0	86.6	71.3
1991	80.4	78.5	78.4	92.2	90.2	70.5
1992	82.1	77.7	82.8	92.0	90.7	67.7
1993	81.3	76.6	81.9	92.2	90.7	64.3

oil and the "other" category, Mofas are regaining share in the U.S. FDI picture. The new development confirms American investors' historic preference for solid majority control, and helps to explain where the huge new investments went during the early 1990s. It was observed earlier that they did not lead to expansion of the base with growing sales and employment as one would expect, but instead went for plant modernization and, obviously, the consolidation of majority ownership. A curiosity is the Mofa role in the "other industries" category with the lowest Mofa share on record and still declining. This is not the place where a vastly superior American technology can be brought to bear. Still, a Mofa share of 60 to 70 percent in this residual market segment is conspicuously low compared to shares in the leading groups (see Tables 8.13 and 8.14).

TABLE 8.13. Industry Shares in Area Affiliate Sales (percentages)

Year	Petroleum	Manufacturing	Trade	Finance*	Services	Other
WORLD						
1957	33.1	41.8	12.8	N/A	2.8	9.4
1966	28.1	48.5	14.4	N/A	N/A	9.1
1967	28.6	48.3	13.4	N/A	N/A	9.5
1968	28.1	49.3	13.4	N/A	N/A	9.0
1969	27.1	50.3	13.6	N/A	N/A	8.9
1970	27.2	50.2	13.8	N/A	N/A	8.7
1971	28.8	49.3	13.8	N/A	N/A	8.2
1972	27.9	50.9	14.2	N/A	N/A	7.3
1973	31.2	48.5	13.4	N/A	N/A	7.2
1974	42.2	40.1	10.5	N/A	N/A	7.1
1975	39.0	41.9	11.4	N/A	N/A	7.6
1977	34.8	38.3	15.2	2.0	1.8	2.0
1982	36.4	37.1	15.6	3.2	2.5	5.1
1983	34.7	38.2	15.7	3.4	2.6	5.3
1984	32.8	39.8	16.3	4.0	2.4	4.7
1985	30.5	34.1	16.6	3.8	2.4	4.7
1986	22.1	46.7	18.9	4.3	3.1	4.9
1987	20.6	47.5	19.2	4.7	3.3	4.4
1988	17.9	50.0	20.0	4.7	3.4	4.2
1989	17.5	49.9	20.0	5.0	3.2	4.2
1990	19.7	48.1	18.9	4.8	3.5	5.0
1991	19.2	48.0	18.3	5.3	3.7	5.5
1992	18.4	48.2	18.6	5.5	3.9	5.2
1993	17.2	48.7	19.3	6.0	4.2	4.7

TABLE 8.13 (continued)

Year	Petroleum	Manufacturing	Trade	Finance*	Services	Other
EUROPE						
1957	33.8	48.5	14.2	N/A	N/A	3.5
1966	23.7	53.7	18.5	N/A	N/A	4.3
1967	24.2	54.3	16.8	N/A	N/A	5.0
1968	23.2	55.6	16.9	N/A	N/A	4.4
1969	21.9	56.6	17.0	N/A	N/A	4.3
1970	21.8	57.6	16.4	N/A	N/A	4.1
1971	21.8	57.6	16.0	N/A	N/A	4.5
1972	20.1	59.2	16.3	N/A	N/A	4.3
1973	19.7	59.1	15.7	N/A	N/A	5.1
1974	23.4	55.7	15.0	N/A	N/A	5.9
1975	24.2	54.4	15.3	N/A	N/A	6.0
1977	24.9	47.3	23.5	1.1	2.2	1.1
1982	31.3	39.8	21.6	1.7	2.9	2.6
1983	29.5	41.2	22.1	1.7	3.1	2.2
1984	28.8	41.0	22.4	2.6	3.0	2.1
1985	27.7	42.6	22.3	2.0	3.2	2.0
1986	18.9	48.1	24.2	2.5	4.0	2.2
1987	17.6	49.2	24.4	2.8	4.0	2.0
1988	15.3	51.2	24.4	3.0	4.1	2.0
1989	15.6	50.9	24.3	3.5	3.8	1.8
CANADA						
1957	15.6	58.0	14.0	N/A	3.5	9.1
1966	11.2	62.3	14.2	N/A	N/A	11.8
1967	12.2	61.4	12.4	N/A	N/A	14.2
1968	12.0	62.0	12.0	N/A	N/A	13.8
1969	12.0	62.5	12.5	N/A	N/A	13.2
1970	12.6	58.6	13.4	N/A	N/A	14.9
1971	12.4	59.8	14.9	N/A	N/A	13.0
1972	12.1	60.0	15.4	N/A	N/A	12.4
1973	15.7	57.8	16.5	N/A	N/A	9.9
1974	18.2	57.3	13.2	N/A	N/A	11.8
1975	18.9	55.6	12.8	N/A	N/A	12.4
1977	18.1	55.4	12.9	4.8	1.5	7.3
1982	23.9	49.3	8.5	5.7	2.1	10.5
1983	23.1	50.2	7.7	5.1	1.7	12.0
1984	22.1	53.1	8.0	4.8	1.4	11.0
1985	18.6	55.8	7.2	5.0	1.4	11.9
1986	13.1	58.4	8.0	5.8	1.6	12.9
1987	13.5	57.5	8.4	6.4	1.9	12.8
1988	11.5	60.3	8.6	6.2	2.1	11.9
1989	12.4	57.1	9.8	6.2	2.4	12.4

Year	Petroleum	Manufacturing	Trade	Finance*	Services	Other
LATIN AMERICA						
1957	33.6	26.9	14.6	N/A	2.5	21.2
1966	34.0	40.9	12.3	N/A	N/A	19.9
1967	30.2	41.8	11.7	N/A	N/A	16.5
1968	29.9	42.5	11.7	N/A	N/A	16.1
1969	27.4	44.1	11.4	N/A	N/A	17.3
1970	27.5	47.0	12.1	N/A	N/A	14.0
1971	29.1	47.7	11.1	N/A	N/A	12.4
1972	22.6	40.4	9.3	N/A	N/A	10.1
1973	29.4	48.6	10.7	N/A	N/A	11.1
1974	40.6	40.3	9.1	N/A	N/A	9.9
1975	40.7	41.9	8.3	N/A	N/A	4.2
1977	37.7	41.5	10.5	4.3	1.6	4.2
1982	40.2	37.9	7.8	8.5	1.5	3.8
1983	42.1	34.3	7.1	10.5	1.5	4.4
1984	36.5	37.5	8.2	12.4	1.7	3.9
1985	30.7	42.3	8.5	12.8	1.5	3.8
1986	27.4	44.1	9.4	13.0	2.0	3.9
1987	23.6	47.3	8.0	14.6	3.0	3.6
1988	21.7	51.3	9.0	12.0	2.9	3.5
1989	20.2	55.4	7.5	10.9	1.8	4.3
LATIN AMERICAN REPUBLICS						
1957	39.7	32.3	N/A	N/A	N/A	28.0
1966	N/A	45.0	12.4	N/A	N/A	N/A
1967	28.0	45.2	11.6	N/A	N/A	15.1
1968	26.7	46.5	11.7	N/A	N/A	14.2
1969	23.9	49.3	10.7	N/A	N/A	15.9
1970	24.2	50.8	11.4	N/A	N/A	13.2
1971	24.1	51.6	11.4	N/A	N/A	12.7
1972	22.8	53.0	11.4	N/A	N/A	12.5
1975	31.0	52.4	9.1	N/A	N/A	7.3
1977	21.7	62.6	9.4	1.0	N/A	5.2
1982	23.9	59.4	8.8	0.8	1.6	5.5
1989	14.9	70.4	7.2	1.6	1.3	4.3

TABLE 8.13. (continued)

Year	Petroleum	Manufacturing	Trade	Finance*	Services	Other
OTHER WESTERN HEMISPHERE						
1966	N/A	7.7	11.8	N/A	N/A	N/A
1967	47.2	7.4	10.5	N/A	N/A	35.8
1968	52.1	7.8	10.9	N/A	N/A	29.8
1969	49.7	6.7	9.2	N/A	N/A	34.5
1970	48.5	6.6	10.6	N/A	N/A	34.5
1971	52.7	5.3	11.4	N/A	N/A	30.5
1972	49.3	5.6	11.8	N/A	N/A	33.2
1975	76.9	2.8	5.2	N/A	N/A	15.1
1977	72.3	1.8	10.2	11.0	N/A	4.5
1982	67.8	1.8	6.1	21.5	1.4	1.2
1989	38.1	2.9	8.0	43.3	3.6	3.7
ASIA						
1957	80.4	13.4	N/A	N/A	N/A	6.2
1966	70.2	17.7	6.1.	N/A	N/A	6.0
1967	68.9	19.4	6.1	N/A	N/A	6.0
1968	66.4	21.8	6.4	N/A	N/A	5.1
1969	66.2	21.6	7.0	N/A	N/A	5.0
1970	64.7	22.4	7.9	N/A	N/A	5.4
1971	66.5	18.5	9.8	N/A	N/A	5.3
1972	66.5	18.2	10.1	N/A	N/A	5.1
1973	71.7	16.6	7.5	N/A	N/A	4.0
1974	83.0	9.9	4.4	N/A	N/A	3.0
1975	79.1	11.7	5.6	N/A	N/A	3.7
1977	80.7	9.0	5.5	0.5	N/A	3.1
1982	58.5	17.9	12.3	1.5	2.2	7.6
1983	53.5	20.8	13.7	1.8	2.7	7.7
1984	50.8	24.1	15.7	2.1	2.3	5.1
1985	47.6	26.4	17.1	2.6	3.9	5.0
1986	35.4	31.9	21.3	4.1	1.9	5.2
1987	33.2	34.1	22.2	5.2	1.8	3.4
1988	28.8	35.8	24.4	6.2	2.0	1.4
1989	25.2	37.2	25.4	7.2	2.2	2.7

Year	Petroleum	Manufacturing	Trade	Finance*	Services	Other
AFRICA						
1957	46.1	26.8	N/A	N/A	2.7	24.4
1966	60.9	26.6	6.1	N/A	N/A	6.6
1967	N/A	25.7	6.1	N/A	N/A	N/A
1968	62.8	23.7	6.0	N/A	N/A	8.0
1969	N/A	24.4	N/A	N/A	N/A	8.7
1970	58.7	25.9	6.9	N/A	N/A	8.5
1971	60.0	25.0	7.0	N/A	N/A	8.0
1972	60.1	26.0	5.2	N/A	N/A	7.3
1973	60.7	25.9	6.7	N/A	N/A	6.7
1974	N/A	N/A	N/A	N/A	N/A	N/A
1975	N/A	23.9	6.4	N/A	N/A	N/A
1977	N/A	13.6	4.4	0.5	N/A	N/A
1982	68.6	18.3	7.4	0.5	N/A	N/A
1989	63.8	22.1	5.7	0.3	2.1	7.6
OCEANIA						
1957	28.6	62.7	N/A	N/A	N/A	8.7
1966	N/A	61.4	8.3	N/A	N/A	N/A
1967	N/A	62.8	6.8	N/A	N/A	N/A
1968	N/A	62.1	6.1	N/A	N/A	N/A
1969	N/A	61.1	N/A	N/A	N/A	N/A
1970	N/A	59.2	7.3	N/A	N/A	N/A
1971	N/A	60.8	6.1	N/A	N/A	N/A
1972	N/A	62.9	6.6	N/A	N/A	N/A
1973	N/A	63.5	9.0	N/A	N/A	N/A
1975	N/A	58.8	9.9	N/A	N/A	N/A
1977	N/A	49.0	16.8	2.8	N/A	N/A
1982	27.8	42.2	11.5	2.9	N/A	N/A
1989	18.9	49.1	20.1	3.2	4.2	4.3

Note: *Includes insurance for all years, banking from 1957 to 1977, and real estate from 1977 forward.

Source: See Table 8.5.

TABLE 8.14. Leading Affiliates (sales – $ billion)

Year	1957**	%	1966	%	1977	%	1982	%	1989	%
All Industries*										
Total	$38.2	100	$97.8	100	$507.0	100	$730.2	100	$1,019.0	100
Canada	11.7	31	23.9	24	84.7	17	108.0	15	173.3	17
Europe	11.2	29	40.5	41	220.2	43	364.4	50	573.3	56
Belg./Lux.	0.4	1	2.0	2	15.4	3	21.9	3	31.5	3
France	1.6	4	5.3	5	28.5	6	41.4	6	70.8	7
Germany	1.8	5	7.7	8	48.0	9	67.2	9	106.4	10
Ireland	N/A	–	0.1	–	1.8	–	4.7	1	11.4	1
Italy	0.8	2	3.2	3	14.1	3	24.5	3	45.3	4
Netherlands	0.5	1	2.1	2	17.1	3	27.6	4	45.4	4
Norway	0.1	–	0.4	–	3.4	1	7.4	1	7.6	1
Spain	0.1	–	0.7	1	5.7	1	8.3	1	23.7	2
Sweden	0.4	1	0.8	1	4.2	1	6.3	1	7.7	1
Switzerland	0.2	1	2.8	3	16.6	3	33.3	5	36.2	4
UK	4.7	12	13.4	14	55.9	11	108.0	15	167.2	16
Lat. Am.	7.9	21	14.3	15	58.2	11	103.9	14	87.0	9
Lat. Am. Rep.	7.5	20	12.9	13	38.8	8	65.3	9	67.7	7
Argentina	0.5	1	1.8	2	3.6	1	5.1	1	4.1	–
Brazil	1.3	3	2.2	2	16.6	3	26.0	4	30.6	3
Mexico	1.0	3	2.0	2	5.9	1	11.3	2	16.4	2
Venezuela	2.4	6	3.2	3	4.7	1	7.2	1	2.7	–
O.W. Hemi.	0.4	1	1.3	1	19.5	4	38.6	5	19.4	2
Bahamas	N/A	–	0.2	–	2.4	–	5.9	1	1.5	–
Bermuda	N/A	–	0.1	–	11.9	2	20.1	3	10.8	1
N. Antilles	N/A	–	N/A	–	2.1	–	7.0	1	2.7	–
Africa	1.2	3	3.2	3	19.0	4	23.6	3	11.6	1
S. Africa	0.6	2	1.3	1	4.6	1	7.8	1	2.7	–
Libya	N/A	–	0.1	–	5.1	1	3.5	–	N/A	–
Nigeria	N/A	–	0.1	–	4.6	1	4.5	1	2.3	–
Asia	3.6	9	9.4	10	94.9	19	91.4	13	128.7	13
Japan	0.6	2	2.1	2	13.2	3	25.8	4	58.4	6
Hong Kong	N/A	–	N/A	–	4.9	1	7.5	1	16.4	2
Indonesia	N/A	–	0.5	1	5.5	1	12.5	2	6.1	1
Malaysia	N/A	–	N/A	–	1.1	–	4.3	1	5.4	1
S. Arabia	N/A	–	N/A	–	N/A	–	9.5	1	3.4	–
Singapore	N/A	–	N/A	–	2.1	–	14.1	2	15.1	1
Taiwan	N/A	–	N/A	–	1.0	–	1.9	–	6.8	1
Thailand	N/A	–	N/A	–	0.9	–	2.6	–	5.5	1
Australia	1.2	3	3.5	4	14.5	3	28.7	4	37.7	4
N. Zealand	0.2	–	0.4	–	1.2	–	2.2	–	3.2	–

Year	1957**	%	1966	%	1977	%	1982	%	1989	%
Petroleum Industries										
Total	$14.5	100	$27.5	100	$198.6	100	$266.3	100	$179.4	100
Canada	2.1	14	2.7	10	15.3	8	25.8	10	21.4	12
Europe	4.4	30	9.6	35	54.7	27	113.7	43	89.5	50
Germany	0.6	4	2.0	7	11.1	6	19.3	7	13.4	7
Italy	0.5	3	1.2	4	4.0	2	8.2	3	N/A	N/A
Netherlands	0.3	2	0.6	2	4.2	2	8.6	3	5.4	3
Norway	0.1	1	N/A	–	2.1	1	5.7	2	5.5	3
Sweden	0.2	1	0.2	1	1.3	1	2.2	1	7.7	4
Switzerland	0.1	1	N/A	–	2.3	1	12.3	5	9.4	5
UK	1.2	8	2.5	9	15.9	8	33.9	13	29.3	16
Lat. America	3.3	23	4.2	15	21.9	11	41.8	16	17.6	10
Lat. Am. Rep.	3.0	21	N/A	–	7.8	4	15.6	6	10.2	6
Brazil	0.5	3	0.6	2	3.8	2	6.9	3	4.7	3
Colombia	0.2	1	0.2	1	0.5	–	1.8	1	1.6	1
Venezuela	1.9	13	2.1	8	0.8	–	0.6	–	0.1	–
Panama	N/A	–	0.1	–	0.6	–	1.5	1	0.7	–
O.W. Hemi.	0.3	2	N/A	–	14.1	7	26.2	10	7.4	4
Bahamas	N/A	–	nil	–	1.8	1	4.4	2	0.4	–
Bermuda	N/A	–	N/A	–	9.0	5	14.8	6	5.4	3
Africa	0.5	3	N/A	14e	N/A	15e	16.2	6	7.4	4
S. Africa	0.2	1	0.4	1	N/A	–	2.7	1	N/A	–
Libya	N/A	–	1.0	4	5.0	3	3.4	1	N/A	–
Nigeria	N/A	–	N/A	–	4.3	2	4.0	2	2.2	1
Asia	2.9	20	6.6	24	76.6	38	53.5	20	32.5	18
Japan	0.3	–	1.2	4	7.3	4	13.6	5	10.5	6
Middle East	1.7	12	3.8	14	59.6	30	9.8	4	5.8	3
S. Arabia	N/A	–	N/A	–	N/A	–	4.0	2	2.9	2
Un. Arab Em.	N/A	–	N/A	–	N/A	–	3.7	1	1.5	1
Hong Kong	N/A	–	N/A	–	N/A	–	2.3	1	1.5	1
Indonesia	N/A	–	0.5	2	4.7	2	10.9	4	5.1	3
Malaysia	N/A	–	N/A	–	0.5	–	2.3	1	2.1	1
Philippines	0.2	1	0.2	1	0.7	–	1.3	–	0.9	–
Singapore	N/A	–	N/A	–	0.6	–	11.0	4	3.9	2
Thailand	N/A	–	N/A	–	N/A	–	1.7	1	2.3	1
Australia	0.3	2	0.5	2	2.3	1	7.8	3	6.9	4

TABLE 8.14 (continued)

Year	1957**	%	1966	%	1977	%	1982	%	1989	%
Manufacturing Industries										
Total	$18.3	100	$47.4	100	$194.2	100	$271.1	100	$509.3	100
Canada	7.9	43	14.9	31	46.9	24	53.2	20	98.7	19
Europe	6.3	34	21.7	46	104.3	54	144.7	53	291.7	57
Belg./Lux.	0.3	2	1.1	2	7.6	4	9.3	3	17.6	3
France	0.8	4	3.1	7	16.0	8	19.3	7	34.6	7
Germany	1.1	6	4.8	10	29.4	15	38.1	14	72.1	14
Italy	0.2	1	1.5	3	6.9	4	10.0	4	23.4	5
Ireland	N/A	—	0.1	—	1.1	1	3.2	1	9.3	2
Netherlands	0.2	1	0.9	2	7.4	4	11.1	4	25.8	5
UK	3.3	18	8.3	18	26.6	14	40.6	15	79.2	16
Spain	0.1	1	0.5	1	4.1	2	6.2	2	18.1	4
Sweden	0.1	1	0.3	1	1.5	1	2.0	1	3.4	1
Switzerland	0.1	1	0.6	1	1.3	1	1.8	1	2.3	—
Lat. America	2.4	13	5.9	12	24.2	12	39.5	15	48.2	9
Lat. Am. Rep.	2.4	13	5.8	12	23.9	12	38.8	14	47.7	9
Argentina	0.4	2	1.3	3	2.5	1	3.2	1	2.7	—
Brazil	0.7	3	1.3	3	11.2	6	17.0	6	24.3	5
Colombia	0.1	1	0.3	1	1.0	1	1.8	1	1.6	—
Mexico	0.6	3	1.5	3	4.7	2	9.4	3	14.2	3
Venezuela	0.3	2	0.7	2	2.8	1	4.8	2	1.9	—
Africa	0.3	2	0.8	2	2.6	1	4.3	2	2.6	—
S. Africa	0.3	2	0.8	2	1.9	1	3.4	1	1.4	—
Asia	0.5	3	1.7	4	8.6	4	16.3	6	47.9	9
Japan	0.2	1	0.7	2	3.1	2	5.9	2	22.4	4
Hong Kong	N/A	—	N/A	—	N/A	—	1.1	—	3.5	1
Malaysia	N/A	—	N/A	—	0.5	—	2.3	1	2.7	1
Philippines	0.1	1	0.3	1	1.0	1	1.7	1	1.7	—
Singapore	N/A	—	N/A	—	0.9	—	1.9	1	7.6	1
Taiwan	N/A	—	N/A	—	0.8	—	1.5	1	4.9	1
Australia	0.8	4	2.2	5	7.2	4	12.2	5	18.9	4

Year	1957**	%	1966	%	1977	%	1982	%	1989	%
Chemical Industries										
Total	$2.4	100	$7.4	100	$32.4	100	$54.8	100	$94.7	100
Canada	0.9	38	1.7	23	4.9	15	7.5	14	12.1	13
Europe	0.8	33	3.4	46	18.7	58	30.7	56	60.1	63
Belg./Lux.	N/A	–	0.2	3	2.1	6	3.1	6	6.7	7
France	0.1	4	0.5	7	2.8	9	4.5	8	9.3	10
Germany	nil	–	0.5	7	3.6	11	6.0	11	10.7	11
Ireland	N/A	–	0.1	1	0.3	1	N/A	–	1.8	2
Italy	0.1	4	0.3	4	1.6	5	2.3	4	6.1	6
Netherlands	N/A	–	0.3	4	2.6	8	4.0	7	8.6	9
Spain	N/A	–	0.1	1	0.8	2	1.6	3	3.1	3
Sweden	N/A	–	0.1	1	0.3	1	0.5	1	0.4	–
Switzerland	N/A	–	nil	–	0.2	1	0.7	1	0.2	–
UK	0.5	21	1.4	19	3.9	12	6.5	12	11.8	12
Lat. America	0.5	21	1.3	18	6.5	20	9.1	17	9.7	10
Lat. Am. Rep.	0.5	21	1.3	18	5.3	16	8.7	16	9.5	10
Argentina	nil	–	0.2	3	0.6	2	0.9	2	0.7	1
Brazil	0.1	4	0.3	4	2.5	8	3.9	7	4.3	4
Colombia	nil	–	0.1	1	0.3	1	0.5	1	0.6	1
Mexico	0.2	8	0.4	5	1.1	3	1.9	3	2.6	3
Venezuela	0.1	4	0.1	1	0.5	2	0.9	2	0.6	1
O.W. Hemi.	nil	–	0.1	1	0.1	–	0.4	1	0.2	–
Africa	nil	–	0.1	1	0.4	1	0.7	1	0.7	1
S. Africa	nil	–	0.1	1	0.3	1	0.5	1	0.5	1
Asia	0.1	4	0.5	7	1.8	6	3.4	6	7.2	7
Japan	nil	–	0.3	4	0.7	2	1.7	3	4.1	4
Philippines	nil	–	0.1	1	0.3	1	0.5	1	0.6	–
Australia	0.1	4	0.3	4	1.3	4	3.3	6	4.6	5

TABLE 8.14 (continued)

Year	1957**	%	1966	%	1977	%	1982	%	1989	%
Nonelectrical Machinery Industries										
Total	$1.9	100	N/A	–	$28.4	100	$40.5	100	$100.3	100
Canada	0.7	37	N/A	–	3.6	13	5.0	12	8.2	8
Europe	1.0	53	N/A	–	20.0	70	27.2	67	66.6	67
Belg./Lux.	nil	–	N/A	–	1.2	4	1.2	3	2.4	2
France	0.2	11	N/A	–	4.3	15	5.6	14	9.9	10
Germany	0.2	11	N/A	–	5.7	20	6.9	17	13.9	14
Ireland	N/A	–	N/A	–	0.2	1	0.8	2	3.5	4
Italy	nil	–	N/A	–	1.6	6	3.0	7	7.9	8
Netherlands	nil	–	N/A	–	1.2	4	1.0	2	5.6	6
Spain	N/A	–	N/A	–	0.3	1	0.8	2	2.4	2
Sweden	N/A	–	N/A	–	0.5	2	0.9	2	2.0	2
UK	0.5	26	N/A	–	4.9	17	6.7	17	18.4	18
Lat. America	0.1	3	N/A	–	1.9	7	3.3	8	5.8	6
Lat. Am. Rep.	0.1	3	N/A	–	1.9	7	3.3	8	5.8	6
Argentina	nil	–	N/A	–	0.3	1	N/A	–	0.8	1
Brazil	nil	–	N/A	–	1.4	5	2.4	6	4.4	4
Mexico	nil	–	N/A	–	0.2	1	0.5	1	0.9	1
Africa	nil	–	N/A	–	0.3	1	0.5	1	0.4	–
S. Africa	nil	–	N/A	–	0.3	1	0.5	1	0.3	–
Asia	0.1	3	N/A	–	1.8	7	3.1	8	17.3	17
Japan	N/A	–	N/A	–	1.5	5	2.3	6	12.0	12
Singapore	N/A	–	N/A	–	0.1	–	0.5	1	3.8	4
Australia	0.1	3	N/A	–	0.8	3	1.4	3	1.9	2

Year	1957**	%	1966	%	1977	%	1982	%	1989	%
Electric/Electronic Machinery Industries										
Total	$2.0	100	N/A	–	$18.7	100	$25.2	100	$39.7	100
Canada	1.1	55	N/A	–	3.2	17	4.1	16	5.6	14
Europe	0.7	35	N/A	–	10.3	55	11.9	47	17.0	43
Belg./Lux.	N/A	–	N/A	–	1.0	5	1.3	5	0.7	2
France	0.1	5	N/A	–	1.2	6	1.1	4	1.7	4
Germany	0.1	5	N/A	–	2.8	15	3.5	14	3.7	9
Ireland	nil	–	N/A	–	0.1	1	0.3	1	0.8	2
Italy	0.1	5	N/A	–	1.0	5	1.3	5	1.2	3
Netherlands	N/A	–	N/A	–	0.2	1	2.4	10	1.3	3
Spain	N/A	–	N/A	–	0.9	5	0.9	4	0.6	2
Switzerland	N/A	–	N/A	–	0.3	2	0.2	1	0.4	1
UK	0.3	15	N/A	–	2.0	11	2.4	10	5.7	14
Lat. America	0.2	10	N/A	–	2.0	11	2.7	11	3.6	9
Lat. Am. Rep.	0.2	10	N/A	–	1.9	10	2.5	10	3.5	9
Argentina	nil	–	N/A	–	0.1	1	0.2	1	2.2	6
Brazil	0.1	5	N/A	–	1.1	6	1.2	5	2.0	5
Mexico	0.1	5	N/A	–	0.5	3	0.9	4	1.2	3
Africa	nil	–	N/A	–	0.2	1	0.2	1	–	–
S. Africa	nil	–	N/A	–	0.2	1	0.1	–	–	–
Asia	nil	–	N/A	–	2.5	13	5.7	23	16.1	41
Japan	N/A	–	N/A	–	0.2	1	0.5	2	2.7	7
Hong Kong	N/A	–	N/A	–	0.4	2	0.6	2	1.4	4
Malaysia	N/A	–	N/A	–	0.3	2	1.3	5	2.1	5
Philippines	N/A	–	N/A	–	0.1	1	0.3	1	0.4	1
Singapore	N/A	–	N/A	–	0.7	4	1.0	4	2.8	7
S. Korea	N/A	–	N/A	–	0.1	1	0.3	1	0.6	2
Taiwan	N/A	–	N/A	–	0.5	3	0.8	3	1.6	4
Thailand	N/A	–	N/A	–	N/A	–	0.3	1	0.6	2
Australia	0.1	5	N/A	–	0.4	2	0.5	2	0.9	2

TABLE 8.14 (continued)

Year	1957**	%	1966	%	1977	%	1982	%	1989	%
Transportation Equipment Industries										
Total	$4.2	100	$11.2	100	$48.9	100	$57.2	100	$114.4	100
Canada	1.5	35	3.9	35	17.3	35	19.0	33	42.5	37
Europe	1.7	40	5.0	45	22.7	46	25.4	45	55.4	48
Belg./Lux.	0.1	2	N/A	--	N/A	--	N/A	--	N/A	--
France	0.2	5	N/A	--	3.2	7	1.3	2	1.6	1
Germany	N/A	--	N/A	--	9.6	20	11.6	20	25.1	22
Italy	N/A	--	0.1	1	0.4	1	0.3	1	2.0	2
Spain	N/A	--	N/A	--	1.3	3	1.6	3	6.9	6
UK	0.8	19	N/A	--	6.7	14	9.0	16	16.7	15
Lat. America	0.4	10	1.0	9	5.2	11	8.2	14	9.9	9
Lat. Am. Rep.	0.4	10	1.0	9	5.2	11	8.2	14	9.9	9
Argentina	N/A	--	0.4	4	0.8	2	N/A	--	nil	--
Brazil	0.1	2	0.2	2	2.1	4	2.9	5	3.8	3
Mexico	N/A	--	N/A	--	1.0	2	2.3	4	5.6	5
Africa	0.2	5	0.3	3	N/A	--	0.9	2	nil	--
S. Africa	N/A	--	0.3	3	N/A	--	0.9	2	nil	--
Asia	0.1	2	N/A	--	N/A	--	0.2	--	1.8	2
Singapore	N/A	--	N/A	--	N/A	--	0.2	--	N/A	--
Australia	0.4	10	0.8	7	2.5	5	3.4	7	4.6	4

Year	1957**	%	1966	%	1977	%	1982	%	1989	%
Trade Industries										
Total	$5.6	100	$14.1	100	$77.4	100	$113.6	100	$204.3	100
Canada	1.9	34	3.4	24	10.9	14	9.2	8	16.9	8
Europe	1.9	34	7.4	53	51.6	67	79.8	70	139.3	68
Austria	N/A	–	N/A	–	1.1	1	1.2	1	2.3	1
Belg./Lux.	N/A	–	0.5	4	4.3	6	4.9	4	7.4	4
France	N/A	–	0.7	5	5.6	7	9.9	9	22.6	11
Germany	N/A	–	0.7	5	6.3	8	6.9	6	14.0	7
Italy	N/A	–	0.3	2	2.8	4	5.0	4	11.4	6
Netherlands	N/A	–	0.5	4	4.2	6	5.7	5	9.7	5
Spain	N/A	–	0.1	1	1.2	1	1.0	1	4.0	2
Sweden	N/A	–	0.2	1	1.2	1	1.8	2	3.5	2
Switzerland	N/A	–	1.9	14	12.6	16	18.2	16	22.3	11
UK	N/A	–	2.0	14	9.7	13	21.4	19	32.9	16
Lat. America	1.3	23	1.8	13	6.1	8	8.1	7	6.5	3
Lat. Am. Rep.	N/A	–	1.6	11	4.2	6	5.7	5	4.9	2
Argentina	N/A	–	0.2	1	0.6	1	0.8	1	0.5	–
Brazil	N/A	–	0.3	2	0.8	1	1.0	1	0.5	–
Mexico	N/A	–	0.3	2	0.7	1	1.1	1	1.3	1
Venezuela	N/A	–	0.2	1	0.8	1	1.1	1	0.5	–
O.W. Hemi.	N/A	–	0.2	1	2.0	3	2.4	2	1.6	1
Bahamas	N/A	–	0.1	1	0.4	1	1.2	1	0.5	–
Bermuda	N/A	–	N/A	–	1.1	1	N/A	–	0.4	–
Africa	N/A	–	0.2	1	0.8	1	1.8	2	0.7	–
S. Africa	N/A	–	0.1	1	0.6	1	1.4	1	0.4	–
Asia	N/A	–	0.6	4	5.3	7	11.2	10	32.8	16
Japan	N/A	–	0.2	1	2.3	3	5.2	5	17.3	8
Hong Kong	N/A	–	N/A	–	1.4	2	3.0	3	8.3	4
SIngapore	N/A	–	N/A	–	0.5	1	1.1	1	2.9	1
Australia	N/A	–	0.2	1	2.4	3	3.2	3	7.4	4

Note: The above data include wholesale and retail for all years except 1982 and 1989, which represent wholesale only.

TABLE 8.14 (continued)

Year	1957**	%	1966	%	1977	%	1982	%	1989	%
Finance*** Industries										
Total	N/A	–	N/A	–	$10.0	100	$23.5	100	51.1	100
Canada	N/A	–	N/A	–	4.1	41	6.2	26	10.7	21
Europe	N/A	–	N/A	–	2.4	24	6.2	26	20.3	40
Belg./Lux.	N/A	–	N/A	–	0.2	2	0.2	1	0.8	2
France	N/A	–	N/A	–	0.2	2	0.3	1	1.2	2
Germany	N/A	–	N/A	–	0.3	3	0.5	2	1.6	3
Netherlands	N/A	–	N/A	–	0.2	2	0.4	2	1.1	2
Switzerland	N/A	–	N/A	–	0.2	2	0.2	1	1.0	2
UK	N/A	–	N/A	–	1.1	11	4.3	18	13.2	26
Lat. America	N/A	–	N/A	–	2.5	25	9.5	40	9.5	19
Lat. Am. Rep.	N/A	–	N/A	–	0.4	4	0.5	2	1.1	2
Brazil	N/A	–	N/A	–	0.2	2	0.2	1	0.4	1
O.W. Hemi.	N/A	–	N/A	–	2.1	21	8.3	35	8.5	17
Bermuda	N/A	–	N/A	–	1.8	18	4.3	18	4.9	10
N. Antilles	N/A	–	N/A	–	N/A	–	3.6	15	2.6	5
UK Caribbean	N/A	–	N/A	–	N/A	–	0.3	1	0.4	1
Africa	N/A	–	N/A	–	0.1	1	0.1	–	nil	–
Asia	N/A	–	N/A	–	0.5	5	1.3	6	9.3	18
Hong Kong	N/A	–	N/A	–	N/A	–	N/A	–	1.3	3
Japan	N/A	–	N/A	–	0.3	3	0.7	3	6.2	12
Australia	N/A	–	N/A	–	0.4	4	0.8	3	1.3	3

Note: ***Includes finance except banking, insurance, and real estate from 1977 onward. Banking is included up to 1977. Real estate is excluded for 1957 and 1966.

Year	1957**	%	1966	%	1977	%	1982	%	1989	%
Service Industries										
Total	N/A	–	N/A	–	$9.1	100	$17.9	100	$32.5	100
Canada	N/A	–	N/A	–	1.2	13	2.3	13	4.2	13
Europe	N/A	–	N/A	–	4.8	53	10.5	59	21.9	68
Austria	N/A	–	N/A	–	N/A	–	0.2	1	0.1	–
Belg./Lux.	N/A	–	N/A	–	N/A	–	0.5	3	1.2	4
France	N/A	–	N/A	–	N/A	–	1.7	9	3.1	10
Germany	N/A	–	N/A	–	N/A	–	1.0	6	2.8	9
Italy	N/A	–	N/A	–	N/A	–	0.6	3	1.0	4
Netherlands	N/A	–	N/A	–	N/A	–	1.4	8	3.0	9
Spain	N/A	–	N/A	–	N/A	–	0.4	2	0.5	2
Sweden	N/A	–	N/A	–	N/A	–	0.2	1	0.2	1
Switzerland	N/A	–	N/A	–	N/A	–	0.6	3	0.8	2
UK	N/A	–	N/A	–	N/A	–	1.4	8	8.2	26
Lat. America	N/A	–	N/A	–	0.9	10	1.6	9	1.6	5
Lat. Am. Rep.	N/A	–	N/A	–	N/A	–	1.0	6	0.9	3
Argentina	N/A	–	N/A	–	N/A	–	0.1	1	N/A	–
Brazil	N/A	–	N/A	–	N/A	–	0.2	1	0.5	2
Mexico	N/A	–	N/A	–	N/A	–	0.2	1	0.2	1
Venezuela	N/A	–	N/A	–	N/A	–	0.3	2	0.1	–
O.W. Hemi.	N/A	–	N/A	–	N/A	–	0.5	3	0.7	2
Bahamas	N/A	–	N/A	–	N/A	–	0.2	1	0.3	1
Bermuda	N/A	–	N/A	–	N/A	–	0.1	1	0.1	–
UK Caribbean	N/A	–	N/A	–	N/A	–	0.1	1	nil	–
Africa	N/A	–	N/A	–	N/A	–	N/A	–	0.2	1
Asia	N/A	–	N/A	–	N/A	–	2.0	11	2.9	9
Japan	N/A	–	N/A	–	N/A	–	0.2	1	1.4	4
Saudi Arabia	N/A	–	N/A	–	N/A	–	1.2	7	0.3	1
Hong Kong	N/A	–	N/A	–	N/A	–	0.1	1	0.5	2
Australia	N/A	–	N/A	–	N/A	–	1.2	7	1.7	5

Notes: *1957 data cover all affiliates. All other years represent Mofa data. **1957 data exclude trade and finance. e = estimate

Sources: FDI census data: 1957, pp. 110-1; 1966, p. 199; 1977, p. 282; 1982, p. 217; 1989, p. 180. *SOCB*, July 1993, pp. 53-4 (1990-1).

Chapter 9

Affiliate Export Sales

LOCAL VERSUS EXPORT SALES

Local sales always were and still are the mainstay of Mofa business. They accounted for a very steady 70 to 75 percent of total affiliate sales from 1957 to the mid-1970s, with the remainder going for exports to the United States and the rest of the world. That firm relationship underwent a pronounced shift in 1974. Local sales declined in relative importance as export sales moved closer to the 40 percent range before settling back to around 35 percent.

The change can be attributed to several factors. First and foremost was the rapid increase in the numbers of affiliates during the 1960s and 1970s, which more than doubled their numbers between 1957 and 1977. Many of the new affiliates were acquisitions with prior export interests. But regardless of whether they were acquired or established, they posed a growing foreign trade potential involving other affiliate organizations and third parties.

In the design of U.S. FDI, they were increasingly assigned supply functions for associated corporations at a rate outpacing their own parents, as well as their trade with foreigners. Data recorded in Table 8.6 and 8.7 clearly shows Mofa exports to affiliates exceeding like sales to foreigners. The 1977 exports of $134 billion to affiliates were 127 percent higher than the $59 billion volume exported to foreigners; 1993 figures show $278 versus $156 billion or transactions with affiliates still running 78 percent ahead of those with foreigners.

In addition, exports from this newly created supply base to affiliates in the rest of the world grew gradually from 30 to 53 percent in overall Mofa sales to associated companies, and from 9 to 13 percent of Mofa sales between 1977 and 1993 (see Tables 8.2 and 8.7), while U.S. parent exports to the same remained practically unchanged at 3 to 4 percent, if measured in the same terms (see Tables 4.16 C and D, 10.16 A and C). Mofas were unmistakably given the mandate to take the leading role in intra-FDI trade, with a secondary mission to not neglect third-party accounts at the same time.

A certain yet unmeasurable element in this picture is posed by the previously made discovery–that U.S. FDI companies are partially owned by foreign business interests, whose business strategies may influence their export behavior in some form or another.

Another major factor is the price of oil which has been identified repeatedly as being responsible for the temporary disruptive oil excess in all U.S. FDI data. Its fourfold jump in the early seventies caused oil affiliates' exports to swell from a 31 percent share in overall affiliate exports in 1970 to almost 50 percent by 1977, owing to an eightfold increase in trade volume from $13 billion to $98 billion. As oil is traded in dollars, both the rise in oil prices and the resultant surge in the dollar's exchange quotation between 1980-85 contributed to the development. It also helped to boost foreign trade figures of oil affiliates disproportionately against their domestic sales which are invoiced in local currencies and thus suffer automatic share reductions as the dollar's purchasing power goes up.

At any rate, the tenfold expansion of affiliate exports, compared to the fivefold increase in their local sales between the mid-1960s and mid-1980s not only mirrors the growing importance of export accounts for Mofa business, it also demonstrates their growing stature as world traders, an aspect to be elaborated upon in more detail further on.

The primary objective of serving local customers may be true for the whole Mofa family, but not necessarily for all its members, and this is exactly what a look at the data reveals. Closer inspection makes it obvious that there are distinctly different sales patterns. Some affiliates cater predominantly to local markets, others derive the bulk of their business from exports and, finally, there are those with a more balanced sales mix.

This observation can be used to establish three affiliate categories by drawing arbitrary dividing lines at the one-third and two-thirds level of their sales. That is to say, the first group of affiliates comprises only those that sell more than two-thirds of their total to local customers, the second where between one-third and two-thirds of all sales are made to the domestic market, and the third includes all other subsidiaries with domestic sales of less than one-third of their total.

Typical for the first group, with at least 65 percent in local sales, are such major world markets as Canada, France, Germany, the UK, Japan, all of South America, and Australia. The Latin American republics are really the leaders of this group, with a share of domestic business averaging above

90 percent. Their high ratio compared to the rest of this group explains their very weak export position observed earlier.

The second group of subsidiaries with a fairly balanced mix of local sales and exports where both fall into a range of one-third and two-thirds of total revenues includes Belgium, Luxemburg, the Netherlands, Norway, and most of the African and Asian countries. With the exception of Belgium, these affiliates are heavily petroleum-oriented.

The third group, with domestic sales running at less than one-third of overall sales, harbors the profit centers of the first order. Some of the subsidiaries in this category generate their sales and profits through physical exports of locally produced raw material, usually oil. Others conduct their international business on the basis of paper transactions, which do not even require the physical movement of the goods involved through the national territory of the affiliate. Paper transactions point to a vexing problem that besets many of these data: that export sales are not synonymous with actual shipments. Making things even worse is the fact that most differences between the two cannot be fully explained with sales of services.

Switzerland, the Bahamas, Bermuda, other islands in the Caribbean, Panama, Hong Kong, and Singapore are typical examples of these profit centrifuges. Invariably, they share the following features: a very high ratio of export to local sales, relatively few people employed, high sales/profit ratios per employee, and business concentrated in oil and trade. As could be expected, manufacturing is conspicuously underrepresented. If affiliate export sales are compared to official merchandise exports of the nation involved, they usually reach unrealistically high shares. In the case of Switzerland, for example, this share would exceed 90 percent. Table 9.1 illustrates to some extent the magnitude of this phenomenon by listing sales and related shipments of goods side by side where they have been published without any possibility to reconcile the information thus offered.

AFFILIATE EXPORT DEVELOPMENTS

Affiliate sales grew vigorously during the period of 1950 to 1982, but turned flat for a five-year period between 1982 and 1986. Induced to a large degree by the strong dollar and world recession, the stagnation effected both domestic and export markets. A renewed upward trend started in 1987 but, by all indications, fizzled out during the early 1990s.

Addressing the above-mentioned discrepancy between sales and actual shipments leads to the superficial impression that the problem is limited to trade with the United States alone, and here visible only for the census years 1977, 1982, and 1989. Beyond that, nothing is offered to explain the

TABLE 9.1. Local and Export Sales by Mofas ($ billion)

Year	Total Sales	Local Sales	%	Exports	%
1950	$21.2e	$15.9e	75.0e	$5.3e	25.0e
1957*	43.8	33.3	76.0	10.5	24.0
1966	97.8	73.4	75.1	24.4	24.9
1967	108.5	81.3	74.9	27.1	25.1
1968	120.8	89.4	74.0	31.3	26.0
1969	134.3	98.1	73.0	36.2	27.0
1970	155.9	114.0	73.1	41.9	26.9
1971	184.4	133.3	72.3	51.2	27.7
1972	212.3	152.5	71.8	59.6	28.2
1973	291.4	204.4	70.1	86.9	29.9
1974	437.7	276.5	63.2	161.2	36.8
1975	458.3	301.5	65.8	156.8	34.2
1977	507.0	313.3	61.7	193.7	38.3
				138.1**	27.2
1982	730.2	477.9	65.5	252.3	34.5
				221.6**	30.4
1984	717.4	456.0	63.6	261.4	36.4
1985	702.8	448.6	63.9	254.2	36.1
1986	720.1	471.8	65.5	248.3	34.5
1987	815.5	539.4	66.2	276.1	33.8
1988	927.9	606.3	65.3	321.6	34.7
1989	1,019.9	690.5	67.7	329.4	32.3
				299.0**	29.3
1990	1,208.3	809.5	67.0	398.8	33.0
1991	1,240.9	823.7	66.4	417.2	33.6
1992	1,291.6	856.7	66.3	434.9	33.7
1993	1,279.1	844.8	66.0	434.3	34.0

Notes: Data from 1966 forward relate to Mofas only. *1957 data exclude finance, insurance, banking, and trade. **Shipments. e = estimates.

Sources: See Table 9.6.

problem's existence or its scope. All of this leaves the uncomfortable possibility that what can be openly observed for the United States could be a hidden problem for affiliate export sales to the rest of the world. A comparative study measuring actual shipments against reported sales in this area has never been undertaken, despite the U.S. experience.

It would be convenient to link the sales/shipment gap to service sales, which are included in the totals, but any attempt to reconcile the two proves futile. To demonstrate the difficulties, 1982 and 1989 Mofa sales and shipments to the United States are cited, which decidedly rule out services as the cause of the problem. The two sets of figures are just too far apart to be connected in any reasonable way. In 1977, when the gap was noticed for the first time, it amounted to a shipment shortfall of $ 55.6 billion. By 1982, there was a difference of $23.2 billion between sales and shipments of goods, a figure that was reduced to a smaller but still significant $16.4 billion in 1989. The good news here is that the problem becomes smaller both in actual dollar terms and relative to total Mofa sales (see Figure 9.1). Such gaping differences in the goods sector require a look at each major export industry and its contribution to the problem as recorded in the next table. Such information is available for the census years 1977, 1982, and 1989. The 1977 data contain sales of services, but their inclusion is not considered to detract from the general picture in any important way (see Table 9.2).

The evidence clearly points to the petroleum affiliates as the major cause of the problem, accounting for 97 percent of the difference in 1977, 69 percent in 1982, and 70 percent in 1989. The rest is shared by manufacturing, trade and all other affiliates. Finance subsidiaries are only guilty by association. Consisting entirely of service selling functions, they are very unlikely to ever export sizeable amounts of tangible goods. For that reason, they are excluded from further consideration here. Manufacturing, trade, and all other affiliates contribute only marginally to the problem. The small difference between sales and shipments here could easily follow from normal time lags between order receipt, processing, invoicing, and actual transport operations.

Finding oil affiliates almost entirely responsible for the baffling discrepancies in Mofa export statistics sheds some light on the problem, but still

FIGURE 9.1. Sales/Shipments to the United States

	Sales to the United States	Shipments to the United States
Total 1982	$76.8	$46.1
Goods	69.3	46.1
Services	7.4	–
Total 1989	114.7	84.3
Goods	100.7	84.3
Services	10.4	–
Investment income	3.6	–

Sources: FDI census data: 1982, pp. 234, 281; 1989, pp. 202, 206, 235. *SOCB*, August 1992, p. 68.

TABLE 9.2. Industry Differences Between Mofa Sales and Shipments of Goods to the United States ($ billion)

	Total	Petroleum	Manufacturing	Trade	Finance	Other
1977						
Sales	$93.6	$70.9	$17.6	$2.2	$0.6	$2.2
Shipments	38.0	16.8	17.7	1.7	0.0	N/A
Difference	55.6	54.1	0.1	0.5	0.6	N/A
1982						
Sales	69.3	36.3	25.8	5.4	0	1.8
Shipments	46.1	15.5	26.4	2.6	0	1.6
Difference	23.2	20.8	0.6	2.8	0	0.2
1989						
Sales	100.7	21.3	68.8	8.7	0	1.9
Shipments	84.3	9.9	65.2	7.5	1	1.6
Difference	16.4	11.4	3.6	1.2	1	0.3

Note: The 1977 data contain goods and services that cannot be separated for the year.

Sources: 1977 FDI census, pp. 318, 352. 1982 FDI census, pp. 235, 282. 1989 FDI census, pp. 202, 235.

leaves important questions unanswered. Thus, it has to be assumed that sales of tangibles, not followed by actual shipments, are the result of tax ploys. This makes sense insofar as most of the discrepancy arises from business conducted with parent companies. In 1977, Mofa sales to the same reached $66.1 billion versus shipments of only $13.6 billion for a difference of $52.5 billion. Their sales to other U.S. customers showed sales of $4.8 billion, $1.7 billion more than shipments of $3.1 billion (1977 FDI census, pp. 323, 357, 361). The 1982 sales to parents were down to $31.4 billion versus shipments of $12.5 billion, which were near their 1977 level. The difference: $18.9 billion. Sales and shipments to unrelated U.S. clients were again more or less at 1977 levels, with $5.2 and $3.0 billion respectively for a difference of only $2.2 billion (1982 FDI census, pp. 226, 287, 290). In 1989, the figures for trade with parents read sales of $15.5 billion, and shipments $7.2 billion, for a difference of $8.3 billion. Oil trade with unaffiliated U.S. customers showed sales of $5.7 billion, shipments of $2.7 billion, for a difference of $3.0 billion (1989 FDI census, pp. 202, 235).

In all years, parents bought substantially more than they actually received from Mofa suppliers. But this again is also only part of a larger picture.

1982 parent sales to Mofas of $51.6 billion and shipments of only $1.8 billion produced a net increase in parental receivables of $49.8 billion. This compares with their net payables to Mofas of $18.9 billion, as shown above. Netted out, both figures leave a sizable surplus on parent books. Was it all profit? How did affiliates finance this debt of $30.9 billion for 1982 alone? A similar situation cannot be established for 1989, because the necessary information is not furnished. It may, nonetheless, be assumed to continue, and it would be interesting to know what the tax ramifications of such transactions are for the United States and other countries.

There is no way to draw a complete picture of these ping-pong transactions, because parent purchases from foreigners are not disclosed. But similar profit strategies may be involved, if parent sales of $48.8 billion to nonaffiliated foreigners followed by shipments of only $9.2 billion are any indication (1982 FDI census, pp. 316, 269, 332).

Known as "triangle transactions" such business practices are common throughout the world. Employed for duty drawback, subsidy, or tax and profit-shifting purposes, they provide a secretive, yet very practical background that goes a long way in explaining the sizable gap between export sales and shipments observed for U.S. FDI companies. For the researcher, it poses a problem in that it prevents a clear definition of the American position in the world trade of goods, which are not maintained on the basis of sales, but actual shipments.

It is an intractable situation, which makes the further discussion of exports an often ambiguous exercise, as affiliate exports to the rest of the world continue to be reported on the basis of sales being equal to shipments–the same formula applied years ago to affiliate trade with the United States. It is probably correct to assume a similar situation to exist here, with a need of revision. Support for this view is furnished by the business done by profit centers described above, which cover business transacted with other countries as well, and offer no realistic connection between affiliate export sales and official country exports reported.

In passing, it may be noted that export shipments to the United States accounted for an estimated 12 percent of overall affiliate sales in 1950, but declined gradually to between 6 and 7 percent in the early 1990s. The subject of affiliate trade with U.S. customers is explored in more detail in another section, and covers the whole U.S. trade picture involving parents, affiliates, and unrelated customers.

Affiliate exports to other world areas followed an exactly opposite course, insofar as exports went from 15 percent of total affiliate sales in 1957, to 19 percent in 1966, 20 percent in 1977, 24 percent in 1982, and a slightly lower 20 percent in 1989.

Affiliate export sales grew from an estimated $7 billion in 1950 to $252 billion in 1982, to $434 billion in 1993. Adjusted for shipments to the United States and sales of services, subsidiary trade in merchandise put affiliates firmly among the leading world exporters, as shown by the 1982 and 1990 comparison with major trading nations (*International Financial Statistics*, YB 1985, *IMF*, pp. 108-9. *Direction of Trade Statistics*, YB 1993, *IMF*, p. 2). The data drive home a point: the offspring has outgrown the parents as so often happens, leaving a mark on U.S. trade relations with the rest of the world. As will be pointed out later on, the growth of affiliate exports was instrumental in shoring up the overall American position in world trade for a long time. But it could not prevent, and actually may have contributed to, the often cited decline in U.S. exports (see Figure 9.2).

The affiliate export position looks even more phenomenal when contrasted with the American trade volume on a more exacting basis of product mix. As affiliates neither produce nor export agricultural or military products of any consequence, they need to be evaluated against revised U.S. exports of comparable industrial products only, which reached $179 billion in 1982 and $359 billion in 1990 (*Economic Report of the President*, January 1993, pp. 368, 459).

Such data underscore the enormous trading power of U.S. affiliates in their own right. Which raises the question of whether the role of FDI, be it American or foreign, in the international scheme of things can be adequately described in economic terms alone. Control over such far-flung networks of production and trade entities certainly empowers corporate strategists and executives to impact deeply on domestic as well as foreign economies, international trade, and political relations at home and abroad.

The U.S. trade deficit furnishes a good illustration of the juncture between FDI and national politics. Concern over this tenacious problem has

FIGURE 9.2. Mofa Exports Compared to Leading Export Nations

Year	1982	1990
Affiliates	$214 billion	$363 billion
USA	211	492
Germany	176	318
Japan	138	207
France	97	227
UK	97	202

Sources: *Direction of Trade Statistic's Yearbook*, *IMF* (various issues), author's own calculations.

led U.S. federal and state governments to initiate a wide range of export promotion programs. But years of concerted efforts, be they through incentives, moral pressure on business, threats of retaliation against real or alleged trade impediments created by foreigners, or massive currency manipulations, have not induced any appreciable improvement in the foreign trade balance; and, really, how could they? As pointed out in earlier discussions, the foreign trade of the United States lies predominantly in the hands of outward and inward direct investment companies who, by all appearances, have the power to actually influence U.S. foreign trade as dictated by corporate profit considerations. That power is beautifully demonstrated by inward investments, which account for the lion's share of the U.S. trade deficit as shown earlier.

A telling indicator for America's contribution to its own trade and economic woes are Mofa exports, which ran at an estimated 50 percent level of U.S. exports in 1950. Today they may well exceed them by close to the margins shown above, even if allowances have to be made for value differences created by the use of sales versus shipment statistics. Given the choice of serving the world market from their home base or through overseas affiliates, headquarter managers, more often than not, preferred the latter. Otherwise, it could not have come to such a trade inversion. But it was bound to happen as a consequence of absent regulatory controls over foreign investments, a maturing domestic economy, strained industrial relations in the home market, the open door policy and development potential of foreign nations, and the particular international profit lures at work during the whole period.

Aiding the process was the long-term appreciation of foreign currencies which led to incremental returns on American capital invested overseas, by letting subsidiary assets and profits grow automatically in terms of dollars. Exchange rate driven profits could be fortified by decreasing subsidiary costs via intercompany supplies in unfinished form, as well as transfer pricing mechanisms. In addition, there were the unique profit opportunities afforded by the judicious use of tax havens, presumably with the tacit, if not deliberate, acquiescence of the American government and tax authorities. In combination, the many manifest advantages of FDI led to cross-purposes of official and investor interests.

AFFILIATE EXPORTS BY WORLD REGION

Table 9.1 provided a summary view of all reported affiliate exports between 1950 and 1993. Up to 1966, all affiliates are covered, but beginning with the 1966 survey, reporting was narrowed down to Mofas only, and from the 1977 census forward, even further narrowed to include only nonbank Mofas.

Additional data are available that provide fairly detailed accounts of U.S. imports from affiliates, which, in reality, refer only to exports reported by the affiliates. Their exports to other world areas do not enjoy the same degree of detail. Thus, it is impossible to get data for specific countries of destination with very few exceptions. This applies both to exports to other affiliates as well as to foreigners and is particularly annoying, because the lack of information cannot even be partially counterbalanced with affiliate import statistics for individual countries.

Practically all affiliates contributed to the growing export volume, even though great fluctuations can be observed for regions and industrial sectors over time. Significant shifts in area weight resulted from the fluid investment picture, causing changes in industrial structure, and political developments. Industries that enjoyed some prominence in the early period were gradually replaced by others as they emerged. A specific case in point was mining and agriculture, whose combined share in overall affiliate exports declined from 21.5 percent in 1957 to 1.8 and 1.6 percent in 1982 and 1989.

In 1957, Canadian and Latin American subsidiaries dominated the field with shares of 19 percent and 31 percent respectively–one-half of the total. Their close runner-ups were European and Asian affiliates with another 17 and 18 percent each. In combination, these areas accounted for no less than 85 percent of global subsidiary exports (see Table 9.3).

By 1989, these relative positions had been reversed. European affiliates ranked as number one with an overwhelming 60 percent of the total, followed by Canada and Asia with 13 percent each, and Latin America with only 9 percent–only one-third its original share. Within three short decades, the share of the Western Hemisphere affiliates had been cut in half, while that of Europe had more than tripled.

The decline of the Latin American affiliates could be misinterpreted without breaking this area down, once more, into its two major components: continental republics and Caribbean islands, officially called Other Western Hemisphere. Separating the two reveals South American affiliates to be the real losers in the export race. Whereas Caribbean subsidiaries held their share of total affiliate exports (inclusive of services) at 5 percent, that of all Latin American affiliates fell from 26 to 4 percent.

Asian affiliates, including those in the Middle and Far East, maintained relatively steady levels in the export development until the early 1970s, when their share suddenly exploded from 16 percent in 1970 to 43 percent in 1974. Initially propelled by the OPEC crisis, they suffered a serious setback at the hands of the same organization which caused their share to

TABLE 9.3. Affiliate Exports by World Region and Leading Countries (sales – $ billion)

Year	1957	%	1966	%	1977	%	1982	%	1989	%
Total	$10.5	100	$24.4	100	$193.7	100	$252.3	100	$329.4	100
Canada	2.0	19.2	3.9	16.1	18.3	9.4	25.2	10.0	46.0	13.9
Europe	1.8	17.1	9.6	39.5	74.6	38.5	135.9	53.8	195.8	59.5
Belg./Lux.	0.1	0.8	0.9	3.5	8.4	4.3	12.5	4.9	17.7	5.4
France	0.1	0.8	0.8	3.4	6.8	3.5	11.3	4.5	18.7	5.7
Germany	0.3	2.5	1.4	5.8	11.8	6.1	19.1	7.6	34.7	10.5
Ireland	N/A	N/A	N/A	N/A	N/A	N/A	N/A	N/A	7.5	2.3
Italy	0.1	1.2	0.5	2.2	2.4	1.3	4.0	1.6	7.6	2.3
Netherlands	0.1	1.1	0.9	3.6	8.9	4.6	15.2	6.0	25.8	7.8
Switzerland	0.1	0.7	1.9	7.7	13.2	6.8	27.7	11.0	26.2	8.0
UK	0.8	8.7	2.9	12.0	17.4	9.0	33.5	13.3	41.9	12.7
Lat. America	3.3	31.5	4.7	19.3	21.4	11.0	41.9	16.6	31.0	9.4
Lat. Am. Rep.	2.8	26.3	3.8	15.5	5.2	2.7	8.4	3.3	14.6	4.4
Argentina	nil	0.4	N/A	N/A	0.6	0.3	0.9	0.3	1.1	0.3
Brazil	nil	0.5	0.2	0.6	1.2	0.6	2.3	0.9	4.1	1.2
Chile	0.3	2.9	N/A	N/A	N/A	N/A	N/A	N/A	0.4	N/A
Mexico	0.2	1.8	0.2	1.7	0.6	0.3	1.2	0.5	5.2	1.6
Peru	0.1	1.2	0.4	1.5	0.2	0.1	0.5	0.2	N/A	N/A
Venezuela	1.8	17.1	1.7	6.9	N/A	N/A	0.1	0.3	nil	N/A
O.W. Hemi.	0.5	5.2	0.9	3.8	16.2	8.4	33.5	13.3	16.3	5.0
Bahamas	N/A	N/A	N/A	N/A	N/A	N/A	5.2	2.1	0.9	0.3
Bermuda	N/A	N/A	N/A	N/A	10.7	5.5	18.7	7.4	10.3	3.1
Cuba	0.3	2.6	N/A	N/A	N/A	N/A	N/A	N/A	N/A	N/A
N. Antilles	N/A	N/A	N/A	N/A	N/A	N/A	6.6	2.6	2.6	0.8
Africa	0.2	2.3	N/A	N/A	7.8	4.0	9.9	3.9	5.0	1.5
Asia	1.8	17.5	3.8	15.7	64.4e	33.2e	35.1	13.9	43.5	13.2
Japan	0.1	0.6	0.1	0.5	1.0	0.5	2.2	0.9	8.7	2.6
Hong Kong	N/A	N/A	N/A	N/A	3.8	2.0	4.5	1.8	9.2	2.8
Indonesia	N/A	N/A	N/A	N/A	N/A	N/A	8.3	3.3	2.7	0.8
Malaysia	N/A	N/A	N/A	N/A	0.5	0.3	2.0	0.8	2.7	0.8
Middle East	1.5	14.4	2.9	11.9	52.1e	26.8e	4.2	1.7	3.1	0.9
Philippines	nil	nil	0.1	0.4	0.4	0.2	0.6	0.2	0.7	N/A
Singapore	N/A	N/A	N/A	N/A	N/A	N/A	11.6	4.6	11.1	3.4
Taiwan	N/A	N/A	N/A	N/A	0.6	0.3	0.9	0.4	2.7	0.8
Thailand	N/A	N/A	N/A	N/A	0.1	N/A	0.4	0.2	1.7	0.5
Australia	0.1	0.7	0.2	1.0	2.1	1.1	3.7	1.5	5.3	1.6

Notes: Data may not add up to 100 percent due to an "International" category not shown. e = estimate.

Sources: FDI census data: 1957, pp. 110-1; 1966, p. 198; 1977, p. 318; 1982, p. 225; 1989, p. 190.

fall straight to 13 percent by 1989–a level even lower than the 18 percent they had enjoyed back in 1957. This is suggested by the sharp reversal in sales volumes by the petroleum affiliates in the Middle East between 1977 and 1982, the same years for which no statistical records of any sort have been published. The fate of these oil subsidiaries, which are officially treated as part of the Asian region, can be reconstructed from the evidence collected in Table 9.4.

Owing to the complete absence of any export statistics for the interim years 1978 to 1981, any explanation of what happened is reasonable conjecture, at best. Well documented is the rapid decline of U.S. FDI in the area mentioned earlier, and it is fair to assume that it occurred in Saudi Arabia alone. Some insight into the history of the U.S. investment in that country is provided by the fate of ARAMCO, the original oil concession-aire founded in 1933, which had a legal life of sixty years. In the beginning, only one American company (Socal) held all the shares. It was later joined by three more U.S. partners, before being nationalized step by step by the Saudi Arabian government during the 1970s.

The original agreement between the American and Arab sides was repeatedly modified to grant Saudi Arabia successively more equitable profit-sharing terms. In 1948, royalties payable to the Saudi government were increased by five cents per barrel on offshore oil with a guaranteed minimum payment of $2 million per year. In 1950, a mutual agreement was reached which subjected ARAMCO to profit sharing for the first time

TABLE 9.4. Export Sales by Petroleum Affiliates from Asia and Middle East ($ billion)

Year	Asian Exports		Middle East Exports			
	Total	Petroleum	Total	Petroleum	To USA	Others
1973	$25.7	$22.9	$19.9	$19.8	$1.1	$18.8
1974	69.2	64.7	57.4	57.4	4.7	52.7
1975	58.6	54.0	48.5	48.4	3.6	44.8
1977	64.3	58.3	51.8*	51.8*	N/A	N/A
1982	35.1	23.0	3.8	3.8	3.6	0.2
1989	43.5	8.3	2.2	2.2	1.7	0.5

Notes: *Middle East petroleum exports were not reported in the 1977 FDI census. The above estimate was derived by deducting local petroleum sales from total affiliate petroleum sales reported. Mofa data only.

Sources: SOCB, February 1977, p. 32 (1973-75). 1977 FDI census, pp. 283, 320. 1982 FDI census, pp. 228-9. 1989 FDI census, pp. 190, 192, 196.

in the form of a regular income tax instead of fixed royalties per barrel produced. A 5 percent export surcharge started in 1970. This piecemeal sharing of income led–as one would expect–to increasing pressures from the Arab side to be granted full participation in the management of their nation's principal resource. The first step in this direction was taken by Sheik Yamani in 1968 when he proposed a new power-sharing concept. It was adopted in 1972 when the concessionary companies signed the "general agreement" with all governments in the Gulf area, which opened the door to a 25 percent Saudi Arabian minority share in Aramco in 1973. Follow-up negotiations increased the Arab share to 60 percent in 1974, and by 1980 nationalization was complete. The protracted negotiations in the beginning followed by rapid gains of concessions from the American partners, and the Arab takeover (fourteen years before it could have been anticipated under the terms of the original concession) indicates that the transition was not a smooth one. It coincided with the first OPEC price explosion (to help pay for the expropriation of ARAMCO?), the cessation of Saudi oil deliveries to the United States in protest against the American support of Israel in the 1973 war, and the assassination of King Faisal in March of 1975 by his own nephew (*ARAMCO and its World*, pp. 152-163, 235-239) (see Table 9.5).

The development of affiliate oil exports from the region to the United States and other markets is interesting in light of this background. Deliveries to the United States, small though they are, were not visibly affected, and may very well have emanated from non-Saudi sources in the region, while those to other areas were virtually obliterated. U.S. oil companies were able to partly make up for the Saudi losses by moving into other oil fields in Europe and Asia, but not without deep changes in the industry's structure (see Tables 8.9, 8.14). Ten years after the calamitous setback, the United States opened a new chapter by returning to the region with a

TABLE 9.5. ARAMCO's Changing Ownership

Company	1933	1936	1948	1973	1974	1979	1980
Socal	100	50	30	22.5	12	11.3	0
Texaco	0	50	30	22.5	12	11.3	0
Exxon	0	0	30	22.5	12	11.3	0
Mobil	0	0	10	7.5	4	6.0	0
Saudi Gov.	0	0	0	25.0	60	60.0	100

Note: Ownership refers to equity shares held.

Source: Embassy of Saudi Arabia, Ministry of Higher Education, Washington, DC 20007.

protective military force. Precipitated by Iraq's August 1990 invasion of Kuwait, it was a welcome occasion to once more establish influence over the oil region whose political instability and vulnerability provided persuasive arguments for long-term U.S. involvement. Strategically necessary in view of Saddam Hussein's survival and Iran's military buildup, the situation is politically convenient, economically promising, and may pave the way for renewed U.S. investments in the Middle East. The $6 billion purchase of U.S. airplanes announced by Saudi Airlines in February of 1994 is another milestone in renewed U.S.-Saudi relations, and one that successfully shut out Europe's airbus competition, at least for some time.

Affiliates in other world areas were actively participating in international trade all along, but were of lesser importance in comparison to their peers discussed so far. This view applies in particular to those affiliates located in Africa and Oceania whose combined share reached hardly 6 percent of the total at their peak during the oil years of the 1970s. Today it is down to the same 3 percent level where it started from during the 1950s.

REGIONAL EXPORTS TO THE UNITED STATES AND OTHER COUNTRIES

Affiliate exports can be viewed from two different angles. One establishes the affiliate perspective, splitting their total exports between the United States and all other countries providing a measure of relative importance of both markets for individual area affiliates. The other is taken from the customer's side and measures each area affiliates' weight in U.S. imports from all affiliates, or similarly, for imports from affiliates by the rest of the world.

There is a relative abundance of data on the subject, as far as the U.S. side is concerned. It also applies to a lesser degree to the rest of the world, where such information is too global to yield anything but a very superficial impression. That is to say, that affiliate exports to a whole region may be found, but equal details for individual countries are usually lacking. This makes it practically impossible to assess the role of affiliates in national imports, be they to affiliates or local nationals.

The situation is aggravated by an even larger information deficit for affiliate imports by area or country, again with the exception of the United States. Comprehensive information on total affiliate imports from affiliates and foreigners alike was published only once. So far, the 1977 census is the only source providing a rare glimpse at such details. A pity, because more information would have been very helpful in establishing affiliate roles in a country's overall trade.

Affiliate export aggregates open the door to a more detailed analysis of the roles played by the regional affiliates over the whole period by showing first actual dollar exports made by area affiliates in total, to the United States (sales and shipments separately), and to other regions (see Tables 9.6 and 9.7)This information is repeated in a follow-up table in terms of percentages providing a quick and convenient measure of area affiliate shares in total affiliate exports, and the relative changes that have occurred over time (see Table 9.8). A final summary review breaks down total area affiliate exports into those going to the United States and all other destinations. It establishes a focus for affiliate exports by major customers, and changes in the mix over time (see Table 9.9).

Measured in terms of sales, affiliate exports to the United States underwent considerable fluctuations. From a 36 percent high of total affiliate exports in 1957, the U.S. share dropped gradually down to an all-time low of 20 percent in 1975, recovered to its previous levels during the 1980s, only to slide again to 32 percent at the end of 1993. Measured in terms of shipments, however, there may have been a true share erosion from 36 percent in 1957 to 21 percent by the early 1990s, if the government interpretation of sales equals shipments establishes a realistic basis for 1957 (see Table 9.6).

Canadian affiliates ran counter to this overall trend by increasing the U.S. share of their exports from 70 to 89 percent between 1957 and 1989 (see Table 9.9). This led to an increase of their position in total affiliate export shipments to the U.S. market from 37 percent in 1957 to 47 percent in 1989 (see Table 9.9).

Latin American subsidiaries, on the other hand, have decreased both the percentage of their export shipments destined to the parent country, down from 52 to 45 percent (Table 9.9), and the share they once held in overall affiliate shipments to the United States, which was reduced from 45 to 12 percent (see Table 9.8). Affiliates in the Caribbean also decreased the percentage of their total export going to the U.S. market by cutting it practically in half, from 33 to 13 percent (see Table 9.9), and yet were able to raise their share in all affiliate export shipments to the same address from 1 to 2 percent (see Table 9.8).

The completely opposite development of affiliate importance for U.S. imports between Canada and South America is partially explained by their differences in affiliate industry structure. Canadian exports consist of 75 percent manufacture's, mainly automotive, and 16 percent petroleum products. For South America, this ratio is practically reversed with 59 percent derived from petroleum exports (which were subject to wide swings in prices), 30 percent from services, and only 11 percent stemming from manufactures.

TABLE 9.6. Affiliate Export Sales/Shipments by Final Destination ($ million)

Year	Total	To U.S.	%	To Others	%
1950	$5,300e	$2,500	47.2	$2,800e	52.8
1957**	10,459	3,770	36.0	6,689	64.0
1966	24,393	6,300	25.8	18,093	74.2
1967	27,176	7,230	26.6	19,946	73.4
1968	31,312	8,574	27.4	22,738	72.6
1969	36,192	9,500	26.2	26,692	73.8
1970	41,894	9,941	23.7	31,953	76.3
1971	51,159	12,794	25.0	38,365	75.0
1972	59,541	14,067	23.6	45,474	76.4
1973	86,953	19,613	22.6	67,340	77.4
1974	161,152	31,801	19.7	129,351	80.3
1975	156,764	31,571	20.1	125,193	79.9
1977	193,711	93,573	48.3	100,138	51.7
		38,000*	19.6	N/A	N/A
1982	252,274	76,780	30.4	175,494	69.6
		46,101*	18.3	N/A	N/A
1983	N/A	48,328*	N/A	N/A	N/A
1984	261,393	89,116	34.1	172,277	65.9
		57,167*	21.9	N/A	N/A
1985	254,247	89,055	35.1	165,192	64.9
		60,301*	23.7	N/A	N/A
1986	248,294	79,979	32.3	168,315	67.7
		57,195*	22.9	N/A	N/A
1987	276,166	88,922	32.2	187,244	67.8
		65,542*	23.7	N/A	N/A
1988	321,574	101,444	31.4	220,130	68.6
		76,042*	23.6	N/A	N/A
1989	329,438	114,719	34.9	214,719	64.8
		84,298*	25.6	N/A	N/A
1990	398,873	123,865	31.1	275,008	68.9
		88,641*	22.2	N/A	N/A
1991	418,164	125,526	30.0	292,638	70.0
		90,152*	21.7	N/A	N/A
1992	434,913	129,236	29.7	305,678	70.3
		84,890*	19.5	N/A	N/A
1993	434,317	138,209	31.8	296,108	68.2
		95,906*	22.1	N/A	N/A

Notes: Mofa data starting with 1966. Export sales include goods and services. *Represents shipments. **Data exclude finance, insurance, banking, and trade. e = estimate.

Sources: FDI census data: 1950, p. 29; 1957, pp. 110-1; 1966, p. 198; 1977, pp. 318, 352; 1982, pp. 225, 235, 281-2; 1989, pp. 191, 201, 256. *SOCB*, August 1975, p. 27 (1967-71); February 1977, p. 32 (1973-75); September 1986, pp. 36-7 (1983); June 1987, p. 37 (1984); June 1988, pp. 94-6 (1984-86); June 1989, pp. 36, 38 (1987); June 1990, pp. 40-1 (1986-88). 1989 FDI census, pp. 190, 253. *SOCB*, August 1992, p. 68; July 1993, pp. 45-6; June 1994, p. 51; June 1995, pp. 39, 40.

TABLE 9.7. Affiliate Exports by World Area of Origin and Destination ($ billion)

Year	All Affiliates To:			Canada To:			Latin America To:			Caribbean To:		
	World	USA	Other	World	USA	Other	World	USA	Other	World	USA	Other
1950	5.3e	2.5	2.8e	N/A	N/A	N/A	N/A	N/A	N/A	N/A	N/A	N/A
1957	10.5	3.8	6.7	2.0	1.4	0.7	3.3	1.7	1.6	0.3	0.1	0.2
1966	24.4	6.3	18.1	3.9	2.9	1.0	4.7	1.8	2.9	0.9	0.4	0.6
1967	27.2	7.2	19.9	5.2	3.7	1.5	4.7	1.7	3.0	N/A	N/A	N/A
1968	31.3	8.6	22.7	6.3	4.6	1.7	4.9	1.9	3.0	N/A	N/A	N/A
1969	36.2	9.5	26.7	7.2	5.4	1.8	5.4	1.9	3.4	N/A	N/A	N/A
1970	41.9	9.9	31.9	8.2	5.9	2.3	5.2	1.8	3.4	N/A	N/A	N/A
1971	51.2	12.8	38.4	9.8	7.2	2.6	5.8	2.4	3.4	N/A	N/A	N/A
1972	59.9	14.4	45.5	10.4	7.9	2.4	6.3	2.6	3.7	N/A	N/A	N/A
1973	86.9	19.6	67.3	13.0	9.8	3.2	9.4	3.8	5.6	N/A	N/A	N/A
1974	161.2	31.8	129.4	15.9	11.4	4.5	18.4	6.4	12.0	8.7	2.7	5.9
1975	156.8	31.6	125.2	17.5	12.7	4.8	19.5	6.7	12.8	16.2	9.2	7.0
1977	193.7	93.6	100.1	18.3	14.7	3.6	21.4	11.1	10.3	10.6	3.5	7.0
*	138.1	38.0	100.1	17.9	14.3	3.6	15.5	5.2	10.3			
1982	252.3	76.8	175.5	25.2	20.8	4.3	41.9	16.4	25.5	33.5	13.2	20.3
*	221.6	46.1	175.5	24.7	20.4	4.3	32.5	7.0	25.5	24.0	3.7	20.3
1989	329.4	114.7	214.7	46.0	40.8	5.1	31.0	18.5	12.5	16.3	10.1	6.2
*	299.0	84.3	214.7	44.7	39.6	5.1	22.8	10.3	12.5	7.1	0.9	6.2

TABLE 9.7 (continued)

Year	Europe To:			Africa To:			Asia To:			Oceania To:		
	World	USA	Other	World	USA	Other	World	USA	Other	World	USA	Other
1950	N/A	N/A	N/A	N/A	N/A	N/A	N/A	N/A	N/A	N/A	N/A	N/A
1957	1.8	0.2	1.6	0.2	0.1	0.1	1.9	0.3	1.6	0.1	nil	0.1
1966	9.6	0.8	8.9	1.0	0.1	0.9	3.8	0.5	3.3	0.2	nil	0.2
1967	10.1	0.9	9.1	1.2	0.1	1.1	4.6	0.4	4.2	N/A	N/A	N/A
1968	11.7	1.1	10.5	1.5	0.1	1.4	5.3	0.5	4.8	N/A	N/A	N/A
1969	13.2	1.1	12.1	1.7	0.1	1.6	6.0	0.6	5.4	N/A	N/A	N/A
1970	17.8	1.3	16.5	1.9	0.1	1.8	6.8	0.5	6.3	N/A	N/A	N/A
1971	20.6	1.6	19.1	2.1	0.2	1.9	10.5	1.1	9.4	N/A	N/A	N/A
1972	24.4	1.8	22.6	2.4	0.2	2.2	13.7	1.5	12.2	N/A	N/A	N/A
1973	31.9	2.4	29.5	3.3	0.5	2.8	26.4	2.8	23.6	N/A	N/A	N/A
1974	43.8	3.1	40.8	6.2	1.5	4.6	69.2	6.9	62.3	N/A	N/A	N/A
1975	50.7	3.1	47.7	4.8	1.8	3.0	58.7	6.3	52.3	N/A	N/A	N/A
1977	74.6	7.8	66.8	7.8	6.1	1.6	63.5e	N/A	N/A	2.2	0.4	1.8
*	71.5	4.7	66.8	6.0	4.6	1.4	N/A	8.9	N/A	N/A	N/A	1.8
1982	136.9	16.6	119.3	10.4	6.5	3.9	35.1	15.6	19.6	3.8	0.8	2.9
*	125.1	5.8	119.3	6.2	2.8	3.4	28.9	9.3	19.6	3.7	0.8	2.9
1989	195.8	27.8	168.0	5.0	3.2	1.8	43.5	20.4	23.1	5.5	1.4	4.1
*	182.3	14.3	168.0	4.1	2.3	1.8	39.6	16.5	23.1	5.4	1.3	4.1

Notes: *Represents shipments. Africa excludes South Africa from 1966-75. Mofa data starting with 1966. e = estimate.

TABLE 9.8. Area Affiliate Share in Total Affiliate Exports (percentages)

Year	Canadian Affiliates To:			Latin American Affiliates To:			Caribbean Affiliates To:			European Affiliates To:		
	World	USA	Other	World	USA	Other	World	USA	Other	World	USA	Other
1957	19	37	10	31	45	24	3	1	2	17	5	24
1966	16	46	6	19	29	16	4	2	2	40	13	49
1967	19	51	8	17	24	15	N/A	N/A	N/A	37	13	46
1968	20	53	7	16	22	13	N/A	N/A	N/A	37	13	46
1969	20	57	7	15	20	13	N/A	N/A	N/A	39	12	48
1970	20	60	7	12	18	11	N/A	N/A	N/A	43	13	52
1971	19	56	7	11	19	9	N/A	N/A	N/A	40	14	50
1972	17	55	5	11	18	8	N/A	N/A	N/A	41	13	50
1973	15	50	5	11	19	8	N/A	N/A	N/A	37	12	44
1974	10	36	3	11	20	9	6	2	4	27	10	32
1975	11	40	4	12	21	10	8	5	4	33	10	38
1977	9	16	4	11	12	10	8	3	5	39	8	67
*	13	38	4	11	14	10	8	3	5	52	12	67
1982	10	27	2	17	21	14	13	5	8	54	22	68
*	11	44	2	15	15	14	11	2	9	57	13	68
1989	14	35	2	9	16	6	5	9	3	60	24	78
*	15	47	2	8	12	6	2	1	3	61	17	78

TABLE 9.8 (continued)

Year	African Affiliates To:			Asian Affiliates To:			Oceanian Affiliates To:		
	World	USA	Other	World	USA	Other	World	USA	Other
1957	2	3	1	18	8	24	1	nil	1
1966	4	2	5	16	8	18	1	nil	N/A
1967	4	1	6	17	6	21	N/A	N/A	N/A
1968	5	1	6	17	6	21	N/A	N/A	N/A
1969	5	1	6	17	6	20	N/A	N/A	N/A
1970	5	1	6	16	5	20	N/A	N/A	N/A
1971	4	2	5	21	9	24	N/A	N/A	N/A
1972	4	1	5	23	10	27	N/A	N/A	N/A
1973	3	3	3	30	12	35	N/A	N/A	N/A
1974	4	5	4	43	22	48	N/A	N/A	N/A
1975	3	6	2	37	20	42	N/A	N/A	N/A
1977	4	7	1	33	N/A	N/A	2	nil	2
*	4	12	1	N/A	23	N/A	N/A	N/A	2
1982	6	8	2	14	20	11	2	1	2
*	3	6	2	13	20	11	2	2	2
1989	2	3	1	13	18	11	2	1	2
*	1	3	1	13	20	11	2	2	2

Note: *Represents shipments.

284

TABLE 9.9. Percentage Share of Area Affiliate Export Sales by Area

Year	Canada To: USA	Canada To: Other	Lat. America To: USA	Lat. America To: Other	Caribbean To: USA	Caribbean To: Other	Europe To: USA	Europe To: Other
1957	70	30	52	48	33	67	11	89
1966	74	26	38	62	44	56	8	92
1967	71	29	36	64	N/A	N/A	9	91
1968	73	27	39	61	N/A	N/A	9	91
1969	75	25	35	65	N/A	N/A	8	92
1970	72	28	35	65	N/A	N/A	7	93
1971	73	27	41	59	N/A	N/A	8	92
1972	76	24	41	59	N/A	N/A	7	93
1973	75	25	40	60	N/A	N/A	8	92
1974	72	28	35	65	N/A	N/A	7	93
1975	73	27	34	66	31	69	6	94
1977	80	20	52	48	57	43	10	90
*	80	20	34	66	33	67	7	93
1982	83	17	39	61	39	61	12	88
*	83	17	22	78	15	85	5	95
1989	89	11	60	40	62	38	14	86
*	89	11	45	55	13	87	8	92

Year	Africa To: USA	Africa To: Other	Asia To: USA	Asia To: Other	Oceania To: USA	Oceania To: Other	All Affiliates To: USA	All Affiliates To: Other
1957	50	50	17	83	nil	100	36	64
1966	10	90	13	87	nil	100	26	74
1967	8	92	9	91	N/A	N/A	26	74
1968	7	93	9	91	N/A	N/A	27	73
1969	6	94	10	90	N/A	N/A	26	74
1970	5	95	7	93	N/A	N/A	24	76
1971	10	90	11	89	N/A	N/A	25	75
1972	8	92	11	89	N/A	N/A	24	76
1973	15	85	11	89	N/A	N/A	23	77
1974	24	76	10	90	N/A	N/A	20	80
1975	38	62	11	89	N/A	N/A	20	80
1977	78	22	N/A	N/A	18	82	48	52
*	77	23	N/A	N/A	N/A	N/A	28	72
1982	63	37	44	56	21	79	30	70
*	45	55	32	68	22	78	21	79
1989	64	36	47	53	25	75	35	65
*	56	44	42	58	24	76	28	72

Note: *Represents shipments.

The European affiliates as the major players among their peers show a picture that is similar to that of the Caribbean affiliates, but on a completely different scale. They slashed the U.S. share of their total exports from 11 to 8 percent (see Table 9.9), but raised their stakes in all affiliate exports to the United States from 5 to 17 percent (see Table 9.8). Among the rest of the affiliates, the ones located in Asia are very similar to their Canadian relatives in that they raised both the share of their total exports to the American market from 17 to 42 percent (see Table 9.9), and their share of all affiliate shipments going in the same direction from 8 percent to no less than 20 percent between 1957 and 1989 (see Table 9.8).

U.S. imports from affiliates, which essentially represent parent demand, saw significant changes in the supply base for the time frame under study. Canada and Latin America furnished 82 percent of the total in 1957, and presumably even more before, but only 51 percent in 1989. Asia and Europe, on the other hand, with a modest 13 percent share in 1957, in 1989 accounted for 42 percent. Aligning the area affiliates in their rank order of importance as suppliers to the U.S. market shows the following picture for 1957 and 1989 (see Table 9.10).

TABLE 9.10. Rank Order in Total Affiliate Exports to the United States

Position	Area	1957	Area	1989
1.	Lat. America	45%	Canada	36%
2.	Canada	37	Europe	24
3.	Asia	8	Asia	18
4.	Europe	5	Lat. America	16
5.	Africa	3	Africa	3
6.	Other	2	Other	2

Source: See Table 9.7.

Affiliate trade patterns with other world areas are poorly documented by comparison, but still sufficient to support a few broad generalizations. Depending on which set of data is used as the basis for judgement, two very different pictures emerge. If export sales are chosen, other world markets may not experience a share growth among total affiliate exports. If, however, shipments become the measurement of choice, these markets commanded an ever growing share of affiliate exports (see Table 9.9).

The leader in affiliate exports to third countries was Europe whose share had grown from 24 percent in 1957 to 78 percent in 1989, followed by

Asian and Latin American affiliates with 1989 shares of 11 and 6 percent respectively, for a combined total of 95 percent. The latter two areas and Canada, however, lost the market shares that Europe's affiliates gained (see Table 9.8). As far as the 1989 importance of these markets for area affiliates exports is concerned, they accounted for about 90 percent of European, 55 percent of Latin American, 55 percent of Asian, and only 11 percent of Canadian overall affiliate exports (see Table 9.9).

Chapter 10

Affiliate Exports by Industry

Few FDI facets can match the fascination of sales and their changes over time by industry, country, and region. Industry aggregates define markets. Company sales establish shares in these markets, and over time, both help to draw a picture of vital trends. Sales thus become the forerunners of investment, messengers of change, fingers that point to the future, indicators of an industry's state of the art, and proof of its competitive capabilities. Trend changes in exports/imports add a special dimension to the picture. Going beyond purely local marketing conditions, they attest to an industry's capacity to meet the toughest international challenges. Records of affiliate exports can tell a number of things:

1. There is the relative size and importance of each industry in the total picture, including goods and services. It is a portrait of the leaders and followers at a given moment, and how they change positions over time. In the case of U.S. FDI, two industries have consistently patronized subsidiary exports since World War II: oil and manufacturing, with a combined share fluctuating between 70 and 80 percent. Addition of the trade industry here leads to a better than 90 percent coverage of all affiliate exports. Lesser industries are represented by finance, insurance, and real estate (1989: 4.6 percent), services (1989: 2.0 percent), and finally, the all other category which includes agriculture, mining, transportation, utilities, etc. (1989: 2.5 percent). Some of these industries played quite significant roles earlier. According to the 1957 FDI census, agricultural subsidiaries alone held a 5.1 percent share, mining and smelting held 16.3 percent, and public utilities held 11.6 percent, for a combined total of no less than one-third of all affiliate exports in those days. By 1989, their share had eroded to an insignificant 1.7 percent on a comparatively meager value increase from $3.5 billion to an estimated $5.5 billion in thirty-two years. In view of the inflation having occurred over those three decades, this hardly suggests any increase in physical volume.

2. Sales data show a growing export orientation, as with few exceptions, industries expand their exports more rapidly than domestic sales. For all FDI industries, exports rose from 24 percent of total sales in 1957 to 34 percent in 1993 (see Table 9.1). These global developments hide, of course, often opposing trends by individual industries such as the petroleum industry, for instance. As usual, it had a very mixed history with export shares of 33 percent in 1957, but only 17 percent in 1993, with an interim high of 42 percent during the oil crisis years (see Table 8.13).

3. The United States is not the most important customer for exporting affiliates in the majority of cases. Overall, subsidiary exports to the United States account for 20 to 30 percent of their total exports. But Canadian subsidiaries, because of their geographical proximity, ship more than 80 percent of their exports there. With less than 10 percent on average, European affiliates are at the other end of the spectrum. As a norm, regional industry sales to the United States rarely exceed 50 percent of their export business (see Table 9.9).

4. The United States seems to have a shrinking affiliate export market compared to other countries. If actual shipments to the United States were used as the measuring stick for the development, they went from 36 percent in 1957 to only 21 percent in 1982 before recovering to 28 percent in 1989. This assumes 1957 data to actually represent shipments, even though they are labeled sales–a common association of terms in those days (see Table 9.9). It is a somewhat misleading impression as further analysis shows, and heavily influenced by the oil industry, but proving the point again, that what holds true for the affiliate universe may not apply to individual industries or countries.

5. There are major differences in export contributions to total affiliate revenues for the various industries. Food affiliates represent the low end of the spectrum with only 16 percent of all operating revenues, while some manufacturing sectors and trade subsidiaries reach levels between 40 and 50 percent, with others falling somewhere in between.

6. Equally pronounced differences appear for the rank order of individual industries by region. European affiliates maintain a virtual monopoly in exports of general manufactures and trade goods, the Asian subsidiaries dominate in electronics, Canada in the automotive sector, and the Caribbean affiliates in the finance field, excluding banks. But what constitutes the rule for a regional industry as a whole may be completely different, and even reversed, when their exports are split between the United States and other world areas as shown in detail in the following pages.

The finer the details of information sought, the more often serious gaps appear in the database. The reason for this is usually protection of individual company interests rather than nonexistence of the data. In some cases, it is impossible to fill these gaps. In others, estimates were introduced if partial information was available which allowed the establishment of reasonable limits within which the actual data must fall. Following established procedure, all information refers strictly to Mofa exports unless otherwise noted. Their discussion will be handled in two parts. In the first, the relative position of single industries among all affiliate exports from a region or country, the regional export mix, will be addressed. In the second, the focus shifts to individual industries and their worldwide export breakdown by region.

INDUSTRY SHARE
IN AREA AFFILIATE EXPORT SALES

Table 10.1 presents the summary view of export sales rather than shipments by geographical area and by major affiliate industry. Based on census information showing actual data at least once for each of the four decades covered, changes in the industrial mix of major area exports become clearly visible. For easier readability, dollar volumes contained in subsequent tables were converted here into percentages with area total exports equaling 100 percent.

PETROLEUM AFFILIATE EXPORT SALES

Affiliate exports of petroleum products grew from $5 billion in 1957 to a peak of $98 billion in 1977 before declining to $46 billion in 1989. Petroleum exports held a fairly constant share between 25 and 35 percent of total industry sales, except during the crisis decade of the 1970s when it rose sharply to 50 percent as a consequence of two different factors.

The most important one was the already cited nationalization of U.S. investments by Saudi Arabia in 1980. As the expropriation was anticipated, it was in the American interest to take out as much oil as possible before relinquishing ownership. This is more or less confirmed by the sharp growth in Saudi oil output occurring between 1972 (5.7 million barrels a day) and 1980 (9.4 million barrels per day), but then falling off sharply to 6.3 million barrels per day in 1982 and 4.4 million barrels per day in 1983 (Embassy of Saudi Arabia, Washington, DC).

Foreshadowing ARAMOC's fall in 1973 was the acquisition of the first 25 percent share in ARAMCO by the Saudis, and more clearly a year later

TABLE 10.1. Industry Share of Affiliate Exports by Region (percentages)

Year	Total	Mining	Pet.	Mfg.	Trade	Finance	Other
World							
1957	100	16.3	47.6	27.9	N/A	N/A	8.2
1966	100	10.2	33.6	36.2	16.8	N/A	3.2
1977	100	2.0	50.7	30.8	13.8	0.6	2.0
1982	100	1.4	37.3	36.4	18.9	3.5	2.4
1989	100	1.1	13.9	58.6	18.6	4.6	2.5
Canada							
1957	100	30.6	6.4	62.6	N/A	N/A	0.5
1966	100	23.3	4.5	61.0	10.4	N/A	0.8
1977	100	N/A	7.6	77.0	6.2	N/A	N/A
1982	100	N/A	16.2	73.0	4.1	0.7	5.9
1989	100	N/A	10.1	82.7	3.5	0.8	2.8
Europe							
1957	100	2.8	20.7	75.7	N/A	N/A	0.7
1966	100	N/A	N/A	58.2	25.2	N/A	N/A
1977	100	N/A	16.8	52.7	26.6	0.3	2.9
1982	100	N/A	24.2	43.8	27.7	0.9	3.4
1989	100	N/A	10.6	61.0	22.8	2.2	3.2
Latin America							
1957	100	24.7	57.6	3.1	N/A	N/A	14.6
1966	100	27.0e	43.8	7.7	14.1	N/A	N/A
1977	100	3.6	64.4	10.9	14.4	N/A	N/A
1982	100	N/A	59.2	11.2	8.5	17.5	3.6
1989	100	N/A	22.0	34.2	8.7	25.2	9.7
Latin American Republics							
1957	100	25.5	63.1	2.9	N/A	N/A	0.8
1966	100	N/A	48.1	8.4	N/A	N/A	N/A
1977	100	N/A	N/A	42.1	23.2	N/A	N/A
1982	100	N/A	16.8	51.1	18.0	0.5	N/A
1989	100	N/A	13.0	70.0	8.2	nil	8.8
Other Western Hemisphere							
1957	100	N/A	29.8	4.2	N/A	N/A	66.0
1966	100	N/A	N/A	6.0	17.0	N/A	N/A
1977	100	N/A	79.4	0.9	11.6	4.8	N/A
1982	100	N/A	69.8	1.2	6.2	21.8	N/A
1989	100	N/A	38.0	1.9	nil	47.8	12.3

Year	Total	Mining	Pet.	Mfg.	Trade	Finance	Other
Africa							
1957	100	77.5	1.6	9.4	N/A	N/A	11.5
1966	100	N/A	N/A	N/A	N/A	N/A	N/A
1977	100	N/A	72.7	N/A	N/A	N/A	N/A
1982	100	N/A	88.5	2.8	2.1	N/A	N/A
1989	100	N/A	73.3	11.8	N/A	nil	N/A
Asia							
1957	100	0.8	92.7	5.3	N/A	N/A	1.3
1966	100	N/A	69.5	N/A	N/A	N/A	N/A
1977	100	N/A	N/A	N/A	N/A	N/A	N/A
1982	100	N/A	65.3	18.5	12.8	0.2	N/A
1989	100	N/A	19.8	46.5	24.3	5.8	3.6
Oceania							
1957	100	N/A	2.0	63.6	N/A	N/A	N/A
1966	100	N/A	N/A	N/A	N/A	N/A	N/A
1977	100	52.5	N/A	N/A	N/A	N/A	N/A
1982	100	N/A	N/A	34.9	10.9	1.0	N/A
1989	100	N/A	19.0	54.1	21.5	0.8	7.6

when the Saudi share shot up to 60 percent (see Table 9.5). It is interesting that the second OPEC crisis which escalated the price of crude from $12 to $34 per barrel coincided with the full takeover of ARAMCO in 1980. Anticipating such a move would turn any inventory of crude oil into a very lucrative investment, besides facilitating the financing of the Saudi nationalization. A very convenient timing, to say the least, if it was not actually and purposefully orchestrated by both sides, in which case, OPEC is getting more credit than it deserves.

After this tumultuous period, exports returned to pre-OPEC crisis levels of about one-third of total sales, with different areas pitching in to make up for the loss of the Middle Eastern supplies. Contributing to the normalization process were the oil glut produced by excessive supplies, official energy savings measures of importer nations and, finally, reduced user demand. The adjustment took time, because retail prices for refined products in many countries were subject to some form of government control and lagged behind spiraling crude prices. A facilitating factor was the decline of the dollar which mitigated upward pricing pressures for many oil importers except the United States (see Table 10.2.)

TABLE 10.2. Petroleum Affiliate Sales ($ billion)

Year	Total	Exports	%	To U.S.	%
1957	$14.5	$5.0	34.3	$1.4	9.9
1966	27.5	8.2	28.9	1.5	5.4
1970	42.4	13.1	30.9	1.7	4.1
1975	178.7	84.9	47.5	15.1	8.5
1977	198.6	98.3	49.5	70.9	35.6
1982	266.3	94.2	35.4	36.1	13.7
1989	179.4	45.9	25.6	22.8	12.7

Sources: 1957 FDI census, pp. 110-1. 1966 FDI census, pp. 199, 201-2. *SOCB*, August 1975, p. 26 (1970); February 1977, p. 32 (1975). 1977 FDI census, pp. 318-9. 1982 FDI census, p. 226. 1989 FDI census, pp. 191-6.

New oil discoveries (North Sea, Asia), political shifts in individual countries (Saudi Arabia, Iran, Libya, Venezuela), and ultimately, OPEC's formation itself largely determined the industry's capricious nature, and caused wide swings in regional exports by affiliates over the years.

Latin American affiliates were the undisputed leaders during the 1950s, when they commanded a 38 percent share of all affiliate exports. By 1982, they were down to 26 percent, well on their way to 15 percent in 1989, very close to their record low of 14 percent in 1977. The displacement of Latin America from first place was speeded by the emergence of new oil sources in Africa, the Far East, and Europe during the 1960s and 1970s, and the extension of OPEC to the region. But despite their setbacks, Latin American affiliates are still important players in America's oil industry.

Such a global view of Latin American affiliates, however, hides extensive regional shifts within the area. They are basically due to the aforementioned existence of the two types of affiliates: the actual oil producers in South America and the traders located in the Caribbean islands. According to the data, continental producers (mainly Venezuela) saw their export share dwindle from 35 percent in 1957 to a little more than 1 percent in 1989, while the island affiliates boosted theirs from 3 to 13 percent. In actual dollar terms and despite the tremendous price explosion, those South American companies sold less oil in 1989 ($0.7 billion) than they did in 1957 ($1.7 billion). Despite its huge oil reservoirs, Mexico never was part of this picture unless the trade in the islands is based on that nation's exports to the United States which is not recorded, but possible. Mexico did and still does not permit foreign participation in its nationalized industry–a principle that is not likely to be abandoned even under the NAFTA accord reached in the fall of 1992.

Close followers of Latin America during the 1950s were the Asian affiliates, including those in the Middle East. It was primarily due to the latter, and emerging European and African companies, that South American affiliates had lost their dominance by the mid-1960s. Asian affiliates rose temporarily from second place to become the leaders during the 1960s and 1970s for the reasons cited, but were displaced by European subsidiaries in 1980 when the Saudi expropriation led to a redistribution of all affiliate shares across the globe. It bestowed an instant first place on European subsidiaries, who played key roles in the exploration and exploitation of the North Sea oil fields. Everything points to their continued expansion beyond the 50 percent industry share which they approached in 1989 (see Table 10.3.)

With that share, European affiliates outdistanced their Latin American and Asian cousins whose combined share of 34 percent in 1989 falls far short of the European mark. All three areas combined made up 80 percent of total petroleum exports for that benchmark year. The rest was split among Canada with 10 percent and Africa with another 8 percent.

Sales by petroleum subsidiaries to U.S. customers exceeded reported shipments by a wide margin, as indicated before. The same applied to parent sales and shipments to foreign markets, which to a great extent were again mere trading transactions not accompanied by shipments. If sales were used to calculate FDI's world trade share, it would most likely result in a gravely distorted picture.

Table 10.5 documents all available information, but does little to shed light on the question of how these enormous discrepancies come about. The partial information provided for 1977, 1982, and 1989 offers no

TABLE 10.3. Petroleum Affiliate Exports (sales – $ billion)

Year	Total	To U.S.	%	To Others	%
1957	$5.0	$1.4	28.0	$3.6	72.0
1966	8.2	1.5	18.3	6.7	81.7
1970	13.1	1.7	13.0	11.4	87.0
1975	84.9	15.1	17.8	69.8	82.2
1977	98.3	70.9	72.1	27.4	27.9
1982	94.2	36.1	38.3	58.1	61.7
1989	45.9	22.8	49.7	23.1	50.3

Sources: See Table 10.2.

further insight into the subject. Officially, the phenomenon applies only to trade connected with the United States. By Department of Commerce definition, similar differences cannot occur for sales and shipments to third countries (either affiliates or foreigners), as they are considered to be identical in nature.

There are two good reasons to question that position. For one, the very same reasoning was used years ago for trade with the United States, until it was proven untenable later on. More important, nonoil-producing affiliates are heavily involved in selling the commodity to third markets. To cite specific examples, Switzerland sold $9.7 billion dollars worth of petroleum products to "other" countries–meaning not locally nor to the United States–in 1982. Affiliates in the Caribbean similarly sold $15.7 billion to third markets; and affiliates in Asia, not including Indonesia and Malaysia, recorded sales of an estimated $9.5 billion during the same year. As nonproducers, these countries sold 37 percent of all affiliate exports for the year, but are very unlikely to have engaged in any shipments, which makes the undifferentiated equation of sales equalling shipments rather unreal for this market segment (1982 FDI census, p. 229). This view is all the more evident, as in the case of Switzerland, for instance. Physical exports of this size would account for an unrealistically high percentage of total Swiss exports, which never have been known to include oil products to any extent (see Table 10.4).

Most of the petroleum trade with the United States covers physical oil products. Services, which are also included in the data cited, did not exceed 2 percent of parent exports in 1982 and 1989 to Mofas and foreigners. Similar data for affiliates indicate somewhat higher service shares with 6.5 percent reported for 1989.

There are more oil mysteries. In 1977, Mofas shipped $12.2 billion more to their parents than they received from them. Similar parent deficits were generated in 1982 ($9.9 billion) and 1989 ($4.5 billion). Shipments between parents and foreigners generated even larger parent payables which amounted to $17.7, $19.6, and $12.8 billion for 1977, 1982, and 1989 respectively. But, such deficits are nothing unusual for a net importer (see Table 10.5).

What is perplexing, though, are sales data that show exactly the reverse relationship between Mofas and parents. In 1982, parents sold $20.2 billion more to Mofas than they bought from them. For 1989, the difference was reduced to only $5.1 billion. While both cases produced a healthy surplus for the U.S. BOP, it raises the questions of how a net importer has enough raw materials to cover such sales volume, or how the affiliates paid for this

TABLE 10.4. Leading Affiliate Exporters–Petroleum (sales – $ billion)

Year	1957	%	1966	%	1977	%	1982	%	1989	%
Total	$5.0	100.0	$8.2	100.0	$98.3	100.0	$94.2	100.0	$45.9	100.0
Canada	0.1	2.6	0.1	2.1	1.4	1.4	4.1	4.3	4.6	10.1
Europe	0.4	7.5	1.2e	14.6e	12.6	12.8	32.9	34.9	20.9	45.5
Belg./Lux.	nil	0.5	N/A	–	0.9	0.9	N/A	–	1.7	3.7
France	nil	0.8	N/A	–	N/A	–	1.1	1.2	N/A	N/A
Norway	–	–	–	–	N/A	N/A	N/A	N/A	3.2	7.0
Switzerland	N/A	–	N/A	–	1.4	1.4	11.0e	11.7	7.5e	16.3
UK	0.1	1.5	N/A	–	5.6	5.7	8.5	9.1	5.1	11.1
Lat. America	1.9	38.3	2.1	25.1	13.8	14.0	24.8	26.3	6.8	14.8
Lat. Am. Rep.	1.7	35.1	N/A	–	0.9	0.9	1.4	1.5	0.7	1.5
O.W. Hemi.	0.2	3.2	N/A	–	12.9	13.1	23.4	25.0	6.1	13.3
Bahamas	N/A	–	N/A	–	N/A	–	4.0	4.2	0.5	1.1
Bermuda	N/A	–	N/A	–	N/A	–	14.4	15.3	5.6	12.2
Africa	nil	–	1.0e	12.2e	N/A	6.0e	9.2e	9.8e	3.7	8.1
Asia	1.7	34.2	3.7e	45.0e	60.0e	61.0e	23.0	24.4	8.7	19.0
M. East	1.5	30.1	2.9e	34.8e	52.0e	53.0e	3.8	4.0	2.3	5.0
Indonesia	N/A	–	N/A	–	N/A	–	8.0	8.5	2.2	4.8
Singapore	N/A	–	N/A	–	N/A	–	N/A	N/A	2.3	5.0
UAE	N/A	–	N/A	–	N/A	–	2.3	2.4	1.3	2.8

Notes: 1957 data do not add up to 100% because of the "International" category, which is not shown but accounts for 17.2% of all oil exports. e = estimate.

Sources: FDI census data: 1957, p. 110; 1966, pp. 199, 201; 1977, pp. 318-322; 1982, pp. 228, 229.

imbalance. At any rate, it is an intriguing sales marathon with a definite yet perplexing purpose. Similar data are not available for 1977.

The observed discrepancies defy easy explanation. Service sales are of little consequence, which leaves only one logical alternative: profit strategies. All of these baffling transactions could easily lead to double counting and unnecessarily inflated trade volumes, if sales continue to be treated as real exports–the current practice in affiliate trade with the rest of the world. Serial selling of the same merchandise along affiliate network lines, before actual shipment is effected, is obvious from the names of the countries involved, because they are not oil producers. Whether or not the same holds true for parent transactions with foreigners in this industry is hard to tell, but definitely should not be ruled out. Statistics on the oil industry are notoriously secretive, and cover more than they reveal–a very effective strategy intended to shroud its profit gambits and the vast shifts in national wealth. Why else engage in such intricate, globe-spanning trading ventures?

TABLE 10.5. Parent and Affiliate Petroleum Sales/Shipments ($ million)

Year	1977	1982	1989
Mofa sales/shipments to U.S.			
Sales	$70,915	$36,567	$22,783
Goods	N/A	36,299	21,282
Services	N/A	268	1,487
Shipments	16,690	15,507	9,940
Difference on Goods	54,225	21,060	12,843
Mofa sales to parents	66,106	31,384	16,584
Mofa shipments to parents	13,629	12,511	7,237
Difference	52,477	18,873	9,347
Mofa sales to other U.S. customers	4,809	5,183	6,199
Mofa shipments to same	3,061	2,996	2,703
Difference	1,748	2,187	3,496
Shipments by foreigners to parents	20,756	36,144	18,187
Shipments by parents to foreigners	3,076	16,558	5,343
Difference	17,680	19,586	12,844
Total parent sales overseas	N/A	119,623	37,740
Goods	N/A	117,788	36,909
Services	N/A	1,835	831
Total parent shipments overseas	4,829	19,370	8,191
Difference on Goods	N/A	98,418	28,718
Parent sales/shipments to Mofas			
Sales	N/A	51,612	21,718
Shipments	1,429	2,622	2,770
Difference	N/A	48,990	18,948
Parent sales/shipments to foreigners			
Sales	N/A	48,818	16,564
Shipments	3,076	16,558	5,343
Difference	N/A	32,360	11,221

Sources: FDI census data: 1977, pp. 185, 319, 357, 398; 1982, pp. 149, 152, 226, 235, 287, 290, 316, 335; 1989, pp. 97-8, 112, 114-5, 191-2, 202, 206, 255, 259, 263.

The data provide other interesting aspects. Measured in terms of dollars, affiliate sales and shipments to the United States, for instance, display very erratic patterns. As a consequence, the U.S. share of total affiliate shipments went from 28.9 percent in 1957 to 18.2 percent in 1966, rose to 38.1 percent in 1977, before falling off to 21.2 percent in 1982 and 14.6 percent in 1989.

In view of the dynamic oil price history, the figures do not allow the conclusion that physical volumes have followed similar courses. The practically stagnant dollar volumes for 1977 and 1982, for instance, suggest a two-thirds reduction in the 1982 tonnage, considering the three-fold price escalation for crude between the two years. There are also major shifts in the supply base for the whole period. Latin American affiliates gradually relinquished their position as the most favored supplier by going from 69 percent in 1957 to only 8 percent in 1989. Asian affiliates including the Middle East apparently were always in second place before advancing to the number one position during the late 1970s. At the latest count, they ranked in fourth place behind the European and African subsidiaries. Canada's performance was quite remarkable with its share jumping to unprecedented levels in 1982 and 1989. So was Africa's role. Even though the sources are not identified, Nigeria and Libya can be assumed to be the two major suppliers from that continent (see Table 10.6).

Of total U.S. oil imports amounting to $44.5 billion in 1977, $15.6 billion in 1982, and $12.0 billion in 1989, affiliate shipments accounted for 38 percent in 1977, 100 percent in 1982, and 83 percent in 1989, the highest observed import shares for any FDI industry group (*Statistical Abstract of the United States* 1984, pp. 840-1; 1989, p. 797; 1993, p. 819).

Affiliate export sales to the American market reached 18 percent of their export totals in 1975, jumped to an incredible 72 percent only two years later, and fell back to 50 percent in 1989 (see Table 10.3). The ups and downs of business with U.S. customers is even more pronounced for

TABLE 10.6. Regional Breakdown of Mofa Oil Supplies to U.S. Market (shipment – $ billion)

Year	All	Canada	Lat. Am.	O.W.H.	Europe	Africa	Asia	M. East
1957	$1.4	$0.1	$1.0	nil	N/A	N/A	$0.2	$0.2
1966	1.5	0.2	0.8	N/A	N/A	N/A	N/A	N/A
1977	16.8	1.3	3.4	3.0	1.8	N/A	N/A	N/A
1982	15.5	3.7	3.5	N/A	1.9	2.5	3.8	1.6
1989	9.9	3.5	0.8	N/A	1.8	2.0	1.4	0.4
(Percentages)								
1957	100	8.9	69.1	3.4	N/A	N/A	16.2	11.7
1966	100	11.3	51.9	N/A	N/A	N/A	19.5e	16.9e
1977	100	7.7	20.2	17.9	10.5	N/A	35.1e	17.2e
1982	100	23.9	22.6	N/A	12.3	16.1	24.5	10.3
1989	100	35.4	8.1	N/A	18.2	20.2	14.1	4.0

Sources: FDI census data: 1957, p. 110; 1966, p. 201; 1977, p. 354; 1982, p. 283; 1989, p. 255.

regional affiliates, who again saw their positions subject to fairly abrupt fluctuations.

Historically, the two most important sellers to the U.S. market have been Latin America and the Middle Eastern part of Asia. Both lost their positions in the end, paving the way for a more balanced share distribution among all major geographical areas. Latin America saw its share drop from almost 70 percent in 1957 to 23 percent in 1989. For the Latin American republics, this was practically a free fall from 65 to 2 percent in three decades. The Caribbean affiliates gained market share where their continental neighbors lost, but were unable to capture the whole difference. There is no way to establish the source of all the oil sold through the Caribbean islands. It is equally impossible to say to what degree their trades involved Latin American supplies. At any rate, the developments have led to the virtual cessation of affiliate production and trading activities in the producing nations. It would be very interesting to see how shifting the latter to the Caribbean islands for profit-parking purposes has impacted the national incomes of South America and the United States. In a final analysis, it was a replay of the Middle Eastern policy to put natural resource management under national ownership.

Europe's advance from an assumed near zero position during the 1950s and 1960s to 22 percent in 1989 was based on the American participation in the oil fields of England and Norway. Canada gained with a 1989 U.S. share which approached that of the European and Latin American subsidiaries (see Table 10.7).

Mofa shipments to parents accounted for the lowest shares in parent sales to the U.S. market among all industries surveyed. This is explained by the fact that Mofas are incapable of providing more than 25 to 30 percent of what the raw material starved parent industry needs (see Table 10.5). Mofa shares reached 19, 4, and 3 percent of parent sales of $89.6 (1977), $402.5 (1982), and $290.7 billion (1989).

MANUFACTURING AFFILIATE EXPORT SALES

Compared to their mundane and sophisticated petroleum cousins, all other industries appear quite parochial, inasmuch as statistical records lack the mysterious intricacies uncovered for the former.

Sales of manufactured goods grew twenty-eight times from $18.3 billion in 1957 to $509.3 billion in 1989. The first number covers all affiliates, while those from 1966 forward relate to Mofas only. To a large extent, the rapid development comes from the industry's export sector, which more than doubled its share of sales from 16 to 38 percent. Business

TABLE 10.7. Leading Affiliate Exporters to the United States–Petroleum (sales – $ billion)

Year	1966	%	1977	%	1982	%	1989	%
Total	$1.5	100.0	$70.9	100.0	$36.6	100.0	$22.8	100.0
Canada	0.2	11.4	1.3	1.9	3.8	10.3	4.3	18.3
Europe	N/A	–	4.0	5.6	8.0	22.0	5.1	22.4
Germany	N/A	–	N/A	–	0.5	1.3	N/A	–
Netherlands	N/A	–	N/A	–	0.3	0.8	N/A	–
Norway	N/A	–	N/A	–	N/A	–	0.8	3.5
Switzerland	N/A	–	0.6	0.8	N/A	–	2.0	8.9
UK	N/A	–	1.5	2.1	3.7	10.0	1.7	7.5
Lat. America	0.8	52.2	8.7	12.3	8.5	23.4	5.2	22.8
Lat. Am. Rep.	N/A	–	N/A	0.9	0.8	2.2	0.5	2.2
Venezuela	0.5	36.6	N/A	–	nil	–	0	0
O.W. Hemi.	N/A	–	8.1	11.4	7.7	21.1	4.7	20.6
Bahamas	N/A	–	N/A	–	0.9	2.5	nil	–
Bermuda	N/A	–	5.4	7.6	3.9	10.7	3.5	15.4
Africa	N/A	–	5.7	8.0	6.1	16.7	2.9	12.7
Asia	N/A	–	51.2e	72.2e	10.0e	27.4e	4.0	17.5

Note: 1957 data do not add up to 100 percent because of the "International" category, which is not shown but accounts for 17.2 percent of all oil exports.

Sources: FDI census data: 1957, p. 110; 1966, pp. 199, 201; 1977, pp. 318-22; 1982, pp. 228, 229; 1989, p. 192.

with the United States, an important part of that growth, has outgrown that conducted by petroleum affiliates both in volume and percent of sales in 1989 (see Tables 10.2 and 10.8).

In 1982, both industries had basically the same overall sales and export volume in terms of dollars. But while manufacturing kept growing, petroleum affiliates were hit hard by the declining oil consumption and related pricing effects typical for a commodity. It is somewhat ironic to witness the scenario unfolding in this way, because the inflationary pressures generated by oil in the earlier period were definitely one major factor propelling the manufacturing sector in several ways. One was the flow of liquidity to less developed areas, where it helped to spawn demand for the industry's products. The ensuing physical volume developing from such new demand was magnified by inflationary pricing across all product sectors. The industry's vigor is a sharp contrast, if not an outright contradiction, to the widely held American notion that manufacturing has passed its zenith (see Table 10.9).

TABLE 10.8. Manufacturing Affiliate Sales (sales – $ million)

Year	Total Sales	Exports Sales	%	Sales to U.S.	%
1957	$18,331	$2,912	15.9	$1,093	6.0
1966	47,375	8,817	18.6	2,679	5.7
1970	78,335	17,432	22.2	5,352	6.8
1977	194,200	59,773	30.8	17,601	9.1
1982	271,099	91,832	33.9	26,244	9.7
1989	509,308	192,676	37.9	70,456	13.8

Sources: 1957 FDI census, p. 110. 1966 FDI census, pp. 199, 201. *SOCB*, August 1975, pp. 26-7 (1970). 1977 FDI census, pp. 282, 319. 1982 FDI census, p. 226. 1989 FDI census, p. 191.

Besides growth, there are other substantial differences between both industries which represent the FDI leaders in investment, sales, and exports. One is the range of industrial activities covered by each. With only three component parts (extraction, refining, trade), the petroleum industry displays a relatively narrow spectrum against the seven major subgroups on the manufacturing side, each of which in turn consists of several subdivisions: food and related products, chemicals, primary/fabricated metals, machinery except electrical, electric and electronic equipment, transportation equipment and, finally, other manufacturing (tobacco, textiles, paper, lumber, rubber, printing/publishing, plastics, glass, stone/clay, instruments, etc.).

Furthermore, unlike the petroleum case, manufacturing actually ships practically all of the goods they sell to their U.S. customers, which saves a great deal of the guesswork and speculation accompanying the petroleum business. It may be recalled that, by definition, the two are synonymous for trade with third countries (see Table 9.2).

Also, in contrast to the strong geographical shifts in petroleum supplies, manufacturing had two leading regional export centers accounting for over 80 percent of all subsidiary exports from the beginning: Europe and Canada. Interesting to note, their combined export shares of 93.1 percent (1957) and 81.7 percent (1989) are much higher than their respective investment shares of 76 percent (1957) and 70 percent (1990) (see Table 1.10).

Europe never lost its leading export position, and actually was able to expand it from the 44 percent in 1957 to 62 percent in 1989 (see Table 10.10), despite its relatively low share in overall manufacturing investment with only 27 and 50 percent for the same years. The unusually strong export performance can be attributed to the preference of U.S. investors for established European companies with extensive export operations to start with.

TABLE 10.9. Manufacturing Affiliate Exports (sales – $ billion)

Year	Total	To U.S.	%	To Others	%
1957	$2.9	$1.1	37.9	$1.8	62.1
1966	8.8	2.7	30.7	6.1	69.3
1970	17.4	5.4	31.0	12.0	69.0
1977	59.8	17.6	29.4	42.2	70.6
1982	91.8	26.2	28.5	65.6	71.5
1989	192.7	70.5	36.5	122.2	63.5

Sources: FDI census data: 1957, pp. 110-1; 1966, pp. 199, 201-2; 1977, pp. 318-9, 321-2; 1982, pp. 226, 228-9; 1989, pp. 191-2, 190-6.

It made sense for two reasons: acquisitions offered U.S. firms direct access to European markets and technology and, at the same time, a foothold in markets established worldwide including Eastern Europe, whose conversion to little known U.S. products could have been difficult, particularly for engineering industries where the metric system is standard. By going this route, investors bought technical and marketing knowledge, as well as measurable market shares, while avoiding major market development and tooling costs–a rationale which also helps to explain the atypically low 21 percent U.S. import share held by the Europeans in 1989 (see Table 10.11).

Canada's situation was different in that 49 percent of all 1989 affiliate exports to the U.S. market were provided from north of the border. The figure represents 92 percent of all Canadian manufacturing affiliate exports compared to only 13 percent in the European case (see Tables 10.10 and 10.11). They were set up originally for the purpose of supplying the North American market. What makes their situation unique is that roughly two-thirds of all exports are concentrated in the automotive sector, which operated as an unofficial free trade area even before the generalized Free Trade Agreement between both nations went into effect on January 2, 1989.

All other world areas combined reached approximately 18 percent of aggregate affiliate exports to the world. Among them was Latin America with a very steady 4 to 5 percent share over four decades. More than 80 percent of their exports were practically shared equally between Mexico and Brazil (see Table 10.10). Both countries did even better in area exports to the United States where they held a combined share of 91 percent in 1989 (see Table 10.11). Mexico's already strongly increasing role as a supplier to the United States is bound to accelerate dramatically with its full membership

TABLE 10.10. Leading Affiliate Exporters–Manufacturing (sales – $ billion)

Year	1957	%	1966	%	1977	%	1982	%	1989	%
Total	$2.9	100.0	$8.8	100.0	$59.8	100.0	$91.8	100.0	$192.7	100.0
Canada	1.3	43.3	2.4	27.2	14.1	23.6	18.4	20.0	38.0	19.7
Europe	1.4	43.8	5.6	63.6	39.3	65.7	59.6	64.9	119.6	62.0
Belg./Lux.	0.1	2.1	0.6	6.3	5.1	8.5	6.6	7.2	12.5	6.5
France	nil	1.5	0.6	6.3	5.2	8.7	6.9	7.5	11.6	6.0
Germany	0.2	8.3	1.2	13.6	10.3	17.2	16.4	17.8	31.5	16.3
Italy	nil	0.2	0.3	3.3	1.8	3.1	2.8	3.1	6.4	3.3
Ireland	N/A	–	0.1	0.6	0.9	1.6	2.8	3.1	6.9	3.6
Netherlands	nil	0.9	0.4	4.8	4.5	7.6	7.4	8.0	17.9	9.3
Sweden	nil	0.2	N/A	–	0.5	0.8	N/A	–	N/A	–
Switzerland	0.1	2.4	0.2	1.1	0.6	1.1	1.0	1.1	0.7	0.3
UK	0.8	28.5	2.1	23.8	8.3	13.9	12.2	13.3	22.7	11.8
Lat. America	0.1	3.6	0.4	4.1	2.3	3.9	4.7	5.1	10.6	5.5
Lat. Am. Rep.	0.1	2.8	0.3	3.5	2.2	3.7	4.3	4.7	10.3	5.3
Brazil	nil	0.4	N/A	–	1.0	1.7	2.1	2.3	4.0	2.1
Mexico	nil	0.3	0.1	0.4	0.5	0.8	1.0	1.1	4.8	2.5
O.W. Hemi.	nil	0.8	0.1	0.4	0.1	0.2	0.4	0.4	0.3	0.1
Africa	nil	0.8	N/A	–	N/A	–	N/A	–	0.6	0.3
Asia	0.1	2.1	0.3	3.4	N/A	–	N/A	–	20.2	10.5
Japan	0.1	2.1	0.1	0.1	0.3	0.5	N/A	–	3.8	2.0
Hong Kong	N/A	–	N/A	–	N/A	–	0.9	1.0	2.4	1.2
Malaysia	N/A	–	N/A	–	0.4	0.7	1.3	1.4	2.0	1.0
Singapore	N/A	–	N/A	–	0.8	1.4	1.7	1.9	6.6	3.4
Taiwan	N/A	–	N/A	–	0.6	0.9	0.9	1.0	2.3	1.2
Thailand	N/A	–	N/A	–	N/A	–	N/A	–	1.6	0.9

Sources: FDI census data: 1957, pp. 110-1; 1966, pp. 199, 201-2; 1977, pp. 318-9, 321-2; 1982, pp. 226, 228-9; 1989, pp. 191-2, 196.

in the NAFTA accord reached at the end of 1992. African exports have been practically nil, due in part to the U.S. withdrawal from South Africa.

Asian affiliates elevated their share of total group exports from less than 1 percent in 1966 to over 10 percent in 1989, and even to 15 percent of U.S. imports. Japan does share in the general development, but surprises with a very low and almost stagnant export position. This is very unusual for one of the foremost and aggressive trading nations, but another key factor behind the smoldering trade disputes with Washington.

Between 30 and 40 percent of all manufacturing exports went to the United States throughout the period (see Table 10.9), and it is interesting to follow the history of the leading countries in this market. Looming head and shoulders above all suppliers are the Canadians, despite the sharp drop in their position from 76 percent in 1957 to 49 percent in 1989. The three

TABLE 10.11. Leading Manufacturing Affiliate Exporters to the United States (sales–$ billion)

Year	1957	%	1966	%	1977	%	1982	%	1989	%
Total	$1.1	100.0	$2.7	100.0	$17.6	100.0	$26.2	100.0	$70.5	100.0
Canada	0.8	75.8	2.0	73.2	12.3	69.6	15.6	59.5	34.8	49.4
Europe	0.2	17.3	0.5	17.4	2.4	13.7	3.6	13.7	15.2	21.2
Belg./Lux.	nil	0.1	nil	1.5	0.1	0.6	0.2	0.7	0.7	1.0
France	nil	0.3	nil	1.0	0.2	1.3	0.4	1.6	1.0	1.4
Germany	nil	1.4	0.1	2.9	0.8	4.6	0.9	3.4	2.4	3.4
Ireland	N/A	–	N/A	–	0.1	0.8	0.2	0.7	0.7	1.0
Italy	N/A	–	nil	1.4	0.1	0.8	0.2	0.6	2.7	3.8
Netherlands	nil	0.2	nil	0.8	0.1	0.8	0.3	1.2	1.6	2.3
Switzerland	nil	1.9	nil	1.4	0.1	0.4	0.1	0.4	0.1	0.1
UK	0.1	11.9	0.2	6.5	0.6	3.2	1.1	4.0	5.4	7.6
Lat. Am.	nil	3.9	0.1	4.8	0.9	5.0	1.9	7.1	6.7	9.4
Lat. Am. Rep.	nil	2.5	0.1	3.8	0.8	4.5	1.5	5.8	6.5	9.1
Argentina	nil	0.7	N/A	–	N/A	–	0.2	0.6	0.1	0.1
Brazil	nil	0.7	N/A	–	0.3	1.7	0.5	1.8	2.1	3.0
Mexico	nil	0.1	nil	0.9	0.3	1.7	0.7	2.7	4.1	5.8
O.W. Hemi.	nil	1.5	nil	1.0	0.1	0.5	0.3	1.3	0.2	0.3
Asia	nil	2.7	0.1	4.0	1.8e	10.0	4.1e	15.5	11.9	16.8
Japan	nil	0.3	nil	0.7	0.1	0.5	N/A	–	2.0	2.8
Hong Kong	N/A	–	N/A	–	0.2e	1.3e	0.6	2.2	1.4	2.0
Malaysia	N/A	–	N/A	–	0.2	1.2	1.0	3.8	1.2	1.7
Philippines	nil	1.2	nil	1.2	0.1	0.8	0.3	1.0	0.3	0.4
Singapore	N/A	–	N/A	–	0.5	3.1	1.2	4.7	4.1	5.8
Taiwan	N/A	–	N/A	–	0.4	2.5	0.7	2.7	1.5	2.1

Sources: See Table 10.10.

strongest affiliate suppliers behind Canada in 1966 were, in rank order, the United Kingdom and Germany (surprising in view of Europe's overall weakness in the U.S. market) and Singapore. All four put together held an 80.5 percent share of affiliate exports in 1977, but saw that decline to a still respectable 66.2 percent by 1989. The Europeans were briefly surpassed by Singapore in 1982, with England able to recoup its former second place by 1989, putting Singapore in third place, and Germany in fourth. Malaysia had all the promise to join Singapore in replacing the Europeans in 1982, but was unable to deliver. Its share actually declined from 3.8 percent in 1982 to 1.7 percent in 1989, demonstrating the volatile investment and sourcing changes FDI has been known for in the development countries. A similar case is found in the Philippines where political shifts in the country leading to the closing of the U. S. Marine base seem to have, at least temporarily, cooled America's interests in the nation (see Table 10.11).

There is no question, however, that this could change quickly. Asia's economies in general are attracting increasing U.S. investments which, for the moment, are highly concentrated in the electrical and electronic equipment and components fields. It all could end in a landslide development if areas like the automotive field were to open up in a similar fashion. The first steps in that direction are already visible in the case of Singapore and Korea, as well as in the growing cooperation between Japanese and U.S. automakers.

Despite their respectable export volume, affiliates have not achieved significant positions in total U.S. imports of manufactures, and they seem to be actually on the decline. Of total imports of $76.6, $170.4, and $396.9 billion, respectively, in 1977, 1982, and 1989 Mofas reached only 22.9, 15.4, and 17.8 percent (*Statistical Abstract of the United States* 1984, pp. 840-1; 1989, pp. 795-7; 1993, p. 819).

These figures have to be interpreted with the same caution used for all FDI information. In 1989, 89 percent of all manufacturing Mofa exports to the United States went to their parents. Nothing is known about the finishing stage of the merchandise when it reached American shores, but it is entirely conceivable that it was only partially finished like parent/Mofa trade going in the other direction, and subject to inscrutable transfer pricing on top.

This latter aspect may also contribute to the fact that Mofa exports to parents have not reached higher shares in their parent's domestic sales, for which the major part may have been imported. Total Mofa sales of manufactures to parents in the amounts of $14.3 (1977), $26.2 (1982), and $61.9 billion (1989) accounted for 2.3, 2.9, and 4.5 percent of parent sales to U.S. customers in the amount of $635, $906, and $1,374 billion for the same census years. The growth in Mofa share here is comforting in view of their weakening overall U.S. import share mentioned above, yet alarming news at the same time, because it illustrates the gradual erosion of the U.S. domestic manufacturing base with the help of these parent companies, whose competitiveness apparently needs to be shored up with imports from their own overseas subsidiaries (FDI census data: 1977, pp. 319, 391, 395; 1982, pp. 149, 316; 1989, pp. 97, 191).

TRADE AFFILIATE EXPORT SALES

After petroleum and manufacturing, wholesale trade affiliates represent the third largest export industry. Retailers are excluded from the review, because of their small size compared to wholesalers (about 10 percent) and their minuscule role as exporters. Wholesaling operations are somewhat difficult to associate with neatly defined product categories. Most data on record refer to only two product groups–durable and nondurable goods, without further detail. The first covers order of importance for industry sales: professional and commercial equipment and supplies (30 percent), motor vehicles and equipment (9 percent), machinery, equipment and supplies (7 percent), electrical goods (7 percent), metals and minerals (6 percent), etc. The second, on the other hand, includes unprocessed farm products (12 percent), nondurable goods, not else classified (13 percent), drugs (5 percent), groceries (5 percent), paper products, and apparel (2 percent) (1989 FDI census, p. M-13). While rather limited in informative value, this split is helpful insofar as it establishes a sales ratio to the United States of 20:80 for nondurables to durables in 1989, whereas exports to other areas are split 51 to 49 percent.

Sales to the United States barely reached 5 percent of total affiliate sales, and up to 15 percent of all affiliate export sales, reflecting their fundamental orientation toward third markets (see Table 10.12). Overall exports were solidly in the hands of the Europeans with a firm share between 70 and 80 percent. Switzerland and the United Kingdom alone held more than 40 percent, with the rest shared by many affiliates, none of which exceeded 10 percent. One might be tempted to attribute the prominent place of the English subsidiaries to the export of oil products, but this is explicitly included in petroleum affiliate statistics. Latin American Mofas face a declining role in this industry, while companies located in Asia are progressing at their expense.

Exports to the United States are patterned in a similar fashion except that the dominant positions of Europe as a whole, and those of the United Kingdom and Switzerland, have been greatly reduced. Actually, Europe has fallen behind Asia. Canada and Japan held 10 percent shares each, and Hong Kong left the United Kingdom behind with a share of 20 against 15 percent. South American traders again suffered a setback in this business, going from 12 to 8 percent.

TABLE 10.12. Trade Affiliate Sales ($ million)

Year	Total	Exports Sales	%	To U.S.	%
1966	$14,066	$4,100	29.1	$504	3.6
1977	64,463	26,737	41.5	2,195	3.4
1982	113,622	47,409	41.7	5,501	4.8
1989	204,295	61,171	29.9	8,860	4.3

Sources: See Table 10.10.

Due to the imprecise nature of the statistical information provided, the motley product groups involved, and the fact that this industry does not exist as a separate entity in U.S. trade publications, its role in overall U.S. imports cannot be measured beyond the impression of a steady growth. Available data, however, can be used to establish their contributions to parent sales in the U.S. market. Mofa sales to parent went from $1.7 billion (1977), to $3.2 billion (1982), and $7.2 billion in 1989. Parent sales in the United States showed the following volumes for the same years: $46.2, $82.6, and $178.3 billion, allowing Mofa shares to advance minimally from 3.7 to 3.9, and 4.0 percent (see Table 10.13).

FINANCIAL AFFILIATE EXPORT SALES

Covered in this section are such financial affiliate exports as nonbank financial institutions, insurance, real estate, and holding companies. The first two establish the backbone of the industry, with a sales share exceeding 97 percent in 1989. In 1977, financing functions provided 31 percent, and insurance 63 percent of industry revenues. By 1982, the constellation had shifted to 42 and 57 percent, and in 1989, both were fairly evenly matched with 48 and 50 percent, respectively. A main function of the financial branch used to be borrowing from international capital markets to finance investment projects of their parents (see Table 10.14).

Tax incentives, as discussed previously, explain why over 60 percent of the industry's foreign trade transactions were historically handled by the Caribbean affiliates, particularly those located in Bermuda and the Netherlands Antilles (see details in Table 2.1), which in turn causes the region's prominence in U.S. FDI statistics. Exports of mainly intangibles by the group have undergone a truly explosive growth that remains unmatched by any of the other industries.

Around 50 percent of the affiliate exports involve the United States, and yet their total 1989 sales were relatively small compared to domestic sales by parents. Actually, Mofa sales accounted for higher relative sales earlier, but then fell quite severely. In 1977, Mofa sales reached 22 percent of parent sales at $46.2 billion, rose to 28 percent in 1982, only to fall back to 13 percent in 1989 on parent sales of $84.0 and $384.4 billion. The global recession may have contributed to the slowdown, but a more likely cause was regulatory obstacles raised by foreigners to fend off the innovative and aggressive American competitors–a major reason behind America's persistent push for more liberalization of international service markets in GATT negotiations.

TABLE 10.13. Leading Affiliate Exporters – Trade (sales – $ billion)

Year	1977	%	1982	%	1989	%
Total	$26.7	100.0	$47.4	100.0	$61.2	100.0
Canada	1.1	4.2	0.7	1.5	1.6	2.6
Europe	19.9	74.5	37.6	79.3	44.7	73.0
Belg./Lux.	1.7	6.5	N/A	–	3.7	6.0
France	N/A	–	3.0	6.3	5.7	9.3
Germany	0.9	3.4	1.5	3.2	2.4	3.9
Netherlands	2.0	7.6	2.9	6.1	4.2	6.9
Switzerland	10.9	40.7	15.1e	31.9e	17.1	27.9
UK	2.5	9.3	10.7	22.6	9.1	14.9
Lat. America	3.1	11.6	3.6	7.6	2.7	4.4
Lat. Am. Rep.	1.2	4.5	1.5	3.2	N/A	–
O.W. Hemi.	1.9	7.1	2.1	4.4	N/A	–
Bahamas	N/A	–	1.1	2.3	N/A	–
Asia	N/A	–	4.5	9.5	10.7	17.5
Japan	N/A	–	1.4	3.0	2.3	3.8
Hong Kong	1.2	4.4	2.2	4.6	5.7	9.3
Singapore	N/A	–	N/A	–	2.0	3.3
Australia	N/A	–	0.4	0.8	1.1	1.8
LEADING AFFILIATE EXPORTERS TO THE U.S.						
Total	$2.2	100.0	$5.5	100.0	$8.9	100.0
Canada	0.4	16.7	0.5	8.8	0.9	10.1
Europe	1.0	44.7	3.5	62.8	3.1	34.8
France	N/A	–	0.1	2.6	0.7	7.9
Germany	0.1	4.6	0.1	2.2	0.1	1.1
Netherlands	nil	1.5	0.1	1.7	0.1	1.1
Switzerland	0.3	15.6	1.0e	18.2e	0.4	4.6
UK	0.3	13.0	1.1	20.5	1.3	14.6
Lat. America	0.3	12.3	0.5	9.6	0.7	7.9
Lat. Am. Rep.	0.1	6.0	0.2	4.1	N/A	–
O.W. Hemi.	0.1	6.3	0.3	5.5	N/A	–
Asia	N/A	24.0e	0.9e	17.2e	3.7	41.6
Japan	N/A	–	0.5	8.5	0.9	10.1
Hong Kong	0.1	4.3	0.3	5.0	1.8	20.2
Singapore	N/A	–	N/A	–	0.6	6.7
Australia	N/A	–	0.1	1.6	0.4	4.2

Notes: Data for 1977 covers wholesale and retail while those for 1982 and 1989 represent wholesale only. The difference for 1982 is $0.3 billion or less than 1 percent.
Sources: See Table 10.10.

Another major contributing factor may be seen in the reduced borrowing operations of the Netherlands Antillean subsidiaries, which used to float investment certificates and commercial obligations at much higher levels in international financial centers in the past, and export the capital thus secured to the United States. The impact of their activities on the U.S. FDI position was discussed in Chapter 2. Here, they reappear in a different context, but their reduced role in affiliate exports to the United States from a high 85 percent in 1982 to 64 percent in 1989 is conspicuous (see Table 10.15).

SCOPE OF INTRA-FDI TRADE

A very large part of global FDI business is conducted among FDI members themselves: parents with affiliates, and affiliates with each other. The previous discussion of total FDI selling activities prevented this fact from coming into sharper focus up to this point. A major obstacle here is the rather poor documentation of intra-FDI trade, making it particularly difficult to assess its magnitude and rate of change over time. Full or partial intra-FDI data cover only four census years: 1966, 1977, 1982, 1989, and estimates for the period 1990 to 1993. This is a small sample for a period of four decades, indeed. Especially so, since available data once more lead back to the same perplexing questions about the wide differences between sales and related shipments of goods mentioned before in relation to all trade involving the United States (see Table 10.16). As mentioned before, the differences appear only for commercial transaction-sinvolving the United States, and cannot be explained with service charges, time lags between booking and shipment, fob/cif (free on board pricing/cost, insurance, freight) quotation differentials, etc., all of which makes acceptance of the official formula of intra-FDI sales and shipments as being equal for the rest of the world very problematic. Despite these familiar issues, there can be no doubt that this trade has reached significant proportions whether measured in terms of sales, shipments, or by necessity, a mixture of both. The existence of these discrepancies forces a simultaneous discussion of intra-FDI sales and shipments, with the latter being a more tangible indicator of these business relationships than the former. This is not only because shipments represent the bulk of this trade, but also because they can be brought into a meaningful relationship with global merchandise trade.

Mofa sales reached 32 percent of total nonbank parent sales in 1982 and 37 percent in 1993. Of all parent sales, only 4 to 5 percent are targeted at Mofas, whereas Mofa sales to parents alone increased from 5 to 9 percent of their overall sales between 1966 and 1993 (see Tables 10.16A and C).

TABLE 10.14. Finance Affiliate Sales ($ million)

Year	Total	Exports Sales	%	Sales To U.S.	%
1977	10,002	$1,198	12.0	$591	5.9
1982	23,526	8,897	37.8	5,401	23.0
1989	51,137	15,149	29.6	7,189	14.1

Sources: See Table 10.10.

TABLE 10.15. Leading Affiliate Exporters – Finance, Insurance, and Real Estate* (sales – $ billion)

Year	1977	%	1982	%	1989	%
Total	$1.2	100.0	$8.9	100.0	$15.1	100.0
Canada	N/A	–	0.2	2.2	0.4	1.7
Europe	0.3	21.4	1.2	13.7	4.3	28.5
Belg./Lux.	N/A	–	N/A	–	0.2	1.3
Netherlands	nil	0.6	0.2	2.0	N/A	–
Switzerland	0.1	10.6	0.1	1.1	0.3	2.0
UK	N/A	–	0.7	7.5	3.0	19.9
Lat. America	0.9e	71.0e	7.3	82.5	7.8	51.7
O.W. Hemi.	0.8	65.4	7.3	82.0	7.8	51.7
Bermuda	0.6	51.2	3.6	40.0	4.9	32.5
Neth. Antilles	N/A	–	3.4	38.3	2.5	16.6
Asia	N/A	–	0.1e	1.1	2.6	17.2
LEADING AFFILIATE EXPORTERS TO THE U.S.						
Total	$0.6	100.0	$5.4	100.0	$7.2	100.0
Canada	N/A	–	0.2	3.5	0.1	1.4
Europe	0.1	16.9	0.6	10.6	2.2	30.6
France	nil	0.3	nil	0.1	nil	–
Netherlands	nil	0.5	0.1	2.1	N/A	–
Switzerland	nil	6.1	0.1	1.2	0.1	1.4
UK	N/A	–	0.3	6.0	1.9	26.3
Lat. America	N/A	–	4.6	85.0	4.6	63.9
O.W. Hemi.	0.4	70.9	4.6	84.7	4.5	63.9
Bermuda	0.3	49.6	1.5	27.3	2.2e	30.6
Neth. Antilles	N/A	–	2.9	54.4	2.1	29.2
Africa	N/A	–	0.1	2.6	0.3	4.2

Notes: *Excludes banking. e = estimate.
Sources: See Table 10.10.

TABLE 10.16. Intra-FDI Business Volume ($ billion)

	Total	Local	Exports	USA	Other
A. Nonbank Mofa Sales* to:					
All Customers					
1966	$97.8	$73.4	$24.4	$6.3	$18.1
1977	507.0	313.3	193.7	93.6	100.1
1982	730.2	478.0	252.3	76.8	175.5
1988	927.9	606.3	321.6	101.4	220.1
1989	1,019.9	690.5	329.4	114.7	214.7
1990	1,208.3	809.5	398.9	123.9	275.0
1991	1,242.6	824.5	418.1	125.5	292.6
1992	1,291.6	856.7	434.9	129.2	305.7
1993	1,279.1	844.8	434.3	138.2	296.1
Affiliates					
1966	18.7	4.6	14.1	4.6	9.5
1977	168.0	34.1	134.0	84.2	49.8
1982	159.9	28.1	131.8	63.6	68.2
1988	226.6	30.9	195.7	82.2	113.5
1989	246.2	39.0	207.2	93.0	114.2
1990	287.7	37.9	249.9	98.5	151.4
1991	296.7	39.8	256.9	98.9	158.0
1992	320.2	42.5	277.7	103.2	174.5
1993	319.7	41.6	278.1	110.3	167.8
%					
1966	19.1	6.3	57.8	73.0	52.5
1977	33.1	10.9	69.1	90.0	49.8
1982	21.9	5.9	52.4	82.8	38.8
1988	24.5	5.1	60.9	81.4	51.8
1989	24.1	5.6	62.9	80.9	53.0
1990	23.8	4.7	62.7	79.4	54.9
1991	23.8	4.8	61.5	78.8	53.9
1992	24.8	5.0	63.9	79.9	57.0
1993	25.0	4.9	64.1	79.8	56.8

	Total	Local	Exports	USA	Other
B. Nonbank Mofa Shipments to Affiliates**					
1966	$18.7	$4.6	$14.1	$4.6	$9.5
1977	114.8	34.1	80.7	30.9	49.8
1982	134.8	28.1	106.7	38.5	68.2
1988	193.9	24.1	169.8	65.5	104.3
1989	216.4	30.9	178.0	71.3	106.7
1990	249.0	31.1	217.9	75.3	142.6
1991	258.7	32.0	226.7	77.6	149.1
1992	283.6	34.2	249.4	84.9	164.5
1993	288.3	36.0	252.3	95.9	156.4
% of Sales to Affiliates					
1966	100.0	100.0	100.0	100.0	100.0
1977	68.3	100.0	60.2	36.7	100.0
1982	84.3	100.0	81.0	60.5	100.0
1988	85.4	78.0	86.6	79.7	91.9
1989	88.0	79.2	89.5	76.7	100.0
1990	86.5	82.1	87.2	76.4	94.7
1991	87.5	80.4	88.3	78.5	94.4
1992	88.7	80.5	89.6	82.3	94.3
1993	90.1	86.5	90.6	86.9	91.8
C. Nonbank Parent Sales to:					
All Customers					
1982	$2,249.9	$2,002.3	$247.6	–	$247.6
1988	2,828.2	N/A	N/A	–	N/A
1989	3,136.8	2,841.1	295.8	–	295.8
1990	3,243.7	N/A	N/A	–	N/A
1991	3,252.5	N/A	N/A	–	N/A
1992	3,330.9	N/A	N/A	–	N/A
1993	3,495.1	N/A	N/A	–	N/A
Mofas					
1982	102.2	N/A	102.2	–	102.2
1989	130.5	N/A	130.5	–	130.5
%					
1982	4.5e	N/A	41.3	–	41.3
1989	4.2e	N/A	44.1	–	44.1

TABLE 10.16 (continued)

	Total	Local	Exports	USA	Other
D. Nonbank Parent Shipments to Mofas					
1966	6.3	N/A	6.3	–	6.3
1977	29.3	N/A	29.3	–	29.3
1982	44.3	N/A	44.3	–	44.3
1988	78.2	N/A	78.2	–	78.2
1989	86.1	N/A	86.1	–	86.1
1990	88.4	N/A	88.4	–	88.4
1991	95.8	N/A	95.8	–	95.8
1992	100.7	N/A	100.7	–	100.7
1993	104.9	N/A	104.9	–	104.9
% of Sales to Mofas					
1982	43.4	N/A	43.4	–	43.4
1989	65.7	N/A	65.7	–	65.7
E. Combined Nonbank Parent/Mofa Sales to:					
All Customers					
1982	2,980.1	2,480.3	499.9	76.8	423.1
1989	4,156.7	3,531.6	625.2	114.7	510.5
1990	4,452.0	N/A	N/A	123.9	N/A
1991	4,495.1	N/A	N/A	125.5	N/A
1992	4,622.5	N/A	N/A	129.2	N/A
1993	4,774.2	N/A	N/A	138.2	N/A
Mofas***					
1982	262.1	28.1	234.0	63.6	170.4
1989	376.7	39.0	337.7	93.0	244.7
%					
1982	8.8	1.1	46.8	82.8	40.2
1989	9.1	1.1	54.1	80.9	47.9

Nonbank parents derive 9 to 10 percent of all sales from export activities, less than half of which goes to affiliates. Mofa data show a much higher export share ranging from 24 to 34 percent and still growing. Their export business is thus three times more important to them than for their parents, and around two-thirds of the sales volume comes from affiliates. Comparing actual dollar amounts, Mofas are selling 58 percent more to affiliates than their parents did in 1989 with $207 vs. $131 billion

	Total	Local	Exports	USA	Other
F. Combined Nonbank Parent/Mofa Shipments to Affiliates:***					
1966	25.0	N/A	20.4	4.6	15.8
1977	144.1	N/A	110.0	30.9	79.1
1982	179.1	N/A	151.0	38.5	112.5
1988	279.0	N/A	254.9	72.4	182.5
1989	302.5	N/A	271.6	71.3	200.3
1990	337.4	N/A	306.3	75.3	231.0
1991	354.5	N/A	322.5	77.6	244.9
1992	384.3	N/A	350.1	84.9	265.2
1993	393.2	N/A	357.2	95.9	261.3
% of Combined Sales to Affiliates					
1982	68.4	N/A	64.5	60.5	66.2
1989	80.4	N/A	80.5	76.7	81.6

Notes: *Includes services. **Excludes services. ***Excludes parent shipments to U.S. affiliated organizations. e = estimate.

Sources: FDI census data: 1966, pp. 83, 197; 1977, pp. 318-9, 340, 395, 398-9; 1982, pp. 225, 230, 235, 268-71, 285-8, 316, 332, 335; 1989, pp. 201, 257. *SOCB*, August 1992, p. 68; July 1993, pp. 44-5; June 1994, p. 51; June 1995, pp. 39-40.

(see Tables 10.16A and C). More widely available shipment data indicate that Mofas actually shipped twice as much material to affiliates than their parents did in the same year with $178 against $86 billion. By 1993, Mofas delivered even 2.4 times as much to affiliates with $252 against $105 billion (see Tables 10.16B and D).

Total intra-affiliate export shipments in turn were split roughly 30:70 between parents and affiliates, which left parents in a much weaker position than indicated by the sales information. More important, the information permits the conclusion that, over the four decades, parents have delegated major supply responsibilities for this business to Mofas–a fact that does not speak well for America's export development strategies. Available data do not permit breaking this intra-affiliate business down into finished and unfinished products requiring more manufacturing steps.

A significant difference in Mofa exports to affiliates in the United States and third countries exists in the fact that actual shipments reach only 75 to 80 percent of their sales to parents, compared to over 90 percent of sales to affiliates in third countries. In the case of Mofa business with the United States, it touches the intractable problem alluded to before, where petroleum transactions show an abysmal gap between sales and shipments. This is not the case in Mofa dealings with third countries, at least not to the same extent, and the differences may safely be assumed to stem from service sales, which are not followed by shipments (see Table 10.16B).

The combined sales volume of parents and subsidiaries from 1982 and 1989, the only years for which this information is available, reached 9 percent of their aggregate sales to the world, and roughly 50 percent of their combined export sales to all accounts. Combined parent and Mofa export shipments to FDI members show levels between 70 and 80 percent of their reported export sales (see Tables 10.16E and F).

Mofa sales to affiliate organizations in the United States, their local markets, and third countries reach between 19 to 24 percent of their total sales for the whole period. The exception was 1977, when the share went up to 33 percent, most likely in connection with OPEC (see Table 10.16A).

Parent/Mofa trade in terms of actual shipments leads to persistent deficits on the Mofa side. During the 1980s and early 1990s, they ranged from $6 to $22 billion annually, but may be narrowing if 1993 data with $9 billion are indicative of a new trend (see Tables 10.16B and D). While specific reasons for the intraorganizational trade imbalances are not evident, they confirm a previously made observation that parent organizations always have contributed in a positive way to the U.S. BOP. The bulk of the deficits stem from oil transactions, as pointed out before and again below.

Subsidiaries are not mere one-way conduits for parent sales to foreign markets. They play too important and active a role as suppliers and trading partners for their parent organizations to justify such a narrow view. Applying in particular to oil affiliates, this also holds true for other industries, albeit to a lesser extent. Affiliates provide an important second foot in the door of overseas markets by serving as a complementary export base for even larger direct parental exports to foreigners, and by reinforcing the foothold of American business there by means of local production.

INTRA-FDI EXPORT TRADE BY INDUSTRY

The preceding observations lead to additional questions concerning intra-FDI trading details for major industries and possible differences between their sales and actual shipments to each other aside from the ever present service factor. While affiliate and parent data alike are available for more years, only information provided for 1982 and 1989 lends itself for this purpose.

Discrepancies of this sort occur in all industries. Some of them naturally, because of time lags between recording of sales on company books and actual shipments of tangible goods as in the case of manufacturing, wholesaling, and all "Other Industries" whose business relates mainly to physical goods. Here, a close match between the numbers can be expected, because the service factor is normally quite small. Oil affiliates should also fall into this group, but for inexplicable reasons do not, as shipments regularly fall far short of goods sold. Services can obviously not be responsible, as Table 10.17 shows them to be too small to fill the gaps.

Sizable differences seen for finance and services industries, on the other hand, have to be expected because of the predominantly intangible nature of their sales transactions.

The petroleum industry is the chief cause of the gross misalignment between sales of goods and actual shipments shown for intra-FDI totals. In the parent case, oil shipments reaching only 5 to 15 percent of petroleum goods sold accounted for 93 and 54 percent of the overall trade difference for both years. Affiliates did somewhat better in 1989 by shipping 77 percent of oil products sold, but the amount of the shortfall reached double the total difference between sales of goods and shipments in 1989.

Intra-affiliate trade data in manufactured goods show a comparatively balanced pattern for goods sold and shipments by parents and Mofas. In both cases, shipments reached shares between 90 and 100 percent as expected. Much smaller than both oil and manufacturing, wholesale trade should get a brief mention. The low shipment to sales ratio for parents is ambiguous. Wholesale affiliates source from parents in different U.S. industries, while the figures shown are on the basis of parents in wholesaling only, which is very limited. If affiliate purchases from all parents are added, shipments approach 100 percent of goods sold. All previous information on intra-FDI business transactions has been summarized in Table 10.18 to show that Mofas are outstripping parents in practically all sales and shipment categories dealing with export activities except sales of services.

TABLE 10.17. Intra-FDI Trade by Industry ($ billion)

Total	Petroleum	Mfg.	Wholesale	Finance*	Services	Other
U.S. Parent to Mofas						
Sales of Goods and Services						
1982 $102.2 1989 $130.5	$51.6 21.7	$42.8 82.3	$4.9 18.2	$1.3 6.3	$0.4 1.4	$1.2 0.5
Sales of Goods						
1982 $98.8 1989 $119.7	50.9 20.7	41.9 79.1	4.9 18.2	0.2 N/A	0.1 0.6	0.8 N/A
Shipments						
1982 $44.3 1989 $86.1	2.6 2.8	38.3 78.9	2.7 2.5	0.2 N/A	0.1 0.4	0.4 N/A
Shipments as Percentage of Goods Sold						
1982 59% 1989 92%	5 14	91 100	55 14	100 N/A	100 67	50 N/A
Mofas to All Affiliates						
Sales of Goods and Services						
1982 $159.9 1989 $246.2	$63.7 35.1	$65.9 156.8	$17.8 33.6	$6.4 12.2	$2.7 5.2	$3.3 3.2
Sales of Goods						
1989 $221.8	33.3	153.3	32.6	nil	0.2	2.4
Shipments						
1982 $106.7 1989 $224.5	27.1 25.8	61.1 151.9	14.2 32.5	1.7 8.3	0.1 3.8	2.5 2.3
Shipments as Percentage of Goods Sold						
1989 101%	77	99	99	NMF	NMF	96

Total	Petroleum	Mfg.	Wholesale	Finance*	Services	Other
Mofas to Parents						
Sales of Goods and Services						
1982 $63.6 1989 $93.0	$31.4 16.6	$22.6 62.0	$3.3 7.2	$4.1 4.0	$0.9 1.5	$0.8 1.7
Sales of Goods						
1989 $84.2	15.5	60.4	7.0	0	0.1	1.1
Shipments						
1982 $38.5 1989 $71.3	12.5 7.2	22.8 57.1	2.1 6.1	0.0 nil	N/A 0.1	N/A 0.8
Shipments as Percentage of Goods Sold						
1989 77%	46	95	87	0	100	73
Mofas to Affiliates in Third Countries						
Sales/Shipments						
1982 $68.2 1989 $153.2	$14.6 18.6	$38.3 94.8	$12.1 26.4	$1.7 8.2	$1.1 3.7	$0.5 1.5
Mofas to Local Affiliates						
Sales/Shipments						
1982 $28.1 1989 $39.0	17.7 11.7	5.0 16.0	2.5 3.9	0.7 5.2	0.6 1.9	1.6 0.4

Note: *Finance, insurance, and real estate.

Sources: FDI census data: 1982, pp. 152-3, 225-6, 268-9, 285-91, 316, 332-3; 1989, pp. 97, 191, 202, 242-3, 258. *SOCB*, October 1991, p. 37.

TABLE 10.18. Summary of Intra-FDI Exports versus Total FDI Exports ($ billion)

Parent Export To:			-----Affiliate Exports To:-----					FDI Total Exports To:		
Total	Affil.	%	Total	Parents	%	Affil.	%	Total	Affil.	%
1966 Sales/Shipments										
$17.8	$6.3	35	$24.4	$4.6	19	$9.5	39	$42.2	$20.4	48
Sales of Goods/Services, 1977, 1982, 1989										
N/A	N/A	N/A	193.7	84.2	43	49.8	26	N/A	N/A	N/A
247.6	102.2	41	252.3	63.6	25	68.2	27	499.9	234.0	47
295.8	130.5	44	329.4	92.9	28	114.2	35	625.2	337.6	54
Shipments, 1977, 1982, 1989										
86.7	29.3	34	138.1	30.9	22	49.8	36	224.8	110.0	49
139.3	44.3	32	221.6	38.5	17	68.2	31	360.9	151.0	41
223.4	86.1	39	299.0	71.3	24	114.2	38	522.4	271.6	52
Sales of Goods, 1982, 1989										
231.0	98.8	43	237.4	N/A	N/A	N/A	N/A	468.4	N/A	N/A
261.3	119.7	45	298.9	84.2	28	106.7	36	560.2	310.6	55
Sales of Services, 1982, 1989										
16.6	3.3	20	14.8	N/A	N/A	N/A	N/A	31.4	N/A	N/A
34.4	10.8	31	24.3	6.1	25	6.0	25	58.7	22.9	39

Notes: Mofa data only. For the year 1966, export sales and shipments were considered one and the same.

Sources: FDI census data: 1982, pp. 225, 235, 268-71, 285-8, 316, 332, 335; 1977, pp. 318-9, 340, 395, 398-9; 1966, pp. 83, 197; 1989, pp. 97-8, 112, 190-1, 201-2, 205-6, 242-3, 253-4.

PART III:
ASPECTS OF U.S. COMPETITIVENESS

Chapter 11

The United States and the World Economy

INTRODUCTION

The following discussion advances a new concept for the definition and measurement of international competitiveness. It is felt that the presently employed method of comparison that is based on national accounts of geographically defined national entities is inadequate because national influence in the world economy is no longer determined by geography, but by national capital control over business activities dispersed throughout the world. The globalization of national economies via expanding direct investments has caused significant changes in national roles and positions in global output of goods and services as well as in international trade. These changes require special recognition if their transformation from the former national industry into global players within the world economy is to become transparent and fully understood.

The time-tested concept of national accounts can be maintained and, actually, will serve the new approach very well with slight adaptations. That is to say, that a nation's employment of industrial resources in the production of gross domestic product (GDP), for local use and consumption, and foreign trade purposes serves as the foundation of the competitive analysis, just as it is done now after conversion of national data into a key currency.

But instead of continuing with this geographically and politically inspired historic model, which may and should be retained for comparative purposes, it will be changed from here on by the introduction of the capital factor, which allows national influence and control over economic activities to extend beyond national boundaries. Capital can be furnished in two forms: foreign direct investments (FDI), and portfolio investments. As the latter is sufficiently different in character from the former, in that it does not aim at control over marketing organizations and their activities, it is excepted from further discussion here.

Under the traditional view of the economic world, the label "Made in . . ." correctly identified the national origin of products because three elements coincided: national territory, ownership of productive resources, and the decision power over their disposition. Today, this view is not matching reality, as global companies progressively integrate the global economy in which the national state appears more and more as a historical footnote.

Capital ownership by national business interests conducting international business activities projects the central decision-making power of that national enterprise into foreign territories. More correctly, it projects a piece of the original national sovereignty into foreign economies. Decisions about what to produce and export are not made at the subsidiary level. They are dictated by parental boardroom fiat, which clearly separates control from national territory of manufacture, distribution, and consumption. Absentee capital control and locus of decision are moving into the foreground, and thus establish a product's "nationality," with the geography of manufacture and shipment becoming only an incidental aspect.

The progressive liberalization and accessibility of global markets change the ways of and outlook on international marketing efforts. The historic view was shaped by an export-oriented mentality, which attached lesser importance to full control over marketing activities beyond national territory all the way up to the end user or consumer. By contrast, FDI emphasizes 100 percent control over the delivery of marketing efforts up to the end market, full and direct ownership of the market share attained with company products, and, at least, partial and legal ownership of the national economy where the affiliates are located. Exports are still important, but secondary to the fully integrated marketing strategy. The emergence of foreign affiliate production and marketing structures also accounts for a growing FDI share in world trade. FDI is the direct extension of a private enterprise into the global market seeking a comparable degree of control over foreign markets that it enjoys at home.

Control now rests on the capital base established in world markets. From a legal point of view, such company is considered to be a national company. From the capital ownership and control point of view, it definitely is a foreign business entity, whose nationality is determined by the principle of majority share held in the total capital invested and management control. Majority-held affiliates (Mofas) make this a clear-cut case, and present little difficulty in accepting the national origin of capital as the determining criterion of a subsidiary's nationality in preference over the geographical location of the enterprise. But this latter notion is still deeply ingrained in students of international business.

The following analysis is an attempt to demonstrate the usefulness of the new concept for the determination of national competitiveness. It proceeds from the traditional, territorial concept of a national economy, to be gradually transformed into the model based on capital control. For convenience's sake, the example of the United States is used, but the principle may be extended to any national economy. Substituting national capital control for geographically defined business ownership enhances the view and appreciation of the true American-controlled share of the world economy. Instead of dwelling on multitudes of companies, industries, or fuzzy measuring techniques, the United States appears as the "USA Corporation," with multiple industrial divisions in a national, regional, and even global market similarly defined.

The measurement of national competitiveness in this macroeconomic fashion is strictly limited, for now, to trend observations for broad industrial sectors as far as U.S. FDI in foreign markets is concerned for two reasons. One is that international databases and statistical methods are not yet sufficiently standardized to allow for more detailed presentations. The other is that FDI activities rarely extend into the public sector of national economies, and their inclusion could lead to grave distortions.

The proposed concept works in opposite ways. American capital flows from the territorial United States to other world areas tend to increase the American share in the world market and global trade by means of direct capital ownership over both, as explained. The influx of foreign capital into the United States, on the other hand, has the tendency to erode that share. In the ultimate analysis, national competitiveness is thus determined by the relative trend developments between these two forces.

THE GLOBAL MARKET

The ongoing discussion of the global market has yet to produce a clear picture of this promising concept. It is poorly defined when searching for concrete evidence of its size, composition, and development trends. The problem lies in the availability, comparability, and reliability of national statistics, which, despite the commendable pioneer work of supra-national or international organizations like the European Community, OECD, IMF, and World Bank, lack the desirable degree of standardization and uniformity. A major contributor to the problem are the multitudes of national currencies with ever fluctuating exchange rates, lack of annually updated time series, mixtures of preliminary and final data, etc. The use of the U.S. dollar as the international standard of measurements guarantees that U.S. economic data are reported reliably and in a meaningful way for a big part of the global economy. But it adds to grave uncertainties and outright distortions of economic facts and trends in other currency areas as all students of the subject can attest.

Thanks to the World Bank, a rather faint but much needed and still useful picture of the world market begins to take shape as provided in Table 11.1. The original data have been grouped into four areas: the United States, Europe, Japan, and all others.

The U.S. share in this traditional view of the world market, composed of the public and private sectors, is expectedly large and ranges between 26 and 32 percent. It may be declining based on the following calculation. At the end of the 1970s the Triad accounted for 68 percent of the global GDP. Applying this share to the whole decade and calculating the missing world figures indicates an average U.S. share of around 30 percent for the 1970s, 28 percent for the 1980s, and 26 percent for the first half of the 1990s.

Unfortunately, Western European figures are a mixture of two incomparable data series. The first part for the period 1970-83 is based on current country data, with the 1980 exchange rate applied to all years. The period 1984-92 is based on current country data converted at current exchange rates. The latter would be preferable for the whole period even though they are heavily affected by the strong relative movements of all currencies involved. The dollar moved up strongly between 1980-85, which is correctly reflected in the rising U.S. share. Its decline after 1985 led to the weaker U.S. position in the world output of value added, and the growing prominence of the Europeans. The same may be said for Japan whose strength is partially owed to the rising yen.

The data indicate that Europe as a whole has moved ahead of the United States. The OECD data cover 18 countries, which is the practical equivalent to the European Economic Area and very close to the future European Union (EU) of 15 nations. For all practical purposes, the values displayed represent the unified European economic bloc for the rest of this century.

Japan's progress against the United States and Europe is phenomenal, and fully confirms the competitive image of that nation. From a share of around 19 percent in 1970, Japan has been able to advance to 58 percent of the United States and 45 percent of the European gross product levels during the early 1990s. The rest of the world is about equal in economic weight to the United States. The world includes mostly developing nations and some of the remaining industrialized nations such as Canada and Australia in the definition of the OECD.

This preliminary scenario sets the stage for the next steps of the investigation into aspects of national competitiveness as briefly outlined in the introduction. This means moving from the traditional geographical interpretation of countries as representative manifestations of their role in the world economy to national capital control over marketing functions across the world instead.

TABLE 11.1. World Gross Domestic Product ($ million)

Year	Total	U.S.	Europe	Japan	All Others	U.S. Share
1970	N/A	$1,009	$1,079	$197	N/A	N/A
1971	N/A	1,095	1,200	225	N/A	N/A
1972	N/A	1,208	1,339	305	N/A	N/A
1973	N/A	1,350	1,522	414	N/A	N/A
1974	N/A	1,461	1,920	459	N/A	N/A
1975	N/A	1,588	2,181	499	N/A	N/A
1976	N/A	1,770	2,183	562	N/A	N/A
1977	N/A	1,975	2,437	691	N/A	N/A
1978	8,476	2,229	2,723	971	3,553	26.3
1979	9,821	2,486	3,172	1,011	3,152	25.3
1970-79	N/A	16,171	19,756	5,334	N/A	N/A
1980	11,118	2,708	3,468	1,059	3,883	24.4
1981	11,438	3,036	3,813	1,169	3,420	26.5
1982	11,322	3,152	4,415	1,086	2,669	27.8
1983	11,564	3,394	4,616	1,180	2,374	29.3
1984	12,018	3,763	2,855	1,265	4,135	31.3
1985	12,455	4,016	2,954	1,343	4,142	32.2
1986	14,515	4,231	4,032	1,986	4,266	29.1
1987	16,363	4,497	4,979	2,409	4,478	27.5
1988	18,250	4,854	5,553	2,898	4,945	26.6
1989	19,077	5,205	5,635	2,871	5,366	27.3
1980-89	138,120	38,856	42,320	17,266	39,678	28.1
1990	21,141	5,465	7,003	2,932	5,741	25.9
1991	21,985	5,610	7,249	3,346	5,576	25.5
1992	23,334	5,920	7,854	3,671	5,629	25.4
1990-92	66,460	16,995	22,106	9,949	16,946	25.6

Sources: World Bank, World Tables, 1994, pp. 28-9. *OECD*, National Accounts, 1960-85, pp. 19, 104-5; GDP at current prices and 1980 exchange rate 1970-85. Europe data are based on current GDP at current exchange rates, 1984-94, as taken from Main Economic Indicators, *OECD*, October 1993, p. 172, December 1993, p. 196, and April 1995, p. 210.

FDI AND THE AMERICAN ECONOMY

FDI was declared earlier to be the rapidly growing strategic market share alternative to exports for building solid and lasting footholds in the world economy. FDI has the big advantage over trading activities of offering any desired degree of control over international marketing which is not afforded by trading activities alone.

For the purpose of this investigation, three questions have to be addressed. The first, about the size of the U.S. national economy in relation to all others in the traditional definition, has been answered by Table 11.1. The second question must establish by how much the influx of FDI capital has reduced the real American ownership and control over its own resources in the domestic economy in accordance with the above definition. The third question follows logically from this sequence of thought, and deals with the degree of America's control and ownership achieved over productive resources in that part of the world lying outside its own geographical boundaries.

In other words, the focus changes from measuring economic output in a national territory to nationally controlled output within the world economy irrespective of political boundaries. Taking the point one step further by studying the relative development speeds of outward versus inward FDI activities allows fairly accurate prognostications about a nation's course in the international competition. Presently, the attention paid to the development of exports from a national territory as another legitimate measure of national economic weight in the world clouds the vision for the importance of FDI in determining a nation's true economic stature in the global market. Two figures will drive this point home. All American merchandise exports amount to about $500 billion at the present. Despite its size, this amounts to only one-third the $1.5 trillion sales volume generated by U.S. outward FDI enterprises. Impressive as exports appear, they do not come close to matching the earnings power of American overseas enterprises.

This is even more evident if it is realized that roughly 23 percent of those exports are in the hands of foreign-owned firms in the United States. Table 11.2 gives a partial answer to questions two and three by showing how foreign business interests operating in the United States have invested more rapidly here than U.S. FDI businesses abroad, resulting in the growth of foreign investment volumes in the United States from 23 percent in 1975 to 81 percent of like U.S. overseas investments by 1993. Similar advances are registered for employment, from 17 percent in 1977 to 70 percent in 1992; sales, from 30 to 77 percent; gross product, from 22 to 73 percent; and assets, from 29 percent to an even higher 104 percent.

TABLE 11.2. Comparative Aspects of U.S. Outward versus Inward FDI ($ billion)

Year	Position*		Employment**(000)		Sales*		Gross Product		Assets*	
	Out	In	Out	In	Out	In	Out**	In*	Out	In
1975	$124.2	$27.7	N/A	N/A	N/A	N/A	N/A	N/A	N/A	N/A
1976	137.2	30.8	N/A	N/A	N/A	N/A	N/A	N/A	N/A	N/A
1977	145.9	34.6	7,196	1,219	$647.9	$193.9	$161.1	$35.2	$490	$144
1978	162.7	42.5	N/A	1,430	N/A	241.5	N/A	42.9	N/A	181
1979	187.9	54.5	N/A	1,753	N/A	327.9	N/A	55.4	N/A	229
1980	215.4	83.0	N/A	2,034	N/A	412.4	N/A	70.9	N/A	291
1981	228.3	108.7	N/A	2,417	N/A	510.2	N/A	98.8	N/A	407
1982	207.8	124.7	6,640	2,448	935.8	518.1	223.7	103.5	752	476
1983	207.2	137.1	6,383	2,547	886.3	536.6	N/A	111.5	751	532
1984	211.5	164.6	6,418	2,714	898.6	596.0	N/A	128.8	760	603
1985	230.3	184.6	6,419	2,862	895.5	632.9	N/A	134.9	835	741
1986	259.8	220.4	6,250	2,938	928.9	672.0	N/A	142.1	931	838
1987	314.3	263.4	6,269	3,224	1,052.8	744.6	N/A	157.9	1,111	944
1988	372.4	314.8	6,404	3,844	1,194.7	886.4	N/A	190.4	1,206	1,201
1989	381.8	368.9	6,622	4,412	1,284.9	1,058.6	319.9	223.4	1,330	1,431
1990	430.5	394.9	6,834	4,735	1,493.4	1,175.9	365.0	239.3	1,559	1,550
1991	467.8	419.1	6,878	4,872	1,541.6	1,185.9	356.1	257.6	1,678	1,753
1992	502.1	427.6	6,660	4,715	1,574.1	1,231.9	361.5	266.3	1,762	1,825
1993	559.7	464.1	6,731	4,722	1,573.9	1,302.1	357.9	290.4	2,053	2,049

Notes: *All nonbank affiliates. **Mofa data.

Sources: **Position:** *SOCB,* August 1991, p.85; August 1992, p. 122; August 1994, p. 131. **Assets:** Benchmark Surveys, 1977, p. 110; 1982, p. 88; 1989, p. M-25. *SOCB,* September 1986, p. 33; June 1987, p. 33; June 1988, p. 90; June 1990, p. 36. **Sales:** Benchmark Surveys, 1977, p. 138; 1982, p. 109; 1989, p. M-25. *SOCB,* June 1987, p. 33; June 1988, p. 90; June 1989, p. 32; June 1990, p. 36; October 1991, p. 29; August 1992, p. 72; July 1993, p. 52; June 1994, p. 54; August 1994, pp. 154, 174-5. **Employment:** *SOCB,* February 1982, p. 41; July 1989, pp. 120-1; October 1991, pp. 29, 34; August 1992, p. 72; May 1993, pp. 93, 102; June 1994, pp. 43, 54; June 1995, p. 32. **INWARD FDI: Position:** *SOCB,* August 1983, p. 35; August 1991, p. 51; August 1992, p. 92; August 1994, p. 103; June 1995, p. 61; **Employment, Sales, Gross Product, Assets:** *SOCB,* July 1994, p. 154; May 1995, p. 63; June 1995, p. 38.

The vigorous advance of U.S. inward FDI began with the decade of the 1980s at a time when U.S. outward FDI slowed its pace after three decades of active expansion. This enabled foreign companies to register strong gains against their American competitors. Their penetration of U.S. industries was most pronounced in the manufacturing sector which at that time was downplayed by such pejorative terms as smokestack or rustbelt industries by the U.S. business community and public. American investment interest at home centered on service industries with higher and thus more promising growth rates.

A curious aspect of U.S. outward FDI is the fact that total employment has not risen in about twenty years and may actually have fallen, but still accommodates an investment volume three times larger and more than double the sales generated during the late 1970s. As the investment position and assets grew faster over the period, the capital intensity per employee has been increasing rapidly. The trend in capital buildup is even more pronounced for inward investors such that in 1992, outward investments concentrated $25,950 in assets per employee versus $38,460 per employee for inward investors–a 48 percent difference.

Sales output per employee displays less noticeable variations. Sales of $23,469 per outward employee contrast with 25,988 for each inward employee–a 10 percent higher level. The economic implications of the 48 percent higher capital investment yielding only a 10 percent higher sales output per employee for foreign investors in the States are difficult to explain without further studies.

Another difference worth mentioning is the output of value added by both investor types. Outward investment produced a 28 percent margin on Mofa sales of $1,299 billion in 1992 compared to a 22 percent margin for all inward affiliates in the United States. This is a significant variation that can be partially explained with different structures of gross profits generated in both world areas. Employee compensation and profit-type components dominate the inward investment results, whereas indirect business taxes and related factors predominate in the generation of the outward investment value added. It may also be that similar profit policies by both investor types are involved here. In order to escape the American tax bite, both are aiming at maximizing their profits outside the United States where they can be legally sheltered in many different tax havens.

INWARD FDI'S ROLE IN U.S. INDUSTRY

After all this foreign investment activity, how much of the U.S. economy is actually foreign-controlled? FDI data provided so far allow a clear expression and measurement of such influence in national production, distribution, employment, foreign trade, other balance-of-payment (BOP) flows, and related subjects. As discussed earlier, the ideal method for establishing these relationships would be to cover majority-owned enterprises, where the local power and authority in the decision-making process is clearly determined by the foreign element. As it turns out, the discussion has to dwell on the much broader combination of both Mofa and minority holdings, because the database does not always allow a clear separation of the two.

Tables 11.3 and 11.4 summarize the impact of inward FDI in terms of percentage share of America's industrial employment, sales, assets, and output of value added. In all cases, foreigners are showing gains against their American competitors. They are most impressive in the manufacturing sector where shares above 20 percent are not uncommon, indicating a competitive edge for the foreign investors. The highest recorded shares are found in the chemical industry with figures above 30 percent.

In the service sector, the opposite holds true. Foreigners seem to have difficulties in making comparable inroads. Shares remain under 10 percent for all industries surveyed in this sector and lack the general buoyancy seen in manufacturing. Actually, judging by the latest available information, further foreign inroads may be more difficult to achieve here. The highest shares recorded were in wholesaling, insurance, and transportation. But even there none broke the 7 percent barrier.

DIMENSIONS OF U.S. OUTWARD FDI

The main features of the American-controlled economy outside the territorial United States are captured in Table 11.2. Comparing this information to similar data by major world regions is difficult, because no coherent or comparable databases have been developed so far that lend themselves easily for this task, with the exception of the GDP information put together by the World Bank and shown in Table 11.1.

Nonetheless, useful perspectives can be developed by comparing outward FDI parameters with the nonagricultural industrial part of the U.S. economy itself, thereby creating a set of comparable and familiar dimensions. This is very legitimate, because the U.S. economy spawned its own FDI effort, and it is interesting to see how it has developed in relation to its parent country.

The decline of Mofa data against similar American economic indicators is significant and unexpected. Yet, it matches the general tenor of findings documented in Chapters 12 through 14, and leads in the same direction.

TABLE 11.3. Industrial Data for U.S. Inward FDI — Employment

Nonbank Affiliate Share of U.S. Business Employment

Year	Total	Mfg.	Retailing	Wholesale	Finance*	Services	Insurance	Transport	Real Estate	Constr.
1977	1.8%	3.2%	0.9%	2.9%	0.3%	N/A	2.3%	N/A	0.8%	N/A
1980	2.7	5.4	2.4	2.7	3.0	0.6%	3.5	N/A	1.5	1.0%
1981	3.2	N/A	N/A	N/A	N/A	N/A	N/A	N/A	N/A	N/A
1982	3.3	N/A	N/A	N/A	N/A	N/A	N/A	N/A	N/A	N/A
1983	3.4	N/A	N/A	N/A	N/A	N/A	N/A	N/A	N/A	N/A
1984	3.5	N/A	N/A	N/A	N/A	N/A	N/A	N/A	N/A	N/A
1985	3.5	N/A	N/A	N/A	N/A	N/A	N/A	N/A	N/A	N/A
1986	3.3	N/A	N/A	N/A	N/A	N/A	N/A	N/A	N/A	N/A
1987	3.7	7.7	3.3	4.7	7.5	1.3	3.7	2.7%	2.3	1.1
1988	4.3	8.9	3.9	4.8	9.2	1.6	5.0	3.7	2.3	1.2
1989	4.9	10.2	4.7	5.1	9.0	1.9	5.6	5.0	2.1	1.3
1990	5.1	11.0	4.2	5.7	5.3	2.3	5.8	6.1	2.3	1.5
1991	5.3	11.6	4.5	5.6	6.2	2.5	6.5	6.1	2.3	1.5
1992	5.1	11.7	4.0	5.6	6.4	2.4	6.5	5.6	2.2	1.5
1993	5.0	11.6	4.2	5.8	5.2	2.0	6.2	6.7	2.1	1.3

Nonbank Affiliate Share in U.S. Manufacturing Employment

Year	Chemicals	Ceramics**	Electric/Electronic	Primary Metals	Rubber & Plastics	Food & Kindred	Instrument	Motor Vehicles	Nonelec. Machines	Fabric. Met. Prod.
1977	17.0%	N/A	4.7%	5.2%	N/A	4.6%	N/A	N/A	1.9%	1.2%
1980	15.2	5.6%	7.6	5.6	5.3%	6.0	7.4%	7.4%	4.6	3.2
1987	26.2	14.5	12.0	12.2	6.6	8.4	7.4	6.6	5.9	4.1
1988	27.2	15.6	13.7	10.6	10.7	10.8	8.2	7.4	7.5	5.9
1989	29.4	18.7	15.7	12.6	11.3	12.3	9.9	8.9	9.9	6.9
1990	30.4	19.7	16.2	14.8	14.5	12.4	11.2	11.2	10.3	7.1
1991	31.4	19.5	17.3	15.4	14.5	12.6	12.1	12.2	10.9	8.0
1992	32.2	20.8	17.2	15.9	14.8	12.0	11.9	11.0	11.2	8.3
1993	32.5	20.5	17.0	16.2	14.3	10.9	12.2	11.5	11.1	8.6

Notes: *Except banking. **Stone, clay, and glass products.

Sources: *FDI in the United States, Review and Analysis of Current Developments*, August 1991, Tables 5-9, 5-18; June 1993, *An Update*, p. 33. *SOCB*, May 1981, p. 46; July 1994, p. 161; May 1995, p. 66. *Statistical Abstract of the United States*, 1979, Table 681.

Three explanations may be offered for this unexpected phenomenon by drawing on discussions in earlier chapters.

One is the decided slowdown in U.S. direct investments during the 1980s with its withering effect on Mofa sales, employment, and output of gross product, whose aftereffects are still clearly in evidence during the early 1990s. The question has been raised before as to whether this situation might have arisen from poor judgement about the global economic potential, which seems most unlikely, or a deliberate decision because of its rational assessment by executive boards. Plenty of good reasons for skepticism existed. Slowing economic growth and even recessionary trends appeared in major FDI markets at that time. Coupled with sharply rising cost levels compared to the United States, which itself faced a major credit crunch with unprecedented interest levels during the early 1980s, cast a dark cloud over profit expectations and demanded utmost caution in investment decisions.

Another possibility mentioned referred to parent companies succumbing to official political pressures to put domestic priorities over and above their corporate plans for further expansion into the world market. The relative decline of Mofa shares in world trade discussed in Chapter 13, and vis-à-vis U.S. exports may be a hint in that direction. However, this runs counter to another observation made, whereby a declining dollar produces a booster effect on affiliate sales and profits, not to mention the quarterly balance sheets.

The third (and least palatable) factor playing a role is that Americans are facing early manifestations of a loss in national competitiveness. Indications of such a dire possibility come to the surface in the following chapters dealing with Mofa growth relative to host economies (Chapter 12), their participation in world trade (Chapter 13), and falling behind in FDI efforts compared to other nations as well as other related factors (Chapter 14) (see Table 11.5).

As usual, there may be a combination of factors at work, but they leave their indelible imprint here in Table 11.1 and further down in Table 11.6. The slow erosion of the American GDP share, whether measured in conventional terms in Table 11.1, or in the proposed adaptation in Table 11.6, definitely portray a U.S. position in the economic world less robust than it used to be.

A clear message is left by the data presented here and elsewhere. The key to a strong position in the global market is not trade, but direct investment. This point is driven home by relating gross product data for U.S. outward FDI to Table 11.6 information in order to fulfill the stated purpose of this investigation, which is getting an impression of the true share of the

TABLE 11.4. Industrial Data for U.S. Inward FDI–GP, Assets, and Sales

Year	Total	Mfg.	Retailing	Wholesale	Finance*	Services	Insurance	Real Estate	Constr.
					Nonbank Affiliate Share of U.S. Business Gross Product				
1977	2.3	3.6	1.2	3.8	2.2	0.5	2.4	0.6	0.5
1978	2.5	3.9	N/A	N/A	N/A	N/A	N/A	N/A	N/A
1979	2.9	4.6	N/A	N/A	N/A	N/A	N/A	N/A	N/A
1980	3.4	5.3	N/A	N/A	N/A	N/A	N/A	N/A	N/A
1981	4.2	7.2	2.3	5.0	4.2	0.7	4.0	2.2	1.0
1982	4.3	7.3	N/A	N/A	N/A	N/A	N/A	N/A	N/A
1983	4.4	7.6	N/A	N/A	N/A	N/A	N/A	N/A	N/A
1984	4.4	7.9	N/A	N/A	N/A	N/A	N/A	N/A	N/A
1985	4.3	7.8	N/A	N/A	N/A	N/A	N/A	N/A	N/A
1986	4.3	8.0	N/A	N/A	N/A	N/A	N/A	N/A	N/A
1987	4.5	10.5	2.4	6.9	16.5	0.9	6.3	3.0	1.2
1988	5.0	11.4	3.0	7.0	17.7	1.3	5.4	2.9	1.6
1989	5.6	13.0	3.3	7.2	18.7	1.4	3.9	3.4	2.0
1990	5.7	13.8	3.4	7.4	6.1	1.7	5.4	3.3	2.2
1991	6.0	14.2	4.2	8.3	6.2	1.7	5.3	3.4	2.6
1992	5.9	13.9	3.5	8.8	5.6	1.8	5.3	2.6	2.3
1993	6.1	—	—	—	—	—	—	—	—

Note: *Except banking.

Sources: *FDI in the United States, Review and Analysis of Current Developments*, August 1991, Tables 5-4, 5-9. *SOCB* June 1990, p. 46; July 1994, p. 154, 160; May 1995, p. 37.

Nonbank Affiliate Share of U.S. Manufacturing Gross Product

Year	Chemicals	Ceramics*	Electric/ Electronic	Primary Metals	Rubber & Plastics	Food & Kindred	Instrument	Motor Vehicles	Nonelec. Machines	Fabric. Met. Prod.
1977	17.5%	—	—	—	—	7.8%	—	—	2.7%	3.3%
1986	32.2	—	—	—	—	8.9	—	—	—	8.0
1987	33.3	—	—	—	—	8.4	—	—	—	7.4
1990	31.9	24.8%	15.6%	19.3%	17.6%	13.8	11.9%	4.9%	10.3	7.9
1991	35.2	24.8	16.3	19.8	13.0	11.7	10.1	7.6	—	9.8

Nonbank Affiliate Share of U.S. Manufacturing Assets

Year	Chemicals	Ceramics*	Electric/ Electronic	Primary Metals	Rubber & Plastics	Food & Kindred	Instrument	Motor Vehicles	Nonelec. Machines	Fabric. Met. Prod.
1977	15.4%	7.3%	5.1%	6.2%	.6%	4.4%	3.3%	.6%	3.7%	2.8%
1986	32.6	24.8	11.6	20.6	5.8	9.6	7.0	2.7	4.9	8.5
1987	31.6	34.3	10.7	19.5	13.6	12.2	8.7	2.8	6.1	9.0
1988	31.3	39.6	15.2	19.9	22.2	N/A	7.5	3.1	9.8	16.2
1989	36.0	38.2	16.2	24.9	24.0	N/A	9.1	4.2	13.1	24.7
1990	42.4	42.3	20.2	29.1	33.1	N/A	11.6	4.7	12.6	19.0
1991	40.4	43.7	21.0	31.5	28.8	N/A	13.5	4.9	13.1	18.7

Nonbank Affiliate Share of U.S. Manufacturing Sales

Year	Chemicals	Ceramics*	Electric/ Electronic	Primary Metals	Rubber & Plastics	Food & Kindred	Instrument	Motor Vehicles	Nonelec. Machines	Fabric. Met. Prod.
1977	14.5%	6.8%	5.8%	6.7%	2.8%	3.8%	3.8%	.2%	3.8%	1.9%
1986	29.2	21.9	12.2	19.0	4.8	6.8	7.1	3.1	5.4	7.6
1987	32.0	24.6	12.6	19.3	10.4	6.7	9.1	2.6	6.7	7.0
1988	30.0	25.9	15.9	19.0	14.7	N/A	8.2	2.7	9.8	11.3
1989	33.3	29.4	16.3	23.3	15.9	N/A	8.7	4.7	13.9	17.4
1990	38.4	32.1	20.0	26.8	21.9	N/A	10.5	5.6	14.4	13.6
1991	37.4	32.9	20.7	27.7	18.7	N/A	13.9	6.1	14.1	14.5

Note: *Stone, clay, and glass products.

Sources: SOCB, May 1988, p. 64; July 1989, p. 131; July 1991, p. 80; May 1992, p. 55; May 1993, p. 98.

TABLE 11.5. The Size of Outward FDI Relative to U.S. Economy

Year	U.S. Nonag. Industrial GDP $ billion	Nonbank Mofa GP $ billion	%	U.S. Nonag. Industrial Employment 000	Nonbank Mofa Employment 000	%
1977	$1,638	$161.1	9.8	$66,125	$5,369	8.0
1982	2,530	223.7	8.8	71,259	5,022	7.0
1989	4,191	319.9	7.6	85,704	5,114	6.0
1990	4,394	365.0	8.3	86,380	5,356	6.2
1991	4,510	356.1	7.9	84,982	5,387	6.3
1992	4,730	361.5	7.7	85,244	5,282	6.2
1993	5,004	357.9	7.2	86,986	5,260	6.0

Note: The data in this table differs from information in Tables 7.8 and 7.9 because of adjustments for foreign ownership.

Sources: *U.S. Data: Economic Report of the President*, February 1995, pp. 286, 324-5. Mofa employment: Benchmark Survey, 1977, p. 294; 1982, p. 244; 1989, p. 216. *SOCB*, September 1986, pp. 36-7; June 1987, p. 36; June 1988, pp. 94-5; June 1989, p. 36; June 1990, pp. 40-1; July 1993, p. 53; June 1994, pp. 48, 55-6; June 1995, pp. 44-5. Mofa GP: Table 11.2.

global economy owned by American business on the basis of capital participation and degree of control. As stated before, Mofa data should ideally be used for this purpose alone, because minority equity holdings are more like portfolio investments. In this study Mofa gross product figures are used for the stated reason, but also because such data for all nonbank affiliates are not furnished. The American involvement in the world economy is thus larger than the data suggest, but do not necessarily point to American control over economic processes.

Certain caveats need to be emphasized at this point in order to avoid misunderstandings and arriving at wrong conclusions. It should be made clear that all information presented on U.S. inward FDI so far relates to the American business sector, while the World Bank information furnishes data on total economic output including the government sector. In order to make sense, the comparison with the U.S. economy rests on industry data alone, exclusive of the public sector, which are directly comparable with all FDI statistics, while global inward and outward FDI economic data relating to World Bank information are measured in their terms, which reduces the American share somewhat.

CONCLUSIONS

The foregoing investigation introduces a novel concept for the measurement of national competitiveness. Being that, it needs further methodological development, testing, and refinement. In the absence of a well-developed international statistical framework, however, that would allow a more direct access to the desired information, it appears to be a workable proposition. The results presented in this study admittedly are often rough approximations, but still carry a convincing degree of informational value, if only for the underlying trends unearthed, rather than the absolute dimensions established.

According to the information provided, U.S.-owned Mofas operating outside the United States reach between 6 and 7 percent of the U.S. industrial value-added not adjusted for the foreign FDI factor. After such adjustment which, after all, is the main goal of this investigation the Mofa share would reach between 7 and 8 percent. They carry slightly more economic weight than foreign-owned affiliates do in the United States, a fact that was established by Table 11.2.

Assuming that the industrial world outside the United States is structured similarly to that of the United States and thus three times larger in volume–a fact that cannot be established with certainty from available international statistics, leads to the conclusion that America's share in the industrial output of the world outside the United States reaches between 2 and 2.5 percent in contrast to the foreign share of 6 percent in the U.S. economy. In addition, the relative stagnation of outward Mofa data in contrast to the dynamic development of foreign businesses in the U.S. economy supports the probability of a stagnant, if not declining market share for U.S.-controlled business in a global context.

The final contribution of this new analytical tool is a revision of the information contained in Table 11.1 (now Table 11.6) for all those years where pertinent inward and outward gross product data are available. The result is presented below in Table 11.6.

The first impression created by the new measuring technique is a generally elevated global market share for the United States, both in the beginning and end of the period. This had to be expected after the discussion of the additive effect stemming from the U.S. outward FDI data. But, the drop in the U.S. share of the world economy is confirmed. While distressing, it seems realistic for several reasons not considered in the above analysis.

One is the movement of the dollar against all other currencies. Since the beginning of the period covered by the above tables, and indeed the whole period under study, the dollar has generally become weaker with a brief

TABLE 11.6. American Share of World Gross Domestic Product ($ million)

Year	World Total	U.S. Revised*	Europe Total	Europe U.S. FDI	Europe %	Japan Total	Japan U.S. FDI	Japan %	All Other Total	All Other U.S. FDI	All Other %	Global U.S. Share
1977	7,300e	1,940	2,437	69.4	2.8	691	3.1	0.4	2,197e	88.6	4.0	28.8
1978	8,476	2,186	2,723	—	—	971	—	—	3,553	—	—	—
1979	9,821	2,431	3,172	—	—	1,011	—	—	3,152	—	—	—
1980	11,118	2,637	3,468	—	—	1,059	—	—	3,883	—	—	N/A
1981	11,438	2,937	3,813	—	—	1,169	—	—	3,420	—	—	N/A
1982	11,322	3,048	4,415	112.6	2.6	1,086	4.6	0.4	2,669	106.5	4.0	28.9
1983	11,564	3,282	4,616	—	—	1,180	—	—	2,374	—	—	N/A
1984	12,018	3,634	2,855	—	—	1,265	—	—	4,135	—	—	N/A
1985	12,455	3,881	2,954	—	—	1,343	—	—	4,142	—	—	N/A
1986	14,515	4,089	4,032	—	—	1,986	—	—	4,266	—	—	N/A
1987	16,363	4,339	4,979	—	—	2,409	—	—	4,478	—	—	N/A
1988	18,250	4,664	5,553	—	—	2,898	—	—	4,945	—	—	N/A
1989	19,077	4,982	5,635	179.8	3.2	2,871	14.9	0.5	5,366	125.2	2.3	27.8
1980-89	138,120	37,493	42,320	N/A	N/A	17,266	N/A	N/A	39,678	N/A	N/A	N/A
1990	21,141	5,226	7,003	213.4	3.0	2,932	14.6	0.5	5,741	128.0	2.2	26.4
1991	21,985	5,352	7,249	217.4	3.0	3,346	16.5	0.5	5,576	122.1	2.2	26.0
1992	23,334	5,654	7,854	217.7	2.8	3,671	15.7	0.4	5,629	128.1	2.3	25.8
1990-92	66,460	16,232	22,106	648.5	2.9	9,949	46.8	0.5	16,946	378.2	2.2	26.0

Notes: e = estimate. *U.S. GDP less foreign share. Affiliate GP see Table 7.6. Data represent a revision of Table 11.1.

338

rebound in the years 1980 through 1985, which may account for the relatively high U.S. share in the 1982 world economy. This led to relative shifts in the database which perhaps do not correctly reflect the underlying country or area developments expressed in their national currencies.

A second factor is the relatively weak development of U.S. outward direct investments vis-à-vis more vigorous investment activities of foreign competitors. As shown in a different section, the fund outflows from the United States were cut by 28 percent during the 1980s, before assuming new life during the early 1990s (see Table 2.6). The end effect of the cross flows of direct investment capital become visible in Table 11.2, where the relative positions of inward and outward investment and their development can be compared. Two recent OECD publications confirm this situation. They show that the U.S. share of the overall inward investment position in OECD countries, reflecting the inroads made by foreigners in the U.S. economy, has risen from 28 to 36 percent between 1980 and 1992, while the U.S. share in the total OECD outward investment position, reflecting U.S. parent efforts, has declined from 50 to 29 percent in those very same years (OECD, *International Direct Investment Yearbook*, 1993 and 1994).

Finally, an observation made earlier contributes to the outward appearance of America's competitive performance. It was noted that the vigorous direct investment activities of U.S. companies, which led to a rapid expansion in the FDI position during the first half of the 1990s was not followed by any visible increase in Mofa sales, output of value-added, or employment. A close parallel development of all should have occured under normal circumstances. A partial explanation is found in the earlier discussion about the FDI accounting practices employed by government statisticians. In Chapter 2, the treatment of the finance subsidiaries in the Netherlands Antilles was given close attention. Their respective fund flows were seen to affect the FDI position negatively until 1984, when their international borrowings amounted to $42.5 billion, reducing the FDI position by the same amount. That amount had shrunk to only $6.3 billion in 1994. The difference between both was gradually added to the FDI position–a purely financial calculation without any effect on the physical FDI in place (see Table 2.1, p. 41). The net effect of these accounting specifics was the addition of $10.5 billion to the FDI position in the 1990 through 1993 period with a neutral effect on their operations.

Table 11.6 revised has the advantage over Table 11.1 in that it introduces the inward FDI effect on the U.S. economy and, at the same time, America's FDI penetration of major world regions. In Europe, where 50 percent of U.S. investment is concentrated, the American share remained very firm for almost two decades. Considering the advanced development status of the region, just holding their own attests to the competitive equality of both sides.

In the revised table, Japan reveals a very small American presence compared to Europe, where the U.S. share in the economy is five to six times larger. While not advancing, it represents a firm foothold in a market that has presented unique competitive constellations not only for the United States, but also other global business interests.

In the rest of the world, which includes important economies as well as the indisputable growth sector of the world economy, the American position has obviously lost significant market share. The best one can say about the situation is that, by all indications, U.S. competitors are building a solid platform here from which to soar in the future.

It must be remembered that the impressions generated by both tables relate to total economies including the public and private sector. This is not the same as measuring developments of the U.S. competitive position in the industrial sector of major nations presented in the next chapter. Invariably, U.S. shares are reaching higher levels in those nations due to more specifically defined economic sectors, in which American industry competes on an equal footing. The data unearthed are thus more meaningful and conclusive in assessing America's true industrial competitiveness.

A final point has to be made which may modify the above picture for U.S. FDI, based on official statistics, rather substantially in the future. The discovery of foreign capital participation in 15 percent of U.S. parent companies could possibly lead to a reduction in U.S. capital control (FDI) over foreign business operation by an equal or even higher amount. But the real situation cannot even be estimated without better information, which will eventually come forth (see Table 4.6).

Chapter 12

U.S. FDI's Role
in Host Country Economies

The assessment of the U.S. economy in a global context as defined in the previous chapter can be expanded to an analysis of its involvement and degree of control in individual economies. This requires very much the same approach employed in the review of the foreign element in the U.S. economy. A better understanding of the U.S. role in host economies can be achieved by establishing relationships with national points of reference which put the American dimension into proper perspective. Faceless statistics turn, all of a sudden, into meaningful indicators of global business activities undertaken by U.S. companies. Their investments, employees, equipment, output of value-added, domestic and international commercial activities leave measurable imprints on a foreign nation's output of goods and services, employment, trade, technology, management, and ultimately its total social fabric.

Macroeconomic points of reference, as employed in the following, are less detailed than in the previous chapter, but still serve as ideal measures of American competitiveness in major world markets. Actually, more so than market shares which, at best, occasionally appear on a very fragmented basis. National account data are readily accessible for most nations over long periods, standardized in their definition, and thus directly comparable among countries. For the following multivariate analysis, major economic aspects of U.S. FDI are pulled together, quantified, and then related to economic benchmarks of selected host countries and the United States. Their relationships are explored in such standard national accounts as Mofa gross product (GP) against national output of industrial and manufacturing GDP, and Mofa employment against national employment. BOP data link Mofa imports and exports with related national foreign trade. Adding net receipts of income and service fees by total U.S. FDI establishes a fairly clear picture of the American impact on the nation's balance of services and the current account as a whole. Owing to the database available, such information can be provided in broad outlines for the census years 1957, 1966, 1977, 1982, and 1989 as a sort of progress report for a period of four decades. Two additional inputs are given by tracing the country's development in the generation of global Mofa GP, and America's share in the country's overall inward FDI where available.

National economic data are assumed to refer to the "private sector," which invariably includes government-owned or mixed enterprises in many countries. For those that are published in national currencies, all dollar-denominated U.S. FDI data were converted into those currencies rather than vice versa to minimize exchange rate distortions. The average annual exchange rates used for this purpose were taken from IMF sources and are shown at the bottom of each country page. As original FDI financial data were probably translated at monthly rather than annual exchange rates upon consolidation for headquarter use, there is a possibility for discrepancies in the values whose significance cannot even be estimated. Despite these minor flaws, U.S. affiliates become visible as integral parts of foreign economies, even if only in very broad outlines.

The information presented in the following tables once again needs some clarification. National data were taken from both international and country sources. As they are established by different methods and classifications, and for very different purposes, they may not be fully compatible with FDI data. Also, estimates have been substituted for missing information where they can be defended as reasonable and appropriate under the circumstances.

One such case is presented by the 1957 affiliate GP estimates which were developed on the basis of sales plus inventory changes less purchases of intermediate goods and services. The 1957 census, however, does not contain any information on inventory movements leaving the numbers lacking in this regard. A margin of error is built into the data which does seem acceptable, especially when weighed against the alternative of losing a crucial base point of reference for this investigation.

A second point concerns the statistical problems of the oil affiliates mentioned before. Owing to their data presentation method, the processing sector cannot be included under manufacturing, as is common practice, nor can wholesale and retail functions be allocated to a country's trade industry. By lumping all oil affiliate data into one account, the statistics prepared by the U.S. Department of Commerce lead to serious understatements of affiliate positions in some foreign manufacturing and trade situations.

No attempt has been made to extend this information beyond the general "all industries" and "manufacturing" categories, because a full compatibility between census data and foreign statistics, which may look similar on the surface, is not assured. All GP data are based on information presented in Table 7.7 and translated at exchange rates provided in the country tables.

As a final note, it needs to be emphasized that 1957 data cover all affiliates, while 1966 data cover gross product figures only. Starting with 1977, all data relate strictly to Mofas as the true representatives of America's competitiveness. These are major conclusions drawn from the analysis:

1. Total Mofa GP is increasingly concentrated in developed countries and economies such as those in Canada, Western Europe, Japan, South Africa, Australia, and New Zealand. Their share grew from 60 percent in 1957 to 82 percent in 1989.
2. These areas accounted for 76 percent of total U.S. FDI in the same year, represented a very large portion–perhaps as high as 80 percent–of the world's economic potential and are, in themselves, a first indicator of America's investment emphasis on the most competitive world economies.
3. Data for thirty-one selected countries playing major roles for U.S. FDI, and thus telling indicators of America's economic viability vis-à-vis its global competitors, show the following developments expressed as changing share positions in industrial GDP of the nation for 1966 through 1989 regardless of interim ups or downs:

    a. Clear gains were registered in nine countries, or 29 percent of the total. They are: Belgium/Luxemburg, Germany, Ireland, the Netherlands, Spain, Switzerland, Norway, the UK, and Singapore.
    b. Steady positions were maintained in another nine countries, or 29 percent of the total. They are: Australia, Brazil, Denmark, France, Italy, Japan, Panama, Sweden, and New Zealand.
    c. Clear losses in position occurred in eleven countries, or 35 percent of all thirty-one nations evaluated. They are: Argentina, Canada, Chile, Colombia, Hong Kong, Mexico, Indonesia, Peru, Philippines, South Africa, and Venezuela.
    d. Two countries could not be measured for lack of pertinent statistics: the Bahamas and Bermuda.

    In summary, the data suggest that U.S. FDI is establishing a growing foothold in 29 percent of the national economies surveyed, while holding its own in another 29 percent for a batting average of 58 percent, in and by itself a good competitive record.

4. U.S. FDI's performance record improves dramatically, if the focus shifts to the most important GP producer, the manufacturing industry, which eliminates the very erratic influence of the oil sector from

the review. Its influence in the total picture is decidedly negative, because oil's 1957 share in total FDI GP reached 40 percent, fluctuated between 32 and 39 percent during 1957 through 1988, but fell back to 24 percent in 1989 on an absolute drop in its GP dollar volume. Manufacturing always produced higher GP figures than oil, fluctuating between 44 and 49 percent for most years, increasing to a high of 54 percent in 1989. This may be regarded as the key measure of America's rank as an international competitor (see Table 7.7).

   a. Now, clear gains are established in twelve countries, or 38 percent of the total including: Australia, Belgium/Luxemburg, Brazil, Chile, Denmark, Indonesia, Ireland, the Netherlands, Panama, Singapore, Spain, and the UK.
   b. Neutral positions appear in ten nations, or 32 percent of total: France, Germany, Hong Kong, Italy, Japan, Mexico, New Zealand, Philippines, Sweden, and Switzerland.
   c. Definitely weaker positions were found in seven economies, or 23 percent: Argentina, Canada, Colombia, Norway, Peru, South Africa, and Venezuela. Seeing Canada appear again on the negative list raises concern in considering the strategic significance of this vital neighboring market.
   d. Similar to point 3.d, and for the same reasons, the Bahamas and Bermuda defied evaluation.

The net result for the manufacturing part of U.S. FDI is an increase in the batting average to 70 percent. In other words, in more than two-thirds of economies researched, manufacturing Mofas were able to hold their own or gain ground against their competitors—an above average performance and clear indication of U.S. FDI's sectoral strength.

5. GP produced by manufacturing Mofas in developed nations clings to a very steady 80 to 84 percent share of total affiliate manufacturing GP throughout the period.
6. Overall manufacturing GP moves between 44 and 54 percent of total Mofa GP with wide variations from country to country.
7. Despite the large global resource deployment, America's share of the total industrial GDP of individual nations is usually rather modest. Of the thirty-one investment countries surveyed, only four exceed a GDP share of 10 percent. They are: Canada, Ireland, Panama, and the Bahamas. In very general terms, the U.S. share of industrial GDP produced by all nations analyzed is estimated to fall

into a 4 to 6 percent range for the period 1982 through 1989, and below 5 percent of total national GDPs, including the public sector.

8. Penetration levels in manufacturing rise significantly above these averages. In ten countries, U.S. FDI reaches more than 10 percent of the national industry's value-added. The deepest inroads were made in three countries with shares exceeding 20 percent: Canada, Ireland, and Panama.

9. In only six countries, 19 percent of those surveyed, the U.S. share of total industrial GDP was clearly on the rise in 1989: Hong Kong, Ireland, the Netherlands, Panama, Singapore, and Spain while stagnating or declining in the rest despite gains over the whole period.

10. FDI shares in national value added are invariably produced with disproportionately low employment ratios vis-à-vis local industries, attesting to advanced technology and management techniques introduced by American investors. In some cases, they signal the existence of very effective profit strategies, as mentioned in connection with such tax havens as Switzerland, the Bahamas, Bermuda, UK islands in the Caribbean, Hong Kong, and various others.

11. On the foreign trade front, the U.S. position is relatively strong. Not many countries among those researched see Mofa exports of merchandise at less than 10 percent. In some cases, its share exceeds 20 and even 30 percent, such as in Canada, Ireland, Belgium/Luxemburg, the Netherlands, the UK, and Singapore. In a number of countries, reported Mofa exports come close to or even exceed official merchandise exports–Switzerland, Panama, and the Bahamas. They are profit centers with many international service transactions which cannot be separated from real merchandise shipments. The case of the oil affiliates is a typical example. Their unrealistic portrayal arises from official accounting practices which treat export sales and shipments as one, a practice hard to reconcile with the ultimate impression created.

12. Mofas contribute positively to the country's trade balance in eight countries (26 percent), negatively in ten (32 percent), in a balanced fashion in five (16 percent), and to an unknown degree in the remaining eight (26 percent). It can be safely assumed that five out of these eight fall under the countries with positive Mofa trade balances: Indonesia and Norway because of their oil exports, the Bahamas and Bermuda as special profit centers and service providers, and Singapore as a major sourcing point for light industrial products as well as being an active tax haven. If correct, the number

of nations with positive Mofa trade balances rises to thirteen (42 percent).

13. Total U.S. FDI's effect on the services balance in the nation's current account is traced under point H. Covering the aggregate flow of distributed earnings, interests, royalties and license fees, and other service fees in their net form after applicable taxes between parents and all subsidiaries, there is a more or less pronounced negative impact on every country's BOP. Percentages shown refer to the negative effect on otherwise positive country balances (– sign), or an additive effect on already negative country balances (+ sign).

14. The thirty-one countries analyzed account for more than 89 percent of total Mofa GP and 89.7 percent of total Mofa employment in 1989. Each country's contribution to total Mofa GP is traced under point I. in Table 12.1 on the basis of information contained in Table 7.7.

15. The existence and growth of U.S. FDI has left its mark on the American economy. Parent shares in the output of U.S. nonagricultural and manufacturing GDP, and related employment shares, are in a persistent decline, indicating competitive weakness. More positive is FDI's impact on the U.S. BOP. Total FDI-related exports were always larger than imports. This is especially true for trade dealing with Mofas with the exception of 1977. Mofa shares in U.S. exports go up vigorously while import shares are declining.

Keeping track of these developments is not merely a matter of academic curiosity. They have aroused nationalistic concerns and political reactions in the past. Servan-Schreiber's warning to the Europeans about an impending American takeover has become widely publicized. His concern was perhaps justified by historic precedents where power politics first led to economic encroachment, then political dependence. The scope and speed of American acquisitions and establishments all over a Europe still struggling to get on its feet after the war did not make this an unrealistic concern at all. Similar caution could, and still can be observed in Latin America. Mexico negotiated very cautiously before committing itself fully to membership in NAFTA. One sensitive issue was the American desire to get a share of Mexico's oil. It did not materialize. Canada, the other signatory party, considered the treaty very carefully before signing. In a landslide election, the protagonist conservative party was all but obliterated on October 25, 1993, by the liberals whose platform called for a renegotiation of the 1987 United States-Canada Free Trade Agreement as well as NAFTA. Even in the United States, opponents questioned the treaty's advantages, its long-term effect on the country's economy, and the demographic changes to be expected from potentially large scale migration of Mexican labor northward. Born as a countermove to the EU, the treaty raises some of the familiar issues seen in connection with the European integration. Despite the debate, the treaty was ratified by congressional vote on November 17, 1993.

The information contained in Table 12.1 documents the extent of America's involvement in major economies. Mofa data represent the slice of these economies that is majority or fully controlled by U.S. capital, and the rate of change in their data over time is a true measure of America's industrial competitiveness in each. The acronym CPI or "Competitive Power Index" was chosen to condense the statement into a single number without any political overtones in a world still sensitive to the issue.

The CPI defines America's role in the industrial sector alone, as U.S. FDI cannot participate in economic activities reserved for the public sector. Theoretically, a CPI could also be developed for the U.S. share in the country's total GNP or GDP but, lacking the element of competitive achievement, it is not very meaningful.

The CPI resembles the market share concept frequently employed in economic reporting. Its intended use differs slightly, however, in that it measures macroeconomic relationships compared to the microeconomic market shares concept. The latter is considered to be more volitile, often subjectively defined, and thus not quite as objective in its application. It provides a steady long-term, overall view versus short-term, partial, and only fleeting impressions.

TABLE 12.1. U.S. FDI Role in Host Country Economy

Country: Canada Currency: $ Canadian billion					
Year	1957	1966	1977	1982	1989
A. Industrial GDP	23.3	46.0	151.7	261.4	476.8
MOFA Gross Product	4.5	8.9	29.5	41.9	60.3
CPI %	19.3	19.4	19.5	16.0	12.6
B. Manufacturing GDP	7.8	14.0	38.5	57.4	112.0
MOFA Gross Product	3.0	5.7	16.1	20.2	33.4
CPI %	38.6	40.9	41.9	35.2	29.8
% of total MOFA GP	66.7	64.0	54.6	48.2	55.4
C. Industry Employ. (000)	5,731*	5,921	8,226	8,889	12,485
MOFA Employment	670	800	916	781	903.5
%	11.7	13.5	11.1	8.5	7.2
D. Manufac. Employ. (000)	1,341	1,646	1,709	1,714	2,126
MOFA Employment	440	545	562	455	454.5
%	32.8	33.1	32.9	26.5	21.4
E. Merchandise Exports	5.1	10.6	46.3	87.9	138.7
MOFA Export Sales	1.9	4.3	19.4	31.1	52.2
%	37.9	40.1	41.9	35.3	37.6
F. Merchandise Imports	5.9	10.9	44.9	72.0	135.2
MOFA Imports Total	1.2	N/A	19.4	N/A	N/A
%	20.2	N/A	43.1	N/A	N/A
G. MOFA Imports from U.S.	0.9	3.5	17.2	23.9	43.9
%	14.5	32.4	38.4	33.2	32.5
H. BOP Balance on Serv.***	N/A	−1,277	−7,238	−13,418	−25,597
U.S. FDI Serv. Balance***	N/A	−911	−2,414	−3,348	−4,322
%	N/A	71	33	25	17
I. Share of Global MOFA GP					
Total	29.2	22.3	17.3	15.2	16.3
Manufacturing	22.0	29.4	21.2	16.4	16.7
J. U.S. FDI Position***	8.8	15.7	35.1	43.5	64.1
U.S. Share of Inward FDI	N/A	N/A	80	78	62
K. Exchange Rate: $Can/$	.9589	1.0811	1.0635	1.2337	1.1578

Note: ***U.S. $ billion.

Source: *Canada Yearbook*, 1967, p. 744.

Country: Belgium/Luxemburg Currency: Bfrs. billion					
Year	1957	1966	1977	1982	1989
A. Industrial GDP	411	799	2,424	3,243	5,227
MOFA Gross Product	7.6	33	159	245	360
CPI %	1.8	4.1	6.6	7.6	6.7
B. Manufacturing GDP	147	294	793	959	1,441
MOFA Gross Product	4.8	20	100	118	216
CPI %	3.3	6.7	12.6	12.3	14.9
% of total MOFA GP	63.2	60.6	62.9	48.3	59.9
C. Industry Employ. (000)	N/A	2,926	3,148	3,137	3,954**
MOFA Employment	35	87	131	127	122
%	N/A	3.0	4.2	4.1	3.1
D. Manuf. Employ. (000)	N/A	1,192	1,057	871	803**
MOFA Employment	N/A	72	99	94	88
%	N/A	6.0	9.4	10.8	11.0
E. Merchandise Exports	178	370	1,454	2,252	3,943
MOFA Export Sales	4	43	301	570	664
%	2.4	11.6	20.7	25.3	16.8
F. Merchandise Imports	189	381	1,530	2,365	3,884
MOFA Imports Total	N/A	N/A	218	N/A	N/A
%	N/A	N/A	14.2	N/A	N/A
G. MOFA Imports from U.S.	N/A	12.9	57.3	106.1	94.7
%	N/A	3.4	3.7	4.5	2.4
H. BOP Balance on Serv.*	N/A	256	2,425	854	2,230
U.S. FDI Serv. Balance*	N/A	−35	−229	−317	−1,023
%	N/A	−14	−9	−37	−46
I. Share of Global MOFA GP					
Total	0.9	1.8	2.8	2.4	2.9
Manufacturing	1.4	2.2	3.9	2.6	3.2
J. U.S. FDI Position*	192	800	4,616	6,646	9,207
U.S. Share of Inward FDI	N/A	N/A	N/A	33e	42
K. Exchange Rate: Bfrs/$	50.0	50.0	35.84	45.69	39.40

Notes: *$ million. **1990.

TABLE 12.1 (continued)

Country: Denmark Currency: Kroner billion					
Year	1957	1966	1977	1982	1989
A. Industrial GDP	24.7	57.3	196.5	311.5	528.7
MOFA Gross Product	0.4	1.0	4.0	11.1	9.1
CPI %	1.6	1.7	2.1	3.6	1.7
B. Manufacturing GDP	8.9	15.9	47.6	75.1	125.3
MOFA Gross Product	0.1	0.2	0.7	1.9	2.7
CPI %	1.1	1.3	1.6	2.6	2.2
% of total MOFA GP	25.0	20.0	17.5	17.3	29.7
C. Industry Employ. (000)	N/A	1,887	1,771	1,648	2,670**
MOFA Employment	N/A	12	16	17	16.9
%	N/A	0.6	0.9	1.1	0.6
D. Manuf. Employ. (000)	N/A	609	503	470	532**
MOFA Employment	N/A	N/A	4	8	6.6
%	N/A	N/A	5.7	6.5	1.2
E. Merchandise Exports	8.1	16.9	60.4	128.1	205.5
MOFA Export Sales	N/A	N/A	3.5	8.3	N/A
%	N/A	N/A	5.7	6.5	N/A
F. Merchandise Imports	9.4	20.7	79.6	138.9	195.3
MOFA Imports Total	N/A	N/A	10.4	N/A	N/A
%	N/A	N/A	13.1	N/A	N/A
G. MOFA Imports from U.S.	N/A	.166	.480	1.258	1.0
%	N/A	0.8	0.6	0.9	0.5
H. BOP Balance on Serv.*	N/A	193	993	−1,465	−3,539
U.S. FDI Serv. Balance*	N/A	−11	−33	−91	−239
%	N/A	−6	−3	6	7
I. Share of Global MOFA GP					
Total	0.3	0.4	0.4	0.6	0.4
Manufacturing	0.2	0.2	0.2	0.2	0.2
J. U.S. FDI Position*	42	247	768	1,155	1,240
U.S. Share of Inward FDI	N/A	N/A	N/A	N/A	N/A
K. Exchange Rate: Kron/$	6.9071	6.9071	6.0032	8.3324	7.3100

Notes: *$ million. **1990.

Country: France Currency: French Francs billion					
Year	1957	1966	1977	1982	1989
A. Industrial GDP	187	429	1,552	2,831	4,940
MOFA Gross Product	2.5	11.7	47.6	80.2	144.3
CPI %	1.7	2.7	3.1	2.8	2.9
B. Manufacturing GDP	79	152	517	822	1,308
MOFA Gross Product	1.2	6.8	30.5	48.8	75.2
CPI %	1.5	4.5	5.9	5.9	5.7
% of total MOFA GP	48.0	58.1	64.1	60.9	52.1
C. Industry Employ. (000)	N/A	14,720	17,741	17,686	21,739
MOFA Employment	110	212	360	293	333.5
%	N/A	1.2	2.0	1.7	1.5
D. Manuf. Employ. (000)	N/A	N/A	5,524	5,078	6,452
MOFA Employment	N/A	167	291	209	190.0
%	N/A	N/A	5.3	4.1	2.9
E. Merchandise Exports	18.9	52.4	319.2	633.1	1,103
MOFA Export Sales	3.2	4.1	33.3	74.0	111.5
%	1.7	7.5	10.4	11.7	10.1
F. Merchandise Imports	22.7	51.3	346.4	758.3	1,217
MOFA Imports Total	N/A	N/A	34.3	N/A	N/A
%	N/A	N/A	9.9	N/A	N/A
G. MOFA Imports from U.S.	N/A	1.4	6.3	14.5	22.6
%	N/A	2.7	2.1	2.9	1.9
H. BOP Balance on Serv.*	N/A	N/A	2,881	3,703	5,031
U.S. FDI Serv. Balance*	N/A	−110	−681	−707	−2,652
%	N/A	N/A	−24	−19	−53
I. Share of Global MOFA GP					
Total	4.3	6.5	6.0	5.4	7.1
Manufacturing	4.9	7.7	8.6	7.4	6.8
J. U.S. FDI Position*	464	1,790	6,490	7,391	16,430
U.S. Share of Inward FDI	N/A	N/A	46	47	56
K. Exchange Rate: Ffrs./$	3.6164	4.9371	4.9136	6.5721	6.3800

Note: *$ million.

TABLE 12.1 (continued)

Year	1957	1966	1977	1982	1989
Country: Germany **Currency: DM billion**					
A. Industrial GDP	196	431	1,000	1,320	1,856
MOFA Gross Product	2.7	12.0	42.1	60.2	67.1
CPI %	1.4	2.8	4.2	4.6	3.6
B. Manufacturing GDP	87	194	414	496	690
MOFA Gross Product	1.8	7.6	28.0	37.2	48.5
CPI %	2.1	3.9	6.8	7.5	7.0
% of total MOFA GP	66.7	63.3	66.7	61.6	72.2
C. Industry Employ. (000)	20,832	23,339	21,102	20,823	27,742
MOFA Employment	185	356	508	502	493.7
%	0.9	1.5	2.4	2.4	1.8
D. Manuf. Employ. (000)	N/A	9,953	8,918	8,468	8,753
MOFA Employment	N/A	285	425	404	383.7
%	N/A	2.9	4.8	4.8	4.4
E. Merchandise Exports	35.9	80.6	273.0	427.8	682.1
MOFA Export Sales	1.1	5.7	27.4	46.4	63.2
%	3.0	7.0	10.0	10.8	9.3
F. Merchandise Imports	31.9	72.2	235.2	376.6	547.6
MOFA Imports Total	N/A	N/A	26.5	N/A	N/A
%	N/A	N/A	11.3	N/A	N/A
G. MOFA Imports from U.S.	N/A	1.2	4.1	6.6	9.8
%	N/A	1.6	1.8	1.8	1.8
H. BOP Balance on Serv.***	N/A	−2.97	−15.39	−19.71	−20.03
U.S. FDI Serv. Balance***	N/A	−.247	−2.15	−1.6	−3.63
%	N/A	8	14	8	18
I. Share of Global MOFA GP					
Total	3.9	8.2	11.2	11.1	11.2
Manufacturing	6.0	10.9	16.8	15.3	14.9
J. U.S. FDI Position***	.581	2.808	11.189	15.463	24.246
U.S. Share of Inward FDI	N/A	N/A	42	48	28
K. Exchange Rate: DM/$	4.2000	4.0000	2.3222	2.4266	1.8800

Note: ***$ billion.

Country: Ireland Currency: Pound billion					
Year	1957	1966	1977	1982	1989
A. Industrial GDP	0.360	0.638	4.516	10.188	16.877
MOFA Gross Product	N/A	0.034	0.400	1.356	3.152
CPI %	N/A	5.3	8.9	13.3	18.7
B. Manufacturing GDP	0.131	0.290	1.198	3.580	7,290
MOFA Gross Product	N/A	0.014	0.254	0.957	2.468
CPI %	N/A	8.8	21.2	26.7	33.9
% of total MOFA GP	N/A	41.2	63.5	70.6	78.3
C. Industry Employ. (000)	N/A	1,058	1,068	1,131	1,090
MOFA Employment	N/A	4.8	23.9	35.1	40.8
%	N/A	0.8	2.2	3.1	3.7
D. Manuf. Employ. (000)	N/A	198	226	232	216
MOFA Employment	N/A	6.0	19.5	31.7	37.4
%	N/A	3.0	8.6	13.7	17.3
E. Merchandise Exports	0.131	0.244	2.518	5.691	14.597
MOFA Export Sales	N/A	.019	.492	2.035	5.180
%	N/A	7.8	19.1	35.8	35.5
F. Merchandise Imports	0.184	0.373	3.091	6.816	12.284
MOFA Imports Total	N/A	N/A	.379	N/A	N/A
%	N/A	N/A	12.3	N/A	N/A
G. MOFA Imports from U.S.	N/A	0.003	0.082	0.357	0.919
%	N/A	1.0	2.7	5.2	7.5
H. BOP Balance on Serv.*	N/A	220	298	−773	−4,515
U.S. FDI Serv. Balance*	N/A	−4	−50	−326	−1,420
%	N/A	−2	−17	42	31
I. Share of Global MOFA GP					
Total	N/A	0.3	0.5	0.8	1.4
Manufacturing	N/A	0.6	0.7	1.3	2.0
J. U.S. FDI Position*	5	71	986	2,031	4,449
U.S. Share of Inward FDI	N/A	N/A	N/A	N/A	N/A
K. Exchange Rate: Pound/$	2.800	2.800	1.9060	1.3965	1.4190

Note: *$ million.

TABLE 12.1 (continued)

Year	1957	1966	1977	1982	1989
Country: Italy **Currency: Lit. billion**					
A. Industrial GDP	12,791	38,265	168,967	468,900	1,017,100
MOFA Gross Product	216	819	5,140	11,537	22,620
CPI %	1.7	2.1	3.0	2.5	2.2
B. Manufacturing GDP	4,022	11,526	58,922	141,000	278,700
MOFA Gross Product	61	358	2,420	5,450	10,492
CPI %	1.5	3.1	4.1	3.9	3.8
% of total MOFA GP	28.2	43.7	47.1	47.2	47.0
C. Industry Employ. (000)	N/A	15,259	16,873	17,168	21,154
MOFA Employment	45	119	179.2	173.4	159.7
%	N/A	0.7	1.1	1.0	0.8
D. Manuf. Employ. (000)	N/A	5,500e	5,648	5,459	4,730
MOFA Employment	N/A	93	145.4	131.1	116.9
%	N/A	1.7e	2.6	2.4	2.5
E. Merchandise Exports	1,594	5,024	39,968	99,247	190,055
MOFA Export Sales	79	338	2,162	5,401	8,662
%	5.0	6.7	5.4	5.4	4.6
F. Merchandise Imports	2,296	5,368	42,429	116,212	209,867
MOFA Imports Total	N/A	N/A	4,987	N/A	N/A
%	N/A	N/A	11.8	N/A	N/A
G. MOFA Imports from U.S.	N/A	83	647	1,208	2,446
%	N/A	1.5	1.5	1.0	1.2
H. BOP Balance on Serv.*	N/A	1,794	2,615	3,063	−8,712
U.S. FDI Serv. Balance*	N/A	−69	−386	−630	−1,927
%	N/A	−4	−15	−21	22
I. Share of Global MOFA GP					
Total	2.1	3.6	3.6	3.8	5.2
Manufacturing	1.4	3.2	3.8	4.0	4.5
J. U.S. FDI Position*	252	988	3,186	4,316	11,057
U.S. Share of Inward FDI	N/A	N/A	N/A	20e	22
K. Exchange Rate: Lit./$	625.0	625.0	882.4	1,353	1,372

Note: *$ million.

Country: Netherlands Currency: HFL billion					
Year	1957	1966	1977	1982	1989
A. Industrial GDP	28.3	56.5	221.2	302.5	396.1
MOFA Gross Product	0.6	2.0	10.3	14.4	28.0
CPI %	2.1	3.5	4.7	4.8	7.1
B. Manufacturing GDP	9.7	20.7	66.7	64.7	95.8
MOFA Gross Product	0.18	0.98	5.5	6.8	16.5
CPI %	1.9	4.7	8.2	10.5	17.2
% of total MOFA GP	30.0	49.0	53.4	47.3	58.7
C. Industry Employ. (000)	N/A	N/A	3,956	3,839	6,155
MOFA Employment	30	58	101.7	104.0	115.5
%	N/A	N/A	2.6	2.7	1.9
D. Manuf. Employ. (000)	N/A	N/A	1,039	922	1,152
MOFA Employment	N/A	40	71.7	69.3	70.5
%	N/A	N/A	6.9	7.5	6.1
E. Merchandise Exports	11.8	24.4	107.2	176.8	229.4
MOFA Export Sales	.4	3.2	21.9	40.6	49.2
%	3.6	13.1	20.4	23.0	21.4
F. Merchandise Imports	15.6	29.0	112.6	170.3	221.4
MOFA Imports Total	N/A	N/A	15.3	N/A	N/A
%	N/A	N/A	13.6	N/A	N/A
G. MOFA Imports from U.S.	N/A	.8	3.3	7.2	7.9
%	N/A	2.8	2.9	4.2	3.5
H. BOP Balance on Serv.*	N/A	466	1,438	−174	1,658
U.S. FDI Serv. Balance*	N/A	−56	−841	−1,560	−2,845
%	N/A	−12	−58	−1,115	−172
I. Share of Global MOFA GP					
Total	1.0	1.5	2.6	2.4	4.1
Manufacturing	0.7	1.5	3.1	2.6	4.5
J. U.S. FDI Position*	191	870	4,534	6,760	18,529
U.S. Share of Inward FDI	N/A	N/A	N/A	38	34
K. Exchange Rate: HFL/$	3.800	3.6200	2.4543	2.6702	2.1200

Note: *$ million.

TABLE 12.1 (continued)

Year	1957	1966	1977	1982	1989
Country: Norway					
Currency: Kroner billion					
A. Industrial GDP	24.1	47.3	155.6	286.7	485.9
MOFA Gross Product	0.35	0.96	8.8	28.7	28.7
CPI %	1.4	2.0	5.7	10.0	5.9
B. Manufacturing GDP	6.9	11.6	36.2	51.9	91.3
MOFA Gross Product	0.14	0.41	0.95	1.7	0.8
CPI %	2.1	3.5	2.6	3.3	0.9
% of total MOFA GP	40.0	42.7	10.8	5.9	2.9
C. Industry Employ. (000)	N/A	1,290e	1,324	1,326	2,049
MOFA Employment	N/A	11.0	17.9	16.6	18.5
%	N/A	0.8e	1.4	1.3	0.9
D. Manuf. Employ. (000)	N/A	384	389	357	317
MOFA Employment	N/A	7.0	6.5	5.2	2.3
%	N/A	1.8	1.7	1.5	0.7
E. Merchandise Exports	5.9	11.2	47.3	113.2	187.1
MOFA Export Sales	.3	N/A	N/A	N/A	23.3
%	4.6	N/A	N/A	N/A	12.5
F. Merchandise Imports	9.1	17.2	68.6	99.7	163.4
MOFA Imports Total	N/A	N/A	6.1	N/A	N/A
%	N/A	N/A	8.8	N/A	N/A
G. MOFA Imports from U.S.	N/A	.05	.4	.5	1.0
%	N/A	.3	.6	.5	0.6
H. BOP Balance on Serv.*	N/A	539	−981	−1,724	−3,556
U.S. FDI Serv. Balance*	N/A	−2	−264	−917	−788
%	N/A	−1	27	53	22
I. Share of Global MOFA GP					
Total	0.3	0.4	1.1	2.0	1.3
Manufacturing	0.3	0.3	0.2	0.3	0.7
J. U.S. FDI Position*	51	194	1,240	2,728	3,447
U.S. Share of Inward FDI	N/A	N/A	N/A	N/A	100
K. Exchange Rate: Kron./$	7.1429	7.1429	5.3235	6.4540	6.9000

Notes: *$ million. e = estimate.

Country: Spain Currency: Pesetas billion					
Year	1957	1966	1977	1982	1989
A. Industrial GDP	437	1,391	7,841	17,971	39,689
MOFA Gross Product	1.4	14.5	153.4	282.0	875.9
CPI %	0.3	1.0	2.0	1.6	2.2
B. Manufacturing GDP	126	402	2,254	5,326	12,039
MOFA Gross Product	1.2	11.7	112.3	203.8	677.6
CPI %	1.0	2.9	5.0	3.8	5.6
% of total MOFA GP	85.7	80.7	73.2	72.0	77.4
C. Industry Employ. (000)	3,461	12.025	12.551	10.989	12,258
MOFA Employment	N/A	50	130.9	113.5	120.0
%	N/A	0.4	1.0	1.1	1.0
D. Manuf. Employ. (000)	1,732	3.136	3.290	2.680	2,737
MOFA Employment	N/A	40	106.3	92.3	93.5
%	N/A	1.3	3.1	3.4	3.4
E. Merchandise Exports	N/A	75.2	775.3	2,258	5,258
MOFA Export Sales	.33	.72	65.4	79.6	684.1
%	N/A	1.0	8.4	8.0	13.0
F. Merchandise Imports	N/A	215.5	1350.6	3,465.6	8,458
MOFA Imports Total	N/A	N/A	89.0	N/A	N/A
%	N/A	N/A	6.6	N/A	N/A
G. MOFA Imports from U.S.	N/A	.342	26.5	43.3	202.3
%	N/A	0.2	2.0	1.3	2.4
H. BOP Balance on Serv.*	N/A	1,428	2,054	5,009	13,562
U.S. FDI Serv. Balance*	N/A	−17	−84	−278	−468
%	N/A	−1	−2	−6	−3
I. Share of Global MOFA GP					
Total	0.2	0.7	1.3	1.1	2.3
Manufacturing	0.4	1.1	2.1	1.9	3.3
J. U.S. FDI Position*	44	373	2,324	2,350	6,454
U.S. Share of Inward FDI	N/A	7	N/A	N/A	22
K. Exchange Rate: Pes./$	41.30	60.00	75.96	109.86	118.38

Note: *$ million.

TABLE 12.1 (continued)

Country: Sweden Currency: Kroner billion					
Year	1957	1966	1977	1982	1989
A. Industrial GDP	49.4	94.1	253.7	434.5	874.9
MOFA Gross Product	0.46	1.1	4.9	11.9	14.4
CPI %	0.9	1.2	1.9	2.7	1.6
B. Manufacturing GDP	16.1	31.3	83.1	129.6	258.8
MOFA Gross Product	0.18	0.615	2.321	3.9	6.5
CPI %	1.1	2.0	2.8	3.0	2.5
% of total MOFA GP	39.1	55.9	47.3	33.1	45.2
C. Industry Employ. (000)	N/A	3,097	2,908	2,813	4,466
MOFA Employment	N/A	25	32.9	30.8	26.0
%	N/A	0.8	1.1	1.1	0.6
D. Manuf. Employ. (000)	N/A	1.054	992	901	977
MOFA Employment	N/A	14	18.9	15.8	13.1
%	N/A	1.3	1.9	1.8	1.3
E. Merchandise Exports	11.1	22.1	85.7	168.1	332.1
MOFA Export Sales	0.05	0.6	3.6	7.0	9.5
%	.4	2.6	4.2	4.1	2.9
F. Merchandise Imports	12.6	23.7	90.2	173.9	315.1
MOFA Imports Total	N/A	N/A	8.3	N/A	N/A
%	N/A	N/A	9.2	N/A	N/A
G. MOFA Imports from U.S.	N/A	0.290	0.846	1.589	3.167
%	N/A	1.2	0.9	0.9	1.0
H. BOP Balance on Serv.*	N/A	−196	−2,456	−3,144	−7,283
U.S. FDI Serv. Balance*	N/A	−26	−113	−147	−247
%	N/A	13	5	5	
I. Share of Global MOFA GP					
Total	0.6	0.6	0.7	0.8	0.7
Manufacturing	0.5	0.7	0.8	0.6	0.6
J. U.S. FDI Position*	109	346	1,160	1,103	1,336
U.S. Share of Inward FDI	N/A	N/A	N/A	N/A	12
K. Exchange Rate: Kron./$	5.1732	5.1732	4.4816	6.2826	6.4500

Note: *$ million.

Country: Switzerland Currency: Sfr. billion					
Year	1957	1966	1977	1982	1989
A. Industrial GDP	28.7	65.4	145.8	196.0	259.9e
MOFA Gross Product	0.25	1.6	4.8	6.5	8.4
CPI %	1.7	2.5	3.3	3.3	3.2e
B. Manufacturing GDP	N/A	N/A	N/A	56.3	74.6
MOFA Gross Product	N/A	0.739	1.079	1.5e	2.0e
CPI %	N/A	N/A	N/A	2.7e	2.7e
% of total MOFA GP	N/A	46.2	22.5	22.5e	23.8e
C. Industry Employ. (000)	N/A	2.997	2.923	3.033	3,561[†]
MOFA Employment	N/A	37	38.8	39.8	40.1
%	N/A	1.2	1.3	1.3	1.1
D. Manuf. Employ. (000)	N/A	1,143	955	944	894[†]
MOFA Employment	N/A	20	15.8	14.7	11.5
%	N/A	1.7	1.7	1.6	1.3
E. Merchandise Exports	6.7	14.2	42.0	52.7	84.3
MOFA Export Sales	.34	8.2	31.6	56.3	16.1
%	5.1	58.1	75.2	106.7	19.0
F. Merchandise Imports	8.4	17.0	42.9	58.1	95.2
MOFA Imports Total	N/A	N/A	6.5	N/A	N/A
%	N/A	N/A	15.1	N/A	N/A
G. MOFA Imports from U.S.	N/A	.437	1.8	1.4	2.0
%	N/A	2.6	4.2	2.4	2.1
H. BOP Balance on Serv.*	N/A	588	3,642	5,753	12,365
U.S. FDI Serv. Balance*	N/A	−72	−506	−572	−2,870
%	N/A	−12	−14	−10	−23
I. Share of Global MOFA GP					
Total	0.4	1.0	1.2	1.4	1.6
Manufacturing	0.5	0.9	0.6	0.7	0.7
J. U.S. FDI Position*	69	1,880	7,182	12,863	21,228
U.S. Share of Inward FDI	N/A	N/A	N/A	N/A	84
K. Exchange Rate: Sfr./$	4.3730	4,3730	2.4035	2.0303	1.6400

Notes: GDP by industry available for 1985 only. Manufacturing GDP for 1982 and 1989 estimated on that year's ratio. [†]1991. MOFA export share out of line due to export sales, not actual shipments. *$ million. e = estimate.

TABLE 12.1 (continued)

Year	1957	1966	1977	1982	1989
Country: United Kingdom **Currency: British Pound billion**					
A. Industrial GDP	17.3	28.8	113.6	208.2	389.9
MOFA Gross Product	0.68	1.7	9.7	22.0	32.1
CPI %	3.9	6.0	8.5	10.5	8.2
B. Manufacturing GDP	6.9	11.2	38.7	58.8	101.0
MOFA Gross Product	0.5	1.1	6.1	9.9	16.7
CPI %	6.8	10.2	15.8	16.8	16.5
% of total MOFA GP	73.5	64.7	62.9	44.9	52.0
C. Industry Employ. (000)	N/A	21,278	19,602	18,629	26,684
MOFA Employment	570	653	925.6	729.3	749.3
%	N/A	3.1	4.7	3.9	2.8
D. Manuf. Employ. (000)	N/A	8,612	7,417	6,004	5,445
MOFA Employment	N/A	567	707.5	516.0	462.2
%	N/A	6.6	9.5	8.3	8.5
E. Merchandise Exports	3.5	5.3	32.0	55.6	93.2
MOFA Export Sales	0.3	1.0	10.0	19.1	22.0
%	9.3	18.1	31.1	34.4	23.6
F. Merchandise Imports	4.1	6.0	36.2	57.0	120.8
MOFA Imports Total	N/A	N/A	6.5	N/A	N/A
%	N/A	N/A	18.0	N/A	N/A
G. MOFA Imports from U.S.	N/A	0.231	1.3	2.3	4.8
%	N/A	3.9	3.6	4.1	3.9
H. BOP Balance on Serv.*	N/A	386	4,149	4,731	4,957
U.S. FDI Serv. Balance*	N/A	−442	−1,405	−3,543	−12,299
%	N/A	−115	−34	−75	−248
I. Share of Global MOFA GP					
Total	11.8	13.0	10.5	17.2	16.5
Manufacturing	18.6	17.8	14.9	17.3	15.8
J. U.S. FDI Position*	1,974	5,421	16,709	27,537	65,524
U.S. Share of Inward FDI	N/A	N/A	N/A	54	40
K. Exchange Rate: Pound/$	2.800	2.800	1.7455	1.7505	1.6400

Note: *$ million.

Country: Argentina Currency: Pesos/Australes billion					
Year	1957	1966	1977	1982[††]	1989
A. Industrial GDP	1.4[++]	34	19,116	135,929	7,346
MOFA Gross Product	0.001	1.5	590.6	14.6	66.7
CPI %	1.6	4.4	3.1	1.1	0.9
B. Manufacturing GDP	0.5[++]	13.5	6,915	41,918	4,924
MOFA Gross Product	0.001	1.2	385.2	9.3	41.2
CPI %	3.4	8.6	5.6	2.2	0.8
% of total MOFA GP	100.0	80.0	65.1	64.1	61.7
C. Industry Employ. (000)	N/A	N/A	N/A	3,741	N/A
MOFA Employment	100	101	95.4	76.3	48.3
%	N/A	N/A	N/A	2.0	N/A
D. Manuf. Employ. (000)	N/A	N/A	N/A	846	N/A
MOFA Employment	N/A	82	81.2	56.8	35.8
%	N/A	N/A	N/A	6.7	N/A
E. Merchandise Exports*	975	1,593	5,652	7,798	9,579
MOFA Export Sales	42	N/A	556	871	1,056
%	4.3	N/A	9.8	11.2	11.0
F. Merchandise Imports	1,310	1,124	4,162	5,337	4,203
MOFA Imports Total*	33[++]	N/A	333	N/A	N/A
%	2.5	N/A	8.0	N/A	N/A
G. MOFA Imports from U.S.*	21[++]	75	186	317	11.6
%	N/A	6.7	4.5	5.9	2.8
H. BOP Balance on Serv.*	N/A	−339	−726	−5,117	−7,014
U.S. FDI Serv. Balance	N/A	−86	−184	−250	−283
%	N/A	25	25	5	4
I. Share of Global MOFA GP					
Total	1.1	1.9	0.9	1.3	0.5
Manufacturing	1.8	3.1	1.3	1.9	0.6
J. U.S. FDI Position*	333	758	1,262	2,840	2,191
U.S. Share of Inward FDI	N/A	N/A	N/A	N/A	N/A
K. Exchange Rate: Pesos/$	0.075	2.074	407.6	0.005[†††]	0.0423

Notes: [++]1955. [††]000 Australes. *$ million. [†††]Australes per U.S. Dollar.

TABLE 12.1 (continued)

Year	1957	1966	1977	1982	1989
Country: Bahamas **Currency: Bahamas dollar million**					
A. Industrial GDP	N/A	N/A	714	N/A	450
MOFA Gross Product	N/A	39	157	209	425
CPI %	N/A	N/A	22.0	N/A	94.4
B. Manufacturing GDP	N/A	N/A	90.9	N/A	N/A
MOFA Gross Product	N/A	N/A	6.0	14	8
CPI %	N/A	N/A	6.6	N/A	N/A
% of total MOFA GP	N/A	N/A	3.8	5.8	1.9
C. Industry Employ. (000)	N/A	N/A	71	N/A	N/A
MOFA Employment	N/A	6.0	6.4	7.7	8.4
%	N/A	N/A	9.0	N/A	N/A
D. Manuf. Employ. (000)	N/A	N/A	4.0	N/A	N/A
MOFA Employment	N/A	1.0	N/A	0.5	0.2
%	N/A	N/A	25.0e	N/A	N/A
E. Merchandise Exports	5	24	2,409	2,451	2,786
MOFA Export Sales	N/A	N/A	2,018	5,213	706
%	N/A	N/A	83.8	212.7	25.3
F. Merchandise Imports	47	142	2,871	3,051	3,001
MOFA Imports Total	N/A	N/A	1,731	N/A	N/A
%	N/A	N/A	60.3	N/A	N/A
G. MOFA Imports from U.S.	N/A	21	78	152	439
%	N/A	14.8	2.7	5.0	14.6
H. BOP Balance on Serv.*	N/A	N/A	−321	479	787
U.S. FDI Serv. Balance*	N/A	−6	−664	−1,369	−528
%	N/A	N/A	206	−286	−67
I. Share of Global MOFA GP					
Total	N/A	0.1	0.1	0.1	nil
Manufacturing	nil	nil	nil	nil	nil
J. U.S. FDI Position*	0	290	997	3,119	4,376
U.S. Share of Inward FDI	N/A	N/A	N/A	N/A	N/A
K. Exchange Rate: $Bah./$	1.0204	1.0204	1.000	1.000	1.000

Notes: *$ million. e = estimate.

Country: Bermuda Currency: U.S. million					
Year	**1957**	**1966**	**1977**	**1982**	**1989**
A. Industrial GDP	N/A	N/A	N/A	N/A	N/A
MOFA Gross Product	N/A	35	398	82	−113
CPI %	N/A	N/A	N/A	N/A	N/A
B. Manufacturing GDP	N/A	N/A	N/A	N/A	N/A
MOFA Gross Product	N/A	1	0	0	1
CPI %	N/A	N/A	N/A	0	N/A
% of total MOFA GP	N/A	2.9	0	0	NMF
C. Industry Employ. (000)	N/A	N/A	28.3‡	31.5	36.3
MOFA Employment	N/A	1	1.8	2.8	2.2
%	N/A	N/A	6.4	8.9	6.1
D. Manuf. Employ. (000)	N/A	N/A	1.1	1.1	1.1
MOFA Employment	N/A	N/A	0	0	nil
%	N/A	N/A	0	0	0
E. Merchandise Exports	N/A	54	39	17	50
MOFA Export Sales	N/A	N/A	10,682	N/A	1,422
%	N/A	N/A	NMF	N/A	NMF
F. Merchandise Imports	N/A	66	186	351	535
MOFA Imports Total	N/A	N/A	N/A	N/A	N/A
%	N/A	N/A	NMF	N/A	N/A
G. MOFA Imports from U.S.	N/A	N/A	16	9	125
%	N/A	N/A	8.6	2.6	23.4
H. BOP Balance on Serv.	N/A	N/A	N/A	N/A	N/A
U.S. FDI Serv. Balance*	N/A	−21	−272	−526	−3,660
%	N/A	N/A	N/A	N/A	N/A
I. Share of Global MOFA GP					
Total	N/A	0.1	0.2	nil	NMF
Manufacturing	nil	nil	nil	nil	nil
J. U.S. FDI Position*	222	143	7,608	11,274	18,387
U.S. Share of Inward FDI	N/A	N/A	N/A	N/A	N/A
K. Exchange Rate: U.S. dollar	1.00	1.00	1.00	1.00	1.00

Notes: ‡1978. *$ million.

TABLE 12.1 (continued)

Year	Country: Brazil Currency: Cruzeiros billion				
	1957	1966	1977	1982	1989[‡‡]
A. Industrial GDP	0.6[++]	37	2,173	45,406	1,312,000
MOFA Gross Product	0.032	1.7	91.7	2,010	49,854
CPI %	5.3	4.4	4.2	4.4	3.8
B. Manufacturing GDP	0.2[++]	13	606	12,396	342,500
MOFA Gross Product	0.018	1.3	73.1	1.718	42,501
CPI %	9.0	9.6	12.1	13.9	12.4
% of total MOFA GP	56.3	76.5	79.6	85.4	85.3
C. Industry Employ. (000)	N/A	5,000e	25,732	33,787	58,729[++++]
MOFA Employment	140	154	353	364	344.5
%	N/A	3.1	1.4	1.1	0.6
D. Manuf. Employ. (000)	N/A	2,100e	6,510	7,790	8,986[++++]
MOFA Employment	N/A	125	296	306	314.9
%	N/A	6.0	4.5	3.9	3.5
E. Merchandise Exports	0.1	3.8	167.1	3,369.0	34,383[*]
MOFA Export Sales	0.004	0.333	16.7	417.4	N/A
%	3.8	8.8	10.0	12.4	N/A
F. Merchandise Imports	0.1	3.3	181.5	3,626.9	18,263[*]
MOFA Imports Total	0.007[++]	N/A	16.5	N/A	N/A
%	7.4	N/A	9.1	N/A	N/A
G. MOFA Imports from U.S.	0.004[++]	0.2	1.0	126.7	1,383
%	4.0	6.1	5.6	3.5	7.6
H. BOP Balance on Serv.[*]	N/A	−469	−5,012	−17,090	−15,087
U.S. FDI Serv. Balance	N/A	−48	−328	−458	−1,252
%	N/A	10	7	3	8
I. Share of Global MOFA GP					
Total	2.5	2.0	4.0	5.0	5.2
Manufacturing	3.3	3.2	7.2	9.6	8.2
J. U.S. FDI Position[*]	835	882	5,695	9,206	13,799
U.S. Share of Inward FDI	N/A	N/A	N/A	N/A	N/A
K. Exchange Rate: Cruz./$	0.08	2.22	14.14	179.51	.003

Notes: [++]1955. [‡‡]Cruzados million. [++++]1988. [*]U.S. dollars million. e = estimate.

Country: Chile Currency: Pesos million					
Year	1957	1966	1977	1982[‡‡‡]	1989[‡‡‡]
A. Industrial GDP	0.65[++]	20.2	249,096	1,102	6,032e
MOFA Gross Product	0.28	2.4	3,488	23.8	113.9e
CPI %	43.1	11.9	1.4	2.2	1.9e
B. Manufacturing GDP	1.0[++]	6.2	62,574	233	1,508e
MOFA Gross Product	0.02	0.2	1,334	6.2	60.9e
CPI %	2.0	3.2	2.1	2.7	4.0e
% of total MOFA GP	7.1	8.4	38.1	26.1	53.5e
C. Industry Employ. (000)	N/A	N/A	2,821	2,943	4,425
MOFA Employment	55	46	8	12	16.5
%	N/A	N/A	0.3	0.4	0.4
D. Manuf. Employ. (000)	N/A	N/A	472	374	646
MOFA Employment	N/A	7	3	6	7.8
%	N/A	N/A	0.6	1.6	1.2
E. Merchandise Exports*	455	817	2,190	3,710	7,049
MOFA Export Sales	300	N/A	N/A	N/A	419
%	65.9	N/A	N/A	N/A	5.9
F. Merchandise Imports*	441	751	2,259	3,528	4,924
MOFA Imports Total	47[++]	N/A	106	N/A	N/A
%	10.6	N/A	4.7	N/A	N/A
G. MOFA Imports from U.S.	40	54	53	63	N/A
%	9.1	7.2	2.3	1.8	N/A
H. BOP Balance on Serv.*	N/A	−292	−586	−2,367	−2,345
U.S. FDI Serv. Balance*	N/A	−125	−15	N/A	−79
%	N/A	4	3	N/A	3
I. Share of Global MOFA GP					
Total	1.7	1.6	0.1	0.2	0.2
Manufacturing	0.3	0.3	0.1	0.1	0.2
J. U.S. FDI Position*	666	765	159	317	1,333
U.S. Share of Inward FDI	N/A	N/A	N/A	N/A	N/A
K. Exchange Rate: Pesos/$	.001	.004	21.529	50.909	167.16

Notes: [++]1955. *U.S. dollars million. [‡‡‡]Pesos billion. e = estimate.

TABLE 12.1 (continued)

Year	1957	1966	1977	1982	1989
Country: Colombia					
Currency: Pesos billion					
A. Industrial GDP	6.0++	69.3	673.4	2,243.3	13,981
MOFA Gross Product	0.62	3.2	19.6	87.2	440.5
CPI %	10.3	4.7	2.9	3.9	3.2
B. Manufacturing GDP	1.9++	14.2	170.7	529.9	3,128
MOFA Gross Product	0.17	1.6	11.8	46.2	170
CPI %	8.9	11.5	6.9	8.7	5.4
% of total MOFA GP	27.4	50.0	69.2	52.1	56.5
C. Industry Employ. (000)	N/A	N/A	2,530	3,065	3,669
MOFA Employment	50	41	40.3	42.4	36.3
%	N/A	N/A	1.6	1.4	1.0
D. Manuf. Employ. (000)	N/A	N/A	647	N/A	841
MOFA Employment	N/A	28	26.7	26.9	19.9
%	N/A	N/A	4.1	N/A	2.4
E. Merchandise Exports	2.0	6.7	89.9	196.6	5,739*
MOFA Export Sales	.213	1.6	6.5	11.0	635
%	10.6	23.9	7.2	5.6	11.1
F. Merchandise Imports	1.8	9.1	74.6	351.0	5,010*
MOFA Imports Total	0.16++	N/A	10.6	N/A	N/A
%	9.1	N/A	14.2	N/A	N/A
G. MOFA Imports from U.S.	0.12++	.945	6.7	15.3	296
%	6.8	10.4	8.9	4.4	5.9
H. BOP Balance on Serv.*	N/A	−175	−315	−810	−1,675
U.S. FDI Serv. Balance*	N/A	−34	−64	N/A	−190
%	N/A	19	20	N/A	11
I. Share of Global MOFA GP					
Total	1.0	0.7	0.3	0.6	0.4
Manufacturing	0.3	0.7	0.4	0.7	0.4
J. U.S. FDI Position*	396	459	662	1,753	1,614
U.S. Share of Inward FDI	N/A	N/A	N/A	N/A	N/A
K. Exchange Rate: Pesos/$	3.798	13.500	36.775	64.085	382.57

Notes: ++1955. *U.S. dollars million.

Country: Mexico Currency: Pesos billion					
Year	**1957**	**1966**	**1977**	**1982**	**1989**
A. Industrial GDP	80.1[++]	264.2	1,711.4	9,055	476,200
MOFA Gross Product	5.2	11.1	46.3	200.8	12,022
CPI %	6.5	4.2	2.7	2.2	2.5
B. Manufacturing GDP	21.3[++]	59.2	443.0	2,037	124,209
MOFA Gross Product	3.0	8.0	37.2	162.4	10,151
CPI %	14.0	13.4	8.4	8.0	8.2
% of total MOFA GP	57.7	72.7	80.3	80.9	84.4
C. Industry Employ. (000)	N/A	N/A	10,772	N/A	N/A
MOFA Employment	180	127	202.8	258.2	327.0
%	N/A	N/A	1.9	N/A	N/A
D. Manuf. Employ. (000)	N/A	N/A	3,277	N/A	N/A
MOFA Employment	N/A	102	171.2	227.8	290.3
%	N/A	N/A	5.2	N/A	N/A
E. Merchandise Exports	9.2	15.0	102.1	1,231.8	22,819*
MOFA Export Sales	2.3	2.0	13.2	65.3	4,348[†]
%	25.3	13.3	12.9	5.3	19.1
F. Merchandise Imports	14.4	20.1	133.0	774.7	23,633*
MOFA Imports Total	1.6[++]	N/A	22.3	N/A	N/A
%	11.2	N/A	16.7	N/A	N/A
G. MOFA Imports from U.S.	1.6[++]	3.0	18.3	131.3	6,735*
%	10.9	15.1	13.8	17.0	28.5
H. BOP Balance on Serv.*	N/A	−6	−833	−13,102	−3,313
U.S. FDI Serv. Balance*	N/A	−94	−183	−446	−948
%	N/A	−1,566	22	3	29
I. Share of Global MOFA GP					
Total	2.6	2.4	1.3	1.6	1.5
Manufacturing	3.3	3.5	2.2	2.9	2.4
J. U.S. FDI Position*	739	1,329	3,201	5,187	8,371
U.S. Share of Inward FDI	N/A	N/A	N/A	N/A	N/A
K. Exchange Rate: $Pesos/$	12.500	12.500	22.573	56.402	2,462

Notes: [++]1955. *$U.S. million. [†]to U.S. only.

TABLE 12.1 (continued)

Year	1957	1966	1977	1982	1989
Country: Panama **Currency: Balboas million**					
A. Industrial GDP	357[+]	630	1,813	3,858	3,933
MOFA Gross Product	23	92	289	433	530
CPI %	6.4	14.6	15.9	11.2	13.5
B. Manufacturing GDP	49[+]	100	234	394	354
MOFA Gross Product	3	5	26	45	182
CPI %	6.1	5.0	11.1	11.4	51.4
% of total MOFA GP	13.0	5.4	9.0	10.4	34.3
C. Industry Employ. (000)	N/A	N/A	471	561	689
MOFA Employment	20	17	15.2	22.4	19.7
%	N/A	N/A	4.7	4.0	2.9
D. Manuf. Employ. (000)	N/A	N/A	49	54	65
MOFA Employment	N/A	N/A	1.0	1.6	2.0
%	N/A	N/A	2.0	3.0	3.1
E. Merchandise Exports	35	90	251	375	297
MOFA Export Sales	33	N/A	750	1,662	N/A
%	94.3	N/A	298.8	443.2	N/A
F. Merchandise Imports	109	235	861	1,569	965
MOFA Imports Total	N/A	N/A	236	N/A	N/A
%	N/A	N/A	27.4	N/A	N/A
G. MOFA Imports from U.S.	N/A	40	79	239	230
%	N/A	17.0	9.1	15.2	23.8
H. BOP Balance on Serv.*	N/A	75	347	583	851
U.S. FDI Serv. Balance*	N/A	−50	−302	−608	−1,436
%	N/A	−67	−87	−104	−169
I. Share of Global MOFA GP					
Total	0.1	0.2	0.2	0.4	0.2
Manufacturing	nil	nil	nil	nil	0.1
J. U.S. FDI Position*	201	847	2,442	4,388	8,857
U.S. Share of Inward FDI	N/A	N/A	N/A	N/A	N/A
K. Exchange Rate: Balboas/$	1.00	1.00	1.00	1.00	1.00

Notes: [+]1960. *$ million.

Country: Peru Currency: Soles billion					
Year	**1957**	**1966**	**1977**	**1982**	**1989**
A. Industrial GDP	N/A	N/A	1,032	16,010	104,445
MOFA Gross Product	2.4	12.5	33.9	700.9	1,058
CPI %	N/A	N/A	3.3	4.4	1.0
B. Manufacturing GDP	N/A	N/A	293	3,275	31,092
MOFA Gross Product	0.4	3.0	6.2	75.4	239.9
CPI %	N/A	N/A	2.1	2.3	0.8
% of total MOFA GP	16.7	24.0	18.2	9.7	44.4
C. Industry Employ. (000)	N/A	N/A	4,827	5,387[+++]	2,200e
MOFA Employment	50	63	20.2	22.4	13.4e
%	N/A	N/A	0.4	0.4	0.6e
D. Manuf. Employ. (000)	N/A	N/A	741	808[+++]	453
MOFA Employment	N/A	18	7.2	5.6	3.1
%	N/A	N/A	1.0	0.7	0.7
E. Merchandise Exports	6	21	145	2,306	3,488*
MOFA Export Sales	2.5	10.2	N/A	387.1	524
%	41.7	48.5	N/A	16.8	15.0
F. Merchandise Imports	8	22	158	N/A	2,291*
MOFA Imports Total	0.77[++]	N/A	11.1	N/A	N/A
%	9.3	N/A	7.0	N/A	N/A
G. MOFA Imports from U.S.	0.65[++]	3.4	7.0	185.0	69*
%	8.1	15.5	4.4	8.0	3.0
H. BOP Balance on Serv.*	N/A	−219	−484	−1,184	−1,103
U.S. FDI Serv. Balance	N/A	−115	−43	−15	−23
%	N/A	53	9	1	2
I. Share of Global MOFA GP					
Total	0.8	1.3	0.3	0.5	0.1
Manufacturing	0.3	0.6	0.1	0.1	0.1
J. U.S. FDI Position*	383	651	1,160	1,985	813
U.S. Share of Inward FDI	N/A	N/A	N/A	N/A	N/A
K. Exchange Rate: Soles/$	19.16	26.82	84.23	697.57	2,666

Notes: [++]1955. [+++]1981. *$U.S. million. e = estimate.

TABLE 12.1 (continued)

Country: Venezuela Currency: Bolivars billion					
Year	1957	1966	1977	1982	1989
A. Industrial GDP	25.6[+]	39.5	140.7	261.9	1,364.6
MOFA Gross Product	6.0	7.2	5.9	10.3	25.8
CPI %	23.3	18.2	4.2	3.9	1.9
B. Manufacturing GDP	4.2[+]	6.8e	24.8	46.8	314.3
MOFA Gross Product	0.3	1.0	3.2	6.0	17.7
CPI %	7.8	14.7e	12.9	12.8	5.6
% of total MOFA GP	5.0	13.9	54.2	58.5	69.2
C. Industry Employ. (000)	N/A	N/A	3,870	4,351	6,115
MOFA Employment	70	68	68.5	67.1	40.4
%	N/A	N/A	2.1	1.5	0.6
D. Manuf. Employ. (000)	N/A	N/A	629	672	1,052
MOFA Employment	N/A	29	48.4	43.1	29.8
%	N/A	N/A	7.7	6.4	2.8
E. Merchandise Exports*	2,366	2,713	10,135	16,443	12,918
MOFA Export Sales	1,799	1,676	N/A	76	36
%	76.0	61.8	N/A	0.5	0.3
F. Merchandise Imports*	1,668	1,188	9,778	11,670	6,920
MOFA Imports Total	179[++]	N/A	1,352	N/A	N/A
%	10.7	N/A	13.8	N/A	N/A
G. MOFA Imports from U.S.*	147[++]	231	1,042	1,365	445
%	8.8	19.4	10.7	11.7	6.4
H. BOP Balance on Serv.*	N/A	−1,062	−2,541	−6,994	−3,471
U.S. FDI Serv. Balance*	N/A	−415	−205	−408	−96
%	N/A	39	9	6	3
I. Share of Global MOFA GP					
Total	11.1	4.4	0.9	1.1	0.2
Manufacturing	1.4	1.3	1.0	1.4	0.3
J. U.S. FDI Position*	2,465	2,136	1,560	2,580	932
U.S. Share of Inward FDI	N/A	N/A	N/A	N/A	N/A
K. Exchange Rate: Boliv./$	3.35	4.45	4.29	4.29	34.68

Notes: [+]1960. *U.S. dollar million. [++]1955. e = estimate.

Country: South Africa Currency: Rand million					
Year	**1957**	**1966**	**1977**	**1982**	**1989**
A. Industrial GDP	4,490+	7,010	28,443	65,191	181,011
MOFA Gross Product	332	330	1,146	2,507	1,830
CPI %	7.4	4.7	4.0	3.8	1.0
B. Manufacturing GDP	1,020+	1,860	6,963	18,320	52,859
MOFA Gross Product	77	148	475	1,088	1,151
CPI %	7.5	8.0	6.8	5.9	2.2
% of total MOFA GP	23.2	44.8	41.5	43.4	62.9
C. Industry Employ. (000)	N/A	N/A	4,575	5,031	5,128*
MOFA Employment	50	70	82.4	83.9	22.7
%	N/A	N/A	1.8	1.7	0.4
D. Manuf. Employ. (000)	N/A	N/A	1,242	1,454	1,431*
MOFA Employment	N/A	57.0	57.5	56.8	16.8
%	N/A	N/A	4.6	3.9	1.2
E. Merchandise Exports	1,340	1,990	8,690	19,250	39,442
MOFA Export Sales	26.5	N/A	243.6	471.3	103.9
%	2.0	N/A	2.8	2.4	0.3
F. Merchandise Imports	1,150	1,710	5,450	20,080	44,446
MOFA Imports Total	N/A	N/A	896	N/A	N/A
%	N/A	N/A	16.4	N/A	N/A
G. MOFA Imports from U.S.	N/A	86	282	563	68
%	N/A	5.0	5.2	2.8	0.2
H. BOP Balance on Serv.*	N/A	−477	−1,995	−3,829	−4,010
U.S. FDI Serv. Balance*	N/A	−70	−152	−314	−132
%	N/A	15	8	8	3
I. Share of Global MOFA GP					
Total	2.6	1.2	0.8	1.0	0.2
Manufacturing	1.4	1.1	0.8	1.0	0.3
J. U.S. FDI Position*	301	490	1,690	2,284	674
U.S. Share of Inward FDI	N/A	N/A	N/A	N/A	N/A
K. Exchange Rate: Rand/$	.7938	.7177	.8700	1.076	2.610

Notes: +1960. *$ million.

TABLE 12.1 (continued)

	Country: Japan Currency: Yen billion				
Year	1957	1966	1977	1982	1989
A. Industrial GDP	14,283[+]	38,085	172,864	262,427	366,611
MOFA Gross Product	(16)	332	825	1,078	2,062
CPI %	NMF	0.9	0.5	0.4	0.6
B. Manufacturing GDP	5,371[+]	12,279	55,412	78,191	116,619
MOFA Gross Product	21	138	395	512	1,058
CPI %	0.4	1.1	0.7	0.7	0.9
% of total MOFA GP	NMF	41.6	47.9	47.5	51.3
C. Industry Employ. (000)	27,232	48,270	52,990	54,399	61,280
MOFA Employment	N/A	54	65.5	82.2	131.6
%	N/A	0.1	0.1	0.2	0.2
D. Manuf. Employ. (000)	8,530	11,780	14,410	14,174	14,830
MOFA Employment	N/A	40	39.9	47.5	74.5
%	N/A	0.3	0.3	0.3	0.5
E. Merchandise Exports	1,032	3,515	21,436	34,748	37,823
MOFA Export Sales	N/A	29.9	257.7	528.3	754.6
%	N/A	0.8	1.2	1.5	2.0
F. Merchandise Imports	1,546	2,701	17,104	30,655	28,979
MOFA Imports Total	21.7	N/A	379.8	N/A	N/A
%	1.4	N/A	2.2	N/A	N/A
G. MOFA Imports from U.S.	N/A	82.1	190.7	358.8	873.9
%	N/A	3.0	1.1	1.2	3.0
H. BOP Balance on Serv.***	N/A	−1.02	−6.25	−15.15	−19.90
U.S. FDI Serv. Balance***	N/A	−.08	−.62	−.87	−3.57
%	N/A	8	1	5	18
I. Share of Global MOFA GP					
Total	N/A	2.5	1.9	2.0	4.7
Manufacturing	0.8	2.1	2.0	2.2	4.4
J. U.S. FDI Position***	.185	.731	4.593	6.636	20.164
U.S. Share of Inward FDI	N/A	N/A	N/A	53	51
K. Exchange Rate: Yen/$	360.8	360.0	269.0	235.0	137.9

Notes: [+]1960. ***$ billion.

Country: Hong Kong Currency: HK$ billion					
Year	1957	1966	1977	1982	1989
A. Industrial GDP	3.9+	8.0	31.3	176.4	454.6
MOFA Gross Product	N/A	N/A	2.5	6.2	22.9
CPI %	N/A	N/A	8.1	3.5	5.0
B. Manufacturing GDP	1.3*	2.9	12.9	36.4	89.6
MOFA Gross Product	N/A	N/A	0.9	1.6	5.9
CPI %	N/A	N/A	7.2	4.4	6.6
% of total MOFA GP	N/A	N/A	36.0	25.7	25.7
C. Industry Employ. (000)	N/A	N/A	1,606	2,068	2,749
MOFA Employment	N/A	N/A	35.3	37.4	58.2
%	N/A	N/A	2.2	1.8	2.1
D. Manuf. Employ. (000)	N/A	N/A	755	847	817
MOFA Employment	N/A	N/A	29.2	22.6	31.1
%	N/A	N/A	3.9	2.7	3.8
E. Merchandise Exports	3.0	N/A	44.8	136.2	570.5
MOFA Export Sales	N/A	N/A	19.241	29.081	68.6
%	N/A	N/A	42.9	21.4	12.0
F. Merchandise Imports	5.298	N/A	N/A	N/A	562.8
MOFA Imports Total	N/A	N/A	5.215	N/A	N/A
%	N/A	N/A	N/A	N/A	N/A
G. MOFA Imports from U.S.	N/A	N/A	1.510	N/A	17.4
%	N/A	N/A	N/A	N/A	3.1
H. BOP Balance on Serv.	N/A	N/A	N/A	N/A	N/A
U.S. FDI Serv. Balance*	N/A	−23	−222	−343	−1,380
%	N/A	N/A	N/A	N/A	N/A
I. Share of Global MOFA GP					
Total	N/A	N/A	0.3	0.4	0.9
Manufacturing	N/A	N/A	0.3	0.2	0.4
J. U.S. FDI Position*	12	126	1,328	2,928	5,314
U.S. Share of Inward FDI	N/A	N/A	N/A	N/A	N/A
K. Exchange Rate: HK$/$	5.880	5.710	4.662	6.495	7.81

Notes: +1960. *$ million.

TABLE 12.1 (continued)

Year	1957	1966	1977	1982	1989
Country: Indonesia **Currency: Rupiah billion**					
A. Industrial GDP	0.4[+]	299.7	17,639	57,770	156,321
MOFA Gross Product	N/A	N/A	1,934	4,210	7,078
CPI %	N/A	N/A	11.0	7.3	4.5
B. Manufacturing GDP	N/A	26.5	1,817	7,482	30,579
MOFA Gross Product	N/A	0	44	97.3	1,770
CPI %	N/A	0	2.4	1.3	5.8
% of total MOFA GP	N/A	0	2.3	2.3	2.5
C. Industry Employ. (000)	N/A	N/A	18,621	57,803	75,851[**]
MOFA Employment	N/A	N/A	45.4	52.0	36.1
%	N/A	N/A	0.2	0.1	0.05
D. Manuf. Employ. (000)	N/A	N/A	4,171	6,022	7,693[**]
MOFA Employment	N/A	N/A	14.5	16.2	6.6
%	N/A	N/A	0.3	0.3	0.1
E. Merchandise Exports[***]	1.0	0.7	10.9	22.3	22.2
MOFA Export Sales	N/A	N/A	N/A	8.3	2.7
%	N/A	N/A	N/A	37.2	12.0
F. Merchandise Imports[***]	0.8	0.5	6.2	16.9	16.3
MOFA Imports Total	N/A	N/A	.2	N/A	N/A
%	N/A	N/A	3.2	N/A	N/A
G. MOFA Imports from U.S.[*]	N/A	10	127	387	151
%	N/A	2.0	2.0	2.3	0.9
H. BOP Balance on Serv.[*]	N/A	−226	−3,336	−7,163	−7,772
U.S. FDI Serv. Balance[*]	N/A	−44	−624	−1,963	−1,125
%	N/A	19	19	27	14
I. Share of Global MOFA GP					
Total	N/A	N/A	2.9	2.9	1.2
Manufacturing	0	0	0.2	0.2	0.6
J. U.S. FDI Position[*]	169	106	984	2,281	2,631
U.S. Share of Inward FDI	N/A	N/A	N/A	N/A	N/A
K. Exchange Rate: Rupiah/$	50e	149.58	415	666.42	1,770

Notes: [+]1960. [***]$ billion. [*]$ million. [**]1990.

Country: Philippines Currency: Pesos billion					
Year	1957	1966	1977	1982	1989
A. Industrial GDP	10.5[+]	19.0	146.1	299.3	860.1
MOFA Gross Product	0.3	0.96	4.1	9.2	21.8
CPI %	2.9	5.0	2.8	3.1	2.5
B. Manufacturing GDP	2.1[+]	3.7	39.3	79.6	233.2
MOFA Gross Product	0.09	0.36	2.1	3.8	13.5
CPI %	4.3	9.8	5.2	4.8	5.8
% of total MOFA GP	30.0	37.5	51.2	41.6	62.1
C. Industry Employ. (000)	3,202	4,757	6,860	9,291	21,849
MOFA Employment	N/A	50	84.9	81.3	60.7
%	N/A	1.1	1.2	0.9	0.3
D. Manuf. Employ. (000)	1,005	1,331	1,515	1,814	2,297
MOFA Employment	N/A	30	61.1	66.4	51.3
%	N/A	2.3	4.1	3.7	2.2
E. Merchandise Exports	0.9	3.2	23.1	42.4	7,747*
MOFA Export Sales	0.05	0.43	2.6	N/A	648
%	6.2	13.5	11.4	N/A	8.4
F. Merchandise Imports	1.3	3.7	31.6	70.6	10,732*
MOFA Imports Total	N/A	N/A	4.0	N/A	N/A
%	N/A	N/A	12.7	N/A	N/A
G. MOFA Imports from U.S.	N/A	0.8	0.98	2.5	250
%	N/A	2.1	3.1	3.6	2.3
H. BOP Balance on Serv.*	N/A	171	11	−556	1,142
U.S. FDI Serv. Balance*	N/A	−38	−73	N/A	−156
%	N/A	−22	−663	N/A	−14
I. MOFA Share in FDI GP					
Total	0.9	0.7	0.3	0.2	0.3
Manufacturing	0.7	0.5	0.4	0.4	0.4
J. U.S. FDI Position*	306	486	837	1,308	1,104
U.S. Share of Inward FDI	N/A	N/A	N/A	N/A	N/A
K. Exchange Rate: Pesos/$	N/A	3.900	7.4028	8.5400	21.737

Notes: [+]1960. *$U.S. million.

TABLE 12.1 (continued)

Year	1957	1966	1977	1982	1989
Country: Singapore					
Currency: Singapore dollar million					
A. Industrial GDP	N/A	3,119	15,198	32,070	57,277
MOFA Gross Product	N/A	N/A	935.2	2,338	4,588
CPI %	N/A	N/A	6.1	7.3	8.0
B. Manufacturing GDP	N/A	481	4,019	8,151	16,503
MOFA Gross Product	N/A	N/A	490.9	1,202	2,833
CPI %	N/A	N/A	12.2	14.7	17.2
% of total MOFA GP	N/A	N/A	52.5	51.4	61.8
C. Industry Employ. (000)	N/A	N/A	903.9	1,140.6	1,525
MOFA Employment	N/A	N/A	38.5	42.6	71.3
%	N/A	N/A	4.3	3.7	4.7
D. Manuf. Employ. (000)	N/A	N/A	245.5	336.0	430
MOFA Employment	N/A	N/A	32.5	31.8	58.9
%	N/A	N/A	13.2	9.5	13.7
E. Merchandise Exports*	N/A	3,168	8,248	20,788	44,675
MOFA Export Sales	N/A	N/A	N/A	11,579	10,862
%	N/A	N/A	N/A	55.7	24.3
F. Merchandise Imports*	N/A	3,825	10,471	28,167	49,674
MOFA Imports Total	N/A	N/A	1,006	N/A	N/A
%	N/A	N/A	9.6	N/A	N/A
G. MOFA Imports from U.S.*	N/A	N/A	343	955	2,219
%	N/A	N/A	3.3	3.4	4.5
H. BOP Balance on Serv.*	N/A	215	1,689	5,466	4,875
U.S. FDI Serv. Balance*	N/A	−3	−105	−266	−648
%	N/A	−1	−6	−5	−13
I. MOFA Share in FDI GP					
Total	N/A	N/A	0.2	0.5	0.7
Manufacturing	N/A	N/A	0.3	0.6	0.8
J. U.S. FDI Position*	N/A	30	516	1,745	3,144
U.S. Share of Inward FDI	N/A	N/A	N/A	N/A	N/A
K. Exchange Rate: Sing.$/$	N/A	3.08	2.338	2.108	1.950

Note: *U.S. dollar million.

Country: Australia Currency: Australian dollar million					
Year	1957	1966	1977	1982	1989
A. Industrial GDP	10,259*	21,729	89,258	166,227	361,656
MOFA Gross Product	412	1,014	5,020	10,171	17,656
CPI %	4.0	4.7	5.6	6.1	4.9
B. Manufacturing GDP	3,180*	6,277	18,726	31,037	57,881
MOFA Gross Product	265	644	2,212	4,338	8,713
CPI %	8.3	10.3	11.8	14.0	15.1
% of total MOFA GP	64.3	63.5	44.1	42.7	49.4
C. Industry Employ. (000)	2,941*	4,824	5,467	5,008	7,728
MOFA Employment	90	161	206.1	199.4	196.6
%	3.1	4.2	3.8	3.3	2.5
D. Manuf. Employ. (000)	1,019	1,207	1,247	1,163	1,236
MOFA Employment	N/A	116	133.1	118.4	102.5
%	N/A	9.6	10.7	10.2	8.3
E. Merchandise Exports	986	2,940	12,041	20,857	46,900
MOFA Export Sales	349	213	1,913	3,673	4,048
%	3.5	7.2	15.9	17.6	8.6
F. Merchandise Imports	754	3,143	12,195	23,104	51,735
MOFA Imports Total	N/A	N/A	2,055	N/A	N/A
%	N/A	N/A	16.8	N/A	N/A
G. MOFA Imports from U.S.	N/A	218	948	1,760	2,556
%	N/A	6.9	7.8	7.6	4.9
H. BOP Balance on Serv.*	N/A	−812	−4,105	−5,922	−14,222
U.S. FDI Serv. Balance*	N/A	−95	−613	−1,029	−1,467
%	N/A	12	15	17	10
I. MOFA Share in FDI GP					
Total	2.9	3.1	3.5	4.5	4.3
Manufacturing	4.2	4.0	3.5	4.3	4.0
J. U.S. FDI Position*	583	1,855	5,823	9,137	14,310
U.S. Share of Inward FDI	N/A	N/A	N/A	33	23
K. Exchange Rate: Austr.$/$	N/A	0.893	0.90	0.99	1.27

Notes: *1958. *$ million.

TABLE 12.1 (continued)

Country: New Zealand Currency: New Zealand dollar million					
Year	1957	1966	1977	1982	1989
A. Industrial GDP	1,851*	4,190	13,675	27,720	60,179
MOFA Gross Product	18.0	99	396	824	1,645
CPI %	1.0	2.4	2.9	2.9	2.7
B. Manufacturing GDP	N/A	N/A	3,472	7,298	12,662
MOFA Gross Product	8.3	40	163	375	504
CPI %	N/A	N/A	4.7	5.1	4.0
% of total MOFA GP	46.1	40.3	41.1	45.5	30.7
C. Industry Employ. (000)	719*	854	1,248	1,293	1,461
MOFA Employment	N/A	13	15.8	16.1	20.9
%	N/A	1.5	1.3	1.2	1.4
D. Manuf. Employ. (000)	210	277	316	313	257
MOFA Employment	N/A	7	10.7	10.1	9.8
%	N/A	2.5	3.4	3.2	3.8
E. Merchandise Exports	279	787	4,125	9,116	14,905
MOFA Export Sales	7.6	N/A	49.4	100.0	125.1
%	2.7	N/A	1.2	1.1	0.8
F. Merchandise Imports	299	723	4,378	10,330	12,491
MOFA Imports Total	N/A	N/A	495.4	N/A	N/A
%	N/A	N/A	11.3	N/A	N/A
G. MOFA Imports from U.S.	N/A	12.9	57.7	143.6	147.2
%	N/A	1.8	1.3	1.4	1.2
H. BOP Balance on Serv.*	N/A	N/A	−802	−1,420	−2,393
U.S. FDI Serv. Balance*	N/A	−13	−17	−86	−132
%	N/A	N/A	2	6	6
I. MOFA Share in FDI GP					
Total	0.3	0.4	0.2	0.3	0.3
Manufacturing	0.3	0.3	0.2	0.3	0.2
J. U.S. FDI Position*	48	110	410	649	1,062
U.S. Share of Inward FDI	N/A	N/A	N/A	N/A	N/A
K. Exchange Rate: N.Z.$/$	N/A	0.719	1.030	1.333	1.670

Notes: *1958. *$ million.

World Currency: U.S.dollar billion					
Year	1957	1966	1977	1982	1989
A. Industrial GDP	N/A	N/A	N/A	N/A	N/A
MOFA Gross Product	16.1§	36.8§	161.1	223.7	320.0
– Developed Countries	9.7	25.4	107.5	164.2	262.4
%	60.2	69.0	66.7	73.3	82.0
B. Manufacturing GDP	N/A	N/A	N/A	N/A	N/A
MOFA Gross Product	7.1§	18.0§	71.6	99.8	173.3
– Developed Countries	6.0	15.2	60.2	78.9	143.5
%	84.5	84.4	84.1	79.9	82.8
– MOFA Manufacturing GP as % of total MOFA GP	44.1§	48.9§	44.5	44.8	54.3
C. Industry Employ. (000)	N/A	N/A	N/A	N/A	N/A
MOFA Employment	3,200§	3,874	5,369	5,022	5,114
– Developed Countries	1,900††	2,770	3,817	3,411	3,580
%	59	72	71	68	70
D. Manuf. Employ. (000)	N/A	N/A	N/A	N/A	N/A
MOFA Employment	1,700§	2,615	3,773	3,358	3,247
– Developed Countries	1,300	2,090	2,754	2,315	2,167
%	77	80	73	69	67
– % of MOFA Employment	53	68	70	67	63
E. Merchandise Exports	112	204	1,125	1,829	2,909
MOFA Export Sales	10.5§	24.4	193.7	252.3	298.9
%	9.4	12.0	17.2	13.8	10.3
F. Merchandise Imports	120	216	1,164	1,922	3,134
MOFA Imports Total†††	6.8§	N/A	102.3	120.9	204.2
%	5.7	N/A	8.8	6.3	6.5
G. MOFA Imports from U.S.	3.0	7.7	35.8	52.8	97.5
% of all MOFA Imports	44	N/A	21	N/A	N/A
H. BOP Balance on Serv.***	N/A	N/A	–32.7	–107.6	–70.6
U.S. FDI Serv. Balance	N/A	N/A	–17.2	–25.0	–59.9
%	N/A	N/A	53	23	85
I. U.S. FDI Position***	25.4	51.8	146.0	207.3	380.1
U.S. Share in World FDI	N/A	N/A	N/A	44	35

Notes: §All affiliates. ††Excludes Japan. †††Excludes imports from nonaffiliates in other countries for 1982 and 1989. ***$ billion.

TABLE 12.1 (continued)

U.S. FDI Parent Role in U.S. Economy Currency: U.S. dollar billion					
Year	1957	1966	1977	1982	1989
A. Non-Farm Industrial GDP	403	644	1,633	2,634	4,414
Parent Gross Product	N/A	N/A	491	796	1,045
CPI %	N/A	N/A	30.1	30.2	23.7
B. Manufacturing GDP	132	217	465	635	966
Parent Gross Product	N/A	N/A	301	421	587
CPI %	N/A	N/A	64.7	66.3	60.8
C. Industry Employ. (000)	52,853	63,900	82,500	89,900	108,300
Parent Employment	N/A	N/A	17,510	18,192	18,765
%	N/A	N/A	21.2	20.3	17.3
D. Manuf. Employ. (000)	17,174	19,214	19,682	18,781	19,442
Parent Employment	N/A	N/A	11,010	10,268	10,127
%	N/A	N/A	55.8	54.8	52.1
E. Merchandise Exports	19.6	29.3	120.8	211.2	362.1
FDI Exports	N/A	19.2	93.2	147.8	231.3
%	N/A	65.5	77.2	70.0	63.9
Exports to Mofas	3.0	7.7	35.8	52.8	97.5
%	15.3	26.6	29.6	25.0	26.9
F. Merchandise Imports	13.3	25.5	151.9	247.6	477.4
FDI Imports Total	N/A	N/A	79.6	106.1	188.9
%	N/A	N/A	52.4	42.8	39.6
Imports from Mofas	3.8	6.3	38.0	46.1	$84.3
%	28.6	24.7	25.0	18.6	17.7
G. U.S. Balance on Services	N/A	−.88	3.85	12.33	23.85
Parent Balance on Services	N/A	4.63	17.16	24.99	59.88
%	N/A	586	446	203	251

Sources: *U.S. GDP: Economic Report of the President*, February 1988, Table B-10; February 1991, p. 286. *U.S. Employment: Economic Report of the President*, February 1991, p. 344; February 1995, pp. 324-5. Exports/Imports (merchandise excluding military): *Economic Report of the President*, February 1990, Table C-20 (1957). *SOCB*, June 1995, pp. 84-5 (1966, 1977, 1982, 1989). Parent data: Gross Product: *SOCB*, February 1983, p. 27 (1977). FDI census data: 1982, pp. 219-20, 247, 300, 303, 309; 1989, pp. 94, 96, 105, 120. Employment: FDI census data: 1977, p. 392; 1982, p. 323; 1989, p. 105. U.S. FDI trade data include parent trade with Mofas and foreigners, and U.S. nonaffiliates with Mofas: 1966 FDI census, pp. 82-4; 1977 FDI census, pp. 395, 398; 1982 FDI census, pp. 332, 335; 1989 FDI census, pp. 112, 116. Services: Benchmark Surveys, 1966, pp. 69, 76; 1977, pp. 81, 95; 1982, pp. 66, 73, 77; 1989, pp. 26, 31, 34. Total United States, IMF, *International Financial Statistics Yearbook* 1993 and 1994. Global FDI data: *OECD Yearbook* 1993, p. 19; 1994, p. 15. Inward FDI: Japan, 1991. An International Comparison, p. 58.

Chapter 13

The U.S. Position in World Trade

The notion of a general American decline in world trade during the postwar period seems widely accepted. So much, as a matter of fact, that it inspires regular and vigorous export promotion campaigns, incentives, and diplomatic support by the American government. This perception is only partially supported by statistical evidence collected in Table 13.1. A real decline can be demonstrated if export levels of the 1950s and 1960s are seen as a normal basis for the calculation. At that time, the United States enjoyed a trade share of 14 to 16 percent against today's 11 to 12 percent. But the first two decades were a transitional period during which the world relied to a large degree on U.S. exports and financial aid to rebuild and modernize their ravaged industries. Eventually, the need for U.S. goods diminished, ushering in a long-term period of trade normalization during the early 1970s. It was also the time when the U.S. trade share started to stabilize, giving way to a very steady U.S. trade share with some obvious, but not dramatic fluctuations. Averaged out, America's export share in world trade showed 11.8 percent for the 1970s, 11.5 percent for the 1980s, and 11.9 percent for the first half of the century's last decade. With such long-term stability, there really is no need to worry about a persistent decline in the U.S. trade share, because it came to a halt two and one-half decades ago. Quite to the contrary, the figures since then are very encouraging and indicate a presently rock-solid position for the geographical United States.

Following the thoughts developed in Chapter 11, national capital ownership and control over business activities in individual country markets, or in a single world market for that matter, should become the real measure of a nation's share in the world economy instead of geographically defined national output, as is the practice now. That line of reasoning applies equally to foreign roles in the output of national GDPs, as it does to international trade. Exports and imports of American Mofas are, therefore,

TABLE 13.1. World Merchandise Trade and U.S. Share ($ billion)

Year	World Exports	U.S. Exports*				Affil. Exports	"Global U.S. Share"
		BOP	%	Revised	%		
1955	$94	$14.3	15.2	N/A	N/A	N/A	N/A
1956	104	17.3	16.6	N/A	N/A	N/A	N/A
1957	112	19.5	17.4	N/A	N/A	$10.5	(26.8)%
1958	108	16.4	15.2	N/A	N/A	N/A	N/A
1959	116	16.4	14.1	N/A	N/A	N/A	N/A
1965	186	26.5	14.2	N/A	N/A	N/A	N/A
1966	204	29.3	14.4	N/A	N/A	24.4	(26.3)
1967	215	30.7	14.3	N/A	N/A	27.2	(26.9)
1968	240	·33.6	14.0	N/A	N/A	31.3	(27.0)
1969	274	36.4	13.3	N/A	N/A	36.2	(26.5)
1970	314	42.5	13.5	N/A	N/A	41.9	(26.8)
1971	351	43.3	12.3	N/A	N/A	51.2	(26.9)
1972	418	49.4	11.8	N/A	N/A	59.5	(26.1)
1973	578	71.4	12.4	N/A	N/A	87.0	(27.4)
1974	849	98.3	11.6	$73.6	8.7	161.2	27.7
1975	875	107.1	12.2	N/A	N/A	156.8	N/A
1976	989	114.7	11.6	N/A	N/A	N/A	N/A
1977	1,125	120.8	10.8	96.9	8.6	138.1	20.9
1978	1,299	142.1	10.9	110.9	8.5	N/A	N/A
1979	1,640	184.5	11.3	141.5	8.6	N/A	N/A
1980	1,990	224.3	11.3	172.2	8.6	N/A	N/A
1981	1,971	237.1	12.0	173.0	8.8	N/A	N/A
1982	1,829	211.2	11.5	151.0	8.3	214.2	20.0
1983	1,805	201.8	11.2	147.9	8.2	N/A	N/A
1984	1,901	219.9	11.6	161.7	8.5	226.4	20.4
1985	1,933	215.9	11.2	159.5	8.3	216.8	19.5
1986	1,985	223.3	11.2	172.6	8.7	213.6	19.5
1987	2,352	250.2	10.6	202.1	8.6	238.5	18.7
1988	2,744	320.2	11.7	250.7	9.1	281.1	19.4
1989	2,963	362.1	12.2	277.8	9.4	282.5	18.9
1990	3,383	389.3	11.5	297.0	8.8	346.3	19.0
1991	3,485	416.9	12.0	320.0	9.2	365.3	19.7
1992	3,729	440.4	11.8	336.5	9.0	382.9	19.3
1993	3,713	456.8	12.3	351.7	9.5	382.2	19.8
1994	4,185	502.5	12.0	N/A	N/A	N/A	N/A

Notes: *Merchandise excluding military. Revised data represent U.S. exports by American-owned companies only.

Sources: World merchandise exports: 1955-86, *UN Yearbooks* 1960-1990, World Trade by Commodity Classes and regions. 1986-94, Direction of Trade Statistics, IMF, *Yearbook* 1993, p. 3; 1995, p. 3. U.S. merchandise exports: 1955-59, *Business Statistics*, 1973, p. 109. 1960-94, Table 1, U.S. International Transactions, *SOCB*, June 1987, pp. 54-5; June 1995, pp. 84-5. Affiliate exports: data from Table 9.5 adjusted for sales of services beginning with 1982 FDI census. Foreign affiliate exports from U.S.: Table 5.1.

treated as bona fide American trade activities in the following, because they are fully controlled by U.S. parent companies, which makes them an integral part of the U.S. economy in a global sense.

Theoretically, the existence and expansion of a large American-controlled production and trade capacity overseas should be assumed to have produced some impact on America's economy and foreign trade proper, as well as on the country's global trade position in the broadest sense over such a long period. The question of what kind of changes were ushered, and what aspects might be judged positive or negative, is addressed by the comments and observations in the following section.

THE HISTORY OF GLOBAL U.S. EXPORTS

The term "global U.S. exports" combines merchandise exports shipped from American-owned factories in the United States with those from Mofas situated in foreign locations, as both signify American control over international trade from a capital-ownership point of view. Exports by foreign majority-owned subsidiaries in the United States are, by definition, excluded here, and purposefully break with the traditional view of what still is commonly referred to as U.S. exports. To demonstrate the practical implications of both measuring techniques, the results of both the traditional BOT accounting and the expanded concept are shown side by side.

Table 13.1 summarizes all information available and integrates global U.S. exports as defined above in relation to world exports by showing separately world exports of merchandise for the period 1955 to 1994, U.S. domestic exports (BOT data in the traditional sense) of nonmilitary merchandise for the same years, the same data adjusted for foreign-controlled U.S. exports from 1974 forward in the revised column, their relevant shares in world trade and, finally, merchandise exports of U.S. Mofas. A final consolidation, imbedded in the "Global U.S. Share," mirrors actual American control over world trade.

Data up to 1974 (in brackets) reflect unadjusted U.S. domestic exports, as the extent of foreign control over the same could not be established for prior years. They are thus exaggerated and do not reflect the actual U.S. share as defined—a fact that has to be remembered when analyzing trends. Starting with 1974, foreign control can be quantified and establishes the fact that 23 to 24 percent of those exports have been in the hands of foreigners since then, and most likely were before that date, already. This effectively reduces the world trade share controlled by U.S. capital from the home country by three percentage points to between 8 and 9 percent, yet leaving it remarkably steady at this level from that base year forward.

While the development of the traditional U.S. trade share is subject to a certain ambivalence as pointed out in the introductory comments, these data do indeed substantiate the claim of a reduced U.S. trade position for at least the last 25 years, but for different reasons. One is the share reduction documented for the traditional BOT trade in relation to the world, but now fortified by the foreign control exerted over U.S. domestic exports.

U.S. affiliates add an exciting dimension to this discussion. Their growth in relation to world exports took them from a market share of 9.4 percent in 1957 to 10.6 percent in 1991. While the data are not entirely comparable, as will be explained below, the rather modest appearance of their performance takes on different meaning when compared to other pieces of information.

One is the fact that affiliate exports have gained world trade share, while U.S. domestic exports have languished or even declined depending on which interpretation of the data is preferred.

More important, Mofa exports compared to total U.S. domestic exports have risen dramatically since 1957, the first year their trading activities were documented. Back then, they reached 54 percent of total unadjusted U.S. merchandise exports. In 1992, that share had advanced to 87 percent.

Even more impressive is the fact that they have exceeded the American-owned share of U.S.-controlled domestic exports in absolute monetary and percentage terms, perhaps as long ago as the late 1960s. It was a feat that is all the more noteworthy, since Mofa exports are structured differently due to the relative unimportance of agricultural and other natural resource commodities in their calculation, which weigh so heavily in U.S. domestic exports, as well as their heavy involvement in the international oil trade.

The data strongly suggest that Mofas have been assigned increasing responsibility for serving export markets including intra-FDI trade or, put differently, they have produced a major substitution effect for U.S. domestic exports. To some extent, this may help to explain why U.S. domestic exports have declined, over the long term as shown in Table 13.1 or, at least, are not growing in world trade. Obviously, the repercussions of these developments reach beyond America's foreign trade sphere alone. They fundamentally also affect the rest of the U.S. economy.

This point was first raised in Chapter 4 dealing with trade between U.S. companies and FDI affiliates. Tables 4.1 and 4.3 summarized all information on this subject, and can now be revisited in a different context. It clearly illustrates Mofas holding a very steady share of all U.S. exports within a very narrow 26 to 27 percent range between 1966 and 1993 (see Table 4.3B). According to Table 13.1, U.S. exports did not grow against world exports for a long time, meaning that total U.S. exports to Mofas also stagnate by the same measure of evaluation. Actually, they have suffered a serious setback by dropping from 3.8 percent of world trade in 1966 to only 2.9 percent in 1993. In a nutshell, U.S. parents are not making maximum use of their Mofas in support of U.S. foreign trade interest, as observed before (see Tables 4.3A and 13.1).

Deepening the argument for a major trade substitution running its course, and to the detriment of American economic interests, is another set of facts surfacing in the discussion of intra-affiliate trade in Chapter 10. Mofa shipments to affiliates in third countries, excluding the United States, have been running not only ahead of U.S. exports to the same in terms of dollars, but also at an accelerating pace since 1966. U.S. exports to Mofas in that year amounted to $7.7 billion against Mofa shipment of $9.5 billion to their peers, or a level 23 percent above U.S. shipments. In 1993, comparable U.S. shipments of $122.8 billion faced Mofa shipments of $156.4 billion, which now exceeded U.S. shipments by 27 percent (see Tables 4.1 and 10.16B).

In the same vein, a comparison of Mofa exports to foreign customers in third countries with parent shipments to the same reveals the following picture: in 1966, U.S. parents shipped $11.5 billion worth of goods to foreign customers versus $86.6 billion of Mofa sales. In 1977, there was still a parent lead of $61.1 billion against a $50.4 billion sales volume by Mofas. In 1982, Mofas surpassed parents for the first time by a small $0.6 billion margin. In 1989, parents were once more in the lead with $129 billion versus Mofa sales of only $100.5 billion. That apparently was the last time they were able to accomplish that feat, because since 1990, Mofas have outsold their parents in this field by small but regular amounts of $2.4, $6.8, $2.1, and $2.0 billion (1990 to 1993) (see Tables 4.6 and 8.8).

Despite their rapid growth, Mofa exports were seemingly unable to prevent a decline in the global U.S. share of world trade, as newly defined. Revised U.S. domestic exports available from 1974 forward combined with affiliate data document a global U.S. share loss from 28 to 20 percent at present. Under the hypothetical assumption that the foreign element in U.S. exports accounted for the same 3 percent share of world trade that it did in later years, the U.S. global share reduction may more realistically be closer to 3 to 4 percentage points instead of the nominal eight points shown in Table 13.1.

Even this picture may be more deceptive than real. Factors contributing to the appearance of an affiliate decline include improvements in the statistical material published, which gradually progressed from undifferentiated sales of goods and services in the early days to a separate accounting for goods and services later on. Mofa data started to appear with the 1966 census, thus covering practically all years shown, but relate to sales of goods and services until 1977, when actual shipment data appeared for the first time for transactions with the United States. The difference between sales and shipments can be phenomenal, as discussed in a different context. In this year alone, it amounted to $55.6 billion or 4.9 percent of world trade, indicating the potential for vastly distorted trade volumes and associated shares before that date. For a realistic evaluation of the global U.S. trade share, 1977 is, therefore, a better base year to use than 1974 which is blown out of proportion by the export sales of oil affiliates after OPEC. Granting this minor concession mitigates the semblance of a major U.S. trade debacle.

In addition, there is also the element of changing finishing stages in exports discussed before and again below. Looking over this list of potential distortion factors in the period before 1977 permits the conclusion that America's global trade share may have been much more stable than suggested by the somewhat superficial impressions generated by Table 13.1.

Uncovering the ambiguities introduced by a gradually evolving database leaves the strong possibility of another major revision for the global American trade share. In earlier chapters, it was pointed out how affiliate exports to the United States reported on a sales basis in the early years had to be adjusted for actual shipments to bring them into line with official U.S. merchandise imports. This resulted in a strongly downward revision of values, as illustrated by the above data for 1977 and thereafter. But affiliate exports to other countries are still reported on the basis of sales and shipments being equal, despite the U.S. experience. How realistic this is will only be determined after the DOC has done more research into the question. If adjustments become necessary here, they can only result in lower U.S. global trade shares, not higher ones. All of these comments and observations are pertinent to the next point as well.

EXPORT DEVELOPMENT BY MAJOR INDUSTRY

Exports by major industrial sector for the whole world and the United States are available for the years 1965 and 1970 to 1993 from U.S. and UN statistics. A common SITC (Standard Industrial Trade Classification) code makes both sources directly comparable. The same cannot be said for affiliate information that was compiled from databases following a different classification, and which had to be adjusted in some areas to correspond more closely with UN data.

While not totally identical in all cases, the data are now reaching a degree of compatibility that makes it possible to draw valid pictures for major industry segments as shown in Tables 13.2 through 13.7. The development of the six product groups reflects the influence of internal and external factors like structural changes in world demand, price fluctuations and inflation, foreign direct investment, the growth of competitive industries, shifts in the ratios of finished/unfinished products traded, politics, and last but not least, the fluctuations of the U.S. dollar. While it is impossible to measure the impact of each on U.S. trade developments in the context of this study, major developments are pointed out where they can be documented.

The dollar's exchange fluctuations, for instance, is a typical example of one such major influence for the whole investigation period. The dollar was steady until 1971, fell for most of the 1970s, experienced a strong revival during the first half of the 1980s, declined after 1985, then oscillated in the years until now. The decline of the U.S. position in global trade shown in Table 13.1 could be as much due to the oscillations of its own currency as to competitive machinations or the alleged loss of technological leadership which are so often cited. On the other hand, the same currency movements influencing U.S. trade interests negatively at home have had the exactly opposite effect on subsidiary trade data as long as their accounting base is a foreign currency. Oil affiliates are largely excepted here, because much of their business is conducted in U.S. dollars.

GROUP I: FOOD, BEVERAGES, AND TOBACCO

The share development of traditional U.S. exports in total world trade of food items, live animals, beverages, and tobacco (SITC, Rev. 2, Rev. 3, 0, and 1) looks quite satisfactory on the surface.

The first impression of a high and steady U.S. trade performance is deceptive, as the bulk of this trade apparently used to be in the hands of foreigners until the beginning of the 1990s. Adjusting the data for this factor cuts the true American share down to half, or even much less. The "revised" column excludes food and kindred products, groceries and related, farm product raw materials shipped abroad by foreign-owned U.S. enterprises, and thus represents the true American-controlled part of this trade, which now reaches only about 5 to 7 percent of world exports instead of the 10 to 16 percent previously seen.

Adding U.S.-owned affiliate exports of foods, beverages, tobacco, etc., raises the global U.S. trade share from 5 to 10 percent in the end, mainly due to the fact that exports from the United States return increasingly into domestic hands. With affiliate trade also on the upswing, a growing global market share for U.S. companies is emerging in a field that is, and should be, of primary concern to a nation blessed with an abundance of agricultural goods.

Unfortunately, this is not all good news. Group I products had a 16.6 percent share in world trade in 1965, but only 8.6 percent in 1993. The group's share in domestic U.S. BOP exports developed more or less in the same direction from 15 percent in 1974 to 9 percent in 1993. While the steady-to-improving global U.S. share performance in this sector is a commendable achievement, it is a negative factor of sorts for the country's overall trade position, because it reflects a solid-to-improving U.S. share in a trade sector of rapidly declining global importance.

Of 1989 Mofa exports in this category, 83 percent came from food and related items (roughly split between bakery goods and beverages) and all other. Tobacco products accounted for another 15 percent. Europe accounted for 84 percent of Mofa exports of food products, with the Netherlands in the lead, followed by Ireland, Belgium, and France (see Table 13.2).

GROUP II: CRUDE MATERIALS (EXCEPT FUELS), OILS, FATS, ETC.

The second major product group covered by UN statistics under the above heading (SITC, Rev. 2, Rev. 3, 2, and 4) is one where U.S. BOP exports held a significant and very steady world trade share between 1970 and 1993 of 15 to 18 percent. Revising these domestic exports to reflect actual U.S. control, however, leads to the conclusion that since the beginning of the 1980s, foreign business interests dominated this sector, which includes mining (excluding coal), agricultural, forestry and fishing, and metals and minerals. A brief reversal lasting from 1988 to 1990 held the promise of U.S. interests recapturing a better than 60 percent share of those exports, but the upward movement could not be sustained. The American controlled share of Group II in the U.S. BOP exports has recovered to around 8 percent of the sector's world volume, but is still down from the 12 to 13 percent held during the late 1970s. Combined with weak and declining affiliate shares of 2 to 3 percent, or only one-third of the U.S. level, it produces a stagnant global U.S. share of around 11 to 12 percent at this moment. This represents a global share reduction of about 25 percent against the position held during the 1970s (see Table 13.3).

Group II products accounted for 12.9 percent of world exports in 1965, but dropped to only 4.3 percent in 1993, leading to a situation completely

TABLE 13.2. Export Group I: Food, Live Animals, Beverages, and Tobacco ($ billion)

Year	World Exports	U.S. Exports BOP	%	Revised	%	U.S. Affil.	%	"Global U.S. Share"
1965	$31	$4.5	14.5	N/A	N/A	$0.5	1.7	(16.2)%
1970	41	5.1	12.4	N/A	N/A	0.8	1.9	(14.3)
1971	45	5.1	11.3	N/A	N/A	0.9	2.1	(13.4)
1972	54	6.6	12.2	N/A	N/A	1.1	2.0	(14.2)
1973	78	12.9	16.5	N/A	N/A	1.3	1.7	(18.2)
1974	95	15.2	16.0	$3.1	3.3	1.5	1.6	4.9
1975	104	16.8	16.2	N/A	N/A	1.6	1.5	N/A
1976	112	17.2	15.4	N/A	N/A	N/A	N/A	N/A
1977	127	15.9	12.5	3.4	2.7	3.7	2.9	5.6
1978	146	20.5	14.0	4.4	3.0	N/A	N/A	N/A
1979	174	24.5	14.1	1.6	0.9	N/A	N/A	N/A
1980	201	30.3	15.1	10.5	5.2	N/A	N/A	N/A
1981	200	33.1	16.5	9.4	4.7	N/A	N/A	N/A
1982	188	26.9	14.4	3.3	1.8	6.0	3.2	5.0
1983	184	26.9	14.6	6.1	3.3	N/A	N/A	N/A
1984	185	27.2	14.6	4.1	2.2	N/A	N/A	N/A
1985	178	22.2	12.5	1.6	0.9	N/A	N/A	N/A
1986	203	20.1	9.9	2.8	1.4	N/A	N/A	N/A
1987	225	22.7	10.1	11.3	5.0	N/A	N/A	N/A
1988	254	30.9	12.1	13.4	5.3	N/A	N/A	N/A
1989	267	35.2	13.2	14.4	5.4	11.6	4.3	9.7
1990	294	36.4	12.4	18.9	6.4	N/A	N/A	N/A
1991	305	36.3	11.9	20.7	6.8	N/A	N/A	N/A
1992	333	40.9	12.3	23.8	7.1	N/A	N/A	N/A
1993	321	40.4	12.6	21.7	6.8	N/A	N/A	N/A

Sources: World Trade by Commodity Classes: *UN Statistical Yearbook*, 1975, pp. 438-485; 1979-80, pp. 452-475; 1983-84, pp. 904-931; 1987, pp. 628-659; 37th Issue, pp. 882-913; 39th Issue, pp. 822-853. *Monthly Bulletin of Statistics*, May 1990, pp. 260-303; May 1991, pp. 260-308; May 1995, pp. 278-33. U.S. data for the years 1980-88: *Statistical Abstract of the U.S.*, 1990, pp. 811-2; 1989: 1991, pp. 811-12. 1992-93, *U.S. DOC, U.S. Exports by 2-digit SITC Product Groups*, 1983-93. Affiliate data: *SOCB*, October 1970, p. 20, (1965); August 1975, pp. 27-29, (1966-73); February 1977, pp. 32-39, (1973-75). *U.S. Direct Investment Abroad*, 1977, pp. 319-353; 1982, pp. 235-282; 1989, pp. 191-256. Data on foreign-controlled U.S. exports: *SOCB*, May 1976, p. 42; May 1981, p. 47-9; November 1983, p. 24; December 1984, p. 30; November 1985, p. 40; October 1986, pp. 35-6; May 1988, p. 65; July 1989, p. 118; July 1990, pp. 134-5; July 1991, pp. 82-3; May 1993, p. 100; May 1995, pp. 74-5.

TABLE 13.3. Export Group II: Crude Materials ($ billion)

Year	World Exports	U.S. Exports				U.S. Affil.	%	"Global U.S. Share"
		BOP	%	Revised	%			
1965	$24	$3.3	13.8	N/A	N/A	$2.3e	9.0e	(23.3)%
1970	33	5.1	15.5	N/A	N/A	3.4	10.3	(25.8)
1971	34	4.9	14.4	N/A	N/A	3.0	8.8	(23.2)
1972	39	5.5	14.1	N/A	N/A	2.5	6.4	(20.5)
1973	58	9.1	15.7	N/A	N/A	3.3	5.7	(21.4)
1974	75	12.4	16.5	8.4	11.2	4.1	5.5	16.7
1975	66	10.7	16.2	N/A	N/A	3.5	5.3	N/A
1976	76	11.9	15.6	N/A	N/A	N/A	N/A	N/A
1977	84	14.2	16.9	9.6	11.9	4.7	5.6	17.5
1978	93	16.8	18.1	11.3	12.7	N/A	N/A	N/A
1979	121	22.3	18.4	14.2	12.4	N/A	N/A	N/A
1980	138	25.7	18.6	10.6	7.7	N/A	N/A	N/A
1981	126	22.7	18.0	6.7	5.3	N/A	N/A	N/A
1982	112	20.8	18.6	7.5	6.7	4.4	3.9	10.6
1983	113	20.0	17.8	8.4	7.4	N/A	N/A	N/A
1984	124	22.2	17.8	10.8	8.7	N/A	N/A	N/A
1985	117	18.2	15.7	7.6	6.5	N/A	N/A	N/A
1986	120	18.3	15.4	7.3	6.1	N/A	N/A	N/A
1987	142	21.5	15.1	9.8	6.9	N/A	N/A	N/A
1988	167	26.8	16.0	16.4	9.8	N/A	N/A	N/A
1989	177	28.3	16.0	16.4	9.3	4.9	2.8	12.1
1990	175	28.2	16.1	16.9	9.7	N/A	N/A	N/A
1991	163	26.6	16.3	13.6	8.3	N/A	N/A	N/A
1992	171	27.2	15.9	13.3	7.8	N/A	N/A	N/A
1993	161	26.1	16.2	13.0	8.1	N/A	N/A	N/A

Note: e = estimate.
Sources: See Table 13.2.

different from that in Group I, inasmuch as U.S. business interests are facing an actual loss of position in a strongly declining world market.

In basic materials (trade represented by Tables 13.2 and 13.3), the overall domestic American position appears to be on the decline against world trade with a share going from 17.2 percent in 1974 to 14.0 percent in 1993. Growth of U.S. control over domestic exports of both groups combined has risen from 22 percent in 1974 to 53 percent in 1993, which translates into a modest share gain in this world market from 6.8 percent in 1974 to 7.3 percent in 1993.

Such superficially positive aspects are of little consequence, as Group II's share in world trade has also declined from 9 percent in 1974 to 4 percent in 1993, resulting in the true American position in the combined world market to slip from the 10 percent level in 1974 to only 7 percent in 1993. For the investigation at hand, it can be concluded that the American position in world merchandise trade is not served well by developments in this combined sector.

Group I and II accounted for 30 percent of total world trade in 1965, but fell to only 13 percent in 1993. In a similar move, the same groups fell from 29 percent in 1965 to 15 percent in total 1993 U.S. exports, broadly reflecting the trend of the world market. The data emphasize the competitive importance of the United States in world trade of primary products. But the relatively strong performance of U.S.-controlled exports in sectors which are anything but high-tech, produce low value-added, and are of sharply reduced importance in world trade besides, should be a matter of concern. Known as "Leontieff's Paradox" after the scholar that first pointed out this peculiar aspect of America's trade, the phenomenon has been familiar for the last three decades (Leontieff, 1968).

GROUP III: MINERAL FUELS AND RELATED MATERIALS

The third export group comprising mineral fuels (oil, coal, gas), lubricants, and related products (SITC, Rev. 2, Rev. 3, 3) is one where small, but steady U.S. domestic exports and world trade shares of about 3 to 4 percent can be observed.

Such modest trade performance of the U.S. proper in world exports is to be expected from a heavy net importer of vital energy resources. What is less self-evident is the fact that even in this industry known for America's technological lead, there still is a rather visible foreign participation controlling roughly one-third of U.S. exports. After revision of total U.S. exports of petroleum and related products for foreign business groups operating in the United States, it appears that American capital controls only 2 to 3 percent of world trade in this group from continental U.S. supply sources, mainly in the form of processed products.

Historically, the United States has controlled substantially more through its network of overseas petroleum affiliates. Their trade shares of up to 60 percent shown during the early 1970s are, of course, totally meaningless as they refer to sales rather than shipments, which for this industry are notoriously far apart. To illustrate this point, the reader is asked to refer to a similar discussion in Chapter 10 dealing with the trade between petroleum Mofas and the United States. Table 10.5 reveals Mofa sales of $70.9 billion exceeding actual shipments by $54.2 billion, or a factor of 3:1, in 1977. Similar data for 1982 and 1989 show more moderate discrepancies, but sales still exceeded shipments by 36 percent in 1982, and 29 percent in 1989. If similar gaps exist for the affiliate trade with third countries, there is much room for error in assessing the true American trade share prior to 1977. What is a real fact, though, is America's actual global share loss from 21.5 to 13.7 percent between 1977 and 1989, with all data measured in common terms of shipments.

The sharp drop originated with the birth of OPEC, as reported earlier, and is linked to the loss of the Saudi oil concessions in 1980. Reduction of the U.S. position in the huge energy trade sector from an estimated 25 to 30 percent during the early 1970s to merely 14 percent or even less for now represents one of the most dramatic upheavals in international business history. Fortunately, it occurred in a market that also fell vis-à-vis world trade, or the damage to America's global trade position would be more serious.

The energy trade's volatility is demonstrated by the following information. Its 1965 share of world trade stood at 9.6 percent. That was six years before the first OPEC crisis. At the time of the second OPEC price increase during the late 1970s, this share increased to 24 percent before settling back to a 8.6 percent in 1993 (see Table 13.4).

In absolute dollar amounts, world petroleum exports stood at slightly less than half a trillion dollars during the early 1980s before taking a nosedive to $261 billion in 1986. Despite a 20 percent recovery since then, the present volume of oil exports is still one-third below those peak years. By comparison, the situation may be more comforting to the energy users as of now, but for the industry's balance sheets and profits it must be almost like total annihilation. Considering the small number of big players here, the world may face another round of concerted activity in the near future just for the purpose of improving the industry's economic stature.

Such erratic movements of the energy trade sector, combined with the calamitous decline of the global U.S. share, lend credence to the weaker global U.S. position in world trade projected for the period 1970 to 1993 in Table 13.1.

Another minor factor contributed to the weakening of the true American-controlled export performance in this sector: the loss of sales of oil and gas field services that amounted to less than one percent of all exports in 1977 (1977 Benchmark Survey, p. 319), 1982 (1982 Benchmark Survey, p. 226), and 1989 (1989 Benchmark Survey, p. 191). These services are excluded from exports after 1977 but are included in all previous years. According to a report on affiliate oil exports, this position was singled out,

TABLE 13.4. Export Group III: Mineral Fuels and Related Materials ($ billion)

Year	World Exports	U.S. Exports				U.S. Affil.	%	"Global U.S. Share"
		BOP	%	Revised	%			
1965	$18	$0.9	5.0	N/A	N/A	$8.2*	45.6	(50.6%)
1970	29	1.6	5.5	N/A	N/A	13.1	45.2	(50.7)
1971	37	1.5	4.1	N/A	N/A	18.1	48.9	(53.0)
1972	43	1.6	3.7	N/A	N/A	21.6	50.2	(53.9)
1973	63	1.7	2.7	N/A	N/A	36.9	58.6	(61.3)
1974	168	3.4	2.0	$3.0	1.8	95.4	56.8	58.5
1975	169	4.5	2.7	N/A	N/A	84.9	50.2	N/A
1976	200	4.2	2.1	N/A	N/A	N/A	N/A	N/A
1977	221	4.2	1.9	3.6	1.6	44.0	19.9	21.5
1978	223	3.9	1.7	3.1	1.4	N/A	N/A	N/A
1979	334	5.6	1.7	4.5	1.3	N/A	N/A	N/A
1980	482	8.0	1.7	7.0	1.5	N/A	N/A	N/A
1981	474	10.3	2.2	8.4	1.8	N/A	N/A	N/A
1982	431	12.8	3.0	11.3	2.6	72.6	16.8	19.4
1983	385	9.6	2.5	8.2	2.1	N/A	N/A	N/A
1984	377	9.3	2.5	8.0	2.1	N/A	N/A	N/A
1985	362	10.0	2.8	9.1	2.5	N/A	N/A	N/A
1986	261	8.1	3.1	6.3	2.4	N/A	N/A	N/A
1987	280	7.7	2.8	6.1	2.2	N/A	N/A	N/A
1988	263	8.2	3.1	6.5	2.5	N/A	N/A	N/A
1989	292	9.9	3.4	7.7	2.6	32.5	11.1	13.7
1990	348	12.2	3.5	9.1	2.7	N/A	N/A	N/A
1991	325	12.3	3.8	8.9	2.7	N/A	N/A	N/A
1992	324	11.2	3.5	7.8	2.4	N/A	N/A	N/A
1993	319	9.8	3.1	6.5	2.0	N/A	N/A	N/A

Notes: *1966 data. The exports were adjusted downward for sales of oil and gas field services, 1977: $0.5 billion; 1982: $0.4 billion; 1989: $0.3 billion.
Sources: See Table 13.2.

without giving any specific data, as one item that fell sharply because of cutbacks in worldwide exploration and development activity (*SOCB*, June 1988, p. 96).

GROUP IV: CHEMICALS

The fourth major export group broken out in UN trade statistics and covering chemicals (SITC, Rev. 2, Rev. 3,5) and related products provides a high degree of compatibility for UN, U.S., and affiliate data.

U.S. BOP exports account for a steady world trade share around 13 to 14 percent. Correction for the foreign control factor lowers this average to the 10 percent level for American-owned businesses, which seems to be in a long-term decline, while foreign business interests are slowly gaining. During the early 1990s, their share amounted to between 30 to 35 percent of domestic exports compared to 15 percent in 1974.

U.S. overseas affiliate exports seem to be holding their own in world trade with export volumes coming close to total U.S. exports, and definitely exceeding the U.S.-controlled exports from the U.S. territory proper. What limited evidence is available seems to support the impression that trade is shifting away from U.S.-based exports into the hands of overseas Mofas. On balance, the U.S.-controlled portion of the global trade appears to hold steady at about 22 to 23 percent.

Putting these data into perspective is the fact that chemicals have expanded their share in total world trade modestly from 6.5 to 9 percent between 1965 and 1993. By just maintaining a solid global position in this group, an important U.S. role in this vital market and participation in its expansion is assured.

A firm global U.S. share in a growing segment of world trade also speaks favorably for the competitive status of U.S. companies. Even though it cannot fully compensate for competitive weakness in the other markets discussed so far, it goes a long way in preventing further erosion of America's position in overall world trade. The other encouraging message here is a solid American performance in high-tech fields represented by pharmaceutical products where the United States is a recognized leader, as well as plastics, synthetics, and basic industrial chemicals (see Table 13.5).

GROUP V: MACHINERY AND TRANSPORT EQUIPMENT

The fifth export group that shows a high degree of comparability for UN, U.S., and affiliate data is that for electric and nonelectric machinery and transportation equipment (SITC, Rev. 2, Rev. 3, 7). U.S. domestic exports include commercial aircraft which are not produced by subsidiary industries.

The gradual decline of total domestic U.S. exports vis-à-vis world trade in this category since the 1970s may have come to an end, but even though it is too early to call the 1993 export results a trend reversal at least it is an encouraging sign. A clear and less encouraging sign, however, is the unmistakable advance of foreign exporters here. American businesses accounted for over 90 percent of U.S. exports of this group during the 1970s and most

TABLE 13.5. Export Group IV: Chemicals ($ billion)

Year	World Exports	U.S. Exports BOP	%	Revised	%	U.S. Affil.	%	"Global U.S. Share"
1965	$12	$2.4	20.0	N/A	N/A	$1.1	9.2	(29.2%)
1970	22	3.8	17.2	N/A	N/A	2.4	10.9	(28.1)
1971	24	3.8	15.8	N/A	N/A	2.6	10.8	(26.6)
1972	29	4.1	14.1	N/A	N/A	3.4	11.7	(25.8)
1973	40	5.7	14.3	N/A	N/A	5.0	12.5	(26.8)
1974	64	8.8	13.8	7.5	11.7	8.3	13.0	24.7
1975	61	8.7	14.3	N/A	N/A	7.7	12.6	N/A
1976	69	9.9	14.3	N/A	N/A	N/A	N/A	N/A
1977	78	10.8	13.8	9.9	12.6	8.7	11.2	23.8
1978	96	13.6	14.2	12.5	13.0	N/A	N/A	N/A
1979	126	18.7	14.8	17.4	13.8	N/A	N/A	N/A
1980	141	20.7	14.7	18.6	13.2	N/A	N/A	N/A
1981	136	21.1	15.5	16.0	11.8	N/A	N/A	N/A
1982	131	19.9	15.2	15.2	11.6	17.4	13.3	24.9
1983	136	19.7	14.4	15.1	11.1	N/A	N/A	N/A
1984	146	22.3	15.3	17.2	11.8	N/A	N/A	N/A
1985	152	21.3	14.0	16.6	10.9	N/A	N/A	N/A
1986	178	22.2	12.5	17.4	9.8	N/A	N/A	N/A
1987	214	25.6	12.0	19.6	9.2	N/A	N/A	N/A
1988	254	31.3	12.3	23.6	9.3	N/A	N/A	N/A
1989	264	36.5	13.8	27.2	10.3	31.5	11.9	22.2
1990	298	38.9	13.1	28.2	9.4	N/A	N/A	N/A
1991	301	42.0	14.0	30.4	10.1	N/A	N/A	N/A
1992	333	44.7	13.4	32.2	9.7	N/A	N/A	N/A
1993	330	45.9	13.9	32.9	10.0	N/A	N/A	N/A

Sources: See Table 13.2.

of the 1980s. During the beginning of the 1990s, that share eroded to around 83 percent. The decline becomes visible in the share reduction of the "revised" U.S. export column from around 17 to 18 percent in 1974 to 12 percent during the early 1990s.

While the figures are telling one story, its meaning is not fully conclusive and requires more detailed research, because an increasing portion of the trade between the United States and Mofas is in unfinished form and subject to transfer pricing to boot, as indicated before.

In 1966, exports of manufactures for further processing reached 51 percent (parents, 53 percent) of all U.S. exports to affiliates. Both ratios had increased to 81 and 80 percent, respectively, by 1989 (see Table 13.8). As nothing is known about transfer pricing mechanisms for these goods, their finishing status, or the ratio of unfinished products in total world trade, it is difficult to assess the relevance of this information.

There is good reason to believe that the U.S. position, with regard to semi-finished merchandise trades, was unique among all competitors in the earlier years. The Japanese as major contestants in this group did not get their U.S. and European assembly and production operations for cars off the ground until the early to mid-1980s, which made their trade share larger because it was largely shipped ready for resale. Similar is the situation of the European car and machinery manufacturers, who still ship much of their products to the U.S. in finished form (see Table 13.6).

What is more important, the group's share in world trade expanded from 24.7 percent in 1965 to 37.5 percent in 1993, establishing it as the largest and most dynamic force behind the development of total international trade and commerce. While the global U.S. share in this category appears to be soft, it is not justified to declare it a real problem for the reasons given above. Further research is needed to establish a firm basis for informed judgement. But there can be little doubt that here is another key area where U.S. global trade interests may nominally have lost up to six percentage points in total world trade since 1974.

Whatever the real loss amounts to after all missing information can be provided, any decline in an area where U.S. technology used to be the world leader is a very worrisome development, and a direct reflection on the country's ability to demonstrate a convincing competitiveness. Areas under pressure include aircraft, watercraft, motor vehicles, and many other types of machinery, including robotics.

GROUP VI: OTHER MANUFACTURED GOODS

The final export group covering other manufactured goods (SITC, Rev. 2, Rev. 3,6 and 8) appears to be another area of concern for America's trade position. This applies not so much to its overall market share which lately appears to return to historic levels, but for the fact that the share of this market under U.S. capital control is in a slow but decisive decline. This observation applies particularly to exports from the U.S. proper, while records of affiliate trade divulge more stability. Earlier research into the trading activities of manufacturing subsidiaries established a much closer correspondence between sales and shipments, suggesting that the total trade history depicted for global American businesses in chemicals,

TABLE 13.6. Export Group V: Machinery and Transport Equipment ($ billion)

Year	World Exports	U.S. Exports				U.S. Affil.	%	"Global U.S. Share"
		BOP	%	Revised	%			
1965	$46	$10.0	21.7	N/A	N/A	$3.5	7.6	(29.3%)
1970	90	17.9	19.9	N/A	N/A	10.5	11.7	(31.6)
1971	104	19.5	20.7	N/A	N/A	12.5	12.0	(32.7)
1972	125	21.5	17.2	N/A	N/A	14.9	11.9	(29.1)
1973	164	27.9	17.0	N/A	N/A	18.6	11.3	(28.3)
1974	206	38.2	18.5	$36.3	17.6	22.1	10.7	28.3
1975	244	45.7	18.7	N/A	N/A	25.6	10.5	N/A
1976	277	49.5	17.8	N/A	N/A	N/A	N/A	N/A
1977	317	51.0	16.1	N/A	N/A	36.8	11.6	N/A
1978	380	60.2	15.8	N/A	N/A	N/A	N/A	N/A
1979	440	71.5	16.3	N/A	N/A	N/A	N/A	N/A
1980	513	84.5	16.5	77.8	15.2	N/A	N/A	N/A
1981	528	95.5	18.1	87.1	16.5	N/A	N/A	N/A
1982	512	87.0	17.0	78.8	15.4	51.4	10.0	25.4
1983	520	82.4	15.8	75.2	14.5	N/A	N/A	N/A
1984	566	89.9	15.9	82.1	14.5	N/A	N/A	N/A
1985	601	94.3	15.7	86.6	14.4	N/A	N/A	N/A
1986	714	95.4	13.3	88.0	12.3	N/A	N/A	N/A
1987	851	110.2	12.7	100.9	11.8	N/A	N/A	N/A
1988	990	135.1	13.6	120.7	12.3	N/A	N/A	N/A
1989	1,058	148.8	14.1	125.0	11.8	109.7	10.4	22.2
1990	1,212	172.5	14.3	142.7	11.8	N/A	N/A	N/A
1991	1,256	187.9	15.0	155.8	12.4	N/A	N/A	N/A
1992	1,361	181.0	13.3	147.6	10.8	N/A	N/A	N/A
1993	1,392	224.9	16.2	191.9	13.8	N/A	N/A	N/A

Sources: See Table 13.2.

machinery and transport equipment, and other manufactures is more realistic than for the oil industry, for example (see Table 13.7).

Total BOP exports from the United States reveal a lackluster performance by oscillating in the 6 to 8 percent range of world trade in this category since the beginning of the 1970s. But, at that time, 88 percent of this trade was in American hands versus only between 65 to 70 percent at the end of the period. The net effect of these two trends is a 2 to 3 percent world market share decline in this product class for the continental American side alone, after adjustment of U.S. exports shipments of primary and fabricated metals, other manufactures, wholesale exports of durable and

TABLE 13.7. Export Group VI: Other Manufactures ($ billion)

Year	World Exports	U.S. Exports				U.S. Affil.	%	"Global U.S. Share"
		BOP	%	Revised	%			
1965	$51	$4.9	9.6	N/A	N/A	$6.4	12.5	(22.2%)
1970	91	7.7	8.5	N/A	N/A	12.9	14.1	(22.6)
1971	98	7.2	7.3	N/A	N/A	15.1	15.4	(22.8)
1972	117	8.1	6.9	N/A	N/A	17.8	15.2	(22.1)
1973	159	11.1	7.0	N/A	N/A	21.9	13.8	(25.8)
1974	213	16.5	7.7	$14.3	6.7	29.8	14.0	20.7
1975	213	16.6	7.8	N/A	N/A	33.6	15.8	N/A
1976	240	17.8	7.4	N/A	N/A	N/A	N/A	N/A
1977	276	18.6	6.7	17.1	6.2	30.2	10.9	17.1
1978	335	21.1	6.3	N/A	N/A	N/A	N/A	N/A
1979	412	26.9	6.5	24.7	6.0	N/A	N/A	N/A
1980	481	38.9	8.1	34.1	7.1	N/A	N/A	N/A
1981	456	37.7	8.3	32.1	7.0	N/A	N/A	N/A
1982	428	33.0	7.7	28.0	6.5	63.0	14.7	21.2
1983	429	30.4	7.1	26.0	6.1	N/A	N/A	N/A
1984	456	31.1	6.8	26.7	5.9	N/A	N/A	N/A
1985	471	29.8	6.3	24.3	5.2	N/A	N/A	N/A
1986	564	31.2	5.5	27.4	4.9	N/A	N/A	N/A
1987	681	37.3	5.5	30.6	4.5	N/A	N/A	N/A
1988	790	48.2	6.1	33.4	4.2	N/A	N/A	N/A
1989	862	59.9	7.0	40.3	4.7	94.5	11.0	15.7
1990	971	70.9	7.3	51.8	5.3	N/A	N/A	N/A
1991	995	76.9	7.6	54.6	5.5	N/A	N/A	N/A
1992	1,083	84.9	7.8	61.9	5.7	N/A	N/A	N/A
1993	1,074	93.5	8.7	60.5	5.6	N/A	N/A	N/A

Sources: See Table 13.2.

nondurable products, and other industry shipments for the share held by foreign companies operating in the United States.

Fortunately, Mofas produce twice the trade volume of their U.S. counterparts–a distinction they share with their sister companies in the mineral fuel group, but they were equally unable to hold their own in world trade. It has to be feared that American interests have actually lost around five percentage points of their world market share in this category which, in turn, contributes to America's overall decline in its global trade position documented in Table 13.1.

The trade group as a whole is important for the development of world trade. Not only because of its size but also due to its share growth from 27 to 29 percent of total between 1965 and 1993 which, once again, puts the American-controlled export achievements very much into the same light as seen in the previous merchandise category. But, unlike the machinery and transport equipment, it is not believed that a significant portion of this product group has been switched to materials requiring further processing. The registered global American decline in this group is, therefore, another problematic situation, because it suggests a solid loss proposition in what is, after all, an important growth market besides harboring truly high-tech product segments.

SHIFTS IN U.S.-CONTROLLED TRADE

Table 13.1 furnish indisputable proof of a general shift in U.S.-controlled exports away from U.S. shores into the hands of FDI affiliates located abroad.

Most likely since the mid-1960s, Mofa exports have outstripped those exports from the United States, creating a wavy pattern of opening and closing gaps between the two, but never seriously challenging the global trade dominance of Mofas. Assuming 1957 parent exports to have stood at 75 percent of all U.S. exports, as documented for later years, would have resulted in affiliate exports reaching two-thirds of their parent volume for that year. Even though 1966 parent data are not available, affiliate exports may have surpassed those of their parents for that year, already. At any rate, affiliate exports were about double those of their parents in 1977, aided by energy prices, before settling back to margins of 58 percent over and above their parent exports in 1982 and 26 percent in 1989.

Measured in comparison to total BOP merchandise exports excluding military goods from the United States, Mofa exports developed from 56 percent in 1957 to 83 percent in 1966, 114 percent in 1977, 101 percent in 1982 and, finally, only 78 percent in 1989. It is a superficially comforting impression that is immediately dispelled by the new measuring standard proposed for this discussion, whereby capital control becomes the mark of true trade ownership. Now Mofa figures reach the same 56 percent level against U.S. exports in the base year of 1957, but then advance to 83 percent in 1966, 142 percent in both 1977 and 1982, 102 percent in 1989, and 114 to 116 percent for 1990 to 1993.

The seesaw pattern is partly due to the distorting influence of the oil affiliates, which are so prominent in the U.S. FDI picture. Another major factor, without doubt, was the dollar's exchange value which began to slip drastically in 1985, giving U.S. exports a competitive boost in world markets. But paradoxically, the trend may have begun with the rising dollar between 1980 and 1985, as it made U.S. exports more profitable than those from affiliates whose currencies were under pressure. The statements' seeming contradiction is also evidence of a previously stated opinion that global U.S. trade may increasingly become a tool of centrally directed corporate and government trade policies and strategies.

A list of other elements to be considered as causes for the changing export ratios definitely should include the accounting techniques employed in measuring affiliate exports. As discussed before in more detail, they are a mixture of export sales and actual shipments for the whole period, which cannot be fully disentangled even for later years, for which improved data are available. For 1982 and following years, they approached actual ship-ment levels, and are thus becoming increasingly relevant to the discussion of their role in world trade (see Table 13.8).

From the trade pictures, assembled Mofas' deputy trade role assigned by parent profit strategies, and manifestly demonstrating substitution of American-based exports, comes into focus. There is also always the other causal factor for the trade inversion over time relating to the frequently cited and deliberately low parent transfer pricing. Such intracompany transactions have the dual effect of lowering U.S. BOP exports, and rela-tively increasing those of the affiliates. Export substitution in a real, physi-cal sense is not necessarily involved, as may be suggested by lowered U.S. export volumes and trade shares, but definitely a growing share of items with lesser upgrading.

Group I and II data may be used as an illustration of this point. Referring to agricultural raw materials and other commodity-type products they show a skewed distribution in favor of subsidiaries that is totally out of line with their reported investment volumes. The affiliate position in world trade stems predominantly from trading activities, not from sale of their own production.

In 1982, for instance, affiliate trade in these two groups exceeded that of their parents by 16 percent, with respective volumes of $11 billion vs. $9.5 billion. In 1974, the ratio had been exactly reversed, with parents exporting twice as much as their subsidiaries: $11.5 billion vs. $5.6 billion. A related factor was the general price decline in exactly those very same commodities represented by Groups I and II, unlike for manufactures. It was probably a major reason why the share of both groups in U.S. exports fell from 29 percent in 1965 to 18 percent in 1989, and further to under 15 percent in 1993.

Lastly, a significant change in the mix between finished and semipro-cessed products took place in America's exports to subsidiaries over the

TABLE 13.8. U.S. Exports to Mofas ($ billion)

Year	Total	For Resale		For Processing		Other	
1. Grand Total							
All U.S. Exports							
1966	$7.7	$3.4	44.2%	$3.1	40.3%	$1.2	15.6%
1977	35.8	20.5	57.3	13.8	38.5	1.6	4.5
1982	52.8	21.0	39.8	27.8	52.7	3.2	6.6
1989	97.5	38.4	39.4	55.9	57.3	3.2	3.3
Parents							
1966	6.3	3.2	50.8	2.5	39.6	0.7	11.1
1977	29.3	18.5	63.1	9.6	32.3	1.2	4.1
1982	44.3	19.4	43.8	22.4	50.6	2.1	4.7
1989	86.1	36.3	42.2	47.7	55.4	2.0	2.3
2. Manufacturing							
All U.S. Exports							
1966	5.3	1.8	34.0	2.7	50.9	0.6	15.1
1977	25.1	12.1	48.2	12.4	49.4	0.7	2.4
1982	34.7	6.6	19.0	26.6	76.7	1.4	4.0
1989	66.5	11.0	16.5	53.9	81.1	1.6	2.4
Parents							
1966	4.3	1.7	39.5	2.3	53.4	0.3	6.5
1977	20.5	11.3	55.1	8.7	42.4	0.5	1.0
1982	28.9	6.3	21.8	21.4	74.0	1.1	3.8
1989	57.7	10.7	18.5	46.1	79.9	0.9	1.6
3. Trade*							
All U.S. Exports							
1966	1.5	1.3	86.7	0.1	6.6	0.1	6.6
1977	8.1	7.5	92.6	0.4	4.9	0.2	2.5
1982	14.1	13.1	92.9	0.5	3.5	0.5	3.5
1989	26.8	25.4	94.8	1.2	4.4	0.2	0.7
Parents							
1966	1.3	1.2	92.3	0.1	7.7	0.1	7.6
1977	7.0	6.5	92.9	0.4	5.7	0.2	1.4
1982	12.8	12.0	93.8	0.5	3.9	0.4	3.1
1989	25.2	24.0	95.2	1.1	4.4	0.2	0.8
4. Grand Total without Trade							
All U.S. Exports							
1966	6.2	2.1	33.8	3.0	48.4	1.1	17.7
1977	27.7	13.0	46.9	13.4	48.4	1.4	4.7
1982	38.7	7.9	20.4	27.3	70.5	2.7	9.0
1989	70.7	13.0	19.3	54.7	77.4	2.2	3.3
Parents							
1966	5.0	1.9	38.0	2.4	48.0	0.6	14.0
1977	22.3	12.0	53.8	9.3	41.7	1.0	4.5
1982	31.5	7.4	23.5	22.0	69.8	1.7	6.7
1989	60.9	12.3	20.2	46.6	76.5	1.1	3.3

Notes: *Includes wholesale and retail for 1966 and 1977; wholesale only for 1982 and 1989.

Sources: Benchmark Survey, 1966, pp. 90-1, 348; 1982, p. 276; 1989, p. 248.

study period, a process which is now practically concluded and, therefore, of lesser importance in the future. Table 13.8 gives a summary view of these developments for the census years 1966 through 1989.

According to these data, exports to affiliates in unfinished form accounted for 40 percent in 1966 and 57 percent in 1989 (see Table 13.8, Grand Total). Included are trade data which exert a strong bias because materials for immediate retail reach around 90 percent for the whole period. Eliminating their atypical influence in the final category of Table 13.8, "Grand Total without Trade," creates a whole new picture shaped mainly by manufacturing. Materials for further processing now are seen to go from 48 percent in 1966 to 77 percent in 1989 on a value basis. What these data say in terms of physical volumes and ratios is not clear as no relevant pricing information is available.

How significant is this point about U.S. trade with Mofas in the international frame of reference? All U.S. exports to these affiliates accounted for 3.8 percent of world exports in 1966, 3.2 percent in 1977, 2.9 percent in 1982, and 3.2 percent in 1989. By a different calculation, those same exports amounted to 26.3 percent of all U.S. exports in 1966, 29.6 percent in 1977, 25 percent in 1982, and 23.8 percent in 1989. Both sets of information indicate a loss of share in total world trade and more pronounced for U.S. exports which, to a large degree, are influenced by the change in the mix toward goods of lesser value-added. The net effect on the U.S. position in world trade is a net reduction of close to one full percentage point. It would be a superficial loss, however, resulting from technical and pricing strategies rather than necessarily from a serious reduction in physical volume needed to support growth in foreign end sales. Once again, a reminder to look beyond export shares and focus on the output of value-added by Mofas as an additional indicator of a nation's status and development trend in the world economy.

Table 13.8 indirectly provides another interesting insight. The "All Other" category references mainly exports of U.S. capital goods to affiliate operations. Their sharp decline in face of a strongly growing FDI stock can only mean a switch from U.S. suppliers to foreign sourcing, in itself perhaps a noteworthy statement about the competitiveness of the American machinery industry.

REVIEW

America's position in world trade can be evaluated on three different levels. First, by measuring the U.S. trade share on the basis of U.S. merchandise exports as reported in the U.S. BOP, which is the traditional definition of a nation's exports. Second, by eliminating foreign controlled exports from the U.S. BOP to get U.S.-controlled domestic exports and related world trade shares. Third, by adding Mofa exports to this refined set of BOP data the true picture of the American controlled share in world trade emerges.

The advantage of using this latter approach is a much more accurate measure of national share in world trade than can be provided by the conventional accounting method based on geographical origin. In order to get additional perspective on the subject matter, world exports are broken down into five broad product categories employed primarily by UN and U.S. databanks. By blending this information mix, the general notion of a universal decline in America's foreign trade, referred to in the opening statement of this chapter, appears in a new light.

First of all, it confirms an apparent weakening of the U.S. trade position, but from a much broader perspective than demonstrated by the U.S. BOP data alone. Second, it helps to pinpoint areas of U.S. strength. It then raises the question of how FDI activities have affected the nation's trade position through the dual effect of an emerging network of foreign affiliates and structural changes in intra-affiliate trade shifting increasingly to raw materials and semifinished products. All of which leads to the key question of how meaningful the demonstration of a nominal decline in the U.S. position really is, especially in the absence of detailed information about similar changes in the composition of overall world trade.

The key point to make here is that international trade share development may be relevant only with simultaneous information about the development of a nation's position in global as well as national production and commerce as provided by Chapters 11 and 12. In a different context, it was demonstrated how exports can exist independently of direct investment until a critical market mass is reached, which requires protective direct investments for competitive or political reasons. Once established, direct investments fundamentally change the nature of related trade from finished to semiprocessed goods and materials, which can generate the mistaken impression of a nation's competitive decline against other international traders. In the absence of complete and detailed international data on the subject, only partial and cautious situation assessments are possible which may be summarized as follows.

Between 1955 and 1993, U.S. exports defined in the traditional BOP sense have lost nominal share in world trade by declining from an all-time high of 17 percent in 1957 to 12 percent during the early 1990s. Most of the decline occurred before the mid-1970s with a very stable 11 to 12 percent level maintained ever since (see Table 13.1).

Data for the U.S.-controlled portion of this trade indicate a reduced but very stable situation at the 8 to 9 percent level between 1974 and 1993, reflecting the situation observed for overall U.S. exports. In other words, about three percent of world trade emanating from the United States is not controlled by U.S. but foreign business interests. These three percentage points translate to between 20 and 25 percent of all continental U.S. exports (see Table 13.1).

Global U.S. exports, or the combined trade volume controlled by American ownership across the world, has slipped nominally from 28 percent in 1974 to 19 to 20 percent during the beginning of the 1990s. This picture is admittedly exaggerated because of trade accounting practices for the affiliate sector during the early years which needed to be revised to match reported Mofa export sales of goods more closely with actual global merchandise trade reported on the basis of actual shipments. This started with the 1977 census, but only for Mofa trade with the United States. The accounting process may now have to be changed in a similar fashion for Mofa trade involving other countries, which still rests on the old formula of sales being equal to shipments. It would most certainly cause deflationary adjustments of Mofa exports, and most of it will stem from the petroleum sector as before.

A further reduction in America's global trade share seems to be inevitable, once more details about the foreign ownership of U.S. parent companies become available. All of the above comments are made on the basis of official U.S. FDI statistics, which do not take such capital participation of an estimated 15 percent of U.S. parents into account. As soon as details on majority-controlled enterprises become known, it will be possible to gauge its impact on the U.S. global trade position more accurately (see Table 13.9).

For the moment, a more realistic estimate for America's true loss should put it into the 2 to 3 percent range for the whole period, after considering all the factors affecting its appearance. The purported decline was thus aided by: constant improvements in the definition of affiliate exports narrowing them down from less useful sales data to a more precise measure of actual and comparable shipments, even though only as a partial correction, maintenance of steady shares in world markets of declining importance (Groups I and II), loss of business through external and uncontrollable factors (Group III), an inability to maintain market share in growth markets (Groups V and VI), which may be conditioned by the change in the finishing mix of U.S. exports to affiliates, and other factors. A truly positive American performance could only be observed in Group IV, chemicals. It is ironic that the soft American performance occurs mainly in

TABLE 13.9. Development of Global U.S. Share in World Trade

Industry Group	Industry Group Share in:						Global U.S. Share in World Trade of Project Group*	
	World Exports		U.S. Exports					
			1977		1989			
	1965	1989	BOP	Rev.	BOP	Rev.	1977	1989
Total	100%	100%	100%	100%	100%	100%	21%	19%
I	17	9	13	3	10	4	6	10
II	13	6	12	8	8	5	18	12
III	10	10	3	3	3	2	22	14
IV	6	9	9	8	10	8	24	22
V	25	35	42	N/A	41	35	27	22
VI	27	28	14	14	17	11	17	16

Notes: *Global refers to U.S.-controlled domestic plus affiliate exports. Revised U.S. data refer to U.S. BOP exports less foreign-controlled exports.

manufactured goods, which happens to be exactly the economic sector that was neglected at home when America turned its attention to the more rapidly growing services industry.

The decline in U.S. BOP export shares translates into a tragic loss of jobs for American workers. If the United States still had the same 17 percent share of world exports flowing from U.S. factories as it held in 1957, its export volume during the early 1990s would be $150 billion larger than it was. Not only would this have taken care of the perennial trade deficits of similar proportions, it would also have meant 3.8 million additional jobs at the ratio of 25,000 jobs for each $1 billion in exports developed by the U.S. Department of Commerce. This calculation for FDI's effect on the U.S. job situation is interesting, because the number of jobs eliminated corresponds so closely to the 5.2 million people employed by Mofas worldwide in the period 1982 through 1993.

METHODOLOGY

As UN export data for world and U.S. exports are classified differently from affiliate data, it became necessary to make certain adjustments in the affiliate data to achieve a better level of comparability. Unfortunately, these changes could not be made for all years due to the lack of details in the affiliate database. The following is a summary of changes effected.

1. Table 13.2 (SITC, Rev. 2, Rev. 3,0 and 1). Included are affiliate exports for agricultural, fisheries, and forestry products plus tobacco for 1977 and 1982. The tobacco products for prior years are included in the "other manufacturing" category for affiliates (see Table 13.7).
2. Table 13.3 (SITC, Rev. 2, Rev. 3,2 and 4) includes affiliate primary metals exports for 1977 and 1982. The same data for prior years are included in the affiliate "other manufacturing" category in Table 13.7.
3. Table 13.7 (SITC, Rev. 2, Rev. 3,6 and 8), referring to all other manufactures, excludes affiliate exports of tobacco for 1977 ($441 million) and 1982 ($1,006 million) and primary metals for 1977 ($1,302 million) and 1982 ($1,573 million). These categories are included for prior years. Affiliate exports of wholesale and, partially also retail establishments, are also included here for all years.
4. Total affiliate exports are stated as sales to "other" foreign accounts up to 1975 including the United States. The 1977 census introduced Mofa shipments to the United States for the first time while exports to other nations continued to include goods and services. The difference for the global trade share because of the service factor is estimated not to exceed 0.2 percent in 1977. From 1982 forward, shipments to the United States and sales of goods only to third countries define actual Mofa merchandise export shipments more accurately than before. The big question overhanging the accuracy of Mofa actual shipments is the government formula of export sales equaling export shipments to third countries. It used to be applied to Mofa business transactions with the United States as well until the 1977 census discovered substantial discrepancies between both values, as discussed previously.

Chapter 14

Synopsis

The second half of the twentieth century opened a historic window of opportunity for the United States. It helped the country to redefine its national purpose and emerge as a very assertive superpower with a clear vision of a new world order under American leadership. It was a major leap forward for a nation that until then had been self-centered and introverted. The United States was a nation occupied with internal consolidation, economic recovery and development, and the realization of the American dream for immigrants.

The period ended a wrenching conflict of the American soul. On one side, the concept of manifest destiny established the nation's god-given mission to bring the American vision of liberty, democratic rights, and the pursuit of individual happiness to a world seemingly devoid of these aspirations. Related proclamations of the Monroe Doctrine and its Roosevelt Corollary provided the United States with the moral justification for getting involved in matters primarily concerning the Western hemisphere, but also beyond. On the other hand, due to its insular location and lack of the necessary logistics, any moral drive to pursue these ideals as a forceful global policy was tempered by the perceived risks involved, in turn fostering a desire to shield the nation by means of self-imposed isolation. The Smoot-Hawley Act of 1930 raised the average U.S. tariff level to over 60 percent at a time when world trade was already sputtering, touching off a wave of protective reciprocity around the world and effectively burying hopes of a return to free trade. Five years later, the Neutrality Act of 1935 sought to further restrict U.S. political, economic, and military involvement with other nations after the experience of World War I, and the growing threat of a new conflagration in its aftermath.

Curiously, it was war that ended this internal conflict only four short years later. Historians still debate whether outside force or political opportunism made the United States enter World War II, but the fact is that America laid out the grand design for its future role with a network of international institutions under its stewardship. International politics would be the domain of the United Nations; the World Bank in conjunction with the Marshall plan would finance the reconstruction of the destroyed nations; the IMF was assigned the supervision of international exchange stability built on the dollar; and GATT would pave the way for free trade.

By design or not, the war was convenient, inasmuch as the United States was challenged to mobilize its vast resources to first defeat its opponents, and then help them rebuild their shattered nations. The latter, and seemingly altruistic step, was a prudent political and economic strategy. It created the Pax Americana: a free world coalition against the common enemy, communism. At the same time, it opened up a mind-boggling economic potential in the newly won spheres of influence. After all, the deeply exhausted nations–friends and former foes alike–belonged to the small circle of highly industrialized nations of their day. This point was certainly not lost on a nation that, at the outset of the war, was still in the clutches of deep economic depression, had the industrial potential to quickly rebuild the free world's economies, and had a history of economic gains after military conquest.

Once gained, the perpetuation of leadership and power demands superiority on practically all fronts–military, scientific, political, economic, etc. Dealing with the latter exclusively, this can be broadly defined as national competitiveness, which is the declared purpose of this present research effort. Investigation of America's economic leadership in the post-World War II period thus dwells on the scrutiny of pertinent developments in the past as the basis for its present position. But can the same research efforts also serve as reliable predictive tools for America's role in future global relations? Rapid changes in the man-made environment clearly point to one fact: progress, however defined, is not a national prerogative. Part of present-day progress is the gradual disappearance of national boundaries, which creates difficulties with the use of clearcut and universally accepted standards of definition, measurement, and interpretation of national roles. Traditional perceptions here are turning out to be ambiguous and thus increasingly useless. What, for instance, is the meaning of the possessive term "American?"

DEFINITIONS

The starting point of this discussion has to be the clarification of the term "American," as used throughout this text. What really does define the American domestic economy? Of all economic activities taking place within the confines of U.S. boundaries, which is the conventionally employed definition? This is very handy, but imprecise in view of the fact that roughly 10 percent or more of U.S. manufacturing is owned and controlled by foreign direct investors, as is more than 20 percent of America's foreign trade, not to mention the billions of dollars invested by foreigners in U.S. public and corporate debt instruments making the country a net debtor to the world. It is quite doubtful that foreign investors would accept any notion of these assets being "American" from an ownership and control point of view. Neither would American businesses accept any serious claim that the huge sums they invested in majority-held overseas manufacturing, trading, and financial facilities represent anything but American property despite their extraterritoriality.

Many of the same problems arise with regard to American control over commercial activities outside the territorial United States. Do exports from U.S. shores constitute its real and only share in world trade? What about foreign trade generated by U.S. subsidiaries operating globally, which today are as large, if not even larger, than those from the United States? Or even more to the point, what nationality can be ascribed to the local value added by the same American overseas affiliates?

The definitional problems raised by these questions point to the presently unclear principle establishing "nationality," which oscillates between territory and ownership. National ownership and control over productive assets freely crisscrossing the globe characterize a world economy in transition, and any dogmatic tie between economic performance and national territory, as if they were synonymous, clouds the vision for the new reality. Turning capital into foreign companies, plants, and employment renders them national entities in a legal sense and by virtue of location, but does not relinquish national ownership control over those assets from a capital point of view.

The uncertainty created by the different interpretations can easily be avoided by establishing defacto capital control over assets and economic activities as the universal and exclusive denominator of national ownership. If the global economy becomes a lasting reality, it is a conceptual advantage to start seeing national capital ownership and control over assets, trade, and investment flows as the only true and realistic basis for measuring that nation's position in the world economy regardless of geographic location. Actually, this should not be more difficult to accept than it is to accept market shares by American businesses in foreign market sectors.

In other words, territory is a poor basis for defining "national roles" in the international economy any longer. But, macroeconomic statistics published by all nations and major international organizations such as the UN, the IMF, World Bank, OECD, etc., are all still based on that traditional yardstick. It is not advocated here to abandon them, despite their one-sidedness, but they need to be supplemented by databanks based on national majority ownership and control over industrial sectors and commercial activities extending beyond national boundaries. In doing so, more flexibility for measurement and judgement about true national roles and competitiveness could be attained, as the presentation of all relevant information in the preceding pages demonstrates.

Accepting that principle as a useful direction for further studies still leaves a number of other problems relating to the international terminology of FDI itself. For the purposes of this study, the technical definition of the U.S. Department of Commerce has been adopted in measuring American activities in this area. It bases cumulative stock data on the historic book value of the original investment, adjusted for annual additions or deletions to the capital stock plus certain valuation adjustments. Flow data associated with periodic capital and income movements, especially the controversial reinvestment part, are established in dollars at given exchange rates, where applicable.

This is not the uniform practice of all countries. The intricacies of FDI accounting and comparability of data published in this area is a key concern of international organizations such as the UN and OECD, among others, and efforts are made to reach a fundamental consensus. Progress is being made and should ultimately lead to full agreement on the accounting principles to be employed by all nations.

Pointing to some basic discrepancies in the measurement of FDI volumes should be helpful for understanding where some of the difficulties arise. In the conventional view, funds leaving a country are defined as bona fide national funds on the basis of their origin. But how should the reality of today's direct U.S. investments being predominantly financed with capital earned abroad be interpreted? Clearly, labeling it U.S. capital is awkward on the principle of geographical origin, which defined the nationality of the original seed capital flow and yet, from a control point of view, it is American in its totality. U.S. accounting principles circumvent this inconvenience by channeling reinvestments through the U.S. BOP as income in the current account and fund exports in the capital account. While technically incorrect to treat them as flow items, because they never cross international boundaries, they now have acquired American citizenship. Interestingly enough, this practice establishes the U.S. BOP as a measuring tool for America's global economy as visualized in Chapter 11.

Some countries follow the American model, others may include reinvestments in FDI position estimates without formal BOP baptism, while still others ignore reinvestments altogether, and base their stock estimates on cumulative capital flows alone. A similar lack of cohesion appears to exist for valuation adjustments, which play such a prominent role in U.S.

FDI statistics. All these comments point to fundamental problems with international FDI statistics and to some degree invalidate their usefulness for precise and comparable measurements among nations. They still serve a purpose, of course, as indicators of trends, and should be complemented by the addition of other FDI parameters such as employment, sales, exports and imports, assets, etc., to establish more reliable measures of real national competitive stature on a national, regional, and world scale, as proposed throughout this investigation.

Such new frames of reference are needed after the unprecedented growth of direct investments which upset the formerly useful territorial definition of competitive national positions. FDI as the incarnation of economic liberalism transforms the world economy from one based on trade in basic raw materials and finished products, and arm's length transactions among loosely connected markets, into one where productive resources and their management move at will into markets for direct control over integrated global marketing efforts by multinationals. In the process, they even alter the nature of international trade in several ways: first physically and financially, but also from an ownership and control aspect. Large and growing portions of trade are now in the form of essential ingredients, components, semiprocessed goods being exchanged between parents and subsidiaries which, in addition, are subject to transfer pricing with unknown consequences for comparative valuations. But they remain under national capital control and ownership until they reach their final market. This is very different from trade among independent foreigners, where all national influence ceases with the passage of title and possession of goods. Between 1977 and 1993, for example, the trade between American FDI members alone accounted for 8 to 10 percent of total world merchandise exports. This is not an insignificant amount, but how can it be related in any meaningful way to trade among unrelated parties at completely different price levels or finishing stages?

Proceeding from this basic discussion to the formal postulate of the study, only majority-controlled investment and commercial activities by American enterprises are measured, in order to reach a true, reliable impression of the country's competitiveness. The investigation covers three distinct, though interrelated topics: the U.S. domestic economy, the U.S. external economy built on direct investments and related commercial activities, and U.S. global control over international trade. By DOC definition, all information usually covers only nonbank enterprises unless otherwise indicated. Portfolio investments are excluded, despite their size, because they lack the element of competitiveness.

AMERICA'S DOMESTIC ECONOMY

In accordance with the proposed definition of a "national" share in the world economy, America's domestic economy is redefined here by challenging the conventional view of the "American economy" as a homogeneous national entity, wholly owned, controlled and shaped by American business interests, and directly comparable to similarly defined national economies around the world. A correction of the geography-centered, narrow view is the central issue of this study in order to create a factual and realistic perception of America's industrial vitality. Two areas of investigation are ideally suited for this purpose: the growth of foreign competition in the U.S. domestic market, and the country's foreign trade.

Data on this subject began to offer more details than just annual changes in the inward direct investment position plus a few general financial figures with the 1977 benchmark survey, but cannot be considered complete in any sense before 1987. This is no major drawback, as FDI in the United States did not develop on any major scale before 1980, when it reached $83 billion. It broke the $100 billion barrier in 1981 ($109 billion), and twice that level only five years later with $220 billion in 1986. Since then, foreign progress has been rapid: $315 billion were reached in 1988, $419 billion in 1991, and $504 billion in 1994. At that rate of growth, inward U.S. FDI threatened to reach and overtake outward U.S. FDI during the 1988 to 1990 period and has definitely changed the profile of the American economy.

Between 1977 and 1993, foreign control over all U.S. business employment advanced from 1.8 to 5.0 percent (see Table 11.3). In a similar fashion, the foreign share of U.S. business gross product advanced from 2.3 to 6.1 percent during the same period (see Table 11.4). For individual industries, both indexes may have reached much higher levels. In manufacturing, for example, foreign control of employment went from 3.2 to 11.6 percent, and value-added from 3.6 to 13.9 percent. Chemicals exceed all other industries with employment, sales, and GP shares between 30 and 40 percent. Wholesaling is one of the nonmanufacturing industries where foreign interests established positions approaching 10 percent.

Overall, foreigners will continue to gain on their American peers, because inward FDI is still vigorously expanding. How serious the foreign onslaught may become is indicated by the very recent revelation that foreign business interests are aiming directly at their American competitors in foreign markets by exerting control at this moment over 15 percent of what used to be depicted as truly and wholly owned American FDI companies not so long ago.

Such explosive growth in foreign control over U.S. business sectors extends also to foreign trade, where an even stronger foreign influence than that suggested by their above shares in the domestic economy becomes evident. They accounted for 22 to 25 percent of all U.S. merchandise exports (see Table 5.2) and about 35 percent of all imports (see Table 5.3). As U.S. trade is in a perpetual deficit situation, it is not surprising to also find foreigners as the main contributors to the trade imbalance. As a matter of fact, they were responsibile for an average 70 to 80 percent of the annual deficits for the last twenty years (see Table 5.5).

For the record, it should be pointed out that U.S. outward FDI's trade balance has always been impeccable, leading to very favorable balances for the country's international payments (see Tables 4.1 and 4.6-4.8). Trade connected with American parents, their affiliates, and unrelated customers of both appears in the U.S. BOP as follows: on the export side, between 60 and 70 percent of all U.S. exports of goods were affected (see Table 4.7). The important development here is, that trade with affiliates has gone up from 15 to 28 percent between 1950 and 1993 (see Table 4.3B), and showed a favorable balance for most years (see Table 4.5), while parent trade with foreigners has declined from 50 to 30 percent (see Table 4.7). A clear-cut signal is that outward FDI is a major distribution channel for U.S. goods, and is still growing in importance. Keeping in mind how trade with affiliates is subject to transfer pricing on top of lower finishing rates makes this trade even more important from a physical aspect than indicated by the value-based ratios. The declining trade with foreigners, on the other hand, is lending support to the contention that subsidiary trading activities substitute to some degree for U.S. parent exports (see Table 4.7).

Imports related to outward FDI trading partners have fallen from 59 to 40 percent of all U.S. imports during the same timespan. This time, both affiliate trade, down from 29 to 20 percent, as well as sourcing from unrelated foreigners, down from 30 to 18 percent, have shared in the decline. Major contributors to the development are the growing (deficit) influence of the foreign companies and the fact that imports from Mofas were greatly damaged by expropriation like that of petroleum affiliates in Saudi Arabia. This sector must be considered not only the main factor in the declining imports from affiliates by the United States but, at the same time, the foremost negative influence on America's declining share in global trade (see Tables 4.8 and 13.1).

Interesting here is the structural fluidity of trade relating to outward FDI companies. Imports connected with U.S. parents and their affiliates developed in the following manner for the two years of 1977 and 1989, with all U.S. imports equaling 100 percent: petroleum 26 to 9 percent; manufactures

48 to 83 percent; trade 7 to 3 percent; all other 5 to 4 percent. All FDI-related exports on the same basis display the following picture: manufactures 84 to 92 percent; trade 6 to 3 percent; petroleum 6 to 3 percent; and all other categories from 3 to 2 percent (see Tables 4.12D and 4.16D).

It is important for the American BOT to see that U.S. parent companies supply less in monetary terms to their affiliates and relative to their sales volumes, than do foreigners with regard to their U.S. subsidiaries. Mofa imports from the United States thus reach only an 8 to 10 percent level of their sales, compared to foreigners in the United States with 15 to 20 percent shares (see Table 5.6). In addition, U.S. parent trade with their affiliates consists to a much higher degree of merchandise requiring additional processing abroad than seen for foreign operations in America. U.S. parent shipments of partly finished goods to Mofas advanced from 40 percent in 1966 to 55 percent in 1989 (see Tables 5.7 and 13.8). The same information for foreign companies reveals much lower shares going from 21 percent in 1980 to 29 percent in 1992 (see Table 5.8).

Of serious consequence for America's economy is the decline of capital goods exports to affiliates, which dropped from 33 percent of all exports to affiliates in 1957 to only 2 percent in 1989. In view of the rapid expansion of the FDI position in that period, it is hard to imagine a more telling statement about the competitiveness of American machinery by American client companies (see page 156).

Equally important is the fact of foreign ownership in about 15 percent of U.S. parent companies. Not only for the entrenchment of foreign business in the more dynamic industrial companies of the United States, but also the extended influence over global output of GDP and trade thus afforded. On the export side, U.S. parent shipments to their foreign owners account for 3 to 4 percent of all U.S. merchandise exports. On the import side, this trade reaches 6 to 8 percent of all U.S. imports. They are deceptively small shares, because these U.S. parents also ship to other foreign customers or source from them besides their parents, but there is no information that would allow quantification of this aspect (see Table 4.6). Hand in hand with this missing link goes another aspect that only turns the above trade data into the visible tip of the proverbial iceberg. Subsidiaries of U.S. parent companies are very large and important world traders in their own right, as mentioned before. Again no details are provided, but whatever they are, they turn up as another competitive trump card for foreign business interests, thereby reducing the actual American foothold in the world economy.

Further indicators for America's competitiveness are provided by tangible evidence in the country's BOP. Two accounts here are of primary interest: the current account with its two major subdivisions of trade in merchandise and services, and the capital account. The ebb and tide movements of aggregate flows, and in particular also of all inward and outward FDI funds, and their resulting balances, serve as clear indicators of the nation's ability to compete–a scoreboard for the battle between domestic and foreign business interests.

Merchandise exports from American soil have grown all along, even though undeniably at a slower pace than world exports which ultimately resulted in a nominal position loss of 5 to 6 percentage points, or even 6 to 8 percent, if only American-controlled exports are counted. In other words, if U.S. exports proper still had the 17 percent share of world trade they enjoyed during the 1950s, they would, theoretically, be $150 billion greater than they are now. In turn, this would translate into 4 to 5 million additional jobs for the United States, but such calculations are very hypothetical. Other factors than the often-implied lack of American competitiveness have entered the picture. Among them are price declines for basic raw materials which still weigh heavily in U.S. trade, profit strategies implemented via transfer pricing, and a major shift from finished merchandise exports to shipments of major ingredients, components, accessories, parts, and semifinished products among FDI members. It was a development that became inevitable with more refined profit accounting, logistics and related cost aspects, local content laws, dissemination of technology, and the growing external integration of the FDI industries themselves. This is not to say that there has not been sectoral weakness and loss, but to turn it into a generalized scenario of gloom and doom would be outright erroneous, if not actually misleading.

Parent companies, as the main protagonists of U.S. trade activities and global competition, have consistently helped to expand overall U.S. exports to affiliates and foreigners alike. Each dollar of sales to their affiliates was matched by $1.88 sold to foreigners in 1982, $1.36 in 1989, and $1.06 in 1993. Also, affiliate purchases in the United States have raised their share of total U.S. exports from 15 percent in 1950 to 27 to 29 percent in 1994, with a peak of 34 percent in 1977 (see Tables 4.1, 4.3, and 4.6).

Less positive is the declining parent share in overall U.S. exports which went from 68 percent in 1966 to 72 percent in 1977, 66 percent in 1982, 62 percent in 1989, and to only 55 percent in 1993 (see Table 4.18). It is not necessarily a clear indication of a competitive problem, however, because of transfer pricing and the change in the finishing status of goods discussed in connection with the parent/Mofa trade. More positive, and an encouraging indicator for parental competitiveness, is the fact that parent companies have been able to expand their domestic share of industry shipments of manufactures from 51.4 percent, to 50.6 percent and 54.8 percent in 1977, 1982, and 1989 respectively. This figure includes foreign-owned parents, and makes the information only partially correct (Adapted from: *Statistical Abstract of the United States* 1985, p. 756; 1990, p. 744; 1992, p. 744, and Tables 4.3, 5.4, 7.12, and 10.18).

Of more serious consequence for U.S. exports and, indeed, the economy itself is the substitution effect created by the existence of U.S.-controlled subsidiaries, which export more than their parents and even the United States itself (see Tables 5.4 and 13.1; Figure 9.2).

Making the case for measuring world trade shares not on the basis of territorial origin of goods, but rather on national capital control, leads to the realization that exports from the continental United States meeting this definition have stabilized their share of world exports while affiliate exports have gone into a relative decline, causing the superficial impression of an absolute American decline in world trade (see Table 13.1). Before reaching a hasty judgement on the development of global values alone, it is necessary to consider the impact of exchange rate fluctuations, inadequacies of the measuring techniques used, transfer pricing in the very intensive intra-FDI trade, as well as the differences in the finishing stages of such exports, which must certainly apply to Mofa trade in much the same way it does in the parent case. Unfortunately, information on this particular point is neither furnished for the Mofa part nor world trade in general, which makes a more precise measurement and evaluation of its impact impossible.

Skeptics question a generally positive attitude toward FDI's role for America's global trade record by citing the fact that domestic U.S. exports have only lost share in world trade. They also argue that shares could be higher without FDI, because lacking foreign production bases, U.S. industry could get foreigners to buy superior American goods and services here. This would allow job creation in the United States instead of job exports. A related debate arises over the purported loss of America's technological edge by sharing it freely with foreigners.

Arguments of this sort contain fleeting elements of truth and deserve serious consideration. However, it is doubtful that without a physical presence in foreign markets and elbow-to-elbow competition, U.S. competitiveness could have been maintained in the long run. The emergence of other nations among the technological elite speaks against this view. By establishing an international foothold, America has helped to bring progress to other countries initially, and in turn has reaped unquestionable advantages from such exposure and international learning experience. FDI may actually have been much more instrumental in fostering American globalism than trade.

On the import side, a similar argument in support of foreign direct investment's importance for U.S. jobs can be made. Parent imports, in total, amounted to 40 to 45 percent of the country's total purchases of foreign goods in 1982 and 1989, while less than 20 percent came from affiliates. It is conceivable that, without subsidiaries, these goods would still be imported from abroad, and quite possibly at a higher price for finished, or at least, upgraded goods. At any rate, they would not contribute to employment and earnings of American enterprises to the same extent. Again, such trade among FDI members differs from trade with outsiders in two fundamental aspects: (a) it is based on transfer prices which tend to be higher than market prices in this case, and (b) it contains substantial amounts of raw materials or semifinished goods requiring further processing–a point that works both ways for exports and imports.

As far as trade in services is concerned, a distinct advantage appears on the American side. Rather than addressing the overall balances, which are favorable for the country, special attention should be given to the relative performance of outward versus inward FDI in the areas of income, royalties and license fees, and other private service fees inflows vs. outflows. Aggregate data for both FDI parties indicate a huge surplus for U.S. outward FDI flows. While annual flows tend to fluctuate substantially, there are years when outward FDI-related inflows, that is, from American companies doing business overseas, exceed inward FDI-related outflows by a factor of 10:1 or even better (see Table 5.9).

Without any question, the benefits accruing to America's current account from activities of her overseas Mofas are not only far in excess of related outflows and thereby a strongly positive factor for the BOP, they are the only force that kept the balance of services positive for the country in most years. After a more detailed discussion of the subject, it turns out to be a rather one-sided impression generated by American BOP accounting practices. A critical review has to question the inclusion of reinvestments in the income flows accruing to both outward and inward FDI data. They tend to exaggerate actual income and capital flows for outward U.S. FDI data and gravely distort actual flows between inward and outward FDI data. Eliminating their influence to make U.S. data more comparable with international statistics, many countries do not include them. This turns the U.S. balance on the services account decidedly less favorable, if not negative. In other words, this minor correction turns the balance on the current account into a deficit similar to the trade account for many more years than previously indicated, with obvious implications for America's perception as an effective and efficient international competitor (see Tables 5.9 and 5.11).

This point about the statistical treatment of reinvestments in U.S. BOP accounting is not a mere whim. Unfortunately, it creates an image of weakness for America's competitive stature in the world economy, but this is essentially the same message given by the official review of America's international investment position discussed below, even though other factors that are not part of the present discussion like mutual public sector flows and portfolio investments, are included there (see Table 14.5).

While American business controls the fortunes of the services account, foreigners have dominated in the BOP's capital account since the early 1980s. Official American statistics create the impression of vastly superior outward FDI capital flows, including reinvestments, in relation to like inward FDI flows. More realistically, both should be measured exclusive of reinvestments to reflect actual flows. Now, it becomes apparent that during the 1970s, outflows exceeded inflows by $17 billion dollars, indicating U.S. gains vis-à-vis their foreign competitors. During the 1980s, however, the flows reversed sharply, with foreigners flooding the American investment scene with capital transfers of $333 billion vs. U.S. outflows of only $31 billion, a difference of $332 billion compared to the official position of only $162 billion. Such differences have a strong long-term impact on the relative competitive ranking of both parties. During the early 1990s, inward FDI continued its onslaught. With actual capital transfers of $227 billion to the U.S. between 1990 and 1994, they doubly outdistanced American overseas engagements of $106 billion (see Table 5.12). Needless to say, it is open to speculation how beneficial the differences are for the capital account, America's economy in general, and the U.S. employment side in particular where outward FDI deserves and gets a lower grade.

Detailed analysis of the relative flows reveals not only vastly different dollar volumes, but more important, totally different investment philosophies and strategies. Most likely motivated by tax considerations, American outward FDI is overwhelmingly financed by retained earnings, whereas foreigners prefer actual capital transfers. What this produces for both, in conjunction with accompanying imports and exports of semiprocessed goods and transfer price manipulations, is the accrual of earnings outside America, where they are subject to often more favorable local tax laws per se, and the existence of tax havens. Retained earnings, for instance, may be taxed at reduced rates compared to those levied on distributed earnings. Here outward and inward FDI interests share a unison of purpose to the detriment of the country's tax base (see Tables 3.10 and 3.11).

As pointed out above, foreigners operating in the United States also use their affiliates much more as export conduits for their own products than U.S. companies use their affiliates as channels for U.S. exports. Foreign-controlled companies in the United States import at advanced upgrading levels and presumably higher prices to protect their profits outside the United States, while U.S. companies export less upgraded merchandise, presumably at relatively low transfer prices for the same profit purpose. This, at least, can be inferred from parent exports at various finishing stages and their relative positions in affiliate sales (see Tables 5.6, 5.7, and 5.8). Again, it is a negative factor for America's liquidity.

In a global context, these foreign inroads into the official U.S. business economy, excluding the public sector, appear rather modest. But there can be no doubt that they were instrumental in reducing America's domestic share of the world economy, in terms of GDP production, from an estimated 27 to 28 percent during the 1970s to less than 26 percent during the early 1990s (see Table 11.1). From the same viewpoint, the foreign share of domestic U.S. exports effectively reduced the American share in world exports by about 3 percentage points from the official–that is conventional– level of 11 to 12 percent to around 8 to 9 percent. Fortunately, there seems to have been no change in that foreign share of domestic exports since 1974, indicating that American enterprises are holding their own against their foreign rivals (see Table 13.1).

The same does not apply to U.S. FDI parents owned to an unpublished degree by foreigners, however. Their 3 percent share in U.S. exports is not increasing but may be slipping according to the limited information published. As this involves only trade with their foreign parents, it says little about their exports to other foreign accounts. On the import side, this trade seems to grow slowly. With a level three times higher than exports, it contributes significantly (about one-third), to the U.S. trade imbalance, and is an indication of firm foreign control here (see Tables 4.6 and 5.5).

A rapidly progressing foreign involvement in the American economy may be viewed as the internationalization of what was viewed as a sheltered domestic domain, until now. It is a logical and fair trade-off for the Americanization of foreign economies mainly affected by U.S. FDI activities and is a vivid demonstration of the globalization process.

AMERICA'S EXTERNAL ECONOMY

The second topic of interest addresses the degree of American capital control over foreign economies via direct investments, which to some extent is the exact reverse of the above focus on foreign influence in the United States. Portfolio investments are excluded from the discussion here because they are not considered to offer particular insights into specific elements of national competitiveness found in their cousins, direct investment and trade. By definition, majority-controlled outward U.S. FDI is viewed as an integral extension of the similarly defined U.S. domestic economy. While the boundaries between Mofas and minority-controlled data are not always clearly drawn, this is not a serious problem, because Mofas constitute 90 percent or more of outward U.S. FDI (see Table 1.12).

The vital elements of all FDI positions are flows of equity and debt capital, reinvestments, and valuation adjustments stemming mostly from asset valuations exposed to currency fluctuations. The fluid combination of these elements may be estimated annually, with periodic surveys monitoring the estimates' correctness, as in the U.S. case. Other nations either follow the U.S. example, conduct annual surveys as a more accurate way of measuring the stock levels, or base their estimates on cumulative capital flows over the years alone. In short, uniformity in methodology or a highly reliable degree of data comparability among nations cannot be assumed a priori, as indicated in earlier discussions.

The U.S. FDI position has grown by leaps and bounds for the research period covering more than four decades. Starting with $12 billion in 1950, America's commitment to global business investments has expanded to over $600 billion in 1994. Interesting is the changing pace of investment activities when measured in terms of $100 billion increments. It took less than twenty-five years from the above base year to pass the first $100 billion mark in 1973. After only seven more years, the $200 billion threshold was crossed (1980). It took another seven years to surpass $300 billion (1987), only three years to reach beyond $400 billion (1990), and only two years each to break the $500 billion barriers (1992) and $600 billion (1994).

Put in a different perspective, half of U.S. FDI's present volume was accumulated in the first thirty-seven years (1950 to 1987), with the other half emerging in only one-fifth of that time (1988 to 1994). Investments underwent major geographical reallocations during the whole period. Directed at what was then the so-called free world, these are the major trends by continent: in 1950 the lion's share of FDI (73 percent) was found in the Americas, including Canada and Latin America; 14 percent in Europe; 8 percent in Asia; and the rest in Africa and the Pacific. In 1994, that distribution had changed dramatically to a now leading share for Europe with 49 percent; 31 percent in the Americas; 14 percent in Asia; and the same 6 percent share for the rest, indicating a decided investment bias for the developed nations (see Table 1.1).

Equally noteworthy is the fact that the expansion was financed with actual transfers of only $190 billion in equity/debt capital from the United States. The remaining two-thirds consisted of reinvested earnings over the four decades plus valuation adjustments. The actual capital export from the United States feeding this growth increased during the first three decades, reached its high during the 1970s, then declined rather dramatically during the 1980s, to recover smartly during the early 1990s (see Table 2.6).

The sharp change in the sources of investment capital abolishes the notion that capital transfers necessary for the start-up period of FDI are indispensable for feeding its growth forever. The history of U.S. FDI definitely refutes this view. Yes, there was a period of about two decades when seed capital exported from the United States primarily fed the global expansion of the investment stock. But it served mainly as a pump primer before it was gradually and decisively replaced by reinvestments. The change can be seen as the result of a natural maturing process, of accounting changes, a loss of interest, or worse, a loss of competitiveness in a still expanding world economy, of tax and profit strategies, or most likely, a combination of all five (see Table 2.2).

Tax and profit strategies may have played an even stronger role in the development of inward FDI in the United States, where they led to a completely reversed situation. Foreigners have financed their investments here to 95 percent through capital transfers and only 5 percent by reinvested earnings (see Table 4.12). In other words, they tended to keep local earnings at a minimum for tax reasons, and consequently produced only insufficient capital for reinvestment.

Dramatic changes can be seen also for investments by industry, where manufacturing and oil held a combined 61 percent share in 1950, manufacturing 33 percent, and oil 29 percent. In 1994, their aggregate share had declined to 46 percent, with manufacturing still maintaining 36 percent, and oil only 11 percent. Big gainers were trade, up from 7 to 11 percent, and most likely also financial institutions, which ended with a 29 percent share against an unknown 1950 base (see Table 1.7).

A rather curious aspect of U.S. FDI is its concentration in Anglo-Saxon countries–a historic affinity according these nations a prominence far beyond their relative economic importance. Over the whole period, they were able to attract between 45 and 50 percent of all U.S. FDI (see Table 1.4), and regularly deliver between 30 and 45 percent of all U.S. FDI income (see Table 3.7).

U.S. FDI investors prefer majority holdings. For the whole period, investments in Mofas constituted 90 percent of all funds committed to FDI (see Table 1.12). Whether minority holdings are a matter of choice or imposed by national FDI controls cannot be answered from available documentation. Foreign investors in the United States seem to similarly prefer majority holdings, but not to the same degree. In 1989, they accounted for 72 percent of assets and 79 percent of total inward FDI employment.

Aside from the economic potential, the outward FDI's insistence on majority ownership may also be responsible for their growing concentration in developed countries which are more accommodating to foreign investors. In 1950, only 48 percent of the investment stock was located in developed areas due to the focus on Latin America. But with the shift to other world regions, Europe in particular, this ratio changed rapidly. By 1957, it had shot up to 55 percent, continued on its way to 68 percent in 1966, 75 percent in 1977, before leveling off at 74 percent for both 1982 and 1990 (*SOCB*, August 1991, p. 81. Table 12, global summary).

Mofas constitute a major economic presence in their own right. Compared to the United States they have produced up to 10 percent of U.S. industrial GDP. In the manufacturing sector their output achieves even higher levels in the vicinity of 25 to 28 percent (see Table 7.8). On the employment side, Mofas show lower levels than intimated by these comparative output levels. All Mofas averaged about 6 percent of total U.S. industrial employment and around 18 percent of like U.S. manufacturing manpower (see Table 7.9). This unique resource/output combination results in a very favorable Mofa performance against U.S. industry in general, and manufacturing in particular (see Table 7.10).

Comparing Mofas to their own parents fortifies this impression of Mofa excellence. As a rule, they reach one-third of their parents' benchmarks in these areas: sales, 33 to 40 percent; employment, 28 to 31 percent; gross product, 29 to 33 percent; assets, 22 to 24 percent; compensation levels in the vicinity of 19 percent; net income 26 to 43 percent, and more than 100 percent of total parent export shipments (see Tables 7.10, 7.12, and 10.18). Reaching one-third the size of parent companies translates into an affiliate equivalent of 8 percent of the U.S. industrial sector, which in turn is saying they are equal in size to the Canadian economy or the Benelux countries. At any rate, they are big enough to rival many smaller national economies in size, and are a clear demonstration of America's true competitive projection into the world economy (see Table 7.8).

Official statistics covering the income produced by American industry emphasize FDI's comparative importance for corporate America. Their overseas investments invariably produce relatively much higher profit levels compared to domestic U.S. business profits than the above macroeconomic indicators would suggest. Including all income categories discussed in Chapter 3, FDI produces profits in the vicinity of 21 percent of like domestic levels. This is a major accomplishment, but not surprising in view of the above productivity record, magnified by a weaker dollar for much of the time (see page 111).

Changing the focus of discussion to economic activities of U.S. majority-owned enterprises, and here specifically Mofa gross product relative to the industrial or total GDPs of foreign nations, produces mixed impressions. Given all the caveats concerning the databases used, a general decline in America's FDI stature appears indisputable, even though its extent may be questionable. In the European market where half of America's FDI resides, the American share appears stable for the period 1977 to 1992. The same may be assumed to hold true for Japan. But there is a decided weakness of America's share in the rest of the world, including some of the most aggressive growth economies. Here America's share in the output of GDP was cut practically in half for the same period. Together with the U.S. domestic GDP information devoid of its foreign part, the American-controlled GDP output in the world economy seems to have fallen from 29 to 26 percent between 1977 and 1992 (see Table 11.6).

This impression is substantiated by observations made for the historic progress of U.S. business pursuits in 29 selected countries harboring close to 90 percent of all U.S. FDI, including the most advanced competitors of U.S. business. In nine countries, American business showed significant gains. Steady positions were maintained in another nine, and clear declines were registered in eleven nations. This picture refers to development of overall industrial GDP output. If manufacturing becomes the basis of comparison, the U.S. performance improves to position gains in twelve countries, a neutral picture in ten, and weaker positions in seven nations. This obvious competitive strength is important in view of the general disinterest manufacturing receives at home in the United States (see Table 12.1). Furthermore, in ten countries, American contributions to the national manufacturing GDP exceed 10 percent. In English-speaking markets, these shares may even go as high as one-third of the national output of manufacturing value-added.

But there are also clear warning signs. Neutral-to-loss positions are about three times higher than tangible gains at the end of the observation period. In some European countries included in the survey, where close to one-half of all U.S. FDI resides, its share of national industrial GDP has declined between 1982 and 1989. The same holds true for Canada, a pivotal investment area.

Can these developments be construed as a general loss of American competitiveness in the world economy? Partially perhaps, but not necessarily in their totality. More likely they are also heavily influenced by the well documented investment apathy throughout the 1980s which appears to have reversed itself during the early 1990s and thus, hopefully, initiating a much needed and more vigorous phase of American economic activity in world markets (see Chapters 11 and 12).

The above information does not include many nations that belong to the fastest growing and very competitive economies of today. Generally speaking, they fall into the "other" group of nations in Table 11.6 where the American participation is weakest–compelling evidence that American investments need to flow more liberally to this sector of the world economy is provided by official FDI data themselves. While the U.S. FDI position is up 60 percent, as are related assets at the start of the 1990s after languishing throughout the 1980s, it did not result in any comparable increase in Mofa output of GP, employment, or net income, as should be expected. Actually, all indicators more or less stagnated during the whole period (see Tables 1.1, 7.7, 7.12, 11.1, and 11.6).

It is a rather perplexing realization demonstrating the need to look beyond published FDI stock data and capital flows, which are beset with all kinds of questions as to the accuracy of measurements themselves, comparability of definitions, and the impact of exchange rates and related valuation factors. Without additional information, the nominal growth in the FDI stock may be of no practical consequence for a realistic assessment of competitive dynamics. This particularly enigmatic situation may be linked to the merger mania gripping the United States during the 1980s and early 1990s. With 7,466 U.S. corporate mergers during the 1970s, 25,159 during the 1980s, and 11,187 between 1990 and 1992 (*Statistical Abstract of the United States*), much of the increased FDI volume may simply have come from foreign affiliates of acquired firms turning statistically into new FDI for tax accounting reasons, without actual and additional capital flows from the United States, explaining why nominal FDI growth did not lead to higher global resource or output shares.

Referring to the information compiled in various sections of the study, and here particularly Table 11.6, it may be estimated that the overall U.S. FDI share in global GDP, excluding the United States, may have gradually declined from 3.0 to 2.1 percent between 1977 and 1992. As the global GDP figures include the public sector, the United States FDI share needs to be adjusted to correspond more closely with global output of industrial value-added. Arbitrarily assuming worldwide industrial GDP to be roughly around the U.S. level of 80 to 85 percent allows the above share estimate to be adjusted and fall into a new range from 3.6 to 2.7 percent. In view of the rising foreign 6 percent share in America's industrial GDP, these opposing trends offer only a slim margin of comfort when assessing their competitive impact. Such comparatively low global U.S. GDP share estimates in

Chapter 11 do not necessarily contradict the 4 to 6 percent share of industrial GDP estimated in Chapter 12 based on a sample of selected national economies, because the latter are based on shares in industrial output against shares in national GDP aggregates.

The point made about capital participation now comes full circle and establishes a forceful need to redraw the picture presented so far. Returning to the recent official disclosure, foreign ownership of U.S. FDI businesses reached 15 percent of parent companies in 1993 (*SOCB*, June 1995, pp. 39, 40). As the extent of ownership is not made public, it is too early to say, or even speculate, what it means for the American presence in foreign economies. Assuming majority control for a moment, it is entirely conceivable that estimates for the U.S. position will have to be revised by similar, or even higher, percentage figures, which would seriously compromise all data presented here, and with it, America's competitive profile (see Table 4.6).

AMERICA'S POSITION
IN WORLD MERCHANDISE TRADE

The third and final subject to be evaluated for a composite picture of America's competitiveness concerns America's global participation in international trade of goods. By definition, this would include exports from the United States proper by capital-controlled American companies, complemented by shipments of majority-controlled FDI affiliates from foreign shores.

This point is addressed in Chapters 9, 10, and 13, where it is clearly established that Mofas export more in actual dollar volume than American-controlled firms from their home country, or even the whole United States itself. Whereas the former have reached and maintained a steady world trade share around the 8 to 9 percent mark for the last twenty or so years, Mofas were instrumental in elevating the truly American-controlled global share of world trade to between 19 to 20 percent. While that position seems firmly established for some time now, there is good reason to believe it may have suffered a small long-term loss (see Table 13.1).

It must be stressed, that such an impression may be flawed due to the imprecise nature of trade statistics in the affiliate sector, and may have to be researched in more depth. U.S. exports have always been measured in terms of actual shipments of goods and thus provide firm and reliable ground for comparison with world merchandise trade in total. Not so with affiliate trade data. Up to 1977, Mofa exports were based on sales, which were considered to automatically equate shipments and also included services. While preparing the 1977 survey, government statisticians discovered enormous discrepancies between reported affiliate sales to the United States and actual shipments recorded by official import statistics. The gap between both amounted to no less than 5 percent of world trade for that year (see Table 9.2 and Figure 9.1).

While Mofa trade statistics with the United States were thus corrected and afford true comparability with all international trade data, there remains the problem with Mofa trade statistics of all other countries and customers, which are still kept on a sales-equal-shipments basis. That this may not be very realistic, just as for the trade involving the United States before 1977, is almost certain. As discussed in Chapter 9, there still are huge differences between sales and shipments reported for Mofa trade with the United States, even at this moment (see Figure 9.1). But now, at least, they are separable for a clearer view. The fact that in the case of Mofa trade with other nations, this separability does not exist, and reported Mofa export sales often reach such high proportions of officially reported national exports, makes an exaggerated situation a very real possibility.

The ambiguous nature of Mofa exports outlined above could actually cast doubts on the decline of global affiliate trade shares and indirectly, those described for the United States. At any rate, the data presented in Table 13.1 have to be approached cautiously. This would apply to all data reported before 1977. Using that year as a more reliable basis for comparison indicates a small American global position loss of 1.5 to 2.0 percent. A more detailed discussion of sectoral strength or weakness leads to the conclusion that U.S. control over world exports is affected by a wide variety of factors including maintenance or growth of share in export sectors of declining importance to world trade (see Tables 13.2 and 13.3 covering basic materials); position loss due to uncontrollable external factors such as expropriation, but also price movements (see Table 13.4 relating to mineral fuels); inability to maintain a foothold in growth markets indicating competitive weakness (see Tables 13.6 and 13.7 for machinery, transport equipment, and other manufactures); and ultimately, clear indications of competitive strength as shown in the chemical sector, despite major inroads by foreign business interests (see Table 13.5).

Despite the mixed picture, the United States is still the number one world trader because of the synergism created by the interplay of U.S. domestic and Mofa exporting capacities. Mofas on their own produce not only higher export volumes than those of the United States proper, they also exceed the levels of many well-known trading nations, which would give them a very high ranking as a trading nation if this were an acceptable comparison, as mentioned before. In addition, they represent a very important force in individual national export sectors, where often American-controlled exports exceed 10 percent, and in seven countries, even 20 percent (see Table 12.1).

Being such an enormous trading power in disguise, Mofas may be faulted for playing some role in the relative weakening of exports from the continental United States. In their defense, it has to said that they are a growing channel for U.S. exports in general, that their parents were still able to expand exports to foreigners, and able to maintain a favorable trade balance at the same time over the entire post-1966 period (see Tables 4.5, 4.6, and 4.10). Also, the continental American share in world trade seems to have stabilized between 1977 and 1994, despite their existence (see Tables 10.18 and 13.1).

Of real interest is intra-FDI trade taking place between parents and affiliates, which accounts for a major portion not only of overall FDI business, but world trade itself. Of all 1989 Mofa sales (which amounted to $1,020 billion), 24 percent or $246 billion were made to other FDI members in the same country ($39 billion), the United States ($93 billion), or third nations ($114 billion) (see Tables 8.6, 8.7, and 10.16). Of these, $216 billion were actually shipped and delivered. In turn, most of the latter (88 percent) consisted of international trade and the $186 billion thus generated accounted for 6 percent of total world merchandise exports (see Tables 10.16, 10.18, and 13.1).

Parent sales to nondomestic affiliates accounted for a relatively small 4 to 5 percent of their total business volume. Of the total 1989 sales amount of $131 billion, only $86 billion were actually shipped to Mofas, revealing one of the baffling aspects of intra-FDI trade defying easy explanation because the huge discrepancy in values does not stem from service sales. The shipments translated into a significant 66 percent of total parent export sales, 39 percent of their related export shipments, and 3 percent of world merchandise exports (see Tables 3.1, 10.18, and 13.1).

Total 1989 intra-FDI sales to the tune of $338 billion thus accounted for only 9 percent of their consolidated worldwide sales. Out of these, $272 billion became bona fide export shipments accounting for a 9 to 10 percent share of total world trade. Parent shares in this trade fluctuated within a fairly narrow band as follows: 31 percent in 1966; 27 percent in 1977; 29 percent in 1982; and 32 percent in 1989 (see Tables 4.16, 10.16, 10.18, and 13.1).

These figures for intra-FDI trade across international boundaries leave about 50 percent of global U.S. FDI exports going to unrelated customers. In itself a remarkable achievement, it opens the eyes to the importance of intra-FDI trade for America's integrated global marketing efforts. That trade amounted to 9.7, 8.3, and 9.5 percent of total world merchandise trade in 1977, 1982, and 1989. Its share obviously persists despite the changing finishing stages of the materials shipped plus the transfer pricing mentioned before, and is in itself a sign of enduring American competitiveness. It further leads to the conclusion that the official American preoccupation with exports of goods and services needs to be refocused to the export of FDI capital as the more solid warranty for maintaining America's global share in the higher margin affiliate retail rather than wholesaling markets represented by foreign trading partners. This appears especially important in view of the growing inroads by foreign capital interests into the United States. As remarked before, the ultimate measure of international competitiveness is the outcome of the tug-of-war between inward and outward FDI.

All trade with affiliates has noncompetitive overtones and is, therefore, in a league by itself when assessing America's competitiveness in international trade. What would happen to America's position in world trade if this trade among affiliates were hypothetically removed from all consideration here, in order to isolate that trade segment where competitive excellence can be clearly demonstrated? This calls for the elimination of all U.S. exports to affiliates on one side, and all U.S. imports from affiliates on the other. U.S. domestic exports under American capital control would have lost $35.8 billion in 1977, $52.8 billion in 1982, and $97.5 billion in 1989 on shipments to Mofas alone. The corresponding effect on world trade share would be a reduction from 8.6 to 5.4 percent in 1977, 8.3 to 5.4 percent in 1982, and 9.4 to 6.1 percent in 1989, or 3 percentage points on average (see Tables 4.16B and 13.9).

Applying the same criteria to Mofa exports would reduce their trade volumes by $80.7 billion for 1977, $106.7 billion in 1982, and $185.5 billion in 1989, leading to a much more pronounced impact on America's total trade position than shown above. The amounts are equivalent to 7.2 percent of world trade in 1977, 5.8 percent in 1982, and 6.3 percent in 1989. The significance of U.S. global trade shares now pared to 12.6, 11.2, and 12.4 percent is very difficult to grasp, because much of the seemingly lost business may have been recaptured by business activities of local Mofas (see Tables 10.1, 13.1, and 17.1).

The many ambiguities introduced by the analysis of FDI-related trade activities speak clearly in favor of using other macroeconomic parameters introduced above as more reliable indicators of any nation's, and in this case, America's true industrial competitive strength.

CRITICAL EVALUATION

Put into a nutshell, America's position as a leading competitor in the global economy depends on its capability to master three key variables: its share in the domestic economy; its share of foreign markets through FDI operations; and its share of global trade in goods and services. Such focus on macroeconomics conveniently limits the number of topics employed for the measurement of national competitiveness, yet adequately covers all aspects necessary for a meaningful evaluation, and thus offers advantages over measurements based on microeconomic parameters so often used for this purpose. The specific advantages of this greatly simplified evaluation process lie in the easy access to widely available, standardized, and harmonized international databanks, in contrast to the multitudes of poorly defined, incomplete, unreliable, and often plainly estimated time series in the second approach.

All these discussions point to the indisputable fact that FDI activities by identifiable national capital interests are a better indicator for trends in national competitiveness today than trade, which used to be the traditional yardstick. Ample arguments speaking for this position have been provided in the foregoing discussions of U.S. FDI, its position, and historic developments.

For one thing, FDI meets foreign competition head-on in its domestic environment. It either survives and prospers, or it succumbs. While the same set of rules applies also to international trade of FDI enterprises, only that portion dealing with unrelated customers allows valid conclusions to be drawn about its real competitive importance, whereas intra-affiliate trade is not necessarily indicative of any competitive achievement per se. It becomes so only indirectly by being linked to the competitive fortunes of affiliated organizations in their individual markets. Expanding on this thought may help to clarify the point made. Of total 1993 U.S. exports to the world, 27 percent ($123 billion) went to Mofas. This leaves $334 billion worth of goods sold and shipped to foreigners, a national achievement that looks quite modest compared to Mofa sales of $1,574 billion in foreign markets. In addition, the latter represents a truly visible American accomplishment, whereas exports to foreigners may totally obliterate such national identity with the passing of title and possession. At any rate, they cannot offer the same degree of control over foreign markets offered by local Mofa business operations there (see Tables 4.3, 11.2, and 14.1). What the foregoing discussion says is that national competitiveness can, ultimately, be gauged quite accurately by the relative growth of inward versus outward FDI macroeconomics in such areas as: sales, employment, gross product, exports, and imports. Data on mutual investment positions are useful, but for reasons given earlier, have to be interpreted with caution, as they do not necessarily correlate closely to operational developments, which lastly determine market shares alone.

TABLE 14.1. Comparative Measures for U.S. Outward/Inward FDI ($ billion)

Year	SALES Outward/Inward		EMPLOYMENT* Outward/Inward		GROSS PRODUCT Outward/Inward		U.S. EXPORTS** Outward/Inward		U.S. IMPORTS*** Outward/Inward	
1993	$1,574	$1,302	$6,731	$4,722	$488e	$290	$115.5	$105.1	$111.3	$198.5
1992	1,574	1,232	6,660	4,715	489e	266	120.3	103.9	109.2	184.5
1991	1,542	1,186	6,878	4,872	478e	258	115.3	96.9	102.8	178.7
1990	1,493	1,176	6,834	4,734	463e	239	106.4	92.3	102.2	182.9
1989	1,285	1,041	6,622	4,440	392e	223	102.5	86.3	97.4	171.8
1988	1,195	886	6,404	3,844	370e	190	94.9	69.5	87.3	155.5
1987	1,053	745	6,270	3,224	326e	158	78.9	48.1	75.9	143.5
1986	929	672	6,250	2,964	288e	142	71.3	49.6	65.6	125.7
1985	895	633	6,419	2,862	277e	135	69.6	56.4	62.5	113.3
1984	899	596	6,418	2,715	279e	129	66.2	58.2	62.5	100.5
1983	886	536	6,383	2,546	275e	111	57.5	53.9	53.2	81.5
1982	936	518	6,640	2,448	290e	103	56.7	60.2	51.4	84.3
1977	648	194	7,197	1,219	201e	35	40.8	24.9	41.5	43.9

Notes: Data cover all affiliates. Gross Profit for U.S. *000s. **All exports to outward FDI affiliates and by inward FDI affiliates. ***Imports shipped by outward FDI affiliates and to inward FDI affiliates. e = estimate.

Sources: Outward FDI: *SOCB*, October 1991, pp. 29-47; June 1994, pp. 42-62; June 1995, pp. 32, 39. Inward FDI: *SOCB*, July 1994, pp. 154-86; May 1995, p. 62. Mofa share in sales, employment, and GP estimated to reach between 80 and 85 percent. Table 11.3.

This leaves the relative performance of outward versus inward FDI as the balancing criterion in the economic contest of the United States vs. the rest of the world. In other words, the decisive question is whether U.S. industry is making inroads into foreign economies faster than its home base in the United States is eroding. The answer to that can be given by drawing on the comparative developments for employment, sales, imports and exports, and GP for U.S. outward and inward FDI, as far as they are accessible. Employment, as the only variable not affected by exchange rate fluctuations, can be considered a crucial guidepost in this evaluation.

Measuring the share variations attained by total U.S. inward FDI against the same data for outward FDI between 1977 and 1993 leads to the conclusion that overall foreign investment interests are gaining on U.S. positions. Foreign operations in the United States went from 30 to 83 percent of outward FDI sales, from 17 to 70 percent of employment, from 17 to 59 percent of gross product, from 61 to 91 percent for U.S. exports to outward FDI affiliates, and from 107 to 179 percent of U.S. imports from outward FDI affiliates (see Table 14.1).

A more tentative conclusion based on the information presented seems to be that foreigners may have strengthened their world trade position by expanding their trading activities with their U.S. affiliates more rapidly than is the case for U.S. trade with outward FDI affiliates, on top of causing a hefty trade deficit for the United States to boot. If details on the 15 percent foreign capital participation in U.S. outward FDI corporations were available, the relative positions of both FDI opponents would certainly look different and, unfortunately, less positive for the American side.

A point to keep in mind is that America's position in global competition is strongly influenced by the fluctuations of the dollar. Any weakening, as documented since 1985, will help maintain the present U.S. lead over inward FDI, while a stronger dollar can only lead in the opposite direction. The above scenario is based on total inward and outward FDI data, including both Mofas and the portfolio-like minority holdings, which are more abundant than Mofa information (see Table 14.1).

Mofa estimates for the period provide additional and useful insight into the relative rate of progress made by both parties. As postulated throughout this study, Mofas form the only legitimate basis for a final judgement on the competitive strength of U.S. industry in its quest for global market share because of the true economic control exerted by them.

The projected picture essentially confirms the findings for the overall FDI situation and may even be less encouraging. Foreign Mofas in the United States had sales of $194 billion in 1977, or 38 percent of the $507 billion reported for outward FDI Mofas. In 1992, inward Mofas had sales of $1,043 billion, or 77 percent of the $1,299 billion reported for U.S. outward Mofas. Similar developments become evident on the employment side where inward Mofas show 1.2 million employees versus 3.8 million for U.S. Mofas abroad, or 32 percent, in 1977. By 1992, the ratio stood at 3.9 to 5.4 million employees for a foreign share of 72 percent. Estimates for the respective Mofa GPs see the inward share increase from 18 percent in 1977 to 60 percent in 1992 (*SOCB*, June 1994, p. 56; July 1994, p. 169, Table 7.12).

It is in the area of GP generation where outward and inward FDI show the most significant discrepancies. Outward Mofas produce a GP level at about 29 percent of sales compared to only 21 percent for inward FDI. This led to 1993 volumes of $358 and $290 billion, respectively, in favor of American-owned Mofas. What accounted for the difference besides differences in upgrading operations, taxation, and profit allocation, mentioned earlier, is difficult to pinpoint. But the inward affiliate data seem to be in line with overall U.S. industrial GDP output. In 1993, inward FDI firms produced $61,000 per employee against $58,000 for all U.S. industries (see Tables 7.1, 7.8, 7.9, 11.2, and 11.5).

The estimated GP output for all outward FDI employees for the same year yielded a figure of $73,000, a level 20 percent higher than for employees of foreign companies in the United States. Similar ratios can be established for comparative Mofa/Parent GP outputs. Despite the fact that parents produce a higher portion of value-added for each dollar of sales, they still fall behind their Mofas on a per capita output basis, which seems to run 7 to 9 percent higher over the 1977 to 1993 period (see Table 7.12).

What the data prove is that outward FDI with similar levels of investment controls more GP output, employment, sales, income flows, and world trade outside the United States than inward FDI does inside. This was a competitive accomplishment achieved with minimal capital exports, compared to the amounts foreign investors transferred to the United States (see Table 5.12). More important than the comparable positions reached, though, are the underlying trends affecting the competitive future of the U.S.-controlled economy in a global context. Foreign influence in America's economy is unquestionably growing. America's position in the world economy and trade based on U.S. and Mofa exports is overtly slipping, but the evidence is ambivalent, and does not permit the conclusion of an outright competitive weakness on the American side for the reasons cited.

These sketchy developments still permit the tentative conclusion that very substantial gains were made by inward Mofas against their U.S. counterparts. In the final analysis, the United States holds an impressive lead over any single national competitor in the race for world market shares. But all the evidence points to a narrowing gap vis-à-vis the global competitors in relentless pursuit of the same goal. The statistics will become even more compelling as regional economic blocks such as EC emerge with consolidated FDI data. It will be a contest of historic importance to be decided, not by relative positions in world trade, but by global control over economic output via majority-held direct foreign investment, which in actual terms commands a growing portion of world trade as it expands.

Given the situation that total outward U.S. FDI employed 6.7 million people, generateed three times more sales than all U.S. merchandise exports combined, accounted for a 30 percent and growing share of U.S. exports, surpassed the total export volume of the United States with its own foreign trade, produced a GP in excess of that of many U.S. states, and contributed between 20 and 22 percent of the national income, its public image is very faint. Official pronouncements on international economic relations reveal a curious preoccupation with trade issues, usually under the aspect of alleged impediments or violations, almost to the point of totally overlooking direct investment. What it practically amounts to is a confirmation of how little FDI's true dimension and importance for the country's economy and global competitiveness is officially appreciated. Putting it differently, U.S. FDI is relegated to only a secondary role behind trade, because it does not equal trade's political potential. Real or imagined trade violations receive broad official attention in the media, and invoke blustery posturing on the GATT/World Trade Organization scene. Threat of trade restrictions or even sanctions are readily vocalized for a wide range of political, economic, or human rights issues. As they normally yield concessions in some form by the other side, they are much more useful as foreign policy tools than FDI, which is much less pliable in this regard.

Official monitoring of America's competitive stature dwells on two sets of subjects considered crucial for America's commercial interests: one quantitative, the other qualitative in nature. Under the first, we find detailed merchandise trade data for wide public consumption. Of lesser interest to the general public are trade in services and developments relating to FDI.

In the second, mostly American-generated initiatives for freer trade, investment, and the protection of intellectual property are closely followed from launch, and tenaciously pursued step by step through international organizations such as GATT, OECD, UN, World Bank, and the IMF to establish uniform ground rules for the advancement of international economics. Backup measures for the global network efforts are bi- and multilateral agreements such as NAFTA and APEC, both of which were taking tangible shape at the end of 1993, not to mention other political and diplomatic avenues such as NATO, the periodic G7 meetings, conflict management processes with regional blocs (EU) or Japan, and the linkage of political issues to trade concessions, trade quotas, etc. In addition, attention is given to changes in the U.S. trade balance for high-tech goods, the country's international investment position, and the dollar exchange rate.

The pronounced trade orientation of America's business and government officialdom manifests itself in the tenacious battle for freer trade, the deliberate depreciation of the dollar as a hidden export subsidy, the lacking support for global market development from more vigorous direct investments in comparison with domestic investment levels, the emphasis on reinvestments rather than capital exports, declining capital exports during the 1980s, and the now decade-long rush into industrial downsizing and cost reduction as a competitive remedy.

None of these policies has fundamentally improved America's economic situation. The trade deficit looms as large and intractable as ever. The depreciated dollar failed to produce the anticipated growth in America's global trade share, and may actually have turned into a deterrent to direct foreign investments by American businesses as the key to more overseas market opportunities.

On the contrary, it invited foreign direct investors to acquire large portions of U.S. industries and markets, stimulated cascading inflows of portfolio investments, and lifted foreign ownership and control over U.S. assets to unprecedented levels. Rising imports at high prices ushered in a period of inflationary pressures for the country's middle class as well as blue collar workers, and a general decline in the standard of living.

All evidence provided so far points to America's dynamic and successful involvement in the international economy over the last four decades. It has turned the country into the world's leading economy, but there is also evidence that just maintaining that position promises to become more and more of a struggle.

Quoting OECD as the authority on FDI positions of its member nations between 1980 and 1992, data shown in Table 14.2 are probably the most reliable available. This qualification has to be made for several reasons. There are often large discrepancies between the organization's data and those furnished by the countries themselves owing to the variations in defining the subject among the twenty-four member nations. As mentioned before, some nations prefer to use only capital flows as registered in the BOP for establishing estimates of their accumulated FDI stock, actually the basis of the OECD data below, while others add reinvestments to them. In addition, all national data are translated from national currencies at year-end exchange rates to the U.S. dollar. Lastly, while including the largest economies in the world, the OECD data are not all-inclusive.

TABLE 14.2. OECD Cumulative FDI Positions ($ billion)

Year	OECD	U.S.	U.S. Share
1980	$440	$220	50.0%
1981	446	228	51.1
1982	439	208	47.3
1983	445	207	46.5
1984	470	211	44.9
1985	559	230	41.2
1986	690	260	37.7
1987	884	314	35.5
1988	1,011	336	33.2
1989	1,250	382	30.6
1990	1,496	431	28.6
1991	1,650	468	28.1
1992	1,693	499	28.9
1993	1584*	549	NMF

Note: *Provisional data.

Source: *OECD, International Direct Investment Statistics Yearbook* 1993, p. 18; 1994, p. 16.

While Table 14.2 indicates a 50 percent U.S. share in OECD FDI for 1980 and 31 percent for 1989, another source pegs the global U.S. share at 42 and 28 percent respectively for the same years (Rugman, 1990). Taking the 1989 OECD data as the most recent and complete pronouncement on the subject indicates the U.S. position to have shrunk by 38 percent since 1980, owing to dedicated investment activities by competitive nations, but also because the weaker dollar resulted in inflationary exchange rate gains for other currencies. Rugman's estimates are similar, but indicate a smaller decline of only 33 percent.

However, even this picture may not be correct. Seven out of the twenty-four countries do not count reinvestments as part of the inward direct investment stock estimated by the OECD on the basis of cumulative capital flows. They are: Belgium/Luxemburg, France, Germany, Iceland, Italy, Japan, and Spain, with a combined stock volume of $380 billion in 1989 (OECD, 1993 Yearbook, p. 16). Hypothetical adjustment of this figure based on the ratio between flow and reinvestment volumes discovered for the United States could elevate that amount to roughly $1.3 trillion, raise the OECD FDI stock to $2.3 trillion, and lower the U.S. share to 16.5 percent for 1989. In the absence of a coherent and complete data series for many member states, the demonstrated weakening of the U.S. FDI is highly probable, but there is no possibility to quantify the relative positions accurately. A possible argument for a lower U.S. share in the investment area is the American global trade share of around 18 to 19 percent which, as indicated earlier, is closely tied to FDI activities.

The investment priorities of America's business world are revealed and underscored by the fact that over the study period less than one percent of the nation's GDP went for direct investments. This applies equally to actual net equity/debt capital flows from the United States and the expanded capital flows, including reinvestments, in accordance with the American accounting practice (see Table 2.5). America's business orientation is still inward rather than international, even though at least three-fourths of today's global economy lies outside the continental United States (see Table 11.6).

A demonstration of how marginal FDI is in relation to other indicators of America's economy, and probably its managerial mind-set, is given by the following data. The cumulative FDI position of $430 billion in 1990 was roughly $80 billion less than the total U.S. business expenditure of $507 billion for new plants and equipment in 1989. Manufacturing alone spent $183 billion, and all other industries, another $324 billion. Comparing manufacturing investment alone to outward U.S. FDI investment volumes for whole decades is quite revealing (see Table 5.12). If the FDI funds actually exported from U.S. shores alone are counted, the gap is overwhelming (*Economic Report of the President*, 1992, p. 357).

The competitive implications of this example, its sharp contrast to the relative developments of inward FDI becoming visible in the country's BOP (see Tables 5.9, 5.11, and 5.12), and other macroeconomic performance indicators compiled in Chapter 11, are difficult to ignore in determining America's position in the world economy. Regardless of whether U.S. BOP flows are measured with or without the reinvestments in the current and capital accounts, the fact of a narrowing income flow and widening capital flow gap between inward and outward FDI not only makes a more active stance by U.S. investors desirable, but mandatory. For the time being, it is clearly a question of America's ability or willingness to compete, notwithstanding the new investment level during the early 1990s (see Tables 5.11 and 5.12).

One trade area monitored closely by the International Trade Administration is the U.S. performance in high-tech goods. Considered a vital indicator of American leadership in the international competitive race, it includes the following product categories: guided missiles and spacecraft; communication equipment and electronic components; aircraft and parts; office, computing and accounting machines; ordinance and accessories; drugs and medicines; industrial inorganic chemicals; professional and scientific instruments; engines, turbines, and parts; plastics and synthetic resins, etc.

Reaching about one-third of total U.S merchandise exports (FAS basis) and 40 percent of exported manufactures, the same categories account for only 20 to 25 percent of much larger merchandise imports (CIF basis) enduring the late 1980s. The impression of a weakening export performance by America's high-tech industries is caused by only three of the ten industries, with important deficits generated by the communications equipment sector, and only minor deficits by professional/scientific instruments and engines including turbines. All other industries show positive balances (see Table 14.3).

Studies by government trade experts describe a general downturn in the U.S. share of worldwide exports of these goods since 1965. Major winners were Japan and East Asian NICs, while European nations seemed to have maintained a status quo. Reasons given include major changes in the world economy, such as accelerated diffusion of U.S. technology, growing foreign R&D investments and modernization of production facilities, relocation of R&D, product innovation, and production processes from the United States to overseas locations (*U.S. Trade Performance 1988*, p. 21).

This latter point agrees fully with observations made earlier about the role of subsidiaries as an extension of U.S. capital into the world market. As indicated then, ignoring this fact may result in grossly misleading information purely by forgetting the role of U.S. subsidiaries in the picture.

TABLE 14.3. Balance of U.S. High-Tech Trade ($ billion)

Year	$	Year	$
1978	14.4	1986	(.7)
1979	20.6	1987	2.6
1980	26.6	1988	8.1
1981	27.4	1989	27.1
1982	24.4	1990	34.1
1983	19.9	1991	36.9
1984	7.7	1992	33.3
1985	5.3	1993	27.2

Note: New series beginning with 1989.

Sources: *U.S. Trade Performance* 1984, pp. 100-1; 1988, pp. 86-7. *Statistical Abstract of the United States*, 1993, p. 810; 1994, p. 820.

There can be no doubt that subsidiaries and U.S. licensees in NICs, for example, have at least a reasonable potential to cause much of the trade turbulence or contribute to the weakening of U.S. domestic exports.

A typical example is the drugs and medicines category, an industry where the United States possesses an undeniable leading position in the world. Official data show the U.S. trade balance shrinking from $1.3 billion in 1982 to $400 million during 1988 through 1989. During that period, exports grew from $2.3 to $4.0 billion while imports jumped from $1.0 to $3.7 billion. The export picture reflects the maturity of firmly established American subsidiaries around the world, which most likely source only absolutely necessary ingredients rather than finished products from U.S. parents. During that period, foreign drug companies established their own foothold in the American market, often by acquisition of former U.S. licensees, which in turn led to strong increases in raw material imports. To interpret this as a general failure of America's industry is difficult to accept at face value.

While it is not possible to measure the relative impact of either development from available data, the mere possibility that they may have the indicated distortion potential is a strong argument in favor of looking at the overall U.S. position in international trade and country markets by giving credit to Mofas, as postulated in previous comments. Without seeing the total picture, wrong conclusions can easily lead to hasty and reactive policy decisions.

A clear-cut American superiority in certain industries (aviation, space, drugs, telecommunication, ordinance, etc.) is established, even in those high-tech areas where trade balances ostensibly grow weaker. The same can be demonstrated for some American low-tech sectors such as agriculture, certain service industries, (most notably financial services), as well as transportation, banking, advertising, and business consulting, among others.

For reasons of initiating and monitoring the development of active American trade policies, a number of organizations were instituted, as mentioned before. One of them was GATT, with its widely publicized rounds of tenacious negotiations often lasting years at a time. GATT's original purpose was the dismantling of tariffs and other barriers shackling international trade. Very successful in the beginning and truly instrumental in boosting world trade, it now appears to be marking time. Reasons put forth all point to the fact that the organization has changed its focus. Reduction of tariff barriers on industrial products, though still a major topic, has given way to the discussion of TRIMS (trade related investment measures), a term principally referring to national development policies of industrializing countries.

GATT's support of a wide range of demands from developing economies is increasingly perceived as a potential cause of serious free trade and investment distortions by industrial nations. Resented in particular are national development policies aiming at the reduction of BOP deficits through acceptance of required export performance by approved investments, import substitution by means of local content targets, restrictive allocation of foreign exchange for imports and repatriation of capital and earnings, and the like. Different in nature, but also intended to curb foreigners, are laws requiring local equity participation, hiring qualified locals instead of foreign managers, training of the local labor force, tranfer of the latest technology, and many more.

Issues raising similar concerns about GATT's role on the part of developing nations include restrictions on the trade in services to prevent exports of confidential, sensitive, or useful technologial information from developed nations. Equally suspect are the determined drive for universal protection of industrial property rights, and related curbs on the trade in counterfeit products, which are considered unduly protective for business interests of develeloped nations. Also, agreements sought or worked out by GATT increasingly take the shape of bilateral concessions, not the multilateral benefits intended, indicating that the original purpose of GATT loses relevance.

For the United States, as one of the founding nations and major supporter of the organization, this means an uncertain future for at least one of its major foreign trade aspirations: the progressive liberalization of agricultural exports. Expressed frustrations by U.S. policymakers over GATT's performance record in this sector are not only an expression of disappointment with its effectiveness, but also a declining American influence in the organization.

U.S. efforts to generate a solid footing for global trade and investments also include the 1984 Trade and Tariff Act which extended the Generalized System of Preferences (GSP) to July 4, 1993. The latter defined the duty-free benefits accorded to more than 140 countries and covered about 3,000 import items.

How beneficial have all American-sponsored GATT projects been for the country itself? A recent OECD study evaluated the economic gains to be derived from the successful conclusion of the Uruguay Round of GATT negotiations. Signed in April of 1994 after seven years of tenacious wrangling and often stalled negotiations, it was heralded as a major victory for the United States, its main protagonist. But America came away with benefits of only minimal economic consequence, and probably totally out of proportion with the effort expended. The study concluded that the cumulative impact for the world economy will amount to a total of $274 billion in additional growth for the next eight years up to the year 2002. Of the total, the EU will get $71.3 billion to generate 1.7 percent in added economic stimulation; Japan, $42 billion (+1.8 percent); EFTA, $38.4 billion (+6.0 percent); the United States, $27.6 billion (+0.4 percent); and the rest of the world, $94.7 billion, with an unknown growth effect.

The clear winner is the EU, as it does or will include almost all of the EFTA members by 2002. The point here is that the much publicized trade gains derived from the GATT round created very little additional stimulus for the developed nations. The projected total gain for the United States spread over eight years will have the same effect as six months' worth of after-tax income generated by U.S. FDI (Welthandel, Das Internationale Wirtschaftsmagazin, April/May 1994, p. 90).

Protection of U.S. intellectual property rights is one area of major concern and attention, where violations are said to cost U.S. industry about $60 billion in revenues annually through patent infringements, counterfeit products, trademark piracy, etc. The United States does not stand alone in this regard as other industrialized nations are equally affected, causing a commonality of interest in erecting sweeping legal safeguards against such practices. While the finger is readily pointed at NICs as the most flagrant violators, negligence in establishing legal rights or efforts to defend them on the part of the originator from industrialized nations may be a contributing factor. Assuming a nation harboring violators of property rights has the requisite protection laws, these cannot be invoked unless a locally registered right has been established by the foreign plaintiff, which is often overlooked where prior rights where established through registration by nationals. It is a painful realization for owners of commercially valuable goods or processes, who are not familiar with or forgot about the need to establish these rights, in all countries where potential harm may arise. There is still a relatively high rate of misunderstanding about legal differences of product and process patents, the implications of "prior use" vs. registration principles embodied in common or code law countries, and the need to invest in costly patent searches as well as the vigorous defense of any infringement.

Property rights, their establishment, and protection is a field rife with contention between developing and industrial nations. The former have even questioned the justification of such exclusive privilege, or its maintenance for extended periods, as a deliberate means of preventing LDC access to much needed technology.

In a related vein, America's industrial and global competitiveness may be highlighted by the share of annual patent and trademark registrations granted to foreign business operations in the United States. Here is a demonstrable advantage, albeit a tenuous one, on the American side. The place at the top is getting crowded with foreigners continually narrowing the gap and approaching the 50 percent mark of annual patent awards. While the numbers indicate a shifting balance in the international output of intellectual property claims and an obvious U.S. need for foreign-held patents, they say little about the fields of application or their relative economic and commercial importance for the U.S. market (see Table 14.4).

It is safe to assume, though, that they are filed in fields where U.S. industry is presently at the cutting edge of technology. The constant race between U.S. and Japanese computer chip makers for market dominance is a typical example, as are foreign inroads in the development of super computers and telecommunication equipment.

Not surprisingly, in view of the above data, foreigners are registering gains in the BOP flows of royalties and license fees. During the 1960s, outflows to foreigners reached 9.7 percent of similar inflows, 11.0 percent during the 1970s, 16.9 percent during the 1980s, and 23.3 percent during the 1990 through 1994 period. The underlying dollar amounts were $1.4 to $14.0 billion, $4.5 to $40.3 billion, $13.8 to $81.8 billion, and $22.8 to $97.8 billion, leaving a comfortable surplus for the United States (see Table 3.12).

In a rather dramatic reversal of fortunes, the United States will end the century the same way it began: as a debtor nation. Up to World War I, the United States was a net borrower from the rest of the world, as can be expected from a nascent industrial nation, turned into a net lender during the war, and slipped back into a debtor position by 1987, according to the latest official statistics. Since then, the international investment position (IIP) has rapidly deteriorated, leaving the country with more than one-half trillion dollars in net debits at the end of 1994 (see Table 14.5).

Attitudes about the real significance of the figures vary depending on whether the observer's beliefs are more conservative or progressive. Granted that a nation's credit rating is more difficult to measure than that of private individuals or corporations, there still is the disquieting coincidence with other factors of potential concern that are impacting the American economy. These factors include:

- very large and persistent trade deficits;
- a very low rate of growth for GDP according to a new series calculated by the DOC (*The Wall Street Journal,* December 21, 1995, p. C1);
- a federal deficit approaching $5 trillion, still roaring out of control but presently the subject of a bitter confrontation between the President and Congress;
- rising unemployment figures;

- a continuing meltdown of industrial employment;
- one of the lowest savings rates in the world;
- swelling state, corporate, and consumer debts;
- uncertain inflation trends;
- very high and unproductive investments for defense even after the end of the cold war;
- a fundamental weakening of the dollar; and
- a declining government willingness to protect private wealth against rising taxation and income erosion for large sectors of the working population.

In combination, all factors should cause developments in the IIP to be viewed with concern.

The IIP is an accounting tool for changes in U.S. claims on foreign countries (assets) against the reverse claims by foreigners on the United States (liabilities) which, in and by itself, turns the IIP into a balance sheet of the nation's competitiveness. Accepting this as a fundamental premise, the trend of the IIP's total as well as subaccount balances takes on special significance.

Inward and outward FDI positions are an important part of the IIP; they help to shape its balances, and thus deserve a closer look. Their appearance differs very much from all pertinent data discussed so far, because for IIP purposes, all FDI information has been measured on a completely different basis since 1990. Rather than being quoted at historical costs as before, the FDI positions now appear only at current cost and market value. The most important consequence of the new measuring techniques is that the values are not only larger, but also exposed even more to annual exchange rate fluctuations of the dollar and other valuation factors, causing a total disconnection between the development patterns of the various FDI values. The difference between inward and outward FDI values at historical costs and market values was $108 and $277 billion respectively for 1994. The present

TABLE 14.4. U.S. Patent Registrations (000s)

	1980	1985	1986	1987	1988	1989	1990	1991	1992
Patents Issued	66.2	77.3	77.0	89.6	84.4	102.7	99.2	106.8	107.4
Foreign Share	38%	44%	45%	47%	47%	47%	47%	46%	45%

Sources: *Statistical Abstract of the United States*, 1993, p. 544; 1994, p. 552.

TABLE 14.5. International Investment Position of the United States ($ billion)

	1950	1960	1970	1980	1990*	1992*	1993*	1994*
NET POSITION	36.7	44.7	67.8	120.6	-291.9	-515.7	-546.3	-680.8
ASSETS								
Government	35.4	36.3	46.6	90.3	256.1	156.2	245.9	244.7
Private	19.0	49.3	118.8	516.4	1,809.7	1,914.0	2,147.6	2,233.0
Outward FDI	11.8	31.9	75.5	215.4	620.0	657.9	706.6	760.9
Portfolio	5.3	9.6	20.9	62.5	228.7	333.8	542.9	538.6
Bank claims	N/A	5.3	13.8	203.9	695.7	668.0	647.7	646.7
LIABILITIES								
Government	N/A	14.2	27.2	176.0	335.4	442.7	516.7	545.3
Private	3.2	26.6	70.4	310.1	1,942.2	2,215.2	2,422.2	2,613.3
Inward FDI	7.9	6.9	13.3	68.4	467.3	498.6	535.8	580.5
Portfolio	4.6	9.9	25.6	74.1	843.2	1,065.6	1,214.5	1,246.4
Bank claims	N/A	7.6	22.8	137.1	631.6	651.0	671.9	786.3

Note: *Includes direct investment positions at current cost versus historic costs for prior years.

Sources: *International Direct Investment, Global Trends, and the U.S. Role,* 1984, Tables 28, 29. *SOCB,* June 1995, p. 60, Table 3.

net position in the IIP could actually approach one trillion dollars owed to the outside rather than the lesser amount shown (see Table 14.6).

Viewed from another angle, 1994 outward FDI valued at current costs reached 31 percent of all U.S. assets held abroad and valued on the same basis. Valued at market, the FDI position went up to 38 percent of comparable total U.S. assets held abroad–in either case, rather significant parts of America's foreign investments, official or private. In the same year, inward FDI reached 22 percent of foreign assets held in the United States valued at current cost, and 27 percent if valued at market. Again, rather important

TABLE 14.6. Valuation of U.S. Outward/Inward FDI ($ billion)

Year	Historical Costs	Current Costs	Market Value
Outward Position At:			
1982	$207.8	$387.2	$226.6
1983	207.2	376.3	274.3
1984	211.5	367.8	270.6
1985	230.3	394.8	386.4
1986	259.8	431.5	530.1
1987	314.3	505.1	590.2
1988	335.9	526.8	692.5
1989	381.8	560.4	832.5
1990	430.5	620.0	731.8
1991	467.8	644.3	827.5
1992	502.1	657.9	798.6
1993	559.7	706.6	1,021.7
1994	612.1	760.9	1,048.4
Inward Position At:			
1982	124.7	176.9	130.4
1983	137.1	184.4	153.3
1984	164.6	211.2	172.4
1985	184.6	231.3	219.9
1986	220.4	265.8	272.9
1987	263.4	313.5	316.2
1988	314.8	375.2	391.5
1989	368.9	435.9	534.7
1990	394.9	467.3	539.6
1991	419.1	491.9	669.1
1992	427.6	498.6	694.2
1993	464.1	535.8	759.5
1994	504.4	580.5	771.1

Source: *SOCB*, June 1995, pp. 60-1.

portions of foreign assets invested in the United States, and an impressive demonstration of how the very same underlying FDI components change their appearance dramatically with a change in the valuation methods employed. All of them are justifiable, as they are designed to serve different purposes. But, in turn, each creates new difficulties and uncertainties by introducing measuring tools that are themselves subject to variable and uncontrollable influences. While historical cost data are fairly straightforward and stable, current cost estimates reflect changes in the average price of FDI tangible assets and exchange rate fluctuations which have reinforcing or offsetting effects. Market valuations are basically subject to the twin effect of changing stock market prices plus exchange rate translations combined with a number of other value adjustments–a combination which occasionally causes them to project trends in direct conflict with developments shown by the other two means of measurement (Footnotes to Table 4, *SOCB*, June 1993, p. 49).

One factor shared by all three evaluation techniques is their uniform portrayal of the U.S. outward FDI position as always maintaining a very solid lead over the inward position. But, by their very design, the current cost and especially the market valuation approaches introduce elements of volatility not present in the historical cost method of valuation.

Another position in the IIP concerns the monetary gold stock. Expressed in terms of market value, it fluctuates with the prevailing gold price, which says little, inasmuch as the price has gone down over time. A better indicator is the stock measured in troy ounces, as provided by the IMF. Between 1963 and 1993, the world stock of reserve gold moved down from 1,149 to 930 million troy ounces. No explanation for the decline is furnished. With 446 and 292 million ounces, the United States held 39 and 31 percent of the total respectively at these two times. Adding Canada's (23 versus 10 million) and Mexico's reserves (4 vs. 1 million), a hypothetical NAFTA balance sheet reaches 41 percent of world gold reserves in 1963 and 33 percent in 1993.

By comparison, the EU held 459 million ounces, or 40 percent in 1963, but also saw its reserves and share drop to 353 million ounces, or 38 percent in 1993. If the rest of Europe were finally integrated, as more or less it is already through the EEA, the union's share would jump by more than 100 million ounces for a 50 percent share of world reserves (*IMF, Yearbook* 1993, pp. 52-3).

Japan tripled its holdings from 8 to 24 million ounces within those same three decades, for a very modest 2.6 percent share. OPEC has gone from 24 to 44 million ounces in the same time frame, owns more gold than Japan, but is clearly outranked by Japan's economic power.

The final set of information is provided by *Fortune* magazine, which has published an annual scoreboard on the 500 largest industrial corporations in the world for many years. It neatly complements the concept of national ownership of the world market advocated to become the ultimate measurement of international competitiveness. The individual companies listed in the original version have been abstracted into number of firms by national origin for the first 100 companies only (see Table 14.7).

The table is a fitting conclusion to the topic of international competitiveness discussed throughout the study by first illustrating and accenting the shifting relationships of the Triad countries among themselves, and within in a global context for the last half century. To what degree are the shifts in national positions the result of truly changing competitive strengths, exchange rate movements or other factors, which have played a major, but mostly unnoticed role throughout the study?

A second aspect is the visualization of Japan's competitive strength. Within thirty years, that country has worked itself into a position equal to two-thirds each of the American and European economies, with no natural

TABLE 14.7. The 100 Largest Global Corporations

Year	1963	1979	1988	1993
NAFTA	67	50	40	33
United States	67	47	39	32
Canada	0	2	0	0
Mexico	0	1	1	1
Japan	3	7	15	23
Western Europe	30	41	40	37
Germany	13	13	12	14
France	4	11	9	6
UK	7	7	5	4
Italy	2	3	4	4
Switzerland	1	1	3	3
Netherlands/UK	2	2	2	2
Spain	0	0	1	2
Sweden	0	0	2	1
Netherlands	1	3	1	1
Belgium	0	1	1	0
Rest of World	0	2	5	7

Sources: *Fortune*, "The World's Largest Industrial Corporations," July 31, 1989; July 29, 1991; July 25, 1994.

resources of its own, and a population of only 30 to 50 percent of either area. The trends underlying the picture indicate the general direction of each area's future place in the global economy. While the data seem to assign North America and Europe still important roles for some time to come, they will be less dynamic than the clearly emerging centers of economic importance.

The third point is the appearance of developing countries in the picture. As far as their prominence rests on major natural resources like petrocarbons (Brazil, Mexico, Venezuela, Kuwait), it is difficult to assign them the same competitive credit as countries drawing their place from a wider range of industries. But the mere fact of developing nations rising to important ranks in this world order cannot be overlooked, nor the ensuing redistribution of power and wealth. This facet recalls the picture laid down in Table 11.6 revised, and referring to the rest of the world, the only area where U.S. participation was shown to be weak. Important competitive forces are taking shape here, best illustrated by the fact that in 1963, all 100 leading companies listed above belonged to the OECD, while in 1993, only 93. Gradual as the shift was over the last thirty years, it must be seen as the modest beginning of a potentially more rapid development as the wheel of progress rolls around the globe. The best way to participate in this future is physically being in the markets where it occurs. The information mosaic unfolding must be viewed and evaluated from many angles, all useful and necessary for determining America's true global position and importance. Detractors may interpret them as evidence of America's economic decline. Pragmatists, more appropriately, see the same information as the result of a normal adjustment process in the formation of a visionary world community with the United States, as a leader and staunch supporter of the process, remaining the primus inter pares.

Appendix

Industrial Classification

Industry Classification in Benchmark Surveys

Census Years	1950	1957	1966	1977	1982	1989
ALL INDUSTRIES	X	X	X	X	X	X
Agriculture, Forestry, Fisheries	X	X	X			
Agricultural production				X		
Forestry				X		
Fisheries				X		
Agricultural services				X		
Agriculture, forestry, fisheries combination				X		
Mining	X	X	X	X		
Metal Mining				X		
Iron	X	X	X	X		
Copper, Lead, Zinc, Gold, and Silver	X	X	X	X		
Bauxite, Other Ores, and Services	X	X	X	X		
Coal and Other Nonmetallic Minerals	X	X	X	X		
Petroleum	X	X	X	X	X	X
Oil and gas extraction		X	X	X	X	X
Crude petroleum extraction (no refining) and natural gas			X	X	X	X
Oil and gas field services		X	X	X	X	X
Petroleum and coal products				X	X	X
Integrated petroleum refining and extraction		X	X	X	X	X
Petroleum refining without extraction				X	X	X
Petroleum and coal products, nec.				X	X	X
Petroleum wholesale trade		X	X	X	X	X
Other		X	X	X	X	X
Manufacturing	X	X	X	X	X	X
Food and kindred products	X	X	X	X	X	X
Grain mill and bakery products			X	X	X	X
Beverages			X	X	X	X
Other			X	X	X	X
Paper and allied products	X	X	X			

Industry Classification in Benchmark Surveys (continued)

Census Years	1950	1957	1966	1977	1982	1989
Manufacturing *(continued)*	X	X	X	X	X	X
Chemicals and allied products	X	X	X	X	X	X
Industrial chemicals and synthetics			X	X	X	X
Drugs			X	X	X	X
Soap, cleaners, and toilet goods			X	X	X	X
Agricultural chemicals			X	X	X	X
Other			X	X	X	X
Rubber and miscellaneous plastic products	X	X	X			
Primary and fabricated metals	X	X	X	X	X	X
Primary metal industries			X	X	X	X
Ferrous				X	X	X
Nonferrous				X	X	X
Fabricated metal products			X	X	X	X
Machinery, except electrical	X	X	X	X	X	X
Farm and garden machinery			X	X	X	X
Construction, mining, and materials handling machinery			X	X	X	X
Office and computing machines			X	X	X	X
Other			X	X	X	X
Electric and electronic equipment	X	X	X	X	X	X
Household appliances			X	X	X	X
Radio, TV, and communication equipment			X	X	X	X
Electronic components and accessories			X	X	X	X
Other			X	X	X	X
Transportation equipment	X	X	X	X	X	X
Motor vehicles and equipment			X	X	X	X
Other			X	X	X	X
Other manufacturing	X	X	X	X	X	X
Tobacco products			X	X	X	X
Textile products and apparel			X	X	X	X
Lumber, wood, furniture, and fixtures			X	X	X	X
Paper and allied products				X	X	X
Printing and publishing			X	X	X	X
Rubber products				X	X	X
Miscellaneous plastics products				X	X	X
Glass products			X	X	X	X
Stone, clay, and other nonmetallic mineral products			X	X	X	X
Instruments and related products			X	X	X	X
Other			X	X	X	X
Transportation, Communication, Public Utilities	X	X	X			
Water transportation	X	X	X			
Communication	X	X	X			
Other	X	X	X			

Census Years	1950	1957	1966	1977	1982	1989
Trade	X	X	X	X	X	X
Wholesale trade	x	x	x	x	x	x
Durable goods				x	x	x
Nondurable goods				x	x	x
Retail	x	x	x	x		
Banking				X	X	X
Finance, Insurance, Real Estate				X	X	X
Banking	x	x	x			
Finance, except banking		x	x	x	x	x
Insurance	x	x	x	x	x	x
Real Estate				x	x	x
Holding Companies	x	x	x	x	x	x
Nonbusiness entities						x
Services					X	X
Hotels and other lodging places					x	x
Business Services					x	x
Advertising					x	x
Management, consulting, and PR services					x	
Equipment rental (ex. automotive and computers)					x	x
Computer and data processing services					x	x
Other					x	x
Automotive rental and leasing						x
Motion pictures, including TV tape and film					x	x
Engineering, architectural, and surveying services					x	x
Health services					x	x
Management and public relations services						x
Other services					x	x
Other Industries	X	X	X	X	X	X
Agriculture, forestry, and fishing				x	x	x
Mining					x	x
Metal mining					x	x
Nonmetallic mining					x	x
Construction		x	x	x	x	x
Transportation, communication, and public utilities				x	x	
Transportation						x
Communication and public utilities						x
Retail trade					x	x
Real estate	x	x	x			

Industry Classification in Benchmark Surveys (continued)

Census Years	1950	1957	1966	1977	1982	1989
Other Industries *(continued)*	X	X	X	X	X	X
Hotels		x	x			
Advertising, related business services		x	x			
Motion pictures	x	x	x			
Services				x		
Other	x	x	x			

Sources: 1950 FDI census, p. 45. 1957 FDI census, p. 94. 1966 FDI census, p. 33. 1977 FDI census, p. 33. 1982 FDI census, p. 37. 1989 FDI census, p. 4.

Glossary

affiliate: See foreign affiliate.

arm's-length pricing: Intracorporate prices set at level of prices charged to unrelated parties under similar circumstances. See also transfer pricing.

Asia: Includes Japan and Middle East, but excludes Turkey.

benchmark survey: Periodic census taken of U.S. FDI companies. The study includes those for 1950, 1957, 1966, 1977, 1982, and 1989.

BOP: Balance of Payments.

BOT: Balance of Trade.

branch: Consists of operations or activities in one location that a person in a second location conducts in its own name, rather than through an entity incorporated in the first location (1982 benchmark survey, p. 4).

branch earnings: Income or profits earned by a branch operation.

CCA: Capital Consumption Allowance.

CIF: Cost, insurance, freight (price quotation including all three).

CPI: Competitive Power Index. Measures share in national or industrial gross product achieved by foreign direct investors.

debt capital: Intercompany loans. See interests and intercompany debt.

dividend: Income on equity investment.

direct investment (U.S. definition): Implies that a person in one country has a lasting interest in, and a degree of influence over the management of, a business enterprise in another country. For the United States, ownership or control by a single person of 10 percent or more of an enterprise's voting securities, or the equivalent, is considered evidence of such a lasting interest or degree of influence over management. Thus, U.S. direct investment abroad is the ownership or control, directly or indirectly, by one U.S. person of 10 percent or more of the voting securities of an incorporated foreign business enterprise or an equivalent interest in an unincorporated foreign business enterprise. "Person" is broadly defined to include any individual, branch, partnership, associated group, association, estate, trust, corporation or other organization (whether or not organized under the laws of any state), and any government (including a foreign government, the U.S. Government, a state or local government, and any agency, corporation or financial institution, or other entity or instrumentality thereof, including a government-sponsored agency). This definition treats an associated group as a single person (1989 benchmark survey, p. M-4).

distributed earnings: Funds remitted for the use of equity capital, dividends. Interests are not included here.

DOC: Department of Commerce.

earnings: Affiliate income after foreign corporate income taxes, but before distribution and related withholding charges. They are income to the U.S. parent, whether they are reinvested or distributed/remitted to the parent.

EEA: European Economic Area. Agreement between the European Community (EC) and The European Free Trade Area (EFTA) to form a single market of nineteen countries in 1991.

EEC: European Economic Community. Predecessor of EC and EU, established in 1957 by Treaty of Rome.

EC: European Community, the successor of the EEC, established in 1965.

EFTA: European Free Trade Area, established in 1960.

equity capital: Ownership capital. In its net form determined by increases minus decreases in parental fund flows. See dividends.

EU: European Union, the successor of the European Community (EC), established in 1992.

Europe: Includes Western Europe, Romania, Turkey, Yugoslavia but excludes other Eastern Europe.

FOB: Free on Board (price quotation).

FAS: Free Along Ship (price quotation).

FASB: Financial Accounting Standards Board Statement. FASBs 8 and 52 are discussed in the study.

fiscal year: Data for foreign affiliates and U.S. parents were required to be reported on a fiscal year basis. The 1989 fiscal year was defined as the affiliate's or parent's financial reporting year that ended in the calendar year 1989. The fiscal year data from the benchmark survey are not comparable with the calendar year estimates of transactions between foreign affiliates and their U.S. parents that appear in the U.S. balance of payments accounts or the with the calendar year estimates of the U.S. direct investment position abroad on a historical cost basis (1989 benchmark survey, p. M-7).

foreign affiliate: A foreign business enterprise in which there is U.S. direct investment–that is, it is a foreign business enterprise that is directly or indirectly owned or controlled by one U.S. person to the extent of 10% or more of the voting securities for an incorporated business enterprise or an equivalent interest for an unincorporated business enterprise. The affiliate is called a foreign affiliate to denote that it is located outside the United States (although the direct investment interest in it is owned by a U.S. person), a business enterprise, and therefore an affiliate, may be either incorporated or unincorporated. Unincorporated business enterprises include branches and partnerships (1989 benchmark survey, p. M-6).

FDI: Foreign Direct Investment.

Foreign Direct Investment: See also Direct Investment. It comes in two variants: outward and inward direct investments. Outward (foreign) direct investments are a record of the investments made abroad by a capital exporting nation. Inward (foreign) direct investments are the record of foreign capital invested in the recipient nation. The measurements of FDI do not follow a universal standard. Some nations measure only actual capital flows to arrive at cumulative investment stock estimates at historical costs. Others combine capital flows with reinvestments to arrive at cumulative stock estimates at historical costs. A third approach combines flows and reinvestments with valuation adjustments of the existing stock. The latest version establishes stock estimates also on the basis of current costs (replacement costs) or market value in addition to the historic cost method–essentially the present U.S. practice.

GATT: General Agreement on Tariffs and Trade.

GAAP: Generally Accepted Accounting Principles.

GP: Gross Product or value-added by upgrading process of goods and services. See also: value-added.

GDP: Gross Domestic Product.

GSP: Generalized System of Preferences.

IIP: International Investment Position (of the United States).

IMF: International Monetary Fund.

income: The term in this study is exclusively used for the U.S. parent share in affiliate profits after foreign income taxes and withholding taxes on distributed earnings. It may also appear in government publications, including FDI benchmark surveys, in reference to income statements of U.S. parents where it reflects total revenues consisting of sales, income from equity investments, capital gains/losses, and all other.

indirect taxes: Includes production royalty payments plus taxes other than income and payroll taxes minus subsidies received.

intercompany debt: Outstanding loan volume from parents to affiliates. Net positions are affected by increases in U.S. parents' receivables less increases in U.S. parents' payables. An increase in U.S. parents' payables is a decrease in intercompany debt and, thus, a capital inflow in the U.S. BOP, and vice versa.

interest: Income on debt capital. Usually quoted net of withholding taxes. Term may also be used to denote general capital participation.

inward FDI: See FDI.

Latin America: Includes continental republics south of United States as well as the island nations in the Caribbean.

LDC: Less Developed Countries.

manufacturing industries: For detailed definition, and changes over time, see preceding section, "Industry Classification in Benchmark Surveys" in the Appendix.

ME: Middle East.

Mofa: Majority-owned foreign affiliate.

NAFTA: North American Free Trade Area. Includes the United States, Canada, and Mexico. Plans are drafted to extend the agreement to rest of the Americas.

N/A: Not available.

NEC: Not Else Classified.

net flows: Any fund flows netted for payments coming in less payments going out.

NIC: Newly industrialized country.

nil: Not significant, not measurable.

NMF: No Meaningful Figure.

Oceania: Australia and New Zealand.

OECD: Organization for Economic Cooperation and Development.

O. W. H.: Other Western Hemisphere/island nations in Caribbean basin.

other direct investment services: Charges for the use of tangible property, and film and television tape rentals. Both receipts and payments are net of (foreign or U.S.) withholding taxes.

outward FDI: See FDI.

parent: A U.S. person (organization) who has direct investment–that is, a 10 percent or more direct or indirect ownership interest–in a foreign business enterprise. Although the U.S. government may have equity investments in a foreign business enterprise, such investment is not covered by BEA's direct investment surveys (1989 benchmark survey, p. M-5).

petroleum industry: Includes extractive and processing activities in the American accounting system. For details see preceding section: "Industry Classification in Benchmark Surveys."

production royalties: Depletion charges levied by some oil-producing nations. Included under indirect taxes.

profits: A term normally avoided in all government publications dealing with FDI. Instead such terms as income, earnings, reinvested earnings, etc., are used.

reinvested earnings: That part of affiliate earnings not distributed to parent organization.

reinvestments: same as reinvested earnings.

retained earnings: same as reinvested earnings.

royalties and license fees: Receipts by U.S. parents from, less payments by U.S. parents to, their foreign affiliates of royalties, license fees, and other fees for the use or sale of intangible property or rights, such as patents, industrial processes, trademarks, copyrights, franchises, designs, know-how, formulas, techniques, manufacturing rights, and other intangible assets or proprietary rights. Both receipts and payments are net of (foreign or U.S.) withholding taxes. Net can also imply parent receipts minus parent payments in some cases (1982 benchmark survey, p. 25).

service industries: For a listing of the various industries included in the American system of industrial classification, and their changes over time, see preceding section, "Industry Classification in Benchmark Surveys."

service charges: Consist of fees for services such as management, professional, or technical services rendered between U.S. parents and their foreign affiliates, whether in the form of sales of services or reimbursements (1982 benchmark survey, p. 25).

SITC: Standard Industrial Trade Classification.

SOCB: Survey of Current Business. Monthly publication of the U.S. Department of Commerce.

subsidiary: Same as foreign affiliate.

third countries: All countries except the United States and outside of the affiliate domicile.

trade industry: Normally includes wholesale and retail operations. But may be restricted to wholesale only where indicated.

transfer price: Pricing of goods and services exchanged in intracorporate transactions. See also arm's-length pricing.

triangle transaction: Physical business transaction between customers in two countries which is invoiced through a third where the profit is made. Normally involves tax sanctuaries.

TRIMS: Trade Related Investment Measures (GATT).

UK: United Kingdom.

Valuation Adjustments: Includes translation adjustments for foreign currency fluctuations against the U.S. dollar affecting translation of affiliate assets, liabilities, revenues and expenses, other capital gains or losses, and other.

value-added: Value-added or created in a product by manufacturing or marketing process. Excludes cost of materials, supplies, packaging, or overhead.

VAT: Value-Added Tax.

withholding tax: Tax on funds remitted such as dividends, interests, royalties, license fees, other service fees, etc.

WTO: World Trade Organization. Formally called GATT.

Bibliography

Abdallah, W. M. *International Transfer Pricing Policies: Decision Making Guidelines for Multinational Companies.* New York: Quorum Books, 1989.

Arabian American Oil Company, *ARAMCO AND ITS WORLD, Arabia and the Middle East.* Washington, DC, 1981.

Baade, R. A. "Are U.S. Direct Foreign Investments the Product of an Offensive-Minded Investment Strategy?" *Management International Review,* Vol.19, No. 4, 1979, pp. 21-30.

Ball, D. A. and McCulloch, W. H. Jr. *International Business,* Fifth Edition. Homewood, IL: BPI/Irwin, 1993.

Bartlett, C. A. and Ghoshal, S. *Managing Across Borders: The Transnational Solution.* Boston, MA: Harvard Business School Press, 1989.

Buckley, P. J. and Pearce, R. D. *"Market Servicing by Multinational Manufacturing Firms: Exporting Versus Foreign Production."* University of Reading, Discussion Papers in International Investment and Business Studies, 1981.

Business Week. McGraw-Hill, Inc., P.O. Box 430, Hightstown, NJ 08520, various issues.

Canada Handbook. Minister of Supply and Services, Ottawa, Canada: Queen's Printer and Controller of Stationery, 1984.

Canada Yearbook. Minister of Supply and Services, Ottawa, Canada: Queen's Printer and Controller of Stationery, 1967 and 1985.

Cateora, P. R. *International Marketing,* Eighth Edition. Homewood, IL: Richard D. Irwin, 1993.

Caves, R. "International Corporations: The Industrial Economics of Foreign Investment." *Economica,* February 1971, No. 38, pp. 1-27.

Diebold, W. Jr. "The United States in the World Economy: A Fifty Year Perspective." *Foreign Affairs,* Council on Foreign Relations, Inc., Vol. 62, No. 1, 1983, pp. 81-104.

Doing Business in Belgium, New York: Price Waterhouse, 1994.

Dollar, D. "Input quotas and the product cycle." *Quarterly Journal of Economics,* No. 3, August 1987, pp. 617-32.

DRT International. *DRT International Tax and Business Guide.* New York: Deloitte Touche Tohmatsu International, 1995 ed.

Drucker, P. F. "From World Trade to World Investment." *The Wall Street Journal*, May 26, 1987.

Dun's Marketing Services, Inc. *Million Dollar Directory.* Parsippany, NJ: Dun and Bradstreet Corp., 1988.

Dunn, R. W. *American Foreign Investments.* New York: Arno Press, 1976.

Dunning, J. H. *U.S. Industry in Britain.* London: George Allen & Unwin, 1976.

_____ *Studies in International Investment.* London: George Allen & Unwin Ltd., 1970.

_____ "Trade, Location of Economic Activity and the MNE: A Search for an Eclectic Approach." In *The International Allocation of Economic Activity*, edited by B. Ohlin, P. O. Hesselborn, and P. M. Wijkman. London: Macmillan, 1977.

_____ "Towards an Eclectic Theory of International Production." *Journal of International Business Studies*, Vol. 11, No. 1, Spring/Summer, 1980.

_____ *International Production and the Multinational Enterprise.* London: George Allen & Unwin, 1981.

Economic Report of the President. Washington, DC: U.S. Government Printing Office, various issues.

Ethier, W. "The Multinational Firm." *Quarterly Journal of Economics*, No. 4, November, 1984.

Foreign Direct Investment, 1973-87. New York: Group of Thirty, 1984.

Fraser, C. and Hite, R. E. "Participation in the International Marketplace by U.S. Manufacturing Firms." *International Marketing Review*, Birmingham, AL: MCB University Press Limited, Vol. 7, No. 5, 1990.

Ghoshal, S. and Nohria, N. "International Differentiation Within Multinational Corporations." *Strategic Management Journal*, Vol. 10, No. 4, 1989, pp. 323-7.

Hamel, G. and Prahalad, C. K. "Strategy as Stretch and Leverage." *Harvard Business Review*, Vol. 71, No. 2, pp. 75-85.

_____ "The Core Competence of the Corporation." *Harvard Business Review*, Vol. 68, pp. 79-93.

Hennart, J.-F. *A Theory of Multinational Enterprise.* Ann Arbor: University of Michigan Press, 1982.

Hymer, S. *The International Operations of International Firms: A Study in Direct Investment.* Cambridge, MA: MIT Press, 1976.

International Monetary Fund. Washington, DC.

_____ *Balance of Payments Statistics Yearbook*, various issues.

_____ *Direction of Trade Statistics Yearbook*, various issues.

_____ *International Financial Statistics Yearbook*, various issues.

Keizai Koho Center. *Japan, An International Comparison.* Japan Institute for Social and Economic Affairs, 6-1, Otemachi 1-chome, Chiyoda-ku, Tokyo, Japan. Annual issues 1989-1995.

Kindleberger, C. P., and Andretsch, D. B. *The Multinational Corporation in the 1980s.* Cambridge, MA: MIT Press, 1983.

Leontieff, W. "Domestic Production and Foreign Trade: The American Capital Position Reexamined." In *Readings in International Economics*, edited by R. E. Caves and H. C. Johnson. Homewood, IL: Richard D. Irwin, 1968, pp. 503-27.

Levitt, T. *The Marketing Imagination.* New York: The Free Press, 1986.

_____ "The Globalization of Markets." *Harvard Business Review,* May/June, 1983, pp. 92-102.

MacMillan, J. and Harris, B. *The American Takeover of Britain.* London: Leslie Frewin, 1968.

Matsuura, Nanshi F. *International Business. A New Era.* New York: Harcourt Brace Jovanovich, 1991.

McCaffrey, R. A. and Meyer, T. A. *An Executive's Guide to Licensing.* Homewood, IL: Dow Jones-Irwin, 1989.

Mikesell, R. F., ed. *U.S. Private and Government Investment Abroad.* Eugene, Oregon: University of Oregon Books, 1962.

Moon, H. C. and Roehl, T. W. "An Imbalance Theory of Foreign Direct Investment." *Multinational Business Review,* Vol. 1, No. 1, Spring 1993.

Ohmae, K. *The Borderless World: Power and Strategy in the International Economy.* New York: Harper Collins Publishers, 1990.

Organization for Economic Cooperation and Development, Department of Economics and Statistics, Paris.

_____ *International Investment and Multinational Enterprises, Recent International Direct Investment Trends,* 1981.

_____ *Controls and Impediments Affecting Inward Direct Investment in OECD Member Countries.* Committee on Capital Movements and Invisible Transactions, 1982.

_____ *Detailed Benchmark Definition of Foreign Direct Investment.* Committee on International Investment and Multinational Enterprises. January, 1983.

_____ *Labor Force Statistics 1962-82.* 1984.

_____ *Trade-Related Investment Measures and the International Investment Process.* Committee on International Investment and Multinational Enterprises. January, 1984.

_____ *The OECD Guidelines for Multinational Enterprises.* April, 1986.

_____ *International Tax Avoidance and Evasion.* April, 1987.

_____ *Multinational Enterprises and Disclosure of Information: Clarification of the OECD Guidelines.* June, 1988.

_____ *National Accounts 1974-86*. Vol. I and II, 1988.

_____ *International Direct Investment Statistics Yearbook 1993*.

_____ *International Direct Investment Statistics Yearbook 1994*. September, 1994.

_____ *Performance of Foreign Affiliates in OECD Countries*. September, 1994.

Pattison, J. E. *Acquiring the Future: America's Survival and Success in the Global Economy*. Homewood, IL: Dow Jones-Irwin, 1990.

Porter, M. E. *The Competitive Advantage of Nations*. New York: The Free Press, 1990.

Robert, M. *Strategy Pure and Simple: How Winning CEO's Outthink Their Competition*. New York: McGraw-Hill, 1993.

Rugman, A. M. *New Theories of the Multinational Enterprise*. New York: St. Martin's Press, 1982.

Scripps Howard. *The World Almanac and Book of Facts*. New York: Scripps Howard Co., various issues.

Servan-Schreiber, J. J. *The American Challenge*. New York: Atheneum House Inc., 1968.

Seymour, D. T. *The Pricing Decision*. Chicago: Probus Publishing Co., 1989.

Statistical History of the United States. U.S. Bureau of the Census. New York: Basic Books Inc., 1976.

Takeuchi, H. and Porter, M. E. "Three Roles of International Marketing Strategy." In *Competition in Global Industries*, edited by M. E. Porter. Boston: Harvard Business School Press, 1991.

Terpstra, V. *International Dimensions of Marketing*, Second Edition. Boston: PWS-Kent Publishing Co., 1988.

United Nations. Sources:

Monthly Bulletin of Statistics, various issues.

Salient Features and Trends in Foreign Direct Investment. New York: Center on Transnational Corporations, 1983.

Statistical Yearbook. 1979-80, pp. 448-75; ibid., 1983-84, pp. 904-31; ibid., 1985-86, pp. 685-702.

Statistical Yearbook for Asia & Pacific. 1969, 1974, 1984.

Transnational Corporations in World Development, Third Survey. New York: Center on Transnational Corporations, 1983.

Transnational Corporations in World Development–Trends and Prospects. New York: Center on Transnational Corporations, 1988.

Yearbook of Labor Statistics. Geneva: International Labor Organization, various issues.

Yearbook of National Accounts Statistics, various issues.

Urquhart, M. C. *Historical Statistics of Canada*. Toronto: McMillan of Canada, 1965.
U.S. Department of Commerce, Washington, DC. Superintendent of Documents, U.S. Government Printing Office, Washington, DC 20402.
Value Line. *The Value Line Investment Survey*. New York: Value Line Publishing Inc., various issues.

Monographs

Foreign Protection of Intellectual Property Rights and the Effect on U.S. Industry and Trade. International Trade Commission. February, 1988.
International Direct Investment, Global Trends and the U.S. Role. International Trade Administration. August, 1984.
International Direct Investment, Global Trends and the U.S. Role. International Trade Administration, 1988.
Selected Data on U.S. Direct Investment Abroad, 1950-76. Bureau of Economic Analysis. February, 1982.
United States Trade, Performance in 1984, and Outlook. International Trade Administration. June, 1985.
United States Trade, Performance in 1988. U.S. Department of Commerce, International Trade Administration. September, 1989.

Benchmark Surveys on U.S. Foreign Direct Investment
(also known as FDI census–terms are used interchangeably by DOC)

U.S. Business Investments in Foreign Countries. Office of Business Economics, 1960.
U.S. Direct Investment Abroad, End of 1950. U.S. Department of Commerce, Office of Business Economics, 1953.
U.S. Direct Investment Abroad, 1966, Final Data. Bureau of Economic Analysis, 1974.
U.S. Direct Investment Abroad, 1977. Bureau of Economic Analysis. April, 1981.
U.S. Direct Investment Abroad: 1982 Benchmark Survey Data. Bureau of Economic Analysis. December, 1985.
U.S. Direct Investment Abroad: 1989 Benchmark Survey, Final Results. Bureau of Economic Analysis. October, 1992.
U.S. Investments in the Latin American Economy. Office of Business Economics, 1957.

Periodicals

Business Statistics, 1973.
Statistical Abstract of the United States, various issues.
Survey of Current Business.

DATA FOR U.S. FDI ABROAD

Information under this heading was taken from *SOCB* issues arranged by topic, unless otherwise indicated.

Benchmark Survey of U.S. Direct Investment Abroad
  December 1985, pp. 37-57, 1982 data
  October 1991, pp. 29-47, 1989 data

Reinvestments
  August 1990, p. 45, 1980-89 data

Sales by Foreign Affiliates of U.S. Companies
  November 1965, pp. 14-24, 1957, 1959, 1961-64 data
  October 1970, pp. 18-20, 1961-65, 1967 and 1968 data
  January 1973, pp. 33-9, 1966 and 1970 data
  August 1974, pp. 25-40, 1966-72 data
  August 1975, pp. 22-37, 1973 data
  February 1977, pp. 29-39, 1966-75 data

Balance of Payments Information
  Table 1. U.S. International Transactions and Exports/Imports
    June 1988, pp. 40-1, 1960-86 data
    June 1991, pp. 44-5, 1960-90 data
    June 1993, pp. 70-1, revised 1983-92 data
    June 1995, pp. 84-5, 1962-94 data

  Table 3. International Investment Position of the United States
    June 1995, p. 60, 1980-94 data

  Table 5. Direct Investment: Income, Capital, Royalties, License Fees, and Other Private Services
    June 1984, p. 59, 1981-83 data
    September 1984, p. 46, 1982-83 data
    June 1985, p. 57, 1982-84 data

September 1985, p. 41, 1983-84 data
June 1986, p. 59, 1983-85 data
June 1987, p. 71, 1984-86 data
June 1988, p. 55, 1985-87 data
June 1990, p. 96, 1987-89 data
June 1991, p. 60, 1988-90 data
June 1993, p. 88, 1990-92 data
June 1994, p. 114, 1991-93 data
August 1994, p. 133, 1989-93 data
August 1995, p. 92, 1989-94 data

Balance of Payments Statistical Supplement Revised Edition, A Supplement to the Survey of Current Business, 1963

U.S. Direct Investment Abroad: Detail for Historical Cost Position and Balance of Payments Flows

Years 1950-76. See "Selected Data on U.S. Direct Investment Abroad, 1950-76," above
November 1972, pp. 21-34, 1971 data
September 1973, pp. 20-34, 1972 data
August 1974, pp. 10-25, 1973 data
October 1975, pp. 43-64, 1974 data
August 1977, pp. 32-55, 1976 data
November 1984, pp. 24-7, 1977-83 data
August 1984, pp. 18-30, 1983 data
August 1985, pp. 30-46, 1984 data
August 1986, pp. 40-73, 1985 data
August 1987, pp. 58-84, 1986 data
August 1988, pp. 42-68, 1987 data
August 1989, pp. 62-88, 1988 data
August 1990, pp. 56-98, 1989 data
August 1991, pp. 81-107, 1990 data
August 1992, pp. 116-44, 1991 data
July 1993, pp. 88-124, 1991-92 data
August 1994, pp. 127-61, 1991-93 data
August 1995, pp. 88-116, 1992-94 data

Gross Product of U.S. Multinational Companies

February 1977, pp. 17-28, 1966 data
February 1983, pp. 24-9, 1977 data
February 1994, pp. 42-63, 1977-91 data

U.S. Multinational Companies: Operations in. . . .

> September 1986, pp. 27-39, 1984 data
> June 1988, pp. 85-96, 1984-86 data
> June 1989, pp. 37-9, 1985-86 data
> June 1990, pp. 31-44, 1987-88 data
> August 1992, pp. 60-78, 1989-90 data
> July 1993, pp. 40-58, 1990-91 data
> June 1994, pp. 42-62, 1991-92 data
> June 1995, pp. 31-51, 1992-93 data

U.S. Multinational Companies: Profitability, Financial Leverage, and Effective Income Tax Rates, May, 1974

U.S. Exports to Foreign Affiliates of U.S. Firms

> December 1965, pp. 12-16, 1962-64 data
> May 1969, pp. 34-51, 1965 data
> December 1972, p. 20, 1966 and 1970 data

DATA FOR FDI IN THE UNITED STATES

Benchmark Surveys

Foreign Direct Investment in the United States, 1980. October, 1983

> Ibid., *1987 Benchmark Survey, Preliminary Results*. July, 1989
> Ibid., *1987 Benchmark Survey, Final Results*. August, 1990
> Ibid., *1992 Benchmark Survey Results*. July, 1994

Foreign Direct Investment in the United States, Review and Analysis of Current Developments. August, 1991.

> Ibid., *An Update*. June, 1993
> Ibid., *An Update*. January, 1995

Periodicals

Survey of Current Business

Foreign Direct Investment in the United States: Details for Historical Cost Position and Balance of Payment Flows

> February 1973, pp. 29-40, 1962-71 data
> August 1973, pp. 51-1, 1971-72 data

August 1974, pp. 7-9, 1969-73 data
October 1975, pp. 36-42, 1971-74 data
May 1976, pp. 35-51, 1974 data
October 1977, pp. 26-44, 1973-76 data
August 1980, pp. 38-51, 1978-79 data
August 1981, pp. 40-51, 1979-80 data
August 1982, pp. 30-41, 1980-81 data
August 1983, pp. 31-41, 1981-82 data
October 1983, pp. 25-34, Highlights from 1980 Benchmark Survey
October 1984, pp. 26-48, 1981-83 data
August 1985, pp. 47-66, 1982-84 data
August 1988, pp. 69-83, 1985-87 data
August 1989, pp. 47-61, 1986-88 data
August 1991, pp. 47-79, 1989-90 data
August 1992, pp. 87-115, 1989-91 data
July 1993, pp. 59-87, 1990-92 data
July 1994, pp. 154-86, 1992 Benchmark Survey Results
August 1994, pp. 98-126, 1991-93 data
May 1995, pp. 57-80, New Investments in 1994 and Affiliate
    Operations in 1993
August 1995, pp. 53-87, 1992-94 data

U.S. Affiliates of Foreign Companies, Operations in. . . .

May 1976, pp. 35-51, 1974 (Benchmark Survey)
July 1980, pp. 32-44, 1977 data
May 1981, pp. 35-52, 1978-79 data
November 1983, pp. 25-34, 1980-81 data
December 1984, pp. 26-47, 1982 data
November 1985, pp. 36-50, 1983 data
October 1986, pp. 31-45, 1984 data
May 1988, pp. 59-75, 1985-86 data
July 1989, pp. 116-39, 1987 Benchmark Survey Results
July 1990, pp. 127-44, 1986-88 data
July 1991, pp. 72-92, 1989 data
May 1992, pp. 45-68, 1989-90 data
May 1993, pp. 89-111, 1990-91 data
January 1994, pp. 34-59, *Characteristics of Foreign-Owned U.S.*
    Manufacturing Establishments

Gross Product of U.S. Affiliates of Foreign Companies, 1977-87
    June 1990, pp. 45-53

Gross Product of U.S. Affiliates of Foreign Direct Investors, 1977-90
November 1992, pp. 47-53

JOINT OUTWARD/INWARD FDI REPORTS

Direct Investment Positions on a Historical Cost Basis, Country and Industry Detail
June 1994, pp 72-8, 1982-93 data
June 1995, pp. 61-8, 1982-94 data

U.S. President's Commission on Industrial Competitiveness. "Trade Ripples Across U.S. Industries." Washington, DC, 1986.
Welthandel. Das Internationale Wirtschaftsmagazin, April/May, 1994, p. 90.
World Bank. *World Tables.* Various editions. Washington, DC: World Bank.
Yip, G. S. *Total Global Strategy: Managing for Worldwide Competitive Advantage.* Englewoods Cliffs, NJ: Prentice Hall, 1992.

Index

Page numbers followed by the letter "t" indicate tables; those followed by the letter "f" indicate figures.

Order Your Own Copy of
This Important Book for Your Personal Library!

U.S. TRADE, FOREIGN DIRECT INVESTMENTS, AND GLOBAL COMPETITIVENESS

_____ in hardbound at $129.95 (ISBN: 0-7890-0085-7)

_____ in softbound at $39.95 (ISBN: 0-7890-0187-X)

COST OF BOOKS_____

OUTSIDE USA/CANADA/
MEXICO: ADD 20%_____

POSTAGE & HANDLING_____
_(US: $3.00 for first book & $1.25
for each additional book)_
_Outside US: $4.75 for first book
& $1.75 for each additional book)_

SUBTOTAL_____

IN CANADA: ADD 7% GST_____

STATE TAX_____
_(NY, OH & MN residents, please
add appropriate local sales tax)_

FINAL TOTAL_____
_(If paying in Canadian funds,
convert using the current
exchange rate. UNESCO
coupons welcome.)_

☐ **BILL ME LATER:** ($5 service charge will be added)
(Bill-me option is good on US/Canada/Mexico orders only;
not good to jobbers, wholesalers, or subscription agencies.)

☐ Check here if billing address is different from
shipping address and attach purchase order and
billing address information.

Signature_____

☐ **PAYMENT ENCLOSED: $**_____

☐ **PLEASE CHARGE TO MY CREDIT CARD.**

☐ Visa   ☐ MasterCard   ☐ AmEx   ☐ Discover

Account #_____

Exp. Date_____

Signature_____

Prices in US dollars and subject to change without notice.

NAME _____

INSTITUTION _____

ADDRESS _____

CITY _____

STATE/ZIP _____

COUNTRY _____ COUNTY (NY residents only) _____

TEL _____ FAX _____

E-MAIL_____
May we use your e-mail address for confirmations and other types of information? ☐ Yes   ☐ No

Order from Your Local Bookstore or Directly from
The Haworth Press, Inc.
10 Alice Street, Binghamton, New York 13904-1580 • USA
TELEPHONE: 1-800-HAWORTH (1-800-429-6784) / Outside US/Canada: (607) 722-5857
FAX: 1-800-895-0582 / Outside US/Canada: (607) 772-6362
E-mail: getinfo@haworth.com
PLEASE PHOTOCOPY THIS FORM FOR YOUR PERSONAL USE.

BOF96